ACTIONS
AND
ACTORS

ACTIONS
AND
ACTORS

Principles of Social Psychology

Murray Webster, Jr.
University of South Carolina

Winthrop Publishers, Inc.
Cambridge, Massachusetts

Library of Congress Cataloging in Publication Data

Webster, Murray
    Actions and actors: principles of social
psychology.

    Includes bibliographical references and index.
    1. Social psychology.   I. Title.
HM251.W343   301.1   74-34106
ISBN 0-87626-006-7

00

For my Godson,
Michael

Contents

Preface

Social psychology has fascinated me more than anything else for as long as I can remember. I want to share that fascination with other people, and that's why I wrote this book. If the topics discussed in these chapters are interesting to you, I will be pleased.

More than most subjects, social psychology seems to depend upon good teachers and good textbooks to make it interesting. In working on this book, I found myself remembering all the things I had promised *not* to do: present a lot of trivial detail with no theory to tie it all together; encourage a solipsism which says you can't really trust knowledge claims; encourage an absolutism which says there is only one correct way to interpret the data; oversimplify complicated ideas; overcomplicate simple ones; criticize a research design when I can't suggest a way to improve it; and so on. But in avoiding past mistakes we often make new ones, and there may well be some of these here.

Generally, this is how chapters are organized: the most basic points come first, and I assume no previous contact with social psychology for them. Towards the end of each chapter are the most advanced topics; in some cases—especially when there are two chapters dealing with the same topic —only advanced students may want to read all the way to the end. My second guiding principle is that theories are crucial. Data are always related to theory—"What does this *mean*?"—and I try to avoid forcing upon the reader a huge number of "findings" from studies.

You will see the first person singular used quite a bit in this book. This is because often there is no single accepted interpretation of known facts. Even when I am very sure my opinion is correct, I want to encourage you to recognize that others—including you—might reach a different conclusion from studying the same facts.

Two people were outstandingly helpful to me in this project. D. Randall Smith probably knows the book almost as well as I do. He clarified my thinking and my writing in many places, compiled much of the bibliography at the end, and kept track of innumerable practical details which go into making a book. I look forward to the day Randy Smith writes a book to replace this one. Sherry Seidel acted as administrative assistant and sociological consultant throughout the formative steps of the book. I learned a lot from her, and I hate to think what the project would have been like without her help and cheerfulness.

Looking back on the three years' work that went into this book, what stands out most are the vast, intangible contributions of those around me while I worked. To paraphrase John Lennon, I get by with a lot of help from my friends. The following deserve special mention.

For Ideas:
Joseph Berger, George C. Homans, Peter H. Rossi, I. Richard Savage, Ralph H. Turner

For Reading and Criticizing Various Parts of the Manuscript:
H. Andrew Michener, Richard Ofshe, Barbara Sobieszek, Neil Smelser, Robert T. Hogan

For Typing and Reducing Chaos:
Janis Litrenta, Pam Skalski, Roseann Bindner, Dorothy Tart

For Patience and Help in Publishing:
Paul O'Connell, Barbara Sonnenschein, William Sernett, Stanley J. Evans

For Concern, Warmth, and Love:
Patricia and Murray Webster, Sr., Sue Poage, Mika Koutsogiannis, Lon D. Russ, Donald R. Howard, Victor G. Wexler, Troll

MURRAY WEBSTER, JR.

Acknowledgments

Chapter 1

Excerpt, p. 19. From Tom Wolfe, *The kandy-kolored tangerine-flake streamline baby*, Farrar, Straus & Giroux, Inc., © 1971, p. 177. Reprinted by permission. Table 1–2, p. 35. From Rohrer, J. H., Baron, S. H., Hoffman, E. L., and Swander, D. V., "The stability of autokinetic judgments." *Journal of Abnormal and Social Psychology*, 49(4)596, Table 1. Copyright 1954 by the American Psychological Association. Reprinted by permission. Figure 1–1, p. 38. From Jacobs, R. C., and Campbell, D. T., "The perpetuation of an arbitrary tradition through several generations of a laboratory microculture." *Journal of Abnormal and Social Psychology*, 52:649–658. Copyright 1961 by the American Psychological Association. Reprinted by permission.

Chapter 2

Tables 2–3, 2–4, and 2–5, p. 63. From Dittes, J. E., and Kelley, H. H., "Effects of different conditions of acceptance upon conformity to group norms." *Journal of Abnormal and Social Psychology*, 53:104. Copyright 1956 by the American Psychological Association. Reprinted by permission.

Chapter 3

Figures 3–4 and 3–5, pp. 80–81. Reprinted from *Conflict and conformity*, by Bernard P. Cohen, pp. 135, 140, by permission of the M.I.T. Press, Cambridge, Massachusetts. Copyright 1963.

Chapter 4

Tables 4–3 and 4–4, pp. 98, 101. From Chowdhry, K., and Newcomb, T. M., "The relative abilities of leaders and non-leaders to estimate opinions of their own group." *Journal of Abnormal and Social Psychology*, 47:51–57, Table 3. Copyright 1952 by the American Psychological Association. Reprinted by permission. Figure 4–1, p. 102. From Schachter, S., "Deviation, rejection, and communication." *Journal of Abnormal and Social Psychology*, 46(April):190–207. Copyright 1951 by the American Psychological Association. Reprinted by permission.

Chapter 5

Figures 5–2 and 5–3, pp. 126, 127. From Berger, J., Zelditch, M., and Anderson, B. (Eds.), *Sociological theories in progress* (Vol. 2), © 1972. Used by permission of Houghton Mifflin Company, publishers.

Chapter 6

Table 6–3, p. 151. From Whyte, W. F., *Street corner society: The social structure of an Italian slum*, published by the University of Chicago Press, copyright 1955.

Reprinted by permission. Table 6–4 and Figure 6–7, pp. 157, 158. From Berger, J., Conner, T. L., and Fisek, M. H. (Eds.), *Expectation states theory: A theoretical research program.* Copyright © 1974 by Winthrop Publishers, Inc. Reprinted by permission.

Chapter 7

Tables 7–7, 7–8, 7–9, and 7–11, pp. 172–174. From Caudill, W. A., *The psychiatric hospital as a small society.* Harvard University Press, copyright © 1958 by the President and Fellows of Harvard College. Reprinted by permission.

Chapter 9

Chart 9–1, p. 231. From Homans, G., *Social behavior: Its elementary forms,* rev. ed. New York: Harcourt Brace Jovanovich, pp. 16–39. Copyright © 1974. Used by permission.

Chapter 11

Figure 11–1, p. 276. From Mintz, A., "Non-adaptive group behavior." *Journal of Abnormal and Social Psychology,* 46:150–159. Copyright 1951 by the American Psychological Association. Reprinted by permission. Figure 11–7 and Table 11–1, pp. 287, 288. From Deutsch, M., and Krauss, R. M., "The effect of threat upon interpersonal bargaining." *Journal of Abnormal and Social Psychology,* 61(2):181–189. Copyright 1960 by the American Psychological Association. Reprinted by permission. Table 11–2, p. 298. From Berger, J., Zelditch, M., and Anderson, B. (Eds.), *Sociological theories in progress* (Vol. 2), © 1972. Used by permission of Houghton Mifflin Company, publishers.

Chapter 13

Table 13–4 and Figures 13–1 and 13–2, pp. 347–349. From Zajonc, R. B., "Attitudinal effects of mere exposure." *Journal of Personality and Social Psychology Monograph Supplement,* 90(2), Part 2:1–27. Copyright 1968 by the American Psychological Association. Reprinted by permission. Table 13–5, p. 356. From Aronson, E., and Mills, J., "The effect of severity of initiation on liking for a group." *Journal of Abnormal and Social Psychology,* 59:177–181. Copyright 1959 by the American Psychological Association. Reprinted by permission. Table 13–6, p. 356. From Schopler, J., and Bateson, N., "A dependence interpretation of the effects of a severe initiation." *Journal of Personality and Social Psychology,* 30:633–649. Copyright 1962 by the Duke University Press. Reprinted by permission.

ACTIONS
AND
ACTORS

A Note to the Reader

The study of any field involves application of effort, energy, and creative thought to a wide range of tasks. This is true of all subjects regularly studied in college, as it is true of social psychology. As a student of social psychology you will face intellectual challenges with respect to the amount of information you can absorb, the ways in which you can assimilate and organize it, the total volume of information you can recall on examinations and in discussions, and the connections you can make between currently accepted explanations in your particular field and the empirical facts. These challenges are quite similar to those faced by a student of any other field, especially to those confronting the student of the physical or natural sciences, which are currently used as models for intellectual activity in social psychology.

The student of social psychology faces an additional task, one which is not so often presented to his colleagues in biology or physics; that is the task of explaining to others exactly what he is studying. A little more than a decade ago when I began studying sociology and psychology, I recall clearly the difficulties that arose during vacation periods when I would return home from college. One inevitable question was, "What are you studying?" or "What's your major?" My friends would report that they were studying mathematics, some branch of engineering, or perhaps a premedical course, and would receive the usual comments on the importance of the subject, or anecdotes from the listener about his own experiences with an allied field. I knew that their responses to my course of study, sociology, would be much different: people would look puzzled while they tried to figure out what a sociologist does, and then they would usually recover with a noncommittal comment such as, "Oh, that's nice." At the time it seemed unfair to me that such a response should be applied to students of people and of societies—especially since unless the listener had actually studied mathematics, medicine, or engineering, there was a good chance that he didn't know what those fields entailed either.

Perhaps because of the tremendous growth in awareness of social and psychological problems, and of the vast findings of sociologists and psychologists, such responses would be rare today. Now the individual who announces his professional or temporary commitment to social psychology is unlikely to be met with puzzled looks. Instead the listener usually takes advantage of the opportunity to ask questions of contemporary issues that are vaguely within the purview of the field: "Isn't it true that black school children have been proved to have lower IQs than white children?" "Don't

1

you think that one of the biggest problems with college students today is that they were raised too permissively, so they think they can get anything just by demanding it?" "What do you think will happen if we continue to make more and more pornographic movies and books openly available?" "Hasn't it been shown that IQ tests are pretty much worthless in assessing children's abilities?" (The temptation always exists to introduce the first speaker quoted to the fourth.) As may be apparent from these examples, the answer the listener hopes for—indeed, the conclusion he probably has unalterably reached long before he asks—is often contained within the question. With the idealism of youth I used to take advantage of my quasi-professional status to claim above-average competence to answer questions such as these, and discussions that were both interesting and animated resulted. Somewhat older now, a bit wiser, and considerably more cautious, I usually try to interpret the question before I decide whether to try to answer it. Questions like the preceding ones usually come only when the listener has a deep personal or emotional involvement in the answer; and to *one* answer in particular. The last question, for example, warns me that the questioner probably is the parent of a child who has just come home with a poor score on a standardized test. I try to change the subject.

Even without trying to justify his existence to others, the student of a particular field should ask himself occasionally, "What am I doing, and why?" To someone for whom this book represents an introduction to social psychology, these questions are especially important. Let us spend a few paragraphs examining such questions and their answers, and some implications of both.

At the broadest level, sociologists study people and their relationships to each other. Psychologists also study people, but they are less interested in groups and more interested in individual functioning, such as individual differences in intelligence or attitudes. Social psychologists study people from both perspectives. We are interested in facts about people that are related both to their individual mental functioning and to their inter-relationships with other people. The definition is broad, but to limit it any more would exclude one or another major section of our field.

At this point the reader may well ask how the activities of social psychologists differ from activities of everyone, for we all study people to some extent. Again the question contains the answer: social psychologists do study the same things as everyone studies, but this could as well be said for engineers, physicists, or musicologists. Any professional specialization constitutes a deeper, more complicated study of phenomena that are studied at least superficially by everyone.

Each person carries around with him a store of what may be called "everyday knowledge"; this is the sort that helps him get through his daily encounters more or less successfully. We know that people generally prefer good news to bad news; that most people prefer compliments to criticism; that doing favors for others tends to be reciprocated; that men expect to shake hands upon meeting, but that women generally do not; that many people are very sensitive to criticism of their expensive possessions such as automobiles; that people with personal involvements in public issues cannot be counted on to make fair judgments of them. Knowledge of this sort is gathered and accumulated by the individual from the moment he begins to interact with others, and it usually helps him in future interactions. Such knowledge helps him to imagine likely consequences of several possible actions he can take and to choose the one that is most likely to bring about the desired response. It helps him to understand others and their actions, both friendly and unfriendly. It helps avoid the strained sort of social situations that can occur through oversights or misunderstandings—or it can help to produce strains and misunderstandings, if that is what the individual wants. We all have a store of this everyday knowledge, and we all use it constantly. My set of information may not be exactly the same as your set of information and I may be more or less successful than you at handling certain kinds of social situations, but we would probably find that we agree on a fair number of the principles we use to guide our everyday interactions. Some people amass a surprisingly large amount of such information; these individuals are the informally recognized "experts" in handling people and social situations. Such expertise is sometimes shared with others in books such as Stephen Potter's *Gamesmanship* or Robert Townsend's *Up the Organization,* and as anyone knows who has read these or similar books, at times it can be amazingly insightful and helpful.

Note that what we are asking about in these examples is either some sort of *prediction* of likely future behavior of others or some *explanation* for past behavior. It can be said that the goals of social psychology are to predict and explain human behavior.

These goals still do not differentiate social psychology from ordinary behavior of all people, however. If we concentrate on the knowledge and especially the *sort* of knowledge that is accumulated, then it becomes possible to begin to distinguish social psychological study from ordinary life experiences.

Taking the same area of interest—studying people and their interrelationships—and the same goals—predicting and explaining human behavior—it is still possible to distinguish the activities and the knowledge of social psychologists *as professional social psychologists* from the activity of all people, and from everyday knowledge. If social psychologists study people, we do it in a particular way. If we have knowledge useful for prediction and explanation, it is a particular sort of knowledge. If our goal is to accumulate knowledge about social behavior, it is only certain types of knowledge. It used to be fashionable in the introduction to a textbook in this field to assert that social psychology is interested in *scientific* knowledge, as opposed to all other kinds. This, it has always seemed to me, unnecessarily diverts attention from the important issues. Sociologists and, to a lesser extent, psychologists have been too defensive about whether their discipline was a "science." Many textbooks and college courses question whether the field is a science in the early chapters or the early lectures, and the answer invariably is: YES. Usually it is explained that the field is a science because the practitioners use scientific methods of observation. This is not a good argument; few students of science would agree that a field is defined by its methods. But what is particularly unfortunate about such an argument is that it tends to discourage people who previously were very much interested in the field. As a result it appears that we are preoccupied with numbers and methods, rather than by the very fascinating actors and actions that really define the field.

Let us leave the question of whether social psychology or this treatment of it is to be a science. The issue is complicated, and the resolution has little to do with the subject matter of the field. Likewise it is misleading to claim that when a social psychologist studies people he does it scientifically, and that the knowledge about behavior that is stored in social psychology differs from everyday knowledge in that the former is scientific.

What is crucial and what seems to me to be frequently overlooked, is that professional study of social psychology is very much concerned with *communicability* of knowledge. To return to our illustrations from everyday knowledge of behavior, we may examine what would be needed to make such knowledge communicable. Remember that the principles of everyday knowledge that I use to guide my actions are probably not exactly the same as those that you use to guide yours. Also note that some persons possess more knowledge than others and that they may attempt to communicate their knowledge. A good place to start examining the distinctive type of knowledge sought in social psychology is to ask what would be required for me to communicate knowledge to you. The methods of study and the types of knowledge possessed by social psychologists are determined by an overriding concern that this information be communicable.

Three things seem especially important to ensure communicability. First, I must be relatively certain that my knowledge is reliable, in the sense that I have observed confirming evidence of some idea on more than one occasion. For example, suppose that I have to ask my father's permission to use the car every time I wish to go out. One day when he is feeling particularly out of sorts and complains about having a "bad day at work" he refuses my request on grounds that I should study. The next day though he still knows nothing about how I am doing in my classes, he seems to be in a good mood and he readily grants my request to use the car. By comparing these two days and the differing results of the same request, I *might* conclude that his answers differed because of a difference in his general mood. However, there is at this point no definite reason to be certain that his mood is the explanation, and so I should be quite hesitant to pass on the information as part of social psychological knowledge. If the same thing were observed repeatedly, with requests approved on "good days," and refused on "bad days," then there is much more reason to believe that his mood is indeed the explanation. There is no point in passing on information based upon a single instance for there are too many possible alternative explanations for one case. The first criterion for knowledge, then, is that it be *reliable;* it should be something that may be observed repeatedly. A finding that appears in more than one study is said to have been *replicated.* Usually, only knowledge that is replicable, that is, reliable, is of interest to social psychologists.

Second, there is no reason for me to give you information that applies only to my relations with my father. While such information might be interesting to me, if it is strictly limited to the sorts of things we do together it is of no use to anyone else. Thus information that is to be communicated must be *general* in the sense that it is neither limited to particular individuals nor to a single time and place setting. If it only happens once or if it happens only in one place, it is not particularly interesting from a sociological or psychological point of view. On the other hand if it is something concerning all people—such as an assertion that all people (or all people in our culture) are more likely to grant any request (or any request that does not directly involve the person who must approve it) after they have undergone pleasant experiences than after undergoing unpleasant ones—then it is a very useful piece of information indeed.

Certainly a unique, nonrecurring fact may be communicated to another person; historians, journalists, and others do this. However, we are interested in *principles,* generalizations about situations that are helpful in making predictions about future cases that in some ways are similar to past ones. The fact that one particular person, my father, is more amenable after a pleasant day than after an unpleasant one has limited usefulness. The principle that all people are more agreeable in similar circumstances has much greater usefulness.

Third, the information must be *integrated;* that is, it must be placed in some sort of context. Unrelated facts are practically useless, for there is no way to know their meaning. This indicates that the principle must be presented in such a way that the recipient can make the knowledge relevant to other instances with which he is acquainted. He must be able to place the new piece of information into the organization of previous information. Until this is possible the new information remains a sort of a curiosity. It is known, but no one is sure what it means, how to explain it, or how to use it. Only when it is shown to be connected to some other information or some other explanation is it truly related. In other words some sort of theoretical organization is necessary before a new idea is completely communicated from one person to another. A new finding or a new principle must be related to some set of principles before it is entirely understood and its significance is apparent.

In this book we shall be very much concerned with developing *reliable, general, integrated* knowledge. Applying these three criteria to the enormous catalog of possible topics and data in social psychology has two further implications. First, we focus on data and information that is established according to the rules governing maximum communicability. Findings that do not replicate or that apply only to a few specific situations will not deeply concern us. Second, we shall constantly be trying to place the findings of social psychology in a theoretical context: to tell what these findings mean, how sociological knowledge relates to psychology and the reverse, how new findings relate to previous findings, and how to reduce a large amount of empirical data to a few general theoretical principles.

At this point it is helpful to introduce terms describing the nature of knowledge and research in social psychology. Knowledge is contained in *sentences* that name the phenomena of interest and tell what we know about them. The purpose of research is either to *establish* knowledge sentences where none exists or to *revise* existing knowledge. (Establishing knowledge is much less common than revising knowledge, for in most areas there are myths and "folk wisdom" regarding phenomena even in the absence of any reliable, general, integrated knowledge.) In either case the basic structure of research is the same: a knowledge sentence is stated and then is subjected to *empirical test*; that is, to a comparison with *data*. On this basis the proposed knowledge candidate is either accepted or rejected. A knowledge sentence subjected to empirical test is called an *hypothesis*. If acceptance of a new hypothesis entails rejection of another hypothesis, knowledge is revised. If nothing previously was known (or believed) about the subject, knowledge is established.

Empirical hypotheses claim that change in one thing will lead to changes in a second thing. For example, "The higher the occupational status of an individual, the greater his influence in jury discussions." The two "things" related are called *variables,* since they are allowed to vary in their values. The value of the first variable (in this case, status) affects the value of the second variable (influence). The variable (status) that produces the effect is the *independent variable*; the one that is affected (influence) is the *dependent variable.* In order to perform an empirical test of a hypothesis, the investigator finds or creates a social situation in which the value of the independent variable is known, and then he examines data to see whether the dependent variable does in fact have the predicted (or hypothesized) value.

You will appreciate that correspondence of independent and dependent variables is never so simple in the empirical world as it is hypothesized to be. Therefore investigators use statistics to tell them how likely they are to make a mistake if they accept a hypothesis on the basis of their observations.[1] If the chance of making an error by accepting the hypothesis is small—usually less than 5 percent—then they say the results are *statistically significant* and accept the hypothesis.

Developed fields use the experimental method for testing hypotheses and because the term is given a wide variety of meanings in common usage, it will help our communication if we give it an explicit definition here. For us:

> An *experiment* is an empirical study in which the investigator identifies and controls the independent variable before data are collected on the dependent variable.

This does *not* mean that in an experiment the investigator has no idea what the outcome will be. If his hypothesis has been formulated carefully, he knows very nearly exactly what the outcome should be. The definition states that he exerts control over the independent variable, and then observes

---

[1] These remarks are intended to give sufficient introduction to these topics to permit understanding of the text; they are far from complete descriptions of statistics.

what effect this control has on the value of the dependent variable. Research in which the independent variable is controlled by Nature rather than by the experimenter is *observational* rather than experimental. Of course there are instances in which experimental control is impractical, impossible, or immoral; in these cases observational research designs are used. Choice of type of research depends upon many factors—not the least of which is the training and familiarity of the investigator—but the reliability of knowledge is completely independent of the type of research that produced it.

Relevance

One basic way to classify disciplines dealing with knowledge is to ask whether they are concerned primarily with knowledge for its own sake or concerned with knowledge primarily for its relation to people. The distinction is a subtle one, since any field must value knowledge to some extent on its own merits; at the same time the knowledge should sometimes be useful for human purposes. The question is, why is knowledge *primarily* sought? Fields differ to the extent that that they seek all knowledge, following up theoretical problems even when no immediate application is apparent; or that they seek to solve immediate problems, bringing to bear whatever knowledge—theory, insight, guesses—is available.

In psychology one group is interested primarily in the knowledge. These are psychologists who develop mathematical models of the behavior of theoretical constructs. At the opposite pole are clinical psychologists, interested in whatever techniques can help a patient regardless of their theoretical status. In sociology we find some professionals very much concerned with theory construction and little concerned with contemporary social problems; others just the opposite.[2]

For some reason social sciences were particularly singled out for criticism a few years ago on grounds of nonrelevance. Presumably this criticism means that these fields were too much concerned with developing knowledge for its own sake, and too little concerned with practical application of what we knew. More recently such complaints are less evident, perhaps because just counting the number of modern sociologists and psychologists dealing with practical problems shows what a majority they constitute in both professions. Social and clinical problems exist not for lack of effort to apply principles to solve them; the reasons are human resistance to introduction of practices based upon what we do know, and the vast areas in which we simply have no theory that can help.

---

[2] In the natural sciences, the distinctions have caused disciplines to separate and to establish their own traditions. Astrology and astronomy, for example, are concerned with the same general subject matter but for very different reasons. Astrological knowledge consists primarily of facts relating star and planet positions to human affairs; astronomy is concerned not at all with relations between the sky and human affairs.

Sometimes a call for relevance in social psychology can be seen as a request for help solving one's personal problems. By this standard a "relevant" course is one that helps a student to get along better with his family and friends. Such purposes certainly are important and any course ought to help them indirectly. But no course is likely to give direct, specific advice. Why not? Because everyone's life is unique—a perfectly singular set of circumstances and experiences. No one course and no single book possibly could deal with every unique individual. The best we can do is to try to provide general principles that can later be applied by individuals to specific cases. The situation is quite similar to the relation existing between physicists and engineers: physicists work to develop general principles of, say, mechanics. Engineers can then apply these principles to specific cases in designing a freeway overpass to carry a particular weight of vehicles in particular conditions of weather, geology, and so on. In genetics theoretical principles of natural selection and competition for survival which Darwin developed are applied to produce larger and more attractive flowers, vegetables, and meat animals. Of course as these examples suggest, the task of application is no less difficult nor less important than the task of developing principles. It is simply different, and different types of problems must be solved.

To argue for either a generalizing or a practical orientation as superior seems silly to me, for both branches of a discipline can learn from the other. Ideally in social psychology as in the natural sciences, people interested in knowledge for its own sake would develop and test theories, clinicians and social problems people would apply them to specific cases. Part of the value of theories lies in their applicability, and part of the value of applied work comes from successful applications and tests of theories.

In order to avoid later misunderstandings, perhaps we should reiterate that this book is primarily concerned with developing general principles of interpersonal behavior and not with any specific applications of them. What principles are developed should be applicable, and part of their value will be realized only when they are applied. However, this book cannot help *directly* with anyone's personal problems, any more than a physicist could be a direct help in repairing a television set. There are books on electronics, and there are some very good books on clinical psychology and social welfare. A social psychologist might hope his students and readers will find the ideas in his courses and in his text helpful in a practical sense from time to time, but he hopes even more that students will appreciate the ideas for their own merit.

On Being Value-Free

Students of social psychology are often told—mistakenly, I believe—that the field they are studying is or should be value-free. Sociologists and psychologists are presented as cold, detached observers and explainers of the way things *are*. How things *might be* or how they *ought to be* are things they never consider. What is surprising is that anyone could seriously propose such a description of students of human behavior. Social psychologists are not value-free nor could they be value-free even if they tried. Moreover, they are good reasons why the field would be worse off if we were to become value-free.

In the best sense of the word, to be value-free means to prevent one's wishes from affecting his beliefs about the way things are. A social psychologist who hopes to find black children's school achievement equal to white children's should not let his hopes affect the data he collects; he should find the same results of measures as another person who wants to find racial differences in achievement would find. In this sense and in this sense only, any investigator of the empirical world should strive to keep his own values out of his research.

But research activities involve much more than data or findings of a study. Almost every other aspect of social psychology is, and should be, intimately involved with the social psychologist's values. The decision to study social psychology, the commitment to increasing empirical knowledge, the belief in certain types of evidence (for example, intersubjectively verifiable evidence over intuition), the particular problems chosen for investigation, and even the interpretation placed upon data collected—all these are affected by values held by the social psychologist. To pretend they are not obscures the way people work and also the structure of the discipline.

Certain values that are developed in empirical researchers serve as primary safeguards against the accumulation of erroneous or misleading information. For example, social psychologists place high value on intersubjectively observable data; they are unlikely to believe someone who claims knowledge based upon something nobody else can observe. This value leads social psychologists to attempt to replicate each other's research, and sometimes, to find errors of procedure that led to false results.

Another value developed in researchers is that raw data are almost sanctified. One never, *never* misrepresents actual data collected in a study (though of course many different *interpretations* may be placed upon the same data). This value is probably enforced more strongly than any other among one's colleagues. Rosenthal tells of a biologist who committed suicide as the result of being *suspected* (wrongly, it turns out) of falsifying his data. When data are presented in research articles, the values of honesty in reporting data and intersubjective verifiability are the main safeguards against accumulation of all sorts of unsupportable or false knowledge claims. Even an investigator who very much wants to see his hypotheses confirmed by research would be outraged if someone suggested that he lie about data.[3]

Few people passively observe the world, taking in information about it as a computer might. The social psychologist who studies environmental in-

[3] In 1974 a cancer researcher was found to have falsified data from skin graft experiments on rats. He was dismissed from his job, and other scientists were quoted as saying the episode endangered the reputation of one of the world's foremost medical research centers.

fluences upon intelligence may hope to learn things to help children who come from impoverished environments; one who studies effects of conformity behavior upon interpersonal liking may want to help people decide when and how much to conform to some groups. A researcher who designs an experiment to test some carefully thought out hypotheses usually cares passionately about whether those hypotheses receive empirical confirmation. Many of the people who have done the most to advance our knowledge of the world are deeply involved in the knowledge they gain. How could it have seemed otherwise?

What we properly ask of social psychologists is that they place their highest value upon gaining and improving knowledge; as part of this goal, fair data collection, honest reports of results, and separation of one's own interpretations from actual numbers observed are crucial. After these, what values the investigator holds are rather unimportant even though in some circumstances they affect his interpretation of the data. As a general rule the investigator should accept a responsibility to stack the cards against his hopes in designing empirical research; that is, to design the most *stringent* possible test of his hypotheses. Then if he finds his ideas confirmed, the evidence is much more impressive than it would be if a weaker test had been designed. Whenever his interpretations of data are likely to be affected by his values, as in studies of socially sensitive or controversial problems, others should demand that the investigator make those values clear from the outset.

Another part of the "question of values" in social psychology is concerned with evaluations—of evidence, of ideas, of research design and conclusions, and of controversial issues. Making evaluations is one of the most difficult tasks people face, but to try to avoid it behind the mask of being value-free is wrong. One thing a course in social psychology should do is to help develop criteria for telling good ideas from bad, good research from bad research, probably true statements from probably false ones, and well supported hypotheses from mere conjecture.

The use to whch knowledge is put or may be put has always been a difficult problem for empirical scientists. I once knew a physicist who refused to work on atomic fission in the 1930s since he believed the knowledge gained would be put to military use. This decision, however, is not one for which the study of physics prepared him. Rather it is a decision made as a citizen, the sort of decision that any other citizen would be equally competent to make. Suppose social psychological knowledge someday enabled a dictator to gain control of the world and to maintain himself in power. This, most of us agree, would be an evil usage of the knowledge of our field. But there is nothing in the study of social psychology that says such a use is more or less likely than the layman thinks it is. A social psychologist who makes a decision not to help collect a certain type of knowledge because it may later be put to uses he disapproves of makes that decision as a citizen, not as a professional social psychologist.

For anyone concerned about the possible eventual misuse of social psychological knowledge, here are some comforting thoughts. First, we have no strong reason to believe in an inherent evil of people, so it is possible that no such potential dictator would emerge in the future. It seems plausible, for instance, that with a lot more knowledge of interpersonal behavior than we now possess, such phenomena as dictatorships may become more and more difficult to establish and maintain. Second, we are a long, long way from possessing even a minimum amount of information that can be used for either good or evil purposes. What we do not know in social psychology is much more than what we do know. Third, any proposed strategies tend to generate their own antidotes; they tell people not only how to acquire power over others, for instance, but how to prevent anyone from succeeding at gaining power. Machiavelli's *The Prince* has been available for centuries now, yet no actual "prince" has successfully employed many of the tactics suggested. Even with a large accumulation of social psychological knowledge, we should have faith in the variety and the ingenuity of human beings to keep the set of things we *don't* know large enough to be interesting and the likelihood of misuse of social psychological knowledge quite small.

To the Chapters

Social psychology is a large field, and it currently appears to be one in which both the numbers of people studying phenomena and the amount of empirical data regarding phenomena are increasing rapidly. It would be impossible to provide a comprehensive picture of the field or of the current state of knowledge in social psychology in any single work; thus some conscious limitations of scope are necessary. In this book we shall be concerned with relations between individuals, the ways in which people in immediate interaction behave, and especially with ways in which the presence of one another influences that behavior. Adopting this viewpoint implies that some areas studied by psychologists will be omitted, including some areas of great theoretical or applied interest. For instance we shall have little to say about effects of strictly individual determinants of behavior, such as individual differences in intelligence, different child-rearing practices, or special experiences of the individual.

These are all important areas, but they are not strictly concerned with interpersonal behavior. Similarly effects of various social structures—bureaucracies, schools, military organizations—have all been studied elsewhere and will be mentioned in this work only when they affect interpersonal behavior. Linguistic development, propaganda, and mass behavior, which all have been made central parts of other treatments of social psychology, are studied here as only *parts* of our interests.

By contrast we will be very much concerned with the ways in which people act in informal associations and in informally organized groups. To some extent all these fields overlap. Any division of the sort described here is bound to be arbitrary and can only be justified pragmatically; a student cannot attend to everything at once.

On the other side of the coin it could be argued that phenomena included in this text are intrinsically very important, and that an understanding of the elementary forms of social interaction is necessary to most studies of other fields of sociology and psychology. As a social psychologist I feel that these topics are important, and even more, that they are fascinating—without such beliefs, I could never have sustained the interest necessary to study them and to write a book such as this.

A feature of studies described will become apparent to the reader of this book: data reported and analyzed here often come from experimental studies of social behavior. Again the choice is partly arbitrary and, like all arbitrary choices, it reflects the background of the author. My training is in experimental social psychology; it is the field I know best, and results from laboratory studies of social behavior are the ones I feel most competent to analyze and evaluate. There are good data from other types of research as well: surveys, participant observation, and other naturalistic studies. At some points we include these data, especially when the phenomena they describe can be related to principles used to analyze experimental studies.

Part I of this text, Chapters 1 through 8, is concerned with basic social processes: ways in which individuals affect each other, how groups affect individuals' attitudes and behaviors, how groups are affected by their members, and what sorts of concepts and principles emerge from early studies in social psychology. These chapters deal with the basic substantive subjects of social psychology: what interpersonal processes are studied, how they are studied, and what knowledge we have accumulated about them. We take up the growth and persistence of social norms, conformity behavior, group effects, and conceptions of task ability and their effects upon social structure.

Part II, Chapters 9 through 14, is concerned with theories in social psychology, the ways we explain and predict phenomena of interest. At present, there are two main *types* of theoretical orientation in social psychology, and within each type, there are a variety of specific theories of particular phenomena. Chapter 9 describes the first type of theory, exchange, and outlines several contemporary exchange theories. Chapters 10 and 11 show applications of exchange theories to specific situations. Chapter 12 describes the second type of theory, consistency, with examples. Chapters 13 and 14 show applications of consistency theories. This section begins with an introduction to criteria for developing acceptable theory in social psychology, and the place of theory in knowledge.

Part III, Chapters 15 through 17, deals with selected substantive topics which are currently receiving systematic attention of several investigators: self-evaluation, justice in social interaction, and issues in experimentation. These topics, interesting in themselves, seem quite likely to be the scene of considerable increases in understanding within the next few years.

We are now ready to begin investigating one of the most varied intellectual areas. Phenomena in social psychology range from the broadest questions of how people think and organize knoweldge to the most specific question of rates of change in accepting others' opinions. The variety of social settings in which these phenomena appear likewise is great: subjects alone in the laboratory working on strange tasks; groups discussing the disposition of a juvenile delinquent; students simulating a theater fire, panic, or a flood; and change of political or social attitudes during college. Social psychologists seem to be everywhere, and they seem to be interested in everything.

As you read summaries of each study, it will help to keep four questions in mind: (1) What are the independent and dependent variables? (2) What are the hypotheses, and were they confirmed? (3) What was the interpretation of results, and is it reasonable? (4) How do these findings fit in with what was known before? Someone else might study the same works and emphasize other features and organizing principles, and in fact being able to come to one's own conclusions about the works is a reasonable goal for any student. However, an uninformed opinion is less help than no opinion at all; an explanation that is not based upon specifiable evidence is unlikely to be received with either sympathy or respect. Thus while it may at times seem that we are examining the finest details of some studies rather than "getting an overall feeling" for them, the effort should be justifiable in terms of being more certain about our conclusions. To return once more to the criterion of communicability, all the work and all the knowledge in social psychology should in principle be explainable to someone who is not familiar with it. The goal of this book is to help equip the reader to explain some things about interpersonal behavior, either to himself for his own intellectual satisfaction, or to other people.

Part I

BASIC
CONCEPTS
AND
PRINCIPLES

1

Norms and
Social Structure

Introduction

One of the basic concepts in social psychology is that of *norm;* it figures in almost any topic in social psychology. Norms are the socially agreed upon rules, the definitions of what is right and proper. The term norm should be distinguished from the common usage *normal* meaning "average" or "typical," as the statistical mean. Sometimes they are the same, sometimes not. Norms tell what people *should* do, not necessarily what they do. It is normal to be between 55 and 80 inches tall in our country, but it is not *normative* in the sense that you should be in this range. It is normative to obey all traffic rules all the time, but it certainly is not normal. Generally speaking behavior following norms is in fact typical—most people follow most norms most of the time—but norms are more than simple descriptions of what people do.

Norm is derived literally from the Latin word for a carpenter's square; it is what you test attitudes and actions against to determine whether they are "right." To distinguish the meaning of norm in social psychology from other uses, we need a "working definition" of the term. A working definition is not so precise as a linguist or a philosopher might require, but it is sufficient for shared understanding among social psychologists. In other words we need a definition we can work with.

Norm: A sanctioned rule governing attitudes and behaviors.

Norms are the rules of society; they tell us what to do and even what to think. Some common norms in our culture tell us to drive on the right side of the street (a behavior), to arise in the morning and to sleep at night (behaviors), to think babies are appealing (an attitude), and to be sad when anyone—even a disliked person—dies (an attitude). Moreover norms have *sanctions* attached to them. By sanctions we mean socially-distributed rewards and punishments that are contingent upon following the norms. If you follow the norms, you get rewarded; if you violate a norm, you get punished. The most common sanction, social approval and disapproval, is distributed more or less subtly, and it usually is very effective.

Norms are both prescriptive and proscriptive; that is, they tell us what to do or think and what *not* to do or think. Certain attitudes and actions are so strongly proscribed that they may be called "norms of nonoccurrence"; things that virtually never occur are governed by these norms. For example incest (however defined) is extremely rare in any culture, so we can say the incest taboo is a proscriptive norm of nonoccurrence. Norms are rules that convey a feeling of "should" or "ought:" they prescribe or proscribe what people believe should be the way things are.

We have a tremendous number of norms, potentially enough of them to govern every waking moment. Yet because most of us learn the norms of our culture quite well, most of the time we are not aware of them. Think for a moment about the variety of rules we have available: "Drive on the right side of the road"; "Extend your right hand upon meeting someone for the first time, *but* do not extend your hand first if you are noticeably younger, or if you are male and the other person is female"; "Tell your friends they look good even when they don't—and in fact, tell strangers they look good even if they look *terrible*." So many rules, and many of them are quite complicated! But we take them for granted, so it is only when something forces us to see a contrast, such as when someone follows different norms, that we are made aware of them.

It is normative in our country to take a bath or a shower about once a day. If you do so much more often or much less often, people think you're strange and tell you so. In other words they distribute negative sanctions to you. Most Europeans think a bath once a week is about right; they say we are drying out our skin, and we say they smell bad. In great-grandmother's day, many people were sewed into long underwear for the winter, so we presume they didn't bathe for months. We accept uncritically the normative belief that education is a good thing. It is amazing how many conferences on education call for "a rethinking of our fundamental assumptions," but never include in this an examination of whether more education is always desirable. Visitors to Sweden a few years ago were treated to the spectacle of watching a whole society adjust to a new norm: they switched, one day, from driving on the left to driving on the right. It must have been memorable.

There is even a normative physical distance that people keep, a rule telling how close to approach one another. Furthermore this norm varies from place to place: South Americans stand closer than we do; the English stand farther apart. Try standing too close to someone; you will quickly see that it makes him uncomfortable, and it will probably feel uncomfortable to you also. Usually the other person will back away a little bit, to re-establish the normative distance. If you again move up, you can maneuver him across the room this way. A South American trying to have a conversation with us would think we were trying to escape him. I once spent a summer in Mexico and found that people would talk louder, almost shout, as I backed away trying to establish the distance where I felt comfortable.

Bauer recently studied racial and sex differences in physical distance. In general, he found that women stand closer than men in our country (about 10 inches for women; 15 for men), and blacks closer than whites (about 9 inches for blacks, 15 for whites). Imagine a black girl talking with a white man, each of them ill at ease simply because they have learned different norms of physical distance.

It is useful to distinguish two types of norms, *explicit* and *implicit*. Explicit norms are directly taught to people; they are openly known or easily learned. Explicit norms may even be written down as are traffic laws or high school codes of conduct. Even though there are a lot of them, explicit norms are relatively easy to learn; people will tell you what they are. Implicit norms on the other hand are much more difficult to learn. These are never written down, and people usually won't tell you what they are even if you ask. Implicit norms are not any less important for being obscure; in fact, they are usually more important than explicit norms. It is difficult enough to learn the explicit norms of a society, but implicit norms are even harder. Probably very few people learn all or nearly all of both sorts, but because both types of norms are sanctioned, the better a person knows them in general the more pleasant life is. Let us consider some explicit and implicit norms in our culture.

Explicit norms govern driving speed; there is, say, a speed limit of 55 mph on an expressway. This norm is easy to learn—it is posted on a large sign. But most police follow an implicit norm that anyone may drive 5 mph over the speed limit without getting a ticket. Moreover, the chances are that people, especially males, can get positive sanctions for driving fast; the aggressive, fast driver is socially rewarded in many parts of our culture. There is an explicit norm of honesty: tell the truth, and do not deliberately mislead people. But when someone invites you to dinner, you should praise the meal even if it was nothing special. An explicit norm says that fighting is bad; an implicit norm says that something is wrong with a child who does not get into fights occasionally. In fact the implicit norm is even more subtle: little boys are expected to fight a bit more than little girls are. Did you ever notice that grade school teachers—who are norm-trainers—punish (sanction) little girls much more severely for fighting than they punish boys?

Both implicit and explicit norms are involved in what we call "manners." Explicit norms govern simple acts of politeness and "common courtesy"; these are taught to children quite directly. More subtle norms, many of them taught only indirectly, function in areas that we say reflect "breeding:" it is much more difficult to specify the set of rules that distinguish "cultured" behavior from "commonness" or boorishness. If you suspect you have violated an implicit norm thus betraying yourself as having poor breeding, and ask someone what you did wrong, you are likely to hear, "If you don't know, there's no point in my telling you." This means, "The implicit norm is too subtle or too difficult for me to explain." What we call "rudeness" can be looked upon as violation of more or less subtle implicit norms of conduct.

Implicit norms of formality often serve to separate people of unequal status and to maintain the inequality. In our culture there is a norm that status inequality should be reflected in form of address: superiors are addressed by title and last name while peers and subordinates are addressed by first name. (Many modern languages even have two words for "you:" a familiar form used to address friends, servants, and children; and a formal one to indicate respect.) Suppose a businessman who is accustomed to

Tom Wolfe is a superb chronicler of contemporary American social history; for many years he has sensitively discerned and entertainingly written about the life styles of interesting or unusual people. Much of the life style of any individual is determined by the norms he follows, and some very subtle norms can be crucial for setting oneself off from "the masses." These norms, as Wolfe demonstrates in the following selection, function to isolate a cultural subgroup of glamorous people from the rest of us as effectively as the cultural norms of China set off American tourists there.

The establishment's own styles—well, for one thing they were too dull. And those understated clothes, dark woods, high ceilings, silversmithery, respectable nannies, and so forth and so on. For centuries their kind of power created styles . . . but with the thickening democratic façade of American life, it has degenerated to various esoteric understatements, often cryptic—Topsiders instead of tennis sneakers, calling cards with "Mr." preceding the name, the right fork.

The magazines and newspapers began looking for heroines to symbolize the Other Society . . . Christina Paolozzi! Her exploits! Christina Paolizzi threw a twenty-first birthday party for herself at a Puerto Rican pachanga palace, the Palladium, and after that the spinning got faster and faster until with one last grand centripetal gesture she appeared in the nude, face on, in *Harpers Bazaar*. Some became Girls of the Year because their fame suddenly shed a light on their style of life, and their style of life could be easily exhibited, such as Jackie Kennedy and Barbra Streisand. (Wolfe, 1965, p. 177.)

being addressed as "Mr." by the secretaries finds himself stranded in a subway breakdown with secretaries. One effect of crisis situations is the breakdown of status inequality: after a few hours everybody is usually on a first name basis. The next morning at the office there is likely to be a rather awkward period while both the businessman and the secretaries try to figure out whether or not to return to the formal forms of address. The same sort of awkwardness can ensue the morning after an office party at which sexual advances (presumably on a first name basis) have been made.

Probably the most difficult implicit norms to learn are those that serve to separate behaviors of people in different social and economic classes. These norms thus provide a strong basis for invidious distinctions—between those who know them and those who do not. The wealthy, the glamorous, and the pretenders to both categories learn a body of implicit norms that serve to insulate themselves from others, and to enable them to recognize other members of their ingroup. "One just doesn't *do* such-and-such."

We have an explicit norm that says you should marry anyone you wish as long as it's "truly love." There are dozens of implicit norms that limit or cancel the explicit norm in a variety of circumstances. For example implicit norms say do not marry someone too different from your own ethnic, racial, religious, or economic background. Marry anyone you truly love—except if she is a Jew (or a *shiksa,* depending on your background). My favorite story illustrating explicit and implicit marriage norms comes from an interview with a famous upper-class English lady. Her nephew had decided he was tired of being a nephew and would rather be a niece. He came to Johns Hopkins Hospital for a sex change operation and after successful recovery, began life as a woman. Eventually he met and fell in love with a garage mechanic, a black man, and they decided to marry. A reporter asked his aunt what she thought of all this and especially of the man her niece had chosen. The reply: "Well, of course the important thing is that they really love each other (the explicit norm). But somehow I can't help wishing (here comes the implicit norm!) that he hadn't decided to marry a Baptist."

In cases where implicit norms conflict with explicit norms, the implicit norm almost always takes precedence. If the explicit norm says to do one thing and the implicit norm says another, social rewards generally are given for following the implicit norm. Think of our traffic example. If in a given area the implicit norm says to drive 10 mph over the speed limit, drivers who know the norm are likely to get angry and rude to a driver who comes in who follows the explicit norm. He holds up traffic and gets negative sanctions for doing so. The fact that we are sympathetic to him because implicit norms are difficult to learn does not in the least diminish the sanctions distributed to a slowpoke. The Baltimore area has an implicit traffic norm I haven't seen anywhere else: it is acceptable to continue going through an intersection for about 5 seconds *after* the light turns red. It can be very important for a newcomer to learn this norm, but he has to learn it by watching others or by trial and error.

Normative values in any culture constantly undergo change, some slowly and some rapidly. When the norms change we wonder how in the world people could have accepted the old norms, just as we wonder how in the world foreigners could have different norms from our own.

Norms regarding war—and particularly norms telling what are socially acceptable feelings to express when talking about war—have changed remarkably for Americans within the last couple of decades. During the years of World War II, war was widely considered if not glorious, at least adventurous and honorable. After a decade of fighting in Vietnam the idea of war lost its appeal, both to those calling themselves "hawks" and "doves": it is a dirty, unpleasant business, and soldiers—even POWs—receive little thanks or esteem from civilians when they return home. The changes in attitude— or what is more pertinent here, the changes in norms that describe *appropriate* attitudes towards war—are striking, and we can see them because they have taken place within a relatively few years.

The changes in normatively-sanctioned attitudes are reflected in words to popular songs. In 1946 Perry Como sold well over a million copies of a song that joked about bombing the Japanese. In 1966 several songs were sold with words that objected to bombing anybody.

"The mores [norms] can make anything right, and can prevent condemnation of anything," Sumner observed in 1906. In one sense this is true. However if Sumner meant this as an assertion about norms, he is not quite correct, I think. The point is that norms *define* what is right; the norms *are* what is right. They are not imposed from outside; rather they reflect the shared beliefs of individuals in a social system. Norms do not justify any behavior. They describe behaviors that people already have decided are acceptable.

Norms Provide Structure

Norms, as we have seen, are sometimes arbitrary; they are culturally relative, and they can sometimes look funny under close examination. But they are not silly. Norms provide the social structure; they give us a way to look at the world and to interpret actions of ourselves and others. One way of looking at different cultures is through their norms. From this point of view, what defines our culture and our ways of living are the explicit and implicit norms that we follow. Learning to be an American, or a student, or a physician means learning the norms of people in each group.

What we call "formal occasions"—formal dinners, formal receptions, graduation ceremonies—are social situations possessing a high degree of normative structure. There are norms, that is, that govern nearly every possible type of action, rules telling every person whom to associate with, how to talk and act, when to arrive, and when to leave. By contrast "informal" occasions are those situations with less structure. One may come and go more freely, dress more as he chooses, and say what he pleases to whom he chooses. (But note that there are still restrictions—only the latitude for choice is wider.) By analogy social structure implies certain limitations on the social action of an individual, just as a physical structure such as an office building implies certain limitations on physical behaviors.

Another distinction between relatively formal and relatively informal situations is that they differ in the number of decisions an individual must make. People such as ambassadors, who are very accustomed to formal occasions, can almost go through them in their sleep. The social structure governs their actions and their appearance so closely that they rarely have to make decisions about anything. All that is necessary is to step into the social structure and to occupy a prescribed position within it for a prescribed length of time.

Becoming aware of the norms, learning a social structure, can most easily be done by deliberate violation of a few suspected norms to see what will happen. Children often employ this means: they will violate one or more norms just to see what will occur. For example if someone asks, "How are you?" a child may decide to violate the norm that dictates simply saying "Fine"; he might say, "I feel lousy." Most of us learn quickly that there is a norm operative here. The result of violating even this simple and relatively unimportant norm can destroy any chance for future interaction between two people. I suspect there are many people in the world who are lonely just because they never learned the implicit norm that says do not tell me the whole truth if I ask how you feel.

Professor Garfinkel at UCLA used to instruct his introductory sociology classes to deliberately violate some norms as an assignment and to note others' reactions to the violations. Some students would go into a large department store adjoining the campus and try to bargain with a salesperson over the price of some major appliance or other expensive item. We have a norm in our country that tells us that prices (excluding autos and houses) are fixed; one does not offer the salesman 20 percent less than the price he asks for a washing machine. It's a simple norm, one not shared in any other American country except Canada; we might think, therefore, that violating it would be dismissed lightly. Not so. The desire to bargain over price typically is met with incredulity and often with suspicion and hostility as well. What good American would try to get a washing machine at a 20 percent discount?

The distinction between implicit and explicit norms is pertinent to difficulties children have learning the norms of their subculture. Because any society has such a wide variety of norms, it takes a long time to learn what they are—that is, what acceptable, appropriate attitudes and behavior are. In our culture it seems to take up to about adolescence for children to learn the most important of the explicit norms. About this time they begin to be treated as semiadults; they also become aware of the implicit norms. Remember that there are far more implicit norms than explicit, and that the implicit are much harder to learn. New challenges are placed upon these people, just about at the time they thought they were finally beginning to understand their society: they learn that explicit norms are not sufficient at all, and there is a whole other set of semisecret rules to be learned. A very common response to this—to learning of the existence of implicit norms —is to try to reassert the primacy of explicit norms. They say that adult society is "hypocritical," meaning of course that it follows a set of implicit norms that sometimes countermands the rules of the explicit norms. Charges of hypocrisy come almost exclusively from people whom we might expect to have trouble learning implicit norms—particularly the young. As these people get older, they seem to become less discontent. We could say that they have "sold out" their earlier values; or we could say that they have learned and have come to some sort of peace with the implicit norms of their society.

Within almost any age group or other subgroup of the population, it is possible to see norm conflict that might be called hypocritical. Is it hypocritical for adults to praise someone's terrible cooking or admire "ugly" clothes? Most adolescents know that it is customary to praise the quality of and to comment upon (with particular phrases that vary from place to place) the unusual quality and potency of marijuana that someone shares with his friends—even if your private opinion is that it is mostly sawdust.

When somebody knows the norms for a particular situation, or what is equally significant, when he *thinks* he knows the norms, they are the sort of thing that it is comfortable to rely upon. It seems to be reassuring to know that one can count on others to behave in a certain way, to know that the situation contains at least a minimum of structure as the result of norms governing interaction. When others violate our normative expectations the world becomes a little less comfortable for us. It is disturbing, and in fact there is considerable documentation of the behavior that accompanies violation of normative expectations. Norm violation produces emotional behavior of some sort, frequently anger.

When a norm has been thoroughly learned by an individual we say it is *internalized,* meaning it has been accepted and "taken in" by the individual so that it becomes a part of him. There is no hard and fast rule just how well a norm must be adopted for us to say it is internalized, but in most cases the degree of internalization is considerable. Once norms are internalized, actors "carry" them about inside themselves; for instance, foreigners carry about and display the internalized norms of their home countries, thus making their behavior noticeably different from our own. An internalized set of norms provides an internalized social structure.

Normlessness

Psychologists stress that people need some way to classify the sense impressions that reach their eyes and ears (and to lesser extent, their organs of smell, touch, and taste) in order for these sense impressions to have meaning. Without some way to classify, say, retinal images and the pressure of sound waves, the world is as William James said, "a bloomin' buzzin' confusion." Optical illusions, such as the famous picture of two faces that turn into a vase or the rabbit that begins to look like an antelope, illustrate the degree to which interpretation affects what we see. What objectively exists in these cases is lines upon a page; what makes these lines have meaning, however, is a mental classification that makes them into an object. One does not look at a drawing and think, "these are lines upon a page," anymore than one looks at a blue shirt and perceives a particular frequency of angstrom units.

Sociologists add that the same process applies to social action: the same arm movement may be a threat to strike, a joking gesture, an innocent twitch, or something else. What makes action meaningful is the categories we use to classify it. One of the major schools in social psychology, symbolic interactionism, studies interpersonal behavior through the classifications individuals use for themselves and others. Most social interaction takes place in terms of symbols: we threaten rather than actually hit someone; we pay in checks instead of money or goods; we let a particular piece of cloth symbolize our country for us, and we direct towards that cloth all the feelings we have towards our country. Although we will not limit ourselves to studying action from the viewpoint of symbolic interactionism, the significance of classification to thought and social action cannot be overemphasized.

Speaking for both sense impressions and any sort of social action we can say *perception without classification is impossible.*

Virtually no interaction is entirely without structure. Almost always there are rules and classifications, though these may be subtle and difficult to discover. Moreover people spend a surprising amount of time trying to learn these norms. At this point we note a general principle and will spend much of the remainder of this chapter elaborating and explaining it.

There is something unpleasant about an unstructured situation. People appear psychologically distressed in situations that lack guides to their conduct. They try to classify, to categorize, both their surroundings and other people with whom they interact. Why do people do this? Because an unstructured situation lacks (normative) guides for our actions. Because the actions themselves have no symbolic meanings. Because unstructured situations are unpredictable, and therefore frightening. Now let us examine these features in more detail.

Newspaper columns of advice may be viewed as instruments of norm-learning for individuals: they provide guides to appropriate attitudes and actions in various social situations. One of the leading columns is titled, "Do the Correct Thing"; a social psychologist might prefer to title this and similar columns, "How to Structure an Unstructured Situation."

Usually these columns deal with implicit norms, for presumably the inquirers would not have to write at all if the issue concerned one of the explicit norms of their culture. Moreover the columns frequently deal with issues in which norms are changing, such as whether to call an unmarried woman "Miss" or "Ms." (Amy Vanderbilt writes one of these columns, and she strongly favors "Miss.") Very often the norms provided in the advice are related to socioeconomic status; that is, they present what members of the upper class do as what is right and proper. Generally speaking, advice on conduct is sought by members of working class or middle class origin, and what they want to know is how people who are wealthier than they lead their lives. (On these grounds we may conclude that Miss Vanderbilt is an excellent person to ask.) When the changes in society are so rapid and of so great a magnitude that "all rules are off," or in other words, when there are few norms which give stable meanings to objects and actions, we have a situation lacking in structure. Sociologists, following Durkheim, have a special term for a lack of structure: *anomie,* or *anomic situations.* Anomic situations, as we noted earlier calling them "unstructured situations," are unpleasant for the individuals involved. During times of increased anomie in entire countries, such as that experienced during either rapid industrialization or economic depression, Durkheim has shown that suicide rates rise. For many of the reasons previously mentioned—the need to simplify the world in order to deal with it, the desire to promote smooth social interactions, the desire to have some shared understandings of what is what—it is easy to understand in an intuitive way why anomie should be unpleasant. We might also expect that if anomic or unstructured situations are unpleasant, then individuals will try to avoid them and may also try to impose some structure on them. It is necessary for social actors to be able to order their perceptions and classifications according to what is often called a *frame of reference*. The frame of reference is a set of norms we use for judging perceptions and people, and it provides the rules by which an individual can partially structure an unstructured situation.

The frame of reference provided may be either objective or social; that is, it may be the sort provided by some measure such as distance or time, or it may depend upon judgments and opinions of others. For example if I want to know whether or not I am likely to be an asset to the track team, I might employ an objective frame of reference and note how many minutes and seconds it takes me to run a mile, comparing this to a table of track records. On the other hand I might employ a social frame of reference: I could ask my friends what they think of my ability. The social psychologist Festinger has theorized that individuals have an innate desire to compare their attitudes and abilities, and that they prefer an objective comparison to a social comparison. If a table of standards is available, people will choose it; if not, they will rely on social comparison standards.

However it has always seemed to me that the social frame of reference is ultimately more significant. How are we to interpret an objective piece of information, such as the fact that someone can run a mile in 5 minutes, 40 seconds, without some social frame of reference? Is this fast or slow? Will it get him on the team? Giving meaning to an objective frame of reference depends on the opinions of others; to social definition, that is.

Ultimately, *there is no reality except social reality*. Put differently, the interpretations that people place upon sense perceptions are the basically significant material for answering the question "What does it mean?" This point is easily appreciated in the case of colors: is that wall blue or turquoise? It should be even more clearly true in the case of opinions: do my political attitudes classify me as a "liberal?" The appreciation of particular types of music or foods—which after all are nothing more than stimuli acting upon receptors of sound, smell, and taste—is almost entirely determined by social norms.

To summarize the points we have considered up to now, we began with the observation that behavior occurs in a social context and that to a greater or lesser extent the social context limits the types of behavior that will occur. The term for the context that limits behavior is *social structure*, and we may speak of situations as possessing more or less structure, roughly equivalent to more or less formality, according to how many norms or rules there are for attitudes and behavior. Any action and any understanding of situations seems to require that an individual perform some simplifying operation upon the myriad of sense impressions he receives from his environment. This simplification is called structuring the environment. We have noted that unstructured situations usually appear to be uncomfortable to the individual. Structuring the environment requires either adapting and using a previous frame of reference or developing a new one for very unfamiliar situations. The frame of reference used may be either objective or social, though it might be argued that only social frames of reference are ultimately useful.

Anyone who has spent time with young children becomes impressed with the extent to which they display opinions and attitudes that we may assume they seldom have the opportunity or the need to act upon. Children who are too young to vote express opinions on political issues and either liking or disliking of well-known political figures. Children who are too young to select their own clothes express strong preferences for certain styles and colors; children who have had little exposure to certain forms of classical music will express strong preferences and opinions regarding some pieces—sometimes including pieces they have never heard.

With very young children these strong likes and dislikes are sometimes pointed out by their parents and cited as evidence that, "He certainly makes up his own mind on things." A slightly sophisticated observer of these phenomena will note that there generally is a high degree of agreement between attitudes and opinions of the child and of the parent. Parents who proudly point to evidence of their child's individualistic decision making seem frequently to cite examples in which the child has come to the same conclusions as the parents. None of this is too surprising nor too unusual: where else could we expect a child 10 years old to get his political opinions if not from his parents? From reading campaign speeches or from editorials in *The New York Times?* We might expect that most people's opinions are formed partially through their own individual seeking of information and partially by adopting the opinions of others. However, since most of us have been told since childhood that we should not allow others' opinions to influence us, most of us would deny—perhaps even to ourselves—that others' opinions affect our own to any significant extent.

Opinion formation and social judgments are instances of structuring unfamiliar situations. Suppose a child who knows nothing about either of two Presidential candidates is asked whom he prefers. From his point of view, this is an unstructured situation. There is no frame of reference to tell him what to answer or even what factors to consider in coming to an answer. But it is embarrassing to admit that you have no answer to a question that someone else considers important. One possible place to get the needed information is from others, and one's parents usually are accessible and very willing to pass on their political opinions.

What is at issue here is not whether a person's attitudes and beliefs are influenced by other people, since all attitudes and beliefs rest ultimately upon information from other individuals. But we can distinguish direct influence from indirect influence: to influence someone's opinions indirectly, we provide him enough information that he can reach his own conclusion; to influence his opinion directly, we tell him what conclusion he should reach.

We have a fairly strong explicit norm stating that only indirect influence over the opinions of others is permissible. The norm is especially strong when it comes to *accepting* influence. Nobody should accept direct influence over his opinions; we should all come to our own conclusions. But the suspicion persists that direct as well as indirect influences exist in people's opinions and attitudes. Is there any way to distinguish between the two types of influence so that we can observe their effects separately?

The Basic Experimental Situation

What we have been describing is one instance of a more general problem, which was of interest to a social psychologist named Sherif. He developed one of the classic experimental settings for studying the exertion of influence, now called the "Sherif experiment." It is an ideal setting to study both direct and indirect influence over individuals' beliefs. As we shall see, the beliefs that develop are normative; that is, sanctioned rules.

The situation Sherif developed for study of the formation and the persistence of norms may be called the "basic experimental situation" for these issues. Often it is the case that a particular problem, or a particular set of problems, is most easily studied in a particular type of experimental setting. It is helpful to learn to recognize the basic experimental setting developed for particular substantive interests in social psychology, and to appreciate (and evaluate) the ways in which it may be modified to study the effects of other factors.

A basic experimental design is one developed for the study of one basic social process. The Sherif experiment is the basic experimental design for study of norm formation, and the Asch experiment is the basic design for study of conformity processes (Chap. 2), and so on. The basic design defines the situation in which the process is studied and the sort of data (dependent variable) observed. Once the basic design is established and the results of basic experiments using the design are known, it may be modified later to investigate the effects of other variables. Modifications of the basic experimental design are introduced as additional independent variables for a familiar situation. Rather than learning a large series of experimental designs that differ only slightly from each other, it is preferable to learn the basic design associated with each set of interests and then subsequent modifications of the basic design.

Sherif was concerned with studying the formation of social norms in an unstructured situation. For this type of study, it is desirable that the norm used not be one that will cause major emotional arousal of people (such as norms governing religious attitudes or sexual behavior), since the effects of emotional arousal could well distort information concerned strictly with norm *formation*. What is desired then is a situation where relatively content-free norms may be studied. The situation selected makes use of a phenomenon known for centuries to astronomers. It is the *autokinetic effect*.

Against a completely dark field, a single point of light will appear to move, describing an erratic pattern of varying size for different people. Because measurement of star movements is vital to much of astronomy, the autokinetic effect is considered highly undesirable by astronomers. However, the autokinetic effect is extremely useful to social psychologists. For a person who does not know the light actually is stationary, the amount of movement he reports constitutes a belief that is remarkably free of objective content. In addition if two or more people report judgments about extent of movement, it becomes possible to study the amount of influence each exerts on others by noting the degree to which their reports coincide or diverge.

In the Sherif experiment one or more subjects are seated in a darkened room that contains a single small light source, such as the tiny flashlights used on key chains. After being allowed to adapt to the dark, the subject is repeatedly shown the light for a few seconds; after each exposure, he is asked to report how far he thought it moved. The light actually is stationary, but the experimenter tells subjects they should expect to see some degree of movement. Reports of all judgments by subjects are recorded, and they constitute the primary data of the experiment. There were 100 light judgments or trials, each of about 2 seconds' duration. At least five findings from these early studies are important to our study of norm formation.

First, individuals' judgments are not completely random. They display regularities that Sherif characterized as specific ranges and norms. For example, an individual could be characterized as displaying a range of judgments of 1–4 in. or 3–6 in.; most of his judgments after the first few trials are within that range. The distance most frequently chosen by the individual, perhaps 2 in. in the first example here and 5 in. in the second, would be called the norm for that individual. (Statistically speaking this would be called the *mode,* or the *modal judgment.* We shall have more to say about the use of the term norm later, but for the present we will follow Sherif's terminology.) The ranges and norms established by individuals alone are not all the same, so that we can say a particular range and norm is characteristic of a particular individual.

Second, the same phenomenon characterizes groups: each group develops a characteristic range and norm of reported judgments. That is, when an individual judges the autokinetic situation in a group of two or three, his judgments usually do not differ greatly from those of other members of his own group. Moreover, the group range and norm are displayed by individuals later when they judge the autokinetic situation alone. In other words the range and norm developed in the group session seem to be *internalized.*

Third, if an individual is exposed to the autokinetic situation in two sessions but in the reverse order—that is, individual alone first and later two or three of these individuals brought together into a group—the different norms formed in the private session tend to converge in the group session. In other words, individuals who previously formed their norms of judgment alone exert some influence upon each other when brought together in a group. However, Sherif reported that groups composed of members who had originally formed different norms did not converge so much in their reported judgments as did groups of individuals who had not previously been in the alone sessions.

Fourth, most subjects in this experiment, when questioned afterwards by Sherif or by one of his research assistants, said that they had made up their minds independently. This we may note is not consistent with the second or third finding; namely, that group members do tend to converge in their reports to a group range and norm.

Fifth, we note a very interesting effect produced by the introduction of *confederates*. A confederate in an experiment is someone who is indistinguishable from a subject except that he has previously been instructed by the experimenter how to behave. Use of confederates is widespread in social–psychological experimentation—we shall see many experiments employing them throughout this book—for confederates allow the experimenter to control some features of interaction between subjects which can be vital to the study. In order to distinguish a regular subject from a confederate, we often use the term *naive subject*. All that is intended by the naive label is that a subject presumably does not know some things about the experiment that a confederate knows. (When the term subject is used alone, it will always mean naive subject.)

Sherif's fifth finding comes from groups of 3 persons, two of whom were confederates. The confederates in these groups were instructed to report particular ranges and norms of judgment; for example, confederates in the first such group were preinstructed to report judgments with a range of 1–3 in. and a norm of 2 in. The naive subject in each group did not know of this manipulation, the intent of which was of course to measure influence exerted in such a group situation.

Naive subjects participated in two sessions of 50 trials each. The first session was the group session with the two confederates reporting as described, and the second session was the naive subject alone. Results from a representative group, the first, are shown in Table 1–1.

Note first in Table 1–1 that there is evidence subjects were influenced by the reports of preinstructed group members. The confederates were reporting judgments of between 1 and 3 inches, with a norm of 2. Column 2 shows that in that group, the naive subject's reports were within the range 1–5 in., with a norm of slightly more than 3⅓ in. Also 41 of 50 reports (82 percent) were within the 1–3 range of the confederates. Column 3 shows that the influence persists into the alone session. Even more interesting, it indicates that confederates were *more* influential upon subject's judgments in the alone session than they were when they were present in the group session. Any interpretation of data from a single subject is dangerous, but the data in Table 1–1 are typical of other groups Sherif observed. Let us consider briefly two facts. First, because reports in the alone session were definitely similar to reports of group members in the first session, we suspect that

TABLE 1–1   Social Influence in Autokinetic Situation

Prescribed	S in Group (Trials 1–50)	S Alone (Trials 51–100)
Range 1–3	1–5	1–4
Norm 2	3.36	2.62
% within 1–3 range	82	94

subjects really believed the amount of movement they reported; that is, they did not simply say the same things as other group members in session 1 in order to avoid appearing different. Later when they were alone, their reports were still consistent with those of the confederates. Second, the fact that individual judgments in the second session were even closer to those of confederates than they were in the first session may indicate some resistance in the first session to appearing to be influenced. This is the opposite argument from the one just considered and rejected. Here we say that a subject in the group session wants to *avoid* saying the same thing as the other group members. He does not want to give an opinion just voiced for fear of appearing to be a copycat. When he is alone in phase 2 this resistance is not important, so he is able to report the judgments he actually believes. The phase 2 judgments were very close indeed to those of group members in the first session. We shall have more to say about these two suggestions.

The alert reader may object that use of the word "norm" in the Sherif experiment appears different from the definition of that word given earlier. Do we want to say that the Sherif experiment shows that individuals and groups tend to develop and to maintain their own *norms?* If so, what are the sanctions? What punishments are allocated for reporting more or less movement than the other group members report, or what rewards can the group members give to an individual who adheres to their norm? Subjects never directly confront each other as they might in a less controlled situation, for example, by saying, "Are you sure that's right?"

Part of the answer to this question is that it is not usually the *actual* distribution of positive and negative sanctions that ensures compliance with norms, but only the *expected* distribution of sanctions. The motorist who is tempted to speed but does not actually do so for fear of receiving a ticket is not forced to obey the law by actual rewards and punishments, but only by those expected. Similarly if we knew that subjects in the group sessions of the Sherif experiment *expected* some reward for compliance to what others said—such as approval, esteem, or liking—and that they *expected* punishment—withholding of social approval—for noncompliance, then we could explain the convergence of reports in group sessions in the second and third findings. At this point of course we have no independent measure of whether subjects actually did anticipate these sanctions, but at least the interpretation seems plausible in the light of other situations that appear to be similar.

What of the individual session? Why do subjects alone tend to develop a range and norm of their judgments? Earlier we said that there is something uncomfortable about an unstructured situation, and this suggests that individuals may try to structure their environments; in other words, that in the absence of norms, individuals will feel uncomfortable and will try to establish some regular patterns for their behavior. Again on strictly intuitive grounds such an explanation appears plausible, and it well could account for the early establishment of individual norms. Discomfort associated with unstructured or anomic situations could well be one of the sanctions serving to create norms in the individual sessions.

An anecdote Sherif presented in early reports of his experiments, but which is unfortunately omitted from later reprints, indicates some support for the conjectures advanced in the last section regarding establishment and persistence of norms. It involves a conscious attempt on the part of a graduate student, a confederate who attempted to manipulate the judgments reported by "Miss X," an undergraduate whom he knew previously and perhaps had dated. In his words:

> Miss X and I (Assistant in Psychology, Columbia University) were subjects for Dr. Sherif. I was well acquainted with the experiment, but Miss X knew nothing whatsoever about it. Since she was a close friend of mine, and I carried some prestige with her, Dr. Sherif suggested that it would be interesting to see if we could predetermine her judgments. It was agreed beforehand that I was to give no judgments until she had set her own standard. After a few stimulations [presumably he means "trials"] it was quite clear that her judgments were going to vary around 5 inches. At the next appropriate stimulation, I made a judgment of 12 inches. Miss X's next judgment was 8 inches. I varied my judgments around 12 inches, and she did the same.

To this point there is nothing new. First, Miss X established her own norm, and then the confederate was able to influence her to change it. He doesn't report exactly how quickly she changed her reports, but apparently it did not take too many trials.

> Then I changed my judgment to 3 inches, suggesting to Dr. Sherif that he had changed it [presumably, the "actual" distance moved]. She gradually [note] came down to my standard, but not without some apparent resistance. When it was clear that she had accepted this new standard, Dr. Sherif suggested that I make no more judgments lest I might influence hers. He then informed her on a subsequent stimulation that she was underestimating the distance which the point moved. Immediately her judgments were made larger and she established a new standard. However, she was a little uneasy with it all, and before the experiment had progressed much farther, whispered to me, "Get me out of here." (Sherif, in Maccoby et al., 1958, p. 230.)

The poor woman! To say that she was "a little uneasy" reveals either a gross understatement or else a surprising lack of sensitivity to her feelings. In any case here we have some rather impressive evidence that, while it is possible to demonstrate influence in this situation, the influence is accompanied by considerable discomfort experienced by the person whose judgments are affected. The discomfort is particularly interesting, for at this point Miss X had no reason to believe that anyone had been deliberately trying to affect her reports nor that there was any witting attempt to distress her. It appears as though the change in perception and report is itself stressful to her, as of course we had suggested it might be in seeking to explain why norms persist when there is no intervention from the experimenter or from his assistant. Later, Miss X said, "I don't like that man" (Sherif), and refused to re-enter the laboratory.

At this point, we leave Miss X and the graduate assistant to work out this and perhaps other problems in their relationship. Before turning to later studies utilizing the Sherif experiment, we may summarize the accomplishments of this fundamental advance in social psychology experimentation.

First, Sherif developed a situation in which to study the processes of establishing and maintaining norms and beliefs independent of their content. The effect is reproducible as will be seen subsequently, in the sense that any competent experimenter can replicate the experiment and will find results similar to those Sherif reported. Second, from results of the experiment there is evidence that both individuals and groups tend to establish and to maintain distinguishable ranges and norms of judgment. Third, there is evidence that interpersonal influence occurs in this experiment, and that it plays an important part in judgments reported. Fourth, there is anecdotal evidence that change of an established norm is unpleasant to the individual, a matter that we shall have to explain more fully in later chapters. Fifth, if we rely on subjects' reports that they were not aware of being influenced, we may conjecture that they actually believed the amounts of movement they reported; and thus that not only their overt behavior, but also their beliefs were influenced in this situation. However on this last point it is desirable to find evidence that is collected under more rigorously controlled conditions.

Variations on the Basic Experiment; Stability Through Time with the Individual

Sherif's original experiment provides evidence that the norms adopted by individuals in this setting tend to persist at least for the time between two sessions on the same day, but it is worthwhile to have data gathered in a study designed more directly to investigate the persistence phenomenon. Two studies that provide such data are by Bovard and by Rohrer and his associates.

A total of 9 subjects participated in the study by Bovard, too few a number to permit much confidence in detailed statistical analyses. Hence, we shall look for trends and general findings in his results. Each subject participated in three sessions of a variant of the basic Sherif experimental situation. In session 1 the subject was alone and judged 50 trials of 5 seconds each. In session 2 one hour later, the subject was paired with a confederate who had been previously instructed to make judgments much different from the range and norm established by the naive subject in session 1. There were 50 trials in session 2, also. To increase the magnitude of influence of the confederate in session 2, he was described as being an expert in judging extent of light movement. In session 3, which occurred 28 days after sessions 1 and 2, the naive subject again judged 50 trials alone just as he had in session 1.

Relevant findings from the study are as follows. First, subjects in the experiment did establish distinctive ranges and norms in session 1 of Bovard's experiment just as they had in the original Sherif experiments. Second, they did shift their norms of judgment in session 2 in the direction of the confederates' judgments, thus indicating some social influence in session 2. Third, if subjects are ranked according to how much movement they typically report (their "norms"), then the rank order of subjects in session 2 correlates highly with the rank order of subjects in session 3. This means that those subjects who reported the most movement in session 2 were also those who reported the most movement in session 3, and similarly, those subjects reporting the least movement in session 2 were also those reporting the least movement in session 3. This third finding has two important interpretations. First, it indicates persistence of a norm through the 28-day interval between session 2 and session 3. This is relevant to our interest in persistence. Second, this finding is a replication of one of Sherif's findings; namely, that social influence (in session 2 here) persists into the "alone" condition (session 3 here). The fourth and final finding to be considered here is that if one compares the correspondence between session 1 (individual norm), session 2 (social norm) and session 3, the latter two conditions are closer. This means that the socially developed norm (session 2) persists in session 3 to a greater extent than the individually developed (session 1) norm.

On the strength of this study, we may reach two more general conclusions regarding the establishment and persistence of norms in this situation. First, it is impressive that the findings on persistence that Sherif noted incidentally have been verified in a later experiment designed more specifically to study them. The replication lends confidence to a belief that persistence of norms is to be expected. Second, the norms, and especially the socially developed norms, established in this situation have been shown to be stable for at least a duration of a month.

Rohrer et al. also studied persistence of norms, using additional modifications of the basic Sherif experimental situation. There are 46 subjects of the college undergraduate male variety favored for this sort of work. They participated in three sessions that roughly corresponded to the three in Bovard's study—session 1 judging alone, session 2 with another individual, and session 3 after some time had elapsed, alone again. However the Rohrer study differs in an important respect from other studies using the autokinetic situation in that actual light movement was used for one of the sessions. In session 1, the light observed actually moved 2 in. for half of the subjects and 8 in. for the other half. Thus in this experiment, judgments reported for the first "alone" session had some basis in objective reality—the light actually did move, and we expect subjects receiving the 2-in. actual movement to report less movement than subjects receiving the 8-in. actual movement. Session 2 and session 3 of this experiment again used the stationary light, so reports of movement in these conditions must be attributed either to effects of memory of a previous session or to effects of social influence. No confederates were used in Rohrer's experiments.

Rohrer called the first session, the one with actual light movement, the T or training session. The second, or X session, involved two subjects and occurred one hour after the T session. The third session, Y, was an "alone" condition and occurred *one year* after the X session. As before, each session consisted of 50 judgments or trials. Note that some subjects saw 2-in. actual movement in the T session and some were shown a light that actually moved 8 in. The X session consisted of one subject who had been exposed to a 2-in. movement and one who had been exposed to an 8-in. movement in the T session, judging together, with a stationary light. The Y session a year later had subjects alone, reporting judgments of a stationary light. Main results of the study are shown in Table 1–2. Subjects are described in columns 2 and 3 as belonging either to the 2-in. group or the 8-in. group, depending upon their treatment in the T session. The most frequent judgment of subjects (in inches) in each of these groups and in each session are shown in the rows of the table.

In interpreting these data, we first note that objective reality did make a considerable difference in norms formed in the T session: those who saw an actual movement of 2 in. reported movement of about 3 in., and those who saw actual movement of 8 in. reported movement of nearly 9 in. Second, there is a basis for saying that a social norm did form in the X session and, in fact, it is remarkably alike for subjects in both the 2-in. and the 8-in. groups. Both reported an average movement of around 6.3 in. in the X session. We also note that this figure is different from both groups' T session judgments, and that it is intermediate to them, indicating influence has been exerted by both members of the pairs in the X session. Third, the norm formed on the first day in the X session appears to persist for a year to the Y session. In fact Rohrer provides exact data on this persistence. For the 2-in. group, the measure of association between X reports and Y reports is .74; for the 8-in. group it is .60. These are quite satisfactory levels of association.[1] Fourth, is it the objectively determined norm or the socially determined one that shows greater persistence? From the figures in Table 1–2 it is difficult to see the answer immediately. But the measure of association between conditions T and Y may be compared to the measures between X and Y to give a better answer. For the 2-in. group, association between T

---

[1] Measures of association range from −1.0 through 0 to +1.0. A 0 indicates absence of association; knowledge of the first measure gives absolutely no information for estimating the second measure. A value of +1.0 is "perfect association"; that is, knowledge of the first measure enables a 100 percent accurate estimation of the second measure. Similarly a value of −1.0 enables perfect estimation, though with the order reversed: a high score on the first measure means a low score on the second measure. For our purposes we simply need to know that association measure values above approximately (+ or −) .55 usually are considered reasonably high, while any value above (+ or −) .20 is probably interesting enough to examine further.

Session	2″	8″
T	3.1	8.7
X	6.3	6.4
Y	5.5	5.1

(Adapted from Rohrer et al., p. 596.)

and Y is .26; for the 8-in. group it is .008. Since the comparable figures for the comparison of X and Y were .74 and .60, we conclude that the social norm is much more stable than the individual, or objective, norm. All of Rohrer's findings thus replicate Bovard's findings, though with different subjects and norms, and a much longer time scale.

Discovering and internalizing norms in more naturalistic settings, such as the proscriptions against stealing or the prescriptions to truthfulness, are sometimes asserted to require strong emotional ties between the person transmitting the norm and the person adopting it. The love and dependency between parents and child are often cited as necessary, for example. However as Bovard and others point out, it appears that at least in this situation such affective ties are not necessary. Even individuals having only minimal contact with each other—such as a subject and a confederate—seem to be willing to accept influence; or to put it another way, to accept the structuring of the environment that another person provides. It is difficult to speculate too much about implications of this line of thought for behavior in natural settings without going beyond the interpretations justified by experimental data. However there do seem to be parallels between effects observed in the autokinetic situation and those observable in everyday interaction, and some of the simple results of these experiments lend themselves well to interpretations of more complex naturalistic settings.

Stability Through Time of Group Norms

So far we have seen that individuals tend to maintain the range and norms of judgments they establish in the autokinetic situation either as the result of their own interpretations of the situation or as the result of influence from others. A broader concern is to what extent groups also maintain their normative beliefs through time, as we know they sometimes do. That is, will groups of individuals also maintain characteristic beliefs or norms through time? Further we may ask whether groups will tend to maintain their norms independently of the original members. That is, to what extent may original members leave a group and new members come in, and still have group members in the future display behaviors originally established? Sociologists and anthropologists often study cultural transmission of norms such as those regarding the proper display of a country's flag, how to act in the presence of a king, and how to prepare and eat certain kinds of foods. The term given to cultural attitudes and behaviors is *institution:* we say for example that the institution of the United States Presidency may be defined in terms of norms regarding appropriate behaviors and attitudes of and towards the President.

> *Institution—1:* a cultural collection of norms regarding a particular practice or object.

(Our definition is numbered "1" because in Chap. 8 we shall define a second way the word is used.) Jacobs and Campbell studied transmission of norms through groups even with replacement of the original members in a variant of the basic experimental situation for the autokinetic effect. They said that their intent was to study "the examples of tenacious adherence to incredible superstition with which anthropologists and students of comparative religion provide us." (Hare et al., 1965, 350–351.) I noted with some amusement that they were primarily interested in the "incredible superstition" they saw in religions of other cultures and other countries, and not in the religions of our own, which are probably based upon Divine Truth. But even without reference to religious beliefs, how norms and institutions are transmitted is worthy of consideration in and of itself.

Jacobs and Campbell assembled groups of 2, 3, or 4 individuals judging the autokinetic situation, and systematically introduced "generations" of groups through replacement of one member at a time. Each generation consisted of every person in the group judging 30 trials, and one individual was replaced at the end of each generation. There were two sorts of groups, control groups and experimental groups.

Control groups contained either one member or three, called, respectively, C–1–0 and C–3–0. The C stands for control, the first number is the total number of members in the group, and the second number—0 in these groups—is the number of confederates in the first generation. There were four types of experimental or X groups: X–2–1, X–3–1, X–3–2, and X–4–3, interpreted similarly to the control groups.

Note that for a group containing a total of 3 members (C–3–0, X–3–1, and X–3–2), since one member will be replaced at the end of every generation of 30 trials, the entire group will be composed of new members after 3 generations. This means that in the X groups, after a number of generations equal to the number of persons in the group, there will be no members remaining who were exposed to the confederates. The experiment was conducted for about 10 generations (9 or 11 for some groups).

In the two control groups, it was established that judgments for this particular experimental room would be around 3 in. The average judgment for the C–1–0 groups was 3.8 for the early generations, and around 2.5 in. for the later generations. The average judgment in the C–3–0 groups began around 4.0 in. and declined to around 2.5 in. Based upon this information, Jacobs and Campbell instructed confederates to report judgments between 15 and 16 in., considerably higher than naive subjects would be likely to report in the absence of social factors.

As we would expect from knowing results of prior experiments, naive subjects in all experimental groups showed considerable effect of the confederates' reports. For example, judgments by naive subjects in the X–3–2 and the X–4–3 conditions, where the effect of confederates was strongest, were around 14 in. in the first generation and declined to around 11 in. by the third generation (after the 2 or 3 confederates had been replaced by naive subjects). However it is possible to distinguish details of the Jacobs and Campbell findings that help to describe the manner in which the confederates' norm was transmitted (see Fig. 1–1).

First, for all experimental groups, there is evidence of considerable effect of confederates while they were still present. Second, judgments in experimental groups tend to decline as confederates are replaced and are indistinguishable from control group judgments by the 6th generation for all experimental groups. Third, the magnitude of original effect of confederates (in the first generation) varies directly with the ratio of confederates to naive subjects. For example in the X–3–2 group, which contained one naive subject and two confederates, the first generation reports of the naive subject were about 14 inches. In the X–3–1 group, which contained one confederate and two naive subjects, the first generation reports of the naive subjects were about 8 inches. Fourth, the number of generations required for the effect of confederates' reports to "die out" also varies directly with the proportion of confederates in the original generation: the greater the original ratio of confederates to naive subjects, the longer the confederates' influence persists after they have left.

Jacobs and Campbell report disappointment and surprise that the norm established by their confederates eroded so quickly. It seems to me, however, that what is surprising is not how quickly the norm eroded, but rather, how long it lasted and how great its effect was while it lasted. Note that by the design of the Sherif experiment there is no opportunity for any subject or confederate to attempt the direct exertion of influence upon another. There is no discussion, no overt attempts at persuasion, none of the careful tutelage and argumentation that we usually associate with learning of institutional norms in a natural setting. All group members do in this experiment is to sit near each other in a darkened room and express verbal judgments. They cannot even give each other strange looks for deviant answers! Standardized training of confederates includes the instruction not to try to exert influence by any other means, such as by snickering at a subject's answers or by making other noises extraneous to the purpose of the experiment. Yet under these conditions, it was possible to elicit reports of between 8 and 14 in. from individuals who would most likely have reported judgments around 3 in. in the absence of social factors. Moreover, the influence of confederates' reports continued in all groups for at least two generations after the time when they were present in the group. Far from this being a disappointing demonstration in terms of strength of effect, I find it impressive in its strength, striking in its persistence of effect; and occasionally frightening in some of its implications for the ways in which beliefs and

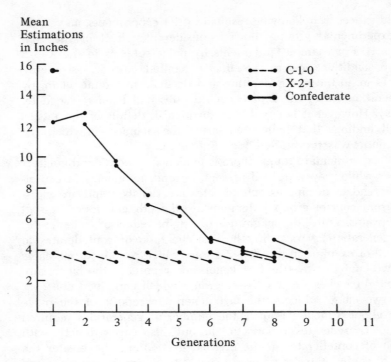

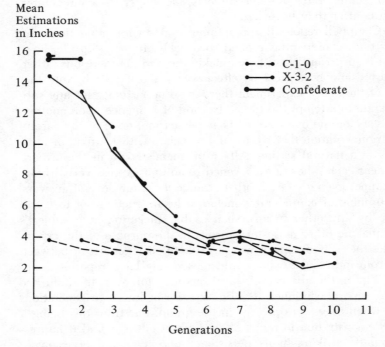

FIGURE 1–1 Transmission of arbitrary norm in two-person *(top)* and three-person *(bottom)* groups. (From Jacobs and Campbell, 1965, p. 345.)

norms can emerge and persist. In the natural setting both active persuasive attempts and sanctions for compliance are considerably greater than they are in this experiment.

Finally, we may return briefly to a question raised earlier, that of punishments for noncompliance to the norm, and rewards for compliance. Why is influence so noticeable in this situation, where the opportunity for distributing sanctions is so very limited and where there is so little reason for any given subject to care how the others feel about the answers he gives? It may sound like begging the question merely to say that this shows the tremendous effect of anticipated approval or disapproval, but at present this seems like the best available explanation. We do know that social approval is very important to individuals (though we all like to think we are less sensitive to it than most other people are), and in this situation there is no very compelling reason for the subject to resist being influenced in his reports by others. Also, we should recall the vaguely stated but nevertheless important need for individuals to structure their environments. The alone conditions of the autokinetic experiments indicate that individuals will tend to structure their reports for themselves, and the group sessions indicate that individuals are very willing to adopt the structure (that is, the judgments) of others.

Some Psychological Processes In the Sherif Experiment

Psychological mechanisms have been referred to rather loosely throughout the preceding review of autokinetic experiments, and some of them constitute crucial parts of our explanations for findings. Thus for example we have considered the possibilities that individuals find unstructured situations uncomfortable, and that they try to structure them. One important implication of this assertion is that subjects in this experiment actually believe the amounts of movement they report, even when they changed their reports to agree with confederates, yet Sherif's subjects studied before claimed they were not being influenced. What is correct?

To some extent this question will always have to be unanswerable: we have few ways of knowing what people truly think other than to ask them or to watch how they behave and then to make reasonable interpretations of their thoughts from their behaviors. But a well-designed experiment certainly can help to confirm (or disconfirm) our interpretations.

Let us formulate three questions for research, and then see how they are answered by findings from an experiment conducted by Hood and Sherif.

First, do subjects really think they see the light move as they report? Second, when subjects change their reports, is this because they have changed their beliefs about light movement, or are they just trying to avoid appearing disagreeable? Third, when subjects change their reports, are they aware of being influenced by confederates or other subjects?

There are at least two possible ways to obtain answers to the first two questions. The first means has already been used in the autokinetic experiments previously discussed. Namely we assume that if individuals were responding only superficially to the situation—that is, without believing either in the original movement or in the changed movement—then they would not demonstrate the behavior in the absence of the social pressures that produced it. If they simply wanted to seem agreeable, for instance, why would they say the same things later when they were alone?

But perhaps, once they began giving a particular answer to the movement question, it was easier to persist in it than to change it. Thus the question of actual belief can be approached in another way in a variant of the basic experiment, in which subjects do not have to make individual judgments before hearing a confederate.

For answering the third question on awareness of being influenced, we may employ a simple means that has been used in one form or another in many studies. After the experiment subjects are asked whether their answers correspond to those of another person. If in fact their answers corresponded a lot but subjects *say* that they did not, then we conclude that influence was exerted; but the subjects were not aware of it.

This, in outline, is the experimental design used by Hood and Sherif to answer the three questions. Subjects were 24 male college students who participated in a two-phase experiment. In phase 1, they simply sat quietly in the laboratory "while their eyes adjusted to the dark," and heard reports being given by a confederate who was presumably already adjusted to the dark. For half the subjects, the confederate gave judgments with a range of 1 to 5 in. and a mode of 3 in.; for the other half, the confederate's judgments were between 6 and 10 in., with a mode of 8 in. After the confederate finished his judgments, he was dismissed by the experimenter and told that his participation in the study was finished. In phase 2, the subject made judgments on 50 trials, with a stationary light. In this experiment, then, subjects made no verbal judgments at all while the confederate was in the room, though they could clearly hear what his answers were. At the conclusion of phase 2, subjects answered several questions related to their perceptions of movement and their perceptions of influence in the situation.

For the first question, whether subjects actually perceive movement in this situation, we need to know both their reports in the situation and some other measure of their impressions. At the end of phase 2, they were asked to estimate the distance that the light "usually" had seemed to move. Subjects in the condition where the confederate's judgments were 1–5 in. said they thought an average of 3.88 in.; those in the 6–10-in. condition estimated an average of 7.00 in. From this it seems reasonable to conclude both that subjects actually did perceive some movement of light, and also that the amount of movement perceived was quite dependent upon the confederate's judgments overheard in phase 1.

For answering the second question, whether influence of the confederate affected beliefs or only reports, we refer first to the above result—it appears that confederate's reports affected subjects' beliefs about movement. We also look at the standard behavioral measure, subjects' reports in the phase 2 of the experiment. The median actual judgment of subjects exposed to the 1–5-in. condition was 3.98 in.; the median judgment of subjects in the 6–10-

in. condition was 6.79 in.; that is, the average judgment by subjects for both conditions is within the range established in phase 1 by the confederate. As a further check on these same issues, we may examine the proportion of subjects' judgments within the range established by confederates, and also, the range of judgments by subjects in the two conditions. This is what the data show: 81 percent of subjects' judgments were within the confederate's range in the 1–5-inch condition, and 71 percent were within the range in the 6–10-in. condition.

Table 1–3 summarizes the findings discussed to this point; with one figure for subjects' actual range of judgment in parentheses to indicate that this is an estimate (the most conservative estimate) from incompletely reported data.

For assessing subjects' awareness of influence, we rely mostly upon their answers to post-experimental questions about the situation. The first finding from the questionnaires is not directly relevant to our third question posed earlier, but it is interesting in itself: of 24 subjects who participated in this experiment, only *one* said he believed the confederate judged the amount of movement accurately. In view of the high degree of correspondence between subjects' judgments and confederate's, this is intriguing indeed!

More directly relevant to the question of awareness, we may ask subjects to estimate what proportion of their judgments in phase 2 were within the range of judgments they overheard in phase 1; that is, the extent to which they think they judged the situation the same way as the confederate had judged it. Since we already know what proportion of their judgments actually were within the confederate's prescribed range, we may compare their estimates of agreement with the actual agreement. In the 1–5-in. condition, *one* subject overestimated the proportion of agreement by 7 percent: he thought that his phase 2 reports were within the phase 1 range of the confederate 7 percent of the time more than they actually were. All the rest underestimated. At the other extreme, a subject in this condition underestimated by 100 percent: he said he thought none of his reports were within the range of the confederate's, though all of his reports actually were. (We should note that subjects were not told what range or norm of judgments they had overheard at the time they answered this question.) In the 6–10-in. condition, the smallest underestimate of overlap was 16 percent; the highest, 80 percent. These yield a mean discrepancy (under-

TABLE 1–3 Results on Subjects' Beliefs and Influence

CONFEDERATE JUDGMENTS		SUBJECT'S REPORTS			
RANGE	MODE	ACTUAL RANGE	ACTUAL MODE	ESTIMATED MEDIAN	ACTUAL WITHIN RANGE
1–5	3	0–10	3.98	3.88	81%
6–10	8	(0–24)	6.79	7.00	71%

(Adapted from Hood and Sherif, 1962.)

estimate of overlap) of 64 percent for the 1–5-in. condition, and of 58 percent for the 6–10-in. condition. Assuming subjects reported truthfully the degree of overlap they perceived, these results indicate that they are very much unaware of the extent to which their judgments had been influenced.

A less precise measure which indicates the same conclusion is obtained by asking subjects to indicate the amount of agreement between their own judgments and the confederate's on a 5-point scale. Two subjects said their judgments were the same as the confederate's between "all of the time" and "some of the time"; eleven said they agreed "some of the time," and the remaining eleven said either "little agreement" or "positively no agreement."

In view of the findings of this experiment, we may conclude several things about psychological processes at work in the autokinetic situation. Most importantly we see that individuals seem actually to believe the amount of movement they report, and that they actually do change their beliefs, not simply their behaviors. Moreover, they seem to be largely unaware of how important the other person really is in forming their own opinions and reports.

From all of these findings, it seems safe to conclude that what is observed in the Sherif experiment represents in important ways the same sorts of processes that occur in naturalistic situations where individuals develop and persist in beliefs about all manner of issues. The simple situation that occurs when a person first becomes aware of a particular other person—say, a political candidate, or a popular leader—and where the person is concerned with deciding whether he favors or opposes the ideas of the person who has just become significant in his consciousness is probably directly analogous to the autokinetic situation. In both there is initial uncertainty and a relative lack of structure about the situation, and in both there apparently is a desire on the part of the individual to find or to impose some structure. The evidence is that in these situations individuals are tremendously susceptible to the influence of others—probably the degree of influence is greater as the situation becomes less and less structured—and also, whatever structure a person places on the situation will tend to persist unless displaced by active intervention of others.

Propositional Inventory on Unstructured Situations

To conclude our investigation of unstructured situations, we will construct a propositional inventory of findings. This is an extremely useful sort of intellectual activity, one which we will repeat from time to time later in the book when the state of accumulated knowledge about a phenomenon or related phenomena warrants it.

A propositional inventory is similar to a list of findings, an attempt to state clearly and precisely "what we know" about a given situation or phenomenon. In other words the person who constructs a propositional inventory is attempting to list all the things which he "knows for sure," or which he believes to be true. By comparison with a list of findings, a propositional inventory is shorter and more abstract. Probably the propositional inventory would not convey much meaning to someone not already quite familiar with details of the phenomenon under consideration. For someone who has studied the phenomenon carefully, a propositional inventory provides much the same information as a good set of lecture notes. It summarizes and condenses enough information that it may be used to recall and to expand upon the pertinent facts. Constructing a propositional inventory and then revising it as more facts become known are early stages in constructing a theory. Thus while even constructing a propositional inventory requires a good understanding of the phenomenon, a complete theoretical understanding of the phenomenon will encompass more than the propositional inventory that preceded the theory.

In constructing the inventory we will place several restrictions on the sentences to be included. First, we require that every statement in the inventory—that is, every proposition—be the sort that we can support by referring to some empirical result. We shall not assert something that we could not support at least partially if someone challenged it, and insofar as possible, we shall attempt not to overgeneralize or to assert more than the data warrant. Second, we require that every proposition be stated as simply and as clearly as possible, consistent with accuracy. Thus we try to eliminate redundancies from the propositions and to use the same words for similar phenomena wherever possible. Third, all propositions must be stated independently of time and place limitations; that is, since we are interested in developing a set of *general* principles regarding interpersonal behavior, we shall not include in the inventory such statements as, "In 1975 subjects in Los Angeles reported an average movement of 4.5 in. in the autokinetic situation." That statement is limited both in time and place; what we are interested in, by contrast, are statements we believe will be applicable (true) within very wide limits of time and place.

With these restrictions in mind, we formulate the following set of propositions, which we intend to apply to any unstructured situation. They are not intended to be a *complete* description of everything that can be observed in an unstructured situation, but they are statements we believe would be supported in any unstructured situation. The relevant evidence for each proposition is given in parentheses following the statement.

Propositions on Unstructured Situations

I. Evolution of Norms
   A. With interaction, the beliefs expressed by the members of a group will tend towards a norm for that group. (Sherif.)
   B. Beliefs expressed by an individual alone will tend towards a norm for that individual. (Sherif.)
   C. In the absence of additional influences, the norms developed by individuals either alone or as members of a group will tend to persist through time to other similar situations. (Sherif, Bovard, Rohrer.)

II. Effects of Norms

A. If an individual who has previously developed his own norm is placed in a group with a different norm, the individual will tend to change his expressed beliefs in the direction of the group norm. (Sherif, Jacobs and Campbell.)

    1. By comparison with an individual who has *not* previously developed a norm, an individual who *has* already developed a norm will initially tend to express beliefs that are more divergent from the norm of the group in which he is placed. (Jacobs and Campbell.)

    2. By comparison with an individual who has *not* previously developed a norm, an individual who *has* already developed a norm will tend to express beliefs that diverge from the group for a longer period of interaction. (Sherif.)

B. If two individuals who have developed different norms are placed in interaction with each other, each will tend to change his expressed beliefs in the direction of the expressed beliefs of the other. (Rohrer.)

    1. Such socially-modified norms, in the absence of additional influences, will tend to persist through time to similar situation. (Rohrer, Bovard.)

III. Influence and Awareness

A. The formation of individual beliefs will be largely determined by reports of others, if this information is available. (Hood and Sherif.)

    1. Individuals tend to underestimate the degree to which their beliefs are influenced by others. (Hood and Sherif.)

B. Changing of an established norm appears to be stressful to the individual. (Sherif; the Miss *X* incident.)

We conclude with two comments about the propositional inventory. Notice that the two propositions in section A of part III have implications for all preceding propositions. These two propositions assert that individuals actually believe what they report, and thus the words "expressed beliefs" in all other propositions are too cautious. This also illustrates one fundamental difference between a propositional inventory and a theory, for the statements in a theory must all be completely consistent with each other. In a propositional inventory, they need not be.

Second, we note that the final proposition in our inventory, B of part III, is stated too vaguely to stand as is. At some point we shall have to return to this statement and reformulate it to increase its precision. However the tension of the Miss X Incident is an important phenomenon. Even though we have only that piece of evidence for its existence, we shall see considerably more in Chap. 3. Thus it is important to note here that we have recognized the tension.

2

Conformity and
Social Influence I

Perception and Misperception; The Social
Enforcement of Norms

In Chap. 1 we spent considerable time examining ways in which people try to understand their environments or, in slightly different words, to impose a *structure* that enables them to interact with the environment. Structure means a set of norms governing behavior, social definitions accepted by individuals in a given set of circumstances, which interpret for them the meanings of various aspects of the environment. In addition and more importantly, norms tell individuals which actions are "appropriate" or likely to be positively sanctioned by others, and which actions carry a risk of censure.

We noted two types of ways to structure an unfamiliar situation, and as a way of beginning to study normative control of behavior, we may look more closely at these. First, an individual in an unfamiliar situation may activate a set of norms he learned previously from other experience or from direct teaching. For example, someone who finds himself at a formal dinner party and who is not certain how to act—which fork to use first, when to begin eating, how much of various foods to take, and so on—may remember what he read in Miss Vanderbilt's column and follow her advice on the correct thing to do. He could remember what he learned as a child from parents, or from previous experience with these dinners while he attended boarding school. To use terms of our discussion in Chap. 1, we say this individual is relying on an internalized frame of reference. He is referring to a learned, or internal, set of categories that give meaning to the situation. Second, in the absence of an internalized frame of reference, we have seen impressive evidence from the Sherif experiments that individuals try to impose a new frame of reference. In other words they try to structure an unstructured situation. In doing this, people are very likely to look to others for the norms. Our hypothetical individual at the formal dinner party, lacking any previous information about how to act, may watch others to see which fork they use first, when they start eating, and so on, and then do likewise himself. He is in effect adopting the structure others have put on the situation, just as subjects in some variants of the autokinetic experiments adopt ranges and norms of behavior they observe from others.

What is important at this point is that both sources of structure, internal and external, contain potential errors in perception for the individual. If he activates a learned set of norms that are inappropriate for the particular situation, then he will not only misunderstand some of the intentions of other people, but he will behave in wrong or inappropriate ways himself. If the frame of reference recalled is not precisely right for the situation—which seems to mean if the frame of reference is not the *same* as most other people are using in the situation—then the individual has a good chance of misunderstanding what people mean, and/or of doing things that look like poor manners to others. Television programs such as Candid Camera have shown some results of individuals activating inappropriate frames of reference in situations. Sometimes these results are funny, but just as often, they can be very unpleasant for one or more of the actors.

On the other hand, if the individual relies on others for his norms, he still may make errors. We have seen, for instance, that individuals will adopt the reported judgments of others in the autokinetic situation—a situation where *any* report of movement is objectively incorrect. At our formal dinner party, watching the wrong person for cues as to how to behave could lead to making the same social errors he makes.

The sort of incorrect information discussed in Chap. 1 leads to unconscious distortion of perception and unconscious exertion of influence. Individuals who report incorrectly the amount of movement in the autokinetic situation probably do believe what they report: they actually think the light moves the amount they say it does. In addition they seem to be unaware that their reports are influenced by what they overhear others reporting in the situation. In this chapter we shall be concerned at least initially, with *intentional* sources of misperception: with attempts by others to make the individual say things that are not true and with individuals knowing full well that others are trying to influence their behavior.

Why should such conscious distortion and conscious attempts at distortion exist? Why should others, either individuals or groups, try to produce distortion in the perceptions and the behaviors of an individual? Perhaps it sounds naive even to ask such a question, though I have never been able to adopt quite such a cynical attitude. It has always seemed to me that the great majority of people try quite hard to make sense of their environments, and that they are all too willing to try to help others do so as well. The norm in the statistical sense seems to be that people try to give accurate information. Just think of the effort most people go to in trying to give directions to some place for example.

But people do try to distort also. An individual who seeks competitive advantage over another may decide that it would help his own cause to give the other false information, to watch him misperceive the situation, or to behave inappropriately in it. People on their own are often concerned with putting on the best possible face, or social appearance for others. We have all heard others who say, "I never can get a good picture of myself!" What is meant by a "good" picture? An accurate one? This doesn't make sense, for we know that cameras record images almost perfectly. More likely what the person means is that the pictures turn out to be not as attractive as he or she would like—perhaps even that the pictures are not as attractive as the subject actually thinks he or she is. Putting on a good appearance for others seems to be a very frequent effort for most people, including, incidentally, a lot of people who say they don't care much about such things. It's pretty difficult to explain why people smile upon meeting friends or acquaintances except for the attractive appearance and friendliness implied (normatively) by a smile. Concern with putting on a good appearance is widespread enough that most psychological and personality tests contain lie scales that help to estimate the extent to which the respondent tries to give socially acceptable answers to questions. It is important for the clinical psychologist to know, both in its own right and for interpreting other scales in the test, how much the individual is willing to distort his answers in order to appear socially acceptable. These are norm-based issues. Social norms tell us what actions and attitudes are desirable, and norms tell us that we should perform those actions as often as possible.

Individual attempts at distortion seem to be based in one form or another on an attempt to manipulate others. If I smile upon meeting you even though I do not feel like smiling, it is because I want you to think I am a pleasant, cheerful person—both socially acceptable qualities—and because I have been told that I am more attractive when I smile. I hope to manipulate your perceptions of me, in other words, and I would also like to have some control over how you act towards me. If I tell you something that isn't true for the purpose of gaining competitive advantage over you, of course again I am trying to affect your behavior.

Collective attempts at distortion are probably of more concern to most people than individual attempts at distortion. We can ignore someone we know who habitually stretches the truth, or who tries too often (and too unsuccessfully) to get us to do things that benefit him. When there is a whole group of others, perhaps an organized group of them, introducing distortions into our perceptions or trying to manipulate our behavior, the situation is much more difficult to deal with. Groups of others are larger and are likely to be more powerful than individuals. They are also likely to contain some extremely clever or highly trained persons who are more adept at distorting information than any single acquaintance would be.

Propaganda and psychological warfare come to mind as collective attempts to manipulate perceptions and behaviors of others, and we tend to become especially upset when governments sponsor large-scale attempts at distortion. The Hitler government refined the "Big Lie" technique: if a claim is preposterous enough and repeated often enough, people will begin to believe it. The huge expenditures of our own government on propaganda dissemination within our country have been widely discussed (and widely deplored). The technique of releasing only partial information on incidents, which came to public attention during the Kennedy administration under the term "managed news," later produced a great "credibility gap" in the Johnson administration, and an "erosion of confidence" in the Nixon White House. Other collectives besides governments have use for the same techniques: advertising, public relations, and lobbying are highly developed strategies for influencing perceptions and behaviors of individuals.

Even more interesting than examples of propaganda or outright lying, however, are cases where there is no immediately apparent rationale for influence. In some cases it is difficult to see either why someone (or some group) should want to affect the behavior of others, *or* why the others' behavior should be influenced. In these situations we can see no immediately obvious reason for the influence processes at work.

What is loosely called *conformity* is a major instance of this sort of situation. It is possible to think of numerous cases in which people all act alike, or in which one set of people act like another set of people, and yet there is no apparent good reason why they should. People follow fads; hula hoops come and go very quickly, certain hair styles and clothing styles sweep the country and then disappear or give way to the next style. High school students all look and talk remarkably alike this year, as they did five years ago or ten years ago. But they certainly do not now look or talk like they did five years or ten years ago. It has been observed that even groups of people who share strong beliefs in individual expression, such as the "hippies" of the 1960s, still found that they liked—presumably on the basis of separate, individual decisions—mostly the same clothes, foods, and hair styles. "Conformity to a nonconformist group" describes such situations, and it seems as accurate as any other generalization. People claim to hold religious beliefs that have little or no direct relation to the ways they live, and yet which are very similar to the beliefs of their friends or associates. Around 80 percent of the people in this country vote as their parents did, which seems a remarkably high percentage unless there is some of what we would like to call conformity involved.

Conformity is a topic that receives wide attention from many branches of study: political science, sociology, history, psychology, and even biology. All these different branches of study use slightly different definitions of conformity, which is natural; the term is applied to a wide variety of situations and by individuals with a wide variety of different interests. As a matter of fact the subject will be approached from several different angles in our own study, beginning with the broadest definition that applies directly to natural situations, moving through a more restricted definition that applies precisely to an experimental setting, and finally to a much broader definition than that with which we began.

Conformity Behavior

To begin the study we need to find some definition of the word *conformity* to be sure that we begin by talking about the same phenomenon. In this case there are dozens of definitions available to choose from without even consulting a dictionary. D. H. Lawrence, who seems to enjoy periodic revivals in movies, wrote about nonconformists in *The Virgin and the Gypsy*. In this usage a nonconformist was one who didn't follow, or conform to, teachings and rituals of the Anglican Church. In the 19th century this was a very frequent use of the term, and it may well be why we currently have the association of nonconformity and freedom of thought and action so strongly fixed in our minds. Yet the meaning of *conformist* for Lawrence is quite similar to modern usage: a person who accepts or adheres to an orthodox set of beliefs.

A social psychologist who reads popularized accounts of the phenomena he studies professionally cannot help but be struck by the frequency with which the term conformity is used as an explanation for something. When conformity is used as an explanation, it is almost always without any explicit definition of the term given or suggested. "People conform," we are told, as if this explains why a certain music style is popular, or why speech patterns and clothing are borrowed from certain movies by large numbers of people. Such loose usage may be satisfactory for some purposes but it is not particularly satisfactory for us. How much do people conform? Under what circumstances do they conform? Do some people conform all the time, or do all people conform sometimes? There is no way to tell exactly what is intended from the sort of usage just given. Not only do we hope to develop a more explicit definition of what conformity *is,* but we hope to explain conformity itself.

Perhaps the most frequent uses of the term imply that conformity is a personality trait; some people are conformists, and some are not. This sort of usage implies that people called conformists are those who habitually follow other people in actions and beliefs. Those called nonconformists generally make these sorts of decisions independently of what others do and think. It is a comparison of the conformist personality versus self-confident individualism, and the usage carries with it strong evaluative connotations. "Be an individual, stand on your own two feet," we tell the child. "Don't be a weak conformist." The strength of this norm may be estimated by asking anyone you know whether he is a conformist or a self-reliant individualist. It could also be judged by the advertising for certain cigarettes (previously, Old Golds; recently, Camels), which promotes the absurd message that consumers should assert their individuality by buying those brands.

A few years ago, the sociologists Riesman, Denny, and Glazer proposed that entire societies may be classified as to whether members are primarily *inner-directed* or *other-directed.* Loosely interpreted, an inner-directed person guides his thoughts and his actions by internalized standards; he is guided in a manner analogous to guiding a ship or an aircraft by a gyroscope. An other-directed person, by comparison, guides his thoughts and his actions by what he perceives others in his social environment expect; he is guided by radar. This classification was used to propose the intriguing idea that American society was becoming more other-directed. The cultural values on self-reliance and absolute moral standards of the past were being replaced by values on flexibility and relative behavior standards. I know of little research testing this idea, and what there is shows disconfirming or contradictory results. Thus we must conclude that at this point the status of the other-directedness hypothesis is indeterminate. But the idea clearly may be related to our present interest in conformity. An inner-directed person conforms to internalized norms, while an other-directed person conforms to current social norms. We might, in addition, expect that an other-directed person would be more successful at learning the implicit norms of his society and especially successful at following changes in implicit norms.

Much earlier, the psychoanalyst Jung proposed introversion–extraversion as one of the fundamental personality orientations of the person. The classification depends upon the individual's report of where he places his primary values. To an introvert, the most important things in life are those occurring within himself: his thoughts, reflections, and subjective enjoyment of ideas. To an extravert, the most important things in life occur outside the body: other people, social situations, acting upon and within the environment. Notice that the popular interpretation of the terms—that introverts are lonely and withdrawn and extraverts are good people at parties—has little basis in Jung's classification.[1] The issue is what the person thinks is most important in life, not how well he can adapt to others. We can imagine, for instance, an introvert who is superbly gifted in social settings simply because he has decided to develop this skill. We can also imagine an extravert enjoying solitary skiing, because of the beauties of the external environment.

Although it is not so clear how Jung's ideas can be adapted to the contemporary interest in conformity, we might make some conjectures. It seems to me that a strong introvert would probably have little interest in, and thus little understanding of, most social norms. Social norms exist in the outside realm and thus are probably of secondary interest to the pleasure he takes in introspection. An extravert would be more likely to learn the social norms, since they exist in the interesting external world. However whether he would choose to conform to them is another question. An extravert seems to have a chance to conform to norms or not to. He knows them better than the introvert, but they may not seem worth following.

Some social psychologists and some laymen have used conformity as a personality trait, but the tendency to view it solely in this way seems to have diminished in recent years. Other interpretations of the same phenomena, especially more social interpretations, have appeared to supplement and even to displace personality and individualistic interpretations. This change of emphasis seems to accompany a more general trend towards awareness of social determinants of behavior, a move away from the older belief that the only source of individual action was to be found within the individual.

As social psychologists and not as clinicians or personality theorists, we shall be interested primarily in situational determinants of conformity. We do not say that there cannot be such a thing as a conformist personality, and we leave it for others to define what would be meant by such a term. However our interest here is going to be in social pressures towards conformity and in interpersonal influence. Though we note clearly that personality questions will not be considered, we shall also see that it is surprising how many interesting findings there are, and how many of the findings may be explained in terms of an interpersonal approach.

---

[1] Another problem, that *extravert* is usually misspelled as *extrovert,* is something we won't go into now.

From an interpersonal standpoint, it seems reasonable to suppose that *everybody* conforms—under certain conditions, and at certain times. The question then becomes, what circumstances surround conformity behavior, and what factors in any situation predispose an individual to conform? Notice that we have not said that individual differences are nonexistent, nor even that they are unimportant; we have said that for the present we are going to put aside questions relating to individual differences and to concentrate on social factors that can affect all individuals.

Let us state a simple definition of what it is that we're interested in, a definition that links *conformity* to concepts already defined and developed earlier.

> *Conformity:* display of attitudes and behavior in accord with the social norms.

Our first definition will have to be modified later in the light of conformity experiments, but it will serve as a good introduction to the field. This particular definition avoids any evaluative aspects of the term; it is not intended to suggest any positive or negative connotations. It explicitly acknowledges that conformity means "conformity to prevailing social norms," and thus that it is relative to a particular situation. Now we may also define the opposite of conformity in these terms:

> *Deviance:* display of attitudes and behavior not in accord with the social norms.

It is important to realize that well over 99 percent of our waking behavior involves conformity to some norms. The thing that makes nonconformity so noticeable is its rarity. Most of the time we conform without even thinking about the rules involved or realizing that there are choices. The psychologist Robert Hogan at Johns Hopkins likes to ask the following question on examinations: "The Marquis de Sade (a) was out of step with his times; (b) primarily conformed to the norms of his times; (c) showed several social maladjustments; (d) all of the above." The correct answer, of course, is (b): even such an unusual person as the Marquis conformed to more than 99 44/100 percent of the norms of behavior of his times. From the time he awoke in the morning, literally thousands of his attitudes and actions were normatively determined. We easily overlook this when we think of the Marquis's very few, but striking, deviations.

Approval/Disapproval

Before we study conformity experiments, a few words about the approval and disapproval directed towards conformity behavior may help to put the term in its proper perspective. The unanimity with which laymen, novelists, humanists, and social psychologists seem to view conformity must be one of the very rare times when these diverse groups of people agree with each other (even among themselves!). Whenever the topic comes up, it is disapproved, regretted, ridiculed. In fact just to use the term *conformity* or to apply the term *conformist* to someone is to disparage him. We "know" so well how people disapprove of conformity that the term itself has become pejorative. It suggests to such thinkers as Nietzsche the idea of slavish submission to others' "will," a weakness and lack of faith in one's own beliefs. Beyond this, conforming has suggested to many others a surrendering of one's individuality, a voluntary merging with an unindividuated mass. One who conforms is thus not even a person anymore; he is less than human for his conformity. Even Asch, the social psychologist who devised the basic conformity experimental situation, quotes Tarde's statement that "Social man is a somnambulist"; he moves through his life as uncomprehendingly and as ineffectually as a sleepwalker.

In the face of almost any unanimous evaluation of something as either good or bad, it seems worthwhile to examine the alternative view. Perhaps aversion to conformity has become overblown in our cultural values, and perhaps it can make people act in ways as undesirable and as unthinking as the automatic conformity they seek to avoid. I have been a member of organizations in which all the members felt that even to vote the same way as someone else was to be a conformist. It was very difficult at times for us to make collective decisions under these circumstances!

What is good about conformity? Well for one thing, a certain amount of conformity makes for efficiency, and it can simplify one's life considerably. This is not only the sort of efficiency that makes the manager of a factory or the political boss of a precinct smile, but the sort of efficiency that allows the individual more free time to do as he chooses. Conformity to some rather simple norms enables an individual to do certain things automatically without having to think about them and waste a lot of time over them. If I know that on days when I teach or lecture I will always wear a jacket and a tie, then when I am dressing I don't have to make so many decisions about my clothing. I can think of my approaching lecture instead. If I am willing to conform to the norm that people walk on the right side of the stairs, I avoid little awkward pauses that waste my time and distract my thoughts from more important matters (to say nothing of the gains if I am willing also to drive on the right side of the road). The fact that large numbers of people are willing to conform to some purely arbitrary hours for eating meals makes it much simpler for them to do other, more important things, such as shopping and conducting business.

Perhaps even more important than the efficiency gains from a certain amount of conformity are what we may call advantages of predictability. You can walk into any American home or apartment and be fairly sure there is a wastebasket in the cabinet under the kitchen sink. Not only is this reassuring, but it is useful information. Conformity to certain norms of behavior enables other people with whom one interacts to predict one's behavior to a certain extent. Knowing the norms governing certain kinds of interaction can in this way lead to a set of shared expectations for behavior, expectations of the sort that will make the interaction run more smoothly. In any interaction, we may say that certain behaviors are going to be *central*

—these are the things that are foremost in the mind of the participants to the interaction, the reason they are together. Other behaviors are going to be *peripheral*—such behaviors as greeting customs, courtesy norms about how things may be said, and so on. A certain amount of conformity to norms governing peripheral behaviors makes both parties to an interaction able to anticipate to some degree the future actions of the other. This, in turn, can free their time and attention for the more important central matters concerning them. It also may help to avoid having the central matters sacrificed due to misunderstandings over peripheral matters.

In summary, norms are the rules of social life. In many ways norms are like rules of a game, and most norms are every bit as arbitary as the rules of any game. People learn them so well that most of us are unaware of all the culturally normative patterns we conform to. We are also relatively ignorant of the fact that many of our normative patterns differ from the perfectly good normative patterns of other peoples. We learn norms, both explicit and implicit, central and peripheral, and most of us conform to most of the norms most of the time.

At this point we will focus consideration upon conformity directly induced in social circumstances; not conformity to norms internalized through long experience. We may conjecture that at some time every norm has to be obeyed through direct social influence before it can be internalized. Thus we study from this point how a pre-existing social norm influences the behavior of individuals who have not yet internalized it. In the remainder of this chapter we limit our attention in two ways. First, we are considering only norms governing *behavior* and behavioral compliance, not norms governing attitudes and beliefs. Second, we consider only norms that are unlikely ever to be internalized. For reasons that will be clear when we study the basic conformity experiment, this is conformity to group norms where the individual would conform little or not at all in the absence of the other group members.

The Basic Experimental Situation:
The Asch Experiment

Suppose that you wanted to study conformity of the kind we have been discussing in a tightly controlled situation. How would you do it? Conformity is a difficult thing to study in any case, for you are almost certain to get little cooperation from your subjects. You cannot simply ask people to tell you about their conformity behavior, or ask them to let you watch them while they conform: they would tell you, not a little indignantly, that they very seldom do conform. Besides, they will tell you it is very difficult to study conformity without specifying conformity *to what;* the issues make a lot of difference in whether an individual conforms. We might expect, for example, that people are more willing to conform to things they consider relatively unimportant—such as peripheral norms—than they are to things that oppose strongly held beliefs.

There are actually two issues that must be faced in designing a study of conformity behavior. First is the issue that Sherif faced in studying development of norms: we are interested in the *process* of conformity, not so much in the particular *content* of any norm to which conformity is produced. Second, if we wish to study direct social influences on conformity, we must be certain that the "behavior in accord with the norm" is being produced by external influences. While our definition of conformity specifies only that behavior follow some norm, the most interesting type of conformity is behavior that would not follow the norm by accident, behavior that does not just happen to coincide with the norm. If we observe a person driving on the right side of the road, we note this as an example of conformity, since it fits the definition of the term. However, there are numerous additional "good" reasons for driving on the right side of the road. More interesting is the person who stops and waits for the green light out in the middle of nowhere at 4:00 A.M. when there is no other car in sight.

In somewhat more abstract terms, an experiment designed to study conformity should incorporate these two features: First, it should be relatively content-free. It should not study conformity to any particular real-life issue, especially not to an issue in which individuals are likely to have deep emotional involvement. Second, the conformity behavior displayed should be clearly distinguishable from behavior that would occur for other reasons. It should be behavior produced by social *influence*.

Solomon Asch developed the basic experimental situation for studying conformity during the 1940s and 1950s. In the first experiments we shall examine, groups of 8 subjects participated. Only 1 of these was a naive subject, however. The other 7 members of each group were confederates. Because the situation and the effects produced in it are so striking, let me describe the experiment as it appears from the point of view of the naive subject.

If you were to be a subject in one of these experiments, you would arrive at the appointed place to find a waiting room with a sign saying "Participants please be seated," and "Please do not talk." There would be 2 or 3 other people your age and sex already there, probably reading magazines and acting relatively uninterested in your arrival, or in each other for that matter. If you were to ask one of them a question, such as what time he was supposed to be there, he would answer you, but briefly. He would not encourage further conversation with you nor would he initiate any conversations. If he were a good confederate, he would look as if he felt exactly the way you felt: a little nervous and expectant about the purpose of the coming experiment, but not eager to discuss it with anyone. One by one, the 3 or 4 remaining confederates would come in and sit down to wait. Even though the confederates probably had gone through this arrival several times already that day, they would try to look as though they were unfamiliar with the surroundings and would show no signs of knowing each other.

When the total number of confederates had arrived, the host experimenter would appear, dressed in a coat and tie or in other "authority clothes," and would ask whether you all were there for an appointment at whatever time it was. Everyone would nod, and he would welcome you. The experimenter would explain that he was going to show the 8 of you to another room for a study and that the room had numbered desks on it. Each person was to draw a slip of paper with a number on it from a box the experimenter held, and the number each person drew would determine the desk he was to occupy in the other room. Everyone would then draw a slip of paper, and you as the naive subject would notice that you had drawn #8. What you would *not* notice is that each of the confederates had also drawn a slip with #8 on it; this is a device to ensure the naive subject occupies desk #8 in the experimental laboratory. You would all go into the laboratory, you would take desk #8, and the other subjects would assort themselves at desks they had previously decided to take.

After everyone was seated, the host experimenter would explain that this was to be a study in perception. He would produce two stacks of white cards, each about 6 by 18 in., and would explain that he intended to show them to the group in pairs. One card of each pair contains a single standard line; the other card contains 3 lines differing in length (see Fig. 2–1). One, and only one, of the 3 lines is exactly the same length as the standard line, and each person would tell which line he thought that was. Everyone would answer in turn, beginning with desk #1. Notice that the point of allocating desk numbers was to get the subject to answer last for every pair of cards or trial, so that by the time he answers, he has heard the answers of every other person.

Then the judging task begins. On the first pair of cards the correct answer is easily discernible, and everyone gives the same, correct answer. The second pair is also easy. Everyone judges it correctly, and at this point you might decide that the task is remarkably simple. As the person at desk #1 judges the third pair of cards, you notice that he is wrong. He picked the

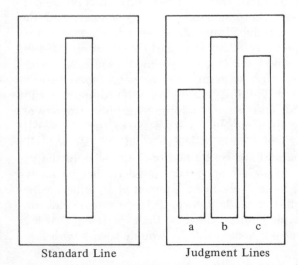

Standard Line   Judgment Lines

a   b   c

FIGURE 2–1 Task for the Asch conformity experiment

first line, when the second one is actually correct. The third cards weren't any more difficult than the first two, but anyone can make a mistake, even at a simple task. But the person at desk #2 also judges it that way, and then person #3 and #4. In fact all 7 confederates make the same judgment, a wrong judgment, and they will do this on most pairs of cards for the session. Out of 18 total pairs of cards, the confederates would judge 12 of them incorrectly and unanimously. Since an error is very easy to detect, we may assume that when the naive subject reports the same judgment as the confederates, he is doing so because of social pressure—he is *conforming* to the norm of the unanimous majority.

How do we know that he is conforming behaviorally to something he doesn't really believe? Could it be the case that the subject makes a mistake on the slides, which happens to coincide with the predetermined answer of the confederates? Or perhaps hearing their judgments disposes him to make a perceptual error, in somewhat the same way that influence is exerted in the autokinetic situation? The answer, to anyone who has seen a set of stimulus cards for the Asch conformity experiment, is that it would be practically unbelievable that someone could misjudge the line lengths. The wrong answers chosen by the confederates are very wrong. The lines Asch used ranged from 1 to 10 in., and discrepancies between the confederates' answers and the correct line ranged from ¾ in. to 1¾ in. With the correct line side by side with both the standard and the confederates' choice, there could be little doubt. Moreover, we have some good, objective evidence that true perceptual errors are not made in the absence of social factors. Asch had 37 subjects judge the same slides alone, without hearing any confederates' judgments. In the absence of social factors, one of these 37 subjects made 1 error, and 1 made 2 errors, an overall mean of .08 errors out of a possible 12.

This is the basic Asch conformity experiment. In later conformity experiments we shall see slight modifications. Discrepancies between confederates' answers and the correct answer become larger in later studies, and the variety of actual line lengths is reduced and standardized. That Asch was able to demonstrate any conformity effect is remarkable in itself. It used to be that whenever I described the Asch experiment, someone would say, "I know it would never work with me. I'd probably spoil the experiment, because I say what I think, no matter who disagrees with me." Perhaps. But Asch did find some conformity in his experiment, just how much we shall see in a moment. I have heard the above disclaimer so many times that I feel certain at least *one* of the persons who has told me that would probably have conformed once or twice in the experiment. In fact if someone in a class announces publicly that he knows he wouldn't have conformed, he is likely to be laughed at by others when the actual amount of conformity is made known. To try to avoid this embarrassment, I usually tell people before I describe the experiment that it is a usual reaction to want to make it known that "it wouldn't work with me— I'm too independent."

How much conformity was elicited in this situation? Of the total number of answers given by subjects on critical trials, about a third, 32 percent, were the same as the confederates' answers. This turns out to be a highly reliable figure, also. Several later experiments using the basic Asch situation have produced total conformity figures between 30–35 percent.

This does not mean that one third of all *subjects* who participate in these experiments conform, nor that all subjects who participate in the experiments conform about one third of the time. The 32 percent is an overall average amount of conformity that is produced in this situation; 32 percent of the total answers made by all subjects conform to the majority answers. Asch found that about 25 percent of his subjects *never* conformed. Although later studies show more variation on this number, at least we may say it is very likely that *some* subjects will never conform in this situation. In fact Asch and later investigators have found that there are wide individual differences in the amount of conformity. Some people never conform, some conform on nearly every critical trial.

Finally we note that in all conformity experiments there is, as we might expect, a high level of tension. Subjects look incredulously at the confederates when they begin giving their wrong answers, they shift around in their chairs and squint their eyes to see whether they can understand how anyone could give that particular answer. They sweat, sometimes visibly, and they fidget, tap on their desks with their fingers, look embarrassed or annoyed, and generally leave little doubt that they are experiencing psychological tension. Sometimes they try to engage the confederates in discussion: "Are you crazy?" "How can you say that?" "What are you saying?"

Something frequently observed during a conformity experiment is a sudden burst of laughter from the subject. It looks incongruous in the situation, and of course it is, from one point of view. The confederates and the experimenter are quite serious, and while the confederates' answers are *strange,* they are not particularly funny. What causes the laughter is tension. Laughter is a tension-relieving mechanism, as much as other behaviors such as shouting, applause, or crying are in other circumstances. One of the most frequent responses to tension in our culture is to laugh unexpectedly. In other stressful situations, people may be laughing loud and long over the most minor incidents or the silliest jokes. Here, where the subject feels both desire to answer correctly and not to appear deviant from the group, laughing is the least disruptive way of relieving the tension.

Just as a social psychologist looks first for norm violation when he sees hostility, so he looks for tension release when he sees incongruous laughter. We do not often think about what makes for laughter, and I wouldn't presume to tell what makes a situation or an act *funny.* Here we consider only laughter when it is difficult to see anything funny in a situation. It is a striking fact of social life that people do laugh at some of the strangest times. In one reported incident, the FBI and some airplane hijackers had a bloody gun battle in a plane full of people; some of them responded to the tension by laughing. An amusing case of tension-relieving laughter was documented by responses to a newspaper interviewer of street corner passers-by.

The question was, "Do you ever laugh while making love?" Almost every-body said they did, at least sometimes. The sole exception answered, "No, I'm married." [2]

We shall return to consider the significance of tension in this experiment later, for it is quite important in constructing an explanation for the con-formity behavior observed. For the present, we simply make two points. First, it is the responsibility of the experimenter to attempt in every way he can to minimize tension felt by the subject in this or any other experi-ment. For the conformity experiment especially, an experimenter typically observes the session from another room, and he is ready to intervene if it appears that the subject feels more tension than he can handle. The subject seldom feels this much tension—I have never seen a conformity experiment terminated for this reason—but it is a possibility, and the experimenter must prepare for it. We shall discuss these issues more fully in the final chapter of this book. Second, the presence of tension in this experiment is convincing evidence that subjects do not misperceive the nature of the task. In other words, the task is unambiguous. They do not, it seems, actually believe that the confederates' answer is the correct one, even when they conform to it verbally.

This awareness of the correct answer is an important point, for it is re-lated to a widespread misconception that the Sherif and the Asch experi-ments reveal the same sorts of processes and the same sorts of effects. Most discussions of social influence lump these two types of studies together, usually under the label "conformity," and proceed to discuss them as if they showed the same things. They do not. This is a fundamental difference between the autokinetic situation and the conformity experimental situation. Here, when the subject accepts influence, he is doing so at the expense of his own private knowledge that the social influence is towards an incorrect answer. It is quite different in the Sherif experiment. Both experiments deal with social influence, but it is a very different sort of influence: over per-ceptions and with little tension in the first case, and over behavior with considerable tension in the second case.

Other Effects in This Situation: Independent Variables Directly Related to Conformity

In this section we shall examine the effects of changing some independent variables upon amounts of conformity produced. Factors to be considered are those we would expect to be related to the amount of conformity.

In the original Asch experiments several independent variables were sys-tematically varied: presence of a "true" partner, presence of a "compromise" partner, and group size. Intuitively we would expect that the first two would

---

[2] Both cases reported in the San Francisco *Chronicle,* 1972.

decrease the total amount of conformity, and that the larger the group, the more the amount of conformity. This is what was observed.

A true partner in this experiment is what it sounds like: either a confederate or a second naive subject who gives the correct or true answer to the stimulus cards. In Asch's experiments he placed the true partner in seat #4, so that he would respond before the naive subject in seat #8. As anticipated, conformity to the majority confederates drops markedly in the presence of a true partner. When the true partner was a confederate, the rate of conformity of the naive subject dropped to 6 percent; when the true partner was a second naive subject, to about 10 percent. The difference between 10 percent and 6 percent is small, but it is possible to construct a simple explanation for it. Why should more conformity be observed when the true partner is another naive subject than when he is a confederate who has been instructed to respond correctly? A few moments thought should provide the answer. If not, consider whether we would expect the naive subject true partner to behave exactly the same as a confederate who has been instructed to be a true partner.

We may ask further, what happens as the result of either late arrival, or withdrawal, of the support of the true partner. Suppose the confederate instructed to be a true partner were to respond with the majority for the first half of the critical trials, and then to begin giving correct answers. Or suppose he were instructed to begin as a true partner, and then to switch to a member of the incorrect majority halfway through the critical trials. In both cases, while the confederate is behaving as a true partner, the amount of conformity displayed by the naive subject is quite close to what was seen in the presence of a true partner throughout the trials. Late arrival of a true partner produced a conformity rate of about 9 percent on the critical trials following his arrival, and withdrawal of the true partner produced a conformity rate of about 28 percent after he "defected" to the majority. These results are summarized in Table 2–1.

We may note for later discussion one more difference in amount of conformity in Table 2–1. In the withdrawal condition, conformity does not go up to quite the level of conformity in the first experiments. It goes to 28 percent, not to 32 percent. Likewise in the late arrival condition, conformity does not drop to quite the level of the true partner condition. It drops to 9 percent, not to 6 percent. We may speculate that these slight differences represent a weak effect of a phenomenon we saw in the Sherif experiment;

TABLE 2–1 Effects Observed in the Original
Asch Experiments

Condition	Overall	True Partner	With-drawal	Late Arrival	S Alone
Overall Conformity (%)	32	6–10	28	9	(.1)*

* % of incorrect responses.

the difference between the withdrawal and the original conditions may be due to a resistance on the part of the subjects completely to abandon the "normative" amounts of conformity they learned during the early critical trials when the confederate was responding correctly.

The most important independent variable studied in the Asch experiments is group size. He asked what the effect would be of varying the number of confederates who constituted the unanimous majority. We would expect that the larger the majority, the more conformity; and this is correct, though only up to a point. Where that point is may be surprising. It turns out that in this experiment, the effect of the confederates increases as their number increases, but only up to 3. In other words in the Asch situation, the amount of conformity effected by a group of 3 confederates is as great as by a much larger group. This is shown in Table 2–2.

It should be noted that the finding that conformity and group size vary directly only up to a majority of 3 applies to this specific experimental situation. A variant of the Asch experiment to be discussed shortly (experiments using the Crutchfield apparatus) produces increases in amount of conformity through groups of 7 or 8. For generalizing the results to natural settings, we may conjecture that a unanimous majority of 3 probably produces almost as much conformity as groups of larger size, but we cannot be sure of the exact size where further increase does not increase conformity— if indeed there is such a point. A group of 3 constitutes a strong influence on the individual's behavior, and this size may be about as large as is needed to elicit conformity on most issues where conformity ever can be elicited.

The finding that a unanimous majority of 3 is as effective as much larger groups has an important consequence for future conformity experiments also. One of the greatest costs, both in time and in money, of the Asch experiment is the large number of confederates employed. As the result of this finding, most later studies which have used the Asch experiment are designed for only 3 confederates. Even at that ratio it still requires the time of three trained confederates to obtain data from a single subject in the basic conformity experiment.

The next major conformity study after the work of Asch was a series of experiments by Deutsch and Gerard, who studied the effects of three different independent variables in various conditions of a modified conformity experiment. The three variables are *group reward* for correct answers, *anonymous or public responses,* and *commitment* to one's answer. We will see what these variables meant in their experiment after describing the overall design.

Subjects were 101 undergraduate students who participated in an experi-

TABLE 2–2 Effects of Group Size on Amount
of Conformity

NUMBER OF CONFEDERATES	1	2	3	4	8	10–15
Amount of Conformity (%)	2.75	12.75	33.3	35.0	32.0	31.25

ment that, like Asch's, had 12 critical trials out of a total of 18. However, instead of responding verbally as in Asch's experiment, subjects registered their answers on a machine called a "Crutchfield apparatus," after the psychologist who developed it. The Crutchfield apparatus is a system of panels, one on each person's desk, with buttons for registering choices and lights to indicate one's own choice and the choices of others. A major advantage of using the Crutchfield apparatus is that confederates are unnecessary. If the experiment contains 4 individuals, all can be naive subjects, for the experimenter can control the feedback through lights so that it appears to each one that the 3 others respond first and that they are choosing the incorrect response.

The Crutchfield apparatus removes the major inefficiency of the Asch design, though it also decreases somewhat the immediate social pressures of actually hearing someone else give his answer. Overall rate of conformity is somewhat lower using the Crutchfield apparatus than in the Asch situation, assuming other conditions are the same.

The effect of the variable *anonymous/face-to-face* was studied by comparing subjects' rates of conformity in the standard Asch experiment to those from an experimental condition using the Crutchfield apparatus. Since the anonymous/face-to-face variable was studied in conditions also involving other variables, it is difficult to assess the precise extent of its effect, but in all conditions, the anonymous condition produced less conformity.

The effect of *group reward* for correct answers may not be obvious at first glance. When the experimenter tells subjects that the group members will all be rewarded for correct answers, the amount of conformity *increases.* For example, in the *group, anonymous, no commitment condition,* 5.8 out of 12 critical trials were conforming responses, or nearly 50 percent conformity. In the comparable *no group, anonymous, no commitment condition,* 2.8 out of 12 were conforming responses, or somewhat less than 25 percent conformity.

Why should conformity increase with reward, when it means conformity to incorrect answers? Probably because implicitly the experimenter is telling the naive subject that what he does in the experiment will affect the outcomes of all people in the room. We said earlier that one possible reason for accepting influence in this situation, or in any other conformity situation, is concern with negative sanctions from the majority. Subjects in the group reward condition were told that what they did in the experiment might cause others to lose money. If a subject stands out by giving nonconforming answers, he is open to all sorts of blame if anything goes wrong later. The interpretation is rather subtle, but it will be an important element for constructing the more complete explanation for what happens in this situation.

The effect of *commitment* to an answer is also revealing. Deutsch and Gerard had 4 degrees of commitment: no commitment, temporary self-commitment, permanent self-commitment, and public commitment. This variable was operationalized as follows. The no commitment condition was the simple conformity experiment, using the Crutchfield apparatus. The temporary self-commitment condition was similar, except that before subjects learned any of the others' answers, they privately recorded what they thought was the correct answer on a magic pad. (A magic pad is the children's toy consisting of a base of black wax covered with two sheets of gray and clear plastic. Anything written on the pad with a plain wood stick shows through in black, but the writing can be completely erased simply by lifting the plastic off the wax.) Subjects in this condition recorded their original decisions on the magic pad, saw the confederates' answers on the Crutchfield panels, and then gave their own answers. Permanent self-commitment meant that subjects wrote their preliminary answers on a piece of paper instead of a magic pad. Public commitment meant writing preliminary answers on a piece of paper, and then at the end of the experiment, signing the paper and giving it to the experimenter.

Because we assume that the answers initially recorded by subjects in the last 3 conditions were very likely to be correct (that is, nonconforming) ones, we would expect that increasing commitment would decrease conformity. In fact this was observed, with overall conformity decreasing from about 25 percent in the *no commitment* condition to about 6 percent in the *public commitment* condition. The degree of effect across all 4 conditions is regularly ordered; that is, no commitment > temporary self-commitment > permanent self-commitment > public commitment.[3]

The effect of a variable which might be called *acceptance by the group* has been studied by Dittes and Kelley. In their experiment groups of 5 or 6 persons first participated in discussion groups before entering the conformity situation. At the end of the discussion, each member rated all other members on "acceptability as a group member," and also indicated the extent to which he personally would like to be a member of that group. Ratings were collected by the experimenter and were reported back to subjects before starting the conformity trials. Of course "acceptability" ratings given to any member were determined not by the actual ratings of the others, but by standardized conditions of the study. Subjects in this experiment used a Crutchfield apparatus, so none of them was a confederate. The conformity phase of the study involved a variety of conformity tasks: judging line lengths, dot estimation, and so on, but the effect of acceptance was quite similar on them all.

Results on the "public dot judging" task may be taken as representative of the effects of this variable. The number of conforming responses out of 12 are given in Table 2–3. Dittes and Kelley also constructed an overall index of amount of conformity in their experiment. Though they do not report exactly how the index was constructed, we may examine the results for the effect of acceptance in Table 2–4.

In both tables, what is significant is that higher acceptance by the group is associated with greater conformity. Since the relationship is not perfectly

---

[3] The > is called an *inequality sign*. It will appear throughout the book, and is read "is greater than." The other inequality sign you should become familiar with is <, read "is less than." Inequality signs are simply a shorthand, just like the equality sign =.

TABLE 2–3   Effect of Group Acceptance on Conformity
Public Dot Judging Task

REPORTED ACCEPTANCE	HIGH	AVERAGE	LOW	VERY LOW
No. conforming responses	7.7	8.2	7.2	6.7

TABLE 2–4   Effect of Group Acceptance on
Overall Conformity

REPORTED ACCEPTANCE	HIGH	AVERAGE	LOW	VERY LOW
"Conformity index"	2.5	3.2	2.5	2.6

regular, it may be easier to see this by averaging the *high* and *average* columns of both tables, and comparing this figure with the average of the *low* and *very low* columns of each table. This is performed in Table 2–5.

The interpretation for direction of effect of acceptance on conformity is related to the explanation offered previously for effect of group reward; namely, anything that increases a subject's concern about sanctions from other members will increase conformity. A subject who has been told he is either high or average on acceptance probably perceives that he has a lot to lose in the way of social approval. A subject told he was rated either low or very low on acceptability probably isn't so concerned anymore with what the others in the group think. After all he has little to lose by refusing to conform to what they say.

The effect of the individual's actual desire to remain in the group, or his *valuation* of the group in this experiment was reported by Kelley and Shapiro. Results for this variable are not so clear as those discussed to this point, but we may examine them for general trends. For subjects told they were low on acceptability, amount of conformity varied directly with their own valuation of group membership. For those told they were high on acceptability, results were mixed. At least for subjects in the low acceptability groups, the effect of valuation of group membership probably could be explained in the same terms we used to account for effects of acceptance and group rewards; namely, a concern with receiving social approval and avoiding disapproval from group members.

Finally, we look at the effect of *responsibility* for the decision upon amount of conformity. Responsibility is an interesting independent variable, for although it is related to amount of conformity in an intuitive way, it

TABLE 2–5   Effect of Acceptance on Conformity

REPORTED ACCEPTANCE	HIGH	LOW
Dot task	7.95	6.75
Overall	2.85	2.55

could be argued either that it should increase conformity, or that it should decrease it. We could, on an intuitive basis, argue that the person who is responsible for making the group's decision will be more likely to accept influence from them, for he is more worried about getting all their approval or disapproval. However we might also argue that the group decision maker might feel more free to deviate from others, either by virtue of his unique leadership position, or because he knows that in this situation, deviance is the best way to increase the number of correct answers the group makes. The question may be resolved empirically.

This experiment involved 25 subjects in a simple modification of the Asch situation. Each subject was a member of a 5-person group with 4 confederates, and answers were given aloud. There were three main differences from the design Asch used. First, the pattern of critical and neutral trials was changed. Except for the first two trials when confederates answered correctly, all other neutral trials were eliminated. The reason for this change is that neutral trials are uninteresting and inefficient—they yield no conformity data. Second, instead of varying the stimuli, all trials used variants of the same set. The standard lines on all trials were exactly the same length, and the 3 choice lines were the same in every trial. They all look like those in Fig. 2–1. However the choice lines were labelled differently: *a, b, c* on one trial, *d, e, f* on another, and so on. Third, for reasons unrelated to our interest here, all subjects went through a ple-liminary test of perceptual ability, the purpose of which was to convince the subject that he was better at this task than the confederates were. The effect of this manipulation was to lower the amount of conformity shown in all conditions, but since it was a constant effect in both responsibility conditions, we need not be much concerned with it.

The major independent variable was manipulated by defining the role of the subject differently, either as being *responsible* for the group, or as being simply one *member* of the group. In all groups, confederates occupied seats #1–#3, with the subject in seat #4. The fifth (confederate) member of the group sat behind the others, and he only recorded answers on a sheet of paper. In the *responsible* condition, the first three confederates were defined as "adviser," and the subject was to make the sole "group decision," which was then recorded by the confederate in back. In the *not responsible* condition, the first 3 confederates *and* the subject were advisers, and the confederate in the back made the group decision himself and wrote it down. Thus in the first case, what was written down depended solely on what the subject said; in the second case, what was written down depended upon the subject *and* the three confederates.

Two pieces of data may be examined from this experiment. First, the total overall proportion of conforming responses in the two conditions may be compared; in the *responsible* condition, this proportion is 39 percent; in the *not responsible* condition, it is 24 percent.

As may be seen, having responsibility for the group decision produces a considerable increase in the proportion of conformity in this situation. Subjects in the condition where they were told that they had all the responsibility for the group decision conformed on 39 percent of the critical trials; subjects told that they were only advisors conformed on 24 percent. Since this condition was quite similar to the basic Asch experiment, we might ask why the latter proportion was not about 33 percent. The answer, of course, is the competence manipulation, in which the subject was told that he had greater ability at the task than the confederates.

The second measure of effect of responsibility is the first trial upon which each subject conformed to the group in each condition. If we expect that subjects are more likely to feel social pressure to conform in one condition than in the other, this might be reflected in the fact that they begin to conform sooner, as well as in their total proportion of conforming responses.

Not only does responsibility for the group decision increase the total amount of conformity (from 24 percent to 39 percent in this experiment), but it also produces earlier conformity. In this experiment, after the second critical trial, 80 percent of the subjects in the *responsible* condition had made their first conforming response; at the same time, only 9 percent of the subjects in the *not responsible* condition had made a conforming response.

Results of this experiment may be explained using approximately the same principles we have used to explain previous results; namely, that subjects in the *responsible* condition were more concerned with avoiding the group's censure than subjects in the *not responsible* condition. However remember that before the experiment was conducted and the results were known, it was possible to make a believable argument that the results might go in the other direction: that subjects might conform *less* and *later* in the *responsible* condition, due to being placed in a position of some authority. This illustrates a phenomenon frequently seen when the topic is of widespread interest: the outcome of a piece of research seems "understandable" or even "common sense" *after* the data are known. If it had worked out some other way, *that* result would have been called common sense. We shall see other examples of this phenomenon in later chapters.

This completes our survey of "direct effects" in the conformity situation. In this chapter we have analyzed social conformity and studied the basic experimental situation devised to study conformity processes. We have also seen some of the major variants on the basic experiment, constructed to study the precise effects of independent variables recognized as important factors affecting whether and how much an actor conforms to the norms established by others. We have not been too much concerned with "indirect effects"—those not regularly expected to affect conformity—nor with constructing a general explanation for social influence phenomena. These more advanced topics are the subject of Chap. 3.

3

Conformity and
Social Influence II

Indirect Effects Associated with Conformity

Here we examine other phenomena that have been noted and systematically studied in some variant of the basic conformity experimental situation. Factors discussed in Chap. 2 are all of the sort that might be expected *on an intuitive basis* to make a difference in this experiment, or that are related to our intuitive definition of conformity behavior. Factors to be examined here are different. They are equally important, and in fact they will be crucial pieces of evidence for the theory to be presented at the end of this chapter, but they are not immediately obvious parts of conformity. Sometimes these factors appear in experiments already reviewed, and it is simply a matter of drawing explicit attention to them. In other cases special modifications of the Asch experiment have been designed to highlight these factors.

First we have *consistency of individuals, and variability between individuals*. Asch reported, and later experimenters also have noted, that there is a certain kind of consistency individuals display in the experiment. There is also variability between individuals—not everyone behaves the same in this experiment. To be more specific, recall that some subjects *never* conform in this experiment; 25 percent of Asch's subjects never conformed, about 16 percent of those in the responsibility experiment never conformed, and in general, an experimenter can expect somewhere between 10 and 30 percent of his subjects never to conform. Second, though subjects begin conforming at different points in the trials, it *usually* is the case that once a subject begins conforming in this experiment, he will continue to do so at least occasionally for the remainder of the trials. Some do not; some conform once or twice and then never conform again. But in general whatever the point at which a subject makes his first conforming response, from that time on there is a tendency to behave consistently. Third, there have been a few experiments in which subjects participate in two consecutive sessions of conformity trials. Sometimes they participate with the same confederates, sometimes with others; sometimes the same task is used for both sessions, and sometimes it differs. Usually in these experiments the investigator reports that subjects who conform in the first session also conform in the second session, and those who do not conform in the first session do not conform in the second session. All of these findings—and remember that there are exceptions to the second and third of them—show both consistency of behavior within individuals, and differences in behavior between individuals.

Second we have *effect of the experimenter,* studied explicitly by Schulman.

This may be one of those findings in the history of science that has been noticed accidentally by many investigators, but the significance of which is realized only rarely. Usually in a conformity experiment the experimenter remains in the laboratory with the confederates and the subject during trials. After he has read instructions to them and the critical trials have begun, the experimenter's work is over until the end of the trials, and he waits in the back of the room where he is less likely to distract the subject's attention from the task. (In most conformity experiments with which I have been associated, the experimenter retires to a desk in the back of the laboratory and either reads a book or writes letters.) By chance Schulman had to leave the laboratory during the critical trials phase of one group in a series of experiments. Afterwards he thought he noticed something strange: amount of conformity for that group was noticeably different from that of other groups in that series. As a consequence of this, he designed a later series of experiments to investigate explicitly whether having the experimenter in the room during critical trials increases or decreases the rate of conformity produced.

His later experiments had three conditions, using a modified Crutchfield apparatus. The first condition was the standard situation: subjects recorded their responses on a panel, and they were told that their responses would be seen by all other subjects and by the experimenter. In the second condition, they were told that other group members would *not* see their answers; only the experimenter would see them. In the third condition, they were told that *only* other group members would see their answers, and that they would be recorded automatically in such a way that the experimenter could never know the answers of any individual subject in the experiments.

Thus what Schulman produced in this experiment was (1) the basic experimental situation; (2) a situation where group members could not see the subject's answer; and (3) a situation equivalent to what had been created accidentally when the experimenter left the room during the critical trials. In condition 2, whatever effect the group had upon the subject's behavior should be weakened, for if subjects believed others could not see their answers, they probably would not be concerned about receiving censure from the group. Condition 3 was designed to allow examination of the effect of the group independent of any effect of the experimenter.

What would you predict? Was there more conformity in condition 1 or in condition 3? The answer—which surprises a good many people upon first hearing it—is that having the experimenter in the room *decreases* the proportion of conformity in the experiment. Out of 26 critical trials, subjects showed an average number of 7.15 conforming responses (about 28 percent) in condition 1, and 12.3 conforming responses (about 47 percent) in condition 3.

Why should the presence of the experimenter decrease total conformity? Because, as we noted earlier, the subject knows that the correct answer is easily discernible. Thus we may infer that he knows the experimenter thinks that he is mis-reporting when he conforms. Remember that the experimenter has told subjects to make their judgments as accurately as possible at the start of the experiment, so when a subject gives a conforming response he probably expects that this will displease the experimenter. He is caught, therefore, between two conflicting demands: one from the experimenter to give correct answers, and one from group members to give incorrect ones. If the experimenter leaves the room, then one source of social pressure is gone and it is easier to give in to group pressure. A question that profitably might be considered further is: Why doesn't conformity go up to 100 percent when the experimenter leaves the room? Are there other pressures upon the subject that keep him from giving *all* conforming answers in this situation? A little thought about this should tell you that there are.

The third and fourth factors associated with conformity are physiological changes accompanying the experience of participating in the experiment. We will not need to go deeply into biological techniques and human physiology, but it is necessary to recognize that the social, psychological, and physiological factors of any situation are interdependent. Here we get an idea of a physiological interpretation of effects of the basic conformity situation.

Generally speaking physiology and psychology reflect each other. Physiological changes—such as those produced by tranquilizers, stimulants, and consciousness-altering drugs—produce psychological changes. Likewise psychological changes can produce physiological changes. For instance, long-term stress can cause ulcers and high blood pressure, and fright causes increase in heartbeat. However, the physiological changes we can measure are not nearly so precise as we think the psychological changes are. For instance, an undetectably small amount of LSD in the blood produces great psychological change. Partly this is because we can make only rather gross physiological measurements on a living organism. What this means is that the investigator who is interested in studying physiological accompaniments of psychological states must be prepared for a certain frustration: he cannot, at least with presently known techniques, make observations either as sensitive or as rapidly as the psychological changes seem to be.

With this caution in mind, let us see what physiological investigators have found. Back and Bogdanoff devised a technique to measure changes in blood chemicals during the conformity experiment. They were primarily interested in getting a physiological measure of psychological tension that we believe accompanies the experimental situation, and with observing changes in tension between different phases of the experiment. Stress causes release into the blood of epinephrine and noradrenaline, two chemicals that essentially prepare the organism for "fight or flight." The heartbeat speeds up, blood supply to the muscles is increased and other processes such as digestion are inhibited. We say that the person is "up" for something. Most importantly for this research, blood sugar level (which roughly determines energy of the individual) is raised through metabolism (breaking down) of some body fat into available starches and sugars. Metabolism of body fat entails release of some free fatty acids (abbreviated FFA) into the blood stream. Thus the level of FFA in the blood is an indirect indicator of presence of epinephrine and noradrenalin; which in turn are indirect indicators of psychological tension. (You begin to see why physiological measures are not so precise as we would like.)

Subjects for the experiment were 32 Duke University ROTC students. As they arrived at the laboratory they were told about the physiological measures to be obtained. A needle that can be left in a person's arm for quite a period of time is used—the researchers assure us that it does not cause much discomfort!—and at several specific times blood samples are drawn. These samples are later analyzed for FFA levels. The four times samples were drawn from these subjects were: (a) immediately after needle puncture; (b) after a ten-minute rest period; (c) during instructions for the conformity trials; and (d) immediately after the conformity trials.

The conformity part of the study used a Crutchfield apparatus, and the task was matching airplane silhouettes—presumably a suitable task for ROTC subjects. There were other independent variables studied here—cohesiveness and ability—but we shall only look at overall relationships involving FFA levels. Table 3–1 gives the overall FFA levels for subjects in this experiment at the four times recorded. (The units are micro-equivalents per liter.) Note that the level drops between the trauma of puncture (time a) and the rest period (time b), during which times subjects presumably got used to the idea of having needles in them. What are more interesting are the increases between (b) and (c), and between (c) and (d). During the instruction period, FFA levels rise considerably again, reflecting anxiety and tension induced as the judging task is described to them. Conformity trials produce another increase, though the increase from the trials is not so great as the increase from instructions. Thus we have some physiological evidence for the tension associated with conformity trials, and, perhaps, evidence that instructions are more tension-producing than the trials.

If we compare FFA increases to conformity, we find that those with *highest* physiological arousal during instructions are those who later conform *most*. However amount of conformity is negatively associated with FFA level at time (d); that is, those who conform *most* show the greatest *drop* in arousal during the experiment. This suggests that a high level of conformity is tension-relieving.

Costell and Liederman investigated closely related physiological changes, and provide more data on physiological changes through time. In addition to release of FFA, epinephrine and noradrenalin in the blood cause a

TABLE 3–1 FFA Blood Levels in the
Conformity Experiment

Time	FFA Level
(a) Puncture	816
(b) Rest	669
(c) Instructions	778
(d) Conformity	791

(From Back & Bogdanoff, 1963.)

number of other physiological changes, including increased sweating. Thus electrical conductivity of the skin may be used as a measure of physiological arousal. The measure Costell and Liederman used is galvanic skin response, or GSR. It is one measure used by the "lie detector" polygraph machine. The greater the tension, the more sweating.

Subjects were 61 male undergraduate students from Stanford University. They used a modified Crutchfield apparatus (giving their answers aloud), and the task was matching pairs of rectangles. The critical trial series was very long, about 80 trials. Groups consisted of 5 individuals, 4 of whom received one set of instructions, and the other member received a different set. Thus the investigators could study effects of the situation upon the minority subject and also upon the members of the majority of 4.

We shall examine only their results for the minority subjects. Results presented deal with GSR levels at different times: before the trials, during critical trials, and during neutral trials after the critical trials. Minority subjects were classified as either "yielding" or "independent," depending upon how many times they conformed during the critical trials. Independent subjects conformed 4 times or less; yielding, 61 times or more. Figure 3–1 shows the general pattern of GSR lever for yielding and independent minority subjects, as well as for control group subjects in which there was no disagreement as to correct answer.

Notice that the control group subjects show a relatively steady GSR level, declining slowly through the trials as, presumably, their familiarity with the situation increased. Independent subjects show a steady increase in GSR or tension through the critical trials and a lesser increase during the neutral trials following them. Yielding subjects show the most interesting pattern: GSR rises early in the critical trials, peaks after about 10 trials, and then declines for the remainder of the critical trials. It increases again with the neutral trials, perhaps indicating a concern with how they behaved during the critical trials. It looks as though yielding subjects may have resisted the

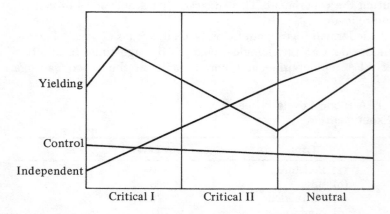

FIGURE 3–1 GSR changes and conformity behavior.
(From Costell and Liederman, 1968.)

group influence for the first few trials while their GSR was rising. Then when they decided to yield, the tension level fell off steadily. The subsequent rise during neutral trials could reflect growing tension as they thought about their yielding, which after all is a counter-normative behavior in our culture.

Notice also that the slopes of the three lines are quite different during the first critical trials period; that is, the changes in tension (GSR) that occur for the three groups of subjects are quite different during the Critical I period. During the second half of the critical trials and during the neutral trials, the slopes do not differ so greatly; thus most of the greatest changes that differentiate groups appear to occur in the first half of the critical trials. Apparently most subjects in every group reach some sort of resolution of the choice dilemma by the second half of critical trials.

On an intuitive level, we may explain these findings as the result of conscious decisions on the part of subjects as to how they are going to act. Presumably a subject becomes quite anxious when first he notices that the others are saying something he doesn't believe is accurate and is in a quandary for awhile about how to resolve the problem. His FFA level and his GSR rise. Some subjects, though by no means all of them, are able to think through the situation and make a firm decision how they are going to behave. They decide "once and for all," that is, either that they are going to conform or they are not going to conform. Once such a decision is made, much of the tension and uncertainty in the situation are gone. It is a question of whether to go along with the majority or not, and it seems that making a firm decision *either way* relieves the tension. The important thing seems to be making a decision, not the content of that decision. Many other subjects in conformity experiments do not seem to make such a decision, however. The typical pattern of responses for them is conforming and nonconforming responses scattered through the series of critical trials. These are subjects we would expect to experience the most tension and to have consistently higher levels of FFA and GSR. In general, most physiological experiments support such an interpretation.

Why Does It Work?
Summary and Further Thoughts

This completes our survey of effects seen in conformity experiments. By no means have we reviewed *all* experiments that have been conducted, for the Asch experiment, like the Sherif experiment, has been employed in an enormous variety of studies. We have, however, seen a representative range of social, psychological, and even physiological effects that have been studied, and we have surveyed a good sample of the more influential work in the field.

Heuristically, it is useful to ask of this experiment, "Why does it work?" Why should people conform to the majority and say something that our best evidence indicates they don't believe? Most people, upon hearing about the experiment, say that they wouldn't conform in the situation. Yet a sizable majority of people who actually find themselves confronted with the situation *do* conform to some extent. We concluded from this that people are not very good at knowing ahead of time how they would behave in a situation in which they never have been. Probably it is also true that subjects who *have* been in the situation are not very clear in their own minds why they conformed. At the end of the experimental trials, subjects are interviewed, both to explain the experiment to them and to learn what thoughts they remember having during the trials. Many different answers usually are produced in these interviews. Some people say they didn't conform, some claim they actually thought the confederates were correct part of the time, and some say they know they conformed, but are not sure why. When the experiment is explained, subjects almost always say they knew all along the confederates' answers weren't correct.

The conformity experiment is an unusual situation, and the more familiar one becomes with the actual running of the experiment, the more puzzling the conformity is likely to become. There are none of the usual attempts at influence one sees outside the laboratory: no arguments, no explicit or clearly implied threats of disapproval, no attempt to claim that the confederates' answers are sensible ones. Subjects who attempt to engage confederates in discussion or even to get them to return unusual or meaningful glances during the trials are disappointed, for confederates are trained to be as neutral as possible.

How does a subject in this experiment define the situation? Recall that it is quite clear that subjects are under considerable pressure in the situation, and that they are tense and uncomfortable. It seems reasonable to believe that the cause of their discomfort is a desire to give correct answers even though everyone around them is giving incorrect answers. Perhaps when a subject conforms on a trial, it is because he has redefined the situation. It has stopped, at least temporarily, being a situation in which he is faced with giving the correct or the incorrect answer. It has become a case of making a fool of himself before the group and risking whatever negative sanctions they might wish to bestow upon him, or a case of going along and being relatively anonymous. These kinds of thoughts are not at all rare in everyday life, and they might well occur during the experiment. Certainly they would be consistent with all the effects we have surveyed in this situation.

Earlier we mentioned the question of awareness, and that awareness of the situation was the major factor that makes the conformity situation unlike the autokinetic situation. There are three types of awareness that apply to both experimental settings, and on all of them the two experiments are very different. First is awareness of group norms. Does the naive subject in the situation perceive that there is a group norm, and what that norm is? The evidence from the autokinetic experiments is that he is unaware of both. In the conformity experiments it is abundantly clear that he is aware. Second, we may speak of awareness of influence when it occurs. When a subject's responses are influenced by those of the group, is he aware that they have been influenced? Again the evidence is that subjects in auto-kinetic experiments are unaware that they give answers that have been partially determined by the group members. Both physiological evidence and subjects' reports after conformity experiments indicate they are very much aware that influence has occurred. Third is awareness that there is a conflict between objective and social stimuli in the situation. Is the subject in the autokinetic experiment aware the confederates are incorrect when they say the light moves, and is the subject in the conformity experiment aware that confederates are saying something that is incorrect? The evidence is that a subject is unaware in autokinetic experiments and most clearly aware in conformity experiments. Because of these three major differences in the situation as perceived by the subjects, we conclude that the experiments are very different, and that they are used to study very different types of phenomena. The autokinetic situation is appropriate for studying development of normative beliefs, for example. The conformity situation is used to study socially enforced normative behavior.

Notice that along the way in this chapter we have narrowed and redefined the meaning of conformity.

The crucial elements in our definition now are:

1. *Unambiguous stimulus.* The judgments the individual is asked to make are such that he knows very clearly what the objectively correct answer is. There can be no doubt, no ambiguity, about it.

2. *Unanimous majority expression.* The individual is faced with a group of others, all of whom say the same thing.

3. *Opposition of sensory and social stimuli.* The individual is in a situation where the majority express opinions that counter his own sense impressions.

4. *Minority of one.* Almost always the individual finds no social support whatsoever for his interpretation of sensory stimuli.

5. *Public expression (usually).* Usually the individual is forced to make a declaration of his belief in such a way that the group members or others will know what is is. He cannot, in other words, remain silent, or abstain. In this way, the conformity experiment is considerably more difficult than many analogous natural situations.

Theoretical Modeling of Social Influence

Now we are to redefine the situation one more time, to describe things in as general a way as possible. Instead of talking about "conformity to the group," or "proportion of incorrect answers," let us say we are interested in *influence in a particular direction.* In other words when someone in the basic Asch experiment gives what we have previously called "a conforming response," we shall now say he gave a response "influenced in the direction of the group." There is no difference in what actually happened in the experiment; the word spoken by the subject is the same. We just agree to look at it differently. If his answer is the same as that given by the group, we will say the response has been influenced towards them.

But we also know from the Schulman experiment that a second direction of influence exists. Subjects act as though they believe that the experimenter "wants" them to give the correct (and usually nonconforming) answer. And of course since the stimulus is unambiguous, we may say that the subject influences himself in the same direction. So there appear to be two directions of potential influence in the experiment: towards what group members say, and towards objectively correct answers.

We might also say that real-life instances of what we generally call "conformity behavior" show a pull in two directions. In natural settings often it is not clear that the group tends to influence the individual towards something that is objectively incorrect, but remember that we have dropped from our consideration any question of whether a response is correct.

If we look at the experiment as a case of influence in two directions, then we see that the individual is in a conflict situation. He is, to use a popular expression, "being pulled in two directions at once," and he must resolve the conflicting demands upon him before he can act. He must, that is, decide whether to give the group's answer or the objectively correct one at every trial of the experiment. It is an inescapable conflict, and it must be resolved—the individual must come to some private conclusion about the conflicting forces before he can say anything. Notice that all we are saying here could just as well be said about any real-life instances of conformity behavior; that is, we could choose to define them as situations of influence in two conflicting directions. We have not changed the situation, or the types of situations of interest; all that we have done is to look at them from a different perspective.

Now that we have partially redefined the situation, we shall make the new definition more precise by constructing a model of it. The type of model to be constructed is called a *representational model,* one which *represents* the situation in a simple way and aids in our understanding of it. For some reason, the term "model" is frequently misused in the social sciences, and all too often it is viewed as something rather mysterious. Taking the word in its loose sense, we all use models of processes every day. When I have to wire a lamp I think of electricity flowing through wires, like water flows through a pipe. The electricity, according to my mental model, is under some pressure just as water is, and it will escape from the wire unless it is insulated. The switch in the lamp cord acts as faucet in a pipe. It can either allow electricity to flow or stop it.

Now in terms of general accuracy, my model of these processes is terrible. Any modern physicist would be horrified if I were to tell him that this is the way electricity is; the concept he holds of electrical phenomena is very different from my model. But this model enables me to do a good job of wiring the lamp. It is useful, for by thinking of electricity in this way, I am able to represent the processes of use to me in the wiring. Within reasonable limits, anything I know to be true of the behavior of water under pressure in a pipe is also true of the behavior of electricity in the wires. This illustrates two criteria for the model we are to construct of the conformity process: it adequately represents the phenomena of interest, and it tells us how to predict likely outcomes of various changes in conditions.

As preparation for the influence model, let us make explicit our final redefinition of the situation. (1) First, we are interested in *choice situations*. The individual is acting to make conscious decisions, in fact, a whole series of such decisions. On each decision he may go with the group or not. This means that he has two options. He cannot choose both, and he cannot refuse to choose at all. It is what is called a *binary* situation. (2) It is a situation of *influence*. There are many sources of influence, but, we can classify them into two types: *towards the group, towards correct answers*. (Since we have decided to omit consideration of correct answers, however, we shall just say that the influence is in two directions—it is easier to think of it by taking the specific case where it is towards the group or towards correct answers, but later we shall see other cases where the terms do not apply.) (3) The situation involves considerable *conflict* for the individual involved. This is shown by observing subjects during the experiment and also by the physiological measures.

A model has been developed for the influence/conformity situation by Bernard P. Cohen. The model is made up of *states and parameters*. In Fig. 3–2, the states are illustrated as circles (#1 through #4), and parameters are illustrated as arrows connecting the states. Let us look at the meaning of both of these.

The model is made up of *states* and *parameters*. In Fig. 3–2, the states are illustrated as circles (#1 through #4), and parameters are illustrated as arrows connecting the states. Let us look at the meaning of both of these.

The four states of the model are intended to correspond to four possible conditions of the individual. We call this a *four-state model*. In other words this model asserts that there are only four possible conditions for individuals in this situation. We speak of individuals being "in" one or another of the states, just as we might speak of a person being "in" a geographical state. (We do not mean that he is physically in the state; rather that we know something about his likely behavior because we know the meaning of each state in the model.)

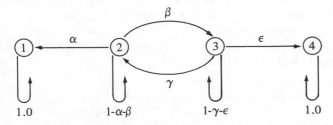

FIGURE 3–2 The conformity model

The first state is *permanent nonconformity* if the model is applied to the basic experimental situation. On any trial of the experiment, if we know that the individual is in state 1, then we know that he is *not* going to conform to the group. State 2 is *temporary nonconformity*. If the individual is in state 2 on any trial of the experiment, we know that he is *not* going to conform. State 3 is *temporary conformity*. If the individual is in state 3 on any trial of the experiment, we know that he *will* conform on that trial. State 4 is *permanent conformity*. If the individual is in this state, we also know that he *will* conform.

Parameters (arrows) show what kinds of changes are possible. On every trial, there is some chance that the individual will move from the state he is in to another state. Arrows show this, and the numbers and Greek letters on the arrows are intended to tell exactly what the chances of a move are. Notice that the two end-states, 1 and 4, have an arrow entering and leaving them, and a probability of 1.0 attached to these arrows. Intuitively this should make sense: State 1 is permanent nonconformity, and state 4 is permanent conformity. Because of the meaning of the word *permanent,* anyone who is in state 1 or state 4 will always be there (for the duration of the experiment or other social situation). Thus the probability of leaving and re-entering states 1 and 4 is 1.0 or a 100 percent probability.[1] Since people who enter these states do not leave them for other states, they are called *absorbing states.* In a way of speaking, they absorb people who enter them.

It is possible to leave state 2 or state 3, however, and the various parameters represent the probabilities of doing this. The probability of moving on any trial from state 2 to state 1 is represented by α, the Greek letter alpha. The probability of moving from state 2 to state 3 is represented by β, the Greek letter beta. The probability of moving from state 3 to state 4 is represented by ϵ, the Greek letter epsilon. And the probability of moving from state 3 to state 2 is represented by γ, the Greek letter gamma. We use Greek letters to represent numbers here for the same reason we use X and Y in algebra: because we do not know yet just what numbers are correct. Subsequently we shall replace the Greek letters with numerical estimates.

Notice that there are arrows leaving and re-entering both state 2 and state 3. This is the way to show that an individual may remain in either of these states on two or more consecutive trials. Since we know that probabilities for all possible events in a situation always sum up to 1.0, we can represent these two parameters without an additional letter. The probability of leaving and re-entering state 2, for instance, is 1 minus the probabilities for other possible moves; namely, to state 1 and to state 3. Now study Fig. 3–2 and be certain that it is also clear why the probability of the arrow leaving and re-entering state 3 is $1 - \gamma - \epsilon$.

---

[1] "Probability" means roughly "the chance that something will occur." For example, to say, "The probability of rain today is 60 percent" means, "Of all days like today, we get rain on 60 percent of them."

Fig. 3.3 gives a more restricted view of the model, one which illustrates its application solely to the conformity experiment. For simplicity, only the change of state parameters are shown; parameters for leaving and re-entering the same state are omitted. In this version of the model, it should be quite clear that the individual who is in either state 2 or state 3 (temporary nonconformity or temporary conformity) is in a conflict state. He feels pressures to be influenced in both directions. By contrast, an individual who is in state 1 or state 4 is in a resolution state. One way or the other, he has resolved the conflict.

The states and the parameters thus make up the model. The goal is to represent a process as simply as possible, in a way that allows us to explain the major findings of interest from the experiments. Suppose, for example, we wondered why it was found that some individuals who conformed for the last trials of the experiment show a drop in GSR. According to the model, what happened with these people is that they moved into state 4, the *resolution* state of permanent conformity, so as a consequence of the resolution of conflict, their GSR levels dropped. We might explain why a single conformity response after several nonconforming responses may be associated with drop in GSR level. The model would say that such an individual was in state 2 during the nonconforming responses, and that because this is a conflict state, tension mounted. When he finally conformed once and moved to state 3, the tension dropped for awhile. In this case the model would also predict that if he stayed in state 3 for any length of time, the tension and GSR reading would begin to rise. The model would explain these findings, in other words, as being consequences of changes or lack of changes of state.

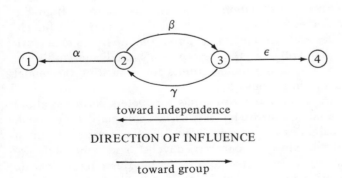

toward independence

DIRECTION OF INFLUENCE

toward group

α = probability of totally rejecting the group

β = probability of changing leaning towards the group

ϵ = probability of totally accepting the group

γ = probability of changing leaning away from the group

FIGURE 3–3 The conformity model as applied to the basic experimental situation

Applying the Model

In order to apply this general model to any specific situation, some way must be found to give numerical values to the parameters. We need some way to tell the size of probabilities of changing states for a given setting in order to apply the model to some data and compare its predictions with the actual findings. Finding these values is called *parameter estimation,* and as the term indicates, we never hope to find the exact true values of parameters. The reason for this is that parameters are theoretical values we might expect to *approach* if we had data from an infinitely large sample of subjects in a perfectly uniform situation. Obviously this is impossible. But we can obtain reasonably accurate estimates of the parameter values.

It is important to note that finding estimates for the parameter is not the whole task of testing the model. We need parameter estimates before the model can make any numerical predictions, and thus before it can be tested by comparison with data at all. However finding precise parameter estimates is not an end in itself, for these do not, by themselves, tell us very much of importance. Parameters are affected in part by assumptions of the model, but also by the specific situation to which the model is applied. For example, having a stern, fatherly experimenter in the room may well increase the parameter values associated with nonconformity (parameters a and γ—see Fig. 3–3), but the precise amount of increase produced in this way is not of interest.

Parameter estimation requires that the model builder have at hand some previously collected data. Some of the techniques of parameter estimation involve rather tricky mathematical procedures, and these are beyond the scope of this book. It is important to know, however, that there are no hard and fast rules for parameter estimation. Even estimates derived from the most sophisticated computer analysis can be altered on the basis of a hunch, if the investigator wishes to do so. The guide here is that he hopes to achieve parameter estimates that will give the best possible predictions of some (already known) data. We shall examine criteria for evaluating the model using parameter estimates in a moment.

Since there are no firm rules about estimating parameters, let us go about trying to get some rough estimates for the basic conformity experiment. We know that all probabilities are between 0 and 1.0 (for events that cannot occur and events that will always occur, respectively), and parameters are probabilities of events, so our estimates must be within this range. What do we know of the experiment that will help us to obtain more precise estimates? First of all we know that a and ϵ must be relatively small. Why do we know this? Because of the definition of parameters: a parameter represents the probability on *each* trial of the experiment that subjects will change state. If a and ϵ were large, subjects would very quickly begin either permanent conformity or permanent nonconformity, much more quickly and much more uniformly than actually occurs in the experiment. For example, suppose that we knew somehow that all of 100 subjects were in state 2 at the first trial of the experiment. If a were equal to, say .40, then after the first trial 40 of the 100 subjects would move to state 1, or permanent non-conformity. After the second trial 40 percent of the remaining subjects in state 2 (those who did not move to state 1 or state 3) would also move to state 1. In a 20-trial experiment all subjects would be responding very consistently (nonconforming) for about the last 15 trials, and we know that this does not occur. Parameters into the absorption states must be quite small.

By comparison, β and γ are larger. Subjects often alternate between conforming and nonconforming responses, and this indicates that parameters for going between states 2 and 3 are relatively large. Finally, we think that for this particular experiment, a should be larger than ϵ. The reason for this is that the total number of subjects who eventually become consistent nonconformers is larger than the total number of subjects who eventually become consistent conformers. The probability of getting into the permanent nonconformity state 1 is greater than the probability of getting into the permanent conformity state 4.

It turns out that some good parameter estimates for this experiment are the following:

$$a = .03 \quad \beta = .12 \quad \gamma = .21 \quad \epsilon = .02$$

These parameter estimates, along with two assumptions of the model, permit the use of a computer to generate the entire process of movement; that is, using these estimates of the parameters and adding two assumptions which tell how the process works, a computer can simulate the process of movement for any number of subjects and any number of trials. The two assumptions are (1) that all subjects begin the experiment in state 2, temporary nonconformity, and (2) that subjects may change only one state at a time.

There are four main statistics the model can generate for use in comparison to actual data: (1) the overall proportion of conforming responses during the experiment; (2) on any single trial, the proportion of subjects who make a conforming response; (3) on any given trial, the proportion of subjects who will show consistent responses (either conforming or nonconforming) for the remainder of the experiment; (4) on any given trial, the proportion of alternations, where an alternation is defined as making a different (conforming or nonconforming) response on that trial from the previous trial. The first three of these statistics are well known, and have been observed before for this situation. The fourth statistic, proportion of alternations on each trial, is determined by the proportion of subjects who (theoretically) move from state 2 to state 3 or from state 3 to state 2 on that trial. Any or all of those statistics could be compared to actual data to test the model. We shall examine only (1) and (2) as examples.

Figure 3–4 shows the proportion of conforming responses predicted and observed on each trial of a 36-trial experiment.

Both predicted and observed curves show the same pattern: they begin with quite a high proportion of correct (nonconforming) responses, drop quickly, and then recover slowly, with the curve rising towards the end of

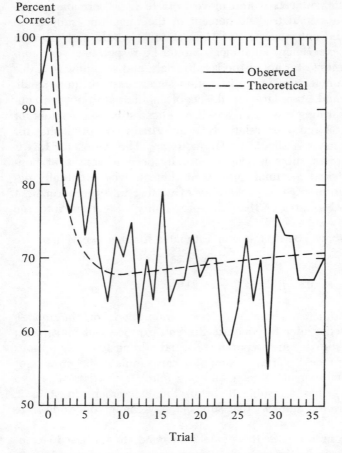

FIGURE 3–4 Comparison of the theoretical and observed mean curves, 36-trial experiment. (From Cohen, 1963, p. 135.)

the trials. In terms of this statistic, the model does a good job predicting the actual data, but from other statistics, it is quite clear that data were needed from an experiment with more trials. At the end of the 36 trials of this experiment, it looked as though not all the subjects had reached the model's two absorbing states. There was still some variance in their behaviors. In view of the small values for α and ϵ, perhaps this was not surprising. However, a 36-trial conformity experiment certainly is a long one.

Figure 3–5 shows the predicted and observed overall proportion of correct answers from 50 subjects in an 80-trial experiment. Note again that the model predicts this statistic quite well. In an experiment with 80 trials, we might well expect that nearly all subjects would reach one of the absorbing states, and this is what the model predicts.

There is one other interesting result of the experiments conducted to test the model. Look again at the curve for proportion of correct responses for the 80-trial experiment in Fig. 3–5.

The curve rises slowly from about the 10th trial to the end, but towards the end of the trials it seems to be slowing its rate of increase. When a curve appears to be approaching some limiting value in this manner, it is assumed that that value, the *asymptote,* is probably the final value the data would reach if the experiment were to continue for many more trials. As such, the asymptote represents the most stable estimate of the true value of particular effects, after the effect of initial experiences—such as getting accustomed to the experimental laboratory—has been overcome. The asymptotic value suggested by the curve in Fig. 3–5 is approximately .76 correct, or 24 percent conforming responses. In many shorter experiments it was found that the proportion of conforming responses approximated .33. We see from the 80-trial experiment that the best estimate of the amount of conformity produced by the basic Asch experimental situation after early

Percent
Correct

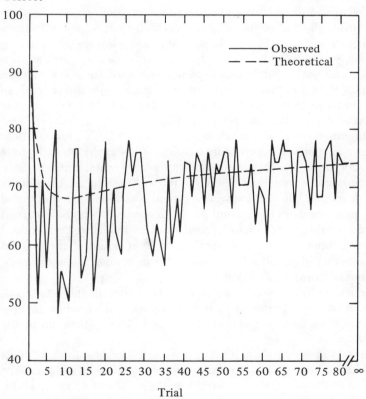

FIGURE 3–5 Comparison of the theoretical and observed mean curves, 80-trial experiment. (From Cohen, 1963, p. 140.)

effects have been overcome is 24 percent, not 33 percent. This fact could not be seen before Cohen conducted his 80-trial experiments, and these experiments would not have been conducted until the model showed the need for them.

Other Applications of the Model

One of our goals in studying this model was to find something which would be of more general application than just to the conformity experiment. At a minimum, we could claim at this point that the model should be applicable to real-life instances of conformity behavior, such as where an individual is urged to conform to peer group norms of illegal behavior, or where someone is confronted with repeated opportunities to violate a norm such as the speed limit. The model should be able to represent such cases with some rather straightforward interpretations of states, parameters, and definitions of the two types of conflicting behavior.

Moreover, the model should be applicable to a large number of situations we would not ordinarily call *conformity situations,* by virtue of the final re-definition we performed early in this chapter. We said we were interested in choice situations, where influence is exerted in two directions, with accompanying conflict and the possibility of a permanent resolution. We thought that these features were characteristic of conformity situations, and in addition, that they are characteristic of many other situations as well. Let us look at a few of these other situations together.

The basic autokinetic situation provides instances that fall within our definition. In Rohrer's experiment for instance, subjects begin the second phase in a situation very much like that for conformity experimental subjects. Subjects in this experiment were first exposed to a pinhole of light which actually moved in a dark room. Half of them were exposed to a 2-in. movement, and half to an 8-in. movement. In the second phase, one subject who had learned the 2-in. movement and one who had learned the 8-in. movement announced public judgments about a stationary, autokinetic light. Each of them could hear that the other's judgments differed from his own, and felt some pressure to be influenced in that direction.

To apply the model in this situation, we would say that all subjects began the second phase of the experiment in state 2, temporarily tending to give the individual response they had previously learned. The application of the model is illustrated in Fig. 3–6.

It is important to understand that being in state 2 means different things to each individual of the pair. To one, it means reporting a judgment of around 2 in., and to the other, it means reporting a judgment of around 8 in.

In this situation we would expect α to be quite small, β to be quite large, γ to be somewhere between α and β, and ϵ to be quite small, but still larger than α. What this represents of course is the empirical observation that very few subjects stuck to their original judgments throughout this phase (by moving to state 1; parameter α). There was considerable alternating be-

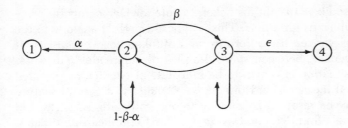

1: Permanent learned movement
2: Temporary learned movement
3: Temporary partner's judgment
4: Permanent partner's judgment

$\alpha < \gamma < \beta$
$\alpha < \epsilon$

FIGURE 3–6 Cohen's model applied to Rohrer's experiment

havior, with some tendency to favor the other person's judgments (β and γ quite large, with β larger than γ); and some few subjects going completely over to the others' judgments (ϵ small, but greater than α).

Bovard's experiment where he used an expert to try to influence subjects who had *not* previously developed an individual range and norm, requires a slightly different interpretation in the model. In his study, we would say that some subjects entered the setting in state 2, and some in state 3; that is, some were disposed from the very start to be influenced by the expert. Because most of the subjects eventually were influenced by the confederate, we would conclude that ϵ was relatively larger in this study than in Rohrer's, and that α was very small indeed.

A very different situation for which the model is most appropriate is democratic voting, where the individual often is placed in conflict between two opposing candidates, or between two issues. Should he vote "yes" or "no" on the proposed school bond issue? In cases like this, the repeated choices may occur at relatively infrequent intervals such as months or years, but in the case of split ticket voting they occur close together. Seen in this way, the voting process is similar to what we see in the laboratory in influence studies. The effect of having close friends or advertising favoring one or the other candidate would be incorporated into the model as a change in values of the parameters.

Application of the model to this situation would draw our attention to a number of features of the voting situation that political sociologists have studied. For example, the voter who is partially persuaded by both sides of an issue and who has friends or acquaintances urging him to vote both ways, is said to be in a *cross-pressure* situation. One way of responding to cross pressures is to vote each way some of the time. For instance, one who believes in schools, roads, public works, and improving garbage collection in his city, yet who is worried about rising taxes is said to be in a cross-pressure situation. He is likely to respond to this by voting for *some* proposed bond issues, and not others, or by voting for, say, school bonds *sometimes*, but not every time. He is also likely to split his ticket; to vote for Democrats for some offices and for Republicans for others. This is almost a perfect analogy to the alternating behavior we see in conformity and autokinetic experiments. It corresponds to movement between states 2 and 3 of our model. The voter in a cross-pressure situation is known to be in a state of conflict, as revealed by several attitudinal measures and interviews. Conflict is a central feature of our model. It may be resolved by moving to one end state, which would correspond to making a firm decision to vote only for Republican candidates, or to vote for all school bond issues no matter what. The voter in a cross-pressure situation is known to take longer to make up his mind about candidates or issues than the voter not in a cross-pressure situation. We could explain this in terms of the model by saying that the cross-pressured voter moves back and forth between states 2 and 3, while the voter not in a cross-pressure situation is probably in one of the nonconflict states 1 or 4. Cross-pressured voters are also less likely to vote than voters not under cross-pressures. In terms of the model, we would say this is explained as being the result of conflict associated with having to make a choice; conflict can be avoided by a psychological withdrawal from having to make the choice (which of course then removes that individual from further consideration in terms of Cohen's model, and also in terms of politics).

It would be instructive to think further about application of the model to the voting situation—for example, what would it mean in terms of the model if the voter had no initial preference between the candidates?—and to other situations. The model is one of wide applicability, and it gives some useful explanations of phenomena when it is adequately interpreted for a particular situation.

General Features of This Model, and of Other Representational Models

Representational models are among the most numerous and the most useful in current sociology. They have been applied to many areas, including:

1. Voting behavior.
2. Mobility—change in social class or economic status over generations.
3. Diffusion of information—describing how a population learns of a news event or a new product.

The model we have selected for study is a particularly good example, since although it is mathematically grounded, it may profitably be studied without much mathematical sophistication. It is related to substantive interests of his text, and, more than many other representative models, it is applicable to controlled experimentation.

Characteristic features of representational models may be illustrated by our model, but they apply to all models of this type. Models, and all theories, are direct outgrowths of propositional inventories like the one we constructed in Chapter 1. The propositions tell what are the most important things we have observed, and the model is constructed to explain the propositions.

First, representational models should give a precise, accurate description of some change process such as the conformity process. In doing this, it is necessary to simplify considerably the situation from the way it appears on first studying it. Some details (such as personality) are omitted, some features that are at first overlooked (such as alternations) are shown to be important. Asch seemed to be concerned with demonstrating that conformity behavior could be produced in the laboratory, rather than with providing the basis for a precise description of the process. The model, by contrast, takes as the starting point the fact that conformity can be produced in the laboratory and seeks to describe more precisely the nature of the phenomenon.

Second, in any representational model there is a process, some series of events that occur. The model provides a way to specify what the entire process looks like in terms of a small number of concepts. The curve representing proportion of conforming responses, the proportion of alternations, and proportion of subjects absorbed at various times; all are features of the influence process. The model of this process enables us to describe all these features in terms of four states, four parameters, and two initial assumptions. Using these features of the model, we can instruct a computer to simulate the process; that is, to provide us with something that looks exactly like the data from an actual experiment. Or using the assumptions and empirical data previously collected, it is possible to obtain parameter estimates for testing and applying the model.

Third, a representational model displays the relation of various aspects of a process to each other. For example, in the voting situation, increasing the strength of cross pressures would mean increasing the β and γ parameter values, and the model tells us what effect this would have on voting behavior.

More generally, in this particular model, we can derive the fact that if all subjects reach an absorbing state (either state 1 or state 4), the proportion of correct responses given will become stable and will not change for the duration of the experiment, no matter how many trials it may continue. This is an interesting result, one which we might expect on intuitive grounds. However, the proportion of correct responses will also stabilize when *not* all subjects are absorbed in any version of this model in which $a = \epsilon$. This result is by no means intuitively obvious.

Fourth, the representational model provides a means of *systematically* studying experimental variations in the conformity situation. More generally, representational models give the investigator some *reason* to make particular sorts of changes in any situation. He does not just change things "to see what will happen," but instead, he makes precisely the changes his model tells him will have a certain specified effect. For example, our model provides a rationale for changing instructions in the conformity experiment to start the subjects in state 3 instead of state 2; the model makes such a change important, and it even will enable us to derive predictions about the effect of such a change.

The use of models in understanding behavior is one of the most powerful tools available to the social psychologist. Representational models are usually constructed at the point that the investigators feel that there is sufficient information (such as a propositional inventory) to begin a precise description of the process. We shall see another example of a representational model later in the book, as well as examples of other types of models.

4

Leadership and
Group Position

The Leadership Personality

Around the turn of the century, the great German sociologist Max Weber described the "charismatic leader." The term entered popular speech, and now it usually is applied to anyone whose life is mildly interesting—politicians and movie stars, for example. But what Weber meant was quite different. A charismatic leader, when the term is correctly used, is an individual of extraordinary personal appeal, someone who can get others to do anything he wants. There are almost no limits to the sphere of influence a charismatic leader can exert over his followers, so long as their cause is successful.

Everyone probably has his own list of leaders he thinks of as charismatic, and so do I. When the term shows up in popular magazines we expect it to be applied only to people we admire, but this isn't necessary. Some of the people I think of as having been charismatic are: President Kennedy, who excited large numbers of previously apathetic Americans and made them really care about political issues for the first time in their lives; Adolph Hitler, who did virtually the same thing for large numbers of Germans a bit earlier; Jesus of Nazareth, who led a group of extremely dedicated followers into a new religion based upon his highly personalistic interpretation of ethical and metaphysical issues; and Governor George Wallace of Alabama. A few years before his Presidential candidacies, Governor Wallace was widely known as an advocate of segregated schooling, a highly unpopular cause among many college students (at least in the North and West), and he undertook a college speaking tour in order to elaborate and defend his beliefs. I heard him address a packed auditorium at UCLA, with an audience of students who were clearly hostile and barely polite to him when he was introduced. By the end of his 45-minute talk, he got a round of applause and even grudging admiration from nearly everyone I talked with on his speech and the way he handled questions. Not that they were converted to his view—this is important: it was not that he convinced his audience that his ideas were right, but rather that he impressed them with himself; clearly the man, not the issue.

The basic premise to a study of leadership personalities and charismatic leaders is that people differ importantly on whether they possess this potential. Weber concluded that it is impossible to identify charismatic leaders in advance, for it is only by observing the size and type of the following (after the fact) that the man was known to possess charisma.

But it is desirable for many reasons to be able to identify potential leaders ahead of time. Businesses want to find future top executives early so as to give them appropriate training and responsibilities (and incidentally, to cut down the time and other investments on those who do not have this potential). The government wants to be able to do the same thing with civil servants for the same reasons. Schools are interested in helping students who could "rise to the top" to do so. And especially, armies are interested in selecting out the potential officers from enlisted men and in evaluating leadership potential from officer candidates. "Join the Army and learn to lead"— but only if you can lead well enough.

If we are interested in identifying future leaders early, we need to decide what it is that will make them leaders. In other words, what are the components of leadership? One list of such traits is given in Chart 4–1. You might want to expand this list or to delete some of the traits, but it comes from people who devote considerable energy to study of leadership: the U.S. Army (Field Manual FM 22-100). This list of traits is not too different from those studied by early social psychologists, including some to be reviewed later in this chapter.

What's wrong with this approach? First, this list, or any similar list we compile, is generally composed entirely of "good" traits, admirable qualities. If this is so, would we want to say that leaders are those who exemplify all desirable qualities, while avoiding undesirable ones? Only with major qualifications, can this question be answered affirmatively. As it stands, let us say that if leaders possess all the good traits and only good traits, why do we need to enumerate them? We could as easily say that leaders are simply supermen, individuals with less than a normal human amount of failings.

Another objection is that if we look at current leaders, such as leaders of countries, major religious figures, and entertainment "leaders," we see too many exceptions to the list of virtuous traits. We can see these people too closely. We see that they are sometimes petty, sometimes less than honest, sometimes cruel. It is much easier to believe that someone far back in history possessed only good traits than it is to believe it of someone whose every waking moment is scrutinized by communications media. To be sure, the media usually help us to maintain our overall evaluation of a well known personality, concentrating on the admirable doings of "good guys" and the reprehensible or foolish acts of "bad guys." But still we can see that some people are leaders who do not conform to any list of leadership qualities we could compile.

CHART 4–1 Leadership Traits

Bearing		Integrity
Courage	{ Physical { Moral	Judgment
		Justice
Decisiveness		Knowledge
Dependability		Loyalty
Endurance		Tact
Enthusiasm		Unselfishness
Initiative		

The third objection to this approach to leadership is the one most important to us; if this objection could be answered, I would be willing to adopt this approach in spite of the other objections. The third objection is that, though some very competent investigators have been investigating the problem of leadership qualities for nearly a century, they have yet to demonstrate any reasonable success at predicting leadership from any measure of traits possessed by individuals. Whatever it is that makes up a future leader, either visible traits or something more intangible and difficult to measure, if we are to adopt this approach, it seems essential to have some demonstrated success at using it to predict leadership. In a way this objection is tied in with the goals of this book, described in the introduction; we want to be able to specify principles that enable us to make predictions in situations of the type we're interested in. Here, we want to predict leadership, and at least so far, the "leadership traits" approach has not demonstrated that it can do this. It is much easier to concoct a *post hoc* explanation for something than it is to produce the set of principles that would have enabled its prediction. If you read some of the accounts of recent Presidential elections, for instance, you might wonder how the outcome could ever have been in doubt—yet for many people, each time the outcome was a surprise.

The argument that leadership is produced when the right man comes along at the right time seems to beg the issue also, unless we could specify both the characteristics of a range of situations and the personal traits that are required to attain ascendancy in each particular situation. That looks like an even bigger task than producing a list of leadership traits. We would also have to produce a list of situational characteristics *and* a cross index for what traits are helpful in which situations. The range of situations in which we can see leadership is huge, and I suspect that the list of personal characteristics that sometimes contribute to attaining leadership would also be huge; it probably would encompass every possible human trait. I think we shall have to look elsewhere for a way to begin building a list of principles regarding leadership, and a place in which we can find some success is examining aspects of situations.

A Situational Approach to Leadership

What we think of as "leadership" is a phenomenon of great complexity since it occurs in so many diverse situations. Perhaps there are not any properties unique to leadership, nor any personal characteristics that all leaders hold in common. If we decide to abandon the trait approach to leadership, what is left to us? Let us say that we shall consider leadership to be a property of a situation, a position within a particular group. In other words we are going to study the *position* of group leadership, not the person who occupies that position.

Leadership is a social position, composed like all social positions of certain rights, responsibilities, and rewards. The higher the social position an individual occupies, the more rights and responsibilities he enjoys. An individual occupying a high social position has greater rights than others; for example, the right to attention of others when he has (or thinks he has) an idea, the right to sanction others for their behavior and not to be sanctioned by them; the right to direct group members' time by choosing group activities; and the right to initiate actions for other members. An individual occupying a high social position also enjoys differential distribution of rewards: approval from others, of positive evaluations of his actions, praise, respect and esteem, and acceptance and security in the group.

These components of the social structure of the group all have one important property: *scarcity*; they are not unlimited in any group. If one person gets more of any one of these components, this means that another person gets less. Why should social rights and rewards be scarce in groups? For certain of these privileges, the answer is that just by the nature of things, not everyone can have the right to choose group activities all the time. However for others, such as respect, approval, and positive evaluations, there is no intrinsic reason why they should be scarce. Why should not every group member enjoy equally high levels of approval from other group members? There is no inherent reason for it, *but* it is almost invariably true that all the components of social position are distributed unequally in groups.

Having described the basic dimensions of social position, let us turn to some findings of empirical investigations of the topic. A good place to begin this investigation is a study by Ferenc Merei, conducted in a nursery school in Germany. This study was primarily concerned with the "power" aspect of leadership. A nursery school is not exactly what we mean by the term in this country, for children studied were between the ages of 4 and 11 years. Teachers and others who have worked with children in this age group have observed that as they become acquainted with each other, they tend to form into groups or cliques for playing. It is possible to distinguish between groups both by the physical groupings of the children and by their characteristic manner of playing with toys and among each other. These two tendencies were noted by Merei and his co-workers: people tend to form into groups, and the groups show specifiable normative patterns of behavior.

A third tendency usually is noticeable in groups and was also observed by Merei and his associates: group members are differentiated by a number of characteristics that we may class together as indicating subordinate —superordinate relationships. In a phrase popular today, group members display a "pecking order." Merei used the following four criteria: giving orders, being imitated in play activity, being older (important in groups of this age range), and being more aggressive. On the basis of these criteria, it was possible to distinguish a single leader for most of the groups.

After allowing the groups to develop and their patterns of dominance to emerge, Merei took the group leaders and put them with other groups. His interest was to study several aspects of the relationship between leader and group, but what is of most interest to us here is what happened to the leaders. Did they again rise to leadership positions, or not? Were they in fact leaders by virtue of some personal traits they brought into any group, or was leadership dependent upon the group in which it became evident? The answer for these groups was quite clear: in every case except one (and it was a rather strange group), former leaders became subordinate members of the new groups. The former leaders stopped giving orders and started accepting them, imitated other group members instead of the other way around, and were noticeably less aggressive than other group members. By the criteria for these children's groups, they no longer were leaders.

There seem to be two reasons why former leaders became subordinate in new groups. First, they were outnumbered; there were 3 to 6 members of these groups, all of whom had developed different normative patterns from the imposed leader (since this is how groups were distinguished from each other). From the conformity experiments we know that a majority of this size should be sufficient to enforce norms, if they choose not to change their own behavior. Second, we may ask why members of the groups weren't likely to change their own normative patterns of play, which, after all, were probably developed through chance. At least a partial answer may be given using what we know of the effect of norms: once norms emerge, there is tension associated with changing them, as we saw in the autokinetic experiment.

Leadership and Conformity to Group Norms

A very famous study of attitude change at college provides a great deal of information regarding some of the determinants of leadership in the sense of prestige or esteem. It was conducted by Theodore Newcomb at Bennington College during the last years of the Depression (1935–1939). Bennington College was and still is a small private school nestled in the beautiful hills of Vermont. Since it is isolated from other communities by geographical location, it provides a good place to study social development of attitudes (and several other social processes) in a situation where outside influences were likely to be minimal.

Only wealthy families could afford to send their children to private colleges during the Depression, and sociologists know that the more wealthy people tend to be more conservative in their political and social beliefs. Most of Bennington's faculty, by contrast, were very liberal by contemporary standards; quite liberal, in fact, even by today's standards. Moreover, everyone at the school was concerned with public affairs: the New Deal, the gathering war in Europe, questions of social and economic policy. In short it was an ideal time and an ideal place to study conflict between the political and social attitudes in which the Bennington students were raised (primarily conservative) and the attitudes prevailing at the new college (quite liberal).

Try to imagine the situation from the point of view of a Bennington woman of the time (the college did not become coeducational until 1968). Since the parents were wealthy, we can assume that, in general, they were not sympathetic to labor unions or social security, they found Communism a greater threat than Nazism, they would have preferred President Hoover to President Roosevelt, and they generally held beliefs which would be lumped together as "conservative."

Our hypothetical Bennington woman graduates from high school—perhaps from a private high school chosen in part because her parents felt that it was a place where she would learn the "right attitudes"—and goes off to college. The college is some distance from her home, and because people didn't travel so often nor so easily in those days as they do now, she is limited almost entirely to other people at Bennington for her friends and acquaintances. In her classes she discovers that professors frequently drop hints that their views differ radically from views she has heard all her life. They adhere to Keynesian economic theories that say the national debt is simply a fiction that will never have to be repaid, they are enthusiastic supporters of President Roosevelt and his policies, some of them even announce that they are members of the American Communist Party. It must have been a shocking experience to hear these professors, whom she was prepared to respect, holding attitudes which all her life she had been told were reprehensible. Even more incredible, the older women students at Bennington, juniors and seniors, seemed to hold some of these attitudes also. We would expect the combination of faculty and older women to influence political and social attitudes in the younger women of Bennington, and in fact this change took place to a considerable extent.

But let us look instead at political attitude as the independent variable, and study its effect upon other things; particularly, prestige or esteem. Do one's political attitudes have consequences for the approval and prestige others are willing to give? Our democratic ideals say that they should not. But we know that political attitudes are *norms*, valued statements of beliefs with sanctions attached to them. So we might expect that holding the normative beliefs would be rewarded.

As a measure of political attitudes (the independent variable), Newcomb administered something called the PEP (Political and Economic Progressivism) scale to all students at Bennington on two successive years. The PEP scale asks respondents to indicate agreement or disagreement with statements of attitudes on issues then current. A high score on the PEP scale indicates a preponderance of *conservative* attitudes. (I think it would more accurately be called the PEC scale: Political and Economic Conservatism.) As a measure of the dependent variable *prestige*, students were asked to nominate 5 others as being "most worthy to represent the college" at a meeting of representatives from several colleges. Because the total enrollment at that time was around 250 and because of their isolation from other communities, it is reasonable to think that the women knew each other well enough to answer such a question. (The dependent variable measured may be *liking* as well as esteem or prestige; probably all these feelings go into any individual's response.)

Table 4–1 is a summary of results, constructed from Newcomb's report of the study. PEP scores, the independent variable, are given as numbers

TABLE 4–1   Number of Choices as a Function of
PEP Scores and Class

93

*Leadership
and
Group
Position*

PROPORTION OF CHOICES	CLASS		
	FRESHMAN	SOPHOMORE	JUNIOR AND SENIOR
Low	73 [0]	71 [0]	69[0]
Medium			58 (15) [12–39]
High	65 (10) [2–4]	64 (8) [12+]	50 (5) [40+]

ranging from 50 to 73 in the first column of each class; the number of students who had the PEP score reported are given in parentheses immediately after the score; and the number of choices received by each student, the dependent variable, is given in brackets. For example, in the bottom of the third column, we see that 5 juniors and seniors who had an average PEP score of 50 received 40 or more choices as "most worthy to represent the college." Where numbers are omitted, it is because they are not contained in Newcomb's report.

Table 4–1 contains a great deal of information; let us begin by making some simple observations. First, we see a general increase in liberal attitudes with increasing time at Bennington. The average PEP score shown in row 1 for freshmen who received no choices is 73; for sophomores it is 71; and for juniors and seniors, it is 69—remember that low scores indicate liberal attitudes. For students receiving a high proportion of choices (row 3), the average PEP score of freshmen is 65; for sophomores, 64; and for juniors and seniors, 50.

Second, we see that juniors and seniors generally received a greater number of choices than freshmen. No freshmen received more than 4 choices, while some juniors and seniors received more than 40. In part we would expect this on the basis of length of time at Bennington, since usually it takes time to build up a reputation and other ties within a community. The difference probably also indicates the effect of relative amounts of status attached to being a freshman or a senior.

The most noticeable effect, as well as the one most important to us, is that high prestige is associated with liberal views at Bennington generally, and within every class. The higher the PEP score, the more likely is a girl to be chosen "most worthy to represent the college." For example, look at column 3, juniors and seniors. Those women who never were chosen had an average PEP score of 69, the most conservative in the column. Those chosen a moderate number of times (12–39) had an average PEP score of 58, while those chosen a high proportion of times (40 or more) had an average PEP score of 50. The same relationship of PEP attitudes and prestige choices may be seen in the freshmen and the sophomore classes. From Table 4–1 it seems that the best advice one could give someone departing for Bennington College in those days would be, "If you want to become recognized and popular, adopt the liberal social and political attitudes."

Some anecdotal evidence from interviews with the Bennington women indicates that it seems like good advice. First, some whom Newcomb classifies as "liberals":

"Every influence I felt tended to push me in the liberal direction: my underdog complex, my need to be independent of my parents, and my anxiousness to be a leader here."

"It's very simple. I was so anxious to be accepted that I accepted the political complexion of the community here. I just couldn't stand out against the crowd unless I had many friends and strong support."

These women seem to have adopted advice similar to ours. Let us look at some who retained their conservative views:

"I always resent doing the respectable thing just because it's the thing to do, but I didn't realize I was so different, politically, from my classmates. At least I agree with the *few* people I ever talk to about such matters[Emphasis added.]

"I wouldn't care to be intimate with those so-called liberal student leaders."

"Probably the feeling that [my instructors] didn't accept me led me to reject their opinions."

Two Groups

The anecdotal evidence just cited seems consistent with the sort of explanation we sketched: political attitudes are important determinants of social success in the group. But there is another factor operating here as well; let us see what it is, from some other "liberals" and "conservatives":

"I came to college to get away from my family, who never had any respect for my mind. Becoming a radical meant thinking for myself and, figuratively, thumbing my nose at my family. It also meant intellectual identification with the faculty and students that I most wanted to be like."

"Of course there's social pressure here to give up your conservatism. I'm glad of it, because for me this became the vehicle for achieving independence from my family. So changing my attitudes has gone hand in hand with two very important things: establishing my own independence and at the same time becoming a part of the college organism."

"I wanted to disagree with all the noisy liberals, but I was afraid and I couldn't. So I built up a wall inside me against what they said. I found I couldn't compete, so I decided to stick to my father's ideas. For at least two years I've been insulated from all college influences."

"Family against faculty has been my struggle here. As soon as I felt really secure here I decided not to let the college atmosphere affect me to much. Every time I've tried to rebel against my family I've found out how terribly wrong I am, and so I've naturally kept to my parents' attitudes."

The idea that college students "rebel" against attitudes and beliefs of their parents has been a popular one for some time, and the second set of these anecdotes supports it. However let us think about the matter in a little more detail, in hopes of finding a more general process at work here. Beyond simple "rebellion," what shows through clearly is that there are two distinct sets of attitudes operating for the women (who show varying degrees of explicit awareness of the sets), which we may characterize as "family attitudes" (conservative), and "Bennington attitudes" (liberal). It is as though there were two groups competing for attention. The physical isolation makes it quite clear why the groups never met directly: when the women were home, such as at Christmas vacation, they brought with them the Bennington attitudes; when they came to Bennington, they brought along their parents' attitudes. The women, then, were in the middle, forced to resolve a conflict that existed between two incompatible sets of attitudes. Becoming a liberal meant (usually) a conscious rejection of parents' attitudes. Remaining a conservative meant turning one's back on others in the Bennington community. Whether all women saw the conflict drawn in such neat terms is doubtful, but for purposes of illustration, we can say that they were faced with this problem. Becoming a liberal meant becoming successfully involved in Bennington life; remaining a conservative meant maintaining close ties to one's parents. There were distinct social consequences of political attitudes. One could have high prestige in the Bennington community, but probably only at the expense of some esteem from one's parents. One could maintain a high standing with one's parents, but it probably would mean giving up the chance at a high position at Bennington.

Some 20 years later, Newcomb again studied the attitudes of these same Bennington women. Instead of measuring political–economic conservatism with the PEP scale, he simply asked them about Presidential votes (or preferences) for past elections. Instead of measuring social integration by asking about who was most worthy to represent the college, he simply asked the women to report on their associates. The follow-up study, conducted by interviewing 130 of the 141 subjects studied for 3 or more years at Bennington, provides some interesting comparisons on persistence of attitudes through the years.

The first thing found in the follow-up study is a remarkable persistence of the (adopted) attitudes from Bennnigton. Table 4–2 compares PEP

TABLE 4–2   Persistence of Political Attitudes

PEP SCORE AT BENNINGTON	1960 PRESIDENTIAL PREFERENCE	
	NIXON	KENNEDY
Most liberal quartile	3	30
Liberal quartile	8	25
Conservative quartile	18	13
Most conservative quartile	22	11

scores of these women from their senior year at Bennington with their 1960 Presidential preferences. Of those in the least conservative quartile at Bennington, 3 out of 33, about 8 percent, preferred Nixon to Kennedy in 1960; of those in the most conservative quartile at Bennington, 22 out of 33, or 66 percent, preferred Nixon.

It should not be inferred, Newcomb says, that the attitudes held at Bennington simply remained unchanged for the next 25 years. Rather, the process of attitude *formation* must be distinguished from processes which serve to *maintain* attitudes. In this case we might expect women who were most conservative at Bennington to seek out friends and associates, including husbands, who held conservative attitudes. The most liberal women would be expected to seek out associates with liberal attitudes. In later years it would be the influence of these consciously chosen associates, rather than the largely unanticipated influence of Bennington, which would account for 1960 political attitudes.

To support this reasoning, Newcomb presents data from 22 women who were identified as clearly liberal at Bennington; only half of them were still identified as clearly liberal in 1960. Of the 8 who were liberal in 1960, only 2 (25 percent) had husbands who were registered Republicans. Of 7 women classified as "intermediate" in 1960, 3 (43 percent) had Republican husbands. Of 3 classified as definitely conservative in 1960, all 3 (100 percent) had Republican husbands. More than half (12) of the originally liberal women identified their friends in the early 1960s as "liberal"; of 16 women identified as conservative at Bennington, 9 described their friends as "conservative." The pattern is that women tended to seek associates whose attitudes were similar to their own. When they did this, their attitudes were maintained by these associates. However when women associated with others whose opinions differed from their own, they tended to change their attitudes in the direction of their associates. What may at first have looked like a surprising persistence of political attitudes turns out, on closer examination, to be actually a persistence only when the initial attitudes are socially supported.

Awareness of Norms

We have raised the possibility that those individuals accorded a high position of prestige at Bennington knew that adopting certain normative attitudes was necessary. A further question is whether all attitudes are important, or only some of them. Perhaps it is necessary to conform only to attitudes that are relevant to the group. If so, we would say that political and social attitudes appeared to be relevant to social prestige at Bennington, but other attitudes, such as opinions on sexual behavior, might not be important. A related question we might raise is whether those individuals who come to occupy a high position of prestige do so because of a general ability to divine others' opinions, or because their sensitivities are attuned to the particular types of issues relevant to the group.

Chowdhry and Newcomb studied the effect of knowledge of group norms in four types of groups to answer these and similar questions. Four groups were studied: a religious club, a political club, a medical fraternity, and a medical sorority. Notice that these clubs fall into two types: those with a relatively narrow focus of interest (political and religious clubs) and those with a relatively broad focus (medical clubs). We would expect considerably more homogeneity of interests and values of the members of a political or a religious club than we would among the members of medical fraternities and sororities. People are attracted to the former type of group *because* of a similarity of interests. They join medical clubs for a variety of other reasons, and their interests and attitudes probably vary widely.

All members of the groups were asked to indicate agreement or disagreement with a series of items. After indicating their own attitudes, they were asked to estimate the proportion of group members who would agree with the item. Items were of three types. Those considered highly relevant to the purposes of the group were called type *A*; those of intermediate relevance, type *B*; and those of little or no relevance, type *C*. Of course what is relevant depends upon the group. Thus for the medical fraternity and sorority, *A* items asked about abortion and euthanasia, admission of women and Jews to medical schools, and the role of professional women. *B* items presumably were of relevance to any students, and *C* items dealt with such general issues as attitudes toward war and the place of the church in society. The same *B* and *C* items were used for all four groups.

Leadership was measured by a combination of four scales, all of which correlated rather highly: (1) Who are the 3 persons who, in your opinion, are most capable of acting as president of your group? (2) who are the 3 persons who, in your opinion, most influence the opinions of the group? (3) Who are the 3 persons who, in your opinion, are most worthy of acting as representatives of this group to a convention? (This is the Bennington question.) (4) Who are the 3 persons in this group with whom you would most like to be friends? Individuals in the highest 20 percent of every group in choices were designated "leaders"; those below were "nonleaders"; and those never chosen were "isolates."

The findings are rather complicated, but I think we can impose some order upon them. First, on *A* items, there were large differences between the ability of leaders and nonleaders to estimate opinions in the medical fraternity and the religious group. Differences were not quite so large, but still appear considerable for both other groups. Second, on the *A* items there were large differences between nonleaders and isolates in every group except the medical sorority. Thus we may conclude that, with the exception of the medical sorority, ability to estimate group opinions on relevant items and group position are positively correlated.

On the *B* items, those of intermediate relevance, there were considerable differences in ability to estimate for the medical fraternity and sorority, but not for the religious group or the political group. This seems to be true when comparing leaders to nonleaders, or nonleaders to isolates.

Finally, on the *C* items, those of most general relevance, there were no important differences in ability to estimate by group position.

We may also look at interesting results with the *B* type items, for in two of the groups (the fraternity and the sorority) group position and ability to estimate *were* related. If we consider the nature of these groups, an explanation may be presented. The fraternity and the sorority were probably constructed much more on the basis of a global agreement on issues among members than the religious or political clubs. That is, for membership in a political club, what is really important is holding the "correct" attitudes on candidates and issues; one's opinions on more general items doesn't matter so much. By contrast, for a fraternity or a sorority, there is not likely to be such a stress on conformity to a few central norms. What is needed for social acceptance is a fairly broad set of ideas where members can agree, such as the *B* items. In other words it probably would be possible to rise to a high position in the religious or the political club on the strength of only a few conforming attitudes. It would be more important to show conformity to more general attitudes in order to rise in a fraternity or a sorority. One would have to be "likeable" on a wider range of topics in the latter; being "a fanatic" on a few would not suffice, as it might in the former type of club. This interpretation seems plausible to me, though it was not made by Chowdhry and Newcomb. The fact that the biggest difference by group position in ability to estimate *B* items was found in the sorority seems to support this interpretation.

One other interesting analysis was performed for these groups. We would expect long duration of membership to be associated with ability to estimate opinions of other members, and it is desirable to see whether the findings just discussed would be more simply explained in this way. In other words if leaders were the ones who had been group members for the longest time, we would say that it was this time difference and not anything else that led to ability to estimate opinions. Table 4–3 presents the average length of membership in the various groups, by position. I have taken data presented by Chowdhry and Newcomb rounded off to the nearest whole month.

On the basis of Table 4–3 it could *not* be said that increasing social position was associated with increasing length of membership; thus Chowdhry and Newcomb rejected this alternative interpretation of the previous re-

TABLE 4–3   Months of Membership in Various Groups, by Position

Group	Leader	Nonleader	Isolate
Religious	12	21	23
Political	5	5	8
Fraternity	34	26	21
Sorority	31	29	25

sults. They write: "Length of membership, in these groups, is not consistently related to leadership and isolation, nor to an individual's ability to estimate group opinion."

This is true, and it is sufficient for their purposes. But I think we can discern a pattern in Table 4–3; it shows up more clearly as the result of rounding off fractions of months. For the religious and the political club, length of membership is inversely related to position. Quite clearly it is possible to come into such a club and rise quickly. For the medical sorority and fraternity, length of membership is directly related to position. One must be a member a long time to rise in the social structure. Since we have already argued that position in the fraternity and the sorority is probably based upon familiarity with a wide variety of norms (the *B* items), it seems reasonable that it would take awhile to learn what they are. For the more homogeneous beliefs of the relatively few directly relevant *A* items in the religious and political clubs, probably a few months would suffice.

Consistent with the notion that leadership in the fraternity and the sorority requires a broad familiarity with a wide range of norms, Chowdhry and Newcomb report that leaders of these groups also tended to have high positions in other groups. This was not true for the religious and political groups. The general principle seems to be: if the group is organized around a relatively small number of normative attitudes, achieving a high position in it requires a very good ability to discern those few attitudes; if there is less specificity of norms, then a moderate familiarity with a broad range of norms is necessary. And both of these principles support the main findings from the Bennington study; namely, that position in the group is a direct function of awareness of, and comformity to, normative attitudes and beliefs.

How does this translate into a prescription for becoming a leader in groups? Could we tell someone that his best bet if he wants to occupy a high group position is to learn the group norms and then to conform to them? Certainly we can advise him or her not to violate norms directly: that way lies rejection and ostracism. But it probably is not particularly satisfying, nor even wise strategy, simply to be a complete conformist either. One of the rewards (components) of high group position is the ability to exert some control over the attitudes and behaviors of others. Someone who plays a perfect conformist is likely to be unsatisfactory as group leader, and he certainly will get little enjoyment from the position. In a few cases it may be possible to rise in a group this way, but most times it is not.

Hollander has proposed the idea of "idiosyncrasy credit" that is earned and accumulated by individuals through conformity to group norms. The idea is that conformity on the part of an individual is noted by others and is rewarded by a slight rise in his group position. At the same time he is given a unit of idiosyncrasy credit: group members become a little more tolerant of him if he chooses to deviate from the norms later. Intuitively this seems plausible: we can think of many instances where we put up with, or even delight in, people whose behavior is distinctly unusual for their groups. Invariably these people already occupy a rather high social position: the deviate of low status is scorned, while the deviate of high status is considered eccentric and interesting. Hollander proposes that this idiosyncrasy credit may also be used to exert influence over group members, to get them to change their attitudes and behavior or even to change the group norms. In view of this idea, perhaps our advice to someone aspiring to a high social position would be *first* be sure to learn the norms and conform to them, and *then* when you see that your conformity has been rewarded a bit, exercise some of your idiosyncrasy credit to influence things your way. I present this advice tentatively, however. Others have argued quite oppositely, to the effect that the only way to become influential is to adopt a noticeably different set of norms and to stick to them persistently. According to this point of view, the best advice would be to try to resist all social influences towards conformity: decide upon the norms you will follow, and stick to them. There is evidence supporting both strategies; probably what is needed now is for someone to study the conditions under which each strategy gives more favorable results.

An alternative view of leadership is provided by such researchers as Stogdill, Homans, and Whyte in some studies we examine in detail in later chapters. This view depends on the observation that people high in group positions *give* other group members more than they *get*. For example, Whyte's study of a street corner gang showed that the group leaders made small money loans to followers. The loans often were never payed back, and they seldom were made in the other direction. Other leaders, such as businessmen and politicians, are able to provide useful things such as jobs and skills to their groups. These individuals also are giving something to the group, and are getting in return a high social position.

What is known about leadership from these various points of view is essentially quite consistent. All students of the topic agree that one cannot become a leader of a group without some rather high level of conformity to its norms. All agree that leaders, once they get in that position, are able to exert influence over the group in many ways, including changing the norms. And if we choose to look at conformity to norms as being rewarding to others in the group, we can see that leaders do give a lot to members. What they get in return is such tangible items as power and influence, and some less tangible (but very important) psychological items such as status and esteem.

Group Enforcement of Norms

The mechanisms by which group members enforce their norms upon newcomers have been hinted at in the Bennington and the Chowdhry and Newcomb studies. They are mechanisms we all use in everyday interaction to show approval or disapproval of peoples' actions: smiles and friendliness for conformity, and criticism or stony silence for deviance. Schachter studied these more directly in discussion groups.

Subjects were recruited to be members of four groups whose purpose was to meet and discuss different issues. There were (1) case-study club, which would discuss social welfare cases; (2) movie club, which would dicuss current films and related matters; (3) radio club, which would learn about broadcasting; and (4) editorial club, which would learn about newspaper editorial work. We shall study only results from group (1) at this time.

The discussion topic was Johnny Rocco. Johnny Rocco is a mythical delinquent who has run into trouble with the law. However there are many extenuating circumstances that could lead one to feel that he ought not to be punished for his actions. Members were asked to discuss Johnny's case, and at the end to decide whether he should be treated with "love and understanding," or whether he should be locked up and the key thrown away. Descriptions of Johnny's case were strongly biased towards the "love and understanding" conclusion. In addition, since subjects of the study were college students, we might suppose that most of them would favor this outcome anyway. Thus a group norm of love and understanding treatment for Johnny Rocco was extremely likely to emerge in these discussions.

Clubs had 8 to 10 members, and their discussions were observed for about 45 minutes each. Of the members, 3 were confederates. One, the *mode*, was instructed to adopt exactly the group's normative stand on Johnny Rocco. The second, the *deviate* (or deviant) was instructed to adopt and maintain just the opposite (to argue for strong punishment). The third, the *slider*, was to begin the discussion as a deviate, but to let the group win him over so that he was like a mode by the end of the discussion.

First let us look at the overall mean ranking members gave each of the confederates on "desirability" as a fellow club member. Table 4–4 shows mean desirability rankings for each confederate in all four groups. (A rank of "1" would mean that the person was the most desirable in the group; a rank of "8" or "10" would be least desirable.) Notice that the deviate is judged least desirable, and the mode is judged most desirable. This is perfectly consistent with the interpretations given for the Bennington results.

Second, group members were asked to select other members for three committees: the executive committee, which was to be important and interesting; the steering committee, which was all right, but less important and less interesting than the executive committee; and the correspondence committee, which was unimportant and uninteresting. The deviate was chosen for the correspondence committee much more than would be expected by chance, and was chosen for the executive committee much less often than chance. This finding closely parallels some of the Bennington results on consequences of deviance.

Third, we may examine patterns of communication towards the deviate in the high cohesive, relevant group. We do this very simply: how much did other members talk to him?

TABLE 4–4 Mean Desirability as Related to Conformity;
High Cohesive Relevant Group

DEVIATE	SLIDER	MODE
6.4	5.0	4.7

The situation is quite similar to the situation of, say, one conservative Republican among a group of very liberal Democrats. Intuitively, several different patterns of communication might be expected. For instance we might expect that nobody would speak to the deviate at all; that is, that he would receive very little interaction during the discussion. Conversely, we might expect that everyone would talk to him; that he would be very high on receipt of interaction. Or we might expect that at first everyone would talk to him, but then that he would receive less and less interaction as time went along. Or finally, we might expect that initially nobody would talk to him, but later everybody would attempt to change his mind. Schachter's study has always been a favorite of mine because once people know how it actually turned out, they say it was common sense. Before they know how it turned out, however, at least four different patterns of interaction sound plausible.

What actually occurred was the third alternative above. Communication directed towards the deviate began at a moderate rate and then rose steadily, presumably as his deviant views became disturbing to other group members. At some time in the third time period the communication peaked, and then very rapidly dropped off. By the end of the session the deviate ranked *last* on receipt of interaction. Fig. 4–1 graphs the pattern of communication to the deviate as a function of time. What Schachter's study suggests is that

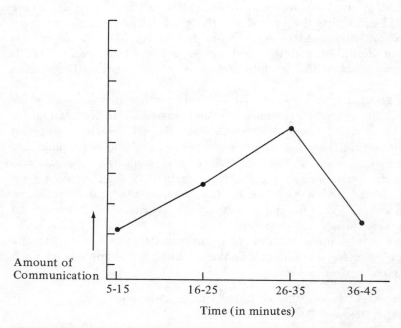

FIGURE 4–1   Mean amount of communication to deviate, High Cohesive Relevant groups. (Drawn from data in Schachter, 1951.)

one almost sure way to end up low in group standing is to adopt a very unpopular (that is, counternormative) stand on some issue. We might expect that an individual possessing unusual persuasive powers would fare a bit better than the average person, but there really is not much chance of changing people's minds on deeply felt issues within the time limits of a single group discussion. In a college environment, discussions of social issues seem to be particularly susceptible to authoritarianism of both the right and the left, and therefore opinions are difficult to change. Whatever the prevailing opinion, speaking against it in a direct manner usually leads to immediate and unpleasant reactions. As a strategy, we might advise someone in the position of Schachter's deviant confederate—that is, someone who wishes to express an opinion vastly different from the prevailing group opinion—to try first to acquire a high social position by expressing the more popular beliefs. Once he has gained the high interaction and influence ratings, then it may be possible to begin to change his public expressions, and with them others' opinions, without suffering the rejection phase Schachter observed. This advice, of course, comes from Hollander's idea of idiosyncrasy credit.

Attribution and Leadership

What we have seen so far is that two major determinants of social position are awareness of, and conformity to, group norms. An individual who is able to discover others' norms and who is willing to conform to them is likely to attain a position of esteem (Newcomb) and power (Merei) in the group. Why should conformity to group norms be so important in determining an individual's position in the ordering of the group? To answer this, we need to consider the relations between some psychological processes and group structure.

A rather simple psychological principle, yet one with tremendous implications, is the *attribution* process, described by Fritz Heider. The attribution process is an assumption, an assertion about the ways in which people think, and some consequences of the assertion in terms of how they behave in a given situation. Though there has been some research directly testing the assertion (and in Chap. 14 we shall study a more advanced theoretical version of the attribution process), this is beyond our interest here. All that we need is to understand what Heider means by "attribution," and how it works. Then we shall see how we can use the concept to explain the phenomena we have observed.

Attribution, according to Heider, is a basic psychological process, characteristic of the ways in which all persons think. It has two major components, a belief in *connectedness*, and a belief in *nonrandomness*, and these need to be examined separately.

Attribution asserts that it is a basic tendency for individuals to see *connections* between observations they make of the world. We tend to believe, Heider asserts, that when we see two or more events occur, they are not simply happenings. There is some sort of association between them. We tend to "look for relations" between events, between persons, or between events and persons. Thus if we happen to have a series of misfortunes befall us, there is a tendency to say that the events are connected somehow: we say that we are having "a run of bad luck." Similar things are believed to "hang together" somehow. If we observe that two people have some trait in common, or even that they are seen together frequently, we tend to see a connection: they are friends, maybe clandestine lovers, or they could be involved in some political conspiracy. There is some connection between them, or more properly, it is a psychological tendency to *infer* connections which we do not observe directly.

Seeing an association and inferring a connection is something we do all the time. If I see a particular person driving a certain car on a couple of occasions, I infer the connection "ownership" between the person and the object. In most such cases the inference will be correct, and it can provide useful information for me in later activities. In other instances such as some of those in the preceding paragraph, my inference would be unjustified. Yet when I make the inference, I have no good guide to how much of the "relatedness" I infer is objectively justified. Heider says that it is a basic fact of human psychology that we tend to impose this association upon our perceptions.

Second, we tend to attribute *nonrandomness* to events and objects, both to those observed singly and to those which occur together. There is imputed a "reason" for what we see, something "behind" the immediately observable. "Every time I wash my car, it rains." "Every time we elect a Democratic President we get into a war." "When a large number of people engage in sinful practices some natural disaster is likely to follow." There is, in other words, some *reason* why things happen the way they do. More properly, there is a tendency to *impute* a reason other than simple happenstance to things, even though we do not have good evidence that any reason exists.

There is also a tendency to attribute nonrandomness to people; that is, a tendency to believe that what they do and what they think "must be" related in some way. Person *A* has been known to approve of anti-union laws, restriction of government powers, and tightening welfare requirements. We do not simply see a series of opinions or votes here. We tend to attribute a more inclusive organization to Person *A:* he is a conservative. There "must be" some reason why he acts as he does. We tend to impute "personality traits" on the basis of observed behaviors, even in the absence of any clinical measures of personality. Perceptions of an individual's behavior are organized so that they become parts of a more general whole, and we impute both present motives and the likelihood of certain future behaviors to others. The principle of attribution states that we tend *not* to see others' behaviors as being either random or unrelated. Rather they are seen to indicate a pattern, which we name if we can.

Most simply, what the principle of attribution asserts is that people have a tendency to feel that many things are connected into a pattern, and that there is some reason for the association. In the absence of information to the contrary, attribution processes are set up which allow the individual to infer connectedness and to impute meanings which he cannot observe to observed behaviors.

As I said, it is such a simple idea and it's so natural to the ways we think, that it may seem unnecessary to draw it out in so much detail. But as I hope to show, attribution can be extremely useful in itself, and it will be even more useful when we explore some further developments of it. Attribution is something we all do, all the time. *Too much* attribution, seeing *too many* causes for events, or seeing *too many* hidden motives in people, is what we call paranoia. But how much is too much? Paranoia, like other psychopathology, seems to be just an extreme form of normal tendencies.

Think of the relation between events and persons, or between observations of behavioral events and particular individuals. Person *A* is seen to do certain things; for example, to behave in conformity with some group norm. A woman college student, let us call her Betty, voices a liberal economic view at Bennington, for example. Strictly speaking, all anyone has observed is one action, speaking the opinion, and the actor Betty. However, the principle of attribution says that an observer will tend to infer more; that the action and the actor are somehow connected and meaningful—that the opinion is "characteristic," or "typical" of Betty—and that it indicates something else about her likely opinions. Attribution says that there is a tendency in this case to assume the existence of a *motive,* a thought out intention on the part of the person. Betty said that, not just because it happened to come into her mind, but because she *wanted* to let us hear that her opinion was such-and-such. Moreover, her liberal view on economics is not a random event, either. It indicates much more, it indicates that her views on politics, social questions, international relations, and so on, are likely also to be liberal. The principle of attribution explains the frequently-noted tendency to "read in" motives on the basis of actions as a consequence of the more general tendency to believe in nonrandomness and connectedness of events and persons.

Let us examine the same hypothetical incident in relation to ideas developed earlier. We have heard Betty voice an opinion, in this case a *normative* opinion; that is, an opinion others in the group *value.* It is an opinion for which sanctions (rewards) will be distributed. It is the opinion others "want" to hear. When they hear it, they tend to infer more than a simple statement. They tend to infer that there is a reason (a motive) for her to say it, *and* that the opinion does not exist in isolation—she will have other opinions of the same (liberal) type, and importantly, these inferred opinions also will be valued ones. So what the principle of attribution does is assert that the consequences of a simple statement of opinion will be far greater than they might logically be expected to be. The person whose image is built up as the result of statements and the principle of attribution will be the one later chosen as "most worthy to represent the college."

We have left out one important part of the explanation: why should anyone care whether Betty has the "right" opinions? Attribution can again be used to provide an explanation, if we make one slight extension of the ideas. Not only will people *tend* to see relations and nonrandomness in their surroundings, but they will *prefer* to see them. It is somehow more pleasant psychologically to perceive things that fit the tendency towards attribution than it is to be confronted with direct evidence that attribution is wrong in a particular case. We would prefer to see things connected in an orderly way. We become uncomfortable or upset when confronted with clear evidence that events are simply random, or that major inconsistencies exist in the world.

In our hypothetical example, if we include two actors, Betty and Sally, and one action, Betty's expressed opinion, we may ask what Sally thinks when she hears Betty's liberal economic opinion. First, she thinks that it indicates a cluster of more liberal political attitudes, and that Betty is also likely to express these sometime in the future. Second, assume for this example that Sally's opinion is also liberal, so the presence of similar attitudes on Betty's part is pleasant. Why? Because in the opposite case Sally would have to recognize the simultaneous existence of some similarity relationship between Betty and herself (they both are Bennington students, and perhaps friends, for example) and some dissimilarity relationship (political and economic attitudes). That would directly counter the *tendency* towards attribution, and also would counter the *preference* built upon that principle.

More generally we may say the following. Upon perceiving an event (the opinion) and a person (Betty), a second person (Sally) will tend to see a reliable connection between the person Betty and the event. Furthermore Sally will *want* to see a connection between Betty and the opinion that is the same as the connection between herself and the opinion. She tends to attribute motives and beliefs to Betty on the basis of an expressed opinion, and she will prefer that Betty's beliefs and opinions be the same as her own. The same general principles could be applied to some results of the autokinetic experiments on norm formation. We said that in general a structured situation was preferred to an unstructured one, and that people seemed to prefer that others structure the situation in the same way (that is, with the same norms) as they themselves did. At least some abstract features of the autokinetic phenomenon and the Bennington situation are similar in this way, and they can be accounted for in terms of the principle of attribution.

If group members prefer to see others displaying the same attitudes as their own, then it seems reasonable that they will try to induce this; that they will want to induce conformity to their valued patterns of beliefs and attitudes. If somebody does display these patterns—if she conforms to the norms, that is—she is likely to be rewarded with a high position in the group. We do not need to assume that the group members approach the situation with such a rational, calculating frame of mind as, "We will reward conformity with a high position in the group." All we need to assume is that they will form their beliefs and actions in accord with the attribution principle. They interpret others' actions this way, and they honestly reflect their own feelings on it. They will say that they feel Betty is fit to represent the college in direct proportion to the extent that they feel Betty displays their own valued attitudes and behaviors. Whichever way we choose to explain it, the consequence is the same.

Now that we have completed our study on emergence of leadership, we can return to the question posed earlier: what advice would you give to someone who wanted to rise to a high position in a group? The evidence is that there are two types of group situations, those with well-established, strongly held norms, and those without. Using terms developed earlier, we say groups are more or less *structured* by having more or less well developed norms. If our hypothetical person is in a well structured group (such as Bennington apparently was), his best bet is to learn the norms and conform to them very well. If he (or she) does not conform, he will be in the position of the deviant in Schachter's experiment: excluded by others. If the group lacks structure (as many committees do at first), it is similar to the autokinetic situation. Then there is some recent evidence that the best thing one can do is to adopt a strong hard line and stick to it, hoping to influence others to that position. This latter is a higher risk strategy, since you might pick a line you cannot get others to agree upon. But it is the only strategy which seems to work—sometimes—in unstructured groups. (If it is an unstructured problem solving group, Chap. 6 can give some other advice.)

Propositional Inventory on Group Position and Conformity

Now we are in a position to summarize our results on determinants of group position. We will concentrate here on structured groups.

The first two propositions have to do with determinants we have seen of high group position. The first one summarizes the findings on attaining a high position, and the second summarizes the findings on required skills.

I. Attainment. Group members will choose others for positions as a direct function of conformity to attitudinal and behavioral norms of the group. (Bennington, Merei, and Schachter.)

II. Ability. The group member who best knows the other members' normative beliefs is most likely to attain a high position. (Chowdhry and Newcomb.)
   A. In groups with relatively homogeneous norms, attaining a high position requires very good knowledge of a small number of norms.
   B. In groups with relatively heterogeneous norms, attaining a high position requires a moderate knowledge of a large number of norms.

The third and fourth propositions have to do more directly with the relative group positions themselves, rather than with the techniques required to attain high position. Both of them are concerned with the maintenance of positions, though in different ways. Proposition 3 has to do with the carryover of high position from one group to another.

III. Transferability

    A. A member who attains a high position in one group with relatively homogeneous norms is unlikely also to attain a high position in a second homogeneous group with different norms. (Chowdhry and Newcomb, Merei.)

    B. A member who attains a high position in one group with relatively heterogeneous norms may also attain a high position in a second heterogeneous group. (Chowdhry and Newcomb.)

The last proposition at this stage states explicitly something which we have observed in these studies, though not drawn much attention to. This proposition will be particularly useful in looking at problem-solving groups in Chap. 6. It states that, in the absence of additional factors, once a power and prestige hierarchy emerges, it tends to be preserved.

IV. Persistence. Once they are established, the relative positions of group members tend to be maintained. (Bennington, Merei.)

    A. This is true even when one member not occupying a high position in the group makes a deliberate attempt to control a greater share of power and prestige. (Merei.)

    B. Members deviating from the group norm tend to be excluded from membership. (Schachter.)

To the statement of Proposition IV we should add the qualifier, "except by the process specified in Proposition I."

This propositional inventory completes our first look at structured inequalities within groups. In Chap. 5 we study the conflict process between the norms of competing groups. In Chap. 6 we restrict interest to problem-solving groups and examine a comprehensive theory of power and prestige relations in informal groups.

5

Groups

Groups and Roles

People spend most of their lives in the company of others, either in the sort of associations we call *groups*—those in which members recognize some commonality with each other—or in simple *collectivities*—associations without the perceived bond, such as a set of people waiting together on the corner for a bus. Here, we are concerned with groups and their effects on people.

When we talk of group membership, we usually talk about the *role* played by an individual, the "part" played in some group. For example, we may say that someone is playing the role of group decision maker or of clown. The word originally was French, *rôle*, meaning the part played in a theatrical sense, and this definition captures much of what social psychologists mean by role. The implication of this theatrical usage is that the role a person is playing at a given moment is not his entire being. The role being played at one time is not necessarily the role that will be played by the same person at another time. Today, in this group of students, John plays the role of "Sophisticated Person with Important Friends." Tomorrow in class explaining his late term paper, he will play the role of "Poor Student with Personal Worries." The roles may or may not be consistent, and neither role by itself fully describes the actor John. He can to a certain extent change roles at will, just as an actor does.

At the same time, it is important to distinguish the social-psychological use of the term role from the theatrical use. A good actor subordinates himself and his personal mannerisms to the role he is playing. He is not expected to *be* the role in any persistent involving sense. We regard it as an insult to our intelligence if an actor tries to convince us he is actually as virtuous, sexy, and intelligent as the parts he plays in movies. By contrast, a role in the social-psychological sense *is* a real, enduring, involving part of the person. One could not tell who the person is without describing some of his characteristic roles and role behaviors. It is "part" of our hypothetical friend John to act sophisticated among friends, and to seek sympathy in class. If we could describe the entire set of group roles an individual adopts, we would go a long way towards telling who he is. People very seldom do anything in which we cannot discern traces of some role or role-related behavior.

As this suggests, usually it is possible to see effects of the group even when the individual is not in immediate interaction with the other members. Some group values are adopted by the individual, learned by him, and incorporated into the way he deals with his environment, even when that environment is different from the group where the attitudes and values originated. We say that the role played in the group has been *internalized,* meaning it has been taken into the individual in a deeply involving sense. When a person learns a new role, there is a period of adjustment before he feels completely comfortable with it, before it is internalized. For example, medical students do not respond immediately the first time somebody calls them "Doctor," for the new role has not been internalized as yet. When they have learned so well "how a doctor should act" that they do not need to think about it, then and only then has that role been internalized. Roles, like norms, get internalized.

Because everybody is a member of many different groups, he plays many different roles. The same man is a *father* to his family at breakfast, an *executive* at the office during the day, a *race car driver* commuting home at night, and perhaps a *marriage counselor* to a friend after dinner. He plays each of these roles and is deeply involved in each. They have been internalized; at various times, he *is* each of the different roles.

It will be helpful to introduce a simple definition of role as it is used in social psychology, a definition that links the concept to other terms introduced and defined previously.

Role: A set of norms associated with a given social position which determine a reasonably consistent set of attitudes and behaviors.

In other words, a role is defined by the social rights and obligations attached to it. A person is expected to play a role in a certain kind of way. Others can observe his performance, decide how good it is, and indicate pleasure or displeasure at it. The person playing the role of suave sophisticate must follow the norms for correct etiquette. Otherwise he risks censure and ridicule and perhaps loss of the right to play that role in the group that has seen him perform poorly at it. It is a curious fact that the same sort of restrictions seem to operate upon undesirable roles. The child who plays the role of scapegoat for others' teasing or jokes seems to share an understanding of the "proper" way to perform the role, and even this role is subject to punishment for not living up to the expected performance.

Formal organizations such as bureaucracies (for instance, large corporations, the Army) are those in which social positions are defined independent of the occupants; that is, in a formal organization, the various roles are defined by descriptions of our rights and responsibilities, but without reference to the particular person who occupies the role. The roles, and the formal organization, can survive replacement of any or even of all of its members. Thus we speak of the president (role) of General Motors without mentioning any particular person. In an informal group, the roles are inextricable from individuals. It is impossible to separate the role from the person playing the role. The study of formal organizations is a separate field in sociology; from now on, when we speak of roles, it will be understood to refer to roles in informal organizations.

Within a given cultural system (such as contemporary American society), many roles come to be known by most of the individuals. It is not necessary ever to fulfill a role to know (or to think you know) how it ought to be performed. We all have a conception of what it means to be a mother, and my beliefs about what constitutes the role probably do not differ very much from yours. Roles thus constitute shared social definitions of appropriate behavior in certain situations.

Generally speaking, people do not like it when norms or expected role behaviors are violated. An attractive, happily married young woman who says she does not want to be a mother—or worse, that she does not even like babies—runs the risk of censure so great that we might think she was guilty of treason.

We may examine some of the reasons for this, using the example of norms defining role behavior. If we observe people getting upset when an individual's behavior is not what was expected according to his social role, we might rightly ask why it would matter to others. Why do people become upset merely upon hearing about someone else whose behavior does not conform to their ideas of appropriate role behavior?

To begin to answer this, let me describe a certain man for you. This man is probably in his 50s, though he could be quite a bit older. He is in very good physical condition. His customary clothing is cotton wash pants and a t-shirt, so you can see that he is not fat or flabby. He works in a college gymnasium and has worked there for the last 20 or 30 years, either in the Department of Physical Education or on the staff of the Athletic Center. For that reason, he knows an enormous amount of things about physical training, treatment of injuries, nutrition, and so on. His manner is gruff, and he frowns or scowls much of the time; however, if you talk with him, you find that he has a heart of gold—he is willing to take however much time you need giving out information, taping injured ankles, and talking about the old days. No one pays much attention to his real name, but everybody calls him Doc.

Do you know him? The chances are pretty good that you do, if you have ever been around a college gym. The reason of course is that nearly every college gym seems to have a Doc. The role exists widely in our culture. If you find yourself in a new gym, you are likely to see such a person. If you want to talk with him, you will know largely how to treat him as a result of knowing this social role (even if his name is not Doc where you are).

As the example suggests, it is comforting to meet Doc. It would be upsetting if he were to violate the normative role expectations we hold for this person. People find life a little bit more predictable when they know the social roles they meet. This predictability is gone when roles are violated, and people become upset. When people interact, a knowledge of, and a conformity to, the role behaviors goes a long ways towards simplifying potentially troubling situations. If I meet someone for the first time, knowing that he is in the role *salesman* and I am in the role *car customer* provides guides to both of our actions. Life is simpler; we can get down to the important matters much more quickly. In this example neither of the actors has to wonder whether the other is going to try to lie to him: it goes without saying that both of us will. Each of us can adjust his actions (and credulity) accordingly.

Knowing the roles involved in a social interaction provides guides to action. It tells a person how to act in an unfamiliar situation. It also tells people how others in the interaction are likely to behave, thus reducing uncertainty even more. Knowing the roles permits each person to have some shared expectations for the behavior of other people. The significance of this point should be clear to anyone who has mistakenly identified a professor as a student, or who has had a plain clothes police officer identify himself suddenly.

The other side of the coin is that if people treat each other entirely in terms of the roles they play, they remove most of the humanizing qualities of individuals. Expecting another person to act exactly in terms of one's conception of the role he is playing is one type of *stereotyping*, which is quite rightly opposed by most of us. Forming an impression of someone only from knowledge of the role he is playing is unfair; he has never been given a chance to show that the negative aspects of the role do not apply to him (nor, of course, is he forced to prove that the positive aspects *do* apply to him).

A place where the advantages of treating others in terms of their roles, as well as the resistance put up by people so treated, shows up very clearly in the interaction between waitress and customer in a restaurant. From the waitress' point of view, each person at the table in her area is alike: a role to be served as quickly and as simply as possible. The waitress does not want to get to know the customers as people. She hasn't time, and even if she did, she probably doesn't think they're very interesting. It is part of the waitress role to be polite, to ask how the customer is feeling today, and what he or she thinks of her food, but she really doesn't want to hear anything more than "fine." The waitress prefers, that is, to reduce the customer to a simple, predictable set of role behaviors. Anything else takes up time and attention, which she doesn't have enough of as it is. From the customer's point of view, he is *not* just like any other diner. He is a person, unusual, if not unique, and entitled to as much of the waitress' attention as he can get. He will try to explain about his diet, he will order food in a highly individual manner, he may even make little jokes with the waitress—anything, in short, to stress how much more of him there is than just the role.

Finding just the right amount of conformity to roles can be a problem. People just beginning to establish their individual identities to themselves and others, such as adolescents, sometimes register strong and emotional protests about being treated as roles: "Don't classify me; I'm unique; I'm an *individual!*" On the other hand, we can see evidence that people try to help others to classify them, by volunteering information that they are members of some group. The usual way to classify oneself (normatively defined, of course) is to say, "I'm *into* . . ."; meaning, "This is what interests me, and you can expect me to be similar to other people you have met who are interested in the same things."

The preferred goal is to find the correct amount of role behavior and the correct amount of individuality in each situation; it is not an easy goal to attain. Someone who limits himself too much to his roles—such as the office worker who sticks too closely to the rules and who has little personal life outside the office—is pitied for not actualizing himself and rejected as uninteresting by most of us. The person who errs on the side of refusing to conform to roles at all—the individual who constantly draws attention to things that have gone wrong, ways in which he or she is just a little bit unique—is a constant drain on our energies. We label this person a hysteric (or a nut), and try to avoid him or her. Roles simplify. Too much conformity to roles oversimplifies and makes the person uninteresting. Too little conformity causes excessive anxiety on the part of others. Finding what is just right is difficult.

A Discursion on Sex Roles

When it first became fashionable for men to wear their hair long, and when women and men began to dress more alike, I saw some very straight people watch while a group of very hip college students walked by. One of the straight group nudged another and said, "You can't hardly tell the boys from the girls," and all of them laughed loud and long at his joke. At the time, it didn't seem particularly funny, perhaps mildly amusing, but no more. From certain perspectives and a fair distance it *was* difficult to distinguish the sexes—but that has always been true of little children, and it never seemed worth much comment in that case.

What makes the incident interesting is that in succeeding years I have heard a version of that joke over and over again. Probably everyone in the country has heard it several times by now, but it always elicits the same loud, long laughter. When a social psychologist perceives laughter in excess of what the situation seems to call for, he looks for tension.

Subjects laugh during the conformity experiment and in other situations when they are tense. Perhaps straight people get tense in the presence of those who do not conform to standard sex roles. Much of the reason for this, I think, is related to our discussion above of the "advantages" of behaving in accord with the norms defining one's social role. In our culture until very recently, sex roles were the most encompassing and most strongly sanctioned of all roles. There were more norms prescribing how one should act as a male or as a female, and the social penalties for violation were stronger, than for any other identifiable role. Knowing the sex of the person with whom you were interacting gave an enormous amount of information about how he or she was likely to think, to act, and to react.

If one believes that men should be strong and women should be beautiful; that men should earn money and women should manage the house; that men are rational and women are governed by emotions; that men are competitive and women are accommodating; that the ideal man is a combination of John Wayne and John Kennedy and the ideal woman is barefoot, pregnant, and chained to the stove; *then* knowing someone's sex tells you nearly everything you need to know. Of course it is disturbing to meet a woman who doesn't try to be glamorous or a man who does; to meet a female business executive who lights her own cigarettes; to meet a man who enjoys cooking—there are no easy rules for how to act towards such a person, nor any social guidelines about how such a person might act towards you. To be unable to classify a new person is to be *anomic*.

Again the problem may lie in finding a desirable level of sex role conformity. I do not want to argue that all sex role behavior is undesirable, for some people feel more comfortable with some of the old norms, while others prefer new ones. It seems clear that sex roles were too sharply differentiated in the past, but whether they should be nonexistent is something I wouldn't presume to judge.

Glazer and Moynihan have reported that Jewish men from traditional families in this country have tremendous difficulties learning to cook. That is "women's work," and they develop enormous psychological blocks against it. They have no such difficulty with sewing, for it is linked with the male role tailor. By contrast, black American males usually have no difficulty learning to cook, but they often cannot learn to sew. The psychological reasons are the same—only the culturally determined roles are different. Sex roles, like all other norms, are quite arbitrary. But they can produce very strong effects on behavior.

Types of Groups

For men in our culture, the occupational role is the one overwhelmingly preferred for identification purposes. If someone asks me, "What do you do?" he does not expect to hear me describe how I shower and dress every morning, or what I do when I have an empty Saturday afternoon to fill. He wants to know what I do that someone else pays me for, and he assumes that I spend the preponderance of my waking hours (at least for five days a week) performing the associated role-determined activities.

If people use group membership and roles to identify themselves to others, we might expect that they use these things as important components of their own self-definition. We say people *identify* themselves as members of this or that group, occupants of these several roles. More psychologically, when a person thinks of himself he is quite likely to think, "I am a member of the group _____"; or, "I play the following role in my family." Family role norms, for example, provide guides to proper behavior during an argument: the father should not back down to one of his children unless he *really* is wrong, he should expect to know more, he should expect to be treated deferentially even when he asserts something with little supporting evidence, and so on. Many problems between parents and children are caused by conflicitng role expectations, as for example, when the father expects the son to act like an obedient child and the son expects to be treated as a young adult.

The most important groups in terms of identifying people and their role behaviors are called *reference groups,* one of the central concepts in social psychology. The reference group is a group to which the individual *refers,* people whom he thinks of in describing himself, and people with whom he can compare his attitudes, beliefs, and behaviors. Some examples of reference groups may be the family, a given school, fraternity members, or members of the same athletic team.

Our working definition is:

> A set of significant others with whom the individual may compare his attitudes, beliefs, and behaviors.

By "significant others" we mean simply that these people matter to the individual. He cares what they think, he wants their approval and agreement. Therefore the idea of a reference group includes the idea of social comparison. The individual compares what he is doing or what he plans to do with what he believes his friends in the reference group would think and do. Because people are closely acquainted with those in their reference groups, they know how members of the reference group *would probably* react to actions they contemplate taking. Members of the reference group thus can function to control the individual's action to a certain extent. He imagines (or expects) approval or disapproval from things he might want to do. The reference group is the "they" in the question, "What would they think if I did this?" To use an example from the last chapter, "What would my friends at Bennington think if I expressed a conservative political attitude?"

Two functions of reference groups have been distinguished by Kelley, Merton, Shils, and others. First, they may function to introduce normative rules for behavior, prescriptions as to how the individual ought to behave if he wishes to avoid some unpleasant sanctions. A television cowboy used to tell his viewers, "A good cowboy takes care of his room and hangs up his clothes." In other words if you want to avoid disapproval of "good cowboys," you'd better do it also. Everyone from fraternity members to Army officers to society ladies has at one time or another told new recruits, "We don't do things like that here."

A second function of reference groups is giving information which, at least analytically, may be distinguished from cases where the information is in the form of sanctioned role behaviors. Someone whose political reference group is Republican would be very much interested in learning how some of the Republican leaders felt about an issue that is not clearly identified as political (such as birth control or the space program) before he developed his own attitude towards the issue. In such a case it is difficult to imagine that the individual expects to be disliked by the Republican leaders if their attitudes differ from his own (after all, they do not know him), but their attitudes on the issue probably will have some influence in determining his attitude.

In any concrete instance, it will be difficult to separate the informational from the prescriptive functions of a reference group; that is, usually it is possible to discern some normative prescription with possible sanction in cases that at first appear to be merely informational. In the example of the preceding paragraph, the individual might think that if his attitude differed from that of the reference group, Republican Leaders, they would dislike him *if* they were to meet him, and this imagined threat of sanction might be called the cause of his forming the attitude they hold. The distinction between prescriptive and informational functions of reference groups, therefore, is not particularly helpful in most cases. Perhaps it would be preferable to think of reference groups exerting more or less probability of sanctioning the individual, since in any case their informational function must be present.

The greatest utility of the concept reference group is this: If you can identify the individual's reference groups, then you can make many very good predictions about his probable attitudes and behaviors by assuming that he will be influenced heavily by these groups. The degree of overlap is very high between the attitudes and behaviors of individuals who use each other as members of reference groups. The group provides the information on what they approve and disapprove, and there usually is some offer of social approval or other sanction for conformity. Then because the individual cares about members of his reference group, he is likely to display the same attitudes as theirs, or those attitudes he thinks are theirs.

When a person has recently acquired a new reference group, or when he aspires to become a member of a group of significant others, then we frequently observe the phenomenon of overconformity to the norms of the group to which he aspires. The most enthusiastic members of a group are those who recently joined: most college jackets and sweatshirts are sold to freshmen, and the most enthusiastic followers of the fraternity rules are the first year members. Similarly the adolescent who aspires to be recognized as an older teenager or adult uses more profanity, boasts more of his sexual adventures than people who actually are having sexual adventures, and generally exaggerates whatever behaviors and attitudes he thinks are displayed by the older group. Few people drink more than those who have recently renounced a life of abstention, and few people proselytize more for temperance than those who have recently given up the use of alcohol.

Before we begin examining some instances of reference groups and reference group phenomena, one caution is in order. Because of the great utility of the concept reference group, there is a corresponding danger of overuse. Suppose we claim that an individual's reference group is political radicals, and someone asks us to support the claim. We reply, "He has all the attitudes of radicals." What now is left to predict? That he will have the attitudes of a radical? We already knew that. In fact we used that information in identifying his reference group. To avoid problems of this sort, we must insist upon an independent means of identifying a person's reference group. We identify the reference group *first, then* we predict that the individual will display similar attitudes and behaviors. The problem of tautologically defining a reference group can be troublesome, and it is not always easy to avoid.

Effects of Reference Groups Upon Attitudes

In the simplest interpersonal setting we have examined, that of the autokinetic effect (Chap. 1), it was observed that norms (of light movement reported) established by a collectivity were similar to later reports of individuals. We might expect that the same sort of influence process would operate in the more complex setting of a natural group, one in which the members felt more clearly some ties of identification with each other. Such a group is the members of a housing unit of graduate student apartments. Residents see each other on the street and interact with each other when they choose to. We shall observe in such a group that the amount of interaction is an important determinant of the degree of group influence over the individual—people we see more often influence us more than those we see infrequently.

One of the great early social psychologists, Kurt Lewin, organized the Research Center for Group Dynamics at Ann Arbor in 1945. Lewin's basic studies have influenced numerous later studies in the way people think about things. The term *group dynamics* indicates that the researcher is interested in some aspect of attitude formation or change, usually the effect of group members upon individual attitudes. Lately the term may also indicate an interest in awareness or training groups (t-groups), though originally it was applied to studies of larger settings. Always, there is a central concern with processes of attitude formation and change.

The most important early study of group dynamics was reported by Festinger et al. in 1950. Westgate and Westgate West were two sets of married students' housing at Massachusetts Institute of Technology, and as usually is the case, residents of the two communities were quite similar to each other in terms of age, amount of education, professional goals, interests, and socioeconomic status. Because of this similarity of background, any differences observed between Westgate and Westgate West would most reasonably be treated in terms other than "previous experience" of the individuals.

Westgate consisted of 9 courts, each with 7 to 13 apartments, and housed 100 families. Courts were U-shaped, as in Fig. 5–1A. Such a placement encourages people to see each other when they come out the front door. Children can play with children from across the court, and parents will meet on the sidewalk as they enter or leave their apartments. One result of such a physical environment, the researchers report, was that members of each court tend to display similar normative attitudes.

Westgate West, the newer set of apartments, had 17 buildings of 10 apartments each, arranged "barracks style" as in Fig. 5–1B. The families,

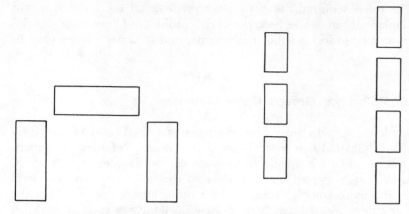

FIGURE 5–1 Physical arrangement of apartments,
Westgate and Westgate West

166 of them, had just occupied the apartments as the study was begun, and so they hadn't had much time to form group norms. Westgate residents had been living there for a year or more, and so group norms already had developed. It was an ideal setting to observe the effect of previously formed norms in Westgate, to compare with Westgate West, and also to watch the formation of group norms in Westgate West.

A tenant organization was formed to promote relations between members and the University and to help see that needs of the residents were met. Residents of both sets of housing units were invited to join, and their attitudes toward joining differed in surprising ways. In Westgate, the U-shaped courts differed markedly on whether their residents would want to join the tenant organization, which was surprising in view of the fact that the population of residents in each court had approximately the same backgrounds and they were randomly assigned to courts. (That is, which court one lived in was determined by factors other than choice of living near friends—availability of apartments, principally.) In Westgate West, attitudes toward the organization were uniformly favorable, but few residents became active members of the organization.

The researchers interviewed residents about the tenant organization, and classified them into two categories on two criteria: in terms of *attitude* and level of *activity,* these are shown in a 2 × 2 table in Table 5–1. (I have condensed the categories from those reported by the authors.) Each person was classified on both attitude and activity, so someone could at least theoretically be "favorable" and "inactive."

Proportions of residents in the two communities by this classification are also shown in Table 5–1. The percentages do not sum to 100 since some intermediate cases are omitted by the researchers.

On the basis of Table 5–1, we can say that residents of Westgate West were both more favorable towards the tenant organization (cell 1), and more active in it (cell 2), than residents of Westgate. This much is hardly sur-

TABLE 5–1   Westgate and Westgate West Residents
Classified on Attitude and Activity

ATTITUDE	ACTIVITY
Favorable	Active
Westgate: 54%	*Westgate: 49%*
Westgate West: 79%	*Westgate West: 62%*
Cell 1	Cell 2
Apathetic or Unfavorable	Inactive
Westgate: 33%	*Westgate: 51%*
Westgate West: 15%	*Westgate West: 37%*
Cell 3	Cell 4

prising: if people are favorable towards an organization, we would expect them to be more likely to be active in it. What is more surprising is if activity and attitude do *not* correspond, and there seems to be some evidence that this is the case in Westgate. About equal numbers in Westgate were active and inactive (cells 2 and 4), but the attitudes were considerably different (cells 1 and 3). Only 33 percent were "apathetic or unfavorable," yet over half were "inactive." Because the people in both residences came from similar backgrounds, finding a difference between Westgate and Westgate West in any respect suggests some factor operative in that environment. It would be consistent with the data of Table 5–1 if there were group standards affecting attitudes in Westgate—activity level would be partially independent of attitudes in that case.

To secure a test of the group standards idea, investigators classified attitudes according to how long residents intended to live where they were. In the absence of any social influences, we would expect that the longer an individual planned to live in the apartments, the more likely he would be to be favorable to the idea of a tenant's organization. Table 5–2 provides relevant data for testing this idea. Tenants who said they planned to move before the following June were classified as short-term; those staying one year or more, as long-term.

The simpler pattern, more favorable attitudes among long-term tenants, was shown again in Westgate West. Of those planning short-term residency,

TABLE 5–2   Proportion Favorable by Expected Term
of Residence

RESIDENCE	SHORT-TERM	LONG-TERM
Westgate	9/16 (56%)	14/29 (48%)
Westgate West	50%	72%

50 percent were favorable to the organization; 72 percent of tenants planning long-term residency were favorable. In Westgate about half the residents, both long-term and short-term, were favorable towards the organization. Thus again it appears that something other than expected individual benefits determines attitudes in Westgate.

What seems most reasonable to conclude at this point is that in Westgate, some group norms operated to produce the result that about half the residents overall were favorable towards the organization—whether or not they were active in it, and whether or not they planned to reside there a long time and to benefit from it. In Westgate West we have no evidence for any such group norm affecting attitudes. One likely reason for the presence of a group norm in Westgate is that the physical layout of the apartments was one that encouraged individuals to meet, to talk together, and to have the opportunity to compare attitudes and to form a group normative attitude.

If group norms did develop within a court, under what circumstances would they *not* be effective? How does it happen that sometimes group influences are resisted by the individual? Perhaps the group within the court was not sufficiently attractive to some members; they did not particularly care what others in the court thought of them or of their attitudes. Perhaps they did not see enough of the other court members even to know their attitudes—this is what we think took place in Westgate West. A third possibility is that if an individual's attitudes differ from those of the majority in the court, it may be that some outsider is influencing him. Maybe he spends enough time with someone from another court or from outside the housing complex so that either he does not know, or does not feel influenced by, the predominant group norm.

These ideas were tested by asking individuals, "Whom do you see most of socially?" and noting whether they named someone else living in the court, or an outsider. In Westgate the smaller the number of in-court choices, the greater the proportion of deviants. In Westgate West there appears a slight tendency for the same finding, but it is much weaker and not strong enough to conclude definitely that it exists. At least in Westgate the more people the individual sees from out of court, the greater the likelihood that his attitude will deviate from the majority attitude within the court. Note that we probably could never get a perfect negative correspondence between number of in-group choices and proportion of deviants, since we would expect that some people who have little contact with others in their residence group will nevertheless form the same attitude as their neighbors without any social influence from them.

Next we may look at the attitude deviants in Westgate to see some features of their social position. From the question just posed we can calculate the mean number of choices each person *gives* to each other person in the court, and the mean number he *receives* from each other person in the court. Since most people name more than one person in response to this question, the average number of choices given and received will be greater than 1. Table 5–3 presents the relevant data on choices given and received.

TABLE 5–3   Choices Given and Received in Westgate
By Deviants and Conformists

SUBJECT TYPE	N	NUMBER GIVEN	NUMBER RECEIVED
Deviant	36	1.25	1.11
Conformist	64	1.53	1.61

By comparing data in the columns of Table 5–3, we see that more choices are given and received by conformists than deviants. This is consistent with what we saw in the Bennington Study in Chap. 4: Those holding deviant attitudes tend to be social isolates. Second, looking at the rows in Table 5–3, we see that deviants give more choices than they receive, while conformists receive more than they give. Though it is not perfectly clear what this difference means, at least on intuitive grounds it seems likely to show that it is more pleasant to be a conformist. These people get chosen by others more than they choose in turn; deviants give more choices than they get. Because the researchers only asked, "Whom do you see?" instead of, "Whom do you like best?" the results probably are not so striking as they could be.

Festinger et al. also present data showing that within a court at Westgate, physical location is an important determinant of interaction patterns. Deviants living at either end of the "U" have considerably less interaction with other court members than deviants living near the center. The physical isolation of corner individuals probably facilitates developing out-court friends, and the deviant attitudes that may be fostered that way contribute to a social isolation. These data would also be consistent with the interpretation given of Table 5–3. In sum, spatial location strongly affects interaction patterns, and interaction strongly affects reference group influence.

Conflicting Reference Groups

Every individual is a member of many different groups, and each group entails a large variety of role-determined behaviors. When the norms of the individual's various groups are consistent, there is no problem for him. If a man's occupational role requires him to be assertive and dominating and his family role requires the same sorts of behaviors, there is no difficulty. On the other hand if his occupational role demands that he be submissive and meek while his family role demands that he be assertive and dominating, the two sets of role behaviors conflict. When the norms are consistent across the various groups of which he is a member, there is no problem. Of course there is also no problem if there is no overlap between groups. But it seldom happens that an individual can completely separate the various roles he performs. It may be easy to separate the occupational role from the family role, but it is probably considerably more difficult to separate the family role from the role played among one's friends. Remember that roles are *internalized*: adopted by the individual and carried around with him. Thus problems arise from incompatible role behaviors.

Most cultures evolve norms to help prevent frequent conflicts between the various roles individuals perform. These norms are concerned with effecting *role segregation*. For example, there is a strong norm which says that a graduate student who is teaching assistant for a section of a course should not date any students in that course. This is an implicit norm, though it is one usually sanctioned quite heavily. Conflict of interest laws represent explicit specification of a role segregation norm: "The president of a corporation should not also be a member of a federal agency that regulates that corporation." Until fairly recently most universities had nepotism rules specifying that a husband and wife could not both be employed in an academic capacity. Now some universities allow both a husband and wife to be employed as members of the same department, so long as neither of them is chairman of that department (and thus in a position to make decisions regarding promotions and salaries).

The most frequent source of role conflict is overlapping membership groups. Everybody is a member of a large number of different groups, and to the extent that he is expected to perform different sorts of roles in each, there will be problems. Even in the absence of formal or informal norms effecting role segregation, individuals will frequently attempt to segregate their various role behaviors. With the increase of employment among women, many women find conflicts between behaviors expected of them in their sex role and behaviors expected of them in their occupational role. In many ways which men seldom have to worry about, women face problems of identifying themselves as professionals, managers, executives, or physicians. An attractive woman who went to graduate school at the same time I did used to refuse to let male graduate students light her cigarettes for her. The reason was simply that she wanted to be taken seriously as a professional sociologist. Her comment on one such occasion indicates clearly an attempt to segregate her roles: "I'm a sociologist, damn it, not a woman!" This was an attempt to tell others that the less apparent of two roles was the relevant one for that interaction.

The great psychologist William James wrote in 1890 that a man has "as many social selves . . . as there are distinct groups of persons about whose opinions he cares." For most people, some overlap and some conflict between various membership groups is inevitable. Additionally, conflict between a person's membership group and his reference group is possible. A person's friends may expect him to do things he believes his reference group would not approve of.

When conflict may be avoided by isolation of the various groups, deciding how to act in a given situation is easy for the individual. When conflict arises it must be settled before any action is possible. In unusual situations the conflict that otherwise might be avoided is forced upon the individual. When the normal social structure is disrupted, as it is for instance, during a natural disaster, an individual may be faced with a conflict between various membership groups that he was able to segregate under more normal circumstances. This is the sort of situation studied by Killian.

Killian's research, conducted through the University of Oklahoma Research Institute, studied the response of survivors of two types of disasters. One was the explosion of ships in Texas City, and the other was tornadoes that struck three different towns in Oklahoma. Individuals who had survived these disasters were asked, "What was the first thing you thought of after the disaster struck?" and "What was the first thing you did?" Interview reports clearly indicate that most individuals faced conflicts between various groups; most frequently the conflict was between helping their family and helping members of the community—a conflict between family role and occupational role. For example, a policeman in one of these towns would be faced with a decision to stay on his job and help a large number of people in the community, or rush home to be sure that his family was safe. A member of a corporation in one of these towns would be faced with a conflict between looking after company property and the welfare of his company and attending to his family. Nearly everyone in such a town would be faced with these conflicts. The only people who might escape would be tourists or others who have no ties, either occupational or family.

From a variety of interview data presented by Killian, it is apparent that the family is the most important group to most people. Conflicts between attending to one's family or attending to one's job usually were resolved in favor of the family. One interesting corollary to this is that individuals we call "heroes" only appeared when their own families were safe. The hero is someone who acts selflessly, who stays on his job while other people are running away, and it is very difficult to become a hero if you're worried about the safety of your own family. Killian's research suggests that the best, or perhaps the *only*, candidates for heroes in natural disaster situations are individuals without close ties in the community. It is an interesting idea, usually overlooked in the popular mythology of heroic adventure.

For people less directly involved in public welfare, such as corporation officials, the conflict between looking out for company property and taking care of injured employees—a conflict between occupational role and humanitarian role—was usually resolved in favor of the humanitarian role. Also during the tornado disasters, telephone workers were on strike in two of the communities. Immediately following the disaster they were allowed by their union officials to return to work but a few days later were expected to go back out on strike. Thus there is a conflict between loyalty to the union or to the townspeople. In this case the conflict was resolved about equally often in favor of each group.

In general Killian's research shows that when individuals are faced with conflict between loyalties to two groups, they tend to resolve the conflict in favor of the group to which they are emotionally closest. People feel closer identification with the family group than with the occupational, closer identification with their humanitarian role than with their job role.

The telephone workers, on the other hand, had human demands on both sides: citizens who needed telephone service, and members of their union urging them to continue the strike. Each group was favored about equally.

The sociologist Cooley distinguished in 1902 between *primary groups* and *secondary groups*. A primary group is characterized by individualized face-to-face interaction. Members of primary groups know each other as individuals. They know each other's idiosyncrasies, and they know each other's histories. By comparison, in a secondary group individuals interact primarily in terms of their roles. For most people the most important primary group is the family. Family members know almost everything about each other, so they are able to treat each other in highly individualistic ways. By contrast, in a large lecture class, much of the interaction between teacher and student is determined by their respective roles. Thus this would be a secondary group. In a large corporation much of the interaction between people is determined by the roles they play; businesses tend to be secondary groups. More precisely, interaction in a large class or in a business corporation tends to be characterized by secondary group patterns. We can use the concepts of primary groups and secondary groups to formulate a principle that gives us a first statement for predicting how conflict is likely to be resolved:

> Conflict between expected role behaviors of two or more membership groups is most likely to be resolved in favor of the primary group.

Conflicting Groups: Abstract Features

Killian's study of conflicting group expectations is significant because, at least in a preliminary way, it points to abstract variables that may be important in a number of situations. The situations described in the disaster study are characterized by four features. First, two groups exist, each group holding different expectations for the individuals' behavior, and these expectations conflict in some cases. Second, in most cases, at least one of the groups is characterized by what we call primary group relations. Third, the conflict is inescapable. The individual is faced *simultaneously* with the conflicting demands from each group. Fourth, in order to act in the situation, the actor has to resolve the conflicting internalized role demands.

When they are described in this manner, situations studied by Killian come to possess much more generality. Situations of conflicting group expectations that display the four features just mentioned occur frequently in the lives of most individuals. An experiment incorporating these features was performed by Richard Ofshe with the goal of isolating more precisely the independent variables of consequency, and making more precise predictions for behavior in these situations. Since he was concerned with studying the effect of conflict, Ofshe created a situation in which two groups existed that held totally opposite expectations for an individual's behavior; that is, of the behaviors possible in the situation no action was expected by both groups. Individuals had to please one or the other. Moreover, since the concern was with studying decision making under situations of conflict, each person was faced with a series of decisions; that is, subjects were expected to choose repeatedly between the expectations of group *A* and the expectations of group *B*.

Subjects were women students at a junior college who volunteered to participate in the study of "esthetic preferences." The experiment had four conditions: (1) no conflict; (2) weak, equal strength conflict; (3) strong, equal strength conflict; (4) unequal conflict. In all cases each subject participated in the experiment by herself, and the task was to decide which of a pair of patterns on a slide was more "pleasing."

In condition 1 the subject was simply asked to indicate her preference. In condition 2 the subject was told that she was one of three persons. The other two individuals were in a different room, and she (the subject) would be asked to indicate a preference for a slide only if the other two individuals had disagreed. The experimenter explained that people find it very unpleasant when people disagree with their choices on this aesthetic preference test. In the weak, equal conflict condition (condition 2) the subject was told that the other two people were students at her school but they were people whom she had never met. In condition 3 the subject was told that the two people in the other room were both *friends* of hers whose names would be revealed to her (and hers to them) at the end of the study. In condition 4 the subject was told that one of the people in the other room was a friend and the other was simply a student at her college whom she did not know. Thus we would expect the amount of conflict felt by the subject to be greatest in condition 3 where two friends had disagreed and were waiting for her to resolve this "highly emotional" issue. In condition 2 there would be some conflict since someone would be upset whichever way she chose, but the people were not friends of hers. In condition 4 somebody would again be upset, either her friend or the stranger.

If we were making predictions for how people would behave in this experiment, there are two things we might expect to find. First, any of the three conflict conditions (conditions 2, 3, and 4) would be expected to induce some psychological tension in the subject since anything she did would please only one of the two reference others. Second, in line with our "primary group principle," we would expect the other described as a friend to be more influential over the subject's behavior than the other described simply as another student. Thus we would examine the data for evidence of psychological tension and for evidence of amount and direction of social influence.

How do people behave when they are in a tension producing situation? One thing we see is that they alternate between one type of behavior and another. Nothing they can do completely satisfies them. We observed this in Chap. 3 with subjects under conflict in the conformity experiments. We would also expect that alternating behavior—that is, choosing the preference of Other #1 this time and Other #2 next time—would be observed in this experiment. Furthermore we would expect that alternating behavior would be greater in the conditions of greater conflict; that is it would be greatest in condition 3, less great in condition 2, and least of all in condition 1. Figure 5–2 presents the probability of an alternation on each trial of this experiment for these three conditions. The alternation data look just as expected. Except for the first block of 15 trials, alternations are greatest in the condition of strong conflict (condition 3), next in condition of weak conflict (condition 2), and least in condition of zero conflict (condition 1).

A second thing we might expect is that psychological pressure or tension would be cumulative; that is, that it would build up over time. Probably the best way to deal with a difficult situation such as the one of the conflict conditions of this experiment is to make perfectly alternating choices—to agree with Other #1 this time and Other #2 next time. The longer a subject agrees with Other #1, the greater would be any sort of tension developing as a result of disagreeing with Other #2. Therefore, the longer the *run length* of choices agreeing with *either* of the Others, the greater the likelihood that on the next trial a subject will change and agree with the second Other. (A *run* is simply an unbroken string of choices of one Other.) We would expect also that, for any given run length, the probability of making an alternation on the following trial would be greater for subjects in either of the conflict conditions than it would be for subjects in the no conflict condition. Although the numbers are not perfectly regular, this is generally what the data show.

Finally, in order to examine our ideas about the relative strengths of influence between a friend and a student, we may compare behavior in condition 3 to behavior in condition 4. Let us arbitrarily designate the friend in

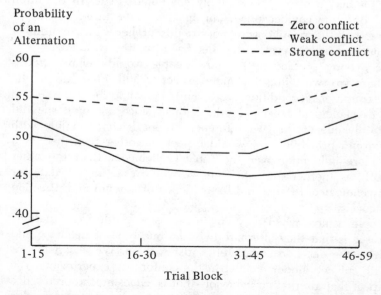

FIGURE 5–2 Probability of an alternation through time

condition 4 as O_1 and the student as O_2. In condition 3, of course, both O_1 and O_2 were described as friends. Now we may examine in each condition the proportion of times that subjects indicate a preference agreeing with O_1. In condition 3 we would expect subjects to be indifferent between O_1 and O_2; they would choose O_1 about half the time. In condition 4 we would expect subjects to choose to agree with O_1 (the friend) more than half the time. Figure 5–3 presents relevant data for this test. As may clearly be seen, both of our expectations were borne out. In condition 3 the overall mean probability of indicating a preference in agreement with O_1 was .49; in condition 4, the overall mean probability of agreeing with O_1 (the friend) was .58. The difference is significant ($p < .05$) by the statistical U test.

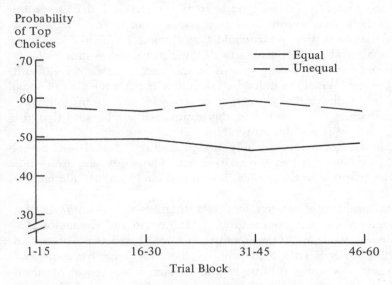

FIGURE 5–3   Regression of top choices through time

Reference Groups and Membership Groups

Reference groups need not be membership groups (and vice versa)—this is a fundamental principle in using the concept reference group. A person may become a member of a group and not care at all what the other members think of his behaviors or his attitudes. This is sometimes the case when a person is given no choice about joining the group, such as when he joins an Army unit. In this case group norms may not be particularly effective determinants of the individual's behavior, although as we shall see, cases where the individual completely ignores the norms of his membership group are unusual.

More frequently we see cases where individuals orient themselves to groups of which they are not members. Then the individual adopts a reference group that is not a membership group. The examples of reference groups given earlier in this chapter were both reference and membership groups. What would a nonmembership reference group be? We have already studied one such case in some detail in Chap. 4: the parents of Bennington students were important reference groups, yet "Bennington parents" was a group no student could join. Some people read newspapers to discover clothing fashions of society leaders, but have no real hope ever of joining that group. A child may orient his behavior and attitudes to the reference group *cowboys* after watching enough television, a reference group that probably never even existed, at least in the form depicted on television. The dress and mannerisms of prestigious older school children—members of varsity athletic teams or auto racers—can serve as reference group norms for children too young to join the groups. In all these cases a definite group of reference others may be identified as exerting influence over individual thoughts and actions in the "what would *they* think if I did this?" manner.

Although analytically it is possible to distinguish reference group effects from the influence of membership groups, in most actual cases it is difficult to separate the two. When the individual definitely is not a member of some group, we might still see that this group exerts reference group influence. When the individual is a member of the group, can we be sure that the influence we observe is *not* due to reference group effects?

In an ingenious and very carefully designed study, Siegel and Siegel were able to separate the two types of effects. The study and its results are directly comparable to the earlier Bennington study on attitude change at college.

The general problem of interest was to distinguish between effects of a membership group and a reference group in formation and change of attitude. The Siegels' study was more focused in interest and more precise in results than the earlier Bennington study, but there are many basic similarities. The Siegels' study was conducted with freshmen women at Stanford University during the early 1950s. To appreciate the features of the research design, we need some familiarity with certain aspects of life at that institution at that time.

All freshmen were required to live on campus in one of the "freshmen dormitories." These dorms are now co-ed, but when the Siegels' study was conducted, all women lived in two large buildings. There were approximately 900 freshmen of whom 300 were women. Dormitories, while certainly not luxurious—especially by today's standards—were habitable and pleasant. As we shall see, they were much more pleasant than some of the upperclass housing available to women.

After freshman year, women move either into an upperclass dormitory or into a "residence house" (at that time, all women undergraduates were required to live on campus). The residence houses, of which there were about a dozen, were large old houses that had originally been sororities. During the 1930s, as the result of some unfortunate incidents, sororities were abolished and the University assumed control of the old houses, but they retained much of their previous character. They were, for instance, on

fraternity row, and their residents saw fraternity men frequently. We shall
call the women's residences "row houses."

Although the row houses and the dormitories all were run by the University, they were very different types of places to live, and they required
very different life styles of residents. Dormitories are large and fairly im-
personal, in some ways like apartments. Houses were small, housing about
30–40 women at any time, and were usually characterized by strong primary
group ties between residents.

By any physical standards, the dormitories were much more desirable
places to live. They were newer and better maintained, uncrowded, and
safer from fire. Houses were old, crowded, and generally decrepit, and most
were in need of major structural repairs. (Early in 1960 the county fire
marshal condemned 22 of the 24 Stanford fraternity houses as unsafe for
human habitation—the women's houses were much worse.) But physical
conditions are not all in making a living place desirable. The houses were generally acknowledged to be more prestigious places to live—the Siegels collected data from students to document this—and women who lived in houses
were thought to be prettier, more sexy, sophisticated, and all around superior to dorm residents. The prestige of houses may have been partially
due to the fact that they were interspersed among fraternity houses, but
there was little support for all of the glamorous myths surrounding the "Row
House dollie." Since the University took over the houses, there was no
selective rush for members, no way to ensure that a given woman either
would or would not enter a given house. Perhaps the major function of the
greater prestige of the houses was a motivating one, to make some women
willing (in fact, eager) to live in the houses.

However, even without selective rush, there were many differences between house women and dormitory women. Of particular interest to us now
is the fact that they typically differed on the *F*-scale measure of antidemocratic tendencies, and also on the *E*-scale measure of ethnocentrism.
Row house women usually scored higher (more antidemocratic and ethno-
centric) on these measures than did upperclass dormitory women. At the
time of the study, the mean *E–F* scale scores of the various living groups
were as follows:

All freshman women: 102
All (upperclass) row house: 90
All upperclass dormitory women: 81

One effect of Stanford during the 1950s, like one effect of Bennington
during the 1930s, was to increase liberal attitudes, producing a general
lowering of *E*- and *F*-scale scores. Thus freshmen typically scored higher
than seniors on these measures. As we might expect, these scales measure
some attitudes of the "Political Economic Conservatism" scale Newcomb
used at Bennington. The Siegels report that their *F*-scale correlated +.55–.75
with the PEC, which is a high degree of association. But what is significant

is not the specific attitudes under study. It is the effect of groups upon individuals' attitudes of any sort, and the *E–F* scale scores were simply convenient attitudes to measure.

The way housing was chosen is another crucial factor in the design of the Siegels' study. At the end of every academic year, all women were given the option of remaining where they lived for another year, or of trying to move (excepting freshmen, all of whom have to leave the freshmen dorms). If a woman chooses to remain, that is the end of it. If she chooses to move, she lists in order of preference three other residences. Then there is a drawing, very similar to a lottery. The lower the number a woman draws, and the fewer other people who choose her first choice residence, the more likely is she to be able to move there the following year. This allocation process is unaffected by any factors other than those mentioned—desire of the house members for a particular woman, for example, is completely irrelevant. Thus for those women entering the drawing, which includes *all* freshmen, the assignment is random with respect to most factors—significantly, the allocation is random with respect to all attitudes, including *E*- and *F*-scale attitudes.

The Siegels studied women who, at the end of a particular academic year, chose as their first choice to move to a row house ($n = 28$). Of course, because of the drawing, not all the women choosing a row house would in fact be assigned to their choice. The fact that they *hoped* to move to a row house enabled the Siegels to infer that the house constituted a reference group to these women. They had some friends there, and they oriented their attitudes towards what they expected would be their new living group associates.

Of the 28 women for whom a row house was their first choice, 9 drew low enough numbers to get it, and the other 19 had to move to an upper class dorm for their sophomore year. For women living in a row house, their reference group and membership group coincided. For those assigned to the dorm, at least initially, reference group was row house and membership group was dorm. Since members of these residence groups typically differed on attitudes measured by *E–F* scales, women in the latter group may have experienced some conflict, particularly when topics related to these attitudes were discussed. Exactly how they responded to this conflict we do not know from the Siegels' data, though we may surmise that they acted in ways similar to what we saw in the Killian and the Ofshe studies.

By the end of sophomore year, some women living in the dorm had decided to remain there; others again entered the drawing in hopes of moving to a row house. (All those who got the row house the first time around chose to stay.) Thus there were 3 groups by the end of sophomore year:

Group *A:* in row house; chose to stay
Group *B:* in dorm; chose to draw out
Group *C:* in dorm; chose to stay

Taking as independent variables choice of row house at end of freshman year and choice of house or dorm at end of sophomore year, and *E–F* scale score at end of sophomore year as the dependent variable, it is possible to see the effects of both reference group and membership group upon attitudes. Table 5–4 presents scale scores for each group of women at the end of both years.

Note first that at the end of freshman year, all 3 groups of women had very nearly the same attitudes, and also that they were identical to attitudes of the entire freshman class. This indicates in both cases an adequate random sampling technique for selection of subjects. Second, we see that all 3 groups of women became more "liberal" during sophomore year; scores decreased for all groups.

The most important group effects show up at the end of sophomore year. The fact that groups *A* and *B* both differ from group *C* (*A, B ≠ C*) shows the effect of *reference* group: women in both of the first 2 groups retained the row house as reference group and maintained correspondingly more "row house-like" attitudes. The fact that group *A* differs from both *B* and *C* (*A ≠ B, C*) shows the effect of *membership* group: women actually living in the dormitory showed a corresponding shift towards more "dorm-like, liberal" attitudes. The fact that group *B* is intermediate to *A* and *C* (*A > B > C*) shows the effect of *conflict* between reference group and membership group for these women, with the reference group "pulling upwards," on scores, and the membership "pulling downwards."

It is tempting also to note that the reference group appears to have had a slightly greater effect upon attitude in the *B* group—91.0 is a tiny bit closer to 99.1 than it is to 82.2—which we would expect if these women had more primary group relations among row house friends than those in the dorm. But the numbers are so close that it would be wise not to take this comparison too seriously. Another interesting datum is the score for group *A* women at the end of sophomore year. It is 99.1, considerably above (less liberal than) the 90 for "all row house" women. Perhaps this was because the "liberalizing" trend continued for all 4 college years in "all row house" women, or perhaps it reflects the "overconformity to the norm" of new group members, which we mentioned earlier. In sum, the Siegels' study ingeniously separates out effects of reference group and membership group upon attitudes. All women in the study began (at the end of freshman year) with row house reference group and displayed row house attitude scores. By the end of sophomore year, those who had lived in a row house (group *A*) still had row house attitude scores. Those (group *B*) who had lived in

TABLE 5–4 *E–F* Scale Scores for Women by Reference
Group and Membership Group, Both Years

Group	End Freshman	End Sophomore
A	103.0	99.1
B	102.1	91.0
C	102.0	82.2

the dorm but who still wanted to move to a row house—that is, whose reference group and membership group differed—had, on the average, intermediate attitudes. Those women (group *C*) who decided to stay in the dorm—that is, who changed reference group to coincide with membership group—showed almost perfect dormitory attitude scores. Both groups have some influence over attitudes; if we know any particular woman's reference group and membership group, we can make a good prediction of her attitudes.

Choosing a Reference Group

Membership in several groups can, as we have seen, cause conflicting obligations upon the individual, but it also entails freedom to choose between the groups. An individual with only a single reference group—for example, a young child with only his parents—has no choice. Either he conforms to the norms of that group or he forfeits whatever social rewards they are willing to offer. With more than one potential set of reference others, the individual has a choice. If he does not conform to what members of one group expect, perhaps he conforms to expectations of the membership of a second group. If a woman at Bennington does not conform to the political attitudes of her parents, they may withhold their social approval, but another group will reward her more liberal attitudes. With reference group influence as in life generally, choice dilemmas and freedom are linked together.

We have been treating group influence in terms of normatively-defined behaviors and attitudes, and conformity or nonconformity to norms. This should suggest that perhaps the Cohen model of abstract features of the conformity experiment may also apply to reference group situations. Our goals are to use the model to codify our knowledge, to clarify our description of the situation and, we hope, to alert us to see new features of situations of reference group conflict.

Recall from Chap. 3 that the model has 4 "states," corresponding to different orientations to the conflicting normative demands of two different groups. Everything to the left of the dotted center line in Fig. 5–4 represents conformity to the norms of group I. Everything to the right represents conformity to the norms of group II. States 1 and 4 represent permanent conformity to the norms of each group, respectively. States 2 and 3 represent temporary conformity to the given group, as well as conflict. An individual in state 1 or 2 has "chosen" group I for his reference group, either permanently (state 1) or temporarily (state 2). States 3 and 4 are similarly interpreted.

Let us see first whether we can apply this model to describe and illuminate the situation of the Bennington woman. Group I will be her parents with their relatively conservative attitudes, and Group II could be either the faculty or the student body at Bennington—or both. Since we are only interested in this one attitude, for our purposes here, they are equivalent.

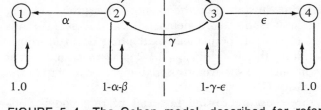

GROUP I
High PEP Scores
High E and F Scores

GROUP II
Low PEP Scores
Low E and F Scores

FIGURE 5–4 The Cohen model, described for reference group conflict

We shall assume that the Bennington woman enters with a predisposition
to have her parents' attitudes. She is thus in state 2. If she were unwilling
ever to consider changing her attitudes, which is also possible, she would
have started in state 1. We know from the model that states 2 and 3 are
conflict states, and that they are characterized by alternating behavior. Thus
we believe that these Bennington women alternated in expressing political
attitudes; sometimes conservative, sometimes liberal. We shall never know
for sure whether this happened since we do not have the relevant observations, but because of the model we are confident it was the case.

For much of the time at Bennington, we imagine most women moved
between states 2 and 3 in their attitudes: alternately holding both views,
but not totally committed to either. Some few, we imagine, may have moved
either to state 1 or 4, but not very many. How do we know it was not very
many? We know that few moved to state 1 since it was the exceptional
woman who graduated from Bennington with her parents' political attitudes. We are reasonably certain that few moved to state 4 because we
know from Newcomb's later study that, unless a woman married a man
with similarly liberal attitudes, she was very likely again to become conservative herself. Of course it is true that we cannot distinguish between
states 1 and 2, or between 3 and 4, with finality. In other words we do not
know for sure whether a Bennington woman who has been consistently
conservative in her attitudes is in state 1 or state 2. (However 30 years is a
long time, so we might take a chance and guess for some that their con-
servativism is permanent by now.)

To apply the Cohen model to the Stanford women we need to consider
separately the three groups (*A, B,* and *C*) distinguished by Siegel and
Siegel. Group I here will be row house attitudes (high *E–F* scale scores),
and Group II will be dorm attitudes (low *E–F* scale scores).

Women of group *A,* who got house membership immediately, present the
simplest case. They probably entered in state 2 (perhaps a few in state 1),
and the overwhelming tendency was to maintain the state 1 or 2 attitudes.
We have no reason to believe that these women ended sophomore year in
either state 3 or 4.

Women of group *B,* who got the dorm but who later tried to move, probably were similar to those of group *A,* but not identical. We do know that these women ended sophomore year in state 1 or 2 (since all still wanted to move to a house), but we also know that their attitudes were, on the average, more democratic by that time than group *A* women. Presumably they spent more time in state 3 on the average than group *A*—they adopted, temporarily at least, some more democratic attitudes. (Perhaps one or two even moved to state 4, permanently adopting dorm attitudes. The only reason for doubting this is a hunch that if a woman underwent such a complete change in outlook, she would probably prefer to stay in the dorm, and would be in group *C*.)

Women in Group *C* are most interesting in terms of the model, since their attitudes "moved" the most. We know that they began sophomore year with the same attitudes as groups *A* and *B,* so they must have been in state 2 at that time. (How do we know they were not in state 1?) By the end of sophomore year, their attitudes had shifted greatly and they chose the dorm (group II) as their reference and membership group. Therefore they were either in state 3 or 4. Practically speaking, we may believe a woman eventually moved to state 4 if she remained (happily) in the dorm for the rest of her time at Stanford, though of course we would want to interview her at graduation to be sure of that.

If we make the simplifying assumption that all women studied, both at Bennington and at Stanford, began in state 2, then we can represent their attitude changes (or attitude maintenance) quite well by applying appropriate values to the parameters α, β, γ, and ϵ. The model then will enable us to make a precise and rigorous description of all the group effects upon attitudes which we have studied. In addition it enables us to be reasonably confident of several effects we did *not* study because no relevant information was provided in the original reports (for example, psychological tension, alternating behavior, and resolution).

Applying the model highlights important features of the situation and explains observed phenomena of interest as being consequences of the unobserved states. It indicates ways in which the Bennington and the Stanford experiences are similar to each other, as well as ways in which they both are similar to the very different Asch conformity experiment. Finally, the model shows that some features of the college situations that may have seemed important at first—such as the PEP and *E–F* scales, the high status of row houses at Stanford, or the "awareness" of influence at Bennington— are, in this sense, irrelevant. Certain features of the situations are enduring; the *influence, conflict,* and *resolution* processes in the model occur independently of the historical setting, the specific attitudes studied, or the exact groups or individuals involved.

In situations where reference group conflict is present (or conflict between membership groups or between reference group and membership group), the situation may be simplified by thinking of Cohen's model and Ofshe's experiment. In the simplest possible way, the model and the experiment highlight essential features of group conflict; hence, they are useful tools for analyzing many, much different sorts, of group conflicts.

6

Power and Prestige

Development of Inequality

The most pervasive feature of social interaction is that, even upon cursory observation, inequality is apparent among the participants. Every known society exhibits *stratification*: a preference ordering of individuals and groups of individuals in terms of power, wealth, and life style. Formal organizations such as modern corporations, and institutions such as the Church are deliberately stratified along explicit criteria (skill, knowledge, experience, or family ties).

At the interpersonal level, we might expect stratification to be less apparent. The "equality norm," stressing essential similarities between people and playing down the importance of differences (especially *evaluated* differences), might prevent a ranking from developing. In fact the opposite is true. There is a great deal of evidence to indicate that *inequality*, not equality, is the most frequent consequence of social interaction. Equality, at the interpersonal level, is a norm of hypocrisy.

In any group of two or more individuals it is possible to determine by appropriate measures *rankings* of individuals, some subordination and superordination of members of the group. People may be ranked on all sorts of scales: in terms of height, race, intelligence, attractiveness, or in terms of overall status. In this chapter we shall study the basic processes in development of inequality among members in terms of *power* and *prestige*. Our attention will be restricted to informal groups, those lacking any structure of explicitly defined roles that are independent of their particular occupants.

People who meet for the first time, even if they begin the interaction as equals, tend to develop various rankings among themselves rather quickly. Even after the briefest of interactions, it frequently is possible to decide that one individual possesses more power and prestige in a relationship than another individual. What leads to this inequality among individuals who began as equals? What are the *conditions* under which inequality emerges, and what determines *which* individuals will come to possess more power and prestige, and which less? In Chap. 4 we considered several possible answers to these questions in groups which possess normative structure. However, since here we are concerned with the emergence of inequality among members who have never previously met, there can be no initial group structure. A somewhat different way of viewing group norms is to say that they describe *valued activities* for the individuals in the group. This suggests that any activity which other individuals find valuable is likely to result in a high social position for the individual actor.

Most of the groups we shall study in this chapter are *task-focused*; groups whose purpose in meeting is to solve some problem. Problem-solving groups constitute a large and important proportion of all groups in society, and they are particularly interesting now because it is quite clear in them what constitutes *valued activity.* In a problem-solving group a valued activity is anything that helps to solve the problem. If the group is composed of members of a conference whose goal is to devise a sales operation, any suggestion that furthers this goal is a valued activity. If the group is a debating team in college, any suggestion that helps to win the debate is a valued activity. If the group is a jury faced with the problem of deciding guilt or innocence of the accused, any suggestion that helps members to reach their decision should be valued. Any individual who helps the group to reach its goal of problem solution is performing a valued activity, and as we shall see, he is likely to be rewarded by being given a high position of power and prestige in the group. We shall define power and prestige in task-focused groups as having the same components as "group position" in Chap. 4: the rights to attention of others, to sanction, to use the group's time, and to initiate group activities; and the rewards of approval, respect, esteem, acceptance, and security.

The Bales Discussion Groups

Emergence of power and prestige differences between initially undifferentiated members of problem-solving groups could be studied in a variety of settings. In fact various researchers have observed the differentiation process in such widely varying settings as high school basketball teams, classrooms, and seminar-type discussion groups. The differentiation processes appear most clearly in what are called *Bales Groups,* named after Robert Freed Bales of Harvard University, who first studied them and who developed the basic research setting.

A Bales group is simply a discussion group, usually composed of individuals who are strangers to each other and who are alike in terms of most visible status characteristics such as sex, age, and race. (In Chap. 7 we shall see what happens in these groups when members are dissimilar in these characteristics.) Typically the members of a Bales group are male sophomore college students—simply because male sophomore college students were readily available when Bales conducted his first researches. The number of members of a Bales group varies from as small as two to as many as twelve or fifteen. Usually the groups studied are intermediate to these two extremes of size, with 5-person groups probably studied most frequently. Members of a Bales group are seated in positions so that they can conduct a discussion comfortably, and also so that they may be observed and identified by researchers who watch the discussion through a one-way mirror. Figure 6–1 shows the arrangement of the laboratory rooms for observing a typical Bales group. Individuals are seated at a table with an identifying number in front of each of them. (The number is usually for

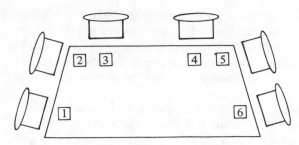

FIGURE 6–1 Table and chair set-up for six-person
Bales group

the researcher's purposes. Individuals, of course, address each other by their
names.) After members have been seated, they are told that the researchers
are interested in observing and analyzing group discussion processes. They
are given a topic to discuss and are told that at the end of the discussion
period—usually about 45 minutes—they will be polled on their opinions of
the topic and of the interaction.

A frequent topic of discussion is the "Johnny Rocco case," described in
Chap. 4. Johnny Rocco is a hypothetical delinquent who has committed a
rather serious crime, but he comes from a difficult background. Bales group
members are asked to read a short summary of his history, to discuss it,
and reach a group decision whether he should be treated with "love and
understanding" or whether someone should "lock him up and throw away
the key." Since the goal of discussion is to enable members to exchange
opinions and reach conclusions on this question, it is clearly a task-focused
group. Note also that the task is one for which there is no single right
answer. The Johnny Rocco case is *ambiguous*: members could reasonably
come to either conclusion. Note also that the task is a *collective* one: it is
both legitimate and necessary for individuals to take each other's opinions
into account in forming their conclusions. For comparison we might think
of a classroom of students all writing answers to the same final examination
—a situation decidedly not intended to be a collective task!

Another topic frequently given to Bales members is to read parts of *Billy
Budd* by Melville. Billy Budd was a seaman accused of striking a superior
officer, a capital offense in the eighteenth century. Again there were miti-
gating circumstances. The task of group members is to decide whether he
should be executed or merely reprimanded for his offense. Again, there is
no clearly right answer.

After explaining the discussion task and observational purposes of the
research to Bales group members, the experimenter leaves the room and
discussion begins, usually with members introducing themselves to each
other. Observers on the other side of the one-way mirror record the ensuing
discussion in considerable detail. Most frequently, interaction is scored in
terms of two general characteristics: who speaks to whom, and the nature of
what he says. Each single complete thought expressed by an individual is
called an *act*, so each act is recorded in terms of "who-to-whom" and in terms

of "content." Who-to-whom is scored using the numbers identifying group members. For example if person #6 directed an act to person #2, the researcher would score this as "6–2." If #2 replied to person #6, this would be scored "2–6." Any act directed towards all the group members is scored with a 0. For example, "Does anybody have any ideas?" by person #3 would be scored 3–0.

Content of each act is scored according to a system of 12 categories developed by Bales and his associates. Figure 6–2 shows the 12-category Bales interaction recording system. Interaction may be scored on a machine that consists of a moving piece of paper divided into 12 rows, each row representing one of the 12 interaction categories. For example if person #1 asked person #4 a question, this would be scored by writing "1–4" in category #7. When interaction recording machines are not employed, the researcher would write 1–4–7 to indicate that person #1 asked person #4 a question. There is one additional rule in scoring a Bales group: the group as a whole cannot *initiate* an act. Thus for example, if everyone in the group spontaneously laughed (category 2), this would not be coded.

The Bales interaction recording system enables researchers to recover a fairly detailed record of the interaction of each group. The record may then be analyzed in terms of the amounts spoken by each individual (his *initiation* rate), the amount each individual is spoken to (his *receipt* rate), and the types of acts initiated and received by individuals. Recording interaction of a Bales group is not so easy as it might appear, and observers require considerable training before they are able to attain a high degree of reliability (interobserver agreement) in their observations. However the basic experimental design has proved to be a most successful means of studying discussion group interaction.

Inequality in Bales Groups

During the course of discussion, members of Bales groups typically differentiate in terms of power and prestige. Long before the end of the 45-minute interaction, it is quite apparent that some members of the group are more influential in guiding the discussion, in getting other members to agree with them, and in making decisions for the group as a whole. Other members participate less, exert less influence, and find that their suggestions are either ignored or are treated as though they were inconsequential or wrong. At the end of the discussion period, members may be asked to fill out questionnaires telling such things as the following: "Who did most to guide the group discussion?" "Who had the best ideas in the group?" "Which group member was most likable?" "Who seemed to show the most leadership?" Typically, there is good agreement among group members in their answers to these questions—questions that deal with various aspects of ability and group structure.

Let us now leave the category system of types of interactions and consider for the moment simply amount of interaction. To do this, all we need to

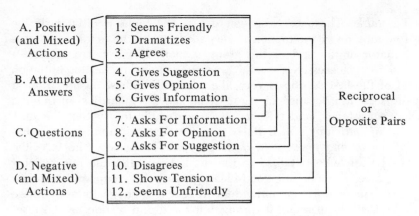

FIGURE 6–2 Categories for interaction process analysis (From Bales, 1970, p. 92.)

examine is the who-to-whom record of interaction. We shall be concerned with how much interaction each individual initiates and how much he receives. Members may be ranked in terms of how much *time* they talk, or in terms of the *number* of acts they initiate. If we examine data from a typical Bales group, we can count on observing some striking regularities of interaction. The first thing we observe is that by these measures there is an *inequality* of members. Most frequently there is a steady progression from highest initiator to lowest, and very seldom do two individuals initiate at about the same rate. Second, if we rank individuals as to receipt of interaction we find that this is also distributed unequally. People talk in different amounts, and they are talked to differentially. Moreover, the ranking on initiation of interaction tends to correspond to the ranking on receipt of interaction; these rankings are *reciprocal*. In other words, those people who talk the most are those who are talked to the most. Those who talk the least are those who are talked to the least. What this indicates is that the popular myth of an individual who talks a lot without being talked to is just that—a myth. In a Bales group, a person talks a lot *because* he has been talked to a lot. In a sense, which we shall specify precisely later, an individual talks a lot because the group *allows* him to do so. It just is not the case that somebody will talk on and on without others wanting him to.

The third finding is even more revealing: most rankings of group members tend to be *consistent*. If the group members are asked to tell who contributed most to the group discussion, who had the best ideas, who did the most to guide the group and keep discussion moving, who seemed to be the leader of the group, or other questions of this sort, the individual most chosen on all these rankings is most frequently the individual who ranked highest on initiation of interaction. (Of course he is also likely to be the individual who ranked highest on receipt of interaction.) The highest initiator is likely also to be chosen by the observers as having been most influential and effective.

The fourth finding is that initiation rates and choices in the questionnaires tend to be *stable*. The actor who emerges as the highest initiator during the first few minutes of interaction is very likely to be the actor who is the highest initiator at the end of the group session. If the group meets for several sessions on successive days, the actor who ranked highest on initiation at the end of the first session is very likely to rank highest on initiation at subsequent sessions. Because of these remarkable regularities—inequality, reciprocity, consistency, and stability—it is reasonable to say that *the rank of initiation of individuals in a Bales group reflects the rank on all components of power and prestige in these groups.* The person who talks the most is the person who is talked to the most. He is also the person most likely to be perceived as having good ideas, guiding the group, and being its leader. Furthermore once an individual attains a high position by these measures, he is likely to retain it throughout the group session or at subsequent sessions if the group meets more than once.

The inequality evident by the end of the group meeting does not always come about smoothly, however. Early in the group's session, there often is a "status struggle" for interaction supremacy. Perhaps because Bales groups usually are composed of college students, nearly all members would like to be the most frequent talker. It is only when some of them are curbed by the reactions of others that the inequality becomes visible and stable. As we shall see, however, the amount of time necessary for differentiation to occur is rather small—sometimes as little as a few minutes, and very seldom is it greater than 10 minutes. (In a moment we shall study conditions surrounding the status struggle. It appears in most Bales groups, but does *not* appear in some other discussion groups, such as juries.)

Very recently Patricia Barchas conducted some Bales groups with an interesting additional variable: before beginning the discussion, group members each consumed about half a bottle of wine. (Who said social research has to be dull?) What would you expect the effect of this independent variable to be? Actually there were two: the power and prestige differentiation emerges more rapidly in these groups, and the stratification (between members) is greater. To explain these results all we need to assume is that the alcohol depresses somewhat the usually high level of competitiveness and perhaps status anxiety of college student subjects. After a little wine they are less concerned with being the highest interactors, less worried about pushing their ideas, than they otherwise would be. Barchas has not completely analyzed the data as yet and there may be other evidence that does not support this interpretation. However it is consistent with other data from Bales groups, and it seems plausible.

One measure by which the highest initiator may *not* rank highest is liking. The individual who talks the most and who is perceived as making the best suggestions and demonstrating the most leadership often is not the best-liked person in the Bales group. The best-liked person then is the second-highest initiator (who also is usually ranked second on other measures as well). Several reasons for this have been proposed, but the simplest seems most convincing. A very high proportion of acts initiated by the highest initiator are in the most task-focused categories (#3, 5, 6, 10). He is making suggestions and tells others when he thinks their ideas are good and bad. Nobody likes to hear that his ideas are bad even when they actually are, and this probably arouses some hostility towards the highest initiator. By contrast, acts of the second highest initiator typically are in social–emotional categories (especially #1 and 2). He is the one who tells a joke at just the right moment to avoid a fight, and who smooths over hurt feelings left behind while the leader pursues the group task goal. Even in a task-focused group, which Bales groups are, someone has to pay attention to the facilitative and emotional needs of the group members. This usually is the function of the second-highest initiator. Attending to the social–emotional needs of the group members is somewhat a thankless function, however, since the "social–emotional leader" forfeits any great control over the group discussion and decision. He is the "nice guy"; liked, but not particularly powerful at task roles.

Lewis has recently shown that development of both a task leader and a social–emotional leader is not an invariable occurrence in Bales groups. Sometimes the task leader is in fact best-liked—the enviable situation of being both powerful and loved. Intuitively we would expect that the less tension generated during the discussion, and especially the less generated by the acts of the task leader, the less the need would be for a second individual to emerge as the social–emotional leader. If the task leader is absolutely ruthless in pursuing his own ideas and his opinions of which ideas offered by others are good ones, he will leave a lot of hurt feelings in his wake. Conversely if he is somewhat more skillful at diplomatic arts, if he can tell another person *politely* to change his line of thought, then he should be able to exercise his influence without needing the efforts of another person to prevent hostile disintegration of the group. What this means is that if the highest initiator recognizes the need to spend some part of his attention on the social–emotional needs of the group members, and of course if he is willing to do so, then the need for a separate social–emotional leader decreases and this second role may not be observable. These needs do exist, and they must receive attention. When the task leader is willing and able to do this, no one else need do so; but if he does not, then someone else must, or the discussion will disintegrate into hostile silence.

One condition particularly promoting a smooth acceptance of differentiation by group members is some sort of *legitimation*. If there is a good reason for one person to claim a high position in terms of interaction and influence, then the need for a social–emotional leader decreases and there is not likely to be either a status struggle or role differentiation. For instance if one individual lets the others know (subtly, of course) that he has some special expertise in the topic under discussion, then it is reasonable to allow him to talk a lot and to take seriously what he says. There usually is little hesitancy on the part of Bales group members to indicate that their special competence lies in just the area of discussion: "We were just studying the Billy Budd case in my Law, Morality, and Ethical Decisions class." In absence of the competence specifically required, a general ability may be sufficient: "I am going to enjoy this discussion, since I have always been good at analyzing cases as president of the Harvard Debating Club." If nobody has either a specific skill or a general ability that is relevant, sometimes it helps just to let the other group members know that you are quite an important person— subtly. At many colleges (including at Harvard during the time Bales did this work) residence halls and fraternities are differentially prestigious. What could be more natural than to introduce oneself as living at Alpha Alpha Alpha, the richest and most desirable place on campus and perhaps in the whole world?

To summarize, both the status struggle and subsequent role differentiation are likely to occur in groups of highly task oriented, completely *undifferentiated* members. If members are initially *differentiated* by some characteristic, then the status ordering emerges very rapidly without a status struggle, and the task leader and social–emotional leader are usually the same individual.

Some support for this interpretation is available from carefully collected and precisely analyzed data on Bales groups reported by M. H. Fisek. He studied 59 3-person discussion groups, initially undifferentiated, to observe the evolution of a power and prestige structure through discussion. Groups met for 45 minutes, during which time the entire discussion was tape-recorded and a record of who-to-whom interaction was made by two observers. Table 6–1 shows the relative amount of participation by each of the three individuals during the final 12 minutes of the group meeting. Overall we can see that a differentiation has emerged in terms of amount of time spent talking. The individual controlling the highest proportion of total discussion in the group contributed about 42 percent of the inter- action. The individual controlling the lowest proportion has about 24 per- cent of the interaction.

However more detailed analyses reveal that groups in Fisek's study fall into two categories: those in which members were initially undifferentiated by participation rate, as is typically reported for Bales groups; and those for which a differentiation was apparent during the very first observational time period. That is, it appeared that for about half the group in Fisek's study members were differentiated at such an early point in the discussion that it was impossible to observe the evolution of a power and prestige structure; the inequality apparently existed from the very outset. Figures 6–3 and 6–4 show the amount of participation through time for both types of groups, the initially differentiated, and the undifferentiated. Notice that during the first time period (3 minutes) members of the undifferentiated subset all are speaking approximately 33 percent of the time. By the end of the session, considerable differentiation is evident. There is also a wide

TABLE 6–1   Participation Rates; Final 12 Minutes

Actor Rank	Participation (%)
1	42
2	36
3	24

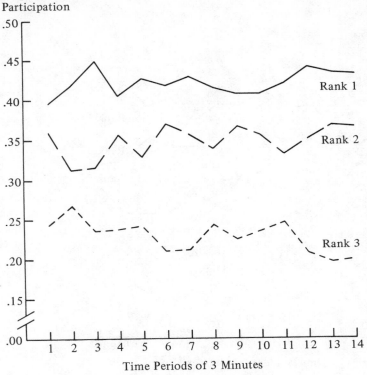

Proportion of
Participation

Time Periods of 3 Minutes

FIGURE 6–3 Participation proportion through time: differentiated subset. (From Fisek, 1971, Fig. 3–8.)

spread between members of the differentiated subset by the end of the meeting. However the differentiation is just as noticeable during the first time period. This suggests that in Fisek's study, and perhaps in many other studies of Bales groups that have not been analyzed according to subsets, the group members differentiate themselves virtually from the first minute of talking.

Why did members of the differentiated subset in Fisek's study sort themselves out so early? In part the differentiation may have been produced by individual differences among members in willingness to participate in discussion. What seems likely to have occurred in most of the groups is that individuals established subordination–superordination relations among themselves almost immediately based on a wide variety of personal characteristics. Fisek's research was conducted in California with college students, and at that time in that place a Southern accent was decidedly a negatively valued characteristic. An individual in a discussion group who revealed a Southern accent was virtually doomed to be headed for the bottom rank on amount of participation in the groups. Other differences among members' dress, residence, speech habits, and even major fields of

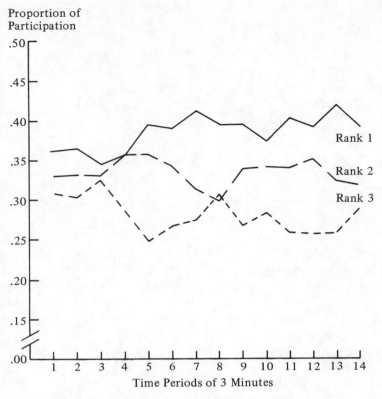

FIGURE 6–4 Participation proportions through time:
undifferentiated subset. (From Fisek, 1974, Fig. 3–9.)

study—perhaps differences that were too subtle to be noticed by the observers could well account for an almost immediate power and prestige
ranking being formed in these groups. Apparently this is just the other
side of what we saw in Lewis' research.

We shall return to the effects of revealing one's social identity external
to the Bales group, and its effects upon group discussion in Chap. 7.

A useful consequence of the *reciprocal, consistent* inequality in Bales
groups is that in discussion groups of this sort (that is, task-focused groups
with a collective task) it is possible to determine the whole power and
prestige structure very simply. All that is necessary is to count how much
each actor speaks. The rank of initiation correlates well with the ranking
of individuals on any other measure of power and prestige we wish (sometimes excluding "liking," which is not a central component of power and
prestige). This means that it is possible very easily to determine the
situational leader of many discussion groups. It is simply the person who
talks the most. If we want to know whose ideas are most likely to be
accepted on a jury, all we need to know is how much each person talks.

If we want to know which individual is likely to be perceived as having the best ideas in a seminar discussion, again all we need to know is how much each person talks. If we want to know which person's ideas will be accepted by the group at the end of the discussion, this too can usually be predicted quite accurately just by knowing how much each person talked during the discussion.

Business conferences and similar discussions sometimes are set up with a belief and an intention that everybody's ideas will be given equal consideration. Yet because these groups are very similar to the Bales discussion groups, we know what is likely to happen: within a short period of time the members will be differentiated as to how much they talk, and this differentiation will reflect beliefs about relative ability and leadership, and will also affect the amount of influence actually exerted over the group members. The evidence is that, so long as the group is primarily task-focused, everybody will *not* participate equally in the discussion, nor will everybody exercise an equal degree of influence.

The technique *brainstorming* is one example of this. The explicit norm is that every member of the group is to say every idea which comes to mind, and everyone's ideas are to be considered equally. In practice what happens is that certain members' ideas are taken very seriously and some are ignored, *and* this differential influence can better be predicted from the status structure of the group than from the quality of ideas. If it is a business organization, for instance, the company president's ideas are far more influential than the ideas of a new junior partner. Many business and other leaders know this, of course, and brainstorming is frequently used to give a facade of democratic participation to decisions already made by the leader. TIME Magazine reported that former Vice President Agnew was chosen in just this way.

An amusing application of ideas from the study of Bales groups is that it should be possible for anyone who is interested in doing so to become leader of a task-focused group. The technique seems relatively straightforward: determine who are the first- and the second-highest initiators in the group, and then systematically support everything the #2 man says. What should happen under these circumstances is that the "supremacy struggle" of early stages will be reactivated. The #1 man and the #2 man will become engaged in heated debate with each other and will ignore the rest of the group. You then can step in and take over leadership of the remaining group members.

Effect of Changes in Size of Bales Groups

Bales has accumulated data from studies of a number of different investigators using the same basic design but varying in the number of group members. Let us examine the effect of group size upon the proportion of group time controlled by each actor; that is, the effect of increasing group size upon the initiation rate of each member of the group. Table 6–2 shows the proportion of the total interaction in the group that is initiated by each member for groups of sizes 3 through 10.

The effect of increasing size is striking. Except for the 4-person groups which are considerably more equalitarian, the person who talks the most controls about 45 percent of the interaction. As the group gets larger, the remaining 55 percent is distributed more and more thinly among the remaining members. In a 3-man group, the #2 man initiates about 33 percent of the interaction, and the #3 man initiates about 23 percent. In a 5-man group, the #2 man initiates about 22 percent of the interaction, the #3 man about 15 percent, and the remaining 15 percent is distributed between the other two people. When the group has 9 members the highest initiator controls about half the interaction, the #2 man about one-tenth of the interaction and so on. What this means is that as the group size increases the *stratification structure* increases also. The difference between any two successive members becomes greater as the group becomes larger. The member ranked highest on initiation (and therefore, on other components of power and prestige) increases in social distance from any other member of the group as the group size increases. The differentiation among members at the bottom of the power and prestige structure is *less* in large groups than in smaller ones, while those at the bottom are "farther away" from those at the top.[1]

Consistency and Reciprocity of Rankings

Some experiments by Bavelas and colleagues reveal the extent to which some components of interaction in Bales-type groups are interrelated. Four-person groups discussed a case in industrial psychology (a problem equivalent to Johnny Rocco), and at the end, indicated their decision regarding disposition of the case. They also filled out questionnaires reporting their opinions of amount of participation, quality of ideas, effectiveness in guiding the discussion, and general leadership ability. There was an additional piece of apparatus: two lights, one red and one green, in front of each member and visible only to him. Members were told that when the observers felt they were making a good point, the green light would go on. When observers felt they were making an error or wasting time, the red light would go on. From our point of view, this means the experimenter was encouraging (green light) or discouraging (red light) the rate of initiation of the "target" individual.

---

[1] Mayhew and Levinger have very recently shown that this effect, increasing inequality with increasing group size, is a phenomenon to be expected even if group members interact completely at random. Thus Michels' famous observation that as groups get larger they tend to be controlled by a smaller and smaller proportion of members (the "iron law of oligarchy") is given a theoretical basis. Inequality develops in Bales groups even faster than it would if members interacted at random, however. The topic of this chapter is the forces which cause inequality to develop as rapidly and as firmly as they do.

TABLE 6–2   Percentage of Total Interaction
Initiated by Each Group Member

147

*Power
and
Prestige*

ACTOR	GROUP SIZE							
	3	4	5	6	7	8	9	10
1	44	32	47	43	43	40	51	51
2	33	29	22	19	15	17	12	11
3	23	23	15	14	12	13	9	8
4		16	10	11	10	10	8	7
5			6	8	9	9	6	6
6				5	6	6	5	5
7					5	3	4	4
8						3	3	3
9							3	3
10								3
	100	100	100	100	100	100	100	100

(From Bales, 1970: 467–470; and 1953.)

The experiment is a particularly interesting one with several conditions. However we may summarize their results as follows: The effect of the green light is to increase the "target's" interaction considerably, even when an initially low interactor is selected for this treatment. This also increases acts directed towards the "target," *and* it improves his rating by self and others on the post-discussion questionnaire. The effect of the red light is exactly the opposite to all these.

These experimental results suggest that it is possible to intervene in the power and prestige structure of the group by manipulating one of the interaction components. Furthermore it shows the degree to which this simple intervention will affect all other interrelated components of the power and prestige structure—even including the perceived quality of a member's performances.

Maintenance of Inequality

One of the four features of the power and prestige order just studied, stability, deserves closer study. Why should it be the case that once a ranking of individuals is established it is unlikely to change? Why should one individual consistently give the best suggestions? What seems more likely, and what in fact appears to be the case, is that once an individual has established a high position in the power and prestige ranking, he tends to have more of a chance to make good suggestions than other people do. Once the group members decide that a given individual makes good suggestions they seem to encourage him to talk more. Once members decide that a given individual makes poor suggestions they seem to discourage his talking and not give him a chance to show that his ideas really are good. We have all seen cases where somebody who is thought to do poorly at a task makes a good suggestion—which other people then ignore. In the Bales group as in seminar discussions, some people's suggestions are met with enthusiasm, and some with indifference or even hostility. A large part of the explanation for the stability of power and prestige structures in Bales-type groups is that the members change their behavior in ways which tend to produce persistence of the inequality. Towards the end of the session if a member low on initiation rank makes a suggestion, it is likely to be ignored, criticized, or subtly discounted—even when it appears to be a good suggestion to the observers.

This "suppression" was observed in the study by Schachter, described in Chap. 4. As we saw then, the deviate received fewer chances to talk than the mode by the end of the session. By contrast the slider received increasingly more chances as he came to express more and more the group-valued ideas.

Stability of the existing power and prestige order of a group is also shown in studies of an entirely different situation. Sherif, White, and Harvey studied summer camp groups of adolescent boys. Their task was for the boys to throw balls at a bullseye target that was covered by a sheet of canvas. Where the ball hit the target was indicated to the experimenters by a light on the back of the target, but the boys could not see where it hit. Before each throw of the ball, experimenters asked each boy how many points he thought he *would* score. After the ball had been thrown and bounded off the canvas sheet covering the target, the experimenter asked each boy how well he thought he *had done,* and they also asked the other boys how many points they thought he had just gotten. The experimenters had previously collected information on the "status structure" (from our point of view, the power and prestige structure) of the groups. They were interested in learning whether ranking within the group affected estimates of performance.

Their findings were that group rank did indeed affect estimates of performance. Furthermore it affected estimates of performance in two different areas: (1) It affected *expectation* of future performance; that is, the estimates the boys made before they threw the ball. (2) It affected *evaluations* of past performance; that is, estimates that all boys made of how many points each throw had won. The higher the group position of a boy, the more likely was he to overestimate his own future performance. Also, the higher the group rank of a boy, the more likely were he and other boys to overestimate the number of points he had just achieved. The previously existing group structure was shown in these studies to be a powerful determinant of perceptions of performance. Individuals ranking high in group structure are believed to do better—both before they have performed and after, in the absence of objective information.

There seem to be two reasons for the stability of the power and prestige structure of the group that emerges. The first is a control process, shown in the Schachter study. Individuals making nonvalued comments are progressively isolated, and in a free interaction situation, this will curtail their frequency of participation. The second is an evaluation process shown by the Sherif, White, and Harvey, and by the Harvey studies: Individuals who have already achieved a high position in the group structure are expected, by that fact alone, to do better at a task than are individuals occupying a low position in the group. Thus behavioral and evaluative aspects of group structures are closely related. Individuals whose performances are evaluated highly tend to occupy high positions in the power and prestige structure of the group. Once individuals are allocated to various power and prestige positions—whatever the basis for the allocation —evaluations of their performances tend to correspond to their relative power and prestige positions.

Maintenance of Power and Prestige in Streetcorner Society

One of the classic studies of interpersonal behavior was conducted during 1937–1941 when William F. Whyte lived with members of an Italian street gang in a Boston slum. As with any field study, this research produces a mine of information. We shall focus on only a small part of it, some anecdotes related to the development and maintenance of social structure.

The Norton street gang was a collection of individuals in their 20s who hung around together. During the time of the research, due to general economic depression as well as to the fact that these were poor people, their activities were strictly limited. Money was not available frequently for going out to dinner or for movies—the major activity was simply to stand or sit around on the street corner and talk. In this setting Whyte came to know the members of the Norton street gang and was able to observe their patterns of interaction.

The leader of the Nortons was Doc. Whyte says, "The Nortons were Doc's gang. The group was brought together primarily by Doc and it was built around Doc" (1943: 3). Doc had a deformed left arm, and he was sensitive about it. He worked hard to develop it, and he became the leader of the Nortons primarily by fighting. He beat their previous leader in a boxing match. We can see here what we saw at Bennington and in other settings: that a high position of power and prestige results as a consequence of performance of valued activities.

Figure 6–5 shows the structure of the Nortons with those individuals higher in power and prestige at the top of the chart. Primary lines of friendship are indicated by lines connecting the actors. I have added the ages of each of the members in parentheses because it shows an interesting feature of the power and prestige structure. With children, age frequently is related to power and prestige; that is, older children in a group frequently occupy higher positions of power and prestige. Older children tend to be better at games, schoolwork, athletics, social skills—that is, they are better at valued activities—than younger children. The Nortons were certainly much older than children, but it is interesting to note that, in

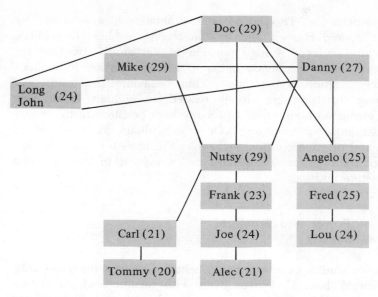

FIGURE 6–5 The Nortons

general, those higher in power and prestige were also older. Konrad Lorenz
has written, "All other conditions being equal, the age of an animal is
very consistently in direct proportion to the position it holds in the ranking
order of its society" (1966, p. 47). Apparently quite a general phenomenon.
Long John's position deserves comment since he was younger than most.
Whyte placed him high in the power and prestige ranking primarily because of his close friendship with the leaders Mike, Doc, and Danny. To
a certain extent, esteem can be delegated.

The famous bowling incident illustrates quite clearly some principles
of maintenance of power and prestige structures. Bowling became a valued
activity for the Nortons. Every Saturday evening in the winter and spring
of 1937–38 they went bowling, and Whyte reports, "[Bowling] became the
main vehicle whereby the individual could maintain, gain, or lose prestige."
(1943: 23). He also called it "the most significant social activity for the
Nortons" (1943: 17).

Bowling is one of the large number of sports where performances is
affected by other factors besides just physical skill. Other sports with this
property are wrestling, track, swimming—all activities where athletes report
that it is important to be psychologically "up" for best performance. The
importance of psychological factors appears to be well understood, and
conscious attempts made to utilize this knowledge are evident in such
widely different contests as boxing (Muhammad Ali) and chess (Bobby
Fischer). Performance is also affected by social factors; for example,
heckling involves control of one's performance by other people. Probably
it is true that it is easier to lower somebody's performance this way than
it is to raise his performance, but the latter is not impossible. I have known
football players who claim that they play better if they hear a lot of noise

from the stands, even though they are not able to understand individual yells.

Alec, who occupied a decidedly low position of power and prestige, decided to raise himself in the group by becoming good at bowling. (Apparently Alec understood the principle that performance at valued activities leads to high positions of power and prestige.) Alec practiced on his own, and he became very good: he achieved the highest single score of any bowler that season. When they went bowling together, Alec usually could beat Whyte, Long John, and most other members of the group. However on Saturdays he always did poorly. Saturdays, you recall, were the days of important bowling—the days when bowling was defined as crucial to the power and prestige structure of the group. Alec said that he had "an off night" on Saturdays; an explanation can be constructed for anything.

The big challenge meet was in April of 1938, and a ten dollar prize was offered for the top three bowlers. Table 6–3 reports a finish order at the important challenge meet. The scores are remarkable. First, we note that Alec lost. This is outstanding evidence of individuals acting to maintain the power and prestige srtucture. He was heckled unmercifully, he began to drink a lot of beer, and he fell apart halfway through the bowling match. He came in last—when on the basis of his ability alone we would expect him to come in first or second.

Mark (7) had no clear relation to the clique. We could not predict his bowling score from the power and prestige ordering in the group.

Joe also bowled a little better than we would expect on the basis of power and prestige ordering. Certainly social factors cannot perfectly predict athletic performance, but we note that his ranking did not threaten the central club leadership of Doc, Danny, and Mike.

Mike "had never bowled well before Saturday night at the alleys became a fixture for the Nortons" (Whyte 1943: 24). Afterwards, he did. In the important bowling match he came in fifth, much better than we would expect him to perform if we didn't know that he was high in the social structure of the group.

Frank's surprisingly low position deserves some comment also. Whyte reports "on his athletic ability alone, Frank should have been an excellent bowler" (1943: 19). Frank was a semipro baseball player, and he had even been offered a contract with a major league team. Why did he do so poorly in bowling? The answer, I think, is quite similar to our explanation for why Long John rated such a high position in the group; namely, esteem can be delegated *or lost* through association. Frank worked with Alec in

TABLE 6–3 Bowling Outcome

1. Whyte	6. Joe
2. Danny	7. Mark
3. Doc	8. Carl
4. Long John	9. Frank
5. Mike	10. Alec

(From Whyte, 1943, p. 21.)

Alec's uncle's pastry shop; he associated with a "social leper," and perhaps as a consequence, the group enforced a low position on him in the bowling match.

In the next chapter we shall take up the issue of why Whyte's bowling score was as high as it was. I think we can explain it with the same set of principles we use to explain Doc's or Alec's scores, but we need some additional theoretical knowledge, to be developed in Chap. 7.

There were postscripts to the bowling incident, which from our point of view were continuing threats to the power and prestige ordering of the group. Alec challenged Long John later and continually beat him in individual bowling matches. Again this is evidence that, in the absence of social factors, Alec was a very good bowler. Why did he choose Long John instead of Doc, Danny, or Mike? Probably because Long John's social position was less secure—it was the result of friendship with the leaders, but he was younger and more vulnerable than they were. In fact Doc had told Alec that before he would bowl him individually, Alec would have to take on, in this order, Long John, Danny, and Mike.

Whyte asked Doc what would have happened at the big bowling match if Alec or, say, Joe had won. Doc replied it would have been called "lucky, a fluke." In other words it would be defined as an unimportant, accidental happening. Attempts would be made to preserve the group members' conceptions of how things "ought" to turn out. Also Doc said they would immediately challenge Alec to a second match and "ruin him."

Whyte reports that, elated by his victory, he pressed his luck and challenged everybody to more matches. Doc told Whyte to take on Long John first, and if he won, then perhaps Doc or Danny would bowl against Whyte. (Most likely, it would have been Danny.) Whyte reports that "urged on by Doc and Danny, Long John won a decisive victory. I made no further challenges" (1943: 22).

Propositional Inventory on Power and Prestige in Informal Groups

Now we are ready to summarize our knowledge of power and prestige structures in informal groups. As a first step towards doing this we construct an inventory of five propositions to summarize information from studies in this chapter and in preceding chapters. After that, we shall be prepared to study a theory explaining these propositions in more general terms.

I. Emergence
Power and prestige ranking is a direct function of an individual's performance in areas of importance to (in relation to valued activities of) the group.

II. Stability
Once a power and prestige structure exists, it tends to persist, unless affected by marked changes in the performance level of individuals.

III. Maintenance

Within limits, performance of an individual is a function of his position in the power and prestige structure of the group.

IV. Cognitions

Beliefs about the performance of any individual will tend to correspond to his position in the power and prestige structure of the group.

V. Consistency

There is a tendency for the various types of ranking (age, ability, esteem, influence, interaction) to be correlated with each other—*and* with the power and prestige ranking of the group.

Expectation States Theory

Many of the findings having to do with power and prestige structures of informal task-focused groups can be explained by what we shall call expectation states theory. The concepts and propositions of the theory are developed and presented in a series of articles by Joseph Berger and associates beginning around 1965. Briefly what they assert is that components of the power and prestige structure of these groups are all distributed in accordance with an underlying structure of performance *expectation states,* which are roughly equivalent to beliefs about task performance ability of the various individuals. The higher the expectation state held for any given individual the more of all components of power and prestige he will be given as the result. An expectation state is a *theoretical construct,* which cannot be directly observed. All we can see are consequences of expectation states; namely, observable components of the power and prestige structure of the group.

To help in understanding the theory, let us apply it to the Bales discussion groups. (It could as well be applied to any other informal task-focused group that we have studied.) Recall that Bales divided interaction into 12 categories. We begin by reducing this number. Categories 7–9 of Bales' scheme may be combined to form the single category *action opportunity.* An action opportunity is a socially distributed chance to perform. For example asking the question, "What do you think about this, Bill?" constitutes giving an action opportunity to the actor Bill. An action opportunity could also be distributed to Bill simply by looking at him meaningfully, or by pausing if he looks as though he wishes to speak.

Categories 4–6 may be collapsed as *performance outputs,* or problem-solving attempts. For example if Bill says, "I think the answer is . . ." this constitutes making a performance output, trying to solve the group's problem.

Any performance output is likely to elicit a *unit evaluation.* This corresponds to categories 1 and 12 of Bales' system. A unit evaluation may be either positive or negative; "I think that's right," or, "I think that's wrong." Any performance output is also subject to *agreement* or *disagreement.* This corresponds to categories 3 and 10. One could agree with somebody's performance output by saying the same thing at the same time, for example. If two actors disagree, one of them may *accept influence,* as in "I think you were right." Relevant task-focused activity in these groups may all be interpreted as instances of one of these components.

In a discussion group such as a jury or a Bales group, an individual is given an action opportunity when he is asked his opinion, or when silence of other members allows him a chance to speak. In a basketball team the same thing happens when a member is passed the ball. An individual makes a performance output when he gives his suggestion, or when he attempts to shoot a basket. Any performance output is likely to receive private and public unit evaluations, and (at least in a discussion group) publicly expressed agreement or disagreement. Finally, in cases of disagreement, the individual who made the performance must decide whether to accept influence ("I guess I was wrong), or to reject it ("No, you're wrong").

The basic assumption of *Expectation States Theory* is that all observable components of the power and prestige structure of the group enumerated above will be distributed in accord with the expectation states held for (and by) the various group members. The higher the performance expectations associated with a given member, the more likely is he to receive an action opportunity, to accept a given action opportunity and to make a performance output, and to receive positive evaluations and agreement from others for any given performance output. Finally in cases of disagreement, the likelihood of rejecting influence is also predicted to be a direct function of the expectation states held.

The way expectation states arise in these groups is through unit evaluations. (We shall see two other ways expectation states are formed in Chaps. 7 and 15.) If person #1 makes a lot of positive unit evaluations of person #2's performance, this will lead, according to the theory, to #1 holding a *high expectation state*, for person #2. If person #2 agrees with this, he will come to hold a high expectation state for himself. They both *expect* that #2 will make good performances in the future. Formation of an expectation state has occurred when an individual moves from saying, "I think he's right," to "I think he has high ability." Once expectation states emerge, they tend to produce stability of the power and prestige structure of the group. The reason for this is that expectation states affect the distribution of the components of the power and prestige structure *including the unit evaluations,* and it is the unit evaluations that determine the expectation states. The process is circular. Once people form ability conceptions of each other, these beliefs tend to persist, and they determine the power and prestige structure of the group.

Expectation states theory thus is designed to explain the findings on power and prestige in the groups we have been studying, as well as to explain the propositional inventory on power and prestige. The explanation may appear deceptively simple. We do not want to explain in a circular fashion the power and prestige structure by expectation states, and then to argue that expectation states exist because we have observed the power and prestige structure. What are needed are independent tests of the theoretical assertions as to how expectation states are produced, and the consequences expectation states have once they exist upon observable interaction. These will be described in subsequent paragraphs.

Expectations are *relative* to any pair of individuals in the group. For convenience we talk only about relatively high or relatively low expectations. Thus if person #1 holds higher expectations for himself than he does for person #2, when he is in interaction with person #2 we say that person #1 holds "high self–low other" expectations. This means that there are four possible states:

high self–low other, written [+ −]

low self–high other, written [− +]

high self–high other, written [+ +]

low self–low other, written [− −]

The [+ −] and the [− +] states are called *differentiated* states. The person holding these states differentiates his expectations for self from those he holds for other. The [+ +] and [− −] states are called *undifferentiated* states. These states indicate the person holds *equal* expectations states for self and for other.

The Basic Experimental Design

Initial tests of expectation states theory were intended to examine three things: First, the idea that a cognitive construct, *expectation state,* gets built up as a result of a series of consistent unit evaluations of performance. Second, the assertion that the particular pattern of expectation states held for (and by) individuals will have important behavioral consequences for features of their future interaction. Third, to demonstrate the asserted cause of stability of the power and prestige structure—namely, the assertion that expectation states, once formed, tend to persist even in the presence of contradictory future information.

As a result of the theoretical work, expectation states theory could be tested in a situation considerably simpler than the situations—such as Bales groups and children's summer camp groups—from which the ideas emerged. In other words because we have a theory which specifies the important independent and dependent variables it is possible to move research to a situation simpler and more highly controlled than the natural situations the theory is designed to explain. One example of the simplification permitted is that expectation states theory is concerned only with task-oriented inter-action. Thus the social emotional aspects of group discussion—those concerned with avoiding hostility and hurt feelings—may be eliminated. The theory simply does not have anything to say about such behaviors. Because of the relative nature of expectation states, the theory may be tested in a group as small as two persons; that is, any assertions of the theory concern relations between two individuals who hold either equal or unequal expectations for each other's performances. The theory says that the group members must be oriented towards solving a problem (task oriented) but it does not specify that any particular task be used. Thus any convenient task may be used to test the assertions of the theory. Finally, although expectation states theory predicts a wide variety of observable behaviors to vary with expectation states—for example, allocation and acceptance of action opportunities, perceptions of ability and leadership, likelihood of receiving agreement and positive evaluations, and acceptance of influence—the theory may be tested by selecting any one of these behaviors for the dependent variable.

The one selected for measurement was *rejection of influence in case of disagreement,* which is predicted to vary directly with the relative level of self–other expectation states. The higher the relative self–other expectations an individual holds, the less likely he is predicted to be to accept influence if someone disagrees with his performance output.

In the basic expectation theory experiments, pairs of subjects entered a laboratory and were seated in separate cubicles so that they could not see each other but both could see two experimenters at the front of the room. Between the two experimenters at the front of the room was a slide projection screen. Each subject and one of the experimenters had in front of him the panel of a machine used to register choices. The purpose of these first experiments was to induce each of the four relative expectation states ([+ +] [+ −], [− +], [− −]), and then to measure their effects upon acceptance of influence.

The experiments consist of two phases, a manipulation phase, and a measurement phase. During the manipulation phase, subjects are given unit evaluations of performance in a manner predicted to lead to formation of a given pattern of expectation states. After each performance, both subjects are told by the experimenter whether they were right or wrong. At the end of 20 trials (performances), total scores are announced for both subjects. Scores given for each of the four expectation patterns are shown in Fig. 6–6. The task for these experiments is completely *ambiguous*: there are no right answers. Thus it is similar to the discussion tasks used in Bales Groups.

In Phase II, subjects work on a second set of problems. This time they both make an initial choice, see each other's choice, reconsider their initial choices, and make a final choice. When they disagree on initial choices, the theory predicts that the expectations held (as the result of Phase I) should affect how likely each subject is to reject influence. Because initial choice communication is controlled by their machines, subjects can be told that

Expectation State	"Correct Answers"	
	Self	Partner
[+ −]	17	8
[+ +]	17	17
[− −]	8	8
[− +]	8	17

FIGURE 6–6 Typical expectation manipulation patterns

their choices nearly always disagree. The proportion of disagreements resolved in favor of self, or $P(s)$, is the main statistic generated by this experiment. $P(s)$ is predicted to vary directly with the *relative* level of self–other expectations.

At the end of phase two of the experiment, subjects again fill out a questionnaire indicating their conceptions of their own and each other's ability. Following this, each subject is interviewed separately by one of the experimenters. There are two purposes to the interview: (1) To be sure that each subject understood and believed all of the crucial interaction features of the situation. For example, that he was task-oriented during the interaction and that he believed the disagreements were real and was concerned with resolving them: (2) To explain the experiment fully to him, including explaining all this information and the necessity of it, and to ask his cooperation in not discussing the experiment with friends of his who might be scheduled to participate later. Following this he is thanked and is paid for his time.

Results From the First Experimental Series

Table 6–4 presents the $P(s)$ data from each of the four expectation state conditions of the initial experiments. As may be seen, the ordering of conditions which would be expected from the relative expectation states held $([+ -] > [+ +] = [- -] > [- +])$ was the ordering observed. Notice that the $[+ +]$ and $[- -]$ states do not produce noticeable differences in this observable behavior. This is consistent with the assertion that it is the *relative,* not the absolute level of expectation states which determines behavior.

Figure 6–7 presents the $P(s)$ curves from this experiment throughout the twenty-two disagreement trials, by blocks of three trials. As may be seen, the relative differences between the four conditions remain constant through time; that is, the $[+ -]$ state is consistently above both equal expectation states and the $[- +]$ is consistently below. These data are as we would expect. One very interesting finding is that in both the $[+ +]$ and the $[- -]$ conditions there is no evidence in Fig. 6–7 of change in expectation states. This is striking given the large number of disagreements used by Berger and Conner for their $P(s)$ measurement. Disagreements

TABLE 6–4   Influence Rejection by Expectation States

EXPECTATION STATE	$P(s)$
$[+ -]$	.78
$[+ +]$	.67
$[- -]$	.65
$[- +]$	.44

(Data from Berger and Conner, 1969.)

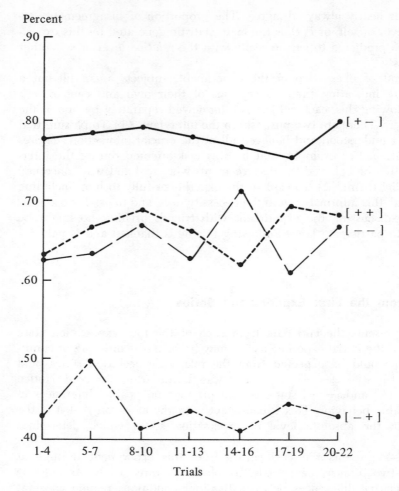

FIGURE 6–7 Proportion of non-acceptance of influence for blocks of three trials. (From Berger and Conner, Fig. 6.)

might reasonably be expected by subjects holding [+ −] expectation states or [− +] expectation states—after all, that is the meaning of the terms: one person performs well at the task and one performs poorly at the task. However when *both* subjects are very good at the task, why should they disagree on so many of the slides? Similarly, if both subjects believe they are very poor at the task they might expect that they would get the wrong answer to most of the slides, but that they would agree on the wrong answer. Thus the fact that there is no evidence of change in expectation states throughout the trials in either of the equal expectation states conditions is consistent with the expectation states theory prediction that only unit evaluations will affect expectations states, since no evaluations of performance were made in phase two. It is as if subjects in the two equal conditions were able to say to themselves, "We disagree on most of these slides, but we're both (correct, wrong)."

Formation of Expectation States

The process of formation of expectation states through interaction, rather than through evaluation by the experimenter, was studied in a variant of the basic experimental design. There were two major differences from the basic design used in the first experiments: (1) the group consisted of three subjects instead of two as before; (2) an unambiguous task was used.

What would we expect in this condition? Because the slides were easy to judge—that is, because people could quite easily tell what the correct answer was—we expect that subjects will eventually form [+ −] expectations for self and any other. Why would we expect all subjects to form [+ −] expectation states? Consider the case where someone disagrees with you and you are sure you are right. If he disagrees with you, then he must be wrong (assuming there are only two possible answers to the question). Thus in this experiment, interaction was controlled in such a way that a subject was very likely to distribute positive unit evaluations to his own performance (initial choice), and negative unit evaluations to the other two individuals' performances. Given enough of these unit evaluations— and 40 is certainly a large number—we would expect subjects eventually to decide that they were doing better than either of their two partners.

In fact this is what the investigators discovered. The $P(s)$ for all subjects in this experiment shows a steady rise throughout the trials. The total amount of rise, about .15, is not particularly great, since rise in $P(s)$ in this experiment will be opposed by "majority effect" of disagreements from *two* other individuals. The majority effect is not of theoretical interest in these experiments (though it would be in Chap. 2), but it certainly would be observable given the 3-person group. However the overall mean $P(s)$ is not the most interesting data from this experiment. What is more interesting is the variance across subjects, because variance gives a measure of the formation process. What we think is going to happen in this experiment is that all subjects will begin with no expectations, they will form [+ −] expectations at different rates, and by the end of the trials all will hold [+ −] expectations. This means that at the beginning of the trials and at the end of the trials, all subjects will hold the same expectation state. During the middle of the trials, because some subjects form [+ −] expectations early and some form them late, there will be essentially two populations of subjects: those holding no expectations, and those holding [+ −] expectations. Presence of two subpopulations within a sample increases the variance. Figure 6–8 presents the variance across subjects throughout the trials of this experiment. As may be seen, the variance begins relatively low, around 2.4, rises to a high of 4.0 around the 20th trial, and then declines as more and more subjects form the [+ −] expectation state.

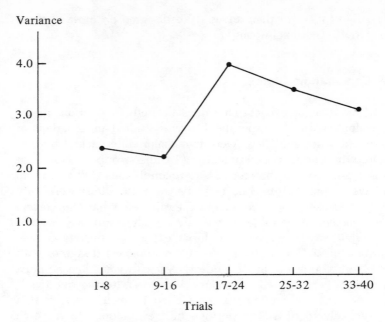

FIGURE 6–8 Variance changes, indicating formation
of expectation states.

Overview of Power and Prestige Differences

Some sort of inequality between members is evident in virtually every social grouping. On the large scale, all societies are stratified in one way or
another. In western industrial societies the stratification system most frequently is closely linked to the distribution of economic wealth. But stratification systems typically are not limited to differences in wealth. Generally
speaking those people in the society who have the greatest amount of
wealth also control the greatest amount of political influence and informal
power. They are also the most likely to exercise a large degree of personal
control over their own lives, and to have access to any of the scarce material,
social, and psychological resources that are available.

Any situation in which individuals meet together for the first time is very
likely to generate a structure of social inequality along some line or another.
Face-to-face interaction seems to produce participation inequality between
actors. The personal characteristics of the participants and their purposes
in meeting are the major determinants of the power and prestige structure.
They are also the major determinants of which characteristics will be considered relevant in establishing the subordination–superordination relationships of the group.

In informal groups the power and prestige structure depends upon the
beliefs of individuals. The power and prestige differentiation emerges only

with the formation of beliefs by the individuals regarding each other, and it persists unchanged only so long as the beliefs of the individual members persist unchanged. Whatever common purposes, whatever common values the group members hold are very likely to determine the ranking they each place upon themselves and upon each other. Performance at valued activities—whether it be expressing the "correct" political attitudes, being the best fighter, giving the most intelligent and well-formulated answers, or harassing the teacher most exquisitely—is by far the most important factor in determining informal power and prestige positions.

In task-oriented groups power and prestige differences between individuals emerge along the lines of *performance expectations* that come to be associated with the group members. Those members who are expected to perform well at whatever the group task is will come to occupy positions of high power and prestige. Those expected to perform poorly will come to occupy low positions within the group structure. The most significant components of the power and prestige structure of problem-solving groups are the following: *action opportunities, performance outputs, unit evaluations, agreement and approval,* and *acceptance or rejection of influence.* All of these components of the power and prestige structure tend to be closely associated; that is, the more that any individual possesses of any one of these components, the more he is likely to possess of all of the others.

Performance expectations form through the interaction process, typically within the first few minutes of the group's meeting. The specific mechanism through which performance expectations form is the unit evaluation process. At the outset of interaction, all members of the group probably offer performance outputs as frequently as they have ideas. These performances are evaluated, and on the basis of these evaluations, members form expectations for the quality of their own and each other's performances. In most ways performance expectations are comparable to conceptions of ability to solve the group's particular problem. Once performance expectations become associated with the members of the group, they tend to persist—people are not very likely to change their minds about the performance abilities of each other. One reason for this is simple resistance to change; there appears to be some effort involved in changing one's mind about other individuals' abilities. Psychological reasons for this reluctance to change opinions may be quite complex. A much simpler reason for the persistence of performance expectations is that, once they exist, they affect the distribution of those components that *determine* them. Performance expectations arise from the distribution of unit evaluations, and existing performance expectations affect the distribution of unit evaluations. Once set in motion this circular process tends to perpetuate itself.

We have reviewed the basic experimental tests of the ideas in expectation states theory, and the major outlines of this explanation have received confirmation. The laboratory experiments to test expectation theory may look very different from Bales groups or Street Corner Society, but the various settings share several crucial similarities. Expectation theory identifies the relevant components of interaction, and therefore it also indicates features of the naturalistic settings which are irrelevant to the emergence and maintenance of power and prestige differences. The experimental tests were designed to incorporate only those features of the situations which the theory identifies as important. Consideration also was given to directing experimental tests towards those assertions of the theory which seemed most problematic; that is, towards those assertions whose accuracy was not self-evident. In Chap. 7 we shall examine related processes in groups of members who are initially differentiated in terms of one or more status characteristics.

7   Status Characteristics

Status Organizes Interaction

Every sociologist and nearly every social psychologist studies *status* in one respect or another. Status, and especially status differences, have been approached from nearly every conceivable theoretical and applied viewpoint. Studies range from investigations into the causes and the structure of stratification in a society through studies of attempts to acquire and maintain prestige, through studies of the effect of various status characteristics upon individual interaction. In fact status effects are so pervasive and they show up so often that it is unwise to undertake any sociological or social–psychological research without asking whether status may affect the observed results.

Because of the volume and the variety of studies involving status, it would be impossible to provide an adequate treatment of them all in a single chapter, or even in a single textbook. We shall not even try. What we shall do is to explore the aspect of status that is particularly important in interpersonal behavior: the effects of status characteristics upon human interaction. The word "status" is Latin. It means *standing,* or more properly, standing in relation to others. The word carries further meanings in both common and professional usage. Nearly always it connotes an invidious (envy-producing) comparison between individuals. Status implies differential ranking, a position in which some individuals are above or below others. When individuals interact, much of their behavior appears to be determined by their relative status positions. This is true in terms of status-determined roles (such as "rich person," "business executive"), as well as in terms of less economically-linked statuses (such as "female," "black person"). Any interaction between individuals is likely to be affected in important ways by status characteristics. Thus there are stereotypical expected behaviors that are associated in our culture with various status roles. Interaction often is *organized around* statuses occupied by the individuals, so if we know their statuses and know the principles linking status to observable interaction, then the behavior becomes understandable.

To begin we need a definition of status characteristic, or as we shall say, *diffuse status characteristic*. We add the term "diffuse" to indicate that the status characteristic is one an individual generally "carries around" with himself. It is "diffused" in the individual. A characteristic, for our purposes, is any property of an individual that may be used to describe him. For example, hair color, height, wealth, sex, and occupation are all characteristics. All that we require in addition for a *status* characteristic is that this property possess differentially evaluated states. Any characteristic differentially evaluated by individuals in the culture is a status characteristic. Thus if it is considered in some way "better" or "more desirable" to be white than black in our culture; or if it is considered in some ways "preferable" to be male than female; then race and sex fit the definition of status characteristics. Because it is quite apparent which state of these characteristics any individual possesses, they are also diffuse status characteristics—they "generalize" throughout the individual, in other words. Our definition, then:

> *Diffuse status characteristic:* any general property of an individual which may be used to describe him and which is differentially evaluated within his culture.

Examples of diffuse status characteristics in our culture are everywhere. Life is easier if you have money; that is, the high state of the characteristic "wealth" is preferable to the low state. Blacks, or in some parts of the country, chicanos, are "last hired and first fired"; that is, white is the high state of the race characteristic, and black or chicano is the low state. In interactions involving rational thought, physical strength, driving ability, and numerous other particular skills, men are expected to perform better than women; that is, male is the high state of the characteristic sex in our culture.

Notice that in discussing diffuse status characteristics we are concerned with people's *beliefs* regarding their desirability or their evaluation. We do not ask whether these beliefs are supported by empirical test, nor whether these beliefs are "right" in a moral sense. Some contemporary social movements such as women's liberation, gay activism, and civil rights movements may be seen as challenges to widely held beliefs regarding differential evaluations of sex, sexual preference, and race (respectively) in our society. To take a well known illustration, women's liberation members deny that there is any objective basis for the widely held beliefs that women are less logical, less dependable, less intelligent than men. They point out that there is no good empirical support for the differential evaluation of the diffuse status characteristic *sex*. But whether the differential evaluation of the characteristic is *justified* is less significant in determining people's interaction than whether it is *believed*. People act upon their *beliefs*, including their false beliefs. Thus the particular evaluation of a characteristic, and even whether a characteristic is in fact evaluated, depend upon historical circumstances and the myths and accurate information in a society.

A second part of these movements is concerned with the morality of differential evaluations of the diffuse characteristics of people. Independent of whether the stereotypes are accurate, one may question whether it is morally supportable to discriminate against individuals for possessing characteristics over which they have no voluntary control. Although morality is a most fascinating subject, here we limit ourselves to concern with the way things *are*. *If* a characteristic is differentially evaluated, no matter that the differential evaluation is inaccurate or morally offensive, it will be considered a diffuse status characteristic and we shall try to predict its effects upon interaction. In Chaps. 8 and 16 we shall investigate aspects of morality.

It has always seemed regrettable to me that proponents of movements concerned with changing discrimination based on diffuse status characteristics seem to feel it is necessary to concentrate their efforts upon only the first part of the objection: to argue that the differential evaluations are *incorrect*. The morality of the discriminatory treatment is decidedly secondary. "One should not discriminate against women in employment *because* in fact they can perform most jobs as well as men," they say. "One should not discriminate against racial minorities in intellectual tasks *because* there is no evidence of racial differences in intelligence." The arguments are heavily pragmatic rather than moral. Perhaps this reflects an assessment by activists that an appeal to "scientific evidence" is more convincing than an appeal to "human worth." If so, it is a shame. Suppose—just suppose, since there is little good evidence on most of these issues—that there were measurable inferiorities of specifiable sorts in certain minority groups. Why wouldn't it be sufficient to say that these do not justify a *general* unequal treatment? To take one simple example, if women cannot perform jobs requiring great physical strength as well as men, does this justify their receiving lower pay at *all* jobs? At most this might justify paying women less for jobs involving strength, but even for those jobs, we typically do not pay weaker or older men less than stronger ones.

It is not difficult to think of examples of diffuse status characteristics; they are all about us. What is difficult is to come up with an example that does *not* fit the definition of a diffuse status characteristic; that is, to find a characteristic of individuals that does not have differentially evaluated states. Hair color certainly won't do; "blondes have more fun." Any sociologist knows that clothing styles are differentially evaluated, as are speech patterns. So far the best I have been able to do in searching for an example of a nonevaluated characteristic is blood type: RH+ or RH−. However I have recently been told that blood type is thought by some people to be associated with race. If that is true, then blood types certainly will not do as a nonevaluated characteristic. Still in the absence of something better, I think that blood type is a candidate for nonevaluated characteristic.

We have been hinting at several features of status characteristics which we will now study with more precision. Status characteristics seem to affect the expectations for performance held by individuals. In some cases it seems that possessing one status characteristic (for example, race) can lend status to a second characteristic associated with the first (for example, hair color). In many cases we expect to find certain behaviors (such as deference or assertiveness) associated with various states of the status characteristic. In the following pages we shall study these effects more closely and try to state them more precisely. As always we shall be concerned to specify the *conditions* under which each of these effects is likely to occur.

Strodtbeck's Jury and Family Studies

Strodtbeck has studied interaction in family and jury settings using observational techniques similar to those developed by Bales. By contrast with the Bales groups, however, members of the groups studied by Strodtbeck are not all status equals.

First, let us examine the effect of the status characteristic *sex* upon interaction in three different types of families. The family types studied were Navahos, Mormons, and Texans. The status of women in these three types of families, according to Strodtbeck, differs markedly. Her position is most favorable in the Navaho family and least favorable in the Mormon family. In the Navaho family, women control economic and decision making rights to a greater extent than men do. After marriage, the Navaho moves in with his wife's parents and works for her father until he has proved himself a responsible person. In case of divorce or separation, the children are considered to belong to the mother. In sharp contrast in the Mormon family, women have almost no rights (or at least this was the case at the time of Strodtbeck's study). Strodtbeck quotes Joseph Smith's *Gospel Doctrine* to illustrate the favored position of the man:

> The father is the head, or president, or spokesman of the family. This arrangement is of divine origin.

In the Texan families, farmers and ranchers, women's position presumably was intermediate to that in the Navaho and Mormon families.

We might expect to find that the status position of the wife is related to the amount of influence she had when disagreements arose with her spouse; that is, we expect the wife to have the most influence in the Navaho family, and the least in the Mormon family. This is what Strodtbeck found. When disagreements arose between husband and wife, Strodtbeck recorded the number of times the wife won the decision. His findings are reproduced in Table 7–1. Clearly the status position of the wife is directly related to the amount of influence exerted in the group.

Because of the similarity of the situation to Bales groups, we might also expect that influence of an individual will be related to the amount of time spent talking. Again the results are clear. If the husband talks more, he wins more decisions (14 out of 19). If the wife talks more, she wins more (10 out of 15). Both sets of findings are consistent with the findings observed in Bales groups *once a power and prestige structure has emerged*

TABLE 7–1 Decisions Won by Wife

Culture	Percent
Navaho	58%
Texan	45%
Mormon	41%

(Adapted from Strodtbeck, 1951: Table 1.)

through interaction. Part of our task later in the chapter will be to construct an explanation for these findings.

Juries are in many ways similar to Bales discussion groups. Members perform a similar task to members of Bales groups (discussion of a problem), they are previously unacquainted with each other, and they must come to a group decision about the problem. Strodtbeck has studied the effects of occupation and sex as status characteristics in jury deliberations.

Because it is illegal to observe actual jury deliberations, he studied "mock juries," designed to be as similar to actual juries as possible. Members were chosen for the mock juries from the same pool as members are chosen for real juries—from the voter registration lists—in Chicago, Minneapolis, and St. Louis. The subject pool for juries is not entirely representative of the society, since very low income people tend not to register to vote, and certain high income groups (for example business executives and professionals) tend to be excused from jury duty. However Strodtbeck's sampling was as representative of American society as a real jury, and it does provide individuals with a variety of diffuse status characteristics.

The first study we shall examine (Strodtbeck and Mann, 1956), shows the effect of the status characteristic sex upon jury interaction. Subjects were recruited and assembled for the study and listened to a tape recording of a trial. After this they were asked to do everything a real jury does; that is, to select a foreman, to deliberate, and to reach a verdict in the case. Twelve of these juries were constructed involving 144 individuals, although data analyses were performed only upon those ($n = 127$) who originated at least five acts during the deliberation. Let us examine the effects of the sex status characteristic upon the same dependent variables in this study as in previous studies: amount of interaction and amount of influence.

The average number of acts initiated by males during the jury deliberation was 162. The average number of acts initiated by females was 91. By a ratio of nearly 2 to 1, men talked more in the jury deliberation. Are they also more influential? For these studies there is no direct answer to the question. However we do have data on answers to the question, "Which group member really helped the group arrive at its decision?" The question probably taps subjective (perceived) influence over the group decision, if not objective (actual) influence. Strodtbeck divided jurors into categories according to whether they initiated *more* than the median number of acts in the deliberation or *less*. The former were called "active"; the latter, "inactive." This classification minimizes the effect of interaction upon perceived influence. Table 7–2 (constructed from data in the original

TABLE 7–2 Proportion Chosen as Influential

	MALES	FEMALES
"Active"	71%	44%
"Inactive"	39%	35%

(From Strodtbeck and Mann, 1956.)

article) presents the proportion of individuals in each category who received more than the median number of votes by this question. Among those individuals classified as "active," males were chosen nearly twice as often as females as having "helped the group arrive at its decision" (71 to 44 percent). Among those classified as "inactive," the difference is considerably smaller, but it is still apparent (39 to 35 percent). Remember that the inactive individuals are unlikely to exert any marked effect upon the jury deliberation. Even with some statistical control for amount of interaction, males are perceived as exerting more influence than females in the jury setting.

A second set of jury studies reported by Strodtbeck reveals the effect of occupational status upon jury interaction. These data are based upon 49 deliberations similar in most respects to those from which the sex characteristic data were drawn. However there are considerably more analyses. Jury members are classified according to their occupation as falling into one of four ranked categories: proprietor, clerical, skilled labor, unskilled labor.

First, let us examine data relevant to the same questions we asked in the first jury studies. Table 7–3 presents the amount of participation in deliberation by occupation and sex. Table 7–3 shows what we saw with married couples; namely that women initiate less interaction in these studies than men. In addition it shows the effect of occupational status. Within either sex there is a perfect rank ordering of amount of participation by occupational status; that is, occupational status and amount of initiation are positively associated.

Table 7–4 presents data on the number of votes received by each individual as being "helpful in reaching the verdict." This measure, like the question used for Table 7–2, probably reflects individuals' perceptions of influence over the group decision. Again males are more likely to be perceived as helpful than females. Holding sex constant, there is a perfect rank ordering of perceived helpfulness by occupational status. By both of these measures, the higher the sex status, or the higher the occupational status, the more likely is the individual to participate in jury deliberation, and the more likely is he to be perceived as being helpful.

The third thing we may examine is selection of a foreman. Jury members select the foreman prior to deliberation, and in some ways the foreman is

TABLE 7–3 Percentage Rates of Participation in
Jury Deliberation by Occupation and Sex of Juror

	OCCUPATION			
SEX	PROPRIETOR	CLERICAL	SKILLED	LABORER
Male	12.9	10.8	7.9	7.5
Female	9.1	7.8	4.8	4.6
Combined	11.8	9.2	7.1	6.4

(From Strodtbeck et al., 1965: Table 2.)

	OCCUPATION			
SEX	PROPRIETOR	CLERICAL	SKILLED	LABORER
Male	6.8	4.2	3.9	2.7
Female	3.2	2.7	2.0	1.5
Combined	6.0	3.4	3.5	2.3

(From Strodtbeck et al., 1965: Table 3.)

comparable to the task leader in a Bales discussion group. Specifically, he
has been chosen (presumably) on criteria of perceived ability and influence.
Table 7–5 shows the effect of occupational status upon jury foreman selection. Proprietors are chosen for jury foremen about twice as often as would
be expected on the basis of their proportional representation in the sample
(18 times actual, when expected was about 10), and unskilled laborers are
chosen about half as often as would be expected on the basis of their
proportional representation (8 times actual, about 15 times expected). By
this measure, the effect of occupational status upon "leadership" is dramatic.

The final piece of data presented by Strodtbeck is even more intriguing.
As a way of measuring perceived qualification for jury duty, jurors were
asked to indicate the occupational status of jurors they would prefer if a
member of their own family were on trial. An index of these responses is
presented in Table 7–6. The numbers in the columns represent the proportional choices of each occupational status, where, if the occupation were
chosen at random, its score would be 100. Thus for example, proprietors
would prefer a jury made up of proprietors by a ratio of about 2.5 to 1
(actually, 2.41 to 1). Laborers would prefer a jury made up of skilled
laborers by a ratio of about 1.50 to 1. For all occupational statuses, the
data in Table 7–6 show a marked preference for jurors of higher status.
Unskilled laborers would prefer skilled laborers first and proprietors second;
skilled laborers, clerical workers, and proprietors would all prefer proprietors on the jury. It seems that people would prefer to be judged, not by
their peers, but by their status superiors.

TABLE 7–5   Occupational Status of 49 Jury Foremen

OCCUPATION	EXPECTED *	OBSERVED
Proprietor	9.73	18
Clerical	15.03	15
Skilled	9.56	8
Labor	14.68	8

* Computed under assumption that foreman will be proportional to portion of sample in the given occupation.
(From Strodtbeck et al., 1965: Table 1.)

TABLE 7–6 Choice of Juror if Member of
Respondent's Family Were on Trial,
Based Upon Occupation Stereotypes
(Pro rata expected is 100)

RESPONDENT'S OCCUPATION	PREFERRED OCCUPATION			
	PROPRIETOR	CLERICAL	SKILLED	LABORER
Proprietor	241	95	51	13
Clerical	206	112	71	11
Skilled	172	55	139	33
Laborer	126	42	147	84

(From Strodtbeck et al., 1965: Table 4.)

Before moving on to studies in other settings, let us review and summarize the findings from Strodtbeck's studies of families and juries. In all studies, the individual who is most influential (or who is perceived as most influential) is also the individual who initiates the most interaction. As in the Bales groups, amount of talking and amount of influence are directly related. Second, for the culture where women may possess a higher status than men, the Navaho, women exert more influence over decisions and talk more than men. In other cultures—the Texans, the Mormons, and residents of large American cities—it is the men who exert more influence. Third, for all groups except the Navaho, not only do men talk more and exert more influence, but they are also perceived as being more helpful during the deliberation. Fourth, in the jury studies, there are several pieces of information to indicate that individuals feel that those of higher occupational status are better qualified for jury duty than those of low occupational status.

How do individuals know the occupational status of their fellow jurors? Actually if you have observed a jury deliberation, it is not hard to tell. Some men appear for jury duty wearing a dress shirt, a tie, and a sport coat; others, a colored sport shirt, open at the neck. Some women appear for jury duty wearing a dress or a suit, and others in a cotton print house dress or slacks and a sweater. Speech patterns are particularly revealing. It should not require more than five minutes of jury deliberation for individuals to identify those who use correct grammar and those who pronounce words carelessly or incorrectly. Cues to the occupational status, and to the status in general, of individuals in our society are numerous. What is more, they are the sorts of cues that most people observe closely and take very seriously. Thus the Strodtbeck studies enable us to describe more precisely and more rigorously the effects of status in the jury setting. However none of these effects should be particularly surprising to anyone who has observed the status structure of American society; nor to anyone, such as a trial lawyer, who is familiar with the action of juries. Very recently, trial lawyers have begun to apply social science to jury selection in hope of gaining more favorable verdicts for their clients. The acquittals of Angela Davis and of John Mitchell and Maurice Stans were attributed in part to this practice. All the implications of this for our legal system are not apparent, but clearly we are a long way from the "trial by a jury of one's peers" described in the Constitution.

Status and Interaction in the Psychiatric Hospital

Caudill studied interactions among the staff of a psychiatric hospital intensively and for an extended period of time. Many of the data were collected in such a way that they may be compared directly to data from some experimental groups we have already examined.

Medical institutions are particularly interesting to sociologists because they provide a setting in which the effects of status differences may be observed quite clearly and quite strongly. There are several reasons for this fact. First, statuses within a medical institution are clearly delineated—everyone knows the status difference which exists between a doctor and a nurse. Second, status differences usually are highly visible—they are indicated in various ways such as differences in dress and in equipment. Third, in contrast with some other contemporary institutions, the status differences in hospitals are considered *legitimate* by participants in the system; that is, there is comparatively little effect of the democratic norm to assert that "all people are basically the same." Individuals recognize, believe in, adhere to, and therefore tend to perpetuate the status differences. Fourth, as a result of these facts, *formal* statuses tend to have strong, direct effects upon *informal* organization. For example, nurses will be deferential to doctors not only within their professional role relationships, but also when they meet outside of them. Senior physicians will expect (and will receive) respect from their junior colleagues in situations well beyond those where professional competence is an issue.

Every morning the staff of the psychiatric hospital (from 13 to 18 persons) met to discuss current events related to the patients and to reach decisions regarding relations between staff and patients. Typical topics of conversation would be reports from the responsible officials of occurrences during the previous evening, and disposition of therapeutic problems raised by the staff and of requests for privileges that had been raised by the patients. Caudill attended 63 such conferences and recorded the interaction in shorthand for later scoring according to the Bales Interaction Process Analysis categories.

First, let us examine the effect of formal status upon amount of interaction in the conference. Table 7–7 shows the average number of acts per conference for five of the status groups (in order of decreasing formal status) head of hospital, senior physician, chief resident physician, resident physician, nurse, and "other" personnel. Notice that—with the exception of chief resident—there is a perfect ordering of amount of interaction by status of the actors' positions. The head of the hospital speaks most frequently, and the nurses and other personnel speak least frequently. The chief resident speaks more than other senior physicians because of the

TABLE 7–7   Index of Average Individual Participation
Per Conference, by Role Group

ROLE GROUP	FIRST 21 CONFERENCES	SECOND 21 CONFERENCES	THIRD 21 CONFERENCES	ALL 63 CONFERENCES
Head of hospital	26.9	28.8	15.1	24.6
Senior physicians	18.0	16.5	14.8	16.6
Chief resident physician	24.8	22.0	19.8	22.2
Resident physicians	15.7	16.5	10.9	14.4
Nurses	4.8	4.7	3.8	4.4
Other personnel	4.4	5.4	4.0	4.7

(From Caudill, 1958: Tables 10.2 and 10.5.)

formal social structure: he is officially the leader of the conferences. Senior physicians and the head of the hospital have much less contact with patients and with the day to day activities discussed at these conferences. It is significant, however, that not even the formal position of leadership at the conference is sufficient to gain the chief resident a higher participation rate than the head of the hospital (except for the third set of conferences). Apparently the status of head of the hospital is sufficiently elevated that he is encouraged and permitted to speak very frequently at the conferences —even though his knowledge of particular events under discussion is likely to be much less than that of the residents and the nurses.

Besides showing the effect of the differences *between* status groups on participation, Caudill examined the effects of status differences *within* several of the status groups. Table 7–8 shows the average participation rate among members of the group *nurses,* composed of supervisor of nurses, charge nurses, and staff nurses. The effects of status in Tables 7–7 and 7–8 are identical: the higher the official status rank of the individual, the greater his participation rate.

Within the single formal status role "doctor," all members of which are equal in official status, there were considerable variations in amount of participation at staff conferences. The resident physicians—those directly

TABLE 7–8   Index of Average Individual Participation
Per Conference, by Subcategory of Nurses

SUBCATEGORY	FIRST 21 CONFERENCES	SECOND 21 CONFERENCES	THIRD 21 CONFERENCES	ALL 63 CONFERENCES
Supervisor of nurses	7.1	6.8	7.6	7.2
Charge nurses	4.2	4.3	3.0	3.8
Staff nurses	0	2.0	0	0.4

(From Caudill, 1958: Table 10.7.)

concerned with patient care and responsibility for running the hospital—show the same sort of participation inequality as may be observed between statuses or within the status "nurse." Table 7–9 shows the average number of acts initiated per conference by each of the five residents. On the average they range from approximately 26 acts per conference for Dr. A to a low of about 7.5 acts for Dr. E. It is interesting to compare the amounts of interaction by each of the five resident physicians to the relative amounts of interaction Bales observed in groups of college sophomores. Table 7–10 compares the *proportion* of total acts initiated by each of the five residents (computed from Table 7–9) to the proportion of interaction Bales reports for a large number of 5-person discussion groups (taken from Table 6–2).

Most interesting, because of the comparison of these groups to Bales groups, we might suspect that the ranking of residents on amounts of participation reflects conceptions of their relative competence to perform their psychiatric tasks. Caudill pursued a similar idea. Sometime after completing his observations, he wrote to each of the senior physicians. This was two months after the residents had completed their year of service. Senior physicians were asked to rank residents in terms of their own opinion of "overall competence," and they were asked not to consult with each other in making the rankings. Table 7–11 shows the ranking of residents given by each of the senior doctors. Compare these ability rankings with the doctors' relative amounts of participation in Table 7–9. Only near the bottom of the rankings—Drs. D and E—is there any deviation from perfect correspondence. As a matter of fact although Caudill does not draw this conclu-

TABLE 7–9 Index of Average Individual Participation Per Conference, by Each Resident

RESIDENT	FIRST 21 CONFERENCES	SECOND 21 CONFERENCES	THIRD 21 CONFERENCES	ALL 63 CONFERENCES
Dr. A	20.9	31.2	25.9	25.9
Dr. B	18.9	19.4	10.8	16.3
Dr. C	17.7	15.3	11.4	14.9
Dr. D	10.3	9.9	5.3	8.5
Dr. E	10.0	7.6	5.3	7.6

(From Caudill, 1958: Table 10.9.)

TABLE 7–10 Initiation Rates, Doctors and College Sophomores

RANK	DOCTORS	SOPHOMORES
#1	37%	47%
#2	23%	22%
#3	17%	15%
#4	12%	10%
#5	11%	6%

TABLE 7–11   Ranking of Residents According to
Seniors' Evaluation of Over-all Ability

Senior Doctor	Dr. A	Dr. B	Dr. C	Dr. D	Dr. E
Dr. Sutton	2	1	3	5	4
Dr. Scott	1	2	3	5	4
Dr. Shaw	1	2	3	5	4
Dr. Sloan	1	2	3	5	4
Dr. Sears	1	3	2	5	4
Dr. Simmons	1	2	3	5	4
Total of ranks	7	12	17	30	24

Coefficient of concordance $= 0.93$ ($p < .005$).
(From Caudill, 1958: Table 10.11.)

sion, it is possible to construct a status-related interpretation of even this reversal: Dr. E possesses the low state of a highly significant status characteristic—she is a woman. Although Caudill does not mention the sex of the
other residents, if we may assume that Dr. D is a male, then we see an effect
similar to the effect of sex in Strodtbeck's jury studies. Apparently possessing
either low (reputed) competence or the low state of a diffuse status characteristic such as sex is likely to lead to lower participation in group problem
solving.

Formal Status and Informal Influence

Torrance studied the interaction effects of formal status in groups of Air
Force bomber crews. A total of 95 3-man crews, consisting of pilot,
navigator, and gunner, were studied. Sixty-two of these crews were *permanent;* men who had worked together previously, and who knew each other.
The other 32 crews were *temporary.* These were formed by taking each man
from a different permanent crew. For example in one temporary group the
pilot was taken from permanent group 1, the navigator from permanent
group 2, and the gunner from permanent group 3.

In an aircraft crew the pilot has the highest authority (even if his Air
Force rank should be lower than that of the other two members of the
crew), the navigator is second, and the gunner is third. In terms of official
Air Force rank, the pilot's formal status usually is highest, the navigator's
second, and the gunner's is lowest. Torrance studied the effects of the formal
status possessed by each man upon interaction in a variety of problems. For
our purposes the problems may be separated into two categories: those
for which rank is *relevant,* and those for which it is not. A relevant problem
is one in which it is reasonable to suppose that the higher ranking man will
posssess greater task ability. A nonrelevant problem is one for which there
is no reason to presume this. Let us first examine the effects of formal status
upon a relevant problem.

The relevant problem involved survival after an aircraft crash, and members of the permanent crews were asked to discuss the problem and to devise escape procedures. Their deliberations were scored according to the Bales interaction analysis scheme, and at the end of the session, individuals were asked how much influence they felt they and the other two individuals had over the crew's decision. Table 7–12 presents the perceived influence of the group members over the final decision.

Two things are apparent in Table 7–12. First (row two), the amount of perceived influence over the decision varied directly with formal status. Pilots exerted most and gunners exerted none. Perhaps even more interesting are the data in rows three and four. In row three we see that navigators and gunners were less in agreement with the decision than pilots. This is to be expected from the relative amounts of influence they exerted over the group decision. However, in row four we see that there is very little difference in amount of satisfaction with the decision across individuals. Apparently gunners and navigators are approximately as satisfied with group decision as pilots. Even though they had less influence over the decision and agreed with the decision less, they seem to feel that it was "satisfactory."

Now let us examine the effect of formal status at nonrelevant tasks. One of the nonrelevant tasks was what is called the Dot Estimation Task. The task is to estimate the number of dots on a white card after studying the card for 15 seconds. The card actually contains 3155 dots, a number which would be impossible to count in 15 seconds. Therefore the task is somewhat *ambiguous;* the correct answer is not at all immediately apparent. Members of the crews are asked, first, to write their own private estimates of the number of dots on a slip of paper. Next they discuss the question and finally, each man again writes his estimate of the number of dots on a slip of paper. In both permanent and temporary crews, the gunners changed their estimates the most as a result of group discussion and the pilots changed their estimates the least. These data again show the effects of formal status upon influence. Remember that the Dot Estimation Test is an ambiguous one, so it is impossible for an individual to be certain that any of his answers is correct.

TABLE 7–12 Effects of Formal Status Upon Influence;
Relevant Task

	PERCENTAGES		
ATTITUDE OR BEHAVIOR	PILOTS	NAVIGATORS	GUNNERS
Made little effort to influence decision	43.8	28.1	55.3
Had most influence on decision	41.7	8.8	0.0
Complete agreement with decision	77.1	59.6	52.6
Complete satisfaction with decision	89.6	86.0	84.2

(From Torrance, 1965: Table 7.)

An unambiguous task is the "horse-trading problem." It is stated as follows:

> A man bought a horse for sixty dollars and sold it for seventy dollars. Then he bought it back for eighty dollars and sold it for ninety dollars. How much money does he make in the horse-trading business?

Again each individual wrote his private answer on a slip of paper, and then conferred to reach a group decision. The correct answer, I trust you have figured by now, is twenty dollars. What is of interest is the proportion of times an individual who had the correct answer *failed to influence* the other two members to accept that answer. In other words, what is examined is the proportion of times that one member of the crew knew the correct answer and yet was unable to convince the other members to accept that for the crew's decision.

In both permanent and temporary crews pilots failed to influence the group to accept the correct decision the least, and gunners failed the most.

In describing the bowling incident in Chap. 6, I told you that we would want to explain the fact that the researcher Whyte came out with the highest score of the entire group. We are beginning to be in a position to explain this fact, and to explain it in the same terms as used to explain the other group members' relative bowling scores. Our explanation for others' scores was that they reflected members' conceptions of standing within the group, or what we now call *status*. Whyte's status within the group is not certain, but the status he brought from outside was much higher than that of the others; they were "corner boys" at a slum in Boston, and he was a Harvard graduate student. Thus from knowing that his external status was extremely high, and from the principle that high status and high performance scores are associated, we would be able to explain the fact that Whyte did so well at that important match.

Status Characteristics and Expectation States

All of the studies reviewed in this chapter have in common the following features. First, they are all groups in which actors are differentiated in terms of one or more diffuse status characteristics. The diffuse status characteristic may be formal rank, sex, age, occupational status, education or even regional origin; what these characteristics have in common is that they are properties of an individual which are (in the particular given groups, at least) differentially evaluated. Second, the interaction situations studied all have to do with some sort of group problem solving. In this way all the groups are comparable to the Bales discussion groups studied in Chap. 6. Third, in every case, it appears that the diffuse status characteristics of individuals organize the interaction in the informally organized groups; that is, people with higher status *on whatever basis* are accorded more power and prestige in these groups. Furthermore this difference takes place whether or not these individuals are *correct* in their decisions, and whether or not their status characteristics are *relevant* to the task being performed. Fourth, there is some evidence that, not only are power and prestige allocated in accord with status, but that the actors involved feel that it is "right and proper" that this should be the case.

The following abstraction may be drawn from all of these studies:

> When a task-oriented group is differentiated with respect to some external status characteristic, this status difference determines the observable power and prestige order within the group whether or not the external status characteristic is related to the group task.

Our goal at this point is to extend the propositions of expectation states theory presented in Chap. 6 so that they will account for these findings and for the abstract summary statement. Notice that the differences in the observable power and prestige structures of these groups could be accounted for *if* we had some reason to believe that members held differentiated expectations for each others performance. In other words if we had a reason to believe that expectations are formed on the basis of external status characteristics (and if we could specify the conditions under which this will and will not occur), then we could explain the findings reported above from all of these groups.

Such an extention of expectation states theory has been developed by Berger et al. The extention asserts, basically, that if individuals are in interaction with each other, and if they possess no other information except the fact of their relative standing on a diffuse status characteristic, then this diffuse status characteristic will be used by the actors to form performance expectations for each other. High expectations will be assigned to the actor possessing high status, and low expectations to the actor possessing low status. Then we may add the basic expectation assumption that expectation states associated with actors will determine the observable power and prestige order among them, and the theoretical extension is complete.

The status characteristic extension of expectation states theory is far-reaching in its applications, for it asserts that people will use status characteristics to organize interaction in problem-solving situations whether or not the status is related to task-performing ability. Thus it asserts that in the absence of knowledge that sex does not matter in jury deliberation ability, jurors will assume that it *does* matter, and will treat each other differentially on the basis of it. In other words, the burden of proof is placed on someone wishing to believe that status is *not* relevant to the particular interaction. This would explain why Strodtbeck found that women talk less and exert less influence in juries than men. Clearly, there is no reason to believe that women are less able jurors than men are. However, there is no evidence that they are *not* less able, or at least we assume that Strodtbeck's jurors were not aware of any such evidence. Thus according to the status characteristics extension of the theory, we would expect jurors to treat each other differentially on the basis of the sex status characteristic—as they do. This same sort of explanation could be outlined for the effect of occupational status in juries, Air Force rank in Torrance's studies and medical speciality ranking in the psychiatric hospital. The "burden of proof" nature of the theoretical extension is its most interesting feature. It is the crucial assumption that enables explanations of most of the status characteristic effects studied.

The first experimental tests of these status characteristics extension are by Moore. The research uses the basic experimental situation for expectation states theory, described in Chap. 6. Subjects were women recruited from a junior college. They were brought into the experimental laboratory separately and were prevented from seeing each other. The status manipulation was conducted by means of describing subjects and their partners. Some of the women were told that their partners possessed higher status than they themselves did, and some were told that their partners possessed lower status. The status characteristic used was one which might be called "academic attainment"; that is, year of education in school.

All status manipulations were performed as follows. In the high status conditions, the experimenter looks straight at both subjects and says, "I see we have with us today one young lady from a junior college, and one young lady from a high school." Thus both subjects are led to believe that the partner is a high school student. In the low status manipulation condition, the experimenter looks straight at both subjects and says, "I see we have with us today one young lady from a junior college, and one young lady from a four year university." Thus each subject is led to believe that her partner is a university student.

Table 7–13 presents the $P(s)$ data, showing the effect of status manipulation. We would expect the $P(s)$ from subjects in the high status conditions to be higher than the $P(s)$ from subjects in the low status conditions, if the theory is to be supported. The data show this is the case.

Since Moore's experiment, there have been many experiments in which several other diffuse status characteristics were used; for example, Air Force rank, age, and sex. In general, results of all these experiments are similar to Moore's. It does not seem to matter what status characteristic is used. What all these experiments show is that, unless actors know for sure that the status difference is irrelevant, they will form performance expectations consistent with the status differences they perceive. Then their actions will be consistent with the structure of performance expectations in the situation, just as we saw in Chap. 6.

TABLE 7–13 Average Effects of Status Difference
On Expectation States

Status	$P(s)$
High	.75
Low	.61

(Data calculated from Moore, 1968, Table 2.)

One diffuse status characteristic that has *not* produced simple results is race. There is ample observational evidence that mixed-race interaction shows almost exactly the same features as other mixed status interaction. Any of the results reviewed earlier in juries, bomber crews, and psychiatric conferences would almost certainly be reproduced if the individuals differed on race instead of other status characteristics. However to date no experiment has demonstrated effects of race in a satisfactory way.

The first expectation experiment using race was reported by Seashore in 1968. Following a procedure very similar to Moore's, she had subjects read a form on which their partners had supposedly already told their race. Since subjects were white junior college women, the high status manipulation consisted of telling them their partners were black college women. The low status condition told them their partners were (white) university students, just as Moore had. *No effect* of the status manipulation was visible in the data. Later, B. P. Cohen and associates repeated the attempt to demonstrate effects of race. Again results are either weak or nonexistent.

Why should this be so? We know that race differences do affect interaction in natural settings. What I think happens in these experiments, however, is that other factors overcome the effects of race. For one thing, when these experiments were run in late 1960s, subjects probably were very much concerned about appearing "not prejudiced." Some of them bent over backwards to be deferential to their supposed black partners. Others, being college students, may honestly not regard race as a status—that is, evaluated—characteristic. And still others may have become so upset by knowing they were being "tested" for prejudice that they behaved erratically. Some data are consistent with all of these conjectures, though of course we do not know for certain just what goes through a person's mind during the experiment.

In sum, there is a large and still growing body of experimental research studying how status differences affect expectations and future behavior. The basic prediction, that actors form expectations consistent with their different states of status characteristics, has repeatedly been confirmed. Effects of race have not yet been demonstrated clearly in the laboratory. My belief is that this is due to special historical circumstances that make racial experiments particularly delicate, not to anything special about race.

Mixed-Race Interaction

The status characteristics *race* and *sex* are of greatest importance in contemporary American society. To date, study of the effects of the sex characteristic upon interaction has not been pursued in any systematic or cumulative manner. However interest in race has existed for a longer period of time, and it is possible at this point to see some cumulative knowledge developing. Katz and his associates (1958, 1960, 1962, 1970) have studied various aspects of interaction in black–white racially mixed groups. In groups composed of two members of each race who were engaged in sessions of cooperative problem solving, Katz reports, "Negro subjects made fewer proposals than did whites, and tended to accept the latter's contributions uncritically. . . . Negroes made fewer remarks than did whites and spoke more to whites, proportionately, than to one another" (Katz, 1970:390). These results again indicate the effect of the race status characteristic upon performance expectations: in these studies, black individuals *behave as if* they have low expectations for themselves and high for whites, and the whites *behave as if* they hold high expectations for themselves, and low expectations for the blacks. These results are even found in groups where all members are matched on intelligence and where the blacks are demonstrated to possess ability equivalent to the whites. By questionnaire reports at the end of the sessions, blacks rate whites higher than themselves on intellectual performance, and say they would prefer whites as future work companions.

In another experiment, Katz and Cohen attempted to train blacks to be more assertive in groups such as these. Subjects were students at a Northern university, engaged in solving a set of problems in 2-man teams. One member of each team was white, and one was black. Even after receiving the "assertiveness training," blacks were deferential towards whites and tended to accept suggestions of whites *even when it was quite apparent that the whites were in error.*

What is particularly interesting about these studies, however, is that at the end of the session the whites tended to downgrade the blacks' performance, and to say that they would prefer not to have them as future partners. Apparently an unintended consequence of the assertiveness training was hostility on the part of whites. The hostility is understandable if we postulate the following chain of events. First, the result of assertiveness training is to raise blacks' expectations for their own performance. As a consequence of raised self expectations, blacks begin behaving more like "high selves": they accept less influence from whites, and they expect that their own answers are more likely to be correct than those of the whites. However, the whites who hold low expectations for blacks based upon the status characteristic, see no reason to change their beliefs. From their point of view, the blacks are behaving inappropriately. Stated differently, the blacks are not allocating components of the power and prestige structure in accord with the expectations held by the whites. What may have been created in the Katz and Cohen experiments, therefore, was a situation analogous to what Bales observed in the discussion groups at the beginning of their sessions: a "status struggle." One result of behaving like a "high self" when these expectations are not shared by others is that they will try to "put the individual in his place"; that is, an attempt will be made to enforce an allocation of power and prestige components on the basis of the expectations each actor holds. When actors differ in their expectations, we see a struggle.

Something of the same sort has been observed by E. G. Cohen and her associates. Cohen's studies are based explicitly upon the status characteristics theory, and are designed to help alleviate undesirable effects of the race status characteristic in interaction. Their goal is to find practical ways to intervene in a situation so as to define race as a nonrelevant characteristic in forming ability conceptions. They hope to break into the status characteristic expectation state process at the "burden of proof" stage and to help overcome the stereotypic behavior which usually follows this stage. Cohen's research involves groups of junior high school aged children, black and white. Children are formed into teams which must cooperate to achieve a team goal. One of the tasks is to assemble a radio crystal set. In this situation if biracial groups are formed and allowed to work on the task, individuals behave as though low expectations were held for blacks' performance and high for whites' performance. In Cohen's first experiments blacks were given "expectation training"; that is, they were given additional information how to perform the task well, information not given to the whites. Measurements of the success of the training indicated that in fact blacks' expectations for their own performance had been improved as a result of the training. However as soon as the groups were integrated, the status characteristic took over: blacks again began behaving deferentially, and whites acted as though this is what they expected blacks to do. This is the same phenomenon observed in Katz's studies. It was quite apparent from the first studies that simply changing blacks' expectations was not sufficient.

In the second studies, the attempt was made to alter, not only blacks' self-expectations, but *whites'* expectations for blacks. In these experiments whites were allowed to observe the additional training being given to blacks, and furthermore, the whites were allowed to observe blacks actually performing well at the task. *Only under circumstances in which expectations were changed for all members of the group was it possible to demonstrate a breaking down of the effects of the race status characteristic.* Cohen's researchers are still continuing as of this writing, but it is quite clear that her strategy of developing techniques based upon the status characteristics theory is promising.

Freese and B. P. Cohen (1973) have recently constructed an explicit version of expectation states theory which accounts well for E. G. Cohen's results. Basically, their theory asserts that individuals form *general expectations* for actors whenever they have information on two or more consistently evaluated characteristics. For example if a person knows he is good at arithmetic and at reading, this is sufficient for him to form high general expectations for schoolwork. Also according to this theory, it is *only when two or more characteristics are inconsistent with a diffuse status characteristic* that the effects of the status characteristic upon expectation states can be overcome.

What this means in practical terms is that if you wish to overcome the effects of status differences, you need to demonstrate at least two performance skills that are inconsistent with the status characteristic. For instance to overcome low expectations formed for black children in mixed-race groups, you need to show that blacks are better than (or equal to) whites on at least two particular tasks. It takes two tasks, they claim, to block the burden of proof process.

Freese and Cohen conducted an experiment in which two performances were "measured," and they were inconsistent with the status characteristic (age) which differentiated actors. The older person did worse at the tasks than the younger, in other words. Results indicate that the burden of proof was blocked effectively in this case.

Overview of Status in Social Interaction

Status value—differences in prestige, esteem, respect, and estimation of "overall worth"—is attached to nearly every characteristic we can think of. Not only do people notice and classify differences in such characteristics as sex, age or place of birth, but they also *evaluate* states of these characteristics. For our culture, it is desirable to be male as opposed to female, relatively young (although not too young), wealthy rather than poor, and employed at a nonmanual occupation. Virtually any characteristic that can be used to differentiate people rather quickly comes to hold evaluated status significance as well as simply descriptive significance. A sociologist looks almost in vain to find a characteristic that is not a status characteristc; that is, one which is not differentially evaluated by actors in some social system. As these examples suggest, precisely *which* state of the characteristic is positively valued differs from one time and one place to another. One of many examples of this may be found in Japan. Before 1940 old age was highly valued; even revered. Since the end of World War II, Japanese have adopted and accentuated the American value placed upon youth.

Status differences between individuals usually generalize beyond the specific areas in which they arise. Thus an enlisted man who meets an officer, even outside of the military, is likely to treat him with deference and respect.[1] Similarly when an individual possessing high status in one area interacts in a different social situation, he is likely to be treated *as though* his outside status were relevant to the immediate interaction. Physicists of deservedly high status for their professional work have been invited to testify on the relative merits of defensive missile systems—a political and engineering issue for which skill in physics provides no special competence. Physicians regularly are called upon to give opinions about problems of nutrition and sexual and marital adjustment—problems for which they have received no professional training—and their opinions are treated as if they really knew what they were talking about. (Some have even written best selling books containing misinformation about social and psychological aspects of sexual behavior.)

---

[1] When I was in graduate school, I used to play table tennis with a friend who was a high school student. He beat me consistently, until one day I explained to him about the bowling incident of Streetcorner Society.

Exactly why status differences generalize beyond specific areas we do not know. Neither do we know with any precision the limits of the phenomenon of generalization of status. Where it will occur and where it won't occur, specific circumstances which are necessary for the generalization to occur, and exactly how far status will generalize are questions that have received little theoretical or empirical investigation.

What is probably the most significant fact about status generalization is that, very often, a *diffuse status characteristic* produces conceptions of task ability. Cases where individuals form ability conceptions based upon knowledge of status characteristics have been documented repeatedly; we have reviewed some of the most important of these studies.

Of many potential applications of the effects of status upon performance expectations, we examined two. Experiments in naturalistic mixed-race groups showed clear effects of the status characteristic *race* upon performance expectations and interaction. Attempts to raise the expectations of blacks in mixed-race groups produces a phenomenon comparable to the "status struggle" observed in early Bales groups. More recent studies that attempt to minimize the "interaction disability" effect of race have shown the necessity for changing not only blacks' expectations for themselves, but also whites' expectations for blacks. Certainly there is a need and an opportunity for more systematic work, guided by theory, in all of these areas.

The Future of Status Characteristics

Of the many candidates for further research on the effects of status characteristics in social interaction let us consider three that have unusually profound implications and are likely to receive attention and partial solution during the next decade. First is the classic sociological problem of the effects of two or more status characteristics upon social interaction. As long ago as 1945 Stuart Hughes formulated the question for sociologists, "How do you treat a black physician?" The question still has not received an adequate answer. In our society, *physician* is the high state of the occupational characteristic, while *black* is the low state of the race characteristic. Does one treat him according to sterotypic beliefs about a black person (that is, expect him to be deferential, unintelligent, violent and unskilled), or does one treat him according to sterotypic beliefs about a physician (that is, expect him to be authoritative, well educated, fatherly and competent)?

Under certain circumstances—particularly when only one of two possible characteristics is activated or when both actors decide to use the same characteristic to guide their interaction—the situation is simplified. When a black physician and a white physician interact within a strictly professional situation, such as consultation over a patient, we may presume that only the professional status will be activated, and thus that they will form no status-based differential expectations in the interaction. On the other hand if these men meet in an informal situation such as a cocktail party or on a jury, we may presume that only the race characteristic gets noticed, since it is the only characteristic that is easily seen. If this is so, then we can use the status characteristics theory to predict the likely form of interaction between the two.

However suppose the black physician does not recognize the race characteristic as relevant during the interaction—he believes, for example, that it has no bearing on fitness for jury duty. If the white physician does use the characteristic, then we have the interesting situation of actors forming inconsistent expectations: the black man has formed equal expectations [+ +] for self and other, while the white man has formed [+ −] expectations for self and other. In this case they have conflicting expectations for what constitutes appropriate behavior on each other's parts. The interaction is likely to be unsatisfactory to each man, though they might find it difficult to explain precisely why they find it so. The black man "expects" to be treated as an equal at the task, while the white man "expects" to be treated as a superior.

Let us make the hypothetical situation even more complicated now by supposing that our white physician is a woman in interaction with a black male physician. Now the following status positions obtain:

	PROFESSION	RACE	SEX
Person #1	high	high	low
Person #2	high	low	high

What form will interaction take in such a situation (one, incidentally, which is far from rare)? In a strictly professional setting, it seems likely that only the first status will be considered relevant, and both actors will treat each other as equals, just as in the first example. But in informal settings, the interaction cues provided by the statuses are ambiguous and contradictory. Equality on profession probably means it will be discounted as a factor affecting interaction between these two persons. Now, if *both* actors decide to activate *only one* status in this situation, *and* if they both decide to activate *the same* status (either race or sex), again there will be no difficulty. One will form [+ −] expectations, and the other will form [− +] expectations, and their behaviors towards each other will be complementary.

But suppose the first person decides that race is relevant to the interaction and tries to assert her "whiteness," and the second decides sex is relevant and tries to assert his "maleness." Or suppose that both of them are aware of the possibility that both race and sex could affect their interaction, but it is not clear that either or both statuses *must* affect interaction. Then we are likely to see an instance of "status struggle," as in the Bales groups—both individuals attempting to gain the upper hand in the interaction.

Attempting to emphasize status characteristics upon which one is high, or to suppress the relevance of those upon which one is low, can certainly be observed in a wide variety of situations. This can be accomplished most directly by telling the other person—tactfully, of course—of one's high standing and of its presumed relevance to whatever is taking place. This may be done either for play (as in "gamesmanship"), or for serious purposes.

In many strictly professional encounters, female physicians face potential difficulties from possessing both a professional and a sexual status at the same time. Often it is difficult for a male patient to comply with a request to undress for examination before a female physician. Female physicians have told me that they learn early in their medical training to emphasize the professional aspects of the encounter and to minimize the effects of their sex. They develop a somewhat distant, clinical, "scientistic" approach to patients. They wear little or no makeup, and they always dress in shapeless white lab coats with stethoscope and other "doctor apparatus" conspicuously displayed. It is interesting to note that the frequent complaint heard regarding women doctors—that they are "cold"—is actually due to their concern for making their patients more comfortable.

We might expect that all actors attempt to emphasize the characteristic on which they were highest, but we would be wrong if we assumed this invariably takes place. Certainly it occurs sometimes, but we simply do not have sufficient empirical evidence to conclude that it always occurs. And in fact there are good reasons to suppose it is not universal. Consider what will happen if someone attempts to make the status characteristic on which he is highest the only relevant one for interaction in a task oriented group. If he succeeds, then everyone will form high performance expectations for him. This may be pleasant for a time, but it carries along considerable responsibility. The individual who has been granted respect, esteem, deference, and so on, by virtue of the high expectations held for him also is expected to perform well. He has responsibility to the group—he is even likely to be delegated a leader, such as jury foreman. Thus the consequences of initially gaining a high position of power and prestige are *potentially* quite unpleasant. One could fall from favor from repeated poor performance, and would henceforth be termed a phony. There are dangers as well as social rewards associated with power and prestige, and individuals in some circumstances may well not wish to accept them. Stated more generally, there is no good empirical or theoretical reason to believe that individuals in interaction will attempt to suppress the relevance of status characteristics on which they themselves are low. In some cases it seems as though individuals will "average" their various statuses to arrive at either an overall status, or an overall level of performance expectations. If this is so and if we can obtain measures of the relative weights and significances of different types of status, then it will be possible to extend the theory to cover situations of two or more diffuse status characteristics. However this task has not yet been accomplished.

A second interesting topic is the ways in which initially unevaluated objects can acquire status value, and how status-valued objects can become unevaluated. The sociologist George Homans wrote in another context, "Men value some of the damnedest things." For status symbols in our society this is entirely true. A large desk in an office may be used to indicate someone's importance within the company. A key to the executive washroom may do the same thing. Around college campuses, considerable status value is attached to the particular parking lot which an individual is allowed to use.

Faculty lots are generally closer to buildings and more desirable than student lots. Once an object has acquired status value—be it a large desk, a washroom key, or a particular parking sticker—it becomes desirable in and of itself, wanted by people whether or not they intend to use it. (Have you ever tried to get someone to give up the key to an office he no longer uses?) How is it that initially nonvalued objects acquire status value? Conversely, how do they come to lose status value? In Chap. 16 we shall return to the issue of status value, and we'll develop some answers. However there remains a wide range of questions for which we simply have no information.

The final question is the precise conditions surrounding the burden of proof process by which a status characteristic comes to be relevant to performance at a specific task. Exactly when will individuals assume that any status characteristic is relevant for the task? Are there different *types* of status characteristics, and if so, are they limited in the types of situations to which they are thought to be relevant. Does the burden of proof process operate *only* in the absence of any evaluative information about relative ability, or does it operate *in addition to* specific task performance information? What is the effect of *equal* status of actors—does it always lead to equal performance expectations? Some of these questions have received partial answers in the studies we have reviewed in this chapter, but as this listing indicates, many more issues remained unsolved.

Perhaps it is appropriate to conclude our study of status effects upon interaction at this point—with an explicit statement that, although we know some things about the effects, there are many more important things that we do not yet know.

8

Socialization

What is Socialization?

"Socialization is the process by which the mewling, puking infant is transformed into the sophisticated young men and women I see sitting before me." That is how George Herbert Mead used to describe the process to his classes at the University of Chicago during the 1920s. It is still the best one-sentence description of socialization I know. Readers of this text, as sophisticated men and women, will appreciate that many factors contributed to their development. But while the end product, the social human, is complex, socialization occurs through well-understood principles of social learning. We begin our study with a brief look at how human socialization is similar to animal development, and how it is different. Then we study learning theories. Finally we examine how learning affects some of the most important areas of human development, beginning with childhood and continuing through adulthood.

When social psychologists talk of socialization, they refer to all the processes that go into making human infants into social beings—everything necessary for the initially unsocial infant to learn to adapt to others, to coexist with them, to understand them and anticipate their actions, and to learn to like or even love others. None of this "comes naturally." Whatever must be learned to get the newborn baby to act and think as its parents and others of the culture think it ought to, makes up the socialization process.

Man creates culture. We studied some elementary processes of culture building in earlier chapters. But culture also creates man, or at least culture creates the overwhelming proportion of what it takes to make up something recognizable as a human being. Socialization is the processes by which culture "gets into" the members of particular groups and subgroups of societies.

The range of human socialization practices and the outcomes of those practices vary tremendously. Almost every culture attempts to minimize the use of violence, and every culture tries to train its young not to marry whatever relatives would be defined as incest. Beyond this, it is difficult to specify any other universal outcomes of socialization. What is most impressive about socialization is the tremendous range of possibilities. Humans seem to be able to learn to become almost anything. All of us, to a far greater extent than we usually think, are products of our cultures. The more complex the culture, the greater the need for both child and adult socialization.

Both the need for and the enormous influence of socialization of humans are consequences of our biological natures. The human infant is uniquely helpless at birth. Our brains develop considerably during gestation, seemingly at the expense of the rest of our bodies. Consequently we need long years of care. During those years we are particularly able to benefit from intentional and unintentional teaching from the social and the natural environments.

For contrast it is instructive to see what happens to humans who are not socialized. There have been a few—fortunately, very few—recorded cases of children who grow up with only minimal contact with other humans. These are *feral children,* meaning "fierce" or "wild." Some feral children appear to have been abandoned when very young and miraculously to have survived in the woods. An excellent description of one such boy in 1749 is given in *The Wild Boy of Avignon,* which was the basis for the 1970 movie *The Wild Child.* More often feral children are unwanted by their parents and live out their early years locked away from the world in attics or isolated rooms, where they receive food but little else.

Kingsley Davis described a girl found at the age of 7. At that time she was barely recognizable as human. She could not speak and showed tremendous fear of strangers and all men. She did not play with objects in the way children usually do. Instead she spent most of her time crouched in a corner.

The story has a happy ending, however. Within 18 months, she could recognize words and sentences, write, and count. Thereafter as often happens with feral children, she progressed rapidly. Unless there is brain damage, feral children learn very rapidly when they are brought out of their impoverished environments. It appears that they make up for lost time, learning very quickly so that they come close to the level of normal children their age.

Humans and Other Primates

Within the past few years, several books by "ethologists" have appeared that attempt to link certain human social behaviors to instinctive and other unlearned behaviors observable in other animals, especially in the apes. Robert Ardrey has argued in *African Genesis* and *The Territorial Imperative* that humans are instinctively aggressive. This instinct leads them to establish and maintain "territory"—a phenomenon that seems analogous to a dog protecting its yard, a street gang protecting its turf, or a suburban homeowner fencing in his backyard. Lionel Tiger and James Fox have argued in *Men in Groups* that the basic social unit, learned in antiquity and transmitted through our genes to the present, is the all-male hunting and fighting band. This seems analogous to the attraction many men feel to their Army units, or perhaps to the closeness felt among gang members.

There are other ethologists who apply similar analyses to other social phenomena. The elements of these writers' arguments are to take a social phenomenon and to compare it to what seems analogous behavior in other animals. Then they ask what function some similar behavior could have fulfilled for primitive men—such as the utility of innate aggression and territorial defense in the hostile jungles of half a million years ago. The argument is completed by saying that since analogous behaviors are visible in several species today, and since some similar behaviors may have been functional (had "survival value") to humans many years ago, it is likely that they are based upon an instinct that has been preserved through natural selection favoring individuals who have the instinct over those who do not.

There is a good deal of controversy surrounding the ethological analyses, and I will leave it to you to assess their status. My own feeling is that the arguments are very weak. They are based on very little observation and often on inaccurate observations of both humans and of the species with which we are compared. Moreover the argument rests at base upon an analogy. Human behavior *looks like* some other animal's behavior. But it only looks like it if you perceive very selectively. If you pay attention to the right things, you will see similarities everywhere. If you concentrate on other things, you will see differences. (Think how easy it would be to argue that humans and apes are "basically" very different in their behaviors.) Finally, the analysis depends upon a conjecture—often plausible, but a conjecture all the same— about how primitive men may have acted. There is so little evidence, and so much conjecture that I do not find the argument persuasive. Also, some authorities in other fields have recently begun to dispute the ethologists. Allard, for example, in *The Human Imperative* shows that there are sound genetic reasons to doubt that instincts of this sort could be transmitted through human genes. The ethologists' ideas are provocative, but at this point they are not well supported, either by evidence, or by other relevant theory.

Konrad Lorenz, who is often called an ethologist but who distinguishes himself from them by careful, systematic observation and by cautious interpretations that do not go beyond what the data or confirmed theories support, tells of some remarkable behavioral parallels between species. Two things should be noted, however. First, the interspecies comparisons Lorenz makes usually do not include humans. Second, the similarities are always of a very abstract nature, not a claim that the same concrete behaviors occur across species. For example, we noted in Chap. 6 that Lorenz observed age and group position often highly associated across species. What the abstract concept "group position" means concretely, however, depends upon the particular group of animals. We have seen several ways to interpret the concept just in human groups. Abstract similarities are not the result solely of observation—they come from the observer's intellectual efforts. We can, in fact, construct a good argument—most stages of it confirmed by experimental test —why age and group position should be associated. We cannot do this with any asserted analogies between contemporary humans and cave men, or between contemporary humans and contemporary apes.

In many ways these ethological writings are similar to the "instinct controversy" that took place in psychology between about 1900 and 1920. At that time, complex behavior patterns that are very probably instinctual were being discovered among several species of animals. Bees dance to indicate food directions, and birds and fish migrate, for example. So it seemed reasonable that human behavior might have an instinctual base as well. We know that a newborn human baby will curl its fingers around someone's finger or a branch (as a chimp will), and that could not be a learned behavior. Unfortunately what happened is that people began to coin new instincts. Every possible action was said to be the result of some recently discovered instinct (even including stamp collecting!). It was eventually realized that this is *naming* behavior, not explaining or understanding it, and the instinct approach fell into disrepute. If we define instincts as *complex, unlearned behavior patterns,* most social psychologists today believe that there are no human instincts.

What we do learn from animal studies (and it can be quite a lot) is that certain abstract phenomena appear in many species including humans, and that these phenomena often behave in similar ways. One important set of studies involves socialization and deprivation of monkeys raised at the University of Wisconsin by Harlow and his associates. Baby monkeys were separated from their mothers and some were raised by surrogate mothers, dummies made of various materials. One finding was that babies preferred a soft terrycloth mother over a hard wire one, even when the latter gave milk and the former did not. (Notice that we do *not* conclude that human babies prefer terrycloth mothers to wire mothers!).

More important to our interest here is what happened to these monkeys raised alone with surrogate mothers. They grew up to be neurotic, in their special monkey way. By adulthood they were afraid of each other, refused to mate or even to play together, and some refused to eat. However when several babies were raised with the same surrogate mother, or when these neurotic babies were introduced to others before adulthood, the deleterious effects were avoided or overcome. Unsocialized monkeys, like unsocialized humans, are probably unable to survive on their own. But they can make up for lost time, if they come to their societies after a period of isolation.

A few zoo keepers and others have tried raising gorilla or chimp orphans in their homes, treating them in most ways as a baby human would be treated. During early months of life, both human and chimp babies are very similar in their needs and in the ways they interact with adult humans. One interesting, perhaps surprising, finding is that for about two years, the nonhuman baby learns faster and better than the human baby. Most skills an infant has to master—the same sort of skills measured for testing human infant intelligence—are mastered more quickly by a chimp.

What is crucial, however, is development of language skills. When the human begins to learn to talk, he very quickly passes the chimp in all other learning as well. Capacity to speak gives the advantage of *inter*acting with the social environment, instead of just acting and reacting. Chimps can learn to recognize a few human words and to "talk" recognizably to a small extent, but they lack the mental and vocal equipment for anything like humans' vocabulary. Language is currently the major known advantage we have over the apes and other animals.

Patricia Barchas has studied interaction in groups of three rhesus monkeys brought together for the first time after capture in the wild. As you might expect, much of their early interaction is concerned with attempts to establish dominance over each other through fighting and acts or threats of violence. After developing a reliable scheme of coding rhesus social interaction in these groups, Barchas observed that most groups evolved a social hierarchy fairly rapidly. We saw this in the Bales groups of humans (Chap. 6), also. In addition Barchas found that her data on evolution of rhesus hierarchies looked very much like Fisek's data on evolution of power and prestige structures in Bales group of college freshmen. The same mathematical model describes the status evolution process in both types of groups about equally well!

Social Learning

We learn: norms; roles; friends, enemies, and how to tell them apart; morality; how to fit into social organizations and still maintain individuality; and more. How do we learn these things? In this area of social psychology we know a good deal.

All learning theories—of which there are a large variety—utilize certain concepts and a few general ideas. As in most fields, much of the work in studying social learning is becoming familiar with meanings of concepts, the *words* used by learning psychologists. In simplest outline, learning theories are concerned with the establishment and the strengthening of links between certain objects and certain actions. Our two concepts name these objects and actions: the object is called *stimulus,* and the action is called *response.* Moreover we speak of cases in which a stimulus provided by the environment is connected to—or "associated with"—a response by the actor. Thus learning theories are often called *stimulus–response theories.* The relationship is often diagrammed as follows: S–R. For example, we say that a red traffic light serves as a stimulus and is followed by a learned response of stopping the car.

Sometimes the basic diagram is expanded to indicate that the effect of any particular stimulus is mediated by past learning of the individual. For example, a given actor may be particularly sensitive to a traffic signal because he has recently received a ticket for running a red light. In this case we include the "organism" in our diagram: S–O–R. Another common variant of the diagram is to note that, at least during the initial learning period, the response is followed by some other action, either a *reward* or a *punishment.* That is how our actor learned to respond to the red light. The reward or punishment is a second stimulus: S–R–S.

Now we add more terminology. Rewards and punishments affect the rate of a particular response. Rewards, or positive reinforcers, increase the rate of response, and punishments decrease the rate. Thus rewards and punishments are two types of stimuli.[1] Other stimuli are neutral. *Learning* or *conditioning* is developing a memory for the association of particular stimuli. For example, an individual is said to *learn* that going through a red light is usually associated with punishment, or he is *conditioned* to stop at red lights.

Stimuli are usually classified into two types: *conditioned stimuli* and *unconditioned stimuli,* and these are represented CS and UCS. An unconditioned stimulus satisfies some need of the organism—most often, hunger—and thus it is "naturally" rewarding. If a particular UCS occurs in conjunction with a particular CS, the individual will learn to associate the two. When this learning takes place, that CS will function in the same way as the UCS originally did. For example, my tropical fish have learned that sight of a yellow can (CS) is associated with food (UCS), and so they get just as excited when they see the can as they do when they taste the fish food. A child learns that a certain tone of voice (CS) from his parent is usually followed by a swat (UCS) and comes to fear that tone. In our traffic light example we actually assumed a fairly long chain of associations. A red light is not punishing in itself, but only by association with getting a ticket. But the ticket is not really punishing either until we associate it with loss of money. How about the money; why should the driver not want to lose money (in terms of learning theories)?

Satiation occurs for most stimuli. At some point what was rewarding becomes less so. For example, a child becomes less interested in candy after he has had some of it. Satiation usually takes place for punishments also. Spanking has less effect in altering behavior if it is used all the time than it does if used infrequently.

Learning of associations between stimuli and responses is *acquisition.* Thus learning is "acquiring a response." If some particular response stops being reinforced, then the stimuli that elicited that response initially will eventually cease to do so. We then say that the response has been *extinguished* and talk of *extinction* of responses. Acquired responses of fear toward the neighborhood bully will extinguish after awhile if other children learn that he no longer can (or will) beat them up.

Both acquistion and extinction of responses are usually shown by figures called *learning curves.* Both types tend to be exponential. This means that at first change occurs very slowly, then more rapidly, and finally levels off. Figures 8-1A and 8-1B show typical learning curves for acquisition and extinction of responses.

In intentional acquisition or extinction, such as when one individual is attempting to train or teach another, we talk about the *reinforcement schedule.* This is the regularity of association between response and reward. Some-

---

[1]A very common error is to equate *rewards* with *positive reinforcers* and *punishments* with *negative reinforcers.* The error is the second part. Correct usage would be to equate *both* positive and negative reinforcement with increase in the rate of some behavior. Punishment is an aversive (unpleasant) event *deliberately* introduced *following* an action. A negative reinforcer is an aversive condition removed by appropriate behavior, thus increasing the rate of that response. Thus, some people acquire the response of using alcohol and other drugs to relieve psychological stress.

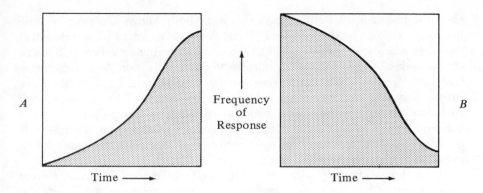

FIGURE 8–1 Typical acquisition and extinction curves

times we reinforce the desired response *continually,* or every time it occurs, such as praising a child every single time he uses the correct fork at the table. Usually, however, the reinforcement schedule is some *ratio,* and there are two types of ratios: *fixed,* and *variable.* On a fixed-ratio schedule, some constant fraction of the desired responses are reinforced. For example, with a 1:3 ratio we would reward the desired response every third time it occurred. On a variable-ratio schedule, sometimes we reward and sometimes we do not. An excellent example of variable-ratio reinforcement is a slot machine, which at least in the short run gives its reinforcement (money) only intermittently for the response of pulling the lever.

Finally we may talk of the *strength of acquisition* of a response, meaning how long it would take to extinguish if it were not ever again reinforced. The longer it would take, the stronger the acquisition. You should remember these two rules: (1) *In general, responses acquired through fixed-ratio reinforcement are acquired more strongly than responses acquired through continual reinforcement.* (2) *In general, responses acquired through variable-ratio reinforcement schedules are strongest of all.* In fact you can teach a pigeon to commit suicide through variable-ratio reinforcement. Using appropriate schedules, you can produce such a strongly acquired response of pecking a target, say, that the calories expended in pecking will exceed the caloric value of grain given as a reward, and the pigeon will starve itself to death. In Las Vegas there are little old ladies who play slot machines all day wearing leather gloves to protect their hands. They are responding to just the same learning principles as the pigeon.

Three basic types of learning are generally recognized: *classical conditioning, operant conditioning,* and *modeling.* In any particular situation it might be difficult to say that only one or only two of the types operate, but analytically they are separate. Using the terms introduced above, let us see what differences there are between types of learning.

Classical conditioning is so named because it is the oldest recognized form of learning. It was studied and described elaborately by the Russian scientist Pavlov in the early decades of this century. In classical conditioning, a CS is repeatedly and deliberately associated with an UCS until the CS can reliably elicit the response elicited by the UCS. Everybody knows the story of Pavlov's dogs, who originally salivated (R) at the sight of meat (UCS). However the meat was always presented in conjunction with ringing a bell (CS), and after awhile the bell alone was sufficient to cause salivation. When Professor Carlsmith lectures on classical conditioning at Stanford, he tells the class, "From now on, you will flinch whenever you hear the term *conditioned stimulus*." As he says the words "conditioned stimulus," he pulls out a blank gun and fires it in the air, making a tremendous noise in the classroom. It produces one-trial learning: for most members of the class, the conditioned response lasts throughout the term!

Classical conditioning, although quite well understood by most people today, is not in fact the most important way that humans are socialized. For intentional training, particularly of young children and of animals, classical conditioning can be important. As children get older and their cognitive capacities increase, operant conditioning and modeling become more significant.

Operant conditioning is a variety of learning that makes use of the same principles as classical conditioning but expands the focus to much more complicated situations. In operant conditioning we do not need to assume intentional training or control over rewards and punishments by another agent. Operant conditioning takes place when an organism emits a range of activities or responses, *some of which get rewarded*. For example, a pigeon can learn that pecking a set of targets in a particular pattern gets rewarded, but no other pattern of pecks does. Operant conditioning is what we often call "trial-and-error learning," and it is extremely important in human affairs. We learn how to treat other people, exactly what clothes to wear for various occasions, how to behave in school, church, and movies through trying out a wide range of actions and finding which are rewarded and which are punished. Operant conditioning differs from classical in that it does not need the terms of UCS and CS. For operant conditioning to take place all we need to assume is that the actor emits a range of acts, some of which get rewarded and some of which get punished. Both nonreinforced and punished acts become less likely to occur in the future, and rewarded acts become more likely. The process of training is called "shaping" of responses, as the learner's actions approximate those desired more and more closely.

B. F. Skinner is the man most prominently associated with operant conditioning. He has produced a tremendous fund of data from experimental studies with animals and humans, and in recent years he has applied this perspective to a wide range of social situations. In *Beyond Freedom and Dignity* he argues that all action is based on previous reinforcement, and it is only through explicit recognition of the rewards and punishments the environment gives us that we can control our own and each others' future actions. The point that operant conditioning works in cases where it is not recognized is a good one, though I do not agree with all of Skinner's other statements.

One good example of unintentional training that may be observed in any suburb is owners teaching their dogs to bark and become nuisances. Barking is decidedly an undesired response, but many people go to the dog whenever he barks "to see what he wants" or even just to shut him up. The attention, of course, is rewarding to the dog, and he soon learns to bark whenever he wants more attention. I have known mothers who train their children to cry in the same way.

Sometimes it is the learner who is unaware he is learning. Verplanck and many others have demonstrated the phenomenon of "unconscious learning," and it is easily reproduced. When I lecture on learning, I get someone to sit across a table from me, and I hold up a set of 20 index cards, one at a time. Each card has two words on it—such as "horse" and "pony"—and I ask the person to look at the card for a minute and then to say one of the words out loud. That is all I say, but actually I am trying to teach a rule. For one set of cards, my rule is to pick the word that begins with a letter from the second half of the alphabet (N through Z). For the second set of cards, my rule is to pick the word that ends with an "s" sound (like "horse"). On each card, if I get the word I want, I nod or say "uh-uh"; if not, nothing. That is a pretty small reward, and most people do not notice they are being selectively reinforced. But I can usually get many more "successes" for the second 10 cards in the set than for the first 10. This of course indicates that the person has learned a rule—usually without knowing he or she is learning anything, and always without being able to tell me what the rule is. Notice that these rules are fairly complicated ones, too.

Modeling or "vicarious processes," or "no-trial learning," is the third type of learning, and the man who has done the most work in this area is Albert Bandura. Bandura began by observing that for many social situations there simply is no chance for either classical or operant conditioning to take place. You just could not learn to drive a car, perform abdominal surgery, or survive military combat if all you relied upon were classical associations of CS with UCS, or operant shaping. These take too long. In cases like learning to drive, the organism faces the problem of what Bandura lightly referred to as "one-trial extinction." In much social learning, the actions required are complex and sequential, and they often involve judgments and choices among a wide range of options. Moreover the complexity of actual situations and necessary responses makes it highly unlikely that any amount of conditioning would prepare the individual for them. In these cases, Bandura says, what happens is that the individual watches someone else perform, and he then reproduces the actions of that model. Actions of the model as reproduced, that is, without either being associated with some UCS, or without ever themselves being rewarded for the individual learner.

Bandura and his associates have studied modeling in children in a wide variety of circumstances and have observed some very complex actions that could not have been learned through conditioning. In one famous study, for instance, children who watched an adult model hit a plastic doll in a particular way and saying particular phrases reproduced this behavior later while playing with the doll in the absence of the model. Children who did not observe the aggressive behavior played with the doll without hitting it or saying the adult's words.

What seems to occur in modeling is that the individual observes some actions on the part of an "attractive" (which we shall define) model. For maximum effectiveness the actions of the model are observed to be rewarded, though this is not always necessary to produce modeling. It looks as though the child imagines himself doing what the model does and imagines himself being rewarded as the model is rewarded. So modeling assumes a rather high level of cognitive development. The learner is able to imagine the complex actions of the model and to reward himself in his imagination sufficiently to acquire the response by himself.

An effective model is generally one the learner finds attractive; that is, someone he wants to be like or someone he admires. The best description of a maximally effective model is "superior, but not too distant." He should be a little older, male (since that sex is considered superior), physically and otherwise reasonably appealing, and observably successful or rewarded. He should seem approachable and warm, not forbidding. Such a model can have considerable effect on other people's actions. These characteristics, you may have noted, are very often found in camp counselors and dormitory advisers. They are sometimes also found in the Army and in prisons, and modeling—often unwanted—occurs here too.

Modeling is tremendously important in socialization, and Bandura's work contributes greatly to our understanding of what shapes people in our society. One controversial topic involving modeling processes is censorship, especially of television.

Traditionally there have been two schools of thought about the effects of watching antisocial or undesirable actions. The older school, with roots in Freudian and other psychoanalytic thought, claims that watching can be "cathartic." It gets these ideas out of your system and thus decreases the actual incidence of behavior. From this point of view, violence and sex in movies and television should decrease violent and sexual activity. The opposing viewpoint is that movies and television produce modeling effects. Censorship, of course, assumes that modeling of violence or sexual activity is more likely than catharsis. But what does the evidence show?

In the case of violence, nearly all the evidence supports an interpretation that modeling is likely and catharsis is not. Much of Bandura's modeling research in fact utilizes violent behaviors, and children copy them readily. Other studies, using films of bloody boxing matches or simulated war also have been shown to increase the disposition to violent attitudes or to actual violence in adult subjects. Goldstein and Arms recently measured violent attitudes of people entering a college football game, and measured again as they departed afterwards. They found a considerable increase in proviolent attitudes from fans of both sides after the game.

In view of the consistent evidence, the amount of violence on television and in movies is frightening. Movies present violence as an acceptable "last resort," the sort of thing which people can turn to when reasonable persuasion fails. When I was young, television cowboys were pretty violent, though now they kill each other less often than they did. But the most violent things I have ever seen are the Saturday morning cartoons on television, the ones aimed at children between 2 and 10 years old.

In the case of sexual behavior, there is considerably less evidence, but what we have seems to favor a catharsis belief. Movies and books with explicit sexual scenes do not seem to increase either the frequency or the unusualness of sexual activity. In fact, readily available pornography is usually associated with a drop in arrests for rape and other sexual crimes. As we have said, however, it is much more difficult to get reliable data on sexual activity than on violence, and to date there are no well-controlled studies which bear on this issue. We should at least note the irony: violence, which we know is modeled, is seldom censored. Depiction of sex, which may be cathartic, is regularly suppressed.[1]

An example of different types of learning may help you to appreciate just how common these processes are in our lives. Let us take a simple example, learning a norm that is almost universal in our culture. We learn quite early and quite strongly not to say unkind things about someone who has died recently. This is true no matter what kind of a person you think he was— do not speak ill of the dead. Imagine a young child who has just learned that a neighbor died. The neighbor was a very unlikeable man. He yelled at children, beat his wife, and called the police to complain about all sorts of minor or imaginary disturbances to the peace. So the child in our example says upon learning of the death, "Good; I'm glad he's gone." It is an honest expression of feeling and seems natural, but his mother becomes upset and tells him very firmly not to say such a terrible thing. That is, to our child, a punishing experience, and he will learn not to say "such a thing" again. This is classical conditioning.

Now imagine instead that the child is a bit older, say ten or so, and he makes the same remark to his friends. Sometimes the comment is well received, but usually they indicate they think it is somehow inappropriate. The child will still learn the norm this way, but by operant conditioning, not classical.

For the norm to be learned through modeling, the child—still older now, and even more cautious—watches in a group to see how people he admires refer to the dead neighbor. He sees that his father, teacher, and other people he thinks highly of force themselves to say kind or neutral things about the neighbor. And as these hypocritical comments gain the models social ap-

---

[1] A large part of the problem, of course, is variance in the legal definition of a sex crime. Places with few restrictions on pornography also tend to permit a wider range of sex practices than places where pornography is suppressed. Thus it may be that making pornography available does increase the rate and the unusualness of sexual activity, but that frequent and unusual activity is not illegal where pornography is available. This state of affairs would be consistent with a modeling, not a cathartic, view.

proval, the child notes this and copies them. The very first comment he makes regarding the death is a bland, "I feel sorry for his poor widow."

To summarize what learning tells about socialization, most socialization of humans is operant conditioning or modeling. Intentional training of people occurs—especially of children—but unintentional training is at least as common for children and much more common for adults. We might think that intentional training is more effective, since the size of reward for desired actions can be controlled, but there are good reasons to believe that unintentional training actually is more effective. Why? Because intentional training usually is accomplished by an invariant link of reward to desired behavior. Unintentional training is more likely to mean a variable-ratio schedule is employed. Thus what we teach our children unintentionally, either by example or by shaping, is what they probably learn most strongly. One case of unintentional training involves learning of implicit norms, which you recall from Chap. 2 are norms that nobody even admits exist. People learn the implicit norms of social and racial prejudice, hypocrisy, and all sorts of other actions very strongly—because of modeling and intermittent reinforcement of responses.

There seems to be a progression from classical conditioning to operant conditioning to modeling in terms of characteristics of the learning. Classical conditioning is best suited to the simplest actions and attitudes, and modeling is best suited to the most complex. On the other hand, what is learned through classical conditioning can be very precise shadings of movement or thought, while modeling produces only an approximation. It is a trade: in one case you can only learn a little at a time, but you learn to reproduce the desired response almost perfectly; in the other you can learn a whole series of responses quickly, but you probably will not reproduce any one of them exactly the way the model did. Through classical conditioning, for example, animals have been taught to discriminate between tones of such similar frequency that you and I probably could not hear any difference between them. By contrast, someone who learns to drive by watching a model will never reproduce all the skills and get all the thousands of minute actions coordinated as well as the model did the first time.

Now let us examine three selected cases of socialization. I will not draw all the links between these cases and ideas of learning theories, but I hope you will try to analyze the cases in those terms as you read.

Some Cases of Social Learning

Sex Roles. How do you know what sex you are? The question is not intended facetiously. I hope that by the time you have read this far you realize that the most important aspects of human sexuality are social–psychological, not biological. The learning theory approach says that we learn what sex we are by processes of intentional and unintentional teaching.

Even before the baby comes home from the hospital, he or she is wrapped in blue or pink blankets, respectively, and from then on is supposed to like one color more than the other.

Secondary sex characteristics—everything except reproductive functions that differentiate males and females in our society—are quite clearly matters of learned preference and habit. The ways parents and other adults treat children—that is, the modeling and the selective reinforcement of actions—are what makes boys grow up to act different from girls.

Meyer and Sobieszek illuminated one crucial link in the assumed process by which children learn what attitudes and actions are appropriate to their sexes. Videotapes were made of two two-year old children, a boy and a girl, playing with a variety of toys, both "girls toys" such as dolls and "boys toys" such as a hammer. The tapes were shown to parent-age adults, and for half the adults the sexes of the children were accurately identified, and for half they were misidentified. The adults were then asked to describe the behavior and the temperament of the children by checking adjectives that might or might not describe them. Some adjectives were stereotypically male (such as "aggressive") and some were stereotypically female (such as "loving"). The sex descriptions of the children had a major effect on the adjectives checked for them, and this effect was stronger than the effect of their actual sexes. What this shows is that social reality of the imputed sex of the child was more important in determining how adults viewed the actions than was the actual sex. Although the exact effects varied considerably in various groups of adults, in general the adjectives checked were those appropriate to the stereotypic image of the imputed sex of the child. Sobieszek has recently replicated the study with adults drawn from a nonuniversity community, and found even stronger effects of this kind.

Becoming a Marijuana User. Long before marijuana became widely popular as a recreational drug, Howard S. Becker described the sequence of events leading to continued usage among professional musicians. If a person is to develop and maintain a liking for the drug, Becker says, a sequence of three events must occur.

First, the person must learn to recognize the physiological and psychological symptoms of marijuana. These effects—dryness of the throat, time distortion, slight vertigo, loss of energy, and hunger—are not particularly strong, and they might easily be overlooked if someone did not know he was smoking marijuana and did not know what to look for.

Second, he must identify these effects as being part of a cluster of symptoms he calls intoxication or "being high," and they must be firmly associated in his mind with use of the marijuana. Otherwise, again, he might not see anything special about the experience and would not be likely to repeat it.

Third, he must define these symptoms as pleasurable. They have to be considered good, different from nausea, for instance, or else no one would continue to use the drug. It is a subtle point but crucial that many experiences are pleasant or unpleasant only because of social definition—in other words, because we have learned to associate them with pleasant or unpleasant stimuli.

When my students are assigned Becker's article now, they often think it must be out of date. A sizeable portion of them smoke marijuana recreationally, and they see no need to read such an article. However, after reading when we discuss the three stages Becker isolates, they are surprised to see their own experiences in reference to Becker's analysis. Somebody was there, telling them to look for the symptoms, telling them what it feels like to be high, and indicating in a variety of ways how much fun it is. Everybody knows stories of someone who kept claiming not to feel anything the first time he smoked marijuana (stage 1), until someone told him to try some test of his perceptions (stage 2), and then everybody told him how much fun it was (stage 3). Similarly people who say they have tried marijuana one time but didn't like like it usually say either that they *didn't* feel any effects (stage 1), that they felt sick (stage 2), or that people laughed at them and made it socially unpleasant (stage 3).

Notice also that Becker's three stages have much wider application than just to marijuana usage. Alcohol and tobacco usage commonly go through the same stages. So does learning to appreciate classical (or rock) music. So probably does any new socially-sanctioned practice.

High School Achievement. James S. Coleman studied subcultures and values in ten Midwestern high schools, and found a striking pattern to the relation between values and achievement. In some of the schools there was the relationship you would expect between ability (various IQ tests) and achievement (grades): students with the highest ability in the school also made the best grades. However in other schools this was not true. What made the difference? One question asked students was "How would you most like to be remembered in school: as an athletic star, a brilliant student, or most popular?" In schools where student values favored being a brilliant student, ability and grades were highly associated. Where students valued athletics or popularity more highly, ability and grade were associated only slightly.

What Coleman's research indicates is that high school students, like the rest of us, strive to achieve at valued activities—and valued activities are not all the same in every subculture. Moreover valued activities of students are not necessarily the same as what the adults who set up the educational system value. The bright students presumably have the most ability to affect their own grades: they can get good grades simply by working harder. But it is only where they also get peer group approval for good grades that they are willing to do this.

Coleman points out that schools, probably unintentionally, have set up social systems in which athletic excellence is more likely to lead to popularity than academic excellence. A person who helps the football team win games brings glory to the whole school, and so indirectly everyone benefits. The person who gets top grades brings glory only to himself and very probably at the expense of everyone else. Highly visible intellectual contests, such as the television program College Bowl and the high school versions in some cities, could help increase the peer group approval of intellectual excellence, but the numbers of people involved and the level of excitement these generate are tiny compared to a good football game. In any case Coleman's study is important for showing that in high schools, as elsewhere, individuals learn the values of their immediate peer group and respond to them—regardless of what the explicit norms of the larger organization may be.

Moral Development

Are there any honest people? We may hope there are, and much of our society is based upon a presumption of honesty, yet the answer to the question as posed is "no." There are honest *actions,* and these actions are made by people. However, few if any of us are honest all the time in all circumstances. There are social situations that are more likely than others to elicit honest actions, and some people are more likely than others to act honestly in many situations, but honesty, like nearly every individual trait that has been posited does not seem to enable us to predict or understand much about human interaction.

The classic study of honesty—in this case, "classic" means both old and good—was reported by Hartshorne and May in 1928–30. They conducted a large variety of studies of honest and dishonest behavior in grade school children, and the overall result of their study may be summarized as follows: honesty is not a trans-situational personality trait of individuals. Rather, honesty and trustworthiness depend upon particular social situations and backgrounds of individuals. Two more specific results of their studies are (1) that children were not honest or dishonest in all types of situations, and (2) usually, honesty is inversely related to desire to excel and to perceived likelihood of getting away with dishonesty.

The research involved a series of ingenious, sometimes almost diabolical, traps to enable observation of cheating when students thought they could not be observed. It showed quite clearly that there is not much point in saying someone is "basically an honest person," since without specifying the situation and the monetary desires of the individual, such a statement has little meaning. Children who want very much to get good grades—particularly those of relatively low ability—will cheat on tests if they think they can get away with it. Poor children are more likely to steal small amounts of money than children from rich parents. The Hartshorne–May studies were enormously influential in directing attention away from studying general "character" to studying situational and motivational properties of honest and cheating behavior.

What do we mean when we think of honest behavior? Honest behavior includes: not deliberately misleading someone; being willing to forego momentary pleasures when we have agreed to do so; not seeking rewards without "earning" them, however that is defined; and following the socially agreed upon rules, such as laws and implicit norms of conduct. This may not include everything you think of as honesty, but these elements would probably be considered important components. Moreover these elements have been studied enough that we know something about how they affect honesty and cheating. Let us look briefly at some results of this research.

Walter Mischel has studied *delayed gratification* in a variety of settings with young children. One of the things we must assume if we believe in a fair world is that honesty "pays off" in the long run; that is, that being honest often means being willing to resist small temptations such as cheating on tests for the long term reward of learning the course material. (We also assume that cheating gets punished in the long run, as when someone is caught after years of income tax evasion. However, delayed punishment was not part of Mischel's studies.)

There is a large number of studies, and Mischel's work is still continuing, so I cannot describe all the details for you. Generally the studies place children in a room containing desirable objects (candy, toys, money) and the experimenter describes social rules by which the children legitimately may reward themselves. Sometimes, for example, children are told to perform some task, and to reward themselves only when they are successful. In other cases children are allowed to choose between a small reward immediately, or waiting awhile for a larger, more desirable reward.

Generally speaking, honesty is furthered considerably if the desired eventual reward is seen to be a sure thing (that is, if "good" behavior is always rewarded), if the reward allocation rule is perceived as "fair" (a topic we take up in Chap. 16), if there is something to do besides sit and look at the reward, and if others in the peer group or models seem to behave honestly.

Mischel's research seems particularly important to me for another reason. Implicitly it deals with social factors which influence the development and exercise of self-control, which is an essential part of the socialization process. People internalize the norms of society, but obviously they do not then invariably follow them. How well the norms are understood, how strongly they are internalized, and other such background factors undoubtedly influence conformity. In addition, however, factors in the immediate social environment are shown here to influence rule following.

John F. Scott has attempted to apply ideas of social learning to analyze the processes of internalizing and conforming to explicit norms such as laws of the society. His analysis places heavy stress on learning through modeling processes, since even the explicit norms are too many and too complex for an individual to learn through classical or operant conditioning processes. In outline the sequence Scott describes is: an individual first learns what the laws are through direct instruction (such as in school) and through observation (modeling) of others' behaviors. However the crucial factor that determines whether or not internalization of norms occurs is whether the individual observes sanctions distributed for conformity. In other words Scott argues that for an individual to internalize the laws of a society—to follow them in the absence of direct coercion—he must either be sanctioned for his own conformity or nonconformity, *or* he must see others being so sanctioned. Since the large number of people and laws makes direct sanction relatively unlikley—not every law violation is observed or punished—internalization depends very heavily upon modeling; that is, seeing others rewarded for following the rules, or punished for noncompliance.

Scott's analysis is provocative, for it accords well with established principles of social learning. And like Mischel's research, it has implications for legal practices. One application that comes immediately to mind is the question of deterrent value of punishments. Does swift, sure, severe punishment deter people from breaking laws? Many social workers would be quick to assure us that there is no deterrent value to punishment; most criminologists would say there is a definite deterrent. But arguments on both sides depend more on emotions than on data. It seems to me a straightforward extension of Scott's analysis to say that short jail terms and easy parole, or dismissal of cases on legal technicalities will increase crime by eliminating the modeling process Scott identifies as crucial; whereas public floggings might cut down on shoplifting. The evidence is not clear-cut, but one recent study by Logan found that certainty of punishment (measured by proportion of arrests that ended in jail) and severity of punishment (measured by length of sentences for comparable crimes) were negatively associated with crime rates in several counties. This result is entirely consistent with results of Mischel's experiments and Scott' analysis.

The question of deterrent value arises most often for murder, however, especially for capital punishment. Here I see some reasons why capital punishment may not serve as a deterrent—and in fact in most states and countries that have abolished the death penalty the murder rate either remains constant or falls. First, the severity of punishment by electrocution as compared to life imprisonment is not at all clear: which is worse? More precisely, which is *perceived* as worse by individuals contemplating murder: We really do not know how potential murderers weigh these punishments at the moment of killing, nor even whether they think they will ever be brought to trial.

More importantly, however, murder seems to differ from most other crimes in that it is committed in an instant of nonrationality. As noted earlier, the effect of socialization in every human society is to minimize use of interpersonal violence, and it is only when this socialization breaks down for a moment that murder occurs. Thus any analysis that supposes a rational calculation of likelihood of punishment or severity of punishment probably is inapplicable to murders. Consistent with this reasoning, Logan's research found very small or nonexistent effects of his two independent variables upon murder rates. (Rape is evidently not a crime of irrationality, for it is affected by punishment in Logan's data.) We might still suppose, however, a deterrent effect for the very small portion of murders that occur coldly and deliberately—the sort which make for good mystery stories, that is.

Development of Moral Action

The most comprehensive modern system for analyzing issues of moral development is embodied in the work of Robert Hogan. According to Hogan, what we term moral behavior depends upon five "dimensions" or factors, each of which may be necessary to produce moral behavior, and all of which together make up what we call a morally mature individual.

The first factor is simply moral knowledge. The individual must learn what it is that others expect of him. In our terms, he has to find out both the explicit and the implicit norms governing behavior with others. Hogan points out that the Hartshorne–May study and many later studies include assessment of knowledge of the rules governing honesty. Knowledge by itself, however, was not sufficient.

Second is internalization of the norms. The individual must come to believe that the rules apply to him or to her. According to Hogan, parents who are warm, nurturant (concerned with the child's physical and psychological needs), and also restrictive or authoritative produce the most completely socialized individuals. Socialization, in the sense of believing that society's rules apply to oneself, may be measured by a scale on the California Psychological Inventory and by several other psychological tests.

Third is what Hogan calls empathy, and it appears to have two components. First is what we have called role learning. The individual must be able to view himself as part of a social context, as playing a role that is interdependent with other roles in his life. Second, the empathic individual possesses the capacity to "put himself in others' shoes"; he is able to imagine how others would feel in situations. In other words he has the capacity to take the role of the other. (This was identified earlier by Mead, in 1934, as essential to social maturity; see Chap. 15.)

Socialization and empathy, as Hogan uses the terms, are independent; a person who is high on one is not necessarily high on the other. For instance a highly socialized person low on empathy is likely to be a rigid rule-follower, unable to make exceptions for anyone. Someone high on empathy but low on socialization is what I would call a pain in the neck: he asks to be understood and loved, but never remembers to return things he borrows, he parks his car across two spaces, and in general demands more than his fair share of others' attention. Hogan feels that developing empathy requires *both* having known empathic models *and* having endured some injustice, ridicule, betrayal, or persecution.

Fourth, the ultimate basis to which a person ascribes moral norms is important, and historically there have been two very different ultimate justifications. The first, which Hogan calls the ethics of conscience, invokes a "higher law," beyond human legislation, which can only be discovered by intuition. The second, Hogan's ethics of responsibility, appeals ultimately to human agreements; laws that are designed however imperfectly to maximize the general welfare. These issues—higher law vs. human law— have been debated for centuries, recently in the case of individuals refusing to comply with the U.S. draft laws for what they considered (on higher law grounds) an immoral war.

In the absence of both socialization and empathy, an individual still may behave morally towards others if he endorses the ethics of responsibility. If he endorses the ethics of conscience in his dealings with others, then he is very likely to treat them in selfish (immoral) ways. Hogan and others have developed a scale to determine individuals' ethical attitudes and have compared scores on it to various other measures. The single adjective that friends used most often to describe those high on ethics of conscience was "rebellious." The adjective most chosen for those high on ethics of responsibility was "thoughtful."

Individuals high on ethics of conscience tend to see others as naturally benevolent. Social injustice for them is produced by evil institutions and is correctable by correcting the institutions. People high on ethics of responsibility tend to see others as essentially selfish and see institutions as designed to protect us from others' selfishness. These different approaches to life, Hogan suggests, are probably learned from parents, in the manner described in Chap. 1. (Incidentally I hope you can appreciate that these different ethical viewpoints can be studied for their psychological and social implications without entering debate as to which is preferable.)

Finally, moral behavior is influenced by the development of a unique set of internalized norms, which are different for every individual who develops them. Hogan calls this autonomy. Even in the absence of socialization and empathy, and with an ethics of conscience, a person still may decide in a particular situation to behave morally just because "I am the sort of person who does not cheat."

Autonomy, Hogan readily concedes, is a troublesome concept, for it is not well defined and could be confused with other concepts such as ethics of conscience. However psychological scales are available for measuring autonomous morality, and they do not seem to be measuring the same things as scales of other psychological characteristics. Moreover it is apparent that many people never achieve a high level of moral autonomy. So long as they are well socialized, empathic, and endorse ethics of responsibility, these people are unlikely to get into trouble with the law. However, if laws change radically or if they move to a country with very different laws, they are likely to be unable to function in potentially moral situations. Unless he develops an autonomous morality, a person is tied very closely to expectations of whatever his peer group happens to be, and it is easy to think of instances where this can lead to trouble.

Life presents continual changes in the situational demands and also the psychological composition of the individual. Moral development, like other development, is measured by the *relative* success the individual has in coping with these changes. Situational factors such as modeling processes and certainty of deferred gratifications are important, as are internal factors—which ultimately are determined socially—such as empathy for others.

After a close study of some elements of moral behavior, it is important to step back and look at the important problems that impel the social psychologist to try to understand the development of morality. It is impressive just how low a level we humans have reached in terms of morality. Hogan defines moral behavior as "rules of conduct which define . . . reciprocal rights and obligations and which prohibit *at least gross acts of malevolence.*" (Hogan, 1973, p. 219; emphasis added.) In personal conversations he points out how much the general level of human morality would be raised if everybody just followed one additional rule such as "Don't kill little children," or "Do not enslave other people."

Adult Socialization and Resocialization

Many people believe that childhood is the only time of learning in a person's life. This is not so. Socialization does not occur all at one time, nor is there anything about the socialization process itself that makes childhood experiences particularly significant. However there are two factors that result in most people's doing most of their learning during early years. One is that there simply is so much to learn: a language, norms, values, cultural meanings of gestures such as smiles, how to walk, and so on. The other is that by about the age of 20, most of us are settled into a social situation and patterns of living that we shall maintain for the rest of our lives. Thus most social learning occurs in the early years. But this is not to say that equal or even greater amounts of learning cannot occur later. If the individual moves to a different country after adulthood, for instance, he has to relearn a large proportion of what he learned as a child. The same thing occurs on a smaller scale if he gets divorced or changes his occupation. The evidence is that learning or socialization can occur equally well at any age.

Adult socialization refers to social learning that takes place in adults, and there are several features that distinguish it from child socialization. First, adult socialization almost always takes place in institutions outside the family. It is the product of basic training in the Army, of going to college and joining a fraternity, or of being sentenced to prison. Second, adult socializing institutions deal with only a strictly limited portion of the individuals' lives. While the family may try to produce a "good person," and the grade school attempts to educate the "whole child"; the purpose of college is to produce some specific vocational skills, and the purpose of the Army is to produce Army officers.

Third, adult socialization almost always has a specific end-point. We know when the process is completed, either successfully or unsuccessfully. There is a particular time, often marked with some ceremony like graduation or a parole hearing, that marks the termination of the socialization process. Fourth, in many cases, adult socialization is begun because the socializee actively desires to change something about himself. He wants to learn another vocation, or he wants to develop the skills and attitudes of an Army officer. Fifth, in some cases but not all, adult socialization involves substitution of a new role for a pre-existing one. For instance, the individual may be undergoing the transformation from *civilian* to *officer,* or from *criminal* to *honest citizen.* When socialization does involve role substitution, it means that the individual has to unlearn his old patterns. Child socialization may involve unlearning also, but probably to a lesser extent than adult socialization.

Dornbusch has provided the classic description of an adult socializing institution, the Coast Guard Academy. Like West Point and Annapolis, the Coast Guard Academy is charged with taking a widely varying group of civilians and transforming them into a uniform group of interchangeable parts ("officers") in the Coast Guard. The process Dornbusch describes could as well be applied to any other (successful) socializing institution. There are six basic stages.

1. *Suppression of existing roles.* As cadets enter the academy, whatever they were in civilian life becomes irrelevant. Differences in wealth are made irrelevant by taking away their money and forbidding them to receive money in mail. Educational and regional differences are not supposed to be discussed, and even their appearance is made as uniform as possible. They all get the same haircut, and they all wear identical clothes—called "uniforms."

2. *Learning skills and an informal code of conduct.* Socializing institutions teach both how to do something, and also how to regard the activity. Cadets have to learn the implicit norms of the Academy, the traditions, how to act around older cadets, and so on. As anyone who has gone to a military academy can testify, these implicit norms are every bit as important as the explicit rules in determining whether the socializee makes it through the system.

3. *Hazing.* There is a deliberate attempt to harass the new cadets on the part of older cadets. Hazing is explicitly forbidden at all service academies, as it is at most college fraternities, in medical schools, and even in Marine Corps basic training. It occurs in all these settings. A very important consequence of hazing is that it produces solidarity among members of the oppressed group. It thus serves to bring the entire entering class of swabs (cadets) closer together. They share common problems, and they can help each other out. Hazing completes the process begun at stage 1. Not only are prior life differences made irrelevant, but individuality and selfishness in the group are unlikely to develop. The swabs are too busy protecting themselves and each other against the hazing.

4. *Clear stages, with increasing rewards.* The socializing institution makes it clear exactly what is needed to advance through the system—earning merit points, passing examinations, surviving through the school year, or whatever it is. Everybody in the system knows just where he is and where he has to go, and each advancement holds out a promise of more rewards. At the Academy, for instance, rewards are more freedom and weekend leaves, relief from hazing after the first year, and the right to haze others during the last year.

5. *Successful models.* Along with the need for clear stages, there must be visible some individuals who have advanced in the system to demonstrate the satisfactions of success and to help others learn how to be successful. Older cadets can serve this function in the Academy; trusties do likewise in a prison.

6. *Rewards and readjustment.* Finally, at the completion of socialization,

individuals are rewarded with whatever the institution has to offer. Cadets are made officers, medical students become doctors, prisoners become free men. In addition to the reward, the institution has to prepare individuals for return to outside society, since the outside is not going to be in perfect tune with the goals of the institution. Coast Guard officers must be made to realize that civilians do not always appreciate them as much they should, and that many details of military precision and appearance will be met only imperfectly by the men in their commands. Similarly, prisoners about to be released have to realize that the outside will present all sorts of temptations to do exactly what they were imprisoned for in the first place, and they have to deal with these. In a way which we shall examine more in a moment, this preparation for "reality shock" on the outside is crucial, for no socializing institution can do a perfect job of preparing individuals to live outside the institution. The changes demanded after stage 6 can be just as great and just as difficult for people as the changes at stage 1.

Institutions and Socialization

Certain organizations exist primarily for purposes of socializing their occupants. For example, schools are created deliberately for teaching certain intellectual and practical skills, as well as middle class values to children. We shall call these *socializing institutions*. To begin we need a definition of "institution."

Institution: An integrated collection of social roles.

Since we have already defined roles in terms of norms (Chap. 4) and norms in terms of rules and sanctions (Chap. 1), we could also say an institution is a set of behavioral norms. Formal organizations such as the Army or business corporation are those in which roles are defined independent of the occupants. Informal organizations and other institutions such as schools, shopping centers, and neighborhoods have roles linked more closely with particular individual occupants.

Institutions vary in the degree of control they exert over their occupants, from those with barely perceptible control such as day care centers to those with a rule for everything, such as mental hospitals and military boarding schools. Those with near total control over the lives of individuals being socialized we shall call "total institutions." Total institutions are designed to provide guides to every little action taken by the individual from the time he awakes until the time he sleeps. To facilitate this control, a total institution is set up to provide all the individual's needs and to screen out any sources of these fulfillments beyond the institution. Letters, money, gifts, expressions of affection, and even definitions of reality are controlled by a total institution.

Erving Goffman provides a detailed, insightful study of a mental hospital, focusing upon the patient's view of his experiences and interpreting his behavior as a reasonable, relatively sane, response to the institution. Since most mental patients are committed involuntarily, either through legal means or through pressures from relatives, the commitment process is very likely to seem a process of betrayal, a conspiracy between trusted relatives and psychiatrists to deprive him of his freedom. Once committed, the most usual response to the betrayal is to deny that it is justified. New patients tell each other and anyone who will listen that they are not "really sick"; perhaps just under pressures, or mistakenly hospitalized.

For our interests now, what is important is that the hospital may be seen as arranged primarily to change the patient's view of himself—from that of a functioning human being with rights and responsibilities to a sick person, incapable of making decisions for himself. The psychiatric record of each patient is composed solely of unusual or bizarre behaviors. No "normal" actions are recorded, for both doctors and staff members have been taught to see the patient in terms of symptomatology. Moreover it is only when the patient begins to see himself in these terms that he is granted privileges such as his own room, better food, or more discretion over use of his time. While the patient insists on describing his past life as if it were normal, the staff of the hospital and sometimes even the other patients see this as a symptom of sickness. When the patient begins to describe his behavior as symptomatic of sickness, the psychoanalyst says he is showing "insight," the staff nurses say he is "settling down," and his relatives say he seems "so much better" when they visit.

In the mental hospital as in any other socializing institution, successful change of the individual's attitudes and behavior depends upon convincing him that the way he acted in previous life was not only different, it was *wrong.* Much the same thing may be seen in meetings of Alcoholics Anonymous, when members stand up to confess their former drunkenness, and begin by telling their names and saying, "I am an alcoholic." Churches that make extensive use of confessions and testimonials also place heavy emphasis on members' denials of their past selves.

Howard S. Becker and Blanche Geer studied many aspects of life in medical school and describe several intentional and unintentional effects of the institution on the students. In "The Fate of Idealism in Medical School," they observe that the overwhelming amount of material students are supposed to memorize in their first two years teaches the students a cynical approach to their studies. Since they cannot possibly learn everything assigned and since much of it is perceived as "irrelevant to the practice of medicine anyway," they concentrate on figuring out and learning those things the instructors are likely to ask about on tests. They study for the tests, that is, and not for the knowledge.

The second two years of medical school, and especially the internship, produce significant changes in students' views of themselves that in many ways are mirror opposites from those Goffman described in mental hospitals. The medical student and intern must learn new attitudes and behaviors appropriate to a doctor, not to a student. He must learn to respond when somebody says, "Doctor," and he must learn to feel comfortable giving orders to nurses and asking patients details of their personal lives. These changes of role and self-concept occur for the most part without deliberate efforts on the part of medical faculty, but they are important effects of most socializing instructions.

Just as some people become doctors, some people become extremely good bureaucrats. They spend a lifetime learning the rules of the organization, and they learn the rules so well they cannot even consider the idea of making individual exceptions. We have all met such people. They tend to cluster in certain government offices; in Maryland, in the Department of Motor Vehicles. These are what Merton has called "bureaucratic personalities," people whose personality structure is easily understood if you know the rules of the bureaucracy where they work. They follow rules rather than do their job; they hide behind procedures rather than get things done; they produce papers rather than make decisions.

Colleges are bureaucracies, and they have at least their share of bureaucratic personalities: the professor who takes points off a term paper with incorrect margins; the secretary insulating the faculty from students; the librarian protecting books for future generations at the expense of current students; the dean who issues statements that "No change has been made in college policy," even when it is clear a major change has just occurred. I have a colleague who brings a copy of *Roberts Rules of Order* to faculty meetings. On a good day he can prevent anything from getting accomplished by inserting "Point of order, Mr. Chairman" often enough. It gives meaning to his life.

In terms from Chap. 2, the bureaucratic personality sees his purpose as enforcing the *peripheral norms* governing interaction. He focuses on what most people take for granted as unimportant *forms* of action, to the exclusion of the *content* which concerns others. It is an overconcern with formality, perhaps caused by the difficulty a bureaucratic personality has learning the peripheral norms most people take for granted. It is frustrating to have to deal with bureaucratic personalities because they can prevent the bureaucracy from doing what it was created to do—bring students and faculty together, license drivers, or whatever the purpose may be.

Since we have all had contact with bureaucratic personalities, it is easy to forget two things. First, bureaucracies, when they work well, are highly efficient and satisfactory ways of meeting goals. In fact there is no form of social organization superior to bureaucracy for coordinating the efforts of large numbers of people. Second, working in a bureaucracy utilizes only a small part of a normal individual's personality, and thus most people need to get away from their work to find friendship and love, artistic gratification, esthetic pleasure, and all the other "human" experiences. So we must not assume that working in a bureaucracy inevitably makes people into "bureaucratic personalities," or even that most people who work in bureaucracies are more rule-following and less creative than people working in other social organizations.

This second point is documented in several careful studies by Melvin Kohn in which he selected two groups of similar individuals, some of whom worked in bureaucracies and some of whom had nonbureaucratic jobs. Interviews with members of both groups showed that bureaucrats tended to value self-direction over unquestioning rule-following; to hold personal standards of morality rather than following the letter of the law; to be quite flexible in dealing with new situations; and to spend leisure time in intellectually challenging pursuits. Moreover the bureaucrats exhibit these traits *more* than nonbureaucrats. *On the average,* then, working in a bureaucracy seems to be associated with just the opposite traits to those of the bureaucratic personality.

Kohn's research is extremely valuable, for it subjects a common overgeneralization to critical examination and shows that the data do not support it. This does not mean that Merton's ideas are wrong, or that bureaucratic personalities do not exist. Rather it shows that bureaucratization of personality is not an inevitable consequence of working in a bureaucracy; it is not even the most common result. To be sure there are bureaucratic personalities, and when we run across them they are likely to leave a lasting impression. Like the crooked cop or the honest encyclopedia salesman, they are exceptions.

What is more, bureaucratic personalities are not really a desirable outcome for the bureaucracy, for they really do not help it attain its goals. When somebody closes a counter exactly at noon even though there is only one more person in line, that has an effect exactly opposite from helping to meet the organization's goals. Overly officious individuals are not likely to be tolerated in well run bureaucracies any more than dishonest policemen are tolerated in a well-run police force.

Life Within the Institution

People can adapt too completely to institutions, especially to total institutions. One of the problems faced by any good mental hospital is the "warm shower" phenomenon: it is easy to get into the institution, but difficult to want to get out. The hospital is a protected, pleasant environment, and the outside world has been threatening and uncertain. Some patients, even when diagnosed as cured, will fake symptoms to continue living in the security of the hospital. At Christmas 1973 there were news reports of a particularly striking example of the warm shower phenomenon. A convict in Iowa who had just completed his years in prison asked the governor, as a Christmas favor, to allow him to continue to stay at the prison. All his friends were there, and he had spent so much of his own adult life behind bars that he didn't feel capable of living on the outside. It was a sad story. I couldn't decide whether I hoped his request would be granted or refused.

For the institution, this over-adaptation is clearly undesirable. The goal of prisons is not to fit people to remain in prisons, and a mental hospital is not intended to produce perfect mental patients. However most institutions can tolerate a small number of their trainees remaining within the system forever. In fact many institutions including the military, schools, and colleges depend upon having some "lifers" to keep things going. Sarge in the comic strip Beetle Bailey is such a person. Sarge has adapted exceedingly well to life in the Army. He knows all the implicit norms, and he feels perfectly at home there. What is more, he would be maladjusted to civilian society if he were forced to return to it. Variations on this same sort of character have been portrayed in movies such as "Soldier in the Rain," "The Americanization of Emily," "Reflections in a Golden Eye," and others. You can also find "professional students" at most colleges: middle aged people who have been enrolled in courses for several decades, amassing credits and sometimes even degrees, but who have no plans to leave.

These lifers are interesting people, for they have adjusted to a very particular, intentionally created society. Rather than spending their efforts confronting challenges produced by random factors in life as most people do, these lifers spend their efforts confronting challenges built by the institutions they live in. They devote their efforts to finding ways to get free Cokes from defective machines; or to procuring contraband or scarce materials (such as nylon stockings or exotic foods) even when there is no particular need for them; or to securing unusual privileges at the college library or swimming pool.

If life is a game for all of us, it looks particularly game-like for the lifer. What he does is to study the system, the social structure which other individuals have designed, and find how to turn it to his advantage in ways the designers never intended. You could regard this either as silly—game playing when he could be confronting "real" challenges on the outside—or perhaps as just another variant of what we all do, operating in a different sphere, but one that is equally challenging and maybe even equally "real."

Summary on Socialization

We have only been able to touch on some of the major themes in socialization in this chapter. The topic deserves, and increasingly is receiving, the attention of separate courses in college.

What I hope to have accomplished in this chapter is to show that most of what we are, most of the characteristics we think of when we use the term "human," can be attributed to what people learn in a social context. Because of biological and psychological frailties at birth, we need a long period of socialization, and during that time we learn whatever we shall later display as our "selves." Much of socialization occurs unintentionally—such as learning of implicit norms—but intentional training is the type most readily observable. Intentional training occurs most often in socializing institutions, such as the school or business bureaucracy. Everything from what sex we are to what foods we like to our ultimate values is the result of our social learning experiences.

Part II

THEORY
IN
SOCIAL
PSYCHOLOGY

Introduction to
Theory in Social Psychology

Chapters 9 through 14 present theories of social psychology. Nothing else is so important as theory in an empirical field, and no other word is so often misused. Before we study particular theories, it will be helpful to consider briefly the uses and some common misuses of the word *theory,* and then to develop our own meaning of the word for future chapters.

What is probably the most common misunderstanding regarding theory is to draw a distinction between *theory* and *fact.* According to this misuse, facts are what we know for sure, the observations of a field—theory is what we think might be true, but without evidence. Facts then are thought to be most important and reliable; theories, we doubt. This view is captured in the phrase, "In theory it ought to work this way, but in reality, it doesn't."

The dichotomy of theory and fact or reality pervades common usage; it is the contrast between the ideal and the actual. Yet it is misleading, in a very fundamental way. Theories of a field are developed from known observations or facts. Existing theories guide empirical research and suggest new facts to observe. In some cases theories will shape the actual observations collected in empirical research. No empirical field divorces its theories from observations. The two are intimately related, and they affect each other profoundly. (Fields without empirical content, such as mathematics or logic, of course are not concerned with any discrepancy between theory and empirical fact.) When the theory and the observations or facts of any empirical field are not exactly the same, this provides a problem for practitioners: much of the efforts of social psychologists are devoted to improving the theories, in the sense of getting theory and facts more closely related. An imperfect theory is not perfectly consistent with accepted observations, and carelessly collected observations will not be perfectly consistent with accepted theory. The discrepancy is not inherent in the nature of theory, however, and it is nowhere near so common as you might suppose from comments such as the one quoted in the last paragraph.

A second misuse of theory, which has lately appeared especially in sociological usage, is to make it a residual category to action. Theorists are people who think about things. Activists and empirical researchers actually do something. Thoughts, analyses, syntheses, insights, and ideas come from theorists; perhaps acts and data come from others. This misusage commonly is linked with the word *theoretician* applied to theorists: "We activists make the changes; the theoreticians will justify them later."

This misunderstanding contains elements of the first misuse; namely, the idea that theory and empirical facts are necessarily divorced. To this, this second usage adds the idea that theorists, or theoreticians, are concerned with moral justification of action. Justification actually has no place in the theories of empirical fields; it belongs in sections of philosophy. What theories do in empirical fields is to tell *how* to do something, not whether it should be done. They tell the activist how to promote the sorts of changes he wants, not whether he ought to want those changes. Theories can also point out likely consequences of particular changes an activist may have in mind—but theories are neutral with regard to moral questions such as whether those changes are desirable. We can imagine a theorist in physics telling a country's leader that a nuclear war could poison the atmosphere and kill most people in the world. This carries a clear moral implication that starting the war is unwise, but there is nothing in the theories of physics that says this—that decision is made on principles other than physical theories.

Theories at their best tell the activist, the engineer, and the empirical researcher what we can do; or what we now know we can do. Theories often are phrased in the negative sense of what we *cannot* do: you cannot continue deficit spending without causing inflation; you cannot attain a high group position and also express deviant views; you cannot get more electric energy out of a dynamo than the mechanical energy put into it. Each of these claims is grounded in theories of some field—economics, social psychology, and physics, in these examples. The negative assertions have their intellectual force from the supporting theories; that is, there is a *reason* (a theory) for each of these "you cannot" statements. The question is not whether action is related to a theory; the question is only whether the activist is aware of theories that could help him choose among various action options.

A third misunderstanding of the word theory is particularly common in social and behavioral fields; it is that theory is largely conjectural, speculative, and unsupported. It is surprising how many social psychologists seem to regard the theories of social psychology in this way: as if our theories were pretty shaky things and rather unreliable in regard to the sorts of understandings we wish we had. Thus we see people speak of the doubtful theories of social psychology, and in the same breath they talk of the "laws of nature" that natural sciences use.

The difference is one of degree, not of kind. Theories of social psychology do the same things for our field as the *laws* of chemistry or of physics do for those fields. What are sometimes called laws of those fields are in fact their theories. The term law simply reflects the fact that the theories of the natural sciences are more developed and more widely accepted than those of sociology and psychology.

Any student who has taken a lab course in physics or chemistry and has worked on problem sets knows that there are two parts to such an assignment. First, you calculate, *using the theories of the appropriate field*, what the outcome of a particular operation *ought* to be; for example, what weight of a particular chemical compound ought to result from mixing and heating other chemicals. This calculation is a prediction based upon the appropriate theory. Second, you actually perform the operation and weigh the result. What next? *Any discrepancy between the calculated (predicted) value and the actual (observed) value is labelled error.* (Your error, that is, not the theory's.) This is marvelously revealing of the high degree of faith in the theory. If the prediction does not conform perfectly to the observation—it couldn't have been that the theory is at fault. By comparison, the same result, failure of prediction, in sociology or psychology, usually leads the researcher to doubt his theory. In our field we seem to have less faith in the theories.

The laws in natural sciences are the same things for those fields as what we call theories in sociology and psychology, and they perform the same functions. We have fewer good theories of human behavior than of the behavior of inanimate objects, but there is no reason to believe that in principle human interaction is any more difficult to understand than the physical aspects of nature. In fact one noted philosopher (Karl Popper, 1957) has argued that human interaction should be simpler to understand than physics. If we assume that people guide their own actions in terms of a few principles (something molecules do not do), then if we can determine those principles, human behavior will become quite simply understandable. Whatever the status of this line of thought, it is good to remember what is meant when we speak of theories of social psychology: these are the things that enable us to make the same sorts of predictions as natural scientists make for their phenomena of interest. It is also good to remember that our goals should be to have theories in social psychology that meet the same rigorous criteria as theories of biology or chemistry or physics.

The Nature of Theory

A good way to study theory in any field is to ask what the theories do for practitioners of the field. In other words what are theories good for? The first thing theories do is to store the knowledge of a field. What we know in any empirical field is simply the set of theories that constitutes that field; no more, and no less. Isolated facts that cannot be linked to any theory are practically useless as knowledge claims—what they mean, how reliable or how believable they are, how they relate to other accepted knowledge, and other such questions cannot be answered unless there is some theoretical backing for an observation. The history of knowledge is rich with empirical knowledge claims that have been dismissed or forgotten because they cannot be related to any theory; books of mysterious facts, such as Fort's *The Book of the Damned* and Von Danieken's *Chariots of the Gods* contain hundreds of knowledge claims that are rejected by most natural scientists on grounds that they cannot be fit in with the accepted theories of their fields. Medical claims, such as using vitamin C to prevent or to cure colds, get rejected by physicians because they cannot be supported by the theories of physiology and biology. (I know, you are probably thinking this indicates that these theories ought to be revised. That is a complex issue that goes beyond the scope of a text in social psychology. Let us just note that unless a knowledge claim can be integrated with accepted theories, either by modifying the theories or the knowledge claim, it is not likely to be taken seriously by most professionals.)

Our knowledge of electricity is contained in theories of electricity. Our knowledge of conformity behavior is contained in theories of conformity. Our knowledge of how status affects interaction is contained in our theories of status-related behavior. The theories of phenomena are the knowledge we have of those phenomena.

The second function of theory is to organize the knowledge of a field. The knowledge sentences are not simply collected and cataloged. They are ordered in terms of importance and in terms of generality or specificity. For instance because of Newton's theories of mechanics, we know that the significant factor determining how long a pendulum takes to swing is the *length* of the pendulum, not its *weight*. This means that the theory can tell us that knowledge of weight of a pendulum is less important than knowledge of length, if we want to use the pendulum for timing something. Because of the theory of status characteristics and expectation states described in Chap. 7, we know that facts regarding relative diffuse status are more important in understanding task-focused interaction than are facts regarding liking among members. We also know that when the group is not task-focused, liking may well be more important to individuals than diffuse status. We know these things because we have a theory that indicates the relative importance of our facts and observations.

The third function of theories is to interrelate knowledge, to show how various bits of knowledge within a field relate to each other, *and* to show how knowledge of one field relates to knowledge of another field. For example, in Chap. 3 we saw how knowledge of conformity behavior in social psychology is related to knowledge in physiology about fatty acids in the blood and sweating responses. We saw, from another perspective, that our knowledge of what happens in the conformity experiment and our theoretical explanation involving tension, must be consistent with physiological knowledge and theories regarding the physiological effects of psychological tension. Knowledge in social psychology has to be related (or at least, it must be relatable in principle) to knowledge in other fields. The knowledge of humans that comes from psychology cannot be too inconsistent with knowledge from biology. Knowledge from sociology cannot be too inconsistent with knowledge from economics and psychology.

Theories as Explanations

A theory of something is simply an explanation of it, and the most common use of theories is to explain. A theory of a given phenomenon is a set of principles sufficient to construct an explanation of that phenomenon. This definition of theory may seem overly simplified and inadequate until you appreciate that the requirements of explanation are more rigorous than the way the term is loosely used. Since we shall call an explanation a theory, the question becomes, "What is an explanation?"

An adequate explanation for our purposes consists of showing that the fact or facts to be explained are special cases of more general principles; that is, we will accept as an explanation the demonstration that our observations are instances of more broad knowledge claims we have already accepted. There are two types of explanation that meet this criterion: *statistical explanation,* and *explanation by general principles.* Statistical explanation consists of showing that the behavior of a single individual or a single group of individuals is consistent with the (already known) behavior of a larger group to which they belong. For example, we could explain the fact that John voted Democratic in a statistical sense by pointing out that John is a Catholic (larger group), and that Catholics tend to vote Democratic. To explain something using a general principle we show that the behavior is an instance of behavior we believe to be true of all people. For example, we could say that John was elected jury foreman *because* he had high socio-economic status, and high status is likely to yield an influential position in a group (the general principle). Statistical explanation and explanation by general principle have the same structure. Both are concerned to show that the fact to be explained is a special case of a more general statement which we already accept. Note that at base, we would probably want to carry any statistical explanation further than is necessary to explain the fact we begin with. Why do Catholics tend to vote Democratic, for instance? To do this, we ultimately would have to construct an explanation by general principles.

It is crucial to remember a point touched upon in Part I; namely, that we never try to explain everything about something. We begin with a given, finite set of facts to be explained and work from there. Thus we would never try to construct an explanation of an entire social situation, for that would mean to explain every possible feature of that situation—an endless task. Furthermore most features of any situation are not too interesting, and we do not want to bother with explaining them. A social psychologist usually would not be concerned with explaining the color shirt worn by everybody in a classroom, for instance; but he might be very much interested in explaining the relative physical distances between people. The only fair task for a theory is to isolate ahead of time the important facts, findings, observations; *and then* to try to explain them.

Explanation by general principle involves three types of sentences, all of them of forms we have seen before. First, there are what we call general principles, or GPs. These are the abstract knowledge claims we will use to try to explain particular observations. Second, there are conditions, or Cs; these are facts or observations we need in our explanation, but are not the facts or observations to be explained. Third, there are observations or Os. These are the sentences we wish to explain.

> GP sentence: *If X, then Y.*
> C sentence: *X exists, or X is true.*
> (rules of logical deduction)
> _____
> *Therefore* O sentence: *Y is true.*

To make all this less abstract, let us examine some general principles, conditions, and observations to see the relations between them. This example is drawn from expectation states theory in Chap. 7, but it should be understandable without having read that chapter. Begin with four GPs we believe to be true.

GP1: The higher the status of any individual, the greater the task–performance ability others will accord him.

GP2: The higher the task–performance ability attributed to any individual, the more chances to interact he will receive from others.

GP3: The more chances to interact any individual receives, the more he will actually interact.

GP4: The higher the task–performance ability attributed to any individual, the more likely he is to be accorded a position of formal authority.

To these we add two Cs, statements of fact about the way the world is, which assert that the "if" clause of the GP has been satisfied.

C1: Proprietors have higher status than clerks.

C2: Males have higher status than females.

Note that neither of these two sentences is necessarily true, in the sense that GPs are; that is, the Cs are true only for a limited historical period, and in certain places. However both Cs assert that the "if" clause of GP1 is satisfied for the respective groups, proprietors, and males.

Having satisfied the condition of the first GP, we can use simple ideas of logic to explain a large number of observations (Os) this way. For instance:

O1: Men talk more than women on juries.

O2: Proprietors talk more than clerks on juries.

O3: Men are more likely to be chosen jury foremen than women are.

O1 is explained by use of C2, GP1, GP2, and GP3; it follows, simply by logical deduction. O2 is explained using C2 and the same GPs. O3 is explained using C2, GP1, and GP4. We have shown that the observations to be explained *follow necessarily* from the GPs and the known Cs. We could in principle use the same strategy to explain a large number of other observations regarding interaction in the jury. Thus we are entitled to claim that our explanation of the Os is in fact more general than simply the list of findings which generated the explanation.

Explanation and Prediction

It is useful to be able to distinguish an adequate explanation, such as the one just constructed, from a *partial* explanation. Partial explanation is far more common than complete explanation, but complete explanation is necessary for developing adequate theory.

Suppose someone offered to explain the fact that his car ran off the road by telling you that one of the front tires blew out: would this constitute an adequate explanation? Or suppose the fact, "John dropped out of college," were explained by "His love life was giving him a lot of trouble"; would that be adequate? A little thought should tell you that neither of these constitutes a complete explanation in the sense described above. These partial explanations consist only of C statements, other facts which occurred before or at the same time as the Os to be explained. To make these explanations complete, we would need to have GPs from mechanics to the effect that a particular type of disequilibrium (caused by the blowout) would force the car off the road. And we would need some GPs from psychology to the effect that a stressful love life makes study impossible and that remaining in college without studying is impossible. Perhaps the GPs are there implicitly when someone offers a partial explanation, but for the sort of complete understanding we require of theories, it is necessary to make all parts of the explanation explicit.

One final misunderstanding remains to be considered in this chapter; that is the idea that *explanations* of phenomena and *predictions* of them differ. We often hear the idea that it is easier to explain something we already know than it is to predict what we have not yet observed. But if we insist upon complete explanations, there is no difference. *The structure of an explanation is exactly the same as the structure of a prediction.* In one case we are given the Os and are asked to come up with a sufficient set of GPs and Cs; this is an explanation. In the other case, we are given the GPs and the Cs, and are asked to derive the Os logically; this is prediction. There is no fundamental difference between an adequate explanatory theory and an adequate predictive theory.[1]

This fact gives us an extremely useful tool for assessing the adequacy of any proposed explanation or theory. Namely, we can ask whether the proposed explanation for a given fact or set of facts would have been

---

[1] You should be aware that this meaning of explanation is not universally shared. However it is the most widely used meaning, and it is the meaning that is most useful in evaluating empirical theories. It is the only meaning we use in this text.

sufficient to predict their occurrence. In order to decide whether a proposed explanation is complete in the sense just described, or to decide whether a proposed theory is adequate, we can ask ourselves whether the theory or the explanation could have predicted the sentence it purports to explain. To return to our two examples, from knowing that a car had a tire blow out, would we be able to predict that the car would run off the road? Of course not; lots of tires blow out without causing drivers any problems at all. From knowing that John's love life was not going smoothly could we predict he would necessarily drop out of college? Clearly that isn't sufficient, for many people have problems of that nature and do not drop out of college. On the other hand, knowing GP1, GP2, and GP3, and adding C2, we could have predicted O1. It follows of logical necessity. Thus we say that those sentences do constitute an adequate or complete explanation for that observation.

Evaluation of Theories

Theories, in the sense of explanations, are formulated in social psychology for almost every observation. Some of these are good theories, and some are not. As previously suggested, in any empirical field one of the major criteria distinguishing a good theory from a poor one is agreement of predictions with observations. However we do not automatically accept a theory that gives good predictions in one area, and we should not always reject a theory solely on the grounds of relatively poor predictions.

One word often applied to theories is "true", in the sense that a true theory is a good one for predicting and explaining, and a "false" theory is not. I hope you will forever remove this word from your vocabulary in discussing theories—or at least that you will reserve use of it to the only area where it is appropriate, the sense of being logically true. A theory never gives absolutely perfect predictions of all facts within its scope, and even if it enabled perfect prediction of all observations to date we have no way to know that it would continue to do so for the future. If it would, it would be true. Since we cannot know this, we ask whether the theory is *useful*. Useful theories are accepted and used until better theories become available.

There are four criteria for acceptance of theories. First is *internal* or *logical consistency*. Are the assumptions of the theory consistent with each other, or does the theory imply two contradictory predictions? Even this simple test can reveal serious inadequacies with some currently accepted theories.

Second is *external consistency*. We have already mentioned this criterion: how well do explanations of our proposed theory fit in with what is already known or accepted in other fields?

Third is *confirmation status*. Compared to the total number of empirical tests that have been performed, how well has our theory been able to predict? Note that any theory will give inadequate predictions some of the time. This is as true in physics today as it is in social psychology, though the instances in physics are harder to see than those of our field. But by counting the confirming and the disconfirming evidence and weighing the "important" evidence (a subjective matter) more heavily, we come to some over-all assessment of confirmation status.

Fourth is *comparison with alternatives*. There has to be some alternative theory explaining the same phenomenon before we reject our first theory. If there is no competing theory, we retain the old one. The only way to reject one theory without simultaneously putting another in its place is to reject the foundations of empirical science. Remember that the next time you hear someone calling for "ignoring the theories and concentrating on the facts." It simply cannot be done. We continue to use any theory until someone offers a more satisfactory (by the four criteria given) alternative.

This introduction to theory is intended as preparation for studying two main lines of theoretical development in social psychology. These are far from the only possible types of theory in social psychology; and in fact they are not the only existing types of theories in social psychology. We shall not try to be encyclopedic, however, and to study every theory that has been proposed for phenomena. The two types to be examined in the next 6 chapters constitute the most widely used, and also the most completely developed, lines of theoretical activity in social psychology at present.

Chapters 9–11 deal with exchange theories. Exchange theories view human interaction in terms of what is being exchanged between people. We see instances of people acting as if they were trading material and psychological rewards with each other, and an exchange theorist analyzes and predicts behavior on this basis. Exchange theorists assume as an article of faith that the basic human motivation is to maximize the rewards and minimize the costs in interaction. This assumption, as we shall see in Chap. 9, is the major distinguishing characteristic of all exchange theories. Exchange theories also offer a distinctive meaning of "rational behavior": rational behavior, to an exchange theorist, means acting in the way most likely to maximize one's gains. Any other type of behavior is "irrational." Exchange theories have been developed with considerable success for predicting behavior of human actors.

The other major line of theory in social psychology is consistency theories. These are studied in Chaps. 12–14. Consistency theories have been developed especially to explain thought processes: how individuals perceive and interpret their environments, how they form and change their attitudes, and similar issues. The basic assumption of consistency theories is that individuals prefer consistency—that is, logical relationships—between their various mental units, or cognitions. To a consistency theorist, rationality means being logical, in the usual sense of the term. Maximizing gain is not necessarily rational. What is important is whether what one does from one moment to the next is logically related, and whether one's actions and ideas are logically consistent. Thus while exchange theories are particularly well adapted for predicting behavior, consistency theories focus upon cognitions. Because exchange theories are somewhat older and more numerous in social psychology, we shall examine them first.

9   Exchange Theories

Human Exchanges

The study of interpersonal behavior took a large step forward in 1958 with the publication of George Homans' paper "Social Behavior as Exchange." From the perspective of more than a decade later it may be difficult to believe, but before this time there was no widely accepted, explicit way of explaining individual action in social psychology. Not that there weren't partial explanations or explanations specific to a single instance; those are always easy to come by. What was lacking prior to 1958 was a single set of principles, generally accepted by practitioners in the field, that could be applied to a wide variety of situations either for explaining them or for predicting likely outcomes. Homans' article provided the first such orientation.

If we want to explain why people act as they do, or if we want to explain why a particular outcome occurred in an experiment, Homans says, why not use the simplest ideas? Why not put forward for our social–psychological explanation exactly the same sort of ideas that we use every day in explaining something? If we want to explain why a person engaged in a particular action, the simplest answer is that he thought it was in his own best interest to do so. Why not develop this sort of common sense explanation and build our theories of interaction around it? This is essentially what Homans suggested should be done. He felt that the best way to look at human interaction was to assume that each individual is concerned with getting as much as he can out of a situation. He assumes, in other words, that individuals act in their own enlightened self interests. When we want to understand why somebody did something, what we need to look for is the interests of the people in interaction. People act in ways calculated to bring them some sort of benefits, and they are consciously concerned with these benefits or gains in choosing their actions. We say *enlightened* self-interest because sometimes actors will be concerned with long-term gains instead of short-term gains. Too much concern with immediate gains in interaction is called *selfishness*. Most people realize that selfishness brings a real danger of long-term loss of friendship and respect.

In a very broad and imprecise way, these ideas have existed for a long time, and they are part of our folk culture about "the nature of human nature and human relationships." We say, after meeting someone, "I got a lot out of talking with him." We ask, when someone proposes a particular action, "What's in it for me?" References such as these indicate at least a rudimentary usage of the ideas of social exchange. We are accustomed to seeing social action *in terms of* what persons have to give and what they can get. The terms we frequently use to describe interaction are analogous to those we use in describing a market economy—people "invest emotional energy" in a relationship, they "give happiness" or "take satisfaction", parents warn their children not to let someone "take advantage" of them— and the elementary concepts of economic transactions are familiar enough that we understand the meanings when others use these terms.

Not only are the ideas of social exchange familiar enough to describe interaction, but (again, in a broad and imprecise way) we actually shape our behavior to accord with some ideas of exchange. Friends who invite us over to dinner expect a reciprocal invitation; we say we "owe" them a dinner. In any one-to-one payment sense this is not true, but over the long run, people who do not fulfill these social obligations do not continue to receive invitations. If a particular neighbor frequently borrows something— say, sugar—from us, we feel rather well justified later in asking to borrow his or her garden hose. Or we might feel we can ask him to do a favor such as feed the dog while we're away for the weekend. Notice how these actions —having sugar when it's needed, giving up use of the hose, taking the time and effort to feed the dog—all seem to have some definite social value attached to them. Giving one of these things somehow entitles the giver to ask for something else in the future. Moreover while there may be some unclarity about the worth of each action, the range of value is well understood. One could not reasonably expect the neighbor who has borrowed sugar once to return the favor by boarding the dog all year; there is too great a disparity between the (unstated) value of the two acts. While we may not explicitly think of the value of such acts most of the time, it is clear that in fact people are guided by such considerations in a wide variety of interactions.

Incidentally we may also note that there is some resistance to exhibiting *too* great a concern for equality of social exchanges, or for the worth of the social or material goods being exchanged. We have the pejorative terms "schemer" and "golddigger" for people who are too open about (or, too unsuccessful at disguising) their interest in what they give and what they get. But most of us would admit that in the long run, we feel favors between individuals ought to "even out." If they don't, we look elsewhere for our friends.

The pervasiveness of ideas of exchange probably is due largely to the prevalence of these ideas in important areas of our socialization. One of the first things a child is taught in cultures such as ours is how to handle money to buy things, or how to trade toys with other children. From early childhood, a child hears adults using the terms of economic transaction to describe human interactions, and this learning is likely to affect the child's ways of conceptualizing things later. And in fact in most cultures, a large part of every person's time is spent in activity which is avowedly economic: working for money, buying or trading objects, bargaining over material objects, working out agreements over nonmaterial goods and services. It seems only natural to carry over and use the concepts and the practices learned for these economic activities into other areas.

As some of the examples indicate, being aware of the exchanges in which one is a part can be a difficult problem at times. Learning to understand the valuables being exchanged is one set of problems, and learning how to bargain effectively and to protect one's own interests are an even more difficult set of problems.

We begin to see that the process of seeking favorable exchanges is not so simple as at first it appeared, and also that exchange theories are not quite so simple mindedly reward-oriented as we might have thought. People are aware of the consequences of their actions, both short-term and long-term. In most cases people are careful not to endanger large long-term benefits (such as respect) for small short-term ones (such as proving a point in an argument, or saving a few cents at a restaurant). This idea, as well as many other qualifications on the basic exchange ideas, will be developed and elaborated in more detail in this and the following chapters. But this basic orienting insight will reappear in many forms: any interaction may be viewed as an exchange, in which one individual is *giving* something to a second, and is *getting* something in return.

The basic ideas in exchange theory, as Homans observed, are far from new. As long ago as Aristotle, thinkers assumed that individuals are concerned with gains and losses in deciding their actions. Homans' article builds upon earlier work, and makes two major contributions to the field of social psychology. First, Homans states explicitly and in a way that can be easily understood the set of ideas he proposes to use in analyzing and explaining behavior. Until an idea is stated explicitly, it is not much help in constructing theories. To assert, as Homans did, *that all human interaction may be explained this way,* and to offer such an explanation is to take a stand and put forth an idea that may be tested empirically.

Homans' second major contribution with this article is less tangible but probably more important. Exchange theories in general, and this article in particular, have attracted the attention of a large number of theorists and experimentalists. Exchange theories provide a focus of interest, a common set of similar research problems, and a foundation for a set of shared understandings about how interaction situations should be analyzed and explained. Exchange ideas appeal to many social psychologists and provide them with a fairly clear way of analyzing situations. Beyond this, the exchange perspective provides an orientation to the *types* of interaction situations considered worthy of analysis. Thus the exchange perspective orients investigators to distinctive types of problems, to a distinctive way of analyzing them and to a distinctive way of predicting and explaining behavior. Currently in social psychology, exchange theories provide the *predominant* world view. The significance of this sort of orienting function in the history of science is not often noted, yet in most fields it is only when a large number of researchers begin looking at a similar set of problems in the same way that the field makes a major advance. Homans' contribution in this area is enormous.

Exchanging Esteem for Help:
The Federal Bureaucracy

The most famous application of Homans' ideas on social exchange is his use of them to analyze interaction in a federal bureaucracy. In addition to providing a clear illustration of the main ideas of the exchange approach, the analysis clarifies the meaning of certain key concepts (such as the sorts of things that may be considered social rewards), as well as the limits within which such commodities may be exchanged. The meaning of a theory is illustrated and amplified through these applications. Familiarity with several situations to which the theory may be applied provides a "working understanding" of the theory—more complete and more useful than simply knowing the abstract concepts and the relations of the assumptions.

The bureaucracy of our "prime example" for exchange theories (first reported by Blau, 1954), was an investigative office staff charged with gathering information and analyzing it for possible prosecution of violations of federal regulations. Agents had the task of visiting and examining business firms and preparing reports on their compliance with the law. Legal matters all involve matters of judgment (they are partially ambiguous, in the terminology of the social psychologist), so it was often difficult to be certain just what to recommend in a particular case. As we might expect, the agents differed in their experience and competence, and they generally agreed among themselves as to how much of these skills they each possessed.

A natural thing to do in a situation characterized by task difficulty, ambiguity, and uncertainty—especially if you perceive yourself to be relatively low on the necessary skills—is to consult with other agents in filling out a report. Even if the agent with whom you consult isn't able to offer much in the way of useful advice, there is some social support just in knowing that someone else has approved the action you intend to recommend. And naturally if you have a choice of several consultants, it is wise to choose the most capable person to give you advice. All of these things regularly were practiced by the agents. Official policy forbade such consultations, but the supervisor was aware that they occurred, and he did not strongly object.

From Homans' point of view, what occurred in the office was an exchange: the expert agents were being asked to give their time and their skills to the less competent. What could the less competent give the experts in return? Several possible goods come to mind (for example, they could buy lunch or give presents), but the most usual thing in such cases is *esteem*. Simply asking for help can convey the asker's admiration for the abilities of the one asked, *and this esteem is a social reward*. Anyone who has some experience in asking for help soon learns the importance of asking for it in the proper manner. If you don't reward the other for his help (a valuable commodity) through deference (which most people value), he is likely to refuse to give it next time, or to extract some other reward (such as money) from you in exchange. People who ask for advice on a personal matter, and then upon receiving it argue with the person who made the suggestion, are in effect denying the deference that is expected. Next time they ask for advice, it will probably be denied them.

Of course, giving help and advice was not all that the expert agents had to do with their time. They had their own reports to prepare, and helping others took time from their work. We might expect them to place some reasonable limits upon the amounts of help they gave, which they did. In exchange terms, two processes are operative here. First, the expert agents were consciously choosing between alternative courses of action: doing their own work, or helping someone else. Giving help to someone else means taking time from one's own work. This points up more precisely just *how much* esteem is needed to entice this help. It must be enough to offset the "costs" of taking time from the expert's own work. Stated differently, the exchange of help for esteem must be *profitable*—more desirable to the expert than doing his own work—or he will not engage in it. Second, the relative value of the esteem changes through time; it becomes less and less valuable to be flattered when one's own work is suffering. In terms of exchange theories, he becomes *satiated,* and the *marginal utility* of additional units of the reward declines. At the same time the subjective value of doing his own work increases as the deadline approaches.

(The objective value probably does not increase so much. The actual professional value of the work is probably about the same no matter whether it is done just barely under the deadline or long before it. But it certainly comes to *seem* more and more important to the person to get it done as the deadline approaches. Anyone who has put off writing a term paper for months, and then stayed up all night just before it was due understands this feeling.)

The central points here are that choices between available alternative courses of action are made in terms of the rewards and costs of each, and that the value of those alternatives changes through time. Now we begin to specify the ideas of exchange theories more precisely and in more detail.

Antecedents of Exchange Theories

The basic ideas in contemporary social exchange theories come from two sources. First, some of the propositions of learning theories are adopted and are interpreted specifically for interpersonal action. Thus exchange theories assume that the actor responds to rewards and costs, and they usually assume that the actor learns through experience which situations are most likely to be rewarding. The second source of social exchange ideas is economic theory. One of the major concerns in economics is to explain why people choose to buy one product rather than another or to invest money rather than to spend it. In exchange theory, one of the prime interests is to explain why people choose one alternative action, or one alternative set of friends, or one alternative situation, over another. The most general answer is that actors attempt to maximize rewards and minimize costs.

Another concept which figures prominently in exchange theories is *marginal utility,* an economic concept with some similarity to the psychological concept *satiation.* The basic idea of marginal utility is that when an individual possesses a certain amount of a given commodity (such as some material good) the value of another unit of that commodity is smaller than it would be if the individual had none. The more food somebody has, the less valuable to him is an additional sandwich. On the other hand if the individual has none of the commodity, and especially if he has not received any for a long time, the value of the first unit of the commodity is likely to be very large. The *value* of alternatives, then, is affected by the individual's history.

Contemporary Exchange Theories

Although it is proper to consider Homans the intellectual father of exchange theories because of his impact on the field, there are at this time a whole family of exchange theories. Some of them develop directly out of Homans' ideas, and some were developed independently by other theorists. But there are certain broad similarities between all members of the exchange theory family.

If we adopt the perspective of exchange theories, we believe that individuals are concerned with obtaining rewards in their actions. The rewards may be material—for example, people are said to be motivated by the desire for money—or they may be intangible and social such as approval or love. In fact in many situations in our society it is quite apparent that people are more concerned with gaining social approval than they are with gaining money. Social approval is a very powerful reward and it is one that affects behavior in a wide range of circumstances. In Homans' terms, it is a very *valuable* and very *general* reward.

The exchange theory point of view also assumes that when we have recently received some quantity of a reward the value of additional quantities of that reward decrease. In other words at some point we become *satiated,* and are less concerned with obtaining more of the reward. Exchange theories generally assert that when an individual contemplates some action, he weighs the rewards and costs of that action against the rewards and costs of an alternative action, and then chooses the one that on balance is more rewarding. In other words he seeks to maximize his total profit in the situation.

Exchange theories are concerned with predicting and explaining *conscious, voluntary* actions. That is, the exchange view assumes that social action is the result of decisions made by individuals, and that the decisions are made for reasons that are known to the actors. Factors such as unconscious motivations, for instance, that figure in psychoanalytic theories, have no place in exchange theories. Actors control their own behavior in terms of goals (rewards) they seek. In addition, exchange theories are intended to apply to situations where actors know, or think they know, the likely outcomes of the various action choices available to them. We do not assume that actors have perfectly complete information before they can make decisions—and in some cases we apply exchange theories where the reward structures are probably too complicated for the actor to calculate them—but before an exchange theory can predict behavior we must assume that the actors have some rough idea of the rewards and costs they are likely to incur. These four characteristics—(1) predicting behavior rather than attitudes, (2) assuming conscious motivations, (3) assuming awareness of likely outcomes of actions, and (4) assuming that social action is voluntary rather than coerced by outsiders or by psychic drives such as neuroses—are shared by all contemporary exchange theories.

Implicit in most exchange analyses of decision making is the idea that actors consider alternative interaction situations and alternative other interaction partners. The idea of *comparison with alternatives* has been developed by Thibaut and Kelley (1959). The comparison level (which they call CL) is defined as a psychological midpoint for outcomes; the point at which an actor is neither satisfied nor disatisfied with his interacton. If the relationship in one situation exceeds the CL, the actor is attracted to that situation; if it provides less, he is repelled. The CL arises by the actor's learning, through his experiences with other people in other situations. The basic idea of the CL is that the individual constantly weighs interaction situations and any available interaction partner with alternatives. At some point when they are about equally attractive, he is indifferent between them. If he is not indifferent, he will choose the interaction situation or the other person who is, on balance, more rewarding. The idea of alternative comparison levels is basic to a large class of mathematical models of decision making, some of which we examine in Chap. 11.

According to the ideas of exchange theory, how do you get somebody to do what you want him to do? Stated differently, in exchange theory how do you exert power over another individual? From the ideas presented above, the answer is fairly simple: You make the action that you want performed profitable; that is, you control rewards and costs so that the individual perceives it is in his own best interest to do what you want him to do. Either you point out to him that you are offering a large reward for doing what you want him to do, or you threaten to impose a large cost for doing something else. If you have enough control over someone's rewards and costs, you can "make him an offer he can't refuse."

An exchange theory analysis of social power claims that a powerful person is one who is able to control most rewards and costs of another person in a situation. Emerson (1962) and Blau (1964) have provided extensive analyses of power relations from this point of view. The basic idea as stated by Emerson is that the amount of power person A has over person B is a direct function of the dependence person B has upon person A for some scarce reward. Stated differently, in a two-person interaction, power and dependence for a reward vary inversely. The more B is dependent upon A for the reward, the greater the power A can exert over B. The extreme example of this idea that comes to mind is a drug addict. If B is dependent upon *A* for his supply of an addicting (or otherwise highly desirable) drug, this fact gives *A* tremendous power over *B*. The same sort of analysis could be applied to individuals in an interaction where the primary reward was social. For example, if *B* wants love from *A* and only from *A*, this gives *A* tremendous power over *B*. In Chap. 10 we shall explore some consequences of Emerson's exchange analysis of power and consider some options that *B* might use to reduce the power *A* has over him.

Another interesting type of situations are those in which individuals decide to team up in one way or another. When both of them desire the same outcome, they may form a coalition to pool their strengths, and divide whatever winnings they get in this manner; or, one individual may decide to trust another to make decisions for him. *Coalition formation* and *interpersonal trust* situations have ben analyzed from the exchange perspective, and we shall examine some of these cases in Chap. 10.

In other types of situations, there is no single available alternative that will satisfy all participants to the exchange. Voting situations, whatever the decision rule—majority, plurality, or unanimity—frequently make it impossible for every voter to realize his preference. In situations of majority rule, fully 40 percent of the voters may not get their preferred outcome, and in plurality situations well over 50 percent may not get their choice. (In cases where unanimity is required, few decisions get made, precisely because of the difficulty of satisfying everyone. This partially explains why unanimity rules are rare. I have served on committees where the norms were that all decisions must be made by consensus. It is invariably a frustrating experience.)

What happens in these collective situations? In Congress there is a tradition of vote trading (called "log-rolling" by political scientists) by which members support each other's favorite legislation. Suppose the Senator from Maine wants strict import quotas on lobsters to protect his state's fishermen, and the Senator from Nebraska wants more money for the Interstate Highway System in the Midwest. Neither Senator has much interest in the other's issue, except that the Maine Senator's bill may slightly increase the cost of lobster for the few people in Nebraska who eat lobster, and the Nebraska Senator's bill may slightly increase gasoline taxes in Maine. From an exchange point of view, for each to support the other's bill entails costs, but these costs are slight. What is important is that his support will probably produce a big reward later: the vote of the other person when his own bill comes up. This logrolling process is the way most measures actually are adopted in bodies which make collective decisions by democratic means.

Coleman has described the process more rigorously and has extended it to sociological applications which meet the following conditions: (1) there are a group of actors and each actor controls amounts of resources (such as votes); (2) there are a series of decisions to be made according to some decision rule (such as majority vote); and the actors do not all "care equally" (have the same *investments* in) the various outcomes of possible decisions to be made. Some similar types of decision making are analyzed in Chap. 10.

Let us begin at the beginning, with a precise and explicit explanation of the ideas of exchange theory as proposed by Homans. Then we shall see what modifications are needed to deal with this wide variety of substantive basic ideas.

Human Exchange: Homans' Propositions

Three years after the original article, Homans (1961) presented an explicit, formalized version of his exchange theory. We have already considered the goals and the advantages of presenting formal explicit theory; here we shall just review some of them. Stating theoretical ideas explicitly forces the theorist to be clear about what he means. Ambiguities of meaning should be reduced, and ideas should be presented as directly as possible. This in turn should reduce misunderstanding of ideas and improve communication. Removing vagueness and unclarity of meanings not only enables more precision of expression, but it also decreases the likelihood that a reader will misunderstand the author's intention. Finally, stating ideas clearly and explicitly facilitates reactions to them. It is easier for others to criticize explicit ideas, and easier to suggest changes, modifications or extensions of the original theoretical ideas. In 1974 Homans revised the original propositions to take account of theoretical and empirical developments in the 13 years since they were first presented. Chart 9–1 presents the later version of Homans' propositions.

CHART 9–1   Homans' Exchange Theory

1. For all actions taken by persons, the more often a particular action of a person is rewarded, the more likely the person is to perform that action.

2. If in the past the occurrence of a particular stimulus, or set of stimuli, has been the occasion on which a person's action has been rewarded, then the more similar the present stimuli are to the past ones, the more likely the person is to perform the action, or some similar action, now.

3. The more valuable to a person is the result of his action, the more likely he is to perform the action.

4. The more often in the recent past a person has received a particular reward, the less valuable any further unit of that reward becomes for him.

5a. When a person's action does not receive the reward he expected, or receives punishment he did not expect, he will be angry; he becomes more likely to perform aggressive behavior, and the results of such behavior become more valuable to him.

5b. When a person's action receives a reward he expected, especially a greater reward than he expected, or does not receive punishment he expected, he will be pleased; he becomes more likely to perform approving behavior, and the results of such behavior become more valuable to him.

(From Homans, 1974, pp. 16–39.)

Proposition 1 is essentially a learning proposition, of the type we studied in Chap. 8. It says that actors tend to increase the frequency of rewarded actions. Proposition 2 also comes from learning theories. It says that actors learn what types of situations are rewarding to them, and that they seek out, or try to produce, that type of situations. Proposition 3 suggests that rewards are *variables;* they have different *values,* with more valuable rewards being the ones most likely to produce the action which gains them. Proposition 4 describes an idea present in both learning theories and in economic theory. After a time, rewards decrease in value. The first 4 propositions form the core of Homans' exchange theory.

Proposition 5, as I'm sure you realize after reading the list of propositions in Chart 9–1, is considerably different in nature from the first four. It depends upon an idea, distributive justice, that we have not defined, and it predicts one outcome of failure of distributive justice. The basic ideas of exchange theory, those contained in propositions 1 through 4, may be considered without the idea of distributive justice. Justice concerns will be taken up separately in Chaps. 10 and 16.

Usually when I present the ideas of exchange theory in lecture, or when I am discussing the ideas of exchange theories with people for the first time, they nod in agreement. The ideas sound so simple, in fact, that they are common sense—people wonder why they need to be said at all. Perhaps you had this feeling upon reading the first sections of this chapter. When I state the propositions explicitly, however, as in Homans' propositions of Chart 9–1, the reactions are very different. People say that they don't always apply. Almost invariably upon first meeting the ideas of exchange theories, people think that they are too commonsensical to require explicit statement. When they are stated explicitly, however, we find disagreements. This is a good illustration of one of the features of explicit theory construction mentioned earlier: it prevents ambiguity in meaning, and it facilitates criticism of the ideas. So long as I present my ideas to you vaguely, incompletely, and intuitively, you are likely to agree with them. When I say exactly what I mean and communication between us is improved, then you can think of exceptions and cases where you disagree with my ideas. This is exactly the point. Much of human behavior and many of our explanations of human behavior seem simplistic and obvious until we state them clearly. At that point we find that what formerly appeared obvious is not at all obvious; what formerly appeared unnecessary to state, in fact requires statement and restatement. But it is only when ideas are stated explicitly and clearly—only, that is, when the theorist takes a stand on exactly what he means—that the ideas can be criticized, reformulated, and improved.

Before we begin to criticize Homans' initial formulation, however, let us be certain that we understand it and can apply it to empirical situations. As an exercise, let us ask what propositions could be used to explain the findings of some previous studies. First, which propositions would we use to explain the findings of the Schachter study summarized in Chap. 4? As you will recall, there are two sets of findings to be explained. First, communication towards the deviate in the "high cohesive relevant" groups initially was very high and then dropped off. Second, in these groups communication to the mode remained constant at a high level throughout the group meetings. The second finding is easier, so let us explain it first. We presume that the verbal acts of the mode were in some sense rewarding to other members of the group. They liked to hear what he was saying. The way to encourage him to speak would be to speak to him. Thus people were talking to the mode to encourage him to talk back to them. We would explain the fact that others were speaking to the mode at a high constant level using propositions 1 and 2. Whoever first allowed the mode to speak found it rewarding. Therefore, by proposition 2, he is likely to encourage him to speak again. By proposition 1, because nearly everything said by the mode was rewarding, all individuals would be likely to encourage him to speak more.

Now let us try to explain the pattern of communication to the deviate. Perhaps initially his unusual ideas were rewarding. They relieved the boredom of the discussion and provided an alternative viewpoint. If this is the case, then by propositions 1 and 2 we would expect a lot of communication encouraging him to speak. However, after a certain period of time, people would get tired of hearing the deviate speak; satiation would begin to occur. By proposition 4, we would expect that his unusual opinions would lose their appeal as time went along. Thus we can explain the initial high level and the subsequent drop of communication towards the deviate, using propositions 1, 2, and 4.

As a second exercise, the reader might attempt to explain the patterns of communication in Westgate and Westgate West. It would also be instructive to note which propositions are needed to explain the differential favorability towards the tenants organization in Westgate and in Westgate West.

Which specific propositions would be needed to explain the example from Blau's federal agency described earlier? Recall that the agents were exchanging help with the work for esteem. Initially, agent A possessed high ability but had no particular abundance of esteem from his colleagues. Agent B possessed lower ability and was willing to give A esteem in exchange for help. How does B know that A is able to help him? If he has asked A for help in the past and has received it, then proposition 2 enables us to predict that B will ask A for help again when he needs it in the future. Proposition 3 is needed to explain why A is willing to help B. A knows that B is willing to give him esteem in return for help and he would like to get this esteem. However because of proposition 4, we would also expect that A will tire of giving B help. In exchange theory terms, A will become *satiated* with esteem after a while, and the relative value of doing his own work instead of Bs will assume greater importance. To state the same idea differently, the attractiveness of the alternative of doing As own work will increase in importance above his CL as he becomes satiated with esteem from B. Also note that in this federal agency, highly competent agents (As) would be expected to exert some power over less competent agents (Bs) in return for their help due to the dependency relationships. The fact that the *A*s wanted esteem from the *B*s would tend to equalize the power relationships.

An Assessment of Homans' Theory

Basically, you recall, a theory constitutes an *explanation* of phenomena of interest. It is a way of showing that a finding (such as the change in a dependent variable) is a special case of more general principles asserted in the propositions. The theory explains specific cases because it tells what we know about social behavior in general. Many specific criteria are applied by philosophers of science in assessing the adequacy of theories, but for our purposes we may think of them in terms of two requirements: (1) The theory should say what it has to say clearly and without possibility of misunderstanding. If it does not, then two different readers will not understand the same things with the same meanings from it. (2) The theory should perform an adequate job of doing what it sets out to do. It should, in other words, do a good job of explaining the things which it claims to be able to explain. The explanation should be thorough, and it should be precise enough to permit us to judge its adequacy from relevant empirical tests. Let us apply these two criteria, *clarity* and *explanatory adequacy* to Homans' propositions.

For clarity, we ask first whether there is a determinate meaning given by the propositions. Are several terms used to convey the same idea, or is the same idea expressed in different terms at different times? Either of these problems decreases the clarity of a theory. Ideally there should be some small set of terms which are used, and these terms either should have very simple meanings so that they may remain undefined, or they should be defined in terms of simple words. Some of Homans' terms such as *stimulus* seem to me to be unnecessarily complicated and also to present no single meaning. The term really is no more precise than *social situation* would be, yet it is certainly more difficult to pronounce and to remember. The idea of a "unit of an activity" seems to me to have no simple interpretation either. Exactly what does it mean: one action, one sequence of actions, or what? Again it is not completely clear, and the theory would be advanced if it were made clear. Proposition 2 seems to be stated in a deliberately complicated way (to say nothing of proposition 5!), and the qualifier "or some similar action" seems a hedge against discomfirmation. What is a "similar" action?

The organization and the interrelation of the propositions is not explicit, and in some cases it appears as though unnecessary ideas are introduced. For example, it is not clear to me under what circumstances, if any, proposition 2 adds anything that has not been stated in proposition 1. Both talk about the effects of amount of total reward. Perhaps it would be possible to eliminate one of these propositions. On the other side, it is true that there are some interaction situations (to be taken up later) for which we do not have sufficient propositions to explain them adequately.

A major problem with exchange theories—and a problem that exists in most psychological learning theories—is specifying exactly the nature of the term reward. As it is usually used, reward is defined tautologically. We know that something is rewarding *because* we observe that the actor is willing to expend effort in order to gain it. At the same time we predict that the actor will expend effort in order to gain a reward. There is no independent definition given of the term reward, and perhaps none could be given. In experimental learning psychology, from which exchange theories take the idea of reward, the most frequently used reward is food. In animal studies of learning, it is standard practice to starve the animals down to 80 percent of their normal body weight before beginning the training trials. Under these circumstances food may be assumed to be a powerful reward indeed. Translating this to the human scale, it would mean starving an individual until he lost, say, 30 pounds. Would he then be willing to perform for a reward of food? You bet he would!

However in most human social interaction, it is not clear that food constitutes the most powerful reward, or even that it is a reward at all. In fact for most situations of interest in social psychology, the relevant reward is probably social approval. Such things as liking, esteem, prestige, or expressions of affection, are probably the major inducements to behavior in most situations studied by social psychologists. However we still do not have the independent measures that would enable us to assert that these things constitute rewards.

If social approval is taken to be the primary reward in social interaction, then we may have an additional difficulty. Social approval is a highly desirable commodity with a very high threshold of satiation. Like money, perhaps even more than money, people seem never to be satisfied with the amount of social approval they have. It may well be, then, that for the major reward of interest to exchange theorists—social approval—one of the basic and essential assumptions of exchange theory—satiation—does not apply. However, at the current stage of theoretical tests, this potential problem is just a conjecture. The best we can do in most cases is to assert that the propositions of exchange theory often allow us to predict behavior *if we may assume* that social approval constitutes a reward for the individual. A major unsolved problem for exchange theories, then, is to constuct an explicit definition of a reward, and to permit independent identification of exactly what does constitute a reward for a given individual.

A second problem with exchange theory which has been discussed by Abrahamson and others, is its explicitly hedonistic nature. The assumptions of exchange theory assume that the individual is motivated primarily, if not exclusively, by self-interest. But perhaps it is the case that important areas of social behavior are unexplainable in these terms; that is, there may be situations in which it is *not* possible to ascribe the person's action to a desire to maximize his own good. Instances of altruism, such as giving to the poor or to charity (when not motivated by income tax considerations) are difficult to explain using exchange theories. There are documented cases of soldiers or others giving up their lives for the benefit of others; how are we to explain such actions from the exchange point of view? One way that is sometimes offered is to assert that these individuals "reward themselves" by the knowledge that they have done a good deed or by imagining social approval from others. This does not seem at all satisfying to me. For one thing, we have absolutely no independent way to ascertain that someone who gives up his life felt rewarded for doing so.

Having noted these exceptions, we must in fairness also note that they are truly exceptional: altruistic acts and giving up one's life for others are very, very rare incidents. For most people, most of the time, behavior can be predicted very well by assuming that they are responding to the rewards and costs of their social situations. Furthermore until people demonstrate that exchange theory is inapplicable to a given class of situations, there is no reason *a priori* to reject it simply because it seems hedonistic. As Homans (1958) wrote, "Before anyone rejects this explanation out of hand for its horrid profit seeking implications, he would do well to ask himself whether he and mankind has ever been able to offer an alternative."

The third objection to Homans' version of exchange theory is one that I believe has considerable merit, but it is one that may be altered in other versions of exchange theory. This is that, as Homans states his propositions, they are not *cognitive*. They do not explicitly assume awareness of the individual, nor do they clearly state that he makes a conscious choice in deciding his behavior. The propositions simply describe relative likelihoods of engaging in certain actions. This objection, at least, could be met by altering the statement of some of the propositions. For instance, instead of saying, "The more similar the present stimuli are to the past ones, the more likely the person is to perform the action," we could say, "The more similar *the individual thinks* the present situation is to the past one. . . ." This change would make the propositions refer to conscious behavior on the part of individuals, which is clearly what we intend in exchange theories. (Skinner, the psychologist whose work heavily influenced Homans, has argued repeatedly that there is no need for cognitive theories, however.)

In spite of the criticisms that have been leveled against exchange theories, in spite of the fact that there are problems with some of the concepts, and in spite of the incompleteness of some of the explanations that may be constructed, exchange theories are enormously useful in social psychology. This is true because they can explain a very wide class of situations, and because in many of these situations they enable very accurate predictions of behavior. They are also useful because of the wide attention they have received from theorists seeking to make the underlying ideas explicit. Versions of exchange theory frequently appear in social psychological literature in which the ideas are stated clearly enough and precisely enough to permit criticism and extensions. Discussion is facilitated because various researchers can understand each other clearly and disagreements become apparent only when a theory is made explicit. Furthermore an explicit theory permits determinate predictions; that is, predictions which are either clearly confirmed or clearly disconfirmed by relevant empirical tests. Consequently it is possible to correct those parts of the theory which produce disconfirmed predictions. Theories grow not by being discarded when they are found inadequate, but by being "patched up." There is a widespread misconception that theories shown to be inadequate are discarded. Far more frequently, and far more wisely, theories that yield disconfirmed empirical predictions are corrected. More precisely, the specific part of the theory (the particular assumptions) that yielded the disconfirmed prediction may be modified.

Very seldom in the history of a field do theories compete with each other to the extent that one and only one theory will survive. Far more frequently a theory is first formulated tentatively (as by Homans in 1958), and various investigators seek to determine its weaknesses and to extend the range of predictions that may be made from it. The progression to a more complete theoretical understanding of phenomena occurs not by *discarding* ideas but by *repairing* them where empirical evidence indicates this is needed. Thus even a theory that receives considerable empirical disconfirmation is useful if the empirical tests show where the theory may be improved. By this criterion, the criticism of Homans' theory itself shows a positive aspect of the propositions.

Exchange Theories as Orientation to Social Interaction

Exchange theories as a set constitute the largest group of explanations and predictions for interpersonal behavior. This means that they have been applied to a wide range of different substantive phenomena. Specific areas of interest range from explaining personal preferences for certain individuals or situations, through analyzing instances of power and influence, through explaining decision making in complex situations. Note that the variety and popularity of exchange theories in social psychology *do not* mean that these theories are the only possible ones (though Homans seems to claim they are), nor even that they are perfectly adequate for the topics to which they have been applied. Exchange explanations are very important in social psychology and in some cases they are very good. But they are not perfect, nor can we know for sure that they will never be replaced by theories of another family.

Although there are many different versions of exchange theories constructed for many different substantive areas of interest, they all share in common certain basic assumptions. All exchange theories subscribe to a core set of underlying beliefs—assumptions—about the nature of human nature and about the proper strategy for analyzing and explaining human behavior. This basic type of assumptions is called *meta-theory*. They are a theory of how to construct theories. The meta-theory is never tested; it is accepted as an article of faith. Rather, one constructs theories (such as Homans' theory) according to the meta-theory, and it is the theories themselves which are empirically tested. Another way to look at this is to say that the assumptions of the meta-theories are so basic, so philosophical, that any empirical test is inadequate either to confirm or to disconfirm them. Meta-theories are assumed to be true before one begins to construct a theory. For instance all exchange theorists accept on faith that human actors are motivated primarily by rewards and costs. But how could they test this assumption empirically? The answer is that they cannot. What *is* done is to construct theories that use the concepts *reward* and *cost,* and then to test these theories empirically.

The meta-theory of a field defines what may be called that field's *orienting strategy*. It orients a group of theorists and the researchers towards work in their field. The orienting strategy constitutes the way that a particular group of investigators (exchange theorists and researchers) view social psychology. An orienting strategy, as we shall use the term, focuses the efforts of its adherents in terms of four distinctive criteria.

First, the orienting strategy provides a distinctive set of concepts and assumptions regarding those concepts. All exchange theorists use the terms *reward* and *cost* in their theories, and all have some version of an assertion that actors are motivated towards rewards and away from costs.

Second, the orienting strategy provides a distinctive set of substantive problems to investigate. It tells, in other words, what issues constitute problems which need to be explained, and which are nonproblems. No exchange theorist regards the search for, or the description of, unconscious motivations as particularly interesting. Exchange theorists are primarily concerned with understanding and predicting individual and social behavior. They are not particularly concerned with predicting such mental processes as attitude changes or how individuals come to acquire preferences.

Third, the orienting strategy provides a distinctive technology for investigating problems. Because exchange theories often are concerned with decision making, basic experimental designs and mechanical equipment used by exchange theorists are those in which choice behavior may be precisely observed.

Fourth, the orienting strategy provides a distinctive definition for solution of theoretical or empirical problems. It tells the investigator when he has in fact achieved a satisfactory solution to the problems of interest. Theoretical problems are solved for an exchange theorist when an adequate explanation for relevant observations regarding behavior has been constructed, according to the criteria presented in the essay that begins Part II of the text. Substantive problems are solved when—and only when—the investigator is able to analyze social situations in terms of the perceived rewards and costs, and is able to show that the observed behavior is actually related to actors' seeking rewards and avoiding costs.

These criteria—the concepts and assumptions, the set of substantive problems, the technology, and the definition of a satisfactory solution to the problems—define the particular orienting strategy, or meta-theory, adopted by exchange researchers. Using these criteria, it is possible to differentiate meta-theories from each other and to recognize a new exchange theory readily. For instance, a new theory may be compared to the exchange meta-theory to see whether it is consistent with these beliefs. If it is, then the theory is an exchange theory; if not, it belongs to some other theoretical family.

The exchange meta-theory is not written down any place. The set of assumptions is so basic that, although exchange theorists probably would agree to them if they were stated, they are not considered worth discussing. They simply are accepted. In order to reconstruct the exchange meta-theory, therefore, one must have a familiarity with most of the current exchange theories. Then it is possible to ask what they all have in common. What basic agreements do these various theorists share, or what is there fundamental philosophical orientation?

Chart 9–2 presents my candidate for a set of exchange meta-theoretical assumptions. Someone else probably would construct a slightly different list of exchange assumptions but I think that the five assumptions in Chart 9–2 would receive a high degree of agreement from current exchange theorists.

Perhaps it will help in understanding the nature and the purpose of meta-theories to compare the exchange meta-theory with two other meta-theories

CHART 9–2 Exchange Meta-Theory: Fundamental Assumptions

---

1. The basic human motivation is to seek (material and social) rewards, and to avoid costs.
    a. People will act in the ways they think will attain these goals.
    b. There is individual variation in perceived rewards and costs ("tastes vary").

2. The values of rewards and costs vary as a functon of time ("satiation") and other factors.
    a. A major task of the theorist is to specify the exact form (e.g., by mathematical modeling) and the determinants of this variation.

3. Humans often act upon the basis of *anticipated* rewards and costs from various courses of action open to them.
    a. A task of the theorist is to conceptualize the calculation of anticipated outcomes.
    b. A task of the theorist is to specify the decision rules used consciously or unconsciously by individuals.

4. Known human action in a given situation may be *explained* by identifying relevant rewards and costs in that situation.
    a. Identifying rewards and costs *as perceived by individuals* is a primary goal of the investigator.
    b. An adequate (acceptable, complete) explanation for an action may be constructed by showing that the action maximized relative perceived rewards.

5. Likely human action in a given situation may be accurately *predicted* using (1) and (2) if the relevant rewards and costs can be identified.
    a. Identifying rewards and costs as *perceived by individuals* is a primary goal of the investigator.
    b. A disconfirmed prediction indicates inaccurate identification of the relevant rewards and costs; not failure of (1) and (2).

---

governing explanations of social behavior. Both these other meta-theories are generally not used by social psychologists at present, but within this century both have had wide acceptance. The first alternative meta-theory tells us to construct religious explanations of behavior. For example, its first assertion (comparable to assertion #4 of Chart 9–2) might be: "Any human action may be explained as being the result of God's will or of God's intervention in the affairs of men." Adherance to this meta-theory would produce explanations of human behavior very different from exchange theories.

The second alternative meta-theory tells us to construct instinct explanations of human behavior: "Any human action may be explained by identifying the basic instinctual drives fulfilled by the specific action." Instinct theories of human behavior also are very different from exchange theories. As with the exchange meta-theory, these alternatives are neither true nor false. With the wisdom provided by historical perspective, we can say that each of these fell into disuse, not because it was false—it could not be tested directly—but because theories constructed consistent with these meta-theories never did a particularly satisfactory job of predicting or explaining human behavior. After a while, social psychologists decided in effect that the religious and instinct meta-theories had been given a fair chance to prove themselves, but had failed. At that point, investigators turn to other meta-theoretical perspectives in the hope that they will prove superior.

The distinction between *theories* and *meta-theories* is a subtle one, and perhaps it will be more completely understood after we examine several specific exchange theories in Chaps. 10 and 11. In Chap. 12 we study a different contemporary meta-theory in wide use: consistency theories.

Some Exchange Theoretical Topics

In the following two chapters we shall consider several topics typically explained by exchange theories. These various substantive areas and their respective theories may be likened to off-shoots from the basic exchange theory ideas. As additional assumptions are added to the core set of ideas (such as Homans'), the meta-theoretical assumptions of exchange have likewise been expanded.

Analyzing and explaining situations of *power* and *influence* has required development of additional assumptions. Recall that the basic orientation of exchange theory analyses of power is to explain them in terms of control of rewards. Some of the power applications we will examine in the following chapter required additional assumptions. Chart 9–3 contains some additional meta-theoretical assumptions of power exchange theories.

Analyzing situations in which individuals make some sort of collective decision or form some sort of alliances requires the basic set of exchange assumptions as well as additional assumptions designed specifically for that purpose. The exchange meta-theory has been expanded for these situations with at least two additional assumptions shown in Chart 9–4.

6. The major means of inducing compliance in individuals is to control their access to some scarce reward.

    a. A task of the theorist is to specify the precise form of the power-dependency relation.

    b. A task of the theorist is to specify observable behavior in situations of unequal power.

    c. A task of the theorist is to specify possible means of altering the power-dependency relation between individuals.

7. Bargaining situations may be analyzed in exchange terms as cases of power-dependence relations (in other words, bargaining situations may be analyzed the same way that power-dependence relations are analyzed.)

8. Collective outcomes may be distinguished from individual outcomes; and they are not always additive. (That is, what is good for each individual may not always be best for the group.)

    a. In case of conflict between collective and individual good, individual good usually is preferred.

    b. A task of the theorist is to specify conditions (e.g., socialization, short run interaction) under which collective good will be preferred.

    c. A task of the theorist is to develop an abstract classification of situations in which collective and individual outcomes are in conflict.

CHART 9–4   Exchange Theories of Decision Making:
Additional Assumptions

9. Individuals may ally themselves with each other to produce a better outcome for each than any one could attain alone.

    a. A task of the theorist is to specify the relevant concerns of individuals in forming alliances.

10. Individuals will choose among a finite set of alternative actions according to the *net gain* anticipated from each.

    a. A task of the theorist is to specify the precise form of the decision making behavior.

The Exchange "Family Tree"

An overview of contemporary exchange theories is given by the meta-theoretical assumptions used in each. This is, in order to gain familiarity quickly with current exchange theories, we may ask which of the meta-theoretical assumptions are employed in constructing each particular exchange theory. Figure 9–1 presents a diagram of some of the major current substantive interests to which exchange theories have been applied, and in some cases, the name of an investigator whose work is representative of a particular area.

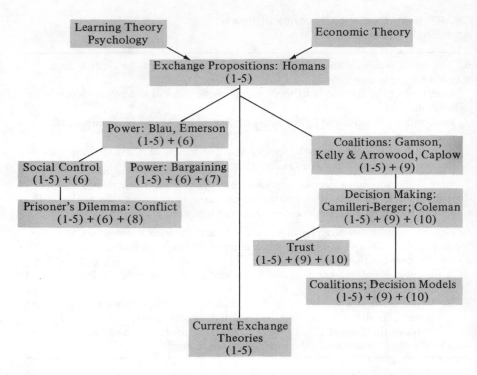

FIGURE 9–1 Intellectual lineage of exchange theories

The original set of ideas Homans used in constructing his version of exchange theory come from behavioral (learning) psychology and from economic theories. These are indicated at the top. Homans' basic version of exchange theory relies upon the first five meta-theoretical assumptions, as is indicated by numbers in the box. Current versions of exchange theory such as Emerson's 1972 theory and Homans' 1974 revision of his theory still rely upon this same set of meta-theoretical assumptions (at bottom). Applying exchange theory to various power phenomena (some of which will be studied in Chap. 10) requires the additional power meta-theoretical assumptions. Similarly, applying exchange theories to various studies of coalition formation and decision making requires adding meta-theoretical assumptions 9 and 10 to the basic set. The same is true of exchange theories of conflict, trust, social control, coalition formation and decision making.

The overview of contemporary exchange theories provided in Fig. 9–1 should be considered only a suggestive guide. There is, of course, no guarantee that the intellectual history of a particular interest will follow in actuality as neatly as it appears to in the diagram, and certainly there are connections between various bodies of researches that are not adequately indicated in the diagram. However so long as one does not expect too strict a correspondence between actuality and its representation, Fig. 9–1 should be helpful in indicating the "place" of topics to be examined in Chaps. 10 and 11.

10 Exchange Research I: Social Interaction

Introduction

In this chapter and the following one, we examine several of the more recent studies that investigate substantive topics from the exchange point of view. Topics range widely across interpersonal behavior: collective decisions, panics and social control, power, trust, individual choice behavior, and coalition formation. This is by no means a complete list. However each topic is important in its own right, each has received empirical and theoretical attention so that we know at least some of the answers as to how and why individuals behave as they do in the particular setting, and each topic illustrates a different adaptation and extension of the basic exchange meta-theory described in Chap. 9. Topics in this chapter are less complex theoretically than those in Chap. 11, but are just as interesting substantively and empirically.

Because each of these settings will be analyzed from an exchange point of view, we assume that individuals' behaviors may be explained or predicted as direct results of their attempts to maximize perceived net gain. The primary tasks of the theorist are to determine the relevant rewards and costs available in each situation, and then to describe as precisely as possible the manner in which individuals attempt to maximize the former and minimize the latter. As we shall see, discovering just what the potential rewards are in a situation is not always a simple matter. Sometimes the rewards are not immediately obvious to the observer, and sometimes even the subjects of an experiment cannot easily tell him the rewards to which they respond. In every application to be discussed, it will be helpful to look for the basic assumptions that individuals seek to maximize rewards (sometimes called "gains"), and to remember that the principal goal of the theorists is to isolate the relevant rewards in each specific situation.

Social Power

One of the simplest and most direct applications of exchange ideas—as well as an application of great intrinsic interest—has been to situations in which social power is exercised. The word *power* is given many different meanings in sociology and psychology: control over the means of production, ability to control votes, influence over the outcome of events, and strength of will enabling the powerful person to guide his own and others' lives. All these meanings have been used by one or another person concerned with power.

Most broadly, power always seems to connote an ability to influence one or more persons to do the will of another person or another group. Essential elements for us to speak of power relationships are: (1) that influence is exerted; (2) that the influence is consciously desired and directed by the powerful individual or group; and (3) that the primary motive of the powerful person is for his own gain. Element 1 is needed to distinguish power situations from situations in which individuals independently engage in the same or similar actions (such as in conformity behavior or coalition formation). Element 2 helps to distinguish power situations from accidental or unintended influence, such as imitation or status-related influence. Element 3 distinguishes power situations from cases in which the good of everybody is at stake, such as behavior regulated by laws.

Within these limits, many explicit definitions of power have been offered, none of them perfectly satisfactory. To me the feeling, if not the exact meaning, of social power is conveyed in the following rather imprecise statement from the German sociologist Max Weber:

> Power is the ability of one individual or group to influence a second individual or group to do something which the second would not otherwise have done.

The definition is not perfectly satisfactory, of course, because in any given situation it may be impossible to be certain what this second individual or group "would have done" if not influenced. Sometimes it is relatively clear, but often it is not. Still, as a working definition, this conveys most elements of what we mean by the term power.

A very useful way to approach the study of power phenomena is through the perspective of exchange theories. Why is one individual able to influence another? It is because the second individual *allows* himself to be influenced. And the only reason why someone would allow himself to be influenced, according to an exchange theorist, is because he perceives it is in his own best interest. In other words, people allow themselves to be influenced when they believe that they can maximize their own rewards (or minimize their own costs) in this fashion. Thus the motivation for allowing someone to exert power is the same as the motivation for wanting to exert power. According to the exchange viewpoint, both the more powerful and the less powerful actors in a power relationship respond to a desire to maximize their own personal gain.

The basic principle therefore is that people can be influenced by controlling their rewards and costs in a situation. How do you get someone to do something you want him to do? You arrange things so that the desired action is in his own best interest—or at least, you make him *think* it is in is his own best interest to do what you want. Emerson (1962) has analyzed social power phenomena in this way, using the notion of *dependency* among individuals. If individual A is dependent upon individual B for something, then A will probably let B exert influence over him in order to obtain that thing. To state the relationship precisely:

$$P_{A>B} = D_{B>A}$$

The power of A over B equals dependency of B upon A.

Linking power and dependency is a very interesting idea, one which has considerable intuitive appeal. We can all think of cases in which Emerson's formulation describes perfectly an interpersonal relationship. More importantly, the formulation begins to give us a general way to analyze and understand power phenomena. Power is exercised for the gain of the powerful person or group. But it also is exercised because of gains accruing to the less powerful individual or group. People *allow* others to exert influence over them because (they perceive) it is in their own best interest to do so. There is no reason that a person has to perform an action in a power situation. The powerful person does not say "You must do X"; but rather, "You must do X *if you want reward R.*"

If a person is dependent upon another for something he wants very much, then the possessor of that commodity has great power over the person who wants it. To maximize power, the reward R should be something of high value. What's more, it should be something that, once given, is rapidly consumed and needs to be replaced. The ideal power situation (for the powerful) is to be the controller of a rare, highly valued, and very short-lived good. Not only is the less powerful individual especially eager to get such a reward, but once he gets it, he uses it up and will need it again. Such things as money, sex, food, and addicting drugs all share these properties. Being the sole source of another individual's addicting drug, for instance, would be expected to give a great amount of power over him. Many romantic entanglements which seem anything but romantic become more understandable when we recognize that love and sex are relatively scarce, highly desired by most people, and once given, they are wanted again in a very short time.

These fairly straightforward ideas on power are directly tested in an exchange experiment by Crosbie. Crosbie formulated the following three hypotheses:

1. The greater the frequency with which Other rewards Ego for compliance, the greater the probability that Ego will comply with Other's directives.

2. The greater the magnitude of reward which Ego receives from Other for compliance, the greater the probability that Ego will comply with Other's directives.

3. The greater the accumulation of the reward which Ego receives from Other for compliance, the less the probability that Ego will comply with Other's directives.

Compare these three hypotheses with Homans' propositions 1, 3, and 4, respectively, in Chap. 9. They are virtual corollaries of the propositions on reward frequency, reward value, and satiation.

The hypotheses were tested in an experiment in which pairs of subjects, college students, bargained over choices of a series of *payoff matrices*. Each subject was given a booklet containing a series of matrices, one matrix on a page for every trial of the experiment. One member of every pair was a confederate, and his instructions were to allow the subjects to choose the row (1 or 2) of the matrix he preferred, and then, on critical trials, to try to induce him to change his choice. The cells of the matrix contained monetary payoffs available to each of the subjects on each trial. Figure 10–1 shows a sample matrix along with instructions to the confederate. Notice that, on this trial, if the subject allows the confederate to influence him, the subject will lose eight cents. This is typical of all payoff matrices in Crosbie's experiment: allowing the confederate to exert power would entail a small monetary loss.

The confederate attempted to exert influence over the subject's choice by offering him a reward. Money would not be a suitable reward, because of what economists call constant high marginal utility; that is, most people's satiation point for money is extremely high. Most people will happily accept virtually any amount of money and still seek more. (Incidentally, it is interesting to note that money is one of very few rewards for which this is true. At least within a short period of time it is not true of drugs or sex, for instance—not for most of us, anyway.) One of the goals of Crosbie's experiment was to observe the phenomenon of satiation and the consequences of satiation upon the ability of an individual to exert power (see his hypothesis 3). Therefore Crosbie used a more practical reward. The confederate was given a stack of notebooks of the kind used to take notes in class lectures and readings. Presumably notebooks are very useful and hence valuable to students up to a point, but nobody wishes to corner the market in them.

The three independent variables are *amount of reward, frequency of reward,* and *accumulation of reward.* Varying the first two of these gives three conditions: (1) High reward, high frequency (HR/HF). In this con-

Subject's Matrix			Confederate's Instructions

Subject's Matrix

Column

		A	B
Row	1	19¢	10¢
	2	11¢	14¢

Confederate's Instructions

Initial choice: column A

Contingency:

If he chooses row 1, ask him to change to row 2.

If he chooses row 2, don't attempt to change him.

FIGURE 10–1 Sample matrix, power experiment. (From Crosbie, 1972, p. 212.)

dition the confederate gave the subject a note reading, "I'd like you to change to row _____. If you do, I'll give you two notebooks." (2) Low reward, high frequency (LR/HF). In this condition the confederate's note read "I'd like you to change to row _____. If you do, I'll give you a notebook." (3) Low reward, low frequency (LR/LF). In this condition the confederate's note read "I'd like you to change to row _____. If you do, I may give you a notebook." (And about half the time in condition 3, he actually did reward a successful power attempt with a notebook.) The possible HR/LF condition was not run, perhaps because Crosbie felt it was less interesting than the first three.

Support for hypothesis (1) requires that the confederate be able to exercise power more frequently in condition 2 than in condition 3. Support for hypothesis (2) requires that the confederate be able to exert power more frequently in condition 1 than in condition 2. And support for hypothesis (3) requires that in all conditions, the confederate become progressively less able to exert power over the subject as a function of the amount of rewards (notebooks) the subject already possesses.

Figure 10–2 shows the proportion of times the confederate was able to exert power over subjects in each of these conditions. In support of hypothesis (1), the proportion of successful power attempts was higher in the LR/HF condition than in the LR/LF condition. In support of hypothesis (2), the proportion of successful power attempts was higher in the HR/HF condition than in the LR/HF condition. In support of hypothesis (3), in all three conditions, the curve representing proportion of successful attempts to exert power shows a general decline through time.

Crosbie's experiment provides a direct test of Emerson's exchange theory

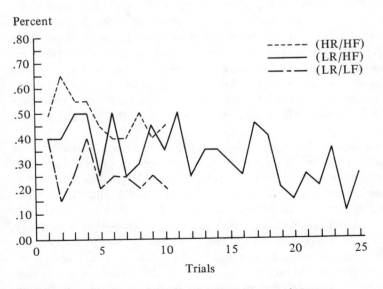

FIGURE 10–2 Proportion of successful reward power attempts. (From Crosbie, 1972, p. 213.)

interpretation of power relationships, with confirmatory results. The greater the reward or the more frequently the reward is made available, the greater the proportion of successful power attempts. Furthermore using a reward (such as notebooks) for which the satiation point is reasonably low, we can observe the predicted decline in power as a direct function of past amounts of reward distribution. Because of the way in which Crosbie constructed his experimental hypotheses, the empirical confirmation applies not only to situations in which power is exerted, but quite directly also to Homans' more general propositions about human exchanges.

What about situations in which the powerful person is able to punish the less powerful for noncompliance? In terms of exchange theory, punishments (losses) are the opposite of rewards (gains), and thus we would expect them to function in an opposite manner; that is, while rewards are quite effective at inducing compliance at first with satiation setting in after awhile, punishments would be relatively ineffective at first until the total loss becomes significant to the individual. Thus we would expect punishments to be increasingly effective through time, at least up to the limiting point where punishments impair the effectiveness of the organism to respond.

Incidentally, behavioral psychologists point out that punishment of unwanted acts seldom is effective for producing an enduring change in an individual's behavior. The reason is not that punishments and rewards behave differently in learning theory or in exchange theory; they don't. In both theories, they behave as exact complements of each other. In fact there is some evidence that punishment is a more efficient way to change behavior than reward. But remember that theories speak of relatively "pure" situations, where the number of independent variables is small. In social situations several alternative actions usually all offer rewards. A behavioral psychologist would say that whatever the unwanted behavior is, it must be providing some gratification (reward) to the individual or else he would not persist in it. While it may be possible to overcome rewards from the behavior by massive punishment for a short time and thus to suppress the behavior, as soon as punishment is withdrawn the rewarding aspects of the behavior will reassert themselves and the individual will begin it again.

As a simple example, imagine a child engaging in the unwanted (from his parents' point of view) behavior of drawing pictures on the wall. The drawing constitutes a reward of some sort. Perhaps it provides gratifying outlet for artistic impulses, or it is rewarding because it allows the child to express hostility towards his parents' authority. It is possible to overcome this reward with a massive punishment such as a spanking—that is, to make the punishments for the act exceed the rewards—but as soon as the punishment stops, the child is likely to respond to the rewards of the act again. Whatever was rewarding about drawing on the wall before the spanking is still rewarding after it. To change behavior in this way, the punishment is only the first step, and it is not sufficient by itself. The second step is to provide the child equivalent rewards from some approved behavior—such as buying him a painting kit, if the reward was artistic expression, or finding some better way for him to express rebellion against parental authority. Punishment can only suppress behavior for a short time. To effect an enduring *change,* some alternative behavior must be found which is just as rewarding as the previous behavior was. For the same reason, hotels—which do not want their customers to use the towels to shine shoes—provide little shoe-shining cloths. A process similar to this one may operate in the case of an adult who steals money from stores or homes: the behavior can be suppressed temporarily by a punishment such as jail, but it is likely to recur when punishment is withdrawn.

However in power situations we sometimes find cases where an individual or a group is in a position consistently to administer punishment to another individual or group. Certain political structures such as absolute monarchies, and certain arrangements such as exist in the military and in some "total institutions" permit constant administration of punishments. When this is the case, we would expect punishment to operate just the opposite way from reward in producing compliance.

Crosbie conducted a condition of his experiment in which the confederate was given what we might call *coercive power* over the subject. In this condition the subject began the experiment with a stack of the notebooks, but the confederate was able to take one notebook away for noncompliance on any trial. As we expected, the successful exertion of power increases rather markedly (from about 35 percent on the first trials to around 60 percent by the 25th trial), and the increase is more rapid towards the end of trials, as the subject's supply of notebooks becomes exhausted.

What options are available to an individual who finds himself dependent upon another, and hence, in the less powerful position, if he finds this arrangement unsatisfactory? From the exchange analysis it seems that he has several possible ways which will help to reduce a power *imbalance* between actors, since we are all a little bit dependent upon everyone else we meet. Emerson's analysis suggests four possible strategies.

First and probably least satisfactory, the less powerful person may conclude the commodity just isn't worth it and decide to do without. Whatever it is the more powerful person is supplying, the costs in terms of self-respect or in terms of what he is asked to do are too high. This alternative is not particularly satisfactory in most cases, however, and it is likely to be employed only as a last resort. If the commodity weren't desirable, the person never would have gotten into the power relationship in the first place.

Love affairs in which power–dependence figure prominently illustrate both the resistance of people to "do without" and sometimes, their reaching a conclusion that "it just isn't worth it." And even in enduring love affairs, tastes change. What seemed a very valuable commodity once upon a time now seems less desirable; this change by itself will reduce power imbalance and require some changes in the relationship. Another possibility within this general category is that the less powerful individual can find a substitute for the highly valuable commodity upon which the power relationship depends. Thus it may be possible to reduce the power of the heroin supplier by deciding that you really prefer methadone. (This is not a perfectly satisfactory solution to the problem of dependency, however, since methadone is probably more addicting than heroin. It is a question of *to whom* the addict wishes to be dependent.)

Second, what is probably the most common method to reduce a power imbalance is to seek alternative sources of the commodity. In a society such as ours it very rarely happens that only one person has what the less powerful person wants, and it may well be possible to "purchase" the commodity elsewhere more cheaply. We implicitly use this principle all the time when we consciously try to produce power imbalances. Animal trainers usually insist that they must work with the animal alone during the training period, since the rewards they have to offer—affection and food, for instance—must be available only from them for the training to be successful. If the owner is allowed on the scene, he is likely to give his pet affection unconditionally, rather than giving it only upon successful performance of some trick. I think this is also one reason why parents are discouraged from visiting their children at kindergarten.

Whatever the reward that is the basis of power imbalance, it can probably be got elsewhere. What is surprising is just how long it takes most people to realize this, once they become aware that they are in an unsatisfactory power imbalance. An exchange theorist would tell us, however, that eventually most people will come to realize where the commodities can be had for the lowest costs, and when they do, specific power imbalances will be reduced or eliminated.

One consequence of seeking alternative sources of the desired commodities is that wherever they are to be had, the individual seeking them will become partially dependent upon the new suppliers. This fact in turn has two consequences. First, it means that for most of us, power–dependency relationships will tend to form with a fairly large number of other individuals, since we will choose many others as suppliers of the goods we need and want. For most people it is not wise to get everything from one other person, since this would make us extremely dependent upon—and therefore subject to the power of—him. Better to give a large number of others each a little power, so that we can employ strategy (1) above occasionally if necessary. Second, the interrelationship of power and dependence means that if an individual wishes to be truly powerful himself, he must control the suppliers of the goods he needs in order to avoid becoming dependent upon any one of them. Kings, especially in medieval times, used such a strategy for their material needs. (A myth persists that this strategy is not satisfactory for love needs.)

The third power-balancing strategy is to employ some coercive force to ensure that one's needs are met. Because governments are extremely dependent upon the domestic suppliers of certain goods (war equipment such as tanks and aircrafts, petroleum fuels, electricity, water), we might expect that the government would be subject to the power of officials of the companies supplying these goods. Of course it is not, since the government can call upon outside coercion to force the suppliers to produce what the government needs. The coercive force probably derives from a power–dependency relationship as well, however. Governments in Central and South America occasionally are reminded that they depend upon the army for the coercive force they can exert upon their citizens and manufacturing companies. Power–dependency relations between countries probably work in the same basic way as they do between a government and its domestic suppliers. However, as the oil-producing countries know, coercive force is less likely to be used in this case.

The possibility of coercive force may lead to an interesting phenomenon known as coalition formation (of which we have more to say later). By himself, a single employee has virtually no power over his company, since the company is not dependent upon him for anything. However if employees collectively organize and strike, it becomes apparent that the company is dependent upon the collective group of them. And hence, a union can exert some power over a company. This possibility, and the fact that it is recognized, often will lead to formation of social relationships between individuals subject to a common powerful individual's will.

The fourth power balancing operation is most interesting of all, because it is the most subtle. The relative power somebody has over you can be reduced if you can gain some power over him. How do you do this? Quite simply by beginning to give him something he wants or needs. If he recognizes the value of what you supply—or, what is the same thing, if he *gets* to like it—then he becomes somewhat dependent upon you for it.

It is a rare relationship when the less powerful person cannot think of *something* to give the more powerful. Sometimes it is simply a case of recognizing what you already are giving him and threatening to withhold it. Lysistrata, who gave us the phrase, "Make love, not war," about 3000 years ago, ended a war by getting Greek wives to withhold sexual favors from their husbands until they stopped fighting. Even in the most extreme case where the less powerful person is hard put to find anything of value he could give the more powerful, there is an out. Remember that social approval is a powerful reward. Status is probably even more powerful. Anyone can begin to grant the more powerful person esteem, respect (or at least flattery), and status—and then threaten to withhold it. Perhaps I need not add that students learned long ago how effective a little flattery is in reducing the power imbalance between themselves and their professors.

If none of these four power balancing options is available to the individual, then we say that he is subject to *absolute power*. But absolute power exists very rarely outside of the laboratory. Most of us have access to one or more power balancing option most of the time. This suggests that, so long as people would prefer not to be in the dependent position, power relationships will tend to be relatively unstable. What a person wants, he is willing to give up some power to get. But he will escape from any dependent relationship eventually if a better "deal" becomes available. The forming, and the reforming, of power–dependence relationships are universal occurrences in an open society.

Whether people invariably would prefer to minimize their dependencies is another question, one which has not yet received systematic investigation. My own suspicion is that they would not always; sometimes it is desirable to give someone else power over your actions. One of the main points of Erich Fromm's *Escape From Freedom* is that freedom always entails making choices, and too much freedom means making too many choices and is bewildering. People often seek to avoid too many choices by giving up some of their freedom. I find Fromm's arguments persuasive and can think of many instances of just that phenomenon. What we do not know in any clear way is just when, *under what circumstances,* people will want to surrender their freedom. When is it desirable to be dependent and let others control our lives? What sorts of decisions do people prefer not to make for themselves?

Trust and Collective Decisions

The concept *trust* figures importantly in nearly every human interaction. What determines when people will trust each other? Which people, or what *kinds* of people, are most likely to be trusted in a given situation? What structural features of situations promote trust between actors, and which structural features act to decrease the probability that trust will develop or be maintained? Obviously these are very general questions, and we will have to focus them somewhat before we can investigate them rigorously. Part of the answers to these questions will come in the next two sections as well as in this section, for interpersonal trust is a complex phenomenon. However here we begin our investigation with an attempt to specify general conditions for trust situations, and within those conditions, to specify some determinants and consequences of interpersonal trust.

Social situations in which trust figures importantly have been analyzed by Deutsch, Gamson, Knox and Kee, and many others. Trust situations seem to be characterized by several key features. Most obviously we speak of one actor trusting another only in cases where the first actor can potentially lose something from his trust. It is absurd to say that the warden of a maximum security jail "trusts" his prisoners not to try to escape, for under most circumstances, the warden could not possibly lose such a bet. Conversely in minimum security institutions, or when a prisoner is out on parole, it becomes sensible to talk of trusting him not to escape. If the prisoner does decide to escape, in cases where he can, the warden has lost his bet. He suffers the indignity and the professional censure that sometimes result from trusting. Notice that if the negative consequences of betrayal are relatively minor for the person betrayed, he usually finds it easier to trust. If the bank accidentally overpays you $1.00 and you report this to them, they probably will trust you for a few days until you return the money. If the amount were $5000, they would probably demand *immediate* repayment.

A second general feature of trust situations is that the actor being trusted must have some freedom to act in a "trustworthy" manner or not. We do not say that the Army trusts an enlisted man to perform his duties, since he has virtually no say in the matter. I used to have a fifth grade teacher who told her class she trusted us to do our assignments, and it always seemed like a misuse of the term. We had almost no freedom to be untrustworthy (as she apparently would use the term), and even if we were, the negative consequences *to her* would be nil.

The third general feature of trust situations is that the actors involved have some interrelated fate; what one does will affect the fortunes of the other. Whether the prisoner escapes affects not only his own future, but less directly, that of the warden: if too many prisoners escape, the warden will be out of a job. But notice too that the warden's decision to trust the prisoner also affects the prisoner's future: he gains some freedom to control his future, and also he gains release from his jail cell. A more precise way to express this intertwining of fates is to say that trust situations are marked by *joint outcomes* for the actors involved. (Figure 10–1 is a *joint outcome matrix* showing gains or *payoffs* to each actor, depending on the behavior of both actors.) The joint outcomes feature of trust situations is a bit more complicated than it may appear at first, but it will turn out to be important for us to understand just how joint outcomes are perceived by the actors.

It may already be apparent to you that our analysis of trust situations will focus upon the rewards and costs of various outcomes. What does each actor get out of trusting or of refusing to trust? When we analyze trust situations in this way, we can use the general ideas of the exchange metatheory to predict that individuals will trust others when they think it is in their own best interest to do so. People trust when they believe that trusting will help them to maximize their gains and minimize their costs. Then the theoretical task becomes to describe when and why—under what circumstances—individuals will think it is in their interest to trust. The second task is to specify consequences of trust: what abstract behavioral effects will we see if one person decides to trust another? Recently, Conviser reported an experiment for which he constructed and tested a formal theory of trusting behavior. Conviser's ideas constitute the basis for our analysis here.

According to Conviser's analysis, there are three general types of situations in which trust figures importantly, and the types of situations are defined by actors' perceptions of desired outcomes. Situations of type 1 are characterized by perceived dissensus on outcomes: the individual believes that Other's first choice outcome is different from his own, as in our warden–prisoner example. Trust is least likely in situations of type 1, but there are instances of type 1 situations in which some trusting behavior appears.

In type 2 situations, actors believe that they have shared goals; that is, they both desire the same outcome. Here we expect trust to be most likely of the 3 situations, since the person who trusts believes that Other wants the same outcome as he himself does.

Situations of type 3 are those in which the individual *does not know* whether he and Other share a joint desired outcome. For example, suppose you are very pressed for time and are about to hand in the last problem set, which will determine your grade in Physics. An acquaintance who is also in the class tells you he is going to drive over with his own problem set and offers to take yours along with him. It may not be altogether clear to you that he desires the same outcome as you do (namely, getting your problem set in on time) in this situation, so accepting his apparently kind offer also involves a strong element of trust. Can we find the important determinants of trusting or not trusting in type 3 situations?

In situations of type 2, we expect actors to be prepared to trust others, although they will still exercise some discretion in deciding whom and when to trust. Imagine for example, a sick person faced with a physician whom he believes to be extremely incompetent. Presumably he prefers not to trust such a physician, even though he believes he sincerely wants to help him get well. In type 2 situations, what determines likelihood of trusting is perceived ability to achieve the shared goal. Or, if the person has a choice of more than one person to trust—such as among two physicians—he is more likely to trust the one he thinks is more competent. In other words, so long as the individual believes the other wants the same outcome as he himself does, the probability of trust is a direct function of perceived ability to achieve that goal.

In situations of type 1, we might at first expect that trust would be highly unlikely. After all if an actor knows that his interests and the other person's are opposed, why should he trust him? But we know that trust does occur in precisely this sort of situation, and the question then is just what it is that produces trust when actors' interests differ. The major determinant seems to be an actor's perceived ability to reward or punish the potential trusted actor in the future. If interaction between actors will continue for some time—as, for example, it usually will between friends or members of the same family or social group—then trust is relatively more likely than if interaction will not persist.

One of the major theories of social control (LaPiere's) asserts that it is just this sort of mechanism in society that usually insures that people will not simply pursue their own selfish ends. In a way what Lapiere says is that people are trustworthy even in cases where they may desire to be selfish because they know that they can be ostracized in the future. Hobbes said much the same thing in 1651. His term was *enlightened self-interest;* that is, self-interest that takes account of possible future rewards and costs.

In situations of type 1, then, we expect to see more trusting behavior when the potential truster knows that interaction will continue for some time than when individuals are about to part company. In accord with this principle, most high schools do not finally release their students for the summer until the student presents some written certification that he has turned in all Library books, gym equipment, and so on. During the year, the school administration may be a bit more trusting. An example of a similar process in politics is vote-trading, or logrolling, in which legislators trade their votes on issues where they have little interest for others' votes on issues of vital importance to them. (See references in Chap. 9 to Coleman's analyses of logrolling and other collective decision-making.)

In type 3 situations it is impossible for the individual to behave rationally

—that is, to seek to maximize his gains—until he can get some notion whether Other desires the same outcomes as he himself does. Put another way, in a type 3 situation it is impossible for an actor to act rationally unless it can be resolved into either a type 1 or a type 2 situation. This means that his task is to try to figure out whether or not he and Other share a desired outcome. The most reliable indicator available to an actor in a type 3 situation is past behavior of Other: the more often in the past Other has chosen an outcome desired by Person, the more likely is Person to believe that the situation is really one of type 2. If you have trusted someone to turn in your Physics problem sets all semester and he has always done so, you are more likely to believe he really shares a joint goal with you than if he has not always turned yours in on time. (Incidentally, this analysis also suggests why the strategy of being reliable all semester and saving up your treachery for the final problem set can be so successful!)[1]

These analyses were tested in 3 conditions of an experiment designed to produce each of the 3 types of situations. In all conditions, pairs of subjects were asked to make a series of choices, and before each choice, to decide whether to let Other make the choice for both of them (the operationalization of trusting). Condition 2 is simplest, so I will describe it first.

In condition 2, subjects were told that one of them possessed much greater ability (or control potential). The prediction, since they both desired the same outcome, was that the person with greater ability would be trusted to make group decisions more often. Table 10–1 shows the proportion of trusting choices by each subject. The high ability actor was trusted more often; about four times as often, in fact.

In condition 1, interests of subjects were opposed. Roughly, if one of them got points, the other lost. The variable of interest here is future interaction. Half the subjects were told they would have a later meeting to discuss how they acted. We would expect these subjects to be more trusting, since they could "get back" later, if need be. Table 10–2 shows that this

TABLE 10–1 Proportion of Trusting Choices:
Condition 2

	Ss ABILITY	N	PROPORTION
	High	21	.12
	Low	19	.50

From "Toward A Theory of Interpersonal Trust," by Richard H. Conviser. Reprinted from *Pacific Sociological Review* Vol. 16, No. 3 (July 1973) p. 391 by permission of the Publisher, Sage Publications, Inc.

---

[1] In racially integrated city councils, a similar phenomenon may be observed. Councilmen of both races frequently view each other with suspicion at first (indicating they perceive a type 3 situation). Later, if they have seen members of the other race vote the same as themselves, trust develops; the situation has resolved into a type 2 situation. On the other hand, if dissimilarity of votes convinces members they are really in a type 1 situation, trust is extremely unlikely and members insist on binding, written agreements for every little detail.

TABLE 10–2   Proportion of Trusting Choices:
Condition I

CONDITION	N	PROPORTION
No future interaction	8	.16
Future interaction	12	.35

(From Conviser, 1973.)

prediction also was sustained. The "future interaction" manipulation produced more than twice as much trusting as the "no future interaction" condition.

In condition 3 subjects were not told whether their interests were the same. But after every block of 10 trials they were told how often they had made similar choices in the past. Agreement was predicted to produce future trusting; disagreement, to produce lack of trust. Table 10–3 shows that this prediction also was sustained. Also in this condition, the data show a steady increase in differentiation of trust, in the direction expected, as a function of time.

TABLE 10–3   Proportion of Trusting Choices:
Condition 3

CHOICE AGREEMENT	PROPORTION *
low	.44
high	.65

* Trials 11–40 only
(From Conviser, 1973.)

Coalition Formation

During the last quarter of the 19th century and the early years of the 20th, Georg Simmel was writing in Germany about conflict, affiliation, and the significance of numbers for social life. Translations of his work began to appear in this country around the turn of the century, but his writings have never attained the degree of influence the quality of his insights and the breadth of his interests deserve. In addition to being one of our most readable sociologists, Simmel provides numerous insights into forms of social life. Because his interest was in abstract social structures and social behavior, the writing is as relevant to groups in our society as it was in his. It would be inappropriate to begin the study of coalitions without tracing interest in the problem and partial solutions to this great thinker.

External threat—whether directed against nations or individuals—produces a recognition of the benefits of forming an alliance with others similar to oneself. The major purpose of the alliance, from an exchange perspective, is to prevent (or to minimize) costs being incurred to the external enemy. At least every two years one or another major figure in the Democratic Party will make a public plea to the various factions to submerge their hostilities (usually called "differences of opinion") and to form an alliance against the external threat Republicans. If rewards are obtainable from the alliance at the same time (such as electing Democrats), so much the better.

For producing close, strong, primary ties, the *dyad* (two members) is ideal. Two can share a degree of intimacy and an understanding that is impossible in any larger group. Each knows the other almost as completely as he knows himself. Each needs the other as much as it is possible to need another person. And each member of the dyad is essential to the social unit: if one member withdraws, the dyad no longer exists. An exchange theorist would point out that each member of a dyad lacks alternative sources for whatever social rewards the other gives him; either these rewards come from the one partner, or they come not at all.

In a *triad* (three members) or larger group, members are somewhat re-placeable: a social unit still exists even if one member withdraws. One simple illustration of this fact is groups of entertainers. If one member of a dyad decides to go out on his own or to retire it becomes impossible to refer to the group anymore; for example, Simon and Garfunkel, Jan and Dean, Rowan and Martin all disappeared in this way. Larger groups are more enduring: The Kingston Trio, The Rolling Stones, Three Dog Night (7 members) all survived replacement of one or more members without changing the basic character of the group. The character of the group goes beyond persistence or nonpersistence of the names. Paul Simon doesn't sound much like Simon and Garfunkel used to sound—which illustrates the essential character of both members of a dyad. By contrast, the current *Supremes* sound to me exactly like the current *Diana Ross*, and both sound exactly like the old *Diana Ross and the Supremes*—the reason is, of course, persistence of the triad even when individual members are replaced.

A social unit of three persons or three nations, a triad, is interesting for another reason: it tends, writes Simmel, towards instability and conflict. The natural tendency within a triad is for two members to align themselves against the third. The third person may become a scapegoat, or he may simply be ostracized from an intimacy developing between the other two. Thus the natural tendency of a triad is to decompose into a dyad and an outsider. Why this happens, under what circumstances it is more or less likely to happen, and what determines which member will be the outsider and which will align themselves, constitute the study of coalition formation.

My own first contact with Simmel was in an introductory sociology class, taken at the end of freshman year of college just before I moved into a different dorm. The new dorm put three persons into two rooms—a perfect situation to test Simmel's prediction that a triad tends to decompose into two against one. People often rebel against the idea that their own behavior is predictable—especially by a man who has been dead for decades!—and I remember resolving that our roommate situation would not deteriorate in this way. I told several of my friends in other residences about this particular idea, and they expressed similar determination. The next year we recalled our resolve and compared experiences. The decomposition occurred in every case—it was easy to specify who was the "outcast"—and it took little more than a month for any of the triads to break down.

This anecdote, like much of Simmel's writing, is suggestive. I could not specify just why these groups decomposed, nor does Simmel offer explanatory propositions telling when and why it should occur. The process of coalition formation, as well as determinants of specific alliances, have been studied in an experimental situation resembling a game. The game incorporates the essential features of coalitions: (1) competition among actors, with the possibility of cooperation between two of them to the detriment of the remaining actor or actors; (2) gain in the competition the only motive for coalition formation (as opposed to things like interpersonal attraction); (3) no norms or other reasons for any coalition to endure beyond the point of its winning—no permanent alliances.

The Basic Coalition Experimental Situation

Vinacke and Arkoff developed the basic situation for studying coalitions, and report the earliest large body of data from this situation. The question is not whether coalitions will form; formation is explicitly encouraged. The question is which coalitions of all those possible will form; and more generally, what principles will allow prediction of likely coalitions under given conditions of the game.

The experiment has subjects play a modified version of pachisi. This is a board game in which each player tries to move his piece through a route of some 67 squares from start to finish before others. Moves are determined by roll of a die, and in the experimental version of the game, each player moves on every roll. Players are assigned "weights" at the start of each game, and each moves a number of squares determined by the die times his weight. For example in a game with three players with weights 3–2–2, if the die roll showed 2, the first player would move 6 spaces (2×3), and the second and third would each move 4 spaces (2×2). The number of players of a game varies from 2 to about 5, but for most studies, it is limited to 3. Winning—reaching "finish" before other players—has some specified gain associated with it. In most cases the prize is 100 points, though of course sometimes the number varies and sometimes points are convertible to money.

There is one other rule: any two players may agree to form a coalition, which must last throughout that game. A coalition has a weight equal to the sum of its members. Therefore if a coalition is formed, on every roll of the die *both* members of the coalition will move *the sum* of their individual weights times the die. In our example a coalition between members with weights 2 each would mean both of them could move four times the die on every throw. Members of a winning coalition decide among themselves how to divide their winnings. Almost always this is decided by bargaining before coalitions are formed. For example, player 3 here might say to player 2, "I'll give you 40 of the 100 points if you form a coalition with me." Player 2 would then, assuming he is sensible, ask the other player 2, "How many points would you let me have if I formed a coalition with you?"

You may have anticipated the next point. In most cases the games are never played, since the winner is determined either by the individual weights or by any coalition that forms. If no coalition forms in a 3–2–2 game, 3 will win. If a 2–2 coalition forms, it will win since both members move four on every roll of the die. (Of course a 3–1–1 game is uninteresting, since coalitions are unlikely. Why?) Once subjects realize that the play is unnecessary, they focus their attention on coalition forming and upon bargaining how to divide any winnings; in other words, upon the same things that are of interest to the researchers.

There are eight types of games studied in 3-person coalition studies, four of which are most interesting (types 1, 2, 3 and 5 in Table 10–4). They are defined by the initial weights of the players. Table 10–4 shows possible types of games for coalition experiments, with both the formal properties of each weight distribution and the numerical weights used. Types 1–6 were produced for the Vinacke-Arkoff experiments; types 7 and 8 have not been studied so extensively. These types form the basis for much of our future discussion of coalition studies. You should satisfy yourself that the numerical weights do indeed meet the formal properties for each type. What sort of coalition would you expect to form most frequently in each case? What sort of implicit principles do you use in deciding which coalitions are most likely? We shall return to these issues presently.

Weights assigned to players at the start of the game clearly produce an inequality among them, and—although as we shall see this is not true in every sense—the inequality seems to be one of power differences. Certainly if no coalition forms, it is clear that the player with greatest weight will win. Thus it is particularly important for players given lower weights to be able to strike a bargain for a coalition. If they cannot do so, they are sure to lose the game. A player with high weight could be relatively in-

TABLE 10–4 Types of Triads for Coalition Studies

Type	Numerical Weights	Formal Properties
1	1–1–1	$A = B = C$
2	3–2–2	$A > B,\ B = C,\ A < (B + C)$
3	1–2–2	$A < B,\ B = C$
4	3–1–1	$A > (B + C),\ B = C$
5	4–3–2	$A > B > C,\ A < (B + C)$
6	4–2–1	$A > B > C,\ A > (B + C)$
7	5–3–2	$A > B > C,\ A = (B + C)$
8	4–2–2	$A = (B + C),\ B = C$

different to forming a coalition, though of course if the "smaller" players look as though they are going to team up, the "big" player must try to break them up.

If we equate weights with strength or power (an assumption we shall modify later), it is easy to think of real-life instances of the various types of games. Assuming low-power members are more eager to form coalitions than high-power members, let us consider some examples and likely outcomes.

Type 1, with all members equal, resembles a classic democratic organization, or informal friendship alliances. Since all members are equal any coalition of 2 will overrule the third member. This type well illustrates Simmel's principle that triads tend to decompose into a dyad and an outsider. But if the only purpose of the coalition is winning or controlling the third member then coalitions formed in such equal-power situations are likely to be unstable and to form and reform among members frequently. Certainly type 1 relations are not desirable in any organization such as a *team* or a committee where a stable authority structure is wanted.

Type 2, with member A superior to B and C but not to both of them together, often exists in work groups and other semiformal organizations. Because of the possibility of overruling A if B and C can agree to form a coalition, this "revolutionary" response seems relatively likely.

Type 3, with two high-power members and one low, could perhaps be found in friendship groups of children. If B and C are older or more popular than A but A continues to hang around with them, what will happen? A would probably be happy to form a coalition with either B or C, but when would either of them want to do this? Probably B or C would want a coalition with A from time to time in order to exert power over each other. A, in such cases, would have the "swing vote" capacity. This is another of Simmel's insights regarding the place of the third person (in this case, A) in a triad: any disagreement between two more powerful members (B and C) works to the advantage of the less powerful (A), since only then are his opinions important. The term is *tertius gaudens,* gains to the third party. In the last two Presidential elections, commentators have discussed the effect of Governor Wallace's supporters on deciding an election between the two major party candidates; this is a clear example of Simmel's *tertius gaudens.* (Note that when one of the major candidates is considerably more popular than the other, the "Wallace vote" becomes inconsequential. It is no longer a type 3 situation.) Another familiar example of a type 3 situation is in some families: in cases of dissension between parents (B and C), each is likely to try to get the sympathy of a child (A) who then becomes quite powerful. I used to know a boy who would move out of his parents' house and into his grandparents' when he was angry. He became very skillful at playing parents and grandparents against each other, and they competed for his company and his loyalty with ever larger presents. Clearly an exchange-theoretic situation!

Type 4 has been mentioned earlier, and you probably recognized that it is uninteresting because there is no reason for a coalition to form. Even if *B* and *C* ally themselves against *A*, they will not win. *A* has no need for any coalition, nor even a need to prevent any coalition. *A* is a very powerful person, it would seem, and this is a good social structure for ensuring stability of power relations. It is too easy to think of instances of type 4 situations, so I will just note that conscious attempts to develop enduring authority structures (as armies or business organizations) often aim to produce a type 4 situation.

Type 5 seems to be most likely to promote a "revolutionary" coalition between *B* and *C*. *A* is only slightly more powerful and could easily be overcome. We might expect that *B* would be particularly eager to form a coalition with *C*, because not only could the coalition dominate *A*, but *B* could dominate *C* in the coalition. Thus a *BC* coalition would make person *B* the most powerful in a type 5 situation.

Type 6 appears to be another good bet for a stable authority structure, with 3 levels instead of the 2 levels in type 4. Again, there is no reason for any coalition to form, because *A* is very powerful. We might expect that *B*'s best bet would be to enjoy his domination of *C*, and to submit to *A*'s domination—to become a good organization man, in other words. Taking a potential troublemaker into an organization, or "co-opting" a potential radical, is a time-tested way of dealing with him. Giving him some power within the organization, as *B* has over *C* here, usually is sufficient to ensure his selling out, or becoming loyal, depending upon your own sympathies.

Now that you have had some time to think about it, what sorts of coalitions did you expect for each of types 1 through 6? Table 10–5 shows the outcomes of 90 games in Vinacke and Arkoff's experiments. In addition to comparing outcomes to your own expectations, compare them to the previous discussion of likely outcomes in the various types of situations.

In most cases, you probably expected the types of coalitions that actually formed. For instance in type 1 we expect all coalitions to be about equally likely. *AB* and *BC* coalitions were about equally frequent, and though *AC* was less so, the difference was not statistically significant. (Note also that players are equal in type 1 situations, so the difference for *AC* coalitions must have been due to chance or to personality factors of the players, not to structural features of the situation.) In type 2 we expect *BC* coalitions to be most likely, and this is the type most often formed. In types 4 and 6,

TABLE 10–5 Outcomes of 90 Coalition Games;
Percent of Coalitions Formed

	GAME TYPE					
COALITION	1	2	3	4	5	6
AB	36	14	26	12	10	10
AC	19	13	44	11	22	14
BC	33	70	17	8	65	9
None	11	1	12	68	2	66

(Adapted from Vinacke and Arkoff, 1957.)

when we thought coalitions to be unlikely, more than two-thirds of the time no coalitions were formed. When coalitions did form in these cases, no pattern favoring one type of coalition over another is evident.

What did you expect for type 5? There are two possible lines of thought here (later we add a third: Kelley and Arrowood; and a fourth: justice), we should make explicit. The first, which we credit to Caplow (1956), is the *minimum power* theory; the second, from Gamson (1961), *minimum resource*. The minimum power theory asserts that members have two primary motivations in choosing coalition partners: First, of course, to win (which explains why people aren't likely to bother forming coalitions in types 4 and 6); and second, to maximize dominance over one's coalition partner. Dominance depends upon the difference in weights of the partners, so that in type 5, A would prefer a coalition with C to a coalition with B since A's own power relative to his coalition partner is maximized in the AC coalition. B, of course, would prefer a BC coalition to an AB coalition since he would dominate only in a BC coalition. C will be dominated in any coalition, but he would prefer a BC coalition to an AC coalition since his relative power would be somewhat higher in a BC coalition. Thus A would prefer an AC coalition, and both B and C would prefer a BC coalition; and from the minimum power theory we would predict that both types would form. (In other words the clear prediction of this theory is that AB coalitions will be less likely than either AC or BC coalitions; Table 10–5 shows that this prediction is supported.)

A minimum resource theory predicts that the smallest coalition necessary to win will form; that is, players will form coalitions only when they can win (the same as the first motive in the minimum power theory), and they will prefer the "cheapest" winning coalition. The reasoning behind this is that players are expected to bargain with each other over division of points in a winning coalition, and in their bargaining, to demand a share of points proportional to their weights. For example in a type 1 situation, players in any coalition would be expected to demand an equal split of the 100 points for winning; in a type 2 situation, player A in an AB coalition would demand a 60/40 split of points since he brings 50 percent more weight to the winning coalition. This means that in type 2 situations, B would prefer a BC coalition to an AB coalition, since in a BC coalition he could demand half the points.

Type 5 situations are the only ones in which the minimum power and the minimum resource predictions differ. We already noted that the minimum power prediction is AC, BC > AB. From the minimum resource ideas, however, we would not expect this. The reason is that C would not be equally happy forming a coalition with A or B. If he forms an AC coalition he will get only about 34 points; if he forms a BC coalition he can demand 40 points. The difference is not large, but over the long run C would prefer the BC coalition—according to the minimum resource theory. The minimum resource theory predicts BC > AB, AC. Closer examination of data in Table 10–5 shows that the minimum resource theory is *better* supported than the minimum power theory, and this conclusion is supported by statistical tests not given here.

How about this idea that players can demand points proportional to the weights they bring to a coalition? Is this a reasonable demand? Perhaps it seems so at first, since a player with more weight might seem to do more for winning than a player with less weight. But Kelley and Arrowood (1960) point out that the advantage of weight often is misleading in a coalition game. In a type 5 game with weights 4–3–2, does A really have more importance, say, than player C? The answer is *no,* but don't feel bad if you didn't see it. The reason is that in a 4–3–2 game, *any* coalition will win, and therefore, *both members of any coalition are equally important.* If C reasoned this way he would come to the conclusion that he is equally important to either A or B: both could win in a coalition with him, and both would lose if C formed a coalition with the other one. In any coalition game except types 4 and 6 (where no coalition except one including A can win), C has *pivotal power:* he can make or break a winning alliance.

Why, then, should he let A demand more points than B could for his help? The answer, according to Kelley and Arrowood, can only be that the true power relations are not obvious to players in a coalition game. If C knew the way things actually are in a type 5 game—that is, if he had gone through the sort of analysis Kelley and Arrowood did—he would not be misled by the apparent significance of weights.

To test their reasoning, Kelley and Arrowood conducted two experiments comparable to type 5 situations. We shall examine results of only their Experiment I. This was the Vinacke–Arkoff type 5, except that players were given very complete instructions about the nature of the game, emphasizing their degree of importance for winning coalitions and also emphasizing that their only concern should be with their own winnings, not with each others'. The expected effect of this instruction was to decrease the illusory significance of weights for coalition partners, making the situation resemble a type 1 game in Table 10–4.

Results of this experiment, with comparable data from the Vinacke–Arkoff experiment, are shown in Table 10–6. Note that the change in instructions, emphasizing the "true" equality of member A, has increased the proportion of coalitions including him. Presumably this is because subjects realize there is no need to grant him more than half the winnings from any coalition. And by comparing Kelly and Arrowood's first three trials to last three, we see that this equalizing effect increases with time.

Overall, Kelley and Arrowood conclude that their analyses indicate sup-

TABLE 10–6 Proportions of Various Coalitions

COALITION	VINACKE–ARKOFF [*] FIRST 3 TRIALS	KELLEY–ARROWOOD EXP. I [**]	
		FIRST 3 TRIALS	LAST 3 TRIALS
AB	10%	23%	30%
AC	22%	27%	29%
BC	66%	46%	41%

[*] weights: 4–3–2, no explanation of power
[**] weights: 4–3–2, full explanation of power
(From Kelley and Arrowood, 1965; p. 580.)

port for the idea that it is players' perceptions, including misperceptions, of the desirability of entering coalitions that determines the likelihoods of forming particular types of coalitions. This conclusion seems acceptable, though with two qualifications. First, Kelley and Arrowood emphasized to subjects that they should be only concerned with maximizing their own winnings. This instruction could partially account for the finding that subjects in their experiment I formed coalitions more nearly at random than did the Vinacke–Arkoff subjects; that is, forming coalitions at random would be expected if subjects were in fact only motivated to maximize their own winnings. As we shall see, there is reason to believe that subjects in both experiments may have had other motives as well, though probably the Kelley–Arrowood subjects were concerned only with their own winnings more often than Vinacke and Arkoff's were.

Second, it is significant that the Kelley–Arrowood experiment I did not produce a true random distribution with 33 percent of the coalitions being of each type. Their data are *closer* to random than Vinacke–Arkoff's for type 5 games so the additional information did work as expected. However the fact that they did not actually reach a random distribution (as in Vinacke–Arkoff's type 1) suggests that some other factor was still operative in determining subjects' coalition choices.

Distributive Justice in Coalition Formation: Indirect Evidence

When players of unequal weights form (winning) coalitions, they are likely to split the points in proportion to their weights. When players of equal weights form (winning) coalitions, they are very likely to split the points evenly. This phenomenon was noted by Vinacke and Arkoff, who commented that it was surprising, and was used by Gamson as a central proposition from which he developed the minimum resource theory. Now we ask why this should be true, and whether it is invariably true or whether it occurs only under certain circumstances. The reason for this phenomenon, we shall see, lies in players' ideas of justice. For the moment, let us stick with a simple interpretation of justice (the term comes from Homans' proposition 5 in Table 9–1) and say that *one concern of coalition players is to produce a fair distribution of winnings*. Each player is primarily motivated to maximize his own winnings, but we assume that this is not his only motive. He also would like to see justice served. Now the question is, "What do players think is a fair distribution of winnings?" Let us use the following working definition:

> Winnings of a player will be perceived as *fair* if (a) among players undifferentiated with respect to evaluated characteristics, winnings are approximately equal; and (b) among players who are differentiated by some evaluated characteristics, winnings are approximately proportional to the distribution of the evaluated characteristics.

Note that we are saying players usually have two separate concerns here:

maximizing personal winnings and producing a fair distribution of winnings. It is usually not possible to satisfy both goals at once, so we expect players to adopt strategies that satisfy one goal one time and the other goal the next. The overall proportion of coalitions formed, as well as the overall winnings of any player, thus will be somewhere in between what we would find if players were pursuing only one or the other of these goals.

There are several fragmentary pieces of evidence that coalition subjects are concerned with promoting a fair distribution of winnings. On the one hand, the unequal distribution of weights provides at least a minimal differentiation of players on an evaluated characteristic; thus, we would expect from part (b) of our working definition of fairness that players would try to promote a slight inequality of total winnings reflecting the unequal distribution of weights. On the other hand, the unequal distribution of weights is not a very strong reason to promote unequal winnings, since players are equated on most of their evaluated characteristics (such as diffuse status characteristics). Thus we would expect part (a) of our working definition to prevent too great an inequality in winnings. Both these effects appear in most coalition experiments.

For instance, look again at the Vinacke and Arkoff data shown in Table 10–5. Some "hopeless" coalitions formed in type 4 (3–1–1) and type 6 (4–2–1) weight distributions. Were players trying to help the low man in these cases? It wouldn't really help C, of course, but it might ease A's guilt feelings about getting too far ahead if he refused to enter any coalitions. Or it might help B's guilt feelings to offer an alliance to C and not to A. Ronald Anderson has analyzed other studies to show the same things more convincingly. Anderson provides evidence of two sorts: efforts to produce equal winnings among undifferentiated players, and efforts to produce unequal winnings among differentiated players, with the inequality of winnings reflecting the inequality among players. These two sets of evidence support, respectively, parts (a) and (b) of our definition of fairness.

The first set of data come from coalition games played using the basic experimental situation with weights 3–3–3, and were reported by Emerson (1962). Notice that a 3–3–3 game is formally equivalent to a type 1 game of Vinacke and Arkoff. The distribution of weights does not introduce any differentiation among players, and therefore our justice principle leads us to look for evidence of attempts to promote equal accumulation of winnings. Emerson's data are particularly relevant to this analysis, since, unlike most coalition studies, players were continually reminded of total winnings. Winnings of every player were posted, and the invidious terms "winner," "runner-up" and "loser" accompanied the point totals. A total of 98 games were played, and the first evidence of efforts to equalize scores is that, of the 84 times when one player was behind in total winnings, 72 times coalitions formed including that player.

Most impressive, however, is the following calculation of division of points among members to a coalition. Table 10–7 shows division of points among players when both members had equal scores, and when their scores were unequal. When partners to a coalition had equal scores, even division of points was nearly inevitable (44 times out of 46). When partners had un-

TABLE 10–7   Division of Winnings,
by Scores of Partners

	DIVISION OF POINTS	
SCORES	EVEN	UNEVEN
Equal	44	2
Unequal	26	26

(From Anderson, 1967.)

equal scores, only half the time did they divide winnings equally, and in the 26 cases of unequal division, *all 26* favored the player who was behind.

The second type of evidence, players promoting inequality of winnings, is found in a coalition experiment which does not use the basic experimental design. For seeing the effects of justice, however, the details of the design are not central. What is central is that the experimenters (Hoffman et al. 1954) attempted to differentiate one member of the triad (who was a confederate) on a relevant evaluated characteristic: intelligence. In one condition (the peer condition) subjects were told that the confederate was their equal in intelligence; in the second (nonpeer) he was described as superior to them. Table 10–8 shows the average number of points given the confederate per trial in each condition, and also the average number of points given the confederate on a trial when he was included in a coalition. In both cases the confederate was allowed to get a higher point total when described as a highly intelligent nonpeer. The finding takes on more significance when we realize that, except as it affects playing ability, intelligence is not connected with fair winnings in an objective sense. The confederate was the same in all cases, and he did not play more intelligently (or bargain for points more strongly) in the nonpeer condition. Thus the differential points given him seem to reflect part (b) of our definition of fairness: he was *given* more points when he was described as more intelligent.

TABLE 10–8   Winnings as a Function of Diffuse
Status Characteristic

POINTS	PEER	NONPEER
Per trial	1.57	2.76
Per coalition	3.51	4.15

(From Hoffman et al., 1954; and Anderson, 1967.)

Distributive Justice in Coalitions: Direct Tests

The idea that distribution of winnings, and therefore the likelihood of specific coalition formation, is affected by players' conceptions of fairness was tested directly in a series of ingenious experiments by Weil. The experimental design differs in concrete features from the basic design developed by Vinacke and Arkoff, but it incorporates the same abstract features well. Weil found that his subjects played in his design in about the same way Vinacke and Arkoff's subjects had.

What Weil eliminated was the pachisi board, since it is seldom actually used in coalition studies anyway. Triads of players were told they would each accumulate points from the throw of the die, and the first player to accumulate 50 points would win each game. Each game was worth 50¢, which would be part of their pay for participating in the study. Players were assigned weights as usual, and a coalition could be formed before any roll of the die. Players always formed a coalition long before the end of all games, usually after a single throw of the die. Players were not told which of the others had which weight in order to minimize the effect of any personal characteristics in bargaining. They only knew the weights were assigned to Player *A*, Player *B*, and Player *C*. Of course each player knew his own letter, as well as the weight assigned to him for the game. After the roll of the die, every player filled out notes on a form similar to this:

———— I make no offers.

———— I offer to form an alliance with player ——, dividing the 50¢
——¢ to me and ——¢ to him.

A coalition could be formed only when two players made reciprocal choices; when they chose each other and agreed on the division of winnings.

All games in Weil's study used either a 3-2-2 (type 2) or a 3-3-2 (similar to type 3) distribution. What is so ingenious about the design is that Weil also controlled the permissible distribution of winnings. In some cases subjects had to split the 50¢ winnings evenly (25¢/25¢), and in some cases they had to split them unevenly (30¢/20¢). Two of the experiments allowed either the 25¢/25¢ or the 30¢/20¢ split, but no other splits. Designs of the 6 experiments are shown in Table 10-9.

Since players in these experiments had no freedom to decide *how* to split the rewards (or only a little freedom in games III and VI), the only decision was *with whom* to offer to split them. From a distributive justice point of

TABLE 10-9   Weights and Agreements in Weil's Study

GAME TYPE	WEIGHTS	AGREEMENTS ALLOWED
I	3-2-2	25/25
II	3-2-2	30/20
III	3-2-2	25/25 and 30/20
IV	3-3-2	25/25
V	3-3-2	30/20
VI	3-3-2	25/25 and 30/20

(From Weil, 1970, Tables 1 and 2.)

view we would expect that the distribution of weights would differentiate players in terms of an evaluated characteristic. Thus players probably would try to see that winnings were allocated consistent with the weights of players. This was possible only by choosing partners to fit the imposed winning distribution. Table 10–10 shows proportion of coalitions of each type observed in the "no alternative" games I, II, IV, and V. The coalition expected from justice prediction is indicated by an arrow for each game. The distribution of coalitions expected on a random basis—that is, with no justice principle or other principle for predicting coalition types—is shown in column 5. In every game the majority of coalitions formed as we would expect from the justice idea, and the difference from chance distribution is considerable.

In games III, and VI players had a little freedom; they could split winnings either 25/25 or 30/20. Table 10–11 shows the outcomes for these "limited alternative" games. Again the sorts of coalitions formed were nearly all of the type expected from the justice idea, and the distribution is far different from a random choosing of partners. In all the games, then, Weil's experiment shows strong evidence that players are trying to produce the type of fair distribution of points we described in the justice principle.

Weil's design is particularly suited to seeing the effect of justice processes at the expense of concern with winnings, because communication between subjects is so limited. Each subject knows that it is important for him to be able to reach an agreement with another subject to form a coalition—if he does not, he will win nothing on that game. Therefore he must ask himself what sorts of offers the other players will accept. One answer is likely to be that they will expect fairness in the offer, and this would lead to making reciprocated offers. This line of reasoning strongly suggests that justice norms exist in society; subjects seem able to figure out what offers will consider fair and will accept.

TABLE 10–10 Coalitions Formed: No Alternative Games

GAME TYPE	WEIGHTS	AGREEMENTS ALLOWED	COALITION		
			TYPE	RANDOM	ACTUAL
I	3–2–2	25/25	3–2(25/25)	66%	37%
			2–2(25/25) →	33%	63%
II	3–2–2	30/20	3–2(30/20) →	33%	100%
			3–2(20/30)	33%	0
			2–2(20/30)	33%	0
IV	3–3–2	25/25	3–3(25/25) →	33%	78%
			3–2(25/25)	66%	22%
V	3–3–2	30/20	3–3(30/20)	33%	0
			3–2(30/20) →	33%	98%
			3–2(20/30)	33%	2%

(From Weil, 1970.)

TABLE 10–11 Coalitions Formed:
Limited Alternative Games

269

*Exchange
Research
I:
Social
Interaction*

GAME TYPE	WEIGHTS	AGREEMENTS ALLOWED	COALITION			
			TYPE		RANDOM	ACTUAL
III	3–2–2	25/25 and 30/20	3–2(25/25)		25%	4%
			3–2(30/20)	→	13%	30%
			3–2(20/30)		13%	0
			2–2(25/25)	→	25%	64%
			2–2(30/20)		25%	0
VI	3–3–2	25/25 and 30/20	3–3(25/25)	→	25%	40%
			3–3(30/20)		25%	0
			3–2(30/20)	→	13%	58%
			3–2(20/30)		13%	0
			3–2(25/25)		25%	0

(From Weil, 1970.)

Summary on Coalition Formation

Because the coalition experiments seem to incorporate abstractly the elementary social processes operating in a wide variety of real-life situations, they have attracted interest from a considerable number of investigators. We have studied the major empirical results of experiments using this setting, and have considered four ways of predicting and explaining the observed outcomes. Minimum power, minimum resources, pivotal power, and justice.

The fourth prediction seems to me the most satisfactory, because it not only accounts well for the results of previous experiments such as Vinacke and Arkoff's, but it also is supported by the direct tests Weil performed. It would be very difficult to explain Weil's results from any of the other 3 types of prediction. Moreover the justice principle is intuitively appealing: we can all think of cases where we have been concerned with fairness (as defined) in playing games—or in life in general.

Here we conclude our study of empirical research guided by the ideas of exchange theory. Studies summarized in this chapter provide direct confirmation for several explicit versions of exchange theories, and indirect confirmation of the exchange meta-theory. In Chap. 11 we continue the study of exchange processes at a somewhat more technical level.

11

Exchange Research II:
Games, Decisions, and Choices

Exchange Theories with Numbers

Quantification of data (using numbers) is a feature of any empirical science, since numerical notation provides the most rapid and clear way to communicate information. The data tables in this and in other chapters illustrate this point. As a field develops, some of its theories are interpreted quantitatively, and because of this, quantified theories make determinate predictions. Any disconfirmation is immediately evident, and an accurate prediction is especially impressive. Both economics and psychological learning theory, the two intellectual "parents" of exchange theories, have become quite thoroughly quantified in recent years. It is only natural that exchange theories should, too. Even in Homans' early propositions (Chap. 9), terms like "frequency of reward," "value of reward," and "satiation" suggest strongly that they refer to numbers. Precisely *which* numbers, and precisely *how* they are interrelated, are questions addressed in this chapter.

Interpersonal Behavior as a Game

One of the ways in which we all, occasionally, regard our interactions with others is as *game-playing*. Long before Eric Berne wrote *Games People Play,* you could hear people refer to "playing games with" someone (meaning deluding him about one's own motives, or controlling his understanding of a situation), or "the game of life." Unstated but always implicit in this sort of speech is the idea of striving to reach some goal. Moreover the goal is *rewarding,* and *costs* may have to be overcome in trying to reach it. Less obvious usually, but still present, is the idea that an individual engaged in game-playing is somewhat selfish. In exchange terms he is primarily motivated by consideration of his own potential gain, and he is not particularly concerned with the conseqences for others as he pursues his goals (unless others' outcomes also affect his own).

A somewhat different use of the word "game" applies in social psychology, and exchange ideas have been adopted very successfully by "game theorists." Some elements that are important in games like Monopoly, such as enjoyment and passing of time, have no place in game theory. Other elements, such as strategies, maximizing one's own gains, and concern with bargaining are central. Game theories provide a distinctive way of looking at behavior, and they adopt a distinctive set of goals. Game theories may

271

*Exchange
Research
II:
Games,
Decisions,
and
Choices*

be constructed for any situation in which we know that the actor or actors are concerned only with maximizing their own rewards; that is game theories assume that the only motivation is to get as much as possible out of the situation. Many situations meet this condition, but it is important to recognize that not every situation does. Game theorists explicitly reject any interest in whether people *should* try only to maximize their own gains. This is a moral issue, they say, and beyond their concern. The first limit to the scope of game theories is that, because they are exchange theories, they are only applied when actors have decided to try to maximize their own gains.

The second scope limitation is more subtle, but I think it is more significant. Game theories cannot ask (or answer) the question whether in fact people *are* primarily concerned with reward maximization. Again it is a scope condition. The game theorist must already be assured that this is the major motivation of actors before he begins to construct his theory. The assumption of reward maximization is never tested. In fact it could not be tested, for it is the first sentence of the exchange meta-theory. The reason I emphasize this point is that in reading empirical tests of game theories you may see the claim made that they test the basic assumption that individuals try to maximize rewards. This is not true. These theories accept on faith that individuals try to maximize their rewards. What is at stake, what is being tested, is the particular *form* of reward maximization predicted by the particular game theory. It never hurts to maintain a healthy skepticism as you read claims for empirical tests. (Likewise it never hurts to ask yourself while reading an exchange theory, "Could some other theory besides an exchange theory better explain this set of phenomena?")

Game theories are concerned with developing strategy, with presenting a set of rules that will help the individual to maximize his rewards. Given that the individual has decided he wants to maximize his own gains and this will be his only motivation, the job of the game theorist is to tell him how to do it. In a social situation where several outcomes are possible, each with its associated rewards and costs, game theory is designed to identify the *optimal strategy:* the actions which are most likely to result in the greatest gain to the individual. Calculating this strategy can be quite a complicated task, since often it is the case that more than one player will use principles of game theories. Then the issue is whether your game theorist is better than their game theorists in telling you how to maximize gains. For instance if you are bargaining over points in a coalition game, presumably a game theorist could help you get more than you could without him. But your opponents also could use principles of game theory against you, and you have to take this possibility into account in planning your own strategy.

Game theories take a wide variety of forms, but they all have in common the properties mentioned: all are exchange theories, all assume that the only motivation is to maximize rewards, and all are concerned with telling the individual how best to maximize his own rewards. Note clearly that game theories make no claim that this is actually how people behave. Actors may or may not adopt an optimal strategy for themselves, depending upon their motivations, awareness of the realities of the situation, and other factors. The game theory tells what *would* be the best strategy. It does not guarantee that people will adopt it.

I knew of a man in the Army in World War II while France was being retaken from the retreating, but still fairly strong, German Army. When you approached a fortified bunker that might or might not be still occupied by the enemy, standard U.S. Army procedure was to announce your presence and call upon the defenders to surrender. If nobody came out with arms raised, you threw a grenade into the bunker to be sure it was unoccupied or to kill the inhabitants. Obviously this is a dangerous procedure. When you call out, you announce your presence to any defenders, and they are most likely to shoot you. This man reversed standard procedure: he threw a grenade in first, then called out for surrender.

From a game theory point of view, this was the optimal strategy, since it minimized his possibility of loss (getting killed). But game theory would not tell us that he was *likely* to do this. To know that, we would need some other theories. Game theory would say that *if* you want to use the optimum strategy, this is the way to achieve it. This example illustrates quite well one circumstance that prevents people from adopting optimum strategies much of the time: norms may oppose it. In this case there are both the official Army norms regarding correct procedures, and unofficial norms against killing people when it is avoidable. There are many situations where the optimal strategy is fairly clear to individuals, yet they do not adopt it. We look first for norms preventing the adoption of such strategies in these cases.

But a game theorist would tell us that people will not continue forever in less than optimal strategies. Eventually with experience and information, people come to realize what the rewards and costs of various options are. And eventually they will choose that course that offers the greatest net profit. Thus we can explain changes in behavior over time if we can show, with a game theoretic analysis, that individuals were coming to adopt an optimal strategy. Part of our analysis of changes in coalition behavior in Kelley and Arrowood's study over time was in these terms: towards the end of the game, players came more and more to realize the "true" state of importance they each had, and to bargain for points in accord with the structural facts of the situation.

All game theories make one basic assumption regarding the calculation of rewards and costs of outcomes. This assumption, though it is usually implicit, is important. When individuals contemplate possible courses of action, the value of the rewards are multiplied by the perceived probability of attaining them to calculate their net value. The same is true of costs: net value is actual value times the subjective probability of incurring the cost. For example if a lottery prize is a million dollars and a million tickets are sold, then $1 apiece would be a good price for the tickets. If they were priced higher, it might be difficult to sell them, and obviously they could not be priced lower. However note that it is *perceived* or *subjective probability* of attaining the rewards which people use. If the individual believes that *his* chances are

273

*Exchange
Research
II:
Games,
Decisions,
and
Choices*

better than the numbers would indicate, for instance if he thinks he is "lucky," then he will pay more than a dollar for a ticket. In game theories:

$$\text{Net value}_A = sp_A\,(rew_A - costs_A)$$

The net value of outcome A is the subjective probability of achieving outcome A *times* the net profit (rewards minus costs) of outcome A.

If this sort of analysis doesn't seem familiar to you, consider some everyday applications of the principle. A high school student deciding whether to do his homework can weight the unpleasantness of being bawled out in class by the probability of being discovered. If he is discovered (outcome) the cost will be high. But the likelihood of being discovered is low, so he decides the chance is worth it. If the probability of discovery were greater, or if the cost were more terrible, he would decide to do the homework.

Have you ever been the driver of a car among hundreds, all trying to leave a parking lot at once? If you have, you know that one thing you have to do is cut into lines of moving traffic. Your choices are "wait" and "go." The opponent's choices are "stop for you" and "refuse to stop." The potential reward for you of deciding to "go" is getting into line. The potential cost is getting your car mangled. The potential reward for him of "refusing to stop" is keeping his place in line, plus probably some ego gratification. His potential cost is getting his car mangled. In most cases the value of the potential rewards to both actors seem about equal: you value getting into line about as much as he values keeping you out. What can vary is the potential *cost* of that alternative. People do not all place the same value on keeping their cars intact. In particular a game theorist would advise you to pick a shiny, new, expensive car to cut in front of. This driver is much more likely to stop to protect his car than is the driver of an old, beat-up wreck. This same sort of analysis may be used to explain why taxi drivers are so successful at getting through heavy city traffic. They worry much less than most of us do about an occasional bent fender.

A somewhat more advanced (and higher risk) tactic is to try to convince the opponent that you and he perceive different payoff matrices. One good way to get across a busy street on foot is to pretend that you don't even see the cars. If this works the drivers won't expect you to stop, since apparently you don't even know there are potential costs associated with your action.

Now let us analyze another social situation, using ideas of game theories.

Panic as a Game

Panics are like earthquakes: they are rare, they affect relatively few people, and their effects upon the normal activities of the world are minimal. Also like earthquakes, panics are very impressive occurrences either to read about or to be involved in; and they have attracted a large amount of study. Finally, most crowd behavior, including panics, is only incompletely understood, the same as is true of earthquakes.

Historically, disease probably has induced more panics than any other cause. Even rumors of plague in towns of the Middle Ages sometimes were sufficient to produce panic and flight into the countryside. We have had several disease-fear panics in this country as well. New Orleans was partially evacuated under panic conditions as the result of yellow fever in 1880. In 1918 an unfamiliar disease swept most of the world, causing sickness and not infrequently, death. No cure except rest was known (or is known for the disease today). Many towns were evacuated in a style reminiscent of the Medieval plague-induced panics, as people sought to protect the very old and the very young members of their families. The disease in 1918 was flu. It has become less virulent in the succeeding decades, and we have become less afraid of it.

The typical panic, the type we most often think about, is the panic that can ensue in any closed space containing large numbers of people. For some reason, say fire, everyone suddenly wants to get out. In our terms every person suddenly perceives that the only possible way to avoid great losses is to get out of that place, and escape becomes the predominant goal. Almost invariably the result of a panic is much worse than whatever threat induced it. The losses resulting from the panic are far greater than any possible losses from the precipitating incident.

The classic description of panic was provided by the vaudevillian Eddie Foy, who described the 1903 fire in the Iroquois Theater in Chicago. The fire started backstage and grew too rapidly to be extinguished. When the first flames became visible to the audience, somebody shouted, "Fire!" and precipitated the panic. People moved from their seats towards the doors, becoming more frightened and more hurried as their numbers grew too great for the aisles. Many of the exits were locked, and stairways from the balcony were too narrow for people to pass. At the doors and at turns in the stairs the crowd was packed too tightly for people to pass, and they began to pile up.

Afterwards, police and firemen found the bodies piled so tightly together that it was difficult to remove them. Flesh was torn from some of them by others' shoes, and Foy reports many faces with heel prints on them. Over 600 people died in a very few minutes there. What makes this particularly tragic is that firemen arrived quickly enough to put out the fire before it reached the audience. Fabric on the first rows of seats was singed; that was all.

This fire resulted in much of the legislation we have in most states today: fireproof theater curtains, plenty of well marked exits, all exit doors opening outwards to prevent people piling up. What are sometimes called "panic bars"—horizontal bars running the width of the door, which can always open the door from inside, even if it is locked—are installed in places where people especially want to avoid panic-related deaths (schools, public buildings).

What is tacitly recognized in these measures is that a panic, once begun, is practically impossible to reverse. Panics occur rapidly, and once they appear it is too late to do much about them. Legal restrictions on buildings are aimed at minimizing deaths that will occur from a panic; primarily by making it easier to get out of the building. The presence of many lighted EXIT signs also probably has a reassuring effect on people who might be tempted to panic if they thought they could be trapped. One thing we want to explain in this chapter is just why these measures usually can prevent panics developing.

Control of panics centers on avoiding them, not upon limiting them once they take hold. Beyond the changes in building structure just described, there is really only one technique: give the people something—almost anything—to do that will distract them from maximizing their gains by panic. In grade schools we have the fire drill procedure, usually involving fairly complex actions. Most of this is unnecessary, and the speed with which a building can be emptied is almost totally irrelevant. So long as people remain orderly and walk to the exits, they are very likely all to get out. What the fire drill procedure does is give people something to occupy their thoughts besides fear of fire. The overriding goal is to prevent individualizing of conduct. In Britain during the blitz bombing of World War II, panic was always a threat; especially at night, when the actual extent of bomb damage could not be seen, people might assume that the end had come, and flee the city. To combat this possibility, elaborate civil defense procedures were established, including a rule to "police your property every 10 minutes for Germans." This gave people something to do, and thus it served a vital purpose during the war. Protected by history, we may smile at such a useless maneuver (in terms of keeping out Germans), but there is good reason to believe that it helped avoid panics.

Panic Simulation: The Mintz Experiment

When a phenomenon is first investigated systematically, often the investigator does not have sufficient information to study the relevant processes in a true experiment. The state of understanding of naturally-occurring panics has never been very complete, for several reasons. Precipitating incidents, such as theater fires, disease, or war, are relatively rare. Also, anyone who happens to be present at an actual panic has several concerns besides making a detailed, systematic observation of what takes place.

However the situation is recognized as having tremendous practical significance, and it suggests interesting theoretical problems as well. The first problem faced by the social psychologist is to explain why people sometimes behave in a way virtually guaranteed to cause the death of some of them, and to explain it in a way that assumes they are trying to maximize net gain. The second problem is to use this analysis to suggest changes in the social–psychological or the physical environment to help avoid panics in the future —or at the least, to show what conditions are most likely to promote panics. (You might be tempted to answer the first question by saying that humans are emotional and irrational. That is not acceptable.)

Mintz investigated some of the important characteristics of a theater fire more than 25 years ago. This study well illustrates a particular type of research, the "partial experiment," or *simulation*. Simulations are useful when the theorist thinks he knows several potentially important independent variables and when the dependent variable is known, but there is no theory to link independent and dependent variables. There is no explicit theoretical justification for deciding to include some variables and not others, and the interrelationships between several independent variables, or between independent and dependent variables, are not well understood. A simulation is a partially controlled exploration of essentially unfamiliar territory.

The apparatus used for Mintz's simulation is shown in Fig. 11–1. Groups of 15 to 21 individuals stood in a circle around the large glass bottle, about the size we now use for a terrarium. Each individual held a string, the other end of which was attached to a cone inside the bottle. The task was to withdraw the cone within a given period of time. If individuals took turns, all the cones could be withdrawn quite quickly—in less than one minute for the 15 to 21 persons in each of his groups. However if two people pulled on their strings at the same time, their two cones would jam the neck of the bottle and then none could be withdrawn. The cones were smooth enough so that if the individuals creating a jam stopped pulling, the way would be free again. Notice the similarities of this situation to a theater fire panic.

The dependent variable is success or failure at pulling all cones out of the bottle within the time limit. Several independent variables were studied: (1) *excitement* induced by confederates whose job was to scream

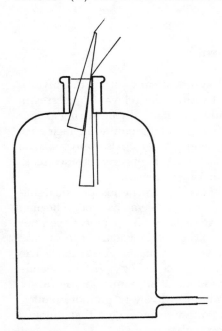

FIGURE 11–1   Mintz apparatus for panic simulation.
(From Mintz, 1951.)

and act upset; (2) *money* rewards for success or fines for failure; and (3) *norms* formed by allowing members to meet and plan an evacuation strategy beforehand.

Results of a simulation can never be clear-cut as those from a true experiment, but it is possible to see a pattern in what happened here. Which of those independent variables would you predict to have some effect here? What effect? The pattern I see in Mintz's data is that only one variable made any difference: reward. With the exception of one group (his PC1), the following seems to be true: *In groups with monetary rewards and fines, jams are produced. In groups without monetary rewards and fines, no jams develop.* Excitement did not produce jams, and being allowed to form norms did not prevent them.

In addition we might suspect that some of the groups without jams actually had a reward for being cooperative. The experimenter told them he wanted to see how well they could work together, and this probably told them he would reward them (with social approval) for not panicking.

What this means, if my interpretation of Mintz's results is correct, is that we see rewards as the major variable in the panic. Groups rewarded (individually) for getting cones out behaved selfishly and panicked. Groups rewarded for being orderly acted this way. Since the simulation was quite true to actual panics, we see that they also may be analyzed in exchange terms.

Do we conclude from our analysis that panics are an inevitable result in situations where the reward structure approximates that of Mintz's study? Most importantly, are panics an inevitable result of theater fires? These conclusions would be a little too strong, but with some qualifications they probably are true. As we noted earlier measures to deal with panic center on *avoidance*. This means designing the situation so that the precipitating causes are unlikely to occur. In terms of game theories the structure must not seem to offer more profit from panicking than from remaining orderly.

Nearly all preventive measures in use center on reducing the apparent potential *costs* of acting in an *orderly* fashion. Theaters and other public buildings are fireproof, and what is equally important, people know that they are fireproof. Automatic sprinkler and other fire-detection equipment is prominently displayed. Patrons are reminded that there are more than enough exits, and all exits are constantly displayed through use of signs and lights. From the stage of the Concert Hall at Kennedy Center in Washington, more than *four dozen* lighted EXIT signs are visible. All commercial airlines go through an elaborate ritual before takeoff to convince passengers that any mishap is extremely unlikely, and that leaving the plane would be very easy and rapid, if necessary.

What is necessary to avoid a panic is to control the situation so that the outcome matrix that exists (or, more precisely, as it is perceived by the actors) does not promote panic. We can specify more precisely just what sort of arrangements must be made in the situation after studying the Prisoner's Dilemma.

The Prisoner's Dilemma

The theater fire illustrates a class of situations game theorists call "mixed motive"; that is, the individual has good (exchange-based) reasons for behaving in more than one way. Frequently as in the theater fire and in Mintz's experiment, the behavior alternatives are incompatible. The actor must choose whether to maximize his own gain directly or to be concerned with the outcome of the entire group. One of the most interesting mixed motive situations, especially from the point of view of social psychology, is the prisoner's dilemma. The prisoner's dilemma describes one of the oldest and most successful interrogation techniques. Its story is as follows.

Two men are suspected of being joint perpetrators of a serious crime. For example, let us say that the district attorney believes both of them to be gang leaders and to have murdered a rival gang member. The two men are incarcerated and are questioned separately. To each of them the district attorney says, "Now, you and I both know you are guilty of murder. However, I probably cannot get enough evidence to convict anyone of first degree murder unless one of you confesses. If you confess, I'll drop charges against you. You will go free. Your partner will almost certainly go to jail for 50 years, so he won't be able to retaliate." At this point the prisoner is likely to ask, "What if I don't confess?" To this the district attorney replies, "If you don't confess, what happens depends on whether the other guy confesses. I'm going to offer him the same deal I'm offering you. If he confesses, you'll go to jail for 50 years and he'll go free." To which the prisoner replies, "What if neither of us confesses?" "In that case I can still get both of you on a charge of possession of an unregistered weapon. You'll probably both go to jail for about a year. That wouldn't be terrible, but you'd be giving up the chance to go free. Furthermore if you're going to confess, you'd better do so quickly, because if both of you confess, then I will prosecute you both for second degree manslaughter and you'll probably go to jail for about 30 years apiece."

Figure 11–2 shows a joint payoff matrix of the various alternatives facing the two prisoners. Obviously the best choice for them would be outcome cell A; that is, for neither prisoner to confess. Their joint outcome would be best in cell A. However there is a powerful feature of the prisoner's dilemma situation which makes it virtually impossible for two rational actors to end up in cell A. In fact if both actors behave rationally, they will end up in cell D; both will get 30 years in jail. Since this is not the most desirable outcome, why is it the most likely one?

Consider the situation from Prisoner A's point of view. His decision is to confess or to refuse. It might appear that A's decision should depend upon B, perhaps involving questions of trust. After all if A knows that B is not going to confess, then A could get the group into cell A by not confessing himself. What is more subtle, however, and more pernicious, about the prisoner's dilemma situation is that if A behaves rationally, *regardless of what B does*, it is to A's advantage to confess. Stated differently, there is no way that a rational actor (in the exchange meaning

	Refuse	Confess
Refuse	A: 1 B: 1 (Cell A)	A: 50 B: 0 (Cell B)
Confess	A: 0 B: 50 (Cell C)	A: 30 B: 30 (Cell D)

Prisoner A (label at left for rows)

*Exchange
Research
II:
Games,
Decisions,
and
Choices*

FIGURE 11–2 Outcome matrix for the prisoner's dilemma

of "rational": gain-maximizing) can choose to refuse. The reason is as follows. If *B* confesses, then *A* must also, in order to avoid his own worst outcome (cell *B*). But if *B* does not confess, *A* is *still* better off confessing than he would be by refusing to confess. If *B* does not confess and *A* does not (cell *A*), *A* will go to jail for a year. If *B* does not confess and *A* does (cell *C*), *A* will go free. Thus *no matter what the other person chooses, it is impossible rationally for prisoner A to choose row 1.* The "dilemma" of the prisoner's dilemma is, then, that if each actor pursues his own greatest gain, the *group* gain is considerably less than it would otherwise be. (Since the actors are interchangeable here, the same dilemma faces prisoner *B*. Check through the logic if this is not clear.)

The prisoner's dilemma illustrates in an extreme form one problem of social control. It simply is not in the prisoner's own interest to refuse to confess. The only successful opposition to the prisoner's dilemma which has been devised is to change the payoff matrix. For example, it is quite clear to members of the Mafia that confession leads to death. This changes the outcomes in Cells *B* and *C*, and it is no longer a prisoner's dilemma situation. However without some change of this sort in the payoff matrix, the prisoner's dilemma is virtually guaranteed to be successful for the district attorney.

The essence of the prisoner's dilemma situation, and of mixed-motive situations in general, is that the individual is faced with a choice of alternative actions. Usually it is fairly obvious that one alternative offers more individual rewards than the others, *but* that alternative will entail costs for others. Finally, choosing rationally to maximize individual gain will actually decrease the net rewards. In some cases it will even threaten the future existence of the group.

Many situations studied under the topic "social control" may profitably be analyzed using the prisoner's dilemma outcome matrix. Social control, as we saw in Chap. 10, is concerned with motivating individuals to behave in "the public interest," however that public interest is defined. For example, getting people to report their deductions honestly on income tax forms, or to obey laws without coercion, are social-control situations. Social-control situations are those in which the individual is faced with a choice between maximizing benefits to himself or sacrificing somewhat to the public good. Thus it would be in a person's own interest to cheat on his income tax (assuming he wouldn't be discovered), but it would be bad for the entire society. It would be in a person's interest to disobey traffic laws, or to steal from stores when he could get away with it; but it would be bad in the long run for everyone else.

To apply the prisoner's dilemma to social control situations, we simply replace one of the actors, say prisoner *B*, with the group, or society. Notice that the same sort of dilemmas persist when we do this: basically, choosing to maximize individual good will be costly for the group, *and,* in a true prisoner's dilemma, it will eventually turn out to be bad (not optimal) for the individual as well.

Situations that encompass many of the aspects of the prisoner's dilemma are easy to find. Consider the case of voting in a democracy. From the individual's point of view, it takes several hours of otherwise useful time to register, to consider the merits of the various candidates and proposals, and actually to go down and cast his vote. The individual knows, in most cases, that the effect of his single vote is very unlikely to influence the outcome of the election. (In spite of what they tell you in high school civics classes, elections almost never are decided by a single vote; and most people realize this.) On the other hand if large numbers of individuals abstain from voting, the consequences for the democratic form of government are disastrous. Somehow enough people must care enough about voting and about the outcome of the election to be willing to devote a large bit of their time to this cause. Largely as a result of this fact, considerable effort is spent to convince people that the political situation is important and is worth their attention. In the United States these measures are successful—at getting 40–60 percent of voters to participate in most elections. In South Vietnam where there are monetary and other costs for nonvoting, voting turnout often exceeds 95 percent. It is all a question of payoff matrices. In the U.S. the payoff matrix for voting is a prisoner's dilemma situation for many people. In South Vietnam where the payoffs are different, the matrix is not a prisoner's dilemma.

Another example of this type of situation is the factory rate buster, a person who produces at a rate higher than the rate of others doing the same work. What rate busting does, of course, is to make other workers look bad. Management may expect everyone to perform at the higher rate. Yet if the individual is paid by the number of pieces he turns out, at least in terms of salary, it is in his own interest to rate bust. The same thing is true of the teacher's pet, a child who lavishes non-normative favors upon the teacher. The only effective way to deal with this problem is in the way LaPiere described: by the efforts of others to distribute sanctions to enforce the output norms and the norms of child–teacher behavior. Stated

281

*Exchange
Research
II:
Games,
Decisions,
and
Choices*

differently, the gains associated with different outcomes must be altered in order to protect the group interest.

All winter long electric utilities companies shower the public with advertising extolling the virtues of electric heat, electric appliances, and all sorts of other ways to increase consumption of electricity. When summer comes and the use of air-conditioning produces a large increase in electric demands, the electric companies appeal to individuals' public spiritedness and ask them to curtail electric uses. Aside from the seasonal inconsistency of the pleas, it should be quite apparent that it is in no one's interest to turn off his air conditioner on a hot day.

Anyone faced with the air conditioner dilemma has the choice to use his air conditioner less (say allowing his home to heat up to 80 degrees), or to try to keep it as cold as possible. He knows that the electric company also has two choices: to keep service at its usual rate, or to decrease the power so everybody will have less. And of course the electric company decision is partially determined by what many individuals do: power will stay at its usual rate *so long as* several people turn their air conditioners down.

Now from the actor's point of view, if electricity is maintained at its usual rate, he is better off to keep his home as cool as he wants it. But suppose through his selfishness and that of his neighbors, the company reduces power. Then his air conditioner won't work so well, and his home will get warm. Isn't he better off if he has already gotten his place down to 60 degrees before power is cut, than if he had been public spirited and let his home get warm first? In addition to these considerations, our actor has good reason to believe that most people have no intention of reducing their consumption. The television announcer who asks you to turn off your air conditioner because there is a power shortage does not seem to be suffering from the heat, even under all those t.v. lights. The businesses downtown are not likely to turn off some of their lights or their electric display signs, nor are they likely to ask their employees to walk up and down stairs instead of using the elevators. In short the contingency tables for not using electricity voluntarily show that there are considerable costs for doing so, and no attendant rewards. Small wonder, then, that few people heed such appeals. As an exercise you might try applying this analysis to some aspects of the petroleum shortage.

Panic as a Prisoner's Dilemma Situation

Roger Brown (1965) has analyzed the case of the theater fire panic in terms of a payoff matrix of the prisoner's dilemma. If an individual is in the audience when a fire breaks out, he is faced with a decision of panicking and running for the exit or of following an orderly withdrawal pattern. Although from the safety of our point of view, we believe that everybody *could* leave the theater easily if nobody panics, this is not exactly the situation facing the individual actually in the theater. He knows that there is *some* chance that *somebody* in the audience will precipitate a panic; *if this happens,* no one will get out after the time the panic occurs. The subjective probability of a panic may seem low, but the costs are enormous. His decision, really, is whether *he* will be the one to cause the panic. You can diagram this situation using a matrix similar to Fig. 11–2. Replace "prisoner *A*" with "individual," and replace "prisoner *B*" with "group." Now replace "confess" with "panic," and "refuse" with "take turns."

Suppose he chooses not to panic. In that case there is some chance that he and the others will be able to escape. But there is also the chance that somebody else will precipitate a panic and in that case he will not escape— even though the person who precipitates the panic probably will get out all right. Now suppose our actor decides to panic and run for the exit. So long as no one else does so, this will be fine for him; he will escape. Some of the others, however, may perish. Suppose he panics and they do also. Probably in that case, he will make it and some of them will not make it. However, it is not a sure thing.

Figure 11–3 illustrates Brown's analysis of panic as a prisoner's dilemma situation. Because of the difficulty of establishing exact numerical values for the payoffs, we use plus and minus signs: the best possible outcome, escaping for sure, we represent by ++; the worst, being trapped for sure, by ——. A single + is used for likely escape, and a single − is used for likely being trapped.

This does not mean that a panic is inevitable, or even that this analysis would lead us to think it is inevitable. The sorts of preventive measures we have mentioned above can often prevent panics. In terms of the payoff matrix, what preventive measures do is to change the gains associated with the choices. For example if fire is unlikely and exits are plentiful, then the relative gains to individual in cell *C* are smaller, and the gains to both individual and group in cell *A* are larger. (Hypothetically, one might also increase the costs to individual in cell *D* by passing a law that precipitators of a panic will be shot. The situation is structurally similar to saying that looters will be shot after natural disasters.)

Recall that a game theorist would say that people are likely to pursue their own individual interests when they can accurately perceive what those interests are. Any social situation that fits the conditions of the

	Group	
	Take turns	Panic
Take turns	I: +	I: − −
	G: + +	G: + +
Panic	I: + +	I: −
	G: − −	G: −

FIGURE 11–3   Prisoner's dilemma analysis of panic. (Adapted from Brown, 1965.)

283

*Exchange
Research
II:
Games,
Decisions,
and
Choices*

prisoner's dilemma, then, is a situation in which a rational actor must choose the selfish alternative. If you are interested in predicting behavior in any similar situation, and if it looks like a prisoner's dilemma when you construct the payoff matrix, then the best prediction for behavior is clear. Actors will choose the alternative offering individual gain, and that alternative will force the group outcome into the less than optimal cell *D*. For example if we had applied this analysis to the Mintz experiment beforehand, it would have been apparent that the money reward conditions of the experiment produced a prisoner's dilemma for players. It would have been clear that those conditions would all produce jams. Likewise if we had constructed a payoff matrix for Mintz's other conditions, it would have been clear that there were no potential rewards for choosing to "rush exit." Consequently it was *not* a prisoner's dilemma situation, and we have no reason to expect players to behave as individuals do in a prisoner's dilemma.

Figure 11–4 illustrates the payoff matrix for players in Mintz's money conditions, using hypothetical monetary *expected* gains for the outcomes. Figure 11–5 illustrates the other conditions, using pluses and minuses for

	Group	
	Take turns	Rush exit
Take turns	I: 10¢ G: 10¢	I: −5¢ G: 15¢
Rush exit	I: 15¢ G: −5¢	I: 2¢ G: 2¢

(Individual — row label on the left)

FIGURE 11–4 Money Reward conditions of Mintz's experiment as a prisoner's dilemma

	Group	
	Take turns	Rush exit
Take turns	I: + + G: + +	I: + + G: − −
Rush exit	I: − − G: + +	I: − − G: − −

(Individual — row label on the left)

FIGURE 11–5 Payoff matrix for Mintz's No Money conditions

either social approval from the experimenter for cooperation, or censure for noncooperation, the only possible regards here are for cooperation. Notice that Fig. 11–4 resembles the prisoner's dilemma of Fig. 11–2. Figure 11–5 does not at all resemble a payoff matrix for the theater fire. Thus the other conditions of Mintz's experiment probably were *not* a prisoner's dilemma for the players.

Formal Properties of the Prisoner's Dilemma

I just said that it is useful to be able to recognize prisoner's dilemma situations, since we know how people are likely to behave in them. In order to recognize a prisoner's dilemma situation, we need to know what they look like; not just instances of them, but *in general*. What properties do all prisoner's dilemma situations have in common?

Scodel and his associates (1958, 1960) describe the abstract properties that define a prisoner's dilemma. It must be a situation in which the individual is faced with making a decision wholly in his own self-interest or in acting in a way partially determined by group interests. It is a mixed-motive situation in that there are rational reasons (rewards) for acting either way, but acting to maximize one's own gains will put both the individual and the group in a worse outcome cell than they would prefer.

Figure 11–6 represents the general case of the prisoner's dilemma situation. Payoffs to actors A and B, contingent upon each of their decisions, are shown in each of the four cells. The situation is a prisoner's dilemma if the following relations between payoffs hold:

1. $X_3 > X_1$

2. $X_4 > X_2$

3. $X_3 > X_2$

4. $2X_1 > (X_2 + X_3) > 2X_4$

It should be evident that the payoffs shown in Figures 11–2 and 11–4 meet these conditions, and therefore that these situations are true prisoner's dilemmas. In Fig. 11–2, because the numbers refer to years in jail, which are punishments or costs, the lower numbers are more favorable. To fit the conditions given above, you would need either to reverse their inequality signs or to interpret them as reading "more favorable than" instead of "greater than." However then the conditions given here are met for the numbers in Fig. 11–2. Note also that we may replace actor B with the group. And we can replace the "confess" alternative with any "selfish" alternative, and "not confess" with any "cooperative" alternative.

As a result of knowing the formal properties of the prisoner's dilemma we are able to specify at least a *range* of permissible values for the less precise interpretation of the theater fire. We know about how much of

Actor B

	Not confess	Confess
Not confess Actor A	A: X_1 B: X_1	A: X_2 B: X_3
Confess	A: X_3 B: X_2	A: X_4 B: X_4

FIGURE 11–6 General case of the prisoner's dilemma. (From Scodel, 1958.)

gains must be perceived by individuals in a theater fire situation in order for it to be a prisoner's dilemma. To put it another way, we know what sorts of relations between the various gains (the Xs) to avoid, if we wish to avoid creating a prisoner's dilemma situation in a new building. Finally and perhaps most important, using the prisoner's dilemma analysis, along with a game theory version of exchange propositions, we are able to construct a rigorous explanation of the outcome of Mintz's and other related studies. People choose the behaviors they do *because* they perceive a payoff matrix like we constructed in Fig. 11–4. This payoff matrix meets the conditions of a prisoner's dilemma, and so long as individuals seek to maximize their own gains, they will choose the "selfish" action alternative.

Bargaining, Commitment, and Threat

The individual in a prisoner's dilemma has no chance to talk to the other individual or to the group, nor try to reach a satisfactory agreement whether to confess or not. In bargaining behavior, by contrast, individuals are allowed to talk and to try to get each other to change their preferred alternative actions. Typically bargaining involves explaining to one's opponent the range of options he has, your own likely behavior if he chooses each option, and the gains for both of you associated with the various possible outcomes.

Although a bargaining situation permits interaction before the choice alternative is acted upon, information does not always flow freely. For one thing actors may try to mislead each other about the gains associated with various outcomes. This strategy was mentioned earlier as sometimes helping you to walk across a busy street. For another thing actors may try to conceal the true size of their expected gains. For example if you believe that a piece of property has oil under it, you do not tell this to the owner while you bargain with him to buy it.

Bargaining situations are those in which both parties have some interest in reaching an agreement. They are better off from reaching an agreement than they would be from a deadlock. However both parties also recognize that several outcomes are possible, and they do not agree as to which is best. Typically the optimal outcome for actor *A* is not the optimal outcome for actor *B*. Thus the task is to find an outcome which is not too bad for both actors. Neither will realize the greatest possible gains in the situation, but at least both will realize some gains.

Bargaining sessions have recently been analyzed by Bartos as consisting of two principal parts: the *main-game* and the *end-game*. The end-game is defined as the last two acts exchanged between the individuals, as when actor *A* says, "This is my final offer," and actor *B* says, "I'll take it." Exactly when the end-game will come in any given bargaining session we do not know until after it is over. It may occur almost immediately, or it may be the climax of an extremely protracted series of interactions. The end-game is identifiable only at the end of the entire bargaining sequence. However the term is a useful one, as we shall see in applying it to bargaining behavior. The first act of the end-game is an offer from one actor, *A*, and the final act is either acceptance or rejection by the other actor *B*.

What is significant is that in the end-game, *a rational actor B will accept any offer from which he stands to make a net gain.* Because the end-game is the very end of the bargaining session, actor *B* is in a take-it-or-leave-it position. Therefore he should accept any offer that gives him any gain whatsoever, no matter how small. Actor *A* must make an offer that contains a net gain for *B* or else it will be rejected. Thus *A*'s rational behavior is to make an offer that *B* will accept. In addition, of course, *A* is concerned to make the smallest offer that entails a net gain to *B*.

The purpose of bargaining during the main-game, according to Bartos' analysis, is for both actors to discover just what gains each of them associates with various outcomes. What each of them is trying to do is to discover the payoff matrix the other believes exists in the situation, so that he can offer the outcome giving the other the smallest net gain. Since each of them knows that is what the other is doing, each of them should try to mislead the other into thinking that his own gains are smaller than they are. If the strategy is successful, at the end-game the opponent may actually offer a more favorable alternative than he thinks he is offering. The greater the uncertainty the actors have about each other's perceived payoffs, the more protracted the main-game bargaining will be.

One strategy that is particularly successful is to convince your opponent that there is some external factor that you cannot change and that limits your ability to make concessions. For example, suppose you are selling your house, asking $55,000. Actually you expect to be talked down by a prospective purchaser, but you do not want to go below $50,000. You would be wise to set some external factor responsible for that floor price, so that you will be unable to change it. When your prospective buyer inquires how much you will accept for the house, you tell him that you must have, at an absolute minimum, $50,000, since you have just bought another house for that amount and you have no other source of money. This tells him there is no point in

287

*Exchange
Research
II:
Games,
Decisions,
and
Choices*

arguing to get you below $50,000. It simply is not in your power to go below that amount. You have already made an outside commitment that requires that money.

I am not particularly good at bargaining, and probably because of that fact I do not enjoy it at all. Buying a new car is a very unpleasant experience for me, since I know I am about to be taken by all these tactics. Even when I protect myself a bit by learning the dealer's cost of the car (*his* outside commitment factor), and even when I arrange to buy the car without haggling over price, it is unpleasant to have to interact with the salesman. I suspect this is due to jealousy. He has skill at an area where I am so lacking.

Deutsch and Krauss have studied the effects of publicly committing oneself to an irreversible decision upon individual and joint payoffs in a bargaining situation. Two subjects were in competition during the experiment. Each subject was told to imagine that she (female subjects) was in charge of a trucking company, either Acme or Bolt in Fig. 11–7. The goal for each of them was to move their truck from "start" to "destination" as rapidly as possible. Each trip was worth sixty cents minus one cent for each second the trip took. Thus if a subject required thirty-five seconds to move from start to destination, her net outcome for that run would be: 60¢ − 35¢ = 25¢. Note that each subject has a choice of two routes. The alternate route will take longer but she is guaranteed to reach the destination. The shorter route involves traveling over a one lane road that can only be occupied by one truck at a time. Therefore if Acme enters the one lane road first, Bolt must either wait until she has come out at the other side, or must take the alternate route.

The independent variable of greatest interest here is possession and use of *threat*. Threat is operationalized as a gate that one or both subjects might be able to lock, thus preventing the opponent from traveling the one lane road.

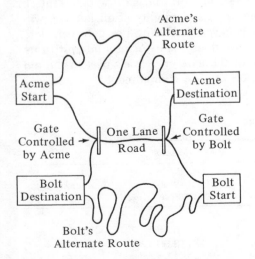

FIGURE 11–7 Trucking routes. (From Deutsch and Krauss, 1960.)

The investigators found that when a subject possesses the potential for threat (that is, when she has access to a gate), she almost invariably chooses to use it. This finding is interesting in itself, but let us look at the effect of a threat upon payoffs to the subjects. Table 11-1 presents the mean actual payoffs in this situation. Row 1 shows the average joint payoff to both subjects depending upon whether none, one, or both of them possess the gate. Row 2 shows the average payoff to Acme (the only subject possessing a gate in the unilateral threat condition) in each of these conditions. Row 3 shows the mean payoff to Bolt, who only possesses a gate in the bilateral threat condition.

First, note in row 1 that the presence of a gate is distinctly disadvantageous to the group as a whole. Joint payoffs are highest in the condition of no threat and lowest in the condition where both players possess the threat. Second, in row 2, notice that possession of the gate does not give an advantage to the actor possessing it. Acme's payoff is greater when she does not possess the gate than it is when only she possesses a gate (column 1 versus column 2). Third, in row 3, note that Bolt does better when only Acme possesses a gate than she does when both of them possess a gate (column 2 versus column 3). The effect of threat in this experiment is striking. It reduces the outcomes to all players—yet they always use it!

How are we to explain the fact that subjects almost invariably decide to use the threat when they have it, especially in conjunction with the evidence that to use the threat decreases *both* individual's outcome? It seems reasonable to assume that a subject playing this game recognizes two sources of potential danger to a rapid completion of the trucking haul. First, there is the danger of an impasse on the one lane road. Second, there may be the danger of the other subject's blocking one's passage by use of her gate.

In the unilateral threat condition, Acme's use of the gate would be readily understandable if we knew that Acme considers the gate a deterrent. In this condition, Acme's only real danger is the possibility of an impasse with Bolt on the one lane road. If Acme believes that using her gate can deter Bolt from taking the shorter direct route, then it is in Acme's interest to use the gate. Thus we would expect use of the gate on Acme's part in the unilateral threat condition. The gate is an outside commitment.

TABLE 11–1   Mean Payoffs by Threat

| | MEANS | | |
VARIABLE	(1) No THREAT	(2) UNILATERAL THREAT	(3) BILATERAL THREAT
Summed Payoffs (Acme + Bolt)	203.31	−405.88	−875.12
Acme's Payoff	122.44	−118.56	−406.56
Bolt's Payoff	80.88	−287.31	−468.56

(From Deutsch and Krauss, 1962.)

289

*Exchange
Research
II:
Games,
Decisions,
and
Choices*

How about the bilateral threat condition? It seems reasonable to believe that this condition constitutes a Prisoner's Dilemma for both subjects. Acme knows that if she does not use her gate there are two dangers: either there will be an impasse with *B*, or *B* may use her gate—or both. If Acme does use her gate, the likelihood of an impasse is reduced somewhat due to the deterrent effect, and in addition, Acme has a bargaining lever (offering to open her gate) in case Bolt decides to use the gate. If Acme perceives potential payoffs such as those in Fig. 11–8, this would explain her behavior. (The exact numbers in Fig. 11–8 are fanciful, since there is no way to know exactly what gains subjects anticipated in this experiment. Remember that gains in the payoff matrix are calculated by subjects' multiplying the money by the probability of actually ending up in each of the outcome cells. The numbers in Fig. 11–8 seem like reasonable expectations for subjects in the Deutsch and Krauss experiment; and if they are reasonable, then we can explain the use of the gate by saying that subjects perceived a prisoner's dilemma situation and were behaving rationally in it.)

| | Acme | |
	No gate	Gate
No gate	A: 15¢ B: 15¢	A: −10¢ B: 30¢
Gate	A: 30¢ B: −10¢	A: 5¢ B: 5¢

Bolt

FIGURE 11–8 Bilateral threat experiment as a prisoner's dilemma

Perspective on Mixed Motive Social Situations

To understand situations in which individuals have interdependent fates and mixed motives, it is necessary to distinguish individual interest from collective interest. In terms of game theories, it is necessary to distinguish outcomes available to an individual from a particular action from outcomes that will occur to a group of individuals from that or a different course of action. When outcomes are about equally favorable, exchange theory leads us to predict that the actor will behave in accord with the "socially desired" outcome. However in many cases, it simply is not in the actor's best (selfish) interest to pursue the collective goals. The reason is that he has no way to be certain that other actors will pursue the collective outcome, except, of course, for unusual instances such as the "Mafia confessions" mentioned previously. We have examined one class of such situations, the prisoner's dilemma. Social situations meeting the formal requirements of a prisoner's dilemma situation probably occur rather frequently. If we can analyze a given situation and show that it does meet the requirements for a prisoner's dilemma, then it is reasonable to expect that most people, most of the time, will pursue their own individual interests and will act accordingly.

In assessing the prisoner's dilemma studies and in placing this approach in perspective, it must be remembered that we have deliberately simplified complex situations. Purposely we have omitted the effects of such factors as internalized beliefs, idealism, ego controls such as conscience, and other factors that tend to promote social stability. My intent has not been to argue that anarchy is likely, reasonable, or preferable in many situations; rather, it has been to show that there are good reasons in terms of exchange theory to expect that *in certain types of situations* individuals are likely to pursue their own interests even to the detriment of the group interests. Most generally we have been concerned to see that behavior that at first appears not to follow the exchange theory prediction of maximizing rewards, in fact is completely consistent with it once the situation is defined correctly.

Models of Decision Making

One way to look at interpersonal behavior is to break down the flow of interaction into single acts by actors; then to consider each single act as the result of a single decision by an actor. Implicitly this approach assumes that the actors are aware of the possible choices they can make, and that they make rational choices—that is, profit-maximizing choices—between the available alternatives. Actors know what they *could* do in a given situation, and they have a good idea of what the outcomes of the possible decisions would be. Then what they *actually* do is determined by some rational decision-making process.

Precisely *how* this choice is evaluated and finally made by actors is the subject of what are called *decision-making models.*

Decision-making models attempt to show by analogy the way actors calculate the net profit of the various options available to them. The reason we say models build an analogy of the process is that we do not need to believe actors go through a complicated mathematical calculation before making a decision. Rather, they behave *as if* they were going through these calculations. Stated differently, by assuming actors actually make these calculations, we hope to be able to predict their behavior—even though we do not usually think that the actors themselves would make the calculations our models require. The "as if" nature of decision models (and in fact, of many theories of human behavior) is rather subtle, but it is important to grasp the idea to appreciate how these theories are constructed. This distinction may become more clear when we discuss the Siegel and Ofshe models a bit later on.

Decision-making models are a type of game theory; that is, they assume that individuals are primarily motivated by desires to maximize rewards and to minimize costs. The only consideration for an actor in a decision-making situation is how to get the most out of his decisions. There are 2 additional conditions in what we shall call a decision-making situation, beyond the conditions already imposed for study of interaction as a game.

First, we assume that actors have a good idea of the outcomes associated with various decisions available to them. In other words actors have enough information to weigh their options. There is nothing unknown about what gains and costs accrue from any of the choices. Of course the actors may not *accurately* perceive the various gains and losses, but they are not uncertain about them. They *think* they know the outcomes of the decision, and that is what they will use to make the decisions. This means that decision-making models explain a later part of the bargaining sequence described previously. During the main-game of bargaining, actors are trying to learn each others' gains. Once these are known, decision-making models may be used to predict actual offers and acceptance or rejection.

Second, decision-making situations are restricted to those in which the actor has a finite set of alternatives. The set of choices is not unlimited. Rather, there are a small, specifiable number of things he can choose to do. In many cases of interest, actors can narrow their options down to 2; for example, to buy a new car, or not to; to quit one's job, or not to. (In fact, one of the best ways of dealing with a complex situation is to reduce it to a large number of small, two-option, or *binary*, decisions. When this can be done, a perviously overwhelming problem often begins to look manageable. Moreover taking little decisions one at a time increases our confidence that each one will be made correctly. Therefore we are less likely to go back over previous decisions again and again, never getting the whole problem solved.) Our working definition of a decision-making situation is one in which:

1. Actors are motivated only to maximize their gains;
2. There are a finite number of action alternatives; and
3. The outcomes associated with each alternative are known to the actors.

In situations that meet these conditions, decision models assume that individual choices are some function of the rewards and costs associated with each alternative. Specifically these models assume that the actor is most likely to choose that alternative offering the greatest net *utility*. The tasks of the model builder are to identify the rewards and costs (or the gains and losses) associated with each outcome, and then to specify as precisely as possible a way to combine these rewards and costs to associate a specific net utility with each outcome.

To calculate the net utility of alternatives, we use one definition from exchange theories and one assumption about the way rewards and costs behave. The standard definition of *profit* of an action or a situation is that it is the rewards of the action or situation minus the costs of that action or situation. Precisely:

$$\text{Profit}_A = \text{rewards}_A - \text{costs}_A$$

In a decision-making situation, the individual is assumed to calculate the net utility (or profit) of the alternatives, and then to be most likely to choose the alternative offering greatest net utility. Net utility of an alternative is calculated by taking its gains (rewards) and subtracting from them the gains of the unchosen alternatives. That is, to calculate the net utility of alternative A, take the gains from A and subtract from them the gains associated with alternatives $B, C, D, \ldots n$. The reason for this is the assumption that, in a decision-making situation, *the rewards of foregone alternatives become costs, and the costs of avoided alternatives become rewards.*

Imagine an individual faced with making a decision between only two alternatives: going to the movies or staying home and studying. The rewards of going to the movies are pleasure and diversion, and the costs are $3.00 admission and a feeling of guilt about not studying. The rewards of studying are increased knowledge and confidence about the upcoming examination, and the costs are boredom and the time involved. This example illustrates the way in which a cost in one alternative becomes a reward in the other: the cost of guilt associated with the movies becomes the reward of satisfaction associated with studying. Now suppose the individual chooses to stay home and study. One of the costs of the movies was $3.00 admission. Since he does not have to pay the $3.00 if he chooses to stay home and study, in calculating the rewards and costs of the studying alternative, we add the $3.00 as a reward associated with studying. *Note that when costs "reverse" to become rewards, their value remains the same.* For most of the rewards and costs we shall use, such as social approval, it is more difficult to attach numerical values to them. However at least we know that their value—whatever it is—is the same, whether it is a cost in one alternative, or a reward in another.

To predict likely behavior in a situation, we assume that an individual's action is a direct function of the gains from each alternative, compared to all the gains possible from all alternatives in the situation. That is, the actor's probability of choosing alternative A is a function of the gains associated with A compared to the gains from all of the finite set of alternatives. More precisely:

$$P_A = \frac{G_A}{G_A + G_B + G_C + \ldots + G_n}$$

For a binary situation (where the actor has to choose between only two alternatives):

$$P_A = \frac{G_A}{G_A + G_B}$$

Incidentally we shall see later that this is not always a strictly optimal strategy, but we need not worry about that now. This basic assumption about

293

*Exchange
Research
II:
Games,
Decisions,
and
Choices*

the probability of choice alternatives is a part of most contemporary decision-making models.[1]

Note that we are focusing upon *gains* (rewards) from alternatives, not upon *net profit* (rewards − costs). This means that in calculating the *net utility* of alternative A, we add the gains of A to the costs of alternatives B, C, D, . . . , n. We do *not* follow the more complicated procedure of adding the quantity (rewards$_A$ − costs$_A$), and subtracting (rewards$_B$ − costs$_B$), then subtracting (rewards$_C$ − costs$_C$), and so on. This approach is not universal. Some decision models *do* calculate net gain using both rewards and costs from all alternatives. However we shall not be concerned with these more complicated models.

An Exchange Theory of Decision Making

These ideas may be stated explicitly. We begin with a set of four undefined terms. These are basic concepts in the theory for which no explicit definition will be given. Later they will be used to create explicit definitions of other terms. The fact that these terms are undefined does not indicate that they are unimportant; they are crucial. But any theory, and any set of definitions, has to start somewhere. At some point it is no longer possible to define everything. That point is where we use undefined terms. The undefined terms of our theory are: *reward, cost, act* (as a noun) *act* (as a verb). These terms will appear in the propositions and will be used to define three more terms. Remember that Homans' term value is a *measure* of rewards and costs.

The propositions of the decision-making version of exchange theory are presented in Chart 11–1. Using simply this set of propositions it is possible to derive many empirical hypotheses involving learning and behavior. For example it is possible to derive hypotheses about the training of animals and about human behavior in simple reward/cost situations.

At this point using propositions 1, 2, 6, and 7, we are able to derive:

Derivation 1: In any decision-making situation, the actor is most likely to try to choose the alternative offering greatest profit.

What we have done with derivation 1 is to show rigorously what is often only suggested; namely, that action in a decision-making situation can be explained *if* we can show that the actor was maximizing his profit.

But in order to predict any actor's behavior, we need to know what value

---

[1] This is known as the Luce choice function in game theories. It is a social psychological assumption about how people act, not a strictly mathematical property of a decision model. It has been quite successful in many different decision-making models applied to fairly unrestricted interaction. Certain special situations—such as conservative investment where the overriding goal is to prevent any possible loss rather than to maximize expected gains—may require use of another function. These special cases are not considered further here.

CHART 11–1   Exchange Theory of Decision Making

ASSUMPTIONS

1. (Basic Motivation)   The actor will act in such a way as to maximize his perceived rewards in interaction.

2. (Basic Motivation)   The actor will act in such a way as to minimize his perceived costs in interaction.

3. (Reinforcement)   The greater the relative proportion of times that performance of a given act has been rewarded in the past, the more likely is the actor to repeat the act in the present.

4. (Satiation, or Marginal Utility)   The greater the absolute amount of any given commodity or rewarding act which the individual has received in the recent past, the less is its reward value to that actor.

5. (Subjective Utility)   The perceived gain or subjective utility of any gain is calculated by multiplying its absolute value times the perceived probability of attaining that gain in any given alternative action.

6. (Unchosen Alternatives)   A reward foregone becomes a cost, and a cost avoided becomes a reward; *and* the absolute value of rewards and costs remains constant across alternatives.

7. (Basic Choice Assumption)   The probability of choosing any given alternative is a direct function of the perceived gains associated with that alternative, compared to the perceived gains of all other alternatives.

DEFINITIONS

1. *Gains* or *utilities* are the subjective value of *rewards* in other exchange theories.

2. *Net utility* or *net gain* of an alternative is equivalent to *profit* in other exchange theories. ($profit_A = rewards_A − costs_A$; $net\ gain_A = total\ utilities_A −$ total utilities of all other alternatives.)

---

he places upon the rewards and costs available in a situation; for example, how much he thinks social approval is worth to him. In addition, we assume that individuals calculate expected utility of alternatives by multiplying their utilities by the probability of attaining the various outcomes (assumptions). We have already informally considered the idea of expected utility. Let us consider a more precise example that uses this concept.

Imagine a gambler facing a situation in which he bets $1 on a sports event against 10-to-1 odds. His expected utility of the outcome "winning the bet" thus is:

$$.1(\$10.00) − .9(\$1.00) = 10¢$$

If he is offered a potential win of $20.00 for a bet of $2.00, and the odds are known to be 5-to-1 against him, the expected utility is:

$$.2(\$20.00) − .8(\$2.00) = \$3.20$$

By our derivation 1, our gambler would prefer the second bet considerably, since its net gain is greater. Now, by adding assumption 5 to derivation 1, we are in a position to tell just *how* the actor will try to maximize his profit:

> *Derivation 2:* In any decision-making situation, the actor is most likely to choose the alternative offering greatest expected utility.

We shall use Derivation 2 for predicting behavior in the choice situations below. Because Derivation 2 only states an ordering (that is, *most likely*) rather than an exact numerical probability (for example, "will choose with probability = .90"), so far we can only predict the ordering of preferences for an individual. Even that is quite an accomplishment, but sometimes we will even be able to make numerical predictions. We can do this in cases in which we have a way to calculate both the gains and their subjective probabilities of occurrence.[2]

Decision Making and Social Influence

Let us now examine a model of decision making in a familiar situation, that illustrates the preceding general points on decision models. The situation is a variant of the basic expectation experiment, described in Chap. 6. The model to predict behavior in this situation is developed by Camilleri and associates. For purposes of constructing and testing the model, the ideas of expectation states theory are not central; however a brief review of the experimental design in Chap. 6 will be helpful. At least you should recall the basic operational measure of expectation state: proportion of disagreements resolved in favor of self, or $P(s)$. Also the basic prediction is that $P(s)$ will vary as a direct function of relative self–other expectations.

To build the model, we note that the subject in this experiment is faced, on each trial, with a binary choice: to change his initial choice in the face of disagreement, or to refuse to change it. We assume that his behavior is a function of the rewards and costs from each alternative behavior. More precisely, choice behavior is assumed to depend upon the perceived probability of attaining gains, minus perceived probability of sustaining losses. Three potential rewards or "utilities," seem crucial in this experiment. First (u_1), the individual is concerned with *self-consistency*. In some sense, it is "costly" or unpleasant to change one's own choice, for this entails admitting that one was wrong. Second (u_2), there is the potential *approval from one's partner* for getting the correct final choice. This gain is irrespective of whether one needed to change the initial choice in order to be correct. Third (u_3), there is *approval from the experimenter* for a correct answer. This occurs under the same conditions as u_2 although its value to the subject may

---

[2] Strictly speaking, since we have not used assumptions 3 and 4 for these derivations, they could be left out of the theory. These assumptions are included here because they would have to be used in decision models designed to show changes in behavior over time, and also to emphasize the relation of this theory to the exchange theories of Chap. 9.

differ. The possibility of receiving the u_2 and u_3 depends upon two things: the ability level of the subject (that is, his relative expectation state) and whether he changes his initial choice. For a subject to change his initial choice if he had very high ability, for instance, would decrease the probability of getting the correct answer. U_1 depends only upon whether the subject changes his initial choice.

The model assumes that behavior, measured by $P(s)$, is a function of the total gains of each alternative. More precisely, we assume that the individual will probably make a "self" resolution when the gains for that alternative outweigh the gains for an "other" resolution. Stated differently, we are using the basic choice assumption, that the probability of choosing alternative A is a function of the gains associated with A compared to the total gains associated with all alternatives. In this experiment we have a binary choice situation: to resolve each disagreement in favor of self or other, and we wish to predict $P(s)$. Since we already know that

$$P_A = \frac{G_A}{G_A + G_B}$$

it is a simple extension to say that

$$P(s) = \frac{G_s}{G_s + G_o}$$

and likewise, that

$$P(o) = \frac{G_o}{G_s + G_o}$$

[You probably saw the last equation before you got to it. Because $P(s)$ is a probability, and because all probabilities in a situation must sum to 1, of course $P(o) = 1 - P(s)$.] Note that the total gains in the entire situation (from both alternatives) determine the denominator in the $P(s)$ equation. Now if we knew the gains perceived from a Self or S response, and the gains perceived from an Other or O response, we could use the $P(s)$ equation to predict the probability of a self response.

What are the gains from both possible actions? They are the sum of the utilities associated with each alternative, u_1, u_2, *and* u_3. Suppose the subject in this experiment decides to make an S response. What utilities will he get? He will certainly get u_1, the gain of being self-consistent. He *might* get u_2 and u_3 (approval from other and approval from the experimenter), but these depend upon his getting the correct answer. Getting the correct answer, in turn, depends upon his ability to do these problems. Since he does not know his ability for sure, we assume that his subjective probability of getting the right answer (and thus of gaining u_2 and u_3) depends upon what the experimenter told him about his ability.

Let a = the subjective probability of making a correct initial choice. Then

297

*Exchange
Research
II:
Games,
Decisions,
and
Choices*

the probability of getting u_2 and u_3 from an S response is a, by assumption 5. The total gains from an S response are calculated using definition 2. They are the utilities from S minus the utilities of 0:

$$S = u_1 + a(u_2 + u_3) - [-\bar{a}(u_2 + u_3)] \quad \text{where } \bar{a} = 1 - a$$

Likewise the total gains from an O response are:

$$O = -u_1 + \bar{a}(u_2 + u_3) - a(u_2 + u_3)$$

Now focusing only on the positive aspects of both alternatives, we know that the utility of S may be represented:

$$G_s = u_1 + a(u_2 + u_3) - [-u_1 - a(u_2 + u_3)]$$

and the utility of O may be represented:

$$G_o = \bar{a}(u_2 + u_3) - [-\bar{a}(u_2 + u_3)]$$

From the basic choice assumption (assumption 7), we have:

$$P(s) = \frac{u_1 + a(u_2 + u_3)}{u_1 + u_2 + u_3}$$

Or in words, the probability of an S response depends upon the positive utilities from an S response, divided by all utilities available from both alternatives in the situation.

Before deriving the exact predictions, we need a description of the experiment. The experimental test of the model involves 12 conditions. Four of the conditions were the four expectation patterns discussed in Chap. 6: [+ −], [+ +], [− −], [− +]. To these, the independent variable *responsibility* was added. In the responsible (R+) condition, the subject was told that only his own final choice would determine the team score. In the not responsible (R−) condition, the subject was told that only his partner's final choice would count. In the equal responsibility condition (R=), both the subject's and his partner's choices would count equally. In general, we expect the effect of responsibility to decrease $P(s)$ in all expectation state conditions, since it increases the likelihood of disapproval from ($-u_2$) for making a wrong choice.

Now note that in the R− conditions, there is no possibility of disapproval from the partner for a wrong choice. More precisely, we say $u_2 = 0$. Given this fact, it is possible to use the $P(s)$ data from one condition to estimate various quantities crucial to the basic $P(s)$ equation. In the [+ +] expectation state, where both the subject and his partner have high ability, it seems reasonable that the subject would think his chance of being correct (reflecting ability, or a) when they disagree is one-half. Therefore, for the [+ +] (R−) condition, $u_2 = 0$, and $a = .5$. Because u_2 is zero in the

$(R-)$ conditions, this utility drops out of the equations, and for them:

$$P(s) = \frac{u_1 + a(u_3)}{u_1 + u_3}$$

Assuming that $a = .5$ for the $[+ +]$ condition, it is possible to solve this equation for an estimate of the *ratio* of u_1 to u_3. Camilleri and Berger use the actual observed data from the $[+ +]$ conditions of the experiment to get an estimate of the numerical value of this ratio, put this number back into equations for the other conditions, and get predictions for the other 9 conditions. Table 11–2 shows the predicted and observed $P(s)$ values yielded by this procedure.

The "fit" of predicted to observed values is quite good, usually within .02, except in the $[- +]$ expectation states conditions. This is frequently an unusual condition, stressful to the subject, and characterized by variable behavior and psychological withdrawal.

Balkwell reviewed this study, and decided that the original model, although a good statement, could be improved upon. He reasoned that the value of a self-consistent response (represented by u_1) would vary in different conditions of the experiment. Specifically, he felt the value of u_1 should vary directly with *ability* (expectation state) and with *responsibility*. The greater one's ability, and the greater one's responsibility, the more it "hurts" to change one's initial choice.

Moreover the value of approval from the partner would vary continuously (and directly) with responsibility. That is, the value of approval (u_2) would be greater in the $(R+)$ conditions than in the conditions of equal responsibility, and, of course it is zero in the $(R-)$ conditions.

Balkwell built a modification of the Camilleri–Berger model incorporating these ideas, and presented independent data testing it. By comparison with the earlier experiments, prediction of all conditions is improved by these theoretical refinements.

As with any theory, mathematical models can always be improved upon. Balkwell's results, though improving the $[- +]$ predictions considerably, still do not show perfect prediction of all data. Perhaps this is due to sample variation in the cells of the experiments, for the samples are not

TABLE 11–2   Predicted and Observed *P(s)*

EXPECTATION STATE	FULL CONTROL		EQUAL CONTROL*		No CONTROL	
	PRED.	OBS.	PRED.	OBS.	PRED.	OBS.
$[+ -]$	.75	.73	.77	.76	.80	.82
$[+ +]$	X	.60	X	.64	X	.71
$[- -]$	.60	.52	.64	.66	.71	.73
$[- +]$	.47	.24	.55	.42	.60	.43

* These data do not appear in the earlier reports. The experiments that generated them are replications at Michigan State University of the original experiments for the equal control conditions carried out at Stanford University.

(From Camilleri et al., 1972, Table 1.)

large. On the other hand it may happen that someone else will come along with ideas that improve predictions even further for this situation. We study another model for this experiment in Chap. 14.

Notice that what is at issue in constructing and testing of models is specifying the precise *form* of the utility maximizing process. We are no longer testing the exchange ideas in the propositions, except very indirectly. Propositions 1 and 2 (p. 294) might be called into question if the predictions from these models were very far from observed data, but this is not the case. Most mathematical model testing, including that of decision models, is the process of specifying as precisely as possible just how it is that individuals seek to maximize total gains in a given situation.

The Camilleri–Berger model is a good one to begin with, since it is a relatively straightforward adaptation of the basic assumptions of decision models. Moreover it has received empirical support in two separate studies, and a degree of theoretical refinement in Balkwell's work—all desirable characteristics of any theory or model. Now we turn attention to a different model, constructed for different purposes, but which reflects the same qualities of empirical confirmation and cumulative theoretical attention.

Siegel's Model of Light-Guessing

During the 1930s and 1940s, an experiment that came to be known as the Humphreys light-guessing experiment attracted wide attention. The reason for its publicity was that behavior in that situation seemed not to be "rational," and this was popularly interpreted as showing that human behavior in general is not rational. The proper question, of course, is whether it is possible to predict and explain human behavior using a set of logically consistent principles. Whether humans are in fact rational is a metaphysical question and unanswerable by the methods of empirical science. Whether behavior can be predicted from rational theories is a simpler question, and at least in successful instances, it is clear what the answer is.

Humphrey's experiment involves having a single subject sit before a pair of light bulbs. For a large number of trials, say 200, he is asked to predict ahead of time which bulb will light up. Sometimes the task is complicated by including the alternatives "both" and "neither," but let us consider the simpler situation for an example. Suppose the light on the right comes on 80 percent of the time and the light on the left comes on 20 percent. We say the probability associated with the outcome "right light" is .80. With the outcome "left light," it is .20. If you were trying to anticipate correctly in this situation as much as possible, what would be the best strategy? After a little thought, you should realize that the optimal strategy is to pick the more frequent event *every single time:* every time you guess "right," you have an 80 percent chance of being correct. No other strategy provides such good odds.

Subjects in Humphrey's experiment do not know the exact probabilities associated with the lights, but after a large number of trials, they certainly must realize which light (called an "event") is more likely. The surprising finding of this experiment is that subjects typically do not adopt the maximizing strategy of choosing the more likely event every time. Instead, they appear to adopt a "matching strategy": if the light on the right has $p = .80$, they soon begin choosing it with $p = .80$.

What does the matching strategy do to a subject's probability of getting the right answer? Suppose the events have probabilities of .80 for right and .20 for left. We already know that if he picks right every time, he will be 80 percent right. Suppose he picks right only 80 percent of the time? Then his overall probability of being correct is the sum of probabilities of being correct for each possible choice. Since probabilities multiply in this situation, his overall proportion of correct answers is

$$(.80 \times .80 = .64) + (.20 \times .20 = .04) = .68$$

This is a considerable decrease. As the probability of one event approaches .50, it gets worse. What would it be, for example, if he adopted the matching strategy when the events had probabilities of .60 and .40? (Your answer should be just over 50 percent correct—about what chance guessing would get him.)

As I said, the matching strategy was widely cited as illustrating the basic irrationality of human behavior. Siegel (1964) saw it differently. After watching subjects in the Humphreys situation, he reasoned that it must become rather boring. Long before 200 or 300 trials have passed, subjects must realize which light appears more frequently, and once they realize this, to adopt a maximizing strategy means they point to the same light in exactly the same way every time. Perhaps they adopt a matching strategy as a way to reduce boredom. Perhaps they are trying to enrich their situation by estimating the exact probability of each event, rather than simply maximizing correct guesses. Correct guesses are so easy to make that they are boring. That is, the utility of a correct guess declines rapidly due to satiation, while the cost due to boredom increases over time (assumption 4 in Chart 11–1).

Siegel formalized his ideas by constructing a decision-making model that incorporates *two* sources of utilities; one for correct answers, and one for what he calls "response variability." The second utility is included because Siegel believed there is some reward in a very boring situation from just varying one's choices sometimes. But note that the effect of the first utility would make the subject want to vary his choices in a way that wouldn't cost him wrong answers—thus he would attempt to vary from choosing the more likely event only when he had a hunch that event wouldn't occur. This, of course, could produce what had earlier appeared to be a matching strategy.

Some very convincing support for the idea that these two sources of utility are present in the light guessing experiment comes from an ingenious variant of the basic experiment. If individuals are motivated by two sources of utility, and if the utilities are gained from different behaviors, then choices should be affected by the relative size of the utilities. Specifically, the more valuable the "correct answer" utility is compared to the "avoiding boredom" utility, the more the choices should approximate a *maximizing* strategy rather than a matching strategy.

This was tested in an experiment with 3 conditions. In condition 1, subjects were instructed to try to guess which light would come on for each of 300 trials. Condition 2 was the same, except that subjects were told each correct guess would win them 5¢—thus increasing the utility of a correct answer. In condition 3, subjects were told that correct answers would win 5¢, and incorrect answers would lose 5¢, increasing the utility of a correct answer even more. In all cases, light #1 came on 75 percent of the time; light #2, 25 percent. Table 11–3 shows the proportion of correct answers by subjects in each condition. Notice that subjects in condition 1 seem to be matching. It is quite clear by condition 3 that subjects are maximizing. The greater the utility associated with correct choice, the more likely are subjects to decide in accord with a maximizing strategy.

This experiment is very clever, since is shows just the sort of effect which would be predicted from the basic idea behind Siegel's model. The experiment also indicates that behavior in this situation *can* be predicted from a rational theory, when the relevant utilities are identified.

The next step is to specify exactly the form in which utilities are combined by subjects in determining their choice behaviors. We need not worry about the derivation and all formal properties of the model; however we do need to know the basic variables it contains. These are:

π_1 = the probability that light i comes on (where i = 1 or 2)

a_i = the marginal utility of a correct choice of light i

b = the marginal utility of choice variability

P_i = the probability subjects will choose light i

The quantity π is of course fixed by the experimenter before the study begins. a is the utility (subjective value) of getting the correct answer for individuals, and b is the utility of varying choices to avoid boredom or

TABLE 11–3 Proportion Choosing Light #1, as a Function of Rewards

Condition	Characteristics	Proportion Choosing 1
1	No payoff	.75
2	+5¢	.86
3	+5¢, −5¢	.95

Light #1: .75; light #2: .25
(From Siegel et al., 1964, p. 15.)

to try to "figure out" the experimental design. Neither of these quantities will be known, nor is it directly measurable in the study. P is the dependent variable. Using the known value for π, plus estimates of a and b, the goal is to predict the observable proportion of choices P.

It turns out that, in a binary choice situation where the utilities of both events are equal—getting the right answer for one event is rewarded the same as getting the right answer for the second event—and where the probabilities of the event sum to one—either one light or the other comes on, but not both lights at once—the model predicts the following proportion of choices for light #1:

$$P_1 = \frac{a}{4}(\pi_1 - \pi_2) + \tfrac{1}{2}$$

And of course,

$$P_2 = 1 - P_1$$

The model was tested in a variety of light guessing experiments, and generally provided good predictions. Table 11–4 shows some typical results.

One application of the model which I particularly like tested it with 1 to 3 year old children. Guessing lights is beyond the normal experience of such young children, so Siegel had them guess repeatedly which of two bottles held a small object. The utility of a correct choice was even varied. Sometimes children got a prize for correct guesses; sometimes not. What is impressive is that the model provides good predictions of behavior even with this subject population. As the researchers note, this vividly illustrates the "as if" goals of model building. Nobody would seriously assert that before children make a decision they go through complicated mathematical calculations required for solving the model's equations. But what is important is that by treating behavior *as if* people went through these calculations, we can predict it quite well. The point is applicable to any theoretical activity. When someone says, "Do you really think people are primarily concerned with maximizing their rewards in a situation?" the proper answer is neither yes nor no. The answer is that, in a surprising number of cases, we can predict their behavior making no other assump-

TABLE 11–4   Three Tests of Siegel's
Light Guessing Model

EXPERIMENT	π_1	PREDICTED P_1	OBSERVED P_1 [*]	ERROR
A	.75	.922	.929	.007
B	.65	.758	.753	.005
C	.70	.842	.862	.020

[*] Final trials in series.
(Taken from Ofshe & Ofshe, 1970, p. 17.)

303

*Exchange
Research
II:
Games,
Decisions,
and
Choices*

tions than that they will behave *as if* they were only interested in maximizing rewards—even where we need some complex mathematics to find out what behavior will maximize rewards.

Utility and Choice in Coalition Formation

Interesting as Siegel's model is, it becomes far more interesting as the result of further work on it by Ofshe and Ofshe. The Humphreys light-guessing experiment is a nonsocial choice situation: the individual is trying to anticipate the behavior of a machine that is programmed ahead of time. However the Ofshes had the insight to notice certain similarities between Siegel's analysis of the light-guessing experiment and social choice behavior in coalition studies we studied in Chap. 10. They argue that the variables and the model of light guessing can be interpreted in such a way that they have direct application to predicting behavior of coalition game players.

A player in a coalition study may be thought of as facing two other players, in a way analogous to a player facing two light bulbs in Humphreys' experiment. The coalition player wants to form a coalition; the Humphreys' subject wants to pick the correct light. If either of them succeeds, he gets *a*, the reward of forming a coalition or of guessing the light correctly. Guessing the light correctly depends upon π, or the actual likelihood that the light will come on. Forming a coalition depends upon reciprocation, being chosen by the player to whom a coalition is offered. Thus the probability of reciprocation may also be represented by π. The Humphreys' subject also gets the utility *b* from response variability; he wants to avoid boredom. What produces a desire for response variability in a coalition player (not always offering a coalition to the same other player)? The answer is that response variability for the coalition player serves the desire for distributive justice or *equity*, as we saw in Chap. 10. Players want to distribute their coalition offers so that all of them will win something in the game. Finally P_1, the probability of choosing light #1, is directly analogous to the probability of choosing to offer a coalition to player #1. This interpretation of the variables is shown as:

π_i = probability of reciprocation from player i

a_i = the marginal utility (winnings) of forming a coalition

b = the marginal utility of equity considerations

P_i = the probability of offering a coalition to player i

Generalizing the Siegel model to a social situation represents an imaginative and daring step. What is claimed here is that behavior in a distinctly social situation may be predicted using the same principles used for predicting nonsocial behavior. There are many large differences in concrete features of the different types of situation. One of the biggest of these is that subjects in the Humphreys experiment know that the sequence of lights is determined before they begin the experiment. How they play will have no effect on which light comes on in the future. By contrast, players in coalition experiments would be expected to think that their behavior *does* affect each others' future style of play. The generalization constitutes a tremendous widening of scope of application of the model, and it makes the model applicable to a far more interesting class of situations (at least to social psychologists) than it was previously.

The Ofshes' generalization was tested in a series of experiments where subjects communicated with each other through teletype machines. The teletypes were used for subjects to transmit offers to potential partners and to receive notification of choices (if any) from potential partners. First, the model was tested in a controlled situation where the probabilities of reciprocated choice could be fixed by the experimenter. In this condition subjects essentially played against a machine. That is, they were trying to guess which other person would choose them in a situation where the probability of a reciprocated choice was previously determined and was held constant. Table 11–5 presents typical results of tests of the model in which the probability of reciprocated choices was controlled. Observed results are very close to predicted. Other experiments, in which instructions were varied to create more or less emphasis upon equity concerns, show just the sorts of results expected from changing the values of b.

The model also was applied to three actual players in a coalition game, who again communicated their coalition offers through teletype machines. To make the test more interesting, players received different amounts of winnings from the possible types of coalitions. Player 1 would receive 10¢ for a successful (reciprocated) coalition from player 2, and 5¢ for a successful coalition with player 3. Players 2 and 3 would receive only 5¢ from any coalitions they could make. The payoff structure of the game is diagrammed in Fig. 11–9. The number on each arrow represents the monetary gain to the player *from whom* the arrow originates, for successfully forming a coalition with the player *to whom* the arrow points.

In this situation, no experimental control was exerted over the value of π, a reciprocated choice. However it is possible to determine estimates of the necessary quantities for solving the model's equations without this, using data from previous experiments. Thus it is possible to predict coalition offers only from knowledge of the payoffs to each player from successful coalition formation. Predictions and the observed strategies are shown in Table 11–6. The behavior predicted by the model is very close to that actually observed.

We might note again the "as if" nature of the model building, as it is

TABLE 11–5 Some Results of Ofshe's Coalition Model

CONDITION	a_1	π_1	PREDICTED P_1	OBSERVED P_1	ERROR
A	5¢	.70	.8619	.8636	.0017
B	5¢	.60	.6818	.6810	.0008

(From Ofshe & Ofshe, 1970, p. 52, 67.)

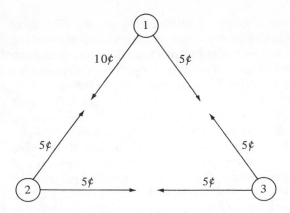

305

*Exchange
Research
II:
Games,
Decisions,
and
Choices*

FIGURE 11–9 Payoffs for coalitions. (From Ofshe and
Ofshe, 1970, Fig. 9–5.)

illustrated by Ofshe's generalization of Siegel's model. An implicit claim here
is that players in a coalition game treat each other, in choosing their partners, "as if" they were choosing lights to guess in the Humphreys experiment. One way to look at the successful predictions made from such an
approach is to say it is encouraging that human social behavior may not be
infinite in its variety. Perhaps most of us do adopt a relatively small number
of strategies for most of our decision making—both nonsocial decisions, and
those involving our human associates.

TABLE 11–6 Predicted and Observed Coalition Offers

	PROPORTIONS		
COALITION OFFERS	PREDICTED	OBSERVED	ERROR
1 to 2	.8896	.8388	.0508
1 to 3	.1104	.1612	
2 to 1	.6817	.6714	.0103
2 to 3	.3183	.3286	
3 to 1	.3183	.3393	.0210
3 to 2	.6817	.6607	

(From Ofshe & Ofshe, 1970, Table 9–8.)

Other Applications of the Siegel–Ofshe Model

Elaine Walster and her colleagues have conducted a large number of studies
of liking and dating choices. One intriguing result that appears repeatedly is
what we may call a "matching phenomenon": dating partners seem to sort
themselves out so that both members of a pair are about equally attractive.
Ugly people seldom date attractive people, that is. (Attractiveness may be
either physical or social, such as being rich). Moreover individuals are asked

to choose a possible date from a group of photographs or descriptions of people; they tend to say they *prefer* others about as attractive as themselves. Even when individuals are paired by the experimenters (through a computer dating service), the matching phenomenon shows up. Those matched on attractiveness say they are more "satisfied" than those mis-matched.

Perhaps it is not surprising that a pretty person would be dissatisfied with an ugly date. But why do we also find that the ugly person with a pretty date is dissatisfied? The answer, I think, comes from another of Walster's findings. In the computer dating study, couples who continued to date were asked how satisfied they were at a later time. At that time the only predictor of satisfaction was attractiveness of partner; that is, the prettier the partner, the more satisfied the individual was, *regardless of matching*.

What does this mean? I think Ofshe's model applies to dating choices as well as to coalitions. Imagine an individual thinking about his potential date. He probably sees two sources of utility from it: (1) the actual value of association, which is roughly measured by physical and social attractiveness; and (2) the negative utility of potential rejection. These are exactly the two utilities of Ofshe's model. Now for a pretty person confronted with an ugly date, the first utility is small. For an ugly person confronted with a pretty date, the second utility is large. Either case promises to be costly, in other words, so our explanation for the dissatisfaction is an exchange one. Now for the couples who continued to date and for whom attractiveness of partner was the only factor in satisfaction: A pretty individual would naturally be more satisfied with an attractive partner than with an ugly one. That part is easy. But if the relationship continues, an ugly person will stop worrying about possible rejection. This means that our second possible utility, which is negative, drops out of the equation.

Not all the steps in my interpretation are confirmed, of course, but it does seem to fit available data. Very recently Huston found, in a situation similar to Walster's, that less attractive partners were concerned about being turned down by attractive ones, and that all individuals expected more rejections from very attractive date prospects than from moderately attractive or unattractive prospects.

Before leaving Ofshe's model, let us consider briefly the predictions it would make in a fairly complex social situation involving five actors. What is most interesting is that using the model to analyze the situation shows that we may expect large changes in individuals' behavior from making relatively minor changes in their social situation.

The situation to be considered has five actors, all interested in forming coalitions, but not in perfect communication with each other. Each of the five actors is only allowed to offer a coalition to a player directly on either side of him. Figure 11–10 represents the structure, with payoffs for successful coalitions shown. Remember that player 1 is only able to communicate with players 2 and 5, and so on for the other players. However the players all have indirect contact with each other. For example, player 1's success at forming coalitions with player 2 depends partially upon whether player 3 offers 2 a coalition. Numbers on the arrows are interpreted as in Fig. 11–10.

307

*Exchange
Research
II:
Games,
Decisions,
and
Choices*

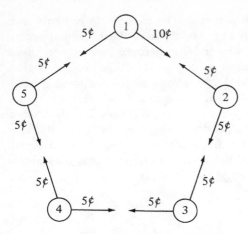

FIGURE 11–10   Five-person modified coalition payoffs.
(Adapted from Ofshe and Ofshe, 1970, Fig. 11.8.)

The only unusual feature of the structure in Fig. 11–10 is that player 1 will receive 10¢ if he correctly predicts that player 2 will choose him on any given trial. All other players receive only 5¢ for any correct prediction.

How would you expect player 1 to distribute his coalition choices in this situation? Your intuitive guess is almost guaranteed to be wrong, as was mine when I first encountered this structure in the Ofshes' book. Player 1's maximizing strategy, which is predicted by the model, is to pick player 2 only 24 percent of the time, and to pick player 5, 76 percent! Figure 11–11 shows the maximizing strategy for each player, as predicted by the model. Numbers on the arrows here represent the probability that the player from whom the arrow originates will pick the player to whom it points.

Next, let us see the effect of another small change in the structure of the utilities shown in Fig. 11–10. Player 4 will be offered 10¢ for a coalition with

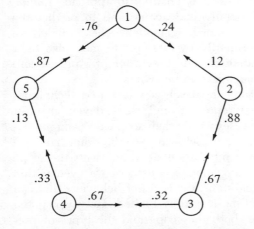

FIGURE 11–11   Maximizing strategy choices of players. (Adapted from Ofshe and Ofshe, 1970, Fig. 11.9.)

player 5, and 5¢ for a coalition with player 3. The changes in rewards and in predicted strategies are shown in Fig. 11–12. Look what has happened to the maximizing choice strategies. Player 5 has become perfectly indifferent between his possible coalition partners, and player 4 has become nearly so. But players 2 and 3 have entered a very strong alliance, choosing each other as coalition partners about 80 percent of the time! How did this happen? I cannot tell you in any simple way—bring 5 people together, offer them the appropriate rewards for coalitions, and see for yourself. The results in Figures 11–9 to 11–12 are striking evidence for the effects of social structural variables upon individuals' behavior. I hope also that they show you some nonintuitive uses of exchange theory ideas.

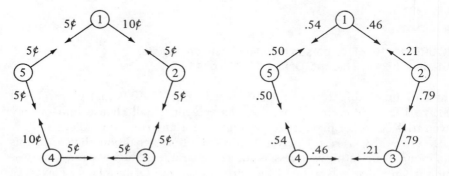

FIGURE 11–12 Reward structure and maximizing strategy. (Adapted from Ofshe and Ofshe, 1970, Figs. 11.9, 11.10.)

Perspective on Human Decision Making

In a surprisingly large number of cases, it is possible to approach human behavior as a series of decisions by individual actors, and to predict the decisions using exchange-based decision-making models. These models all assume that actors are motivated primarily by attempts to maximize their perceived rewards, or utilities, in situations, and they attempt a precise and accurate description of the utility maximization behaviors.

Decision-making models utilize some relatively sophisticated techniques for predicting behavior, and thus they represent the furthest development of the basic exchange meta-theory. For cases within their scope, decision models often can make very precise predictions of behavior. On the other hand we must remember that not every human interaction situation meets the scope conditions for applying decision-making models. Furthermore even within situations that do meet the scope conditions, the types of behaviors that can be predicted by the models at this time is strictly limited. However, if the past is any indication of the future, both the scope and the types of predictable behaviors will be expanded as the result of continued theoretical efforts and empirical tests.

12 Consistency Theories

General Introduction

One of the oldest presumptions about human behavior is that people are, or should be, or would like to be, *consistent*. We say someone's behavior, "Doesn't make sense," when he acts inconsistently with his expressed attitude. If we hear someone say he dislikes classical music and then later learn that he attends the symphony regularly, we also say this doesn't make sense. The two actions are inconsistent and therefore incomprehensible. On the other hand, in many criminal trials the prosecuting attorney attempts to prove that commission of the crime would be consistent with the attitudes and previous actions of the accused. If he can demonstrate this, then jury members are more likely to decide that the accused actually did commit the crime.

We presume, as a general principle, that individuals tend to be consistent in their actions. Moreover we presume that behavior tends to be consistent with individuals' attitudes and beliefs. And finally, we presume that there is a tendency for all the various attitudes and beliefs held by people to be consistent with each other. These ideas, stated more precisely, are fundamental to a major line of theoretical explanation in social psychology we call consistency theories. As a first statement of these theories, we present the "consistency principle":

> An individual will seek consistency among his various attitudes and beliefs among his various actions, and among his attitudes and his actions.

Consistency theories assume, in addition, that individual behavior is a direct function of seeking consistency. That is, these theories predict and explain behavior by assuming that individuals will do whatever is necessary to promote the consistency principle, and that they will avoid actions that would produce inconsistency.

Consistency theories offer an alternative *type* of explanation to social exchange theories. Many of the same actions can be explained either using an exchange theory or using a consistency theory. We shall see later that for some phenomena it is easier to construct a consistency explanation than an exchange explanation; for others, the reverse is true.

It will become apparent that explanations constructed according to the consistency principle seem farther from common sense than exchange explanations, and therefore more practice is needed to become familiar with consistency explanations. We readily say, "I got a lot out of meeting him," or, "That was a valuable discussion for me." Both expressions are rooted in the exchange meta-theory, and they sound perfectly familiar and understandable to us. Now suppose somebody said, "This is an imbalanced situation for me," or, "Talking with him arouses feelings of dissonance." Would you know what he meant? These expressions are rooted in the consistency meta-theory, and when that meta-theory becomes more familiar, these sentences will make sense as easily as the exchange-based expressions.

The ideas of consistency theories are considerably newer; they are only about 25–30 years old, while some of the fundamental ideas in exchange theories go back as far as Aristotle. (The exchange theory ideas borrowed from economics are at least 200 years old, and the ideas borrowed from behavioral psychology are at least 70 years old.) The relative newness and unfamiliarity of consistency theories means that their particular strengths and weaknesses are not so well known as those of exchange theories. It also means that consistency theories are developing and changing rapidly.

Heider's Balance Theory

All contemporary consistency theories grow from some basic observations reported by Fritz Heider in 1944 and 1946. He began by noting that people tend to believe their friends hold the same attitudes as they themselves hold. There is a tendency for me to believe that my friends hold the same political attitudes I do, that they like baseball if I like baseball, or conversely, that they dislike baseball if I dislike baseball: a belief that, in general, my friends and I agree about most things. To a certain extent my perceptions are based on reality. One of the reasons I choose my friends is that we do not have a large number of disagreements about important matters. But even in cases where I do not know my friends attitudes, Heider says, there is a tendency for me to believe that their attitudes are the same as my own.

Starting from this simple observation, Heider began a series of *thought experiments* to test the idea and to explore its usefulness. A thought experiment is simply an imaginary version of a real experiment. The investigator thinks of various situations—that is, he mentally manipulates an independent variable—and asks himself what outcome he would expect—that is what effect this would have upon the dependent variable. Heider thought of various combinations of attitudes and actors, and asked himself what the likely resolution would be in each situation. As a result of these thought experiments, he discovered two other tendencies. First, not only is there a tendency to believe friends hold attitudes similar to one's own, but people sometimes get upset when they are forced to confront the fact of a difference. If I do not know my friends' political preferences in a given election, there is a tendency for me to believe it is the same as my own. If later I learn that their preference is not the same as my own, I am likely to become upset. Second, no such tendency is apparent for enemies or for strangers. There is no reason to believe that an individual would be upset to know that a stranger or an enemy has different political attitudes. In fact for enemies, the opposite may be pleasing. There are several people I know whose political attitudes differ from mine, and I consider this proof of my own wise judgment.

Heider's first statement of his balance theory differs only slightly from our consistency principle. The notation system Heider used talks about individuals p and o (for person and other) and of objects x and y. For cases where there are three individuals the letters are p, o, and q. For three objects, we would use the letters, x, y, and z. The balance principle is the following:

Taking a unit of p, o, and x, or of p, o, and q, the relations between any two are interdependent with the other relations in the unit in specifiable ways. Specifically, there is a psychological tendency to arrange the units in a consistent or *balanced* fashion.

Heider's point is that units may be classified as being either *balanced* or *imbalanced,* and that balanced units differ from imbalanced units in important ways. For now, as for Heider at this early stage of his inquiry, we shall not specify exactly what makes a unit balanced or imbalanced. Instead we simply consider examples of balanced and imbalanced units. This is a *denotative definition:* defining something by pointing to instances of it. Heider distinguishes two types of relations that can exist between the entities of a unit: *affect* (or emotional) *relations*, such as liking or disliking; and *unit relations*, such as ownership, similarity, or closeness.[1] Affect relations are represented by L for positive affect (liking), and −L (disliking) for negative relations. For unit relations there is no negative form. One either owns or does not own, and there is no such thing as "negative ownership." (This last point was only determined later, as the result of experimental research, but since it is crucial to balance theory, we had better learn it at the outset.)

Using this notation, Figs. 12–1 and 12–2 show some units that Heider considered to be balanced, and some which Heider considered to be imbalanced. The first unit of Fig. 12–1 is read "p likes o, o likes q, and p likes q." This is a balanced unit consisting of three individuals, all of whom like each other. The second example, "p likes o, o likes x, and p owns x," would also be balanced. For example, p and his friend o both like p's car (x).

The first unit in Fig. 12–2, "p likes o, o does not like q, and p likes q" is imbalanced. If p likes o and q, it is in some sense disturbing for p to know that o does not like q. Generally speaking we want our friends to like each other. The second unit is likewise imbalanced. P likes o and p

---

[1] Unit relation is a residual category: any relation which does not involve emotion (affect) is a unit relation.

p+Lo   p+Lo
o+Lq   o+Lx
p+Lq   pUx

FIGURE 12-1   Some balanced cognitive structures

owns *x*, but *o* does not like *x*. To use our earlier example of a car, it is in some sense disturbing for an individual to know that his friend does not think much of his car. (In places where the automobile is an object of religious devotion—such as in Southern California—the distress caused by an imbalanced unit of this sort can be extreme!) The consequences of imbalance, no matter what the specific nature of the imbalance in the unit, are the same: psychological tension, actions attempting to change the imbalanced situation, or some sort of psychological distortion (such as pretending it doesn't exist). Imbalanced units are psychologically unpleasant and unstable. Balanced units are stress-free and stable.

Logically, in terms of the ideas involved, if not chronologically, Heider's observations on balanced and imbalanced relations are direct outgrowths of the attribution principle, which we studied in Chap. 4. You will recall that the principle of attribution asserts that when an individual *p* observes the actions of a second individual *o*, *p* tends to see some *connection* between the various actions. Not only does he see a connection between the actions, but he tends to believe they are *nonrandom*. There is some reason for the actions, such as a motive or intention on the part of *o*. To state the attribution principle in the terms introduced here, *p* tends to form a cognitive unit consisting of himself, *o*, and their respective attitudes and actions. You might find it helpful to review the discussion of attribution at this point. Now in addition to the tendencies described by the attribution principle, Heider asserts a tendency for actors to *prefer* balanced cognitive units.

Heider discusses 15 different types of balanced cognitive units, along with some familiar behavioral attempts to produce balance in initially imbalanced situations. Let us briefly consider each of these instances as a thought experiment. The cases may be grouped into categories of similarity, interaction, familiarity, ownership and benefits.

Similarity of p and o. (1) if *p* and *o* are similar in some way, *p* will tend to like *o*. This could be represented in the following way: *pLx, oLx,* (therefore) *pLo; or pUo,* (therefore) *pLo.* If *p* and *o* have a similar attitude (*x*) in common, there is a tendency for them to like each other. Studies of the

p+Lo   p+Lo
o-Lq   o-Lx
p+Lq   pUx

FIGURE 12-2   Some imbalanced structures

selection of marriage partners and formation of friendship choices all support this general assertion. Computer dating services rely on the assertion when they match people on the basis of similarities of interest. (2) If p and o are dissimilar, p tends to dislike o. Hostility and fear towards members of an out-group (xenophobia), are common instances of this principle. The bad guys in adventure stories usually look or act bizarre, predisposing us to dislike them. Bad guys in Dick Tracy, for example, have been physically grotesque for many years now. Assuming we are not grotesque (or at least not so grotesque as Fly-face and his cronies), we should dislike them. (3) If p likes o, there is a tendency for p to believe that he and o hold similar attitudes. This is the observation Heider started with. People tend to distort their perceptions of the attitudes of others depending upon whether they like these others. Note that what happens here is a reversal of the process in case (1): individuals tend to distort their perception so that they can believe their friends share their beliefs.

Interaction. (4) if p interacts with o, p will come to like o. This is one of the famous assertions of social psychology. Numerous instances may be found, yet we still cannot give a completely satisfactory explanation for it, nor specify adequately the *general conditions* under which it occurs. Interaction promotes liking—most of the time. In order to get two people to like each other, the best thing to do is to find some pretext for forcing them to interact. (As I said, it doesn't always work. You might just promote a fight this way. However it's a pretty good bet that interaction leads to liking.) (5) If p likes o, there is a tendency for p to try to interact with o. This extremely common phenomenon would be seen, from Heider's point of view, as the individual taking action to try to promote a balanced unit. Note that (4) and (5) are also complements of each other. (6) If p dislikes o, there is a tendency for p to avoid interaction with o. Again a very common situation, which may be explained as a result of actions taken to balance the cognitive unit. Compare this to case (5). (7) If p likes o, and interaction with o is blocked, p will feel psychological discomfort. What happened here is that circumstances have prevented producing a balanced cognitive unit. Heider asserts that the outcome will be some sort of psychological tension. Examples of this are nostalgia (longing for a situation that no longer exists), homesickness, and idealized romantic love, which by definition occurs only when it is impossible to realize.

Familiarity. (8) If p is familiar with o, then p will tend to like o. Sometimes this principle is simply a restatement of the idea that p tends to like a similar o, or that p tends to like an o with whom he is in contact. Yet in some cases, simple *familiarity* can be shown to produce liking. Heider cites a case in which liking developed for a familiar x. Subjects, none of whom understood Russian, learned to recognize some Russian words. When they were presented a much longer list of Russian words containing those with which they were familiar and asked to rate their liking for the sound of each, there was a tendency to like more the words with which they were more familiar. Zajonc replicated this study with a number of variants and found the same result, as we shall see in Chap. 13. This phenomenon is intriguing, and it deserves further study. (9) If p is unfamiliar with o, p will tend to dislike o. Again distrust of the unfamiliar; xenophobia. Common examples of this are fear of new situations and fear of the dark. (10) If p likes o, p tends to become familiar with o. We seek out situations and people we like, *and* we try to get to know all about them. The incredible number of details of the private lives of entertainers which their fans manage to discover and remember well illustrates this principle.

Ownership. What happens in cases of ownership is particularly interesting, because there are some exceptions to the general tendency towards consistency. (11) If p owns x, there is a tendency for p to like x. To use my favorite example again, one can observe a strong tendency for people to like the brand of car that they drive. In the case of adults we might assume the direction of causation to be reversed: people buy the brand of car they like. However for their children this clearly could not be the case. A child has little control over the make of car his parents buy, yet we can observe among older children a strong preference for their parents' make of car. (12) If p likes x, there is a tendency for p to own x. This is the reverse of (11). But also ownership presents one of the exceptions. If p owns x, and p likes o, it is not always true that p wants o to like x. *Sometimes* it's true. It is balanced to believe that our friends like our possessions. However we do not want them to like our possessions *too* much. I would not want my friend to like my car so much that he took it away from me. The same process works for actors: most people would not find it balanced if their friends were *too* fond of their spouse or their lover. Thus the cognitive unit *pLo, pUx, oLx* may, in some cases, not be balanced. The exception seems to be produced by cases of exclusive ownership; that is, where only one person may possess an object, or where the relationship between two actors by definition precludes a third actor. Thus I would like my friends to like my possessions *up to the point* that they will take them away from me. And it is only because of the norms surrounding love relationships in our culture that the balance principle does not work for these. Other cultures in which it is a sign of hospitality to offer guests one's wife for the evening illustrate the balance principle perfectly well. (For spouse or lover, we should refer to "exclusive unit relations," rather than to "exclusive ownership," to avoid the rather demeaning suggestion that people own each other. Structurally, there is no difference.)

Benefits. (13) If p likes o, there is a tendency for p to engage in actions that benefit o. People give gifts to friends, do favors for loved ones. Not too surprising, perhaps, but another example of action motivated by a desire to produce a balanced cognitive unit. This case is one element of consistency theories so familiar to us that we are amazed when it doesn't occur. (14) If p benefits o, there is a tendency for p to like o. This case, the complement of (13), is considerably more interesting. It argues that sentiments follow actions. Not only are we nice to people we like, but we come to like those people whom, for various reasons, we are nice to. We shall see an interesting instance of this case a bit later. (15) If *p* likes *o*, there is a tendency to believe that *o* benefits *p*. This example illustrates the assertion that cognitive distortion may be used to produce a balanced unit. It is rather the opposite of paranoia: here, *p* believes *o* is benefitting him, when actually *o* may not do this at all.

These are 15 examples of the sort of thought experiment Heider conducted as he was formulating his balance theory. What we did was to imagine a situation, such as *pLo, oLq*, and then to ask what sort of relation *p* and *q* would be likely to have. After considering several instances of situations, which we then grouped into situations involving *similarity, interaction, familiarity, ownership, and benefits*, we can begin to look for abstract features they all have in common. Because Heider had already done this work for us, we said that what all our predicted outcomes have in common is that they are resolutions that produce a balanced or a consistent cognitive unit.

How did you react to the 15 cases as you read through them? Most people seem to have either or both of two responses to the cases. The first is to think of exceptions; cases where the "tendencies" Heider talks about do not occur. For instance any of us, with a little thought, could come up with counter-instances to (1)—similarity leads to liking—or to (5)—liking leads to attempts to interact. We can all think of people who have seemed very similar to us, yet towards whom we were indifferent or even hostile. Perhaps there was something else about the person that made him dislikable, or perhaps we see in him something we dislike in ourselves.

What a counter-instance shows is that we have stated the 15 cases a little too strongly; or what is more significant, *unconditionally*. That is, up to now we have not specified the general conditions under which we expect these balance tendencies to appear, and conditions under which they will not. Specification of these conditions is an important task for consistency theories, and in many cases, later versions of Heider's theory do include explicit statements of conditions.

The second response a few people have to these conditions is to say, "These tendencies aren't rational; sensible, mature individuals do not think this way, or at least they learn to control these tendencies in themselves." Perhaps, but this objection overlooks two facts. First, any theory is a simplification of reality. Theories such as consistency and exchange deal with general tendencies that occur in many settings. Any of these settings has special features that modify the effects dealt with in the theory. In other words people never behave exactly as the theory says they do. But what a theory does is tell us approximately how they behave most of the time. Second, people seem not to like having their own actions predicted. They object that they do not always respond to rewards or to desire for consistency. But if they do not, we can still make pretty good predictions of behavior and attitudes by assuming that they act "as if" the theory were correct.

Heider's Theory: Summary

The 15 cases just described all share certain properties. First, all speak of some sort of *cognitive unit,* which consists of *actors p, o, q* and *objects x, y,* and *z.* Actors and objects to Heider are both called *entities.* In addition to entities, every cognitive unit consists of *relations* which are either *affect relations* L (such as liking) or *unit relations* U (such as ownership). Only L relations may be positive or negative.

The cognitive unit has the property of being either *balanced* or *imbalanced.* For a dyad consisting of two actors, the unit is balanced if all possible relations between the two entities are of the same sign: either positive or negative. For example, the case where *p* and *o* have positive liking for each other, and are similar to each other, is balanced. Triads are balanced if: (1) all three relations are positive; or (2) two relations are negative and one is positive. A triad would be imbalanced if two relations are positive and one is negative. The case of a triad in which all relations are negative (such as *p, o* and *q,* all of whom dislike each other) is rather ambiguous. In most cases, we expect such a triad to disband. If it does persist—if for some reason these unhappy people cannot escape each other—we think this triad would be imbalanced.

From Heider's balance assertion we expect the following consequences. First, if a situation is balanced, it will tend to be stable. It is in the nature of things that balance and balanced units tend to persist. Second, if an incomplete structure becomes completed, it will tend to be completed in a balanced fashion. Our example in which friends assume (in the absence of information) that they hold similar attitudes (case #3) illustrates this consequence. Third, if the situation is imbalanced, it will tend to become balanced. Some of the relations between the entities will change, either by direct action or by cognitive distortion of some sort. These three assertions should apply to, and partially explain, all of the previous 15 cases we have considered. It would be helpful to go back and review each case to see which of these three principles it illustrates. At this point we are down to three principles which may be illustrated in a wide variety of concrete situations. In the next section we shall examine an even simpler set of principles for the same job of explanation.

It is important to keep in mind here the distinction between a cognitive unit and a social structure. The cognitive unit is one individual's representation of the social structure, and in most cases we expect a fairly close correspondence between it and the actual social structure. However the two are not the same thing.

The cognitive unit is how the social structure looks to one individual, usually to *p.* We say that consistency theories are *p*-centered, or *p*-centric.

This means that the cognitive unit reflects *p*'s selection as to what to observe in the social structure, and it also reflects any errors in his perceptions. Many interesting applications of consistency theories focus on cases where *p* distorts the "objective reality" of the social structure in order to produce a balanced cognitive unit. Individuals sometimes distort their understanding of the world in order to make it seem more consistent than it is. Of course it is not a deliberate distortion in the sense that *p* sets out to delude himself; nevertheless, in some striking cases, individuals appear to misperceive all kinds of information—*and* to misperceive it in a way that increases the consistency of their perceptions.

Formalized Balance Theories

Cartwright and Harary undertook to develop an explicit, formal version of Heider's balance theory. Their work produces a vast simplification of the theory presented by Heider, and in addition, it permits application of the theory to a far wider range of situations than those Heider considered.

Formalization means *translation* of the ideas of the theory into a system where formal structure governs the assumptions. A formal system is one in which there are rules governing the form of statements, but not their content. One example of a formal system is Aristotelian logic, in which there are rules governing the way in which statements may be made. Other examples are simple algebra and other versions of mathematics. The rules do not tell us *what* to say but rather they tell us *how* to say it.

The formal system Cartwright and Harary use for Heider's theory is known as *graph theory*. Graph theory is a set of rules which determine how one may construct a two-dimensional graph. With proper interpretation, this set of rules is strikingly similar to the set of psychological principles which Heider deals with (believe it or not!). Constructing a graph according to the rules of graph theory enables us to draw a picture of the cognitive structure of the individual which Heider referred to as a unit.

We begin with two undefined concepts, *point*, and *path*. The point is equivalent to the entity in Heider's system; *p, o, q, x, y, z*. The path is equivalent to the affect or unit relation in Heider's system, and is represented by either an arrow or a bracket. An arrow represents an affect relationship (such as liking), and we place a plus (+) or a minus (−) sign on it to indicate positive or negative affect. A unit relation (such as ownership) is represented by a bracket. There is no need to add a plus or a minus sign since the absence of a unit relationship ("does not own") is represented by not drawing the bracket. Thus affect relations may be positive or negative; unit relations are positive or absent.

Table 12–1 illustrates the coordination of the Cartwright–Harary formalization to Heider's original theory. In addition to paths and points, Cartwright and Harary speak of whether a cycle is balanced or imbalanced, and they define the difference between balanced and imbalanced cycles. A cycle is

TABLE 12–1   Correspondences Between Heider's and
Cartwright and Harary's Balance Theories

HEIDER	CARTWRIGHT AND HARARY
Entity (*p, o, q; x, y, z*)	Point (p, o, q; x, y, z)
Relation	Path
Affect (liking): + or −	Line or arrow: + or −
Unit (similarity): + or absent	Bracket: + or absent
Cognitive Unit	Graph
[No equivalent concept]	Cycle: + or −
Balance: denotative definition	Balance: explicit, nominal definition

any set of paths connecting points which begins and ends with the same point; that is, any complete loop that may be traced within the graph. As you trace the loop, note the (+) and (−) signs on the paths [remembering that all unit relation brackets are (+)]. If the total number of (−) signs is *even,* counting zero as an even number, then the cycle is balanced. If the total number of (−) signs is *odd,* then the cycle is imbalanced. Now the entire graph, representing the cognitive unit, is balanced only if all possible cycles within the graph are balanced. Of course a graph containing only 3 points contains only one cycle. In a moment we shall consider more complex graphs with more than one cycle. What is significant here is that we now have an explicit definition of "balance":

> A cycle is balanced only if it contains zero or an even number of − signs. The entire graph is balanced only if no cycle within it is imbalanced.

Using these concepts, we may represent the relations between points graphically as in Figs. 12–3 and 12–4. The graphs in Fig. 12–3 represent the same entities and relations as those in Fig. 12–1. Points in Fig. 12–3 are given the same names as entities in Fig. 12–1, and paths in Fig. 12–3 have the same signs as relations in Fig. 12–1. In the first graph *p* likes *o* and *p* likes *q.*

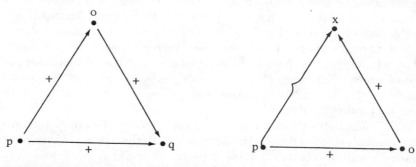

FIGURE 12–3   Balanced cognitive structures

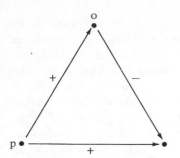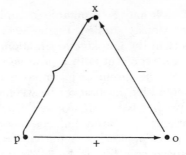

FIGURE 12–4   Imbalanced cognitive structures

These affect relations are represented by arrows from *p* to *o* and from *p* to *q* with plus signs on them. Also *o* likes *q*; this is represented similarly. In the second graph of Fig. 12–3, *p* has positive affect for *o* and *o* has positive affect for *x*. Also *p* owns *x*. The graphs of Fig. 12–4 would be similarly interpreted; they represent the imbalanced cognitive structures of Fig. 12–2.

The assumptions of graphed balance theory are the same as those in Heider's version. First, an imbalanced graph tends to change in some way towards a balanced graph. Second, if balance-restoring change is blocked, the individual will feel psychological tension. Note that the graphs only represent one individual's (*p*'s) view of the world; the theory is *p*-centric.

In addition to increasing the precision and clarity of the concepts and the theory, the Cartwright and Harary formalization makes Heider's ideas far easier to use. The reason for this is that the graph provides a simple way to represent any cognitive unit, and an easy way of calculating balance or imbalance of a structure. Finally, there is the concept *vacuous balance*. Any incomplete cycle, such as would exist if *p* simply did not know the relationship between two entities, is considered to be balanced. Thus either graph in Fig. 12–4 could be made balanced by removing any of the paths connecting points.

In addition to providing a precise, clear version of the concepts and ideas of balance theory, the formalized version yields at least two major advances over Heider's ideas. First, using graphs to represent cognitive structures enables a quick, easy calculation whether a given structure is balanced. All we need to do is to count the positive and negative signs of each possible cycle. With a little practice it may easily be seen that both graphs in Fig. 12–4 are imbalanced. It is far less easy to see this by inspecting Fig. 12–2. Second, the formalized version of the theory permits us to consider much larger cognitive structures than Heider's theory does. In Heider's system we are limited to structures consisting of no more than three entities and three relations. In the graph version of balance theory there is no limit to the number of entities or relations between them which may be considered. And in addition, it is a simple matter to calculate whether even a very large and complex cognitive structure is balanced.

After some practice with samples of relations similar to those in Figs. 12–3 and 12–4, it may be profitable to apply balance theory to some situations we have previously studied. Figure 12–5 represents the possible perceptions of a subject in the autokinetic situation. The subject is attracted to the group, which we represent with a positive sign on the affect line from p to o. He associates the group in his mind with a given range of judgments; this is represented by the bracket between o and x. What balance theory enables us to predict is the sign on a third line between p and x representing p's evaluation of the norm. Balance theory says that *if* p evaluates x, he is more likely to complete his cognitive structure in a balanced fashion than an imbalanced one; that is, he is likely to evaluate x positively, a $(+)$ sign on the px bond.

Let us try a more complex case now. Figure 12–6 represents the situation of the Stanford women studied by Siegel and Siegel in Chap. 5. In order to simplify discussion numbers have been added to the paths. First (1), there is a positive affect relation between p and o_1, who represent the row house women: p is attracted to them. At the same time (2) p holds the same attitudes as the row house women, and positively evaluates these attitudes. This is represented by brackets between o_1 and x, and between p and x. But (3) p finds herself with a unit relation ("living with") to o_2, the dorm women. And finally (4), p becomes aware that the dorm women disapprove authoritarian attitudes. At this stage, p's cognitive structure is obviously imbalanced. The cycle p–o_2–x is imbalanced. Would it help for p to change the arrow connecting p and x to minus; that is, to dislike authoritarian attitudes herself? I hope it is clear that it would not, for this would simply produce a different sort of imbalance in the cognitive structure: the p–o_1–x cycle would be imbalanced. Achieving balance in this difficult situation requires the woman to employ the technique of vacuous balance. She must dissolve *either* the p–o_1, or the p–o_2 unit relation. In other words she must break off her association, either with the dorm women, or with the row house women. If she breaks the connection with the dorm women by drawing into a row house (the p–o_2 bond), then she may maintain her authoritarian attitudes. On the other hand if she changes the affect relation to the row women (p–o_1) to negative, and changes her evaluation of authoritarian attitudes (p–x) to negative, these two changes will also produce a balanced cognitive structure.

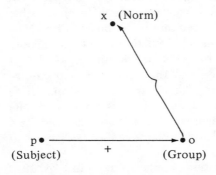

x $\bullet$ (Norm)

p $\bullet$ ————————→ $\bullet$ o
(Subject)   +   (Group)

FIGURE 12–5   Autokinetic effect

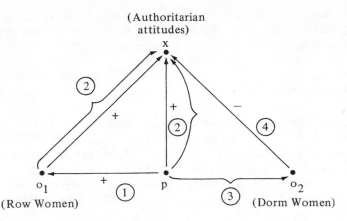

FIGURE 12–6 Balanced theory representation of Siegel and Siegel group effects

These changes represent, respectively, women in groups *B* and *C* of Siegel's study.[2]

As an advanced exercise, you might attempt to construct balance graphs to represent the situation of the subject in the Asch conformity experiment, and to represent the "Miss *X* incident" described in Chap. 1. It can be done, and it provides a good explanation for the different directions of influence over Miss *X*'s judgments, and for the discomfort she felt in this experiment.

The distinction between affect relations (lines) and unit relations (brackets) in graphed balance theory is primarily a notational convenience. Unit relations behave the same way as positive affect relations in determining the balance or imbalance of a graph, and if we wanted, we could simply represent them this way. For most purposes, however, it is helpful to keep the graphic representation of relations distinct; it is easier to interpret the graph in substantive terms if we have preserved the nature of relations by using both arrows and directed brackets. For most uses of balance theory in the remainder of this and other chapters, we shall represent unit relations with brackets and affect relations with + or − lines.

Heider's theory was the first statement of principles directed explicitly towards issues of consistency and inconsistency, so it seems reasonable to credit him with having the earliest influence on this line of thought in social psychology. Not that the ideas were unheard of before: William James, George Herbert Mead, and especially Kurt Lewin all had written about consistency in one context or another. However Heider was the first to investi-

---

[2] Cognitive distortion—for example, changing the o_2 to *x* relation to (+) by convincing herself that dorm women actually liked authoritarian attitudes—would also balance this graph. We presume such distortion was not possible for the women in this study, due to close interaction with the dorm women. Notice also that the common response of denial—refusing to think about authoritarian attitudes and thus dissolving the *px* relation—would not be satisfactory, for the graph would still be imbalanced.

gate types of balance and imbalance, and the social psychological consequences of each, directly. Just as we say Homans is the father of exchange theories, so Heider is the father of consistency theories.

Newcomb's A-B-X System

Newcomb has proposed the set of theoretical ideas most closely related to Heider's and especially to the Cartwright–Harary formalization. Most of the situations are described in terms equivalent to Heider's, and in most cases the same predictions would be made. Even the graphs used to represent cognitive structures in both systems appear much the same, but the notation Newcomb uses is different: actors are represented as A or B instead of p and o (objects are still X and Y).

But the major difference between the theories is that Newcomb introduces the idea of *strengths of relations,* rather than the simpler $+$ and $-$ used in Heider's system. Thus a positive relation between actors A and B could be $+1$, $+2$, or $+3$ (larger numbers do not appear in Newcomb's work). For Heider these would all be simply $+$ relations, and thus, equivalent. The idea of strengths of relations is certainly important in describing interpersonal relations, and Newcomb is able to show some interesting results of using the idea.

A second difference between Newcomb's and Heider's systems is that Newcomb deals with *asymmetric* relations between actors. For example, actor A's feeling for B might be $+3$, while B's feeling for A is only $+1$. This situation is illustrated in Fig. 12–7. (Note that Heider's system could not express this asymmetry.) In Newcomb's system such an asymmetry is imbalanced and will tend towards symmetry. We hope B will come to like A as much as A likes B. However it would also balance the system if A came to realize that B is not so very likable after all ($+1$). An even unhappier case for A is illustrated in Fig. 12–8: A is fond of B but B has a dislike for A. (Figure 12–8 may not be the worst possible case; probably an AB bond of $+3$ and a BA bond of complete indifference, which we could represent by 0, would be even unhappier for A.)

The third difference between Newcomb's and Heider's systems is that

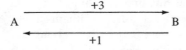

FIGURE 12–7 Asymmetric positive relations

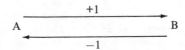

FIGURE 12–8 Asymmetric opposite relations

Newcomb concentrates on affect relations and has very little to say about unit relations. What is significant in Newcomb's analyses is how actors *feel* about things, not how they are structurally associated with things. Thus when we graph a relation using Newcomb's theory, we use only straight lines to connect actors and objects. Because positive affect and unit relations are equivalent in Heider's system, this change does not introduce any different results if we want to make predictions from an A–B–X graph. A unit relation between p and x for Heider is an AX line with $+1$, $+2$, or $+3$ on it for Newcomb.

The possibility of asymmetric relations between two actors, and the use of strengths of relations between actors and objects, leads Newcomb to focus upon interaction as a way of reducing imbalance. For example, suppose we have the situation of Fig. 12–7, with A and B holding asymmetric but positive feelings for one another. However both A and B hold strong positive ($+3$) feelings for an object X: in this case both A and B are extraordinarily fond of peanut butter. This is illustrated in Fig. 12–9a. A likely outcome is illustrated in Fig. 12–9b: when B learns how much A loves peanut butter, B decides that A must really be a good person. (If you find this case implausible, imagine the X is a political attitude, or a religious conviction. Such cases are numerous; we shall study one in Chap. 13.)

However the notion of strengths of relations is a tricky one, and to date it has been impossible to codify any set of general rules for predicting how cases in Newcomb's system will be resolved. Suppose, for instance, that A and B in Fig. 12–9 had both been mildly fond ($+1$) of peanut butter: would we expect this to have any effect upon the AB or the BA relation? If so, what effect? Or suppose A and B both had a slight dislike (-1) for peanut butter: would this have any effect upon their feelings for each other?

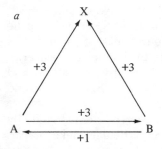 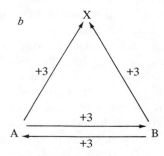

FIGURE 12–9 The effect of peanut butter on inter-personal relations

Festinger's Cognitive Dissonance Theory

By all odds, the most important and influential consistency theory in the last decade has been Festinger's Theory of Cognitive Dissonance. We will briefly look at the major ideas of this theory, and then try to represent them in terms of the balance graph diagrams.

Dissonance occurs, according to Festinger, when an individual simultaneously holds two cognitions such that from the first cognition, the obverse of the second cognition logically follows. Dissonance only applies to situations in which the individual has already made some decision. It occurs *after* the decision to act has been reached. Before making a difficult decision the actor feels tension or discomfort, but he does not feel dissonance. Dissonance is strictly a post-decision phenomenon.

Dissonance faced by the individual after he has made a decision is presumed to be a psychologically motivating state. The emphasis is upon the individual's *doing* something. Dissonance is unpleasant, and the individual will take steps to reduce it. What is of interest then is just how the dissonance may be reduced. The most famous example of dissonance reduction is the case of a cigarette smoker. Suppose an individual has made a conscious decision to smoke. This is his first cognition. The second cognition comes from newspaper stories saying that cigarette smoking causes cancer. If we make certain simple assumptions about the nature of thought and behavior, we would assume that these two cognitions stand in an inverse logical relation to each other. What can the individual do? Obviously he could stop smoking (or stop reading newspapers). More likely what he will do is to try to increase the number of cognitions favoring the decision he has already made. He will tell himself that the evidence is not particularly strong that smoking causes cancer, he will seek out other friends who have made the same smoking decision he has made, and he will remind himself constantly of the many pleasures of smoking cigarettes.

I once saw the president of a cigarette manufacturing company interviewed on television. He was asked how he felt about producing and selling what was widely thought to be a dangerous product. He replied that he didn't think it was dangerous, and he added that there exists no "experimental data from research on humans" to link smoking and cancer. (You can imagine what sort of research that would be!) Furthermore he and all his children had smoked from two to four packs of cigarettes a day since they were 16. Although I do not want to dispute the sincerity of his beliefs, I concluded that he illustrated (1) cognitive distortion and (2) seeking similar friends; both of which Heider and Festinger would predict on the basis of their theories.

Early support for these ideas came from research summarized by Festinger indicating that *after* deciding to buy a particular make of car, people read the advertisements for that make more than they read advertisements for competing makes. Since the commitment has already been made and the individual has already bought the car, there would seem to be no informative value in further reading of the advertisements. Dissonance theorists explain this situation in the following manner. Buying any car is a difficult decision and one in which the individual is likely to experience dissonance. Buying a new car should be an especially dissonant situation because cars are so expensive. Stated baldly, no car is worth what it costs. After buying a particular make of car, the individual is likely to suffer dissonance from the two cognitions: "I bought brand X car," and "Brand X isn't really very good; maybe brand *Y* is better." He combats dissonance by reading ads for his car that reassure him and tell him of its many virtues. Dissonance reduction is a mechanism for producing greater satisfaction with a decision that has already been made.

Situations studied by dissonance theorists may usually be represented simply in graphic form. The standard situation is one in which the individual is committed to an action or an alternative that is associated in his mind with strong negative consequences. In other words there is a strong unit relation between the individual and some act, and there is also a strong unit relation between that act and some consequence for which the individual has strong negative feelings. Figure 12–10 is a graphic representation of the situation faced by the cigarette smoker who is worried about cancer. What he frequently does in this situation is to think of all the pleasurable things associated with smoking; all the things he likes about it. This is represented in Fig. 12–11. As this example illustrates, dissonance reduction is most frequently effected by increasing the total proportion of balanced cycles in the individual's cognitive structure, so that *on the average,* he is satisfied.

A particularly interesting application of the ideas of dissonance theory can be made to political brainwashing. Up to and including World War II, American soldiers taken prisoner were famous for noncooperation with their captors and escape attempts. In the Korean conflict Americans made few attempts to escape, and in Vietnam they made none. What did the North Koreans and North Vietnamese do to produce this state of affairs? How were they able to effect the high degree of collaboration, and the infrequent but occurring ideological changes? What we know about their techniques can be subjected to a dissonance analysis.

According to this analysis, brainwashing may be effected in the following manner: a prisoner, long deprived of food, cigarettes, candy, and most other gratification, is offered a very small reward for signing a false confession. For instance he may be offered three cigarettes for signing a confession that will result in punishment or death to some of his friends. If he succumbs to this offer, he becomes the victim of enormous dissonant

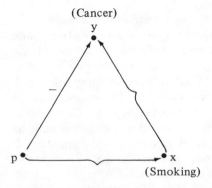

FIGURE 12–10 Smoking and dissonance

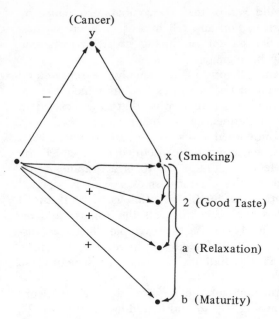

FIGURE 12–11   Smoking and dissonance reduction

feelings. The two cognitions "I signed a false confession for three cigarettes," and "that confession will hurt my friends" are dissonant. If the reward had been large—for example, a million dollars—it probably would not be so difficult for him to live with it. But since he has done it for only three cigarettes, he must find some way to reduce the dissonant feelings. One of the few dissonance reduction mechanisms available to the prisoner in this case is to decide that his fellow prisoners really are not his friends; that is, to change the sign on the affect relation between himself and the other prisoners. The two cognitions then become "I signed a false confession for three cigarettes," and "that confession will hurt my enemies"— not dissonant. This change may frequently occur after confessions are signed for small rewards.

Cases considered under the framework of cognitive dissonance are virtually always those in which the individual p perceives some strong, and unbreakable, bond (unit relation) between himself and an act x. At the same time, either x is something he disapproves of (a negative px affect relation), or x is unalterably linked by unit relation to something else which p disapproves of (as in Fig. 12–10). Thus cases of dissonance may be analyzed the same as imbalanced graphs for the Heider and Cartwright–Harary system. There is one restriction upon how the imbalance may be resolved in dissonance situations: the px bond is unbreakable, meaning p cannot convince himself he actually did not commit the act.

The ideas in dissonance theory have received careful scrutiny, both from proponents and from those seeking to disconfirm the theory. From our point of view, what is most significant is that controversies that previously surrounded dissonance theory (at least up until 1970; interest in the topic seems to have waned a bit since then) led to some interesting unexpected findings, and to some limitations on the original very broad claims for the theory. Apparently dissonance is not an all-pervasive phenomenon: not every decision produces dissonance, and the conditions under which it appears have received some carefully scrutiny. We shall see some of these empirical results and consequent theoretical modifications in Chap. 13.

Heider's $p–o–x$ theory (including the Cartwright–Harary formalization), Newcomb's $A–B–X$ theory, and Festinger's theory of cognitive dissonance constitute the major theories of cognitive consistency. They vary in the types of situations to which they are usually applied, and in some cases they vary in the predictions they would make for specific situations. For example, situations that are asymmetric and therefore unstable in Newcomb's system would be balanced and therefore stable in Heider's.

Yet these consistency theories have far more similarities than differences. Most often they all are applied to three-entity cognitive structures (such as $p–o–x$ or $p–o–q$) and are concerned with analyzing consequences of inconsistent relations between them. The two substantive assumptions of Heider's theory, (1) that imbalance produces unpleasant psychological tension; and (2) that imbalanced structures tend to change in the direction of balance—are in general agreement with assumptions from other consistency theories.

Recent Attribution Phenomena

Heider's attribution principle continues to attract attention of theoretical and empirical investigators, and a considerable body of the consistency literature has grown from this tradition. What are sometimes called "attribution theories" are not theories so much as a set of fairly coherent empirical investigations. Social psychologists interested in attribution phenomena study cases in which individuals seem to add elements to their cognitive structures; for example, cases in which individuals make assumptions and inferences about each other on the basis of limited information. A typical case of attribution would be for the actor to know that someone votes Republican, subscribes to the *National Review,* and drives an expensive American car. On the basis of this information, the actor might also suppose that this person favored American involvement in Vietnam; that is, an attitude on Vietnam is *attributed* to this person after knowing a certain amount about him.

To relate attribution studies to the other theories of cognitive consistency, we can say that these are cases in which individuals spontaneously complete incomplete cognitive structures. The individual knows someone's relations to various objects (in our example, positive affect or unit relations to Republicans, *National Review,* and expensive car), and from this information, the individual assumes that another element (attitude on Vietnam) exists *and* that that person has a positive affect for it.

Although attribution phenomena have not received a high degree of conceptualization to date, it is clear that these investigators assume some significant modifications in earlier consistency theories. For Heider, for example, it is not permissible to assume that individuals will add elements to their cognitive structures. Heider's and others' versions of balance theory state that *if* a new element is added to the cognitive structure, the relations connecting the new element will tend to form in a balanced fashion. However these theories definitely *do not* say there is any (theoretical) reason to believe that the new element will be added. Contemporary attribution ideas do make this assumption. They assume, in other words, that individuals tend to constantly expand their total store of knowledge—not just by adding cognitive elements, but by adding them in a way consistent with previous elements. In our example we would not expect from attribution ideas that the hypothetical person would oppose American involvement, therefore. Elements are added, *and* they are added in a balanced fashion. What presently is lacking from attribution studies are explicit statements of which sorts of information will be added to the cognitive structure, and statements of conditions under which one sort of information is more likely than others to be added. Why should our hypothetical individual infer attitudes on Vietnam, for instance? Because he is interested in other people's attitudes on the war, because someone asked him to conjecture about it? Attribution research does not, at present, give any way to answer these questions.

The tendency to attribute characteristics to individuals certainly is widespread; most of us do it all the time. One reason for it is that it helps us to structure unfamiliar situations: we "create" knowledge about the world which we may need later. An intelligent use of attribution—if that adjective can be appropriate here—is based upon empirical regularities we have already observed in the world: Perhaps our hypothetical individual has seen that most people having the characteristics named also favored American involvement in the war. In this way attribution in a person's day to day activities is quite similar to what scientists do when they generalize their results. The important thing to remember, for the layman as well as for the social psychologist, is just where the attribution or the generalization came from: what he has actually observed to be the case, and what he figures is *probably* also the case.

Person Perception and Information Processing

Suppose you know that your friend John gets grades of A in reading, arithmetic and spelling. Is this sufficient for you to decide that he is overall a good student? And what would you predict about his grades in computer programming or business management? As another example, suppose you know that a hypothetical person Tim is very intelligent, politically conservative, cruel to animals, and wonderfully kind to his wife. What sort of person would you say he is, in one word? There is a significant and growing body of research dealing with questions like this one. It is usually referred to as *person perception* or *impression formation,* and the major theoretical perspective applied is *information processing models.* These models and the cases they attempt to explain constitute the most advanced version of consistency theories.

From an information processing point of view, the individual is seen as being constantly confronted by stimuli in the world, each stimulus containing bits or units of information. The individual selects some bits of this information and ignores other bits; the first theoretical task is to specify which types he will ignore and which he will consider relevant. Next the individual may combine the bits of information to reach an overall conclusion, or he may perform some relatively complicated operation upon the bits so that some of them are more important than others, and some get dropped out of his cognitive structure. Describing just how the individual processes the large amount of available information is the overall task of information processing models.

The most interesting questions arise when information seems to be inconsistent, such as when an individual is told he is intelligent by one friend and unintelligent by another friend, since inconsistent information usually leads to inconsistent cognitive structures, and these must be resolved somehow in inconsistency theories. But even the case of consistent information is interesting; for example, suppose two dozen people all tell you the same thing about Tim: at what point are you unable to absorb any more information about him, and what will you do with the surplus?

Information processing theories are, like all consistency theories, quite recent developments in social psychology. We shall examine some research designed to aid in description of the most general *form* of the information utilization process, as well as to test some models which assume a rather complex mathematical combination of information. Chapter 14 is devoted to the uses of information processing models in social psychology. During the next few years you may expect to come across quite a few information processing theories, all of them derived from the general ideas of consistency theories.

Other consistency theories (for example, Osgood–Tannenbaum's "congruity theory," and Rosenberg and Abelson's "Symbolic Psycho-logic") have been proposed and applied to specific situations. (For a good exposition and comparison of various consistency theories, see Taylor, 1970, Chap. 2.) But—as is also true of the various exchange theories—what is more useful than learning the distinctions between different theories is to learn what they all have in common. Thus we limit our study here to these four branches of the general consistency approach.

The View of Self in Balance Theories

Often it is convenient to be able to represent the way an individual regards himself in balance diagrams. This can be useful for studying, self-evaluation, or for representing a general level of satisfaction with oneself in situations.

What we need is a way to represent the feelings an individual has when he regards himself as an outsider, the way he thinks he looks from the outside. In cases where an individual is consciously aware of himself we say that p is an object of orientation to himself.

Figure 12–12 shows a single actor p with himself as object of orientation. P as an object is represented by p', and any relations that might exist between p and any other actor o may exist between p and p'. In the diagram of Fig. 12–12, there is a positive affect bond between p and p'; this could indicate a positive self-evaluation, satisfaction with self, or any other positive sentiment relation the actor might feel towards himself.

In his original theories Heider assumed that the affect relation between p and p' would be positive; that is, $p + Lp$. In most cases we expect this to be true. But there are times when a person regards himself in a negative way, such as when he thinks he did something wrong or was momentarily unable to do some task well. A negative relation between p and p' may also represent a more enduring negative view of self; for example, a person who thinks he is generally worthless or is generally unintelligent would also be represented as in Fig. 12–12, but with a negative p to p' bond. Cases of an enduring, global dissatisfaction with self produce some unusual and interesting outcomes—both in balance diagrams, and substantively. Let us briefly examine two instances of an enduring negative p to p' sentiment relation.

Figure 12–13 shows an individual p (whose name is Martha), who generally has low regard for herself. She sees herself in an enduring social relationship such as marriage with an o (whose name is George), as shown by the unit relation between p' and o. For someone like Martha, it will be unpleasant and tension-producing if o shows any sort of positive affect towards her—this is what George is doing in Fig. 12–13, as shown by the positive affect relation between o and p. What this means theoretically is that, for an individual who does not think well of herself, any show of positive feeling (such as affection) from an other will produce an imbalanced cognitive structure, leading to psychological tension. We might predict that Martha in this situation will suffer whenever George is nice to her. As the tension builds up she will periodically vent with emotional outbursts directed against George: a strong negative bond from p to o would balance the structure. What poor George does by being nice to Martha is to produce exactly the sort of psychological conditions that lead to hostility and the mysterious (to George) attacks upon himself!

The second case of interest is an individual who dislikes himself or herself, which again we represent with a negative p to p' affect bond. This time, our p acts out the self-dislike by all sorts of self-harmful behaviors: p is a masochist. What sort of person would we expect p to be attracted to for companionship and perhaps something deeper? From balance

FIGURE 12–12   P as object of orientation to himself

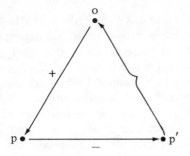

FIGURE 12–13   The George and Martha phenomenon

theory we predict that any person will act in such a way as to try to produce a balanced cognitive structure. Figure 12–14 shows such a masochistic *p,* who has found a sadistic *o*—and who presumably is balanced, if not entirely happy.

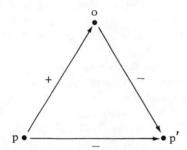

FIGURE 12–14   The masochist and the sadist

Some General Issues in Consistency Theories

(1) The relations between attitudes and behavior have traditionally occupied much of the attention of social psychologists. Most often they have been interested in measuring people's attitudes so that they could predict their behaviors; for example, measuring political attitudes in order to predict voting. One thing consistency theories assert is that the direction of causality can be reversed; that is, it is possible to observe behaviors and use them to predict changes in attitudes. Reversing the usual "attitude leads to behavior" sequence to "behavior leads to attitudes" is one of the most intriguing features of consistency theories. What the theories claim is that, in certain cases, the way individuals act will affect the way they regard the objects of their actions. If I am inconsiderate of someone, a consistency theorist would say this act by itself is very likely to make me think less of that person. If I treat someone like a criminal, I am likely *as a result* to come to think of him as evil. If I am cruel, I can come to hate those to whom I am cruel. This idea has tremendous implications

for interpersonal relations, several of which have been described by the psychologist Weinberg. Using the "behavior leads to attitudes" sequence, imagine the effects of too much secrecy and self-protectiveness: one likely result is a vicious circle of increasing paranoia. Treating people as if they were untrustworthy may lead to a belief that they cannot be trusted. As you treat people, so you come to believe they are—at least sometimes.

(2) Most frequently, consistency theories are useful for understanding actions that are directed towards reducing or eliminating *cognitive* inconsistency. When the cognitive structure of the individual is correctly described, for example, with an accurate balance graph, then it is possible to predict behavior in a straightforward manner: the actor is likely to engage in whatever action will reduce his cognitive inconsistency. Of course it is crucial that the theorist set up a balance diagram which *accurately* reflects *p's perceptions* of the situation—not the way the situation might look to an outside observer. What we are predicting is the individual's attempts to make his view of the world consistent. Thus what we need to know is how the individual thinks things look. Put another way: consistency theories are concerned with *p's* subjective view of his social situation, and are not directly concerned with the "objective facts" of that situation.

Suppose we have constructed a balance diagram that accurately reflects an individual's view of his social circumstances, and the diagram is imbalanced: what do we predict will happen? Well, we predict the individual will feel tension, and that he will act to decrease the imbalance. But just *how* will he act to decrease imbalance? What will he do? In many cases there are several different ways he could try to reduce imbalance, and a general problem with consistency theories is that they do not tell us just *which* mode of imbalance reduction will be preferred.

Often, particularly in fairly complex social situations, there are a variety of changes that would produce a balanced structure. The individual may act to change his own behavior or the behavior of someone else. He may change his attitude about something or he may attempt to change someone else's attitude. He may cognitively misperceive or distort the true attitudes of someone else. He may simply "not think about" part of the situation, he may produce a general distortion of his own and others' perceptions of the situation. But which of these modes of imbalance reduction will he take, if he has a choice between several?

What we would need to answer that sort of question is a set of principles that specify exactly *which* path of balance restoration is likely to be followed in *what particular types* of situations. At present we do not possess such a set of principles. Balance theories therefore are *indeterminate* with respect to many predictions we would like to make.

One possibility is that attitudes are easier to change than unit relations: perhaps individuals can change how they regard things more easily than they can change relations (distort beliefs about relations, or actually change them by behavior) such as "ownership" or "similarity." Moreover perhaps it is easier to change one's perceptions of others' attitudes than it is to change one's own attitudes. Yet as soon as we consider these possibilities, exceptions come to mind. There are attitudes people hold (if our own, we like to call them "convictions") we would not change for anything— or at least we would take behavioral action to change some unit relations before changing these attitudes. Perhaps we shall someday be able to state a set of principles governing when people will attempt to produce balance by changing attitudes, and when they will try to change unit relations. When this can be done, the determinacy (precision) of balance theory predictions for many situations of interest will be considerably increased.

(3) Another problem with contemporary consistency theories is the issue of degrees of balance. Intuitively we suppose that some sorts of imbalance are more disturbing than others, but there is presently no generally accepted way to represent this in balance diagrams. If a perfectly satisfactory way to represent degrees of balance is developed, it also may solve the problem of predicting resolution of imbalance. That is, it may be possible to specify what modes of imbalance resolution are likely by predicting that individuals will first try to reduce large imbalances, then smaller ones, and so on. Three general ways of dealing with degrees of balance have received the most attention of consistency theorists. Although at this time none of these methods has solved the problems completely, each seems to offer promise of a partial solution, perhaps to be perfected by future work.

The first suggestion (Fig. 12–15) is to assign differential weights to relations, as Newcomb does in his A–B–X theory. Suppose that a young man likes to wear his hair long. He also has a grandmother of whom he is very fond who detests long hair. If we know that the affect relation to Grandmother is very strong (+3) and that Grandmother's affect relation to long hair is very strong (−3), we might predict that the "less weighted" relation

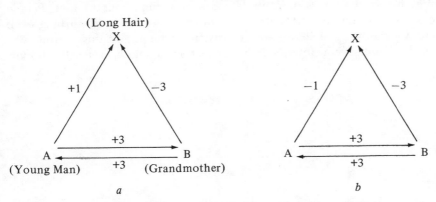

Imbalanced structure (A) is resolved in (B) by A deciding he is not in favor of long hair. Note that B is still asymmetric, since the BX relation has greater weight (−3) than the AX relation (−1). Thus we predict some further change beyond that shown in B.

FIGURE 12–15 Differential weighting

(+1 to long hair) will change. The young man will decide that he does not like long hair, or at least it is not worth upsetting Grandmother over it. Variants of this method have been proposed by Abelson and Rosenberg (1958), Harary (1959), McGuire (1966), and Triandis and Fishbein (1963).

A second possibility is to consider "degrees of balance" as calculated by various systems. For example, dissonance theory presupposes that it is the proportion of imbalanced cycles to balanced cycles which determines relative comfort or discomfort of the individual. A cognitive structure consisting of a single imbalanced cycle and a large number of balanced cycles would be considered relatively satisfactory for the individual (see Figs. 12–10, 12–11). Variants of this idea have been proposed by Cartwright and Harary (1956), Harary et al. (1965), Feather (1966), and Morrissette et al. (1966).

The third possibility considers psychological distance from the actor as being the most important factor. If two people I know only distantly dislike each other, that is less troubling to me than if two of my close friends dislike each other. Given that an imbalanced cycle exists, the degree of tension it produces is inversely related to the distance of the cycle from p. Figure 12–16 illustrates a cognitive structure with an imbalanced cycle (q–r–s) which is quite distant from p. Presumably, according to this way of calculating degree of balance, this is less tension-producing than an imbalanced p–o–r cycle would be. Variants of the distance idea have been proposed by James A. Davis (1967) and by Norman and Roberts (1972).

Each of the three proposed ways to calculate degrees of balance has been applied successfully to some cases, but none of the ways has been successful for all cases. For instance, possibilities 2 and 3 (proportion of balanced cycles and distance) will certainly be affected by possibility 1 (weighting relations). Even one imbalanced cycle among many, or even one very distant imbalanced cycle, will be very disturbing to the individual if the entities involved (actors or attitudes) are very important to him. People whose opinions and actions matter very much to us can be disturbing even when everybody else behaves in a consistent fashion, and this is true even when there are several intermediate connecting people between the impor-

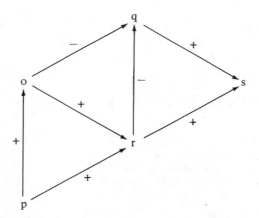

FIGURE 12–16   Distant imbalance

tant people and ourselves. Similarly a person whose whole attention is taken up with a single cycle (possibility 1) is going to be disturbed in that cycle even if the relations between entities are all quite weak. So it goes.

(4) Before leaving this general discussion, I would like to mention one additional topic: When is inconsistency pleasing? Generally we assume that people do not like inconsistency—that it produces tension—and most experience certainly bears this out. But Heider (1958) noted quite early that a world in which every cognitive structure was balanced would become boring. In fact, he argued, one of the main reasons Russian writers are so engrossing is that their works are filled with dozens of minor inconsistent relations between characters. Computer date matching, which I mentioned as a practical application of the consistency ideas, also illustrates this problem. Of the people I know who have tried computer-arranged dates, those who were dissatisfied most always said it was because their dates were dull. The two people quickly found out they agreed about almost everything (thanks, of course, to the computer matching them on this basis), and they had nothing to talk about.

Perhaps cognitive inconsistency is like danger: We like a little bit of it in our lives—not too much, and never out of control, but just a little. Stanton (1967) and Harary (1963, 1966) have analyzed plays in terms of degree of balance for the characters. What seems to happen is that imbalance is evident at the outset of the plot, and that it rises during the first half of the story. Imbalance, and presumably with it the audience's tension, reaches a maximum at about the point we call the climax of the play, and drops off rapidly to a low point or to zero by play's end. This sort of imbalance, like the tension of a good theatrical or movie performance, is pleasant. Is it pleasant in itself, or is it pleasant when it is over? ("It feels so good when I stop beating my head against the wall.") I don't know the answer to that question, but I suspect too much consistency may be similar to the boredom of always picking the right answer in the Humphreys light-guessing experiment. *Usually* we try to reduce inconsistency, just as *usually* we seek to maximize rewards. And in general, heaven knows, events in the world make it difficult enough to get rewards or to get consistent relations. But for the fortunate few who have all the rewards they want, and all the cognitive consistency they could hope for, it may become boring. One of those interesting little unexplored areas of human nature is just what happens when our normal motives all get satisfied. (This is a social psychologist's way of saying that most of us would be maladjusted in paradise.)

Exchange and Consistency Explanations

You surely have realized that some of the cases we have been analyzing using consistency theories could also have been analyzed in terms of rewards and costs; analyzed, that is, with one of the exchange theories. If in fact we could analyze most social situations using either an exchange or a consistency approach, wouldn't life be simpler if we learned only one set of theories? Why not concentrate on the exchange theories and try to explain everything in terms of rewards and costs? Since we are already familiar with this approach, it would be easier than mastering the very different ideas the consistency theorists have. Conversely someone who had studied consistency explanations first, reading this chapter before Chaps. 9–11, might prefer to analyze the world in consistency terms and never learn about exchanges.

There are two reasons, I think, why you will want to be familiar with both exchange theories and consistency theories. First, in a relatively new field such as theoretical social psychology, a variety of different types of explanation are proposed for phenomena. Each explanation has its proponents, and the proponents usually argue that their theory candidate is markedly superior to its competitors. Since the proponents of theories are advocates, it is necessary for someone else (that is, for *us*) to judge the merit of their claims. We need to understand their theories before we can judge for ourselves how satisfactory they are at explaining phenomena of interest to us.

Second, the proponents of exchange and consistency theories have not all been totally successful at explaining all phenomena. Sometimes an exchange explanation seems simplest and most adequate, and sometimes a consistency explanation seems preferable. In fact the proponents of consistency theories tend to focus on situations for which no simple exchange explanation is satisfactory, and vice-versa. For instance, the dissonance (consistency) theorists have conducted a large proportion of their investigations in areas where people seem to prefer *less* rewarding situations, or where people seem to give *more* compliance for *smaller* rewards. This is not to say that exchange theories could never explain dissonance phenomena; only that the exchange explanations offered seem cumbersome and implausible, compared to the dissonance reduction explanation.

Generally speaking, exchange theories have demonstrated considerable success at predicting peoples' *behaviors* in cases where the definition of the situation favors maximizing rewards. For instance, in decisions involving a person's career, one of the implicit norms is that he should consider how to maximize the financial and other rewards to be had from his various options. Therefore we ordinarily consider first an exchange based decision making model to predict behavior in this case. When the norms favoring maximization are explicit, we can be even more confident that an exchange theory can be developed to predict behavior. For example in competitive or in gambling situations, the norms explicitly tell the individual not to worry about anything except winning and his chances of winning: exchange theories are made for this sort of case.

Consistency explanations, on the other hand, seem to have been most adaptable to situations involving individuals' *cognitions,* such as their perceptions and misperceptions, their subjective definitions of situations, and especially, their attitudes. Perhaps this is not surprising, since the strategy of constructing a consistency explanation involves trying to describe the individual's cognitive structure, how the world looks to the actor. The way behavior is predicted is to assume that individuals' behaviors are direct consequences of their trying to achieve and to maintain cognitive consistency. But what the consistency theorists are always concerned with is what the actor *thinks* about the social situation in which he finds himself. Just as the more developed exchange theories, mathematical models of decision making, are tested by telling subjects to try to maximize their rewards, so the more developed consistency theories, information processing models, are tested by telling subjects to try to find some integration of the information bits they are given. Each theory, therefore, is developed and tested in an experimental situation favorable to the occurrence of the basic processes the theorist assumes.

Chart 12–1 gives the meta-theory behind contemporary consistency

CHART 12–1 The Consistency Meta-Theory

1. Considering a cognitive structure consisting of two or more entities (actors or objects) and two or more relations (affect relations or unit relations) between the entities, it is possible to identify balanced and imbalanced states of the structure.

   a. Whether a structure is balanced depends solely on the nature of the system of relations.

   b. A task of the theorist is to specify as precisely as possible the properties which differentiate balanced structures from imbalanced.

2. Balanced structures are always preferred to imbalanced structures.

   a. A task of the theorist is to specify the motivating consequences (such as tension, dissonance) of imbalance.

   b. Individuals will act, either cognitively or behaviorally or both, to change imbalanced structures in the direction of balance.

   c. Balanced structures are stable.

   d. A task of the theorist is to specify the likely modes, and their most likely ordering, of attempts to reduce imbalance.

3. Cognitive structures must be considered from the viewpoint of the individual of interest *p*-centric).

   a. Imbalance may be reduced by cognitive distortion.

   b. A task of the theorist is to specify likely modes of balance-producing distortion.

4. Some cognitive structures are more balanced than others.

   a. A task of the theorist is to find ways to measure the relative balance of two or more structures (degrees of balance).

5. Under certain circumstances individuals will complete cognitive structures by adding one or more elements (usually objects) associated with already existing actors and objects (attribution).

   a. When this occurs, the relations between previous and attributed elements will be formed so as not to reduce the balance of the total cognitive structure.

   b. A task of the theorist is to specify the form of the attribution process, and the conditions under which it occurs.

6. Environmental stimuli may be considered as bits of available cognitive information, and individuals may be considered as information processing systems.

   a. A task of the theorist is to identify useful (relevant) sources and types of information for individuals.

7. Many bits of information are utilized to form a relatively small set of cognitions regarding actors and objects.

   a. A task of the theorist is to specify as precisely as possible the form of the "information reduction" process.

theories. Future theoretical work may make some modification and extension of these statements necessary.

Figure 12–17 gives an overview of the main lines of thought which rely upon the consistency meta-theory as an orienting strategy. The basic ideas, which are also the older ones, appear at the top with groupings near the bottom indicating more recent work in this area. As in the exchange family of theories the meta-theoretical assumptions adopted by each group of investigators is indicated within the box representing that line of investigation.

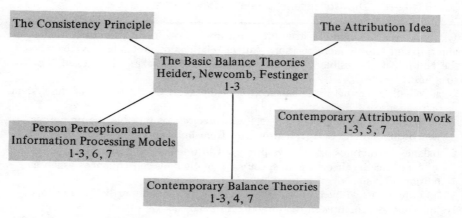

FIGURE 12–17 Consistency theory groups

13

Consistency Research I:

Direct Applications

General Introduction

Like exchange theories, the ideas of consistency theorists have generated considerable empirical research. The earlier studies, conducted during the 1950s, were aimed at testing the most basic of the consistency ideas: that individuals prefer balanced to imbalanced situations, and that imbalanced situations produce tension and attempts to change towards balance. Most of the research testing the general consistency orientation has produced confirmatory results. As a consequence of the early confirmation, as well as because consistency theories have been stated precisely, more recent research has been aimed at developing and refining the basic ideas. In a number of cases it has been possible for investigators to specify with considerable precision both the independent social variables that produce consistency or inconsistency, and the exact outcome that is predicted in a given situation. The precision of prediction as well as the cumulative development of the theory may be traced directly to the explicitness and the rigor of the consistency theories.

In this chapter we shall examine studies related to three major areas of research: tests of the general ideas, tests of predicted balance effects in interpersonal attraction, and some of the dissonance research. All of these areas share in common the basic ideas of the consistency meta-theory. However it is quite apparent that these general ideas have been adapted and modified for a wide variety of differing interests.

Direct Tests of Basic Ideas

The basic ideas of consistency theories have been tested in a variety of situations. Most tests involve asking subjects to imagine various social situations and then to report their responses to them, rather than actually creating the social situations and observing their responses. There are both advantages and disadvantages to this strategy. The advantages are that it is easier to manipulate independent variables symbolically—that is, simply by asking subjects to imagine situations—than it is to manipulate independent variables in a concrete, actual social situation. In addition because subjects are able to imagine a variety of different social situations within a short period of time, this procedure is more economical of their efforts than an actual experimental study would be. The major disadvantage of this type of research is the possibility that subjects may be unable to imagine accurately the situations, or to describe their own likely reactions. People may not know how they would behave in an actual, concrete situation when they are asked to imagine it. Fortunately results from other studies using actual situations are quite consistent with results from studies using imaginary social situations.

Jordan (1953) conducted one of the earliest and most influential studies of consistency ideas. The basic idea under test was the assertion that imbalanced situations are tension-producing. The measure of tension used was "pleasantness," which we would expect to be inversely related to the degree of psychological tension in a situation. Subjects were asked to imagine that they were members of various types of *p–o–x* social structures. Relations between the points of the structures were either affect relations (like or dislike) or unit relations. Thus subjects were asked to imagine themselves as *p* in several social situations in which their own relation with *o* and relations with *x* were given. Both types of relations, L and U, were employed in this study, and both types could be either positive or negative. (Recall from Chap. 12 that we said only L relations could be + or −; U relations are positive if they form and are otherwise absent. You will see the reasons for this from Jordan's data.) Situations were described to subjects using ordinary language. For example, a situation of *p+Lo*, *o+Lx* and *p+Ux* would be, "I like *o; o* likes *x;* and I own *x*." With three entities and four possible types of relations between each, there are 64 possible types of social situations or cases.

The dependent variable, tension, was measured by asking subjects to indicate how they felt about each situation, choosing points on a ruler to indicate feelings. One end of the ruler, numbered "10," was labelled "extremely pleasant." The other end, numbered "99," was labelled "extremely unpleasant." The numberings were intended to permit a quantitative measure of subjective unpleasantness, but we shall be concerned only with classifying situations as pleasant or unpleasant. A situation with a mean rating of 54 or below will be pleasant; a rating of 55 or above, unpleasant.

Table 13–1, constructed from Jordan's data, shows the effect of the independent variable balance/imbalance upon the dependent variable pleasant/unpleasant. As expected, more of the 32 balanced cases are pleasant than unpleasant. Note, however, that the support for the

TABLE 13–1 Tension as Affected by Balance

	BALANCED	IMBALANCED
PLEASANT	21	15
UNPLEASANT	11	17

(Adapted from Jordan, 1953.)

predicted effect of imbalance is quite weak: 17 cases were considered un-pleasant, and 15 were considered pleasant. This rather weak support was improved by adding several ad hoc assumptions about the "potency" of various social situations. None of these assumptions seems particularly per-suasive, however. And since the potency assumptions were added to account for the results after the data were known, none of them had received any independent test or support.

Runkel (1956) reanalyzed Jordan's data a few years later, dropping from analysis the cases that included a —U relation. The —U relations would be something like, "You do not own x," or "O has no connection with x."

Table 13–2 presents Runkel's calculation of pleasantness for Jordan's data with —U cases dropped from analysis. The prediction is much im-proved. Only 4 cases of 27 fail to fall into the expected cells. Jordan's data provide one of the earliest direct tests and partial confirmations of the ideas of balance theories. Runkel's reanalysis provides a clear instance of modi-fication and clarification of theoretical ideas as the result of empirical research. The Cartwright–Harary graphed formulation of balance theory incorporates this result by omitting U relations unless they are positive.

Two studies illustrate the asserted tendency for individuals to believe that balance structures exist in the absence of information regarding balance or imbalance of the structures. Kogan and Tagiuri studied groups of naval enlisted men who lived together for a long enough period to form acquaintanceships and friendships. They studied relations between mem-bers of p–o–q structures by asking subjects to describe their own friends and other people's friendship choices on the ship. These investigators found two results that would be expected from consistency theories. First, there was a greater than chance tendency for individuals to believe that their friends were friends of each other. That is, in those cases where p had a positive affect relation to both o and q, there was a greater than average tendency for p to believe that o and q had a positive affect relationship also. This would be expected from balance theories since to believe the opposite (a negative affect relation between o and q) would create an imbalanced structure. Second, not only was the tendency to believe balanced struc-tures greater than *chance*, but it also was greater than *actual* choices. For example if p had a positive relation to both o and q, he often was likely to think that o and q had positive affect for each other when in fact, o and q

TABLE 13–2 Jordan's Data, Excluding —U Cases

	BALANCED	IMBALANCED
PLEASANT	10	0
UNPLEASANT	4	13

(Adapted from Runkel, 1956.)

both reported that they disliked each other, or that they did not know each other. This distortion also would be predicted on the basis of the ideas in balance theories.

Morrissette (1958) conducted a similar study using college students as subjects. Subjects were asked to imagine hypothetical social situations involving either three or four persons of which they themselves were one. In Morrissette's study as in the Kogan and Tagiuri study, subjects were told the nature of some of the affect and unit relations between points and then they were asked to predict affect relations between persons where they were not given. Afterwards subjects were asked to rate the degree of tension they would feel in each of the hypothetical social situations. Results of Morrissette's study were generally consistent with those of Jordan and of Kogan and Tagiuri. Subjects tended to complete the structures in a balanced fashion if that were possible, and in cases in which neither positive nor negative affect relation would balance the structure, the tendency was to make the structure as near balanced as possible. In addition, ratings of tension clearly showed greater tension in the imbalanced social structures than in the balanced structures.

More generally, the results of these studies indicate support for the asserted tendency to distort perception in the direction of balanced structures. People tend to perceive balance more than it actually exists, and they tend to perceive balance when they do not have any objective basis for doing so.

A different experimental situation used to study balance effects has been developed by DeSoto (1960, 1968). The assumption that balanced structures are in some way preferable to imbalanced structures suggests that there is some sort of psychological resistance to forming a cognition involving imbalance. If this is the case, then we would expect individuals to have more difficulty learning relations in a social structure when those reactions produce imbalance than when the relations produce balance. For example, it should be more difficult to remember that John likes Jim and Jim dislikes John than to remember that John and Jim are friends.

The situation involving learning as the dependent variable for measuring a consistency preference constitutes an advance in objectivity over asking subjects to rate the pleasantness of a situation. A subject might claim that a situation is pleasant even without believing it, but it is more difficult to fake ability to learn various structures. Difficulty can be measured objectively (by how long it takes to learn it, proportion of subjects remembering it incorrectly, and so on).

Subjects in DeSoto's studies are presented with a large number of social situations in which all affect and unit relations between points are given. Subsequently they are asked to report the nature of the relations between the points they had earlier studied. DeSoto's results show, first, that balanced structures of all sorts are consistently easier to learn than imbalanced structures. Subjects also say that they are better able to remember balanced structures, and they make fewer errors in reproducing the structures when they are asked to. Second, in some cases subjects have been asked to recall structures in which not all of the relations are given. In Cartwright and

Harary's terms, subjects were asked to learn some vacuously balanced structures. Results of these studies suggest (although not conclusively) that completely connected structures are easier to learn than incomplete structures. Remember these interpretations all depend on the assumption that *tension* interferes with *learning* a social structure.

Attitude Similarity and Attraction

One of the many problems faced by the director of a college dormitory—and by others in similar responsible positions such as prison wardens—is to assign individuals to rooms in such a way as to minimize potential conflicts. When I was a college freshman, roommates were assigned solely on the basis of height. The belief apparently was that individuals of noticeably different height were more likely to get into fights than those of approximately equal height. Using this single criterion suggests that the authorities at that time were unaware of any other means of promoting harmony between individuals who were forced into close contact. Nowadays it is customary at many schools for dormitory residents to indicate a preference for smoking or nonsmoking roommates.

What other criteria besides height and use of tobacco might be used in roommate selection? Is there knowledge in social psychology that could be applied for this very practical purpose? The development and maintenance of friendship choices has been studied extensively by Newcomb in a college dormitory. The dormitory was a small residence at the University of Michigan in which, for two consecutive years, a small number of entering freshmen were given free room and board in return for allowing social psychologists to make an intensive study of their adjustment to the university and to each other. Let us look at some of their findings on the relationship of attitudes and interpersonal attraction.

Consistency theories would lead us to expect that those individuals holding similar attitudes would be more likely to become friends than individuals holding dissimilar attitudes. This prediction may be tested by tabulating two of the many measures available from the study. The first measure is a set of philosophical value statements (called Spranger values) and the second is the degree of friendship attraction reported by individuals. Table 13–3 shows the relationship between level of agreement on values and level of mutual attraction in dyads. Of those dyads whose agreement level

TABLE 13–3 Value Agreement and
Interpersonal Attraction

| | ATTRACTION | |
AGREEMENT LEVEL	TOP HALF	BOTTOM HALF
Top half	44	25
Bottom half	24	33

(Adapted from Newcomb, 1963, Table 8.)

was in the top half for the group, 44 were also in the top half of attraction. Only 25 were in the bottom half of attraction. For those whose agreement on values was in the bottom half, the pattern was reversed. Twenty-four of these dyads reported attraction in the top half, and 43 reported attraction in the bottom half. These measures were taken in the 14th week, after the individuals had had ample time to get to know each other and each other's beliefs. We would expect that earlier in the semester, individuals would not know each other's values, and consequently, that friendship choices might not be so highly associated with attitude similarity.

Newcomb also reports two significant changes during the first semester acquaintance process. First, during early weeks of the study, individuals show a great tendency to believe that those whom they like, like them. On the basis of consistency theories this distortion is understandable. By the 15th week, after individuals have had the chance to interact, their estimates of reciprocal friendship choices are more influenced by reality. In a significant number of cases, individuals report that their friendship choices are not reciprocated. Of course, for various reasons we would expect that the proportion of nonreciprocated friendship choices would never be very high.

The second trend visible in Newcomb's data is an increase through time in the stability of individuals' judgments of who their friends are. Residents of the house were asked to rank all other residents in terms of attractiveness as friends each week during their first semester living together. Comparing rankings from any two weeks (for example, the ranking in the first week compared to the ranking in the second week) shows that, the later in the semester this comparison is made, the higher the degree of association between the two rankings. The association between week 1 and week 2 was only .51; the association between week 14 and week 15 was .88. In other words during the semester, residents of the house came to hold relatively stable ideas of the rankings of all other residents in terms of whom they liked.

Newcomb also discusses the possibility that authoritarianism, as measured by the F-scale, might be associated with tendencies toward cognitive consistency. One of the characteristics of highly authoritarian people is reported to be a low degree of tolerance for ambiguity. Therefore we might expect that when high authoritarians are asked to estimate others' attitudes, they will show greater distortion in the direction of balance than low authoritarians. Newcomb reports some evidence of this tendency in his data. However available measures of authoritarianism do not provide the high degree of reliability which we would like to have confidence in such a finding. Also, some of Byrne's research has shown no tendency for authoritarianism to be associated with preference for balance. In view of these facts we must conclude that the tendency—if it exists—is not well documented.

A more recent study was conducted by Griffitt and Veitch in which experimental control was exerted over the independent variable *interaction* that Newcomb studied in the natural setting. This study has 13 adult males live together in a simulated fall-out shelter 12 feet by 24 feet. Results on attraction here closely parallel those Newcomb found. Similar attitudes led to liking and desire to "keep" the member who was similar. Also, over time both "keep" and "reject" choices tended to become reciprocated, indicating that pairs of individuals generally produced balance cognitive structures.

Other studies by Byrne's research team have investigated the effect of racial prejudice upon the tendency for attitude similarity to breed liking. White subjects who had been classified as "prejudiced" according to an attitude measure rated blacks as attractive when they held similar attitudes to those of the subject, and unattractive when their attitudes were reported to be different. In the first study the similarity—attraction relation was independent of degree of racial prejudice. In a later study there was an interaction: prejudice was related inversely to attraction, and attitude similarity was related directly to attraction.

Another interesting study showed that heterosexual attraction was strongly influenced by attitude similarity. Subjects were asked to rate the attractiveness of various pictures of individuals after being given information that their attitudes were either similar to those of the subject or dissimilar. The pictures had previously been rated for attractiveness of the model by the research team. (Admittedly this is not a perfectly objective rating, but we hope that their judgments were reasonably accurate.) The results show that attitude similarity was much more important than physical attractiveness (if the researchers' estimates were accurate) in determining overall attractiveness for subjects. In general those models reported to have similar attitudes to the subject were rated as attractive by the subject. Those reported to hold dissimilar attitudes, as unattractive.

Many of the studies dealing with interpersonal attraction have found that it is influenced by a complex set of factors; this is what we would expect. However all of the studies show that attitude similarity is extremely important in determining attractiveness of other individuals. It is not the only determinant of attraction, but it is always one of the determinants, and a very important one at that. If we know that someone's attitudes are similar to ours, there is a very good chance that we shall like him—regardless of what else we know about him, and regardless of prejudicial feelings we may hold. If we know that someone's attitudes on "important matters" are dissimilar to ours, it will be quite difficult to like that person well—regardless of what other factors may exist that recommend him or her to us.

Does simple familiarity lead to liking? The first case of Heider's thought experiments which we considered in Chap. 12 postulated that p tends to like a familiar o, but so far we have had little to say about this case. With the direction of causation reversed, it becomes readily understandable: we become familiar with people we like. But can it work the other way as well? Some of the most interesting applications of balance ideas come from the assertion that attitudes and actions are intimately related, and that a change in either one will produce a specifiable change in the other. If we like a particular o, we tend to associate with him, *or* if we associate with a particular o, we tend to come to like him.

At first glance, this process might seem the same as the Newcomb study where attitude similarity led to interpersonal attraction. However in Newcomb's study, the individuals began with both of them having positive affect relations towards a particular attitude x. In a cognitive unit where both p and o have positive relations to x, we would expect a positive p to o bond to be more likely to form than a negative p to o bond (because the latter would produce an imbalanced structure). Now we are considering a simpler situation: the cognitive structure contains only p and x, and we are saying that a positive bond from p to x is more likely to form than a negative bond. There is nothing in balance theories that would lead us to expect this to be true.

Still we might expect that in many cases familiarity does lead to liking, both of objects and of other actors. Many people seem to have an initial dislike of new clothing or furniture and to come to like it with the passage of time. Some people we do not like at first come to seem more likeable as time goes by and we become familiar with their habits. Zajonc has investigated this process more systematically and has produced some very impressive evidence that simple familiarity does lead to liking.

The first evidence favoring the familiarity–liking hypothesis comes from comparing liking for various objects with the frequency of usage of the words naming them. Word frequencies have been tabulated by psychologists and linguists, so we know with considerable accuracy just how often many words appear in written English. Liking of the objects named by the words was established by Zajonc by asking large numbers of college and high school students to rate on a 7-point scale how much they liked the objects in each category.

The categories of objects were extremely varied: countries, cities, trees, fruits, vegetables, and flowers. Note that it is not necessary for tests of this hypothesis for the students to have any actual experience with the objects evaluated. One can have an opinion about how much he likes, say, Chicago without ever having been there. In fact the hypothesis speaks only about how often the student has probably seen the word "Chicago," not about any experiences he may have had with the city.

Table 13–4 presents the word frequency and the liking ratings for objects. Support of the hypothesis requires a positive correlation between the frequency and the liking of words in each category. The correlations are positive and extremely high: .89 for countries, .85 for cities, .84 for trees, .81 for fruits, .85 for vegetables, and .89 for flowers. The more often a word appears in the language we use, the more we seem to like the thing named by the word.

But how about the problem of deciding which produces which? For instance, perhaps we use the word corn a lot because we like corn, not the other way around. To rule out this alternative interpretation, Zajonc designed a series of experiments to study liking of previously unfamiliar objects. Three different types of objects were used for these studies: nonsense words described as being Turkish; characters that resembled Chinese

TABLE 13–4 Frequency and Liking Ratings for Various Objects

COUNTRIES	f	APR	CITIES	f	APR	TREES	f	APR
England	497	2.67	Boston	255	2.75	pine	172	4.79
Canada	130	3.33	Chicago	621	3.08	walnut	75	4.42
Holland	59	3.42	Milwaukee	124	3.83	oak	125	4.00
Greece	31	4.00	San Diego	9	4.25	rosewood	8	3.96
Germany	224	4.92	Dayton	14	5.75	birch	34	3.83
Argentina	15	6.08	Baltimore	68	6.08	fir	14	3.75
Venezuela	9	6.58	Omaha	28	7.08	sassafras	2	3.00
Bulgaria	3	7.75	Tampa	5	7.08	aloes	1	2.92
Honduras	1	7.92	El Paso	1	7.50	yew	3	2.83
Syria	4	8.34	Saginaw	2	7.58	acacia	4	2.75

FRUITS	f	APR	VEGETABLES	f	APR	FLOWERS	f	APR
apple	220	5.13	corn	227	4.17	rose	801	5.55
cherry	167	5.00	potato	384	4.13	lily	164	4.79
strawberry	121	4.83	lettuce	142	4.00	violet	109	4.58
pear	62	4.38	carrot	96	3.57	geranium	27	3.83
grapefruit	33	4.00	radish	43	3.13	daisy	62	3.79
cantaloupe	1.5	3.75	asparagus	5	2.33	hyacinth	16	3.08
avocado	16	2.71	cauliflower	27	1.96	yucca	1	2.88
pomegranate	8	2.63	broccoli	18	1.96	woodbine	4	2.87
gooseberry	5	2.63	leek	3	1.96	anemone	8	2.54
mango	2	2.38	parsnip	8	1.92	cowslip	2	2.54

f = frequency of usage; APR = average preference rating.
(From Zajonc, 1968.)

words; and human faces. In all cases subjects were shown a long series of words (or characters, or faces) in which some were shown more frequently than others. They were then asked simply how "good" each seemed to them, or how favorable they felt towards it. Figure 13–1 shows the goodness or favorability as a function of frequency of exposure. For all three types of stimuli, the more often subjects have seen it, the more they like it on the average. The evidence is strongly supportive of the familiarity leads to liking hypothesis, and it is difficult to think of any alternative interpretation of these results.

After Zajonc's first report, other investigators studied the familiarity-liking process in other situations and found essentially the same results. For instance, Schick, McGlynn, and Woolam found that familiar comic strips (*Peanuts*) were liked better and thought funnier than the same strips redrawn with unfamiliar characters. Zajonc and Kreveld found that abstract art to which subjects were frequently exposed was "liked better" than those seen only a few times. Saegert, Swap, and Zajonc found that subjects got to like experimenters to whom they were frequently exposed better than those

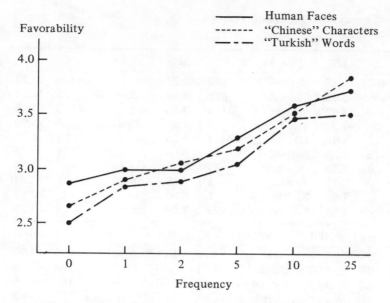

FIGURE 13–1 Frequency and liking of three types of objects. (Adapted from Zajonc, 1968, Figs. 2, 5.)

with whom they had few encounters. Stapleton, Nacci, and Tedeschi found the same thing with liking for confederates, and others have recently replicated the results using sounds and music. Apparently the phenomenon is a very general one!

A possible partial explanation of these findings is that novelty and new situations are tension-producing for individuals. For instance, regardless of what people say, most of us really don't like surprises of any except the most mild sort. There is something unpleasant, perhaps threatening, about a new situation. Perhaps the unpleasantness wears off through repeated exposure, so that we can only be truly comfortable in the presence of very familiar surroundings and very old friends. Some of Zajonc's data support this point of view. Subjects were shown the "Turkish" nonsense words in a long series. Some words were shown only once, some 2 times, others 5, 10, or 25. Galvanic Skin Response (GSR) measures were taken from subjects as an indication of psychological tension and arousal of the central nervous system. (See Chap. 2 for discussion of the GSR, and description of how these measures are obtained.)

What is of interest is the GSR for the *last* time each word is exposed. To support the idea that tension is associated with novelty, we should find that the more often the word has been shown, the lower the GSR for that word at its last showing. Figure 13–2 shows the GSR on the last exposure of words. As can be seen, there is a perfect negative relationship between frequency of exposure and tension.

Results of these experiments are striking because they are strong and they are all consistent with the general idea that familiar things are more liked than unfamiliar. They are intriguing for two reasons: first, because we do not have a perfectly adequate theoretical explanation for them; and second, because we can think of numerous examples of the phenomena he is studying. Many people seem to show a great resistance to new things—new ideas, new actions, new acquaintances—at first. Sometimes, the newness is overcome with familiarity, and the new becomes the accepted and liked thing —though it is possible to think of persons who never have adapted to one change or another.

It has always seemed to me that one difference between popular and classical music is that popular music often is likeable on first hearing, but eventually becomes less and less interesting. Classical pieces, in contrast, often seem unpleasant at first hearing and become more and more appealing with repeated listenings. Perhaps this is because popular music is so much simpler than classical. There is nothing much new and unfamiliar about a new rock record; hence, nothing to produce tension. As a matter of fact, it is standard practice for any singer who has had one hit record to release a second one that sounds almost like the first: similarity to a familiar and

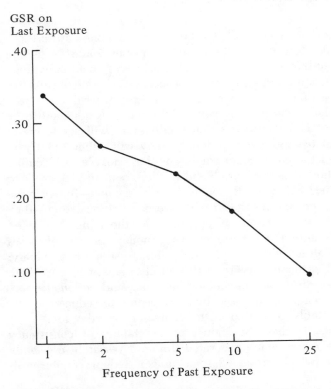

FIGURE 13–2 GSR as a function of familiarity. (From Zajonc, 1968, p. 21.)

liked song. Classical music, with its vastly more complicated structure and tonal patterns, may well be tension-producing at first. If the listener sticks with it, however, the familiarity may lead to liking. The same sorts of processes seem to occur historically, as well as for individuals. Several classical pieces we now think of as great, including works of Stravinsky and Wagner, were received with open hostility when they were new. By contrast the rock music of the 1960s which we thought was great then now sounds either too simplistic or too pretentious (or both).

If it is generally true that familiarity leads to liking, then efforts directed solely towards making products well known should be quite effective. A politician who is fortunate enough to have an opponent who is relatively unknown would be wise never to mention him by name—a strategy followed to the letter by Presidents Johnson in 1964 and Nixon in 1972. Those in charge of propaganda to sell a new program or idea should try for maximum exposure of their ideas. Those in charge of propaganda opposing the new idea should try to suppress publicity for it.

Research on Cognitive Dissonance

Simultaneous awareness of two inconsistent facts regarding one's attitudes or behaviors—for example, "I am basically an honest person," and, "I lied in reporting my income to the government"—can be disturbing to an individual. In an extended discussion of this sort of inconsistency, Festinger proposes and develops the idea that awareness of the inconsistency produces a psychological feeling called *cognitive dissonance*. Dissonance is assumed to be unpleasant, and thus it is a motivating state. Individuals will act to try to reduce their dissonant feelings. Most generally, they will either (1) try to change one or more of the inconsistent cognitions—for example by deciding either, "I am not an honest person" or, "I did not lie about my income"; or (2) try to change their behaviors to remove the dissonance—for example by stopping the lying; or (3) engage in what we call "rationalizing"—they will think of as many other reasons as possible why the lying is justified (everyone else cheats also; the government uses money for evil purposes anyway; if I reported all my income, I couldn't affort to support my family; and so on). These three dissonance reduction mechanisms may be called, respectively, *cognitive distortion, behavior alteration,* and *rationalization.* All three mechanisms regularly are used by most people to reduce the dissonance which is inevitably generated in the course of everyday life.

Cognitive dissonance is the best known of the family of consistency theories. It was also the one which generated the most research—especially during the 1960s—and which produced some unexpected or counterintuitive results.

Figure 13–3 depicts the basic situation for a dissonance problem. In this situation, the most direct way for p to remove inconsistency is to change

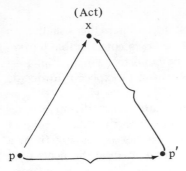

FIGURE 13–3   Basic cognitive dissonance situation

the negative bond between p and x to positive: to decide, that is, that whatever he did must be all right. Dissonance theory often focuses on attitude change from negative to positive as the result of seeing oneself linked to some previously disfavored act.

Counterattitudinal actions and essays. Fig. 13–3 represents the case of an actor who has done something he does not believe in, committed an act he does not approve of. The graph is imbalanced, so we presume the actor feels tension and pressure to change his attitude. (Most dissonance research deals with cases in which all the unit relations are unchangeable; that is, situations where the actor p cannot deny that he (p') committed the act x.) Now suppose p has been induced to commit the act by giving him a large amount of money, as in Fig. 13–4. This time the money is associated with all sorts of other pleasant things, which means that the majority of cycles in the cognitive structure are balanced. This fact, in turn, makes the situa-

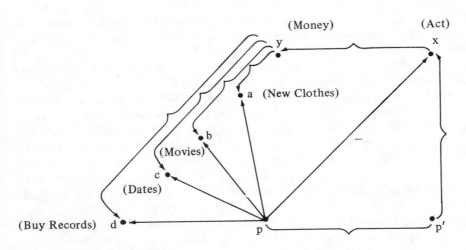

FIGURE 13–4   Dissonance situation with large incentive

tion in Fig. 13–4 less unpleasant or dissonant for p than the situation in Fig. 13–3. In other words, in Fig. 13–3 p is subjected to considerable tension which can only be resolved if he changes the px bond to $(+)$. In Fig. 13–4 the tension is much less, so there is much less reason to expect p to decide he approves of x.

This is an abstract description of the counterattitudinal dissonance research. Subjects are induced to perform some act which they disapprove of (such as saying something they do not believe), either by paying them a very small sum of money, or by paying them a large amount. Subjects paid a small sum are thus placed in the situation of Fig. 13–3: suffering considerable dissonance, which can only be resolved by changing their attitudes towards x. Subjects paid a lot of money are in the situation of Fig. 13–4: much less dissonance, so less reason to change their attitudes.

The first experiment of this sort was reported by Festinger and Carlsmith (1959). Subjects were required to perform an experimental task of crossing out some numbers on large sheets for a period of one hour—decidedly a dull task. At the end of this time they were asked to tell a confederate, who presumably was another subject about to perform the same task, that it was in fact an interesting and rewarding experience. Subjects were given either a \$1 or a \$20 incentive for saying that the task was interesting. Then they were asked how interesting they actually found the task to be.

We would expect that subjects offered \$20 would feel considerably less tension or dissonance than those paid \$1: \$20 is a lot of money, and it could constitute justification for telling the lie. Therefore little attitude change is necessary to reduce dissonance. This is what Festinger and Carlsmith found: subjects offered the \$1 incentive gave their private opinion of how interesting the task was, and it was much more favorable than the private opinion of subjects paid \$20 for performing the same act.

Cohen (1962) tested the same basic ideas in a different setting. After a student disturbance at Yale University, he asked students to write an essay favoring the actions of the police—an attitude we may assume most students did not favor. Subjects were paid 50¢, \$1, \$5, or \$10 for the essay writing task, and as predicted, private attitudes were inversely related to the amount of the monetary inducement offered.

On the other hand, Rosenberg (1965) attempted to replicate the Cohen study at Ohio State University, asking students to write an essay favoring keeping Ohio State from playing in the Rose Bowl (to which they had been invited that year). Rosenberg had the essay written for one experimenter, and then private students' attitudes measured by a second experimenter. His results were the opposite of Cohen's: the *greater* the inducement, the *more* favorable the attitude towards keeping the football team out of the Rose Bowl. These findings are more easily explained from an exchange theory than from dissonance reduction: people do what they are paid to do; the more they are paid to change their attitudes the more they change their attitudes.

Carlsmith et al. conducted an experiment combining features of the original Festinger and Carlsmith experiment and the later essay-writing studies. Subjects performed the dull number-crossing task, and they were induced either to tell another subject that it was interesting, or to write an essay saying the task was interesting. They were paid either nothing (control condition), 50¢, $1.50, or $5.00 for falsely describing their attitudes. As before, private attitude measures towards the task were collected following their false descriptions. Thus there are two independent variables: face-to-face description, or essay writing; and amount of inducement.

Table 13–4 presents some of their results on private favorability towards the experiment, with negative numbers indicating an unfavorable attitude, and positive numbers indicating a favorable attitude. The results are remarkably consistent. In the face-to-face condition, the dissonance prediction is supported: size of inducement and attitude favorability are inversely related. In the essay condition the exchange prediction is supported: size of inducement and attitude favorability are *directly* related.

The authors interpret these results as follows. College students, they say, are quite accustomed to writing essays that they do not agree with. They have learned that often it is necessary to write a term paper reflecting the professor's point of view, not the student's, in order to pass a course. Everyone knows that essays may not reflect the writer's attitudes. Therefore the essay condition of this experiment probably did not produce much dissonance for the students. By contrast, college students place considerable value upon being honest in face-to-face interaction. Thus this condition of the experiment did produce considerable dissonance for subjects. In the face-to-face condition dissonance predictions were supported. In the essay condition other forces (namely, exchange processes) were at work and produced opposite results.

I leave it to you to decide whether this explanation is convincing. On the one hand we must note that some links in the explanation are untested; for example, the assertion that students do not find writing a counterattitudinal essay dissonant. On the other hand it certainly is consistent with good research design and our understanding of the world to assume that when one particular process (in this case, dissonance) does not occur, results are determined by another process (in this case, exchange).

When Prophecies Fail. One of the earliest studies of dissonance was reported by Festinger, et al. They joined a religious interpretation group who believed that the world was to end at midnight on a particular day.

TABLE 13–4   Mean Ratings on "Fun and Interesting"

CONDITION	INDUCEMENT			
	NONE	50¢	$1.50	$5.00
Face-to-Face	−2.71	1.81	−1.62	−2.19
Essay	−2.14	−1.80	3.24	3.95

(Adapted from Carlsmith et al., 1966, Table 1.)

As the appointed hour approached, members of the group met for prayer and perhaps to be rescued by people from flying saucers.

What is striking is the way these people dealt with the eventual disconfirmation of the central belief of their religion: instead of abandoning the religion, they redoubled their efforts to seek converts, and their own faith in the (appropriately revised) prediction of the imminent end of the world was strengthened.

I have not included this study and some later attempts to replicate it because they do not illustrate principles of dissonance theory as well as some of the later studies we did examine. However it should be relatively easy for you to construct an explanation for the way these religious people reacted to disconfirmation in a fashion similar to explanations constructed for other dissonance phenomena.

David Halberstam, an excellent journalist and contemporary historian, but apparently not acquainted with Festinger's theory, has written regarding American involvement in Vietnam:

> Dealing with the military, . . . both Kennedy and Johnson would learn, was an awesome thing. The failure of their estimates along the way, point by point, meant nothing. It did not follow, as one might expect, that their credibility was diminished and that there was now less pressure from them, but the reverse. It meant that there would be an inexorable pressure for more—more men, more hardware, more targets. . . . (*The Best and The Brightest,* 1972, p. 220).

Severity of Initiation. For many years in this country, it was traditional for college fraternities to subject new members ("pledges") to difficult, unpleasant, and demeaning initiation practices ("hazing"). Occasional deaths resulted from choking while attempting to swallow goldfish, and unknown numbers of psyches were damaged temporarily or permanently through intentionally cruel procedures. Still on most college campuses, fraternity membership was actively and eagerly sought by the vast majority of male college students. Moreover in most cases, once the initiate progressed beyond the hazing stage, there was a high level of enthusiasm and morale—what social psychologists call "cohesiveness"—among the members. Fraternities flourished, members and alumni developed and maintained close ties, and the expressions of loyalty to the fraternity were frequently extraordinary. For many college students, fraternity membership was by far the most satisfying experience of their four years in college.

One might expect that the high level of cohesiveness among fraternity members was the result of a selective process. No one would go through the rigors of the hazing procedure unless he had an almost fanatical desire to be a member of the fraternity. Those who were merely indifferent would never put up with the hazing and would drop out. (One could make the same argument for *volunteers* subjected to basic training in the military.) However a dissonance explanation is a bit more subtle. It postulates that the relationship could as well work in the reverse direction;

that is, enduring the hazing could actually increase feelings of attraction towards the fraternity. The argument may be sketched as follows. Admittedly the hazing is an unpleasant procedure for the pledge, and thus he is faced with the problem of justifying to himself why he would endure it. Dissonance is created from the combination of facts that hazing is unpleasant, and that he has willingly subjected himself to it. The only way to reduce the dissonance (short of dropping out of the fraternity) is to change his attitude towards the group; that is, to decide that the group is so extremely attractive that the hazing is in some sense "worth it." Because of the postulated dissonance reduction mechanism, we would expect that the more severe the hazing, the more dissonance the individual would have to resolve, and consequently, the greater would be his eventual attraction to the group.

Aronson and Mills (1959) conducted an experiment to test the preceding idea. Subjects for the experiment were 63 college women, freshmen and sophomores who had volunteered to participate in "a discussion of the psychology of sex." Each subject was assigned to one of three conditions: control group, mild initiation, severe initiation. As she arrived for her scheduled appointment, the subject was met by an experimenter who explained that he was interested in investigating features of discussion groups, and that he had chosen sex as the topic of discussion in order to make the experience interesting. But there was one drawback, he reported to the subject: sometimes people feel embarrassed and are too inhibited to discuss sex freely. Then he asked the subject whether she felt *she* would be able to discuss. Invariably she showed her sophistication by saying yes.

Women in the control group were immediately sent to the second phase of the experiment. Women in both of the "initiation" groups were then told they would have to prove their lack of inhibitions by reading a list of sexual words aloud to the male experimenter. In the "mild initiation" condition, the words the subject read were noncontroversial; such words as "male," "female," "love," and so on. In the "severe initiation" condition, the subject read a list of obscene words. (The investigators do not report the exact words on the list, so we will have to take their word for it that the words were obscene.)

In all three conditions the woman was then sent to a small booth and asked to put on a pair of earphones. She was told that the other members of her group were in similar booths with microphones and earphones and that they had already begun their discussion of sex. She was requested simply to listen to the discussion for a period of time to familiarize herself with the topic before joining in. The other discussants existed merely as tape recorded voices. The recording was an unbelievably dull discussion of secondary sexual behavior of animals—such topics as whether male dogs are more aggressive than female dogs. After listening to the discussion the subject was asked to indicate on various measures how well she liked the other group members, and how much she had enjoyed her first participation in the discussion group. The prediction was that the more unpleasant the initiation the greater dissonance would be induced by participating in the group, and subsequently, the *more attractive* the subject would have to decide the experience had been in order to be worth it.

The results of the study are shown in Table 13–5. Both the discussion and the other participants were rated about equally in the control condition and in the mild condition. In the severe initiation condition both the discussants and the participants were rated considerably more attractive, thus confirming the hypothesis. Aronson and Mills conclude that the results support the dissonance reduction process. Because the finding is striking, it has attracted wide attention and some criticism, some of which we shall examine briefly.

Schopler and Bateson (1962) interpreted the results of the Aronson and Mills experiment, not in terms of dissonance reduction, but in terms of a *dependency* they assumed subjects felt towards the experimenter. In other words Schopler and Bateson felt that the results of the Aronson and Mills experiment could better be explained by an exchange-based interpretation than by a consistency theory. Their interpretation, in brief, is that the severe initiation condition demonstrates to subjects that the experimenter has considerable power over them. He forces them to do something unpleasant. The subjects' response to this is to try to increase the experimenter's dependency upon them by giving him something they think he wants; namely, liking for his experiment. This is a type 3 power a balancing operation discussed in Chap. 10. They tested this interpretation by conducting an experiment including *control, severe,* and *severe disparage* conditions. The control and severe conditions were quite similar to those of Aronson and Mills. In the former, there was no initiation, and in the latter, subjects read aloud a passage from Henry Miller's *Tropic of Cancer* (thought to be quite sexual in the 1960s). In the third condition, subjects underwent the initiation, but the experimenter told them he thought they would probably not like the group. The intent of this instruction was to remove the giving of liking as a power balancing mechanism. Table 13–6 shows the mean liking ratings for these three conditions. What is significant for Schopler and Bateson is that subjects rated the discussion and the other participants lower in the disparage condition than they did in the severe condition, and also lower in disparage than in the control condition.

TABLE 13–5 Mean Liking Ratings by Severity
of Initiation

	INITIATION		
	NONE	MILD	SEVERE
Discussion	80.2	81.8	97.6
Others in Group	89.9	89.3	97.7

(Adapted from Aronson and Mills, 1959, Table 1.)

TABLE 13–6   Mean Liking Ratings

	INITIATION		
	CONTROL	SEVERE	SEVERE/ DISPARAGE
Discussion	39.2	47.8	37.1
Others in Group	59.7	62.9	59.5

(Adapted from Schopler and Bateson, 1962, Table 3.)

They interpret this as showing that, when power balancing operations are ruled out, subjects like the group as a direct function of the pleasantness of the initiation. The *severe disparage* condition was unpleasant to subjects, and consequently, they liked it least.

Gerard and Mathewson, two supporters of dissonance explanations, disagreed with the Schopler–Bateson interpretation of the effects of severe initiation. We will compare results in only two of their conditions. In the *mild* condition, subjects' initiation consisted of receiving a weak electric shock. In the *severe* condition, the initiation was a strong electric shock. In terms of dissonance theory, these treatments should be roughly equivalent to a mild and severe initiation using sexual words; that is, liking should be greater in the severe shock condition than in the mild shock condition. An exchange prediction would be the opposite (degree of shock and liking inversely related). Table 13–7 presents the mean liking ratings for a mild shock and a severe shock condition of this experiment. As may be seen, the dissonance prediction is well supported: liking and severity of electric shock are directly related. It is quite difficult to come up with an exchange-based explanation of this outcome.

A Perspective on Dissonance Controversies.   As you may have concluded, dissonance ideas have produced an enormous amount of research, of which the two sets described here are typical. Dissonance research also has produced an enormous amount of controversy, of the type described for each of these experimental designs. The severity of initiation experiments have been subjected to a variety of alternative interpretations: the finding that severity and liking are positively related has been explained in many ways which do

TABLE 13–7   Mean Liking Ratings
by Severity of Shock

	INITIATION	
	MILD	SEVERE
Discussion	11.0	27.0
Others in Group	11.5	31.1

(Adapted from Gerard and Mathewson, 1966, Table 1.)

not use the ideas of dissonance at all. For instance, perhaps women in the severe condition felt relieved to get into the dull discussion after the embarrassment of the initiation. Perhaps they felt proud of themselves for having withstood the severe initiation. Perhaps they actually found the severe initiation titillating, and thus enjoyed the experience more, and so on. These interpretations and many others that do not use the ideas of dissonance or cognitive inconsistency have been put forth, and a number of researchers have spent much effort either trying to support or to refute the dissonance explanations.

What is significant about these controversies, I believe, is that the disputing parties implicitly adopt different meta-theoretical orientations to the work. Dissonance theorists adopt the consistency meta-theory, and the critics adopt the exchange meta-theory. The alternative interpretations of dissonance experiments all are in terms of seeking to maximize some sort of rewards, while the dissonance explanations are all in terms of seeking cognitive consistency. But meta-theories, you will recall, are orienting strategies. They are accepted on faith, not subjected to empirical test. Thus there is no single "right" way to interpret these (or any other) experiments.

In large measure, the participants to debates of this sort talk past each other. They see the world in different ways, and they have different views of human actors. Exchange theorists see social situations in terms of available rewards and costs, and they assume that actors try to maximize their rewards. Dissonance researchers see social situations in terms of consistent or inconsistent sets of cognitions, and they assume that actors try to promote as much consistency as they can. Neither point of view is wrong, and neither is true. Perhaps one or the other type of theory will enable more predictions of situations we are interested in, and if so, then that is the type of theory we should use. But we should not become engaged in fruitless debates about whether one or the other type of theory is correct, or "really" describes what occurs in these experiments. Both are correct within their scope conditions, and each describes what occurs in terms of the reality which it recognizes. To see the world in terms of rewards and costs is no more or less real than to see it in terms of consistent and inconsistent cognitive structures.

Attitude formation and change, interpersonal attraction, and dissonance reduction constitute the major types of situations for which consistency theories have been shown useful. If you understand how consistency principles are used in each type of case, you have a good grasp of much of the important work in social psychology. But although most of the studies reviewed in this chapter were conducted within the last 15 years, in a sense they are the older ones of the field. In Chap. 14 we see the most active current areas of research in consistency-related issues.

14   Consistency Research II

Introduction and Overview

Consistency research in the 1970s seems to be developing along three major lines: *attribution, person perception,* and *information processing.* Although there are important differences in the problems studied and in theoretical perspectives of the researchers, there also are many similarities. Most important of the similarities is the fact that all of these studies are conducted in accord with the basic assumptions of the consistency meta-theory.

Attribution research is the most theoretical of the three. You recall that all consistency theories can be traced to Heider's formulation of the "attribution principle" (Chap. 5), describing how people sometimes attribute motives to others. Contemporary attribution research is intended to extend Heider's original insight, explore situations in which it does and does not apply, and then attempt to develop a more complete theoretical understanding of how and why the process works.

Person perception research begins with an interesting substantive question rather than a theoretical issue. We know that people form impressions, often very complete impressions, of others after very brief meetings. How do they do this? That is, what social cues become salient, and how do people combine various bits of information to reach an overall assessment of someone's personality? We are only beginning to understand just how the person perception process works. But what this research does show clearly is that the process usually involves making great "leaps of faith"—that is, coming to a firm conclusion about supposed personality traits never actually observed. For example if you tell me that Person X is *intelligent* and *dishonest,* I am quite likely to conclude he is also *rude*—a trait I haven't observed.

Information processing is one way to view people in interaction. It treats people *as if* they were mechanisms to receive, process, store, and then utilize information. This viewpoint suggests studying human intelligence in terms originally developed to analyze how computers operate. The most useful feature of this viewpoint is that mathematical models can be developed to describe how information processing works. Information processing models thus do for consistency theories what decision models do for exchange theories: they give very precise predictions from explicit models in certain kinds of situations. Also, though it is too early to be sure, information processing models may be useful for both attribution and person perception phenomena.

Heider's original formulation of his balance theory included what he called the *transitivity assumption*: Individuals will tend to complete incomplete cognitive structures in a balanced fashion. For instance if I know that someone (*o*) has conservative views on political and social issues, I am likely to assume that he is also a religious person. It may be because most of the religious persons I know are conservative, or it may be because several prominent conservative politicians also are religious. But for whatever reason, I infer something about *o* on the basis of absolutely no direct information. (The choice of attitude here is completely arbitrary. I could as well have concluded that *o* is an atheist. What matters is that I form some conclusion.)

Put in terms of balance theory, the transitivity assumption says that I will tend to put an *x* called "religious attitudes" into my cognitive structure, and will put a unit relation between *o* and *x*. The transitivity assumption thus is a direct outgrowth of the principle of attribution we studied in Chap. 5. However the Cartwright and Harary formalization of Heider's theory changes the transitivity assumption quite a bit, and the change is incorporated in all other contemporary balance theories. What they said is that *if* an incomplete structure is completed, it will tend to be completed in a balanced fashion. The idea that individuals *will* tend to complete incomplete structures is dropped.

Eliminating the transitivity assumption simplifies the theory and removes the necessity for stating special conditions upon when it will and when it won't work; thus it was helpful. However it certainly is true that sometimes individuals behave in accord with the transitivity assumption: they seem to seek out information beyond what they already have, and they infer or assume information which they cannot observe. Within the past few years there has been a revival of interest in just such situations.

The two primary interests have been to determine conditions under which attribution phenomena occur and to describe the attribution process in more detail than previously. Attribution research is one of the newest areas of empirical investigation conducted by workers in the consistency tradition, and it is not possible to ascertain just whether the work will become systematic and cumulative enough to yield useful results. However the phenomena studied are interesting and important aspects of social behavior, so we shall examine some of them.

What is most often attributed to actors is motives: *p* observe *o* engage in a series of actions, and on that basis he attributes to *o* an underlying motive. It is not simply that *o* did acts *x, y,* and *z;* there is a general motive possessed by *o* that produced *x, y,* and *z and* is likely to produce other specific acts in different situations. Motives are inferred (or attributed) on the basis of actions, and future actions are predicted (or attributed) on the basis of the inferred motives. Moreover at least in some cases, individuals evaluate the inferred motives and behave in ways calculated to establish and maintain a favorably evaluated "social identity."

When are individuals most likely to attribute motives to actors on the basis of observed actions? Suppose that two men go off into the woods on a hunting trip, and only one of them returns safely. The returnee says that there was a terrible accident and his partner was killed. For the moment we do not know the nature of the accident. Under what conditions are we most likely to infer intentionality to the acts of the survivor, to say that he deliberately committed murder? In other words when are we most likely to attribute a motive?

Jones and Davis have examined this question in light of the attribution principle, and there appear to be five principle conditions that increase the tendency to attribute motivation. Let us consider each of them in turn.

(1) Attribution is more likely if an act has *unique effects* than if it has multiple and ambiguous effects. The greater the number of consequences and the less clear the relation between the act and the consequences, the less likely is attribution to take place. In our example if the dead man had been shot, attribution would be more likely than if he had fallen from a cliff as the result of his partner's negligence. It seems somehow "more obvious" to us that a shooting is motivated because being shot has more unique effects than an act of negligence; that is, there are many possible reasons for negligence besides a desire to kill someone, and the results of negligence are not at all so clear-cut as the results of shooting someone. We are more likely to attribute a motive when an act has a few simple, direct effects than when it has complex, multiple effects.

(2) The greater the *control over an act* possessed by the actor, the more likely is attribution to occur. In our example if we knew that the survivor was an expert marksman or very experienced at living in the wilderness, we assume that he has considerable control over the outcome. In general the more skillful the actor is at performing the act, the more likely is attribution to take place. By contrast if we see someone performing an act with an obvious lack of skill, we are more likely to dismiss it as a random occurrence and not a reliable basis for attributing a motive.

(3) The greater the *importance of the effect* to *o*, the more likely is attribution to take place. If the death of the partner were a very significant event in the life of the survivor—for instance, if he were a beneficiary in the dead man's will, or if he wanted to marry his wife—then we are quite likely to attribute a motive to the death. As this example suggests, if the event is significant in a positive way—that is, if *o* stands to benefit from the effect— we are more likely to attribute than if the effect is negative to *o*. However this is not always necessary; attribution can occur also for significant negative events. We usually are more likely to attribute a motive between two friends—assuming they may have had a fight—than we are between two perfect strangers. In our example if the two persons had never met each other prior to the tragedy, attribution of a motive to murder would be less likely than if they were well acquainted and often went hunting together.

(4) An act that is *congruent with past behavior* is much more likely to serve as the basis for attribution than an act that is unrelated. We are much

more suspicious of the man who "accidentally" has lost another hunting partner the year before than we are of the man who loses his first. Similarly if a woman's husbands seems all to die of mysterious causes, we begin to infer that there must be some reason—to attribute, that is, a motive to her. If our survivor had in the past exhibited some other signs of hostility or aggression towards the dead partner, we would be more likely to think the death was deliberate. Inconsistent acts, which we say are "out of character," are more likely to be put down as random occurrences and dismissed.

(5) *Social desirability* of effect can play a large part in attribution processes, independently of whether the actor stands to make a direct gain from the effect. If the outcome of an act produces social approval for the actor, we are more likely to attribute a motive than if it does not. The person whose manners are too perfect, who always says exactly what other people want to hear, we call a "phony." We attribute, in other words, to that person a desire to impress people. We assume that his motivation is to gain respect and admiration, and we think he is not willing to earn it by the actual behaviors. (Interestingly enough, an actor who has a motive to impress people can usually avoid being termed a phony by inserting an occasional negatively evaluated act or by occasionally revealing some weakness of his. What this does is to break down the tendency to attribute the motive to impress others.) In our hunting example if the person killed were thoroughly disliked by the survivor's friends and associates, we would be more likely to attribute a motive than if everyone would mourn his passing. Although it sounds macabre we can imagine a person responding to a general belief that the world would be better off without so-and-so. Our being able to imagine this means that we are more likely to attribute under circumstances of social support for the act than under circumstances of no social support.

A helpful way of looking at the attribution process is to observe that it helps the individual to make sense out of what he observes in the world about him. Put differently, attribution helps to structure unstructured situations. Instead of seeing an unconnected series of events and acts, the individual attributes a common motive to the acts of each actor, and he uses this hypothetical motive to develop expectations regarding that actor's likely future behaviors. When attribution occurs—especially if the individual does not make too many errors of attribution—it helps enormously with the tasks of choosing appropriate future actions. Attribution makes the world more orderly and predictable, and often it provides guides for the individual's future actions.

Attribution researchers believe that the process always tends to occur in situations that are incompletely defined. The individual seeks out additional information to complete his cognitive structure, inferring elements and relations necessary to do this. The five social conditions just discussed affect the likelihood that any attribution will take place. Then the precise *form* of attribution which occurs depends on other, special circumstances. That is, the situation the actor finds himself in will affect the type of attribution he is likely to make.

One major effect is whether he will attribute causation of an act to something within himself or to something within his environment. When something goes wrong (or goes right), is it my fault, or did it occur through the actions and motives of others? Duval and Wicklund (1973) investigated this question through two ingenious experiments. In both it was shown that the tendency to attribute causation to oneself is negatively affected by the degree of attention one must pay to the outside environment. In other words the more the individual directs his thoughts inwards, the more he will tend to attribute actions to himself.

In both experiments individuals were given short descriptions of situations, such as the following:

> *You're driving down the street about 5 miles over the speed limit when a little kid suddenly runs out chasing a ball and you hit him.* (Duval and Wicklund, 1973, p. 22.)

They are then asked what proportion of responsibility they feel they have for the event. In the first experiment subjects were asked to respond to 10 such sentences in either of two conditions. In the "turntable" condition they were asked at the same time to hold one finger at a point on a revolving turntable while they answered the sentences. In the control condition there was no additional task beyond the sentences. We might reasonably expect that the effect of the turntable task was to distract much of the subjects' attention outside themselves, and this should in turn lessen the degree of attribution to themselves. In the control condition, about 58 percent of the responsibility was perceived to be the subjects'; in the turntable condition, only about 50 percent was attributed to self. The difference, while not great, is in the expected direction, and it is statistically significant.

In the second experiment a different manipulation was used to control internal/external thoughts. In one condition the subject sat facing a large mirror, and in the control condition the mirror was absent. The mirror, we might suppose, focuses the subjects' thoughts, and hence, attribution, inwards. This time both positive and negative events were presented to examine whether positive or negative outcome events are more likely to be attributed to self. Table 14–1 shows the mean percent of causality attributed to self for both positive and negative events in the two conditions of this experiment. The effect of the internal/external manipulation is very much in evidence, and it does not matter whether events had a positive or a negative

TABLE 14–1   Attribution and Outcomes

Condition	% to Self
Mirror—Positive	60.00
Mirror—Negative	60.20
No Mirror—Positive	49.91
No Mirror—Negative	51.09

(Adapted from Duval and Wicklund, 1973, p. 27.)

outcome. The attribution to self of both positive and negative events is about 60 percent in the mirror condition, and about 50 percent in the no mirror condition.

These experiments, as well as many others we shall not examine, indicate quite clearly that the strength and the direction of attribution can be affected by situational variables. Individuals tend to attribute motives and causes in accord with the 5 general principles listed above, but the specific form of the attribution is affected by the immediate social situation.

Once actors attribute motives to each other, these motives affect many other social processes such as trust, competition, status effects, and modeling. An example of how attribution affects modeling is an experiment reported by Alexander and Weil. They described two hypothetical persons, Al and Bob, who played a series of games similar to the prisoner's dilemma. Al was consistently cooperative and Bob was consistently aggressive. As almost always happens in real life cases of this game, the cooperative player ended up with very few points, while Bob did very well indeed. In condition 1 Al's actions were described positively (cooperative, friendly, considerable) while Bob's were negative (exploitative, greedy, treacherous). In condition 2 Al was gullible, spineless and submissive, while Bob was clever, intelligent and practical. This was for the same actions, remember; only the attributed motives differed.

Then subjects actually played the same games as Al and Bob supposedly had. Results showed about three times more cooperative behavior in condition 2! What this shows is that modeling is strongly influenced by the positive or negative attributed social identity or potential models.

The work of contemporary attribution researchers may turn out to be especially important in understanding simple social processes if they are able to describe the "situational identity" formation process in detail, and to specify the conditions under which actors will prefer one identity or one action to another. Studies such as this one by Alexander and Weil point towards such answers, but obviously there is considerable empirical and conceptual work for investigators in the future. Some of these issues have also been studied by cognitive psychologists interested in impression formation, and we now turn to this approach.

Person Perception: Attractiveness

When individuals form impressions of others, they usually reach broad conclusions on the basis of very limited information. As in attribution, often they must infer the existence of some trait that is not directly known, and usually both traits are evaluated. For example, we may know that Mussolini was a Fascist who insisted on total obedience from party members and *on that basis* assume he was also cruel to his family. (He wasn't.) We attach negative evaluation to "Fascist," and we assume the existence of the also negative trait "cruel."

Thus some simple person perception situations are quite similar to attribution. They differ from attribution, however, in that attribution is always from an *action* to a *motive*. Person perception may follow this, but in addition it involves inferences from an *action* to a second *action* (as our Mussolini's example), and from one *motive* to a second *motive*, and from a descriptive *trait* to a second descriptive *trait*.

One trait that figures importantly in many situations is physical attractiveness. We sometimes think that attractive persons (however that is defined) have an easier time of it in life than unattractive persons. Good things seem to happen more often and more easily to attractive people. All this, of course, in distinct contrast to the explicit hypocrisy norm that appearance is nobody's fault, and you shouldn't hold ugliness against someone. (Did you know that several cities still have laws against "being ugly in a public place?")

If attractiveness is an advantage, and it is, why should this be true? Part of the answer seems to be that we tend to perceive attractive people as possessing more positively evaluated traits than unattractive people; that is, if we see a person with pleasing appearance, we are more likely to think this is a "good" person than if we see an ugly person. Some examples of this follow.

Dion asked observers to read teachers' descriptions of several types of aggressive behavior (such as seven-year-old children throwing a snowball containing ice chunks at someone). Each description was accompanied by a picture of a child, either attractive or unattractive, who supposedly did the aggressive act. After reading and seeing the pictures observers were asked their opinion on such questions as: (1) How likely do you think it is that this child did something similar in the past? (2) How likely is it that he or she will do it again? (3) How serious is the act? (4) How much punishment should he or she receive? When the same act was accompanied by an attractive picture for some observers and by an unattractive picture for others, we can see the effect of attractiveness alone. *On all four measures,* attractive children were perceived more favorably than unattractive; that is, they were seen as less likely to have done the act before and less likely to do it again, the act was less serious and deserved less punishment.

Dion, Berscheid and Walster showed college students pictures of other college age people and asked them to make several guesses about the people in the pictures. Attractive people were thought to be: less likely to get divorced, more likely to have happy parents, more likely to find "deep fulfillment" in their social and occupational roles, more likely to be successful at work, and more likely overall to be "happy."

Later Dion and Berscheid showed that the process operates in children as young as four. These children liked their attractive classmates more, and thought they were more likely to be independent and less likely to get into trouble than their unattractive classmates. Sigall and Landy asked male college students to evaluate essays, both well written and poor, by female college students. A picture of the essay's supposed author was attached, sometimes an attractive author and sometimes an unattractive one. Regardless of the actual quality of the essay, it was graded more highly when supposedly written by an attractive person.

Why do we observe these far reaching effects of attractiveness? For one thing, appearance is the most readily apparent trait of an individual so it is reasonable that it will affect much of person perception. At least as important in most cultures including our own, there is only a narrow range of what we consider attractive, and it is considered very important to be within this range. So appearance is easy to observe and strongly evaluated for us. It is not too surprising that we use perceived attractiveness in forming impressions, nor that "prettiness" is thought to go with other traits we value positively. In a moment we shall return to this question and explore it in more depth.

Information Processing

Now let us complicate person perception by including information on several traits instead of one. Typical research of this sort presents individuals with a list of adjectives purported to describe someone—usually including sex, occupation, race or religion, and several personality traits—and then asking respondents to check what they think of the hypothetical individual on a series of different descriptive terms—such as friendly/hostile, good/bad, active/passive, and so on. The goal is to find a simple model which can describe how individuals use all this information to reach a conclusion about the hypothetical individual. The test is trying to predict the impression from a variety of models that describe different ways of processing information. The specific model being tested reflects the investigator's beliefs about just what people do with the diverse bits of information available to them in social situations.

Most work in impression formation assumes that actors will follow either of two means of dealing with information. Either they will add it all up, or they will average it. Showing how information is used is the task of information processing models. Investigators who construct these models thus have been occupied with answering the question whether an additive or an averaging model does the better job of predicting the data. Triandis and Fishbein are associated with additive models, and N. Anderson is associated with averaging models.

Below is a typical term J (for *judgment,* the dependent variable) of a simple averaging model (adapted from Anderson, 1968):

$$J = C + \Sigma w_k s_k$$

As noted J is the dependent variable we wish to predict; C is some constant (with which we need not be concerned); and $\Sigma w_k s_k$ means that we sum up (Σ) the importance or weight (w) of information bit k times the *scale value* (*s*) of information bit *k*. In other words we take the scale value (how positive or negative the description is), multiply it by a number (which indicates how important that information is to the individual), and then sum up all these weighted bits.

Two variants are possible of Anderson's model given here. *First,* if we impose the restriction that all the weights must add up to 1, then we have, not only an averaging model, but a *weighted averaging* model. We force the model to incorporate the idea that weights given to the individual bits of information are relative to each other: the importance of any bit is determined by comparing it to the subjective importance of all other bits. Second, if instead of making all *weights* add up to 1 we make each weight equal 1, then the model becomes an *additive* model. Multiplying each *s* by 1 is the same as simply excluding the *w* term from the equation, so the model is an additive one which asserts that individuals simply add up all available bits of information.

Whether additive or averaging (or weighted averaging) models do the better job of describing the impression formation process has not been determined with finality. Triandis and his associates seem to prefer additive models, and Anderson and others prefer averaging models. There is considerable empirical support for both types at this point, so we are not in a position to choose between them: [1] What this suggests is that *in certain types* of impression formation situations individuals' attitudes are best predicted by an additive model, and in other types, by an averaging model. Specifying general conditions under which each type of model is preferable thus would constitute a considerable advance in understanding. One recent article by Triandis et al. (1966) concludes that for subjects from three different cultures—Indian, Japanese, and American—an additive and an averaging model seemed about equally satisfactory.

Evaluated Characteristics and Expectation States

Three general findings stand out from our review of person perception studies. First we have seen that the simple variable *physical attractiveness* affects perceptions of numerous other traits of actors. Second, when individuals know several traits of an individual, they process this information somehow to reach an overall impression of him. Third, the information processing occurs in a way related to cognitive consistency processes, but the exact form of it—for example additive or averaging—is not known. Our task now is to bring these findings together and explain them with a familiar perspective.

---

[1] More of the current research supports averaging models rather than additive. However this may be due to the large number of bits of information—sometimes as many as 20— used. When only a few traits are known, individuals seem just to *add* them in forming an impression. When they must deal with 20 traits, they need to *average* them.

Let us begin with attractiveness. We know that it is an evaluated characteristic of individuals, and thus that performance expectations may form for a wide range of other attributes from attractiveness. From this perspective the burden of proof process causes individuals to form expectations for any other evaluated characteristic—such as criminality, occupational success, or quality of essay writing. Recognizing that attractiveness is an evaluated characteristic allows us to apply expectation states theory from Chap. 7 to explain most of the effects of physical attractiveness.

When we turn to impression formation when two or more traits are known, the situation is more complicated. Now we are faced with the question of how individuals combine known evaluated characteristics before the burden of proof process works to produce an overall impression of the individual. To the burden of proof process in expectation states theory we need to add an information processing model, perhaps one of the variants of Norman Anderson's, or perhaps some other model.

Berger and Fisek conducted an experiment to find just what sort of information processing model could be developed for expectation states theory. At this preliminary stage the investigators were not trying to test an explicit model. They simply wanted to see what *type* of model was most satisfactory. When an individual has more than one piece of information available, he may either ignore some of it, or use it all and combine it somehow. The first process assumes an *elimination model* and the second assumes a *combining model*.

The design had pairs of subjects in the basic expectation experiment (described in Chap. 6) receive either high or low evaluations on two characteristics. Through the burden of proof process they then had to form expectations for a third ability. Results of the experiment show clearly that a combining model is adequate for this situation, and an elimination model is not.

These experiments isolate the general form of the information utilization process, but they do not describe it precisely; that is, no explicit models of the process are presented. Consequently the next step is to generate and test several specific models of the information utilization process and to try to determine what the exact form of the combining process is. Many different combining models can be imagined.

For example, take the situation of a high school student going out for the football team. After the first day of practice he receives evaluations of his performance from two sources, his coach and a friend of his who is also trying to make the team. The coach, who is a high ability evaluator, can either tell the player that he performed well (a positive evaluation) or that he played poorly (a negative evaluation). Compared to the coach, the player's friend its a low ability evaluator, and he can give the player either a positive or a negative evaluation also. The question is, how does the player use the information he receives from these two sources to come to some idea about his ability to play football? Consider the following six models of information processing.

(1) The Single Source Model. The player could choose to ignore some of the information he receives about his playing ability. Since his friend doesn't know as much about football as the coach, the player may not pay any attention to what his friend says and use just the information the coach gives him. This model assumes that people use a "selective rejection" process in using available information.

(2) The Single Source Given Disagreement Model. This model has two parts. If both the coach and the friend tell the player the same thing (say that he performed poorly during practice) then the player would add up both pieces of information. However, if the friend and the coach disagreed on their evaluations of the player (for example, the coach told him that he played poorly while the friend told him that he did a good job) then the selective rejection process would operate and the player would ignore information from the low ability evaluator (the friend).

(3) The Simple Additive Model. This model is the simplest. The player could just add up all the information he receives from both sources. Thus even if the coach and the friend disagreed on their evaluations of his performance, the player would use both in forming his opinion of his ability.

(4) The Simple Averaging Model. Suppose the friend spoke to the player before the coach did and therefore the player felt that the friend's evaluation was more important. In other words the most valuable evaluation the player receives is the one he gets first, and while the second evaluation has some effect on his final opinion of his playing ability, it is not so important to the player as the information he gets first. This model assumes that each additional unit of information is decreased in importance by every previous unit.

(5) The Averaging Given Disagreement Model. This model also has two parts. If the coach and the friend disagree on their evaluations of the players performance, then the player will average the two pieces of information together as model 4 predicts. If both the coach and the frend gave negative (or positive) evaluations, then the player would just add the two pieces of information together as in model 3.

(6) An Operator Model. The five models discussed to this point all assume that the player gives equal weight to both positive and negative evaluations received from the two sources; that is, a negative evaluation from the coach is just as important to the player as a positive evaluation from the coach.

However, our player may feel that a positive evaluation means more than a negative evaluation from the coach. Thus he would give more *weight* to the opinion if the coach told him he did a good job than if the coach told him he played poorly. The same could be said for the player's processing of the evaluation he receives from his friend—a positive evaluation is more important to him than a negative evaluation. Operator models assume that individuals perform a fairly complicated mathematical operation upon information before using it, multiplying the opinion by what the player thinks of its source.

Models 1 and 2 are explicit statements of Berger and Fisek's "elimination" model; 4–6 are different versions of their "combining" model. Model 4 is similar to Norman Anderson's simple averaging model; 3 is the additive model; and 6 is one weighted averaging model set up to predict the $P(s)$ data of an expectation theory experiment. An overview of models is given in Table 14–2.

An experiment conducted by Roberts, Sobieszek and myself was designed to test each of the models of information processing just described. The experiments used the basic experimental setting for expectation states research (described in Chap. 6) with one important difference. Because subjects view an experimenter as a high ability evaluator, it was necessary for subjects to receive their evaluations from another source. The subjects were told that they were being evaluated by a third "subject" (actually just a tape recorded voice) in the next room and that "subject" was described as having either a high ability or a low ability.

TABLE 14–2   Form of the Six Models

Model	Typical Form
1. Single Source	$P_{H+L+} = P_o + E_{H+}$ and $L_+ = L_- = 0$
2. Single Source/Disagreement	$P_{H+L+} = P_o + E_{H+} + E_{L+}$ and $\{L_+ = 0 \mid H_-\}$ or $\{L_+ = 0 \mid H_+\}$ or
3. Simple Additive	$P_{H+L+} = P_o + E_{H+} + E_{L+}$
4. Simple Averaging	$P_{H+L+} = \dfrac{P_o + (E_{H+} + E_{L+})}{k}$
5. Averaging/Disagreement	(model 3 and model 4)
6. Simple Operator	$a_{L+}[a_{H+}(P_o)] = P_{H+L+}$

k = number of evaluations
H = High ability evaluator
L = Low ability evaluator
$+,-$ = Are positive or negative evaluations
P_{H+L+} = $P(s)$ where H and L give positive evaluations to subject.
P_o = $P(s)$ observed in experiment with *no* evaluations at all
$a_{H+}(P_o) = P_{H+}$ or $a_{H+} = \dfrac{P_{H+}}{P_o}$
(Adapted from Webster et al., 1972.)

The experiments have 5 conditions, dependent upon the ability of the evaluator (high or low) and the nature of the evaluations (positive or negative) he gave to the subjects in that condition. These are shown in Table 14–3. Note that these experiments include condition 3 where the subject received evaluations from two high ability sources who disagreed on their evaluations, (the case if the football player was told by the coach that he played well while the assistant coach told him he played poorly).

Each model makes somewhat different predictions for *P(s)* of these experiments. In Table 14–4 you can see the actual *P(s)* as well as predictions from each of the six models.

Two models are considerably better than the others at predicting the actual *P(s)* values from these experiments: the simple additive model (#3) and the averaging given disagreement model (#5). The distributions of subjects, not shown here, give no evidence for two populations, as would be required to support models #1 and #2. Model #5 is very slightly superior to #3 on the grounds of accuracy of prediction, and on those grounds we might be tempted to accept it. However model #3 is conceptually far simpler than model #5. When two models predict the data with approximately equal accuracy, and this is the case here, then on theoretical grounds of simplicity and clarity, we prefer the simpler model. Overall model #3 does a good job of predicting the data—almost as good as model #5—and it is a much simpler set of ideas. Therefore, overall, we prefer model #3.

TABLE 14–3   Information Conditions:
Webster et al. Experiment

	EVALUATORS' ABILITY		EVALUATORS' OPINIONS OF S	
CONDITION	#1	#2	#1	#2
1. H[+]L[+]	High	Low	High	High
2. H[+]L[−]	High	Low	High	Low
3. H[+]H[−]	High	High	High	Low
4. H[−]L[+]	High	Low	Low	High
5. H[−]L[−]	High	Low	Low	Low

TABLE 14–4   Predicted and Observed *P(s)* Values:
Six Models

CONDITION	OBSERVED	# 1	# 2	# 3	# 4	# 5	# 6
1. H[+]L[+]	.80	.79	.81	.81	.72	.81	.82
2. H[+]L[−]	.75	.79	.79	.73	.68	.68	.71
3. H[+]H[−]	.67	.63	.63	.63	.63	.63	.58
4. H[−]L[+]	.57	.46	.46	.48	.55	.55	.47
5. H[−]L[−]	.42	.46	.40	.40	.51	.40	.41
Mean error of prediction	.048	.044	.036	.060	.032	.052

(Adapted from Webster et al., 1972.)

From these experiments we conclude that the selective process rejected by the earlier experiments is indeed inadequate to represent the process under the scope conditions of expectation states theory. In this respect our results are consistent with those of the Berger-Fisek experiments. However the combining process they seemed to imagine is described by our model #4 (simple averaging), and this is not the most satisfactory model in the later experiments. Therefore these results are better viewed as a refinement of their ideas. As we noted earlier, this may reflect the fact that subjects were not given too much information—so much that they would have to average it.

Still, none of these 6 models was taken from an explicit theory—they were simply representations of intuitively plausible ways that people are asserted to think. If they were consistent with a theoretical rationale, they would be even more persuasive and much more useful.

Kervin (1974) has constructed an explicit version of expectation states theory and a model consistent with that version, which *do* enable prediction of expectation patterns based upon any number of units of evaluated information. Because the model is complex, we shall not study it in detail. However we shall note that it has two parts.

The first part is an information processing model, and it deals with the ways in which units of information are combined to yield a single pattern of expectation states associated with actors. The information combining model assumes a weighted averaging process. In this it is similar to Anderson's model presented earlier in the chapter, and is more complicated than any of the six models previously tested. However reaching a particular pattern of expectations on the basis of evaluative information is only one part of the way towards predicting behavior: this model only describes individuals' *cognitions* about a situation, without telling how they will behave. Remember that we said consistency theorists typically do not predict specific behaviors. They simply assume that behavior will be determined by the individual's efforts to achieve or to improve consistency.

Exchange theorists, by contrast, are very much concerned with predicting behavior (and little concerned with what's happening in the actors' minds). Thus Kervin also constructed an exchange-based decision-making model to predict actual behavior in the experiment on the basis of expectation states. There are two stages in the prediction: first, the information processing model tells what expectation patterns will be produced from the particular information available; and second, the decision-making model predicts what choice behavior (disagreement resolution) will be observed as a function of these expectation states.

Kervin applied his model to data from all experiments described above with good results: in most cases, he was able to predict behavior as well as or better than the original investigators could. He also applied the models to data reported by Camilleri and Berger (see Chap. 11) for this experimental situation, and again, Kervin's models enabled very good predictions of actual behavior. Finally he conducted independent experimental tests of these models, and predicted and observed *P(s)* figures again were very close.

As I warned you at the outset, serious work in information processing models is only beginning, and many problems remain to be dealt with. For instance, though we know that combining models are more satisfactory than elimination models, we still do not know for sure what type—additive or averaging —is preferable in all cases. Before leaving the topic, I would like to indicate four topics that seem to be good candidates for further theoretical and empirical exploration.

First, information processing models have been concerned almost solely with *formation* of cognitions, not with *change* in existing beliefs. Perhaps people do not change existing ideas in the same way as they form new ideas —that is, the same models may not be applicable in the two cases. For instance suppose someone has a very negative attitude towards a particular actor: at least intuitively, it seems likely that he will ignore considerable favorable information before changing his opinion. If so, that would better be described by a selective model than by a combining model—though all our empirical work indicates that combining models are superior for predicting how beliefs form.

A different possibility for the situation of change is that it occurs only after individuals are given more information, and then it occurs very suddenly. Perhaps individuals who have formed opinions stick to them through considerable contradictory information *up to a point*—but then they abruptly reverse themselves. Changes in political or religious philosophy sometimes seem to provide very dramatic examples of this sort of process. One might call this a *quantum* change, reminiscent of analogous changes observed in physics; or perhaps Rosenberg's less elegant term "spasmodic" would be more apt here. In any case if this is actually the way people think, it will require a pretty complicated model to describe the process with any accuracy.

A second issue is whether similar information has as much value or "weight" to the individual as dissimilar information. Suppose you are trying to form an impression of someone or are trying to form performance expectations for him. If several dozen people all tell you about the same thing, it seems likely that you won't give too much weight to any one of them. Now suppose that the 51st person you ask has a very different opinion from all the rest: wouldn't you pay more attention to him than you did to person #50? Intuitively it seems likely that we all would do this—the deviant person often gives valuable information we cannot get from most other persons. We could name this the *prodigal son model*.

Third, the question of whether some topics that look very different in concrete features might turn out to be quite similar in terms of abstract modeling, is intriguing. Recall that in Chap. 10 we found structural similarities between light guessing, play in the coalition games, and perhaps even dating choices. Features of all these situations could be represented quite well by the same model.

Studies of occupational mobility, both intergenerational and intragenerational, often are conducted to decide whether an additive model or an operator model better represent factors in eventual occupation. Additive models simply add up such background factors as father's occupation, education, quality of schooling in order to predict an individual's eventual job. Operator models assume that these factors interact in some way—for example that good schooling doesn't affect one's chances much unless one's father also was highly educated or rich. Intuitively, operator models seem more satisfactory for this situation, but in fact additive models have turned out to be more generally satisfactory. This suggests that perhaps a wide range of social phenomena may be adequately represented by some modification of the addictive models described above. (See Shelley, 1974, and Webster et al., 1974, for discussion of some related issues in information processing.)

The final issue is one I cannot even describe very well, yet which I think I see often. This is that people frequently seem to have an initial resistance to any new information at all. For example, if you tell a person something and then try to support it with two "good reasons," it is my impression that the first reason you offer is much more likely to be disputed than is the second one. Another example: if you suggest one of two things to someone, it often seems as though he would prefer the second alternative offered. There seems to be in other words an immediate initial resistance to anything new, a resistance which is not so obvious for the second and later things presented. What this could suggest for information processing models is that individuals may naturally give less weight to the first piece of information in a series than they do later units—regardless of what sort of information the initial piece is. If people do this, why? And does it happen as generally as I think it does, or what are the particular circumstances under which it appears?

As you can appreciate, the topic of how individuals accept and use information is a broad one, and it contains some fundamental issues about how people think. I hope this brief introduction to the information processing approach to studying human interaction suggests both the difficulties of the task and its great potential payoffs in understanding.

Part III

SOME CONTEMPORARY TOPICS

Introduction to
Some Contemporary Topics

Part III is devoted to topics selected from the range of interests currently under active investigation in social psychology. Three criteria are primary in deciding which topics from the tremendous range being studied should be included. First, these are all interesting issues. Each topic is important enough that it would be worthwhile to think about it and discuss it informally at a social gathering, or perhaps even in a social psychology class. Second, each is receiving considerable attention from researchers. Thus we may expect understanding to increase in each of these areas within the next few years. Finally, each of these topics is fairly complex in itself, but each gives promise of being analyzable using the concepts and principles developed in the first two parts of this book.

Chapter 15 describes issues relevant to other self-referring ideas, especially self-evaluation. It is an introduction to the way social psychologists view the development of ideas relating to oneself. Chapter 16 deals with how we get ideas of fairness in social situations—fair wages, fair prison sentences, fair treatment of minority and majority actors. Chapter 17 deals with issues of interest primarily to people who, like readers of this book, are acquainted with experimental social psychology. The experiment as a social situation has recently been studied in its own right; sometimes the results of these studies shed light upon more naturalistic social situations, and sometimes they remind experimenters to think of their experiments in the same way they think of nonexperimental social behavior.

It should be apparent that this selection of topics, like any selection, is arbitrary. Given practical limits on space and reader's time, I have tried to include those issues that will be most worthwhile, using these criteria. But this means I am relying upon guesses—educated guesses, since I try to keep up with the research journals, but guesses still—for including topics. My guess is that these topics will become even more important in the next few years, and that therefore an introductory text should introduce readers to them. Either as a social psychologist or as an informed citizen, I hope you will find these introductions useful in the future.

As I noted, each of these topics is incompletely understood. The phenomena are "recognized" as important, but just how they work, and what they are related to in our social environment, cannot be perfectly explained yet. The phenomena are complex, but if the more basic work of Parts I and II is valuable, it should prove its value by giving us a place to start and the tools needed to attack these issues.

15

The Social Self

General Introduction

Self-awareness is a part of every healthy individual's personality. Ideas the individual holds regarding himself are so important and so pervasive a feature of social life that it is difficult to understand individual behavior in social situations without taking these ideas into account.

Self-referent ideas function in three broad areas. Most generally they tell the individual who he is in relation to others. This function is fulfilled largely in terms of role specifications, naming the various groups of which he is a member and specifying his role in each of them. A quarterback for a football team may think of himself as the "task leader" who makes decisions and guides the actions of other members. A woman may think of herself in her role as mother to her children, and also as a grade school teacher to other peoples' children. A fraternity pledge may be acutely aware that he is the newcomer to the house, and that he has special duties and (perhaps) rights as a consequence of that fact.

The second important function of ideas the individual holds about himself is to motivate, limit, and direct his behavior. In most situations, we say the individual is *self-conscious,* meaning that he pays attention to what he does and imagines the effect of his actions upon other people. He also imagines their subsequent reactions to him based upon his actions. In this respect ideas regarding the self function in much the same way as reference groups (see Chap. 5) do. Instead of asking, "What would they think of me if I did this?" when contemplating a particular action, the individual can ask, "What would I think of myself if I did this?" Such a question can result in a motivation as in, "I would be very proud if I could win a prize," or it may function to inhibit an action as, "I am not the sort of person who would cheat on a test." Effects described in these examples may be distinguished from effects of internalized reference groups in that they do not need to be tied to a specifiable group of others. If the individual thinks, "I am an Army Officer and Army Officers do not kill civilians," this is action controlled by an internalized reference group. On the other hand if he thinks, "I am a good person and I do not kill civilians," the control mechanism is just as apparent, but there is no particular reference group involved. (You might compare this self-referent control to Hogan's dimensions of moral action in Chap. 8.)

Third, every individual holds ideas regarding evaluations of himself and of his abilities. These ideas may be specific, related to a single ability such as spelling or mathematics; they may be more general, as overall intelligence or problem solving ability; or they may be even more general so that no single measurement would be sufficient, as in being a good person. Evaluative ideas the individual holds regarding himself function partially in each of the first two areas. When an individual tells who he is, almost invariably he thinks of some description involving competence, or abilities relative to other people. In performing situations where the individual exercises choice over whether to perform and what task to attempt, ability conceptions play an important part in determining how he behaves. If someone is a poor chess player, then unless he is foolish, he would not attempt to play against Bobby Fischer. For related but obverse reasons, Fischer probably would not want to play him either. The inexpert skier and the beginning golfer are both likely to spend time waiting for their more proficient companions in the bar at the ski lodge or the country club.

Evaluative ideas occupy a central part in most peoples' self-conceptions, and they have received much attention from social psychologists. In most cases when a social psychologist discusses self-concept, he is really talking about evaluative aspects of the self. Part of the reason for this undoubtedly is pragmatic: several techniques have been devised to measure the determinants and consequences of evaluative ideas. But there are several other reasons for the emphasis upon evaluations in studying the self-concept. Self-evaluation has received considerable theoretical attention, and thus this research may fit into a shared intellectual context. Moreover in many social situations that are important in their own right (such as schools, businesses, and sports), what is of greatest interest is the way the individual decides how good he is, and the subsequent behavioral effects of whatever decision he reaches.

Where do individuals get their ideas of themselves and of their own abilities? What are the effects of others' opinions and of objective experience in determining and modifying self-evaluative ideas? Are all other people equally effective or ineffective in influencing the individual's self-evaluation? What are some of the direct effects of the ideas held by an individual regarding himself and his abilities? These and many other questions have been studied more or less systematically by theorists and by empirical researchers in self-evaluation.

The prevailing views on the development and the nature of the self-concept place heavy emphasis upon the effects of interaction between individuals. The individual's ideas regarding himself are largely determined by the experiences he has with other people. Both what they tell him regarding what sort of a person he is, and how he perceives and interprets (or misperceives and misinterprets) are of major importance.

An older view, the developmentalist or biological view, holds that the individual's self-concept develops and matures in a way analogous to the development of the physical body organs. Developmentalist ideas seem to have been held by Freud and other early psychoanalysts. This view also appears in the work of a few contemporary psychiatrists and ethologists. According to this view the personality structure is determined in major ways by inborn instincts, motives, or personality traits. Thus the problem faced by the individual as he matures is to find an acceptable reconciliation between his inherent drives (usually, aggressive and sexual) and the demands of society. By contrast, according to the social or *interactionist* view, any self-referent ideas, and any combination of personality characteristics that are apparent in an individual may be traced to previous interaction with others.

If we draw each of these arguments in its most extreme form, they may be summarized as stressing either the primary importance of inherent patterns for the developmentalists, or as stressing the infinite malleability developing from a *tabula rasa* for the interactionists. Between the two extremes there are shades of difference, but most students of the subject acknowledge at least the importance—if not the primary importance—of social experiences in forming the self-concept. To me, all available evidence shows a tremendous importance of social interaction, and no significant support for unlearned or inborn traits.

The interactionist view argues that the self is a consequence, primarily, of others' opinions and actions. The individual learns who he is and how good he is by observing the way others treat him and what they say. This means that self-concept is very much dependent on a social comparison process. The individual compares himself to other individuals or to objective standards and formulates a tentative hypothesis regarding his own level of abilities. Then he compares his opinion with the opinion of others to arrive at a more precise conception of his own abilities. Besides the social comparison process the interactionist approach stresses the fact that there is some cognitive representation of the self. That is, the individual carries around a mental picture of himself and of his abilities, and some parts of this picture (for example, level of spelling ability) can be reproduced whenever the individual wishes. Finally, the interactionist view of the self regards the cognitive representation as being more or less stable. The individual's ideas about his abilities tend not to change unless he is confronted with contradictory information, and his ideas about his general ability are carried from one situation to another. Thus the high school student who learns that he can solve algebra and calculus problems well comes to conceive of himself as having high mathematical ability. When he comes to college he is very likely to expect to do equally well at analytic geometry and other college mathematic courses. (The famous "Freshman Crisis" at many colleges is produced in large measure by the individual's discovery that nearly everybody else in his classes also was thought to be superb in high school. For many people it is a threatening blow to their self-concept to discover they are no longer at or near the top of their classes.)

Through The Looking Glass and the Significance of Others

An early statement of the basic ideas of the interactionist view of self-concept was formulated by Charles Horton Cooley. Writing around the turn of the century, Cooley presented what came to be known as the "looking-glass self":

"Each to each a looking-glass
Reflects the other that doth pass."

As we see our face, figure,. and dress in the glass, and are interested in them because they are ours, and pleased or otherwise with them according as they do or do not answer to what we should like them to be; so in imagination we perceive in another's mind some thought of our appearance, manners, aims, deeds, character, friends, and so on, and are variously affected by it. (Cooley, 1902, pp. 183–4.)

The central idea here is that the individual sees himself in the looking glass or mirror of other peoples' attitudes and opinions. His ideas of who he is and of his abilities are directly dependent upon his perceptions of other people's ideas regarding him.

It is a simple idea, but it has enormous implications for the study of the self. Others influence not only the individual's overt behavior, but even the way he thinks of himself, and the sort of person he imagines himself to be. What might be thought of as the most personal, private ideas the individual has, Cooley asserts, are actually developed in social interaction.

When the idea is stated as directly as Cooley does, it might seem to remove self thoughts from the individual's personal control. But every individual's personal history is unique, and the complete set of thoughts that comprise his self-concept is therefore also unique. A self that forms through thousands of separate interactions with hundreds of different people can hardly be said to be under the constant control of others. It is at least as unique, and at least as personal as a self that might be formed as the result of combinations of the 48 human genes.

George Herbert Mead, who taught social psychology at the University of Chicago for many years, was particularly concerned with the process of development of the self, and he adopted and extended Cooley's ideas. Mead stresses the tremendous importance of interaction with others and also the importance of physical activity in developing the self-concept. What is particularly important, according to Mead, is for the individual to learn to see himself as others see him—that is, to see himself as an object. As an infant matures he learns that his parents treat him differently at different times. What he must then learn is that there is some personal reason for the differential treatment of him: he somehow affects their actions toward him. He must imagine how he looks to them in order to come to understand why he is treated well sometimes and is punished other times. By discovering this fact, the infant gains an enormously liberating force: for the first time he is able to manipulate his environment by his own actions so that he can partially determine how other people treat him. The infant can gain attention by crying. If he smiles, adults will smile back at him. He can, in other words, control the behavior of others to a certain extent. This would not be possible, Mead asserts, without learning first to view the self as an object.

Mead's famous example of the development and uses of self-awareness is learning to catch a baseball. In order successfully to catch a ball, it is necessary for the catcher to be able to imagine himself in the place of the person throwing the ball to him. He has to think for a moment about how far away he is, about the wind and physical obstacles surrounding himself, and about his posture and his athletic ability. Only by being able to *take the role of the other* is one actor able to coordinate his actions to those of another actor. Cooley had partly anticipated this point when he wrote that being able to see oneself from the outside was probably the single most important part of what we call "intelligence."

A second idea introduced by Mead is the "generalized other." This is the set of attitudes and opinions that comprise the total community of which the individual is a member. He sees himself as a generalized, or a typical, member of the community appears to see him. As a sort of "average" other person, the generalized other is expected to be more influential in developing the individual's self-concept than is any particular other. This means that if a researcher is highly esteemed by most members of the relevant academic community, he is likely to have a high opinion of his own ability even though he knows that one or two of his colleagues thinks his work contains errors.

The great Baltimore psychoanalyst Harry Stack Sullivan built further upon the ideas of Cooley and of Mead. In studying development of self-concept and self-esteem in children Sullivan introduced the term "significant other" to denote those whose treatment of the child was particularly influential. While the child is very young and remains in the home most of the time the only significant others are his parents. He is very likely to form his self-concept entirely in terms of what he perceives his parents say about him. Later such other people as teachers and friends will be significant others also. The basic idea here is that certain others are unusually important in influencing the individual's self-referent thoughts.

To summarize the ideas of the early interactionist theorists, Cooley argues that the individual's self-concept is a direct result of his perception (or misperception) of the attitudes and opinions of others. Mead introduces the ideas that the individual must learn to view himself as an object and that he should be able to view himself in the way the generalized other views him. Sullivan extends the idea of different types of others with his concept of the significant other, an individual whose attitudes and opinions are particularly important.

As an exercise in applying these ideas, it is revealing to consider cases when we think we are alone in a room and then discover someone else is in there with us. The immediate reaction of most people is to go through a mental review of their actions for the last few minutes: What was I doing while I thought I was alone? Did I do anything silly or embarrassing? Did I pick my nose, or have a stupid look on my face? Was I looking at myself in the mirror? The central concern here is how we appear to others, and in point of fact, we *were* looking at ourselves in a mirror: the mirror of their imagined opinion. Another instructive example is to recall how difficult it can be at times to tell ourselves that we really do not care at all about how a particular person regards us—to be willing to appear foolish or disreputable in the eyes of someone. Most of us, most of the time, monitor ourselves and try to control the "social identities" we present to others.

Early Research in the Social Self

The ideas of Cooley, Mead and Sullivan have been recognized as extremely important for at least 75 years in social psychology. However it is only within the past 15 years that any considerable amount of research has come out of this theoretical tradition. Partially this is due to the persuasiveness of the theorists and to the intuitive plausibility of the ideas; they seem good enough not to require empirical support. But more importantly the earlier lack of research may be related to the difficulty of operationalizing the variables and the asserted links between them. How do you measure someone's self-concept, or even his self-evaluation? The importance of the self and the self-image are so great that the researcher is likely to be concerned about intentional or unintentional distortion of reports by his respondent. How do you operationalize the significant other, or the generalized other? And how do you measure the relative influence of each of them over the individual's self-referent ideas?

One of the earliest, as well as one of the most direct tests of the ideas in the social self was conducted by Miyamoto and Dornbusch. They administered questionnaires to individuals, either in small college classes, or in small college living groups. Each person was asked for ratings on the following four characteristics: intelligence, self-confidence, physical attractiveness, and likeableness. Respondents were asked to perform this rating three times for themselves, and once for every other member of their group. The four ratings were as follows:

1. Rate yourself as you actually are.

2. Rate yourself as other members of your group would rate you.

3. Rate yourself as *most people* rate you.

4. Rate every other member of your group.

Analyses of data were performed by comparing each individual's self-rating to each of the other three ratings. The researchers found, first, that the individual self-conception (1) was very close to his perception of his rating by others in the group (2). This finding is consistent with the basic idea of the social self; namely, that the self-concept is a direct function of others' opinions. Second, the self-rating (1) was more closely associated with *perceived* ratings of others (2) then it was with *actual* ratings of others (measured by 4). This finding indicates that some distortion in perception of others' opinions occurs. Both of these findings are consistent with Cooley's looking-glass ideas.

Third, the self-rating (1) was closely associated with the perceived rating by the generalized other (3), *and* the association between (1) and (3) was even closer than the association between (1) and (2). This is what we would expect from Mead's assertion that the generalized other is the most important determinant of the self-concept. The Miyamoto and Dornbusch study thus provides the first strong empirical basis of support for the central ideas in the interactionist self tradition.

Moore replicated essential features of the Miyamoto and Dornbusch study using a very different subject population. Moore's subjects were 114 married people (57 couples) who were asked for descriptions on sixteen personality trait items. Respondents were asked:

1. Describe yourself.

2. Describe your spouse.

3. Describe yourself as you think your spouse would describe you.

Moore's results confirmed the first two findings of Miyamoto and Dornbusch: self-description (1) was highly associated with actual description by other (2), and it was even more highly associated with perceived description by other (3). In addition Moore's study provides some data relevant to Sullivan's concept of the significant other. Moore felt that the *greater* the number of potential alternative evaluating others, the *less important* should be the opinion of any given one of those others. The idea was tested by comparing the association between (1) and (3) for women who held jobs outside the home, and for those women who did not. This analysis showed that perceived ratings by spouse were more important in determining self-concept for unemployed women than for employed women. Presumably women employed outside the home have access to several important ("significant") evaluating others, while full-time housewives are less likely to have access. Moore's results thus replicate important results of the Miyamoto–Dornbusch study, and extend them in the direction of providing evidence for a more precise specification of the sources of self-concept.

The effect of extensity of interaction was studied more systematically by Reeder et al. Subjects, 54 enlisted men at a military base who were members of small work groups, were asked to rank the members of their group, including themselves, on "leadership," and "most efficient and useful worker." Next they were asked to estimate the rankings each other man in their group would make. Thus information was available on the same three variables as the earlier two studies:

1. Self rank.

2. Objective group rank.

3. Perceived group rank.

Findings of the Reeder research were generally consistent with those of

Miyamoto and Dornbusch and of Moore, and with the ideas of the looking-glass self.

The effect of extensity of interaction was also systematically examined in this research. Reeder et al. hypothesized that those individuals whose self rank was greatly discrepant from the evaluations of them by others might have access to a greater *number* of alternative evaluating others. They constructed an index of the number of alternative others using the following variables: level of education, marital status, urban or rural background, age, and military rank. Those with more education, who were married, from urban backgrounds, older and of higher rank were presumed to have greater extensity of interaction outside their work groups. By dividing the sample according to extensity of interaction the hypothesis was supported: Those individuals with greater extensity of interaction (by this measure) were also those who showed greater discrepancy between self-rank and ranking by others.

In a preliminary way this analysis begins to operationalize the idea of a significant other, since it suggests that for some respondents other members of their work groups were not particularly significant. Although there have been several other studies utilizing variations of this basic research design, their results do not extend appreciably beyond those of these three studies. The basic idea of the looking-glass self, that the self-concept is heavily influenced by others' opinions, receives good general empirical support. In addition there is considerable empirical support for the assertion that not all others are equally significant in determining the self-concept, although studies using this basic design do not explicitly specify the characteristics of a significant evaluating other. There is also support for the idea that the generalized other, or others with whom the individual has the most interaction, tend to be the most important influences upon the self-concept.

Experimental Research on the Interactionist Self

In this section we shall review several studies that involve experimental *control* over an independent variable. The most frequently used independent variable is the nature of evaluations given the individual by others. The dependent variables, various types of self-evaluation, sometimes are measured by subjects' reports, and sometimes measured by their behavior in situations. In general the experimental research assumes that the looking-glass idea is correct, and primary attention is directed toward describing more precisely *how* and *under what conditions* the self-evaluation is affected by others.

Backman et al. (1963) conducted an experiment which demonstrates the possibility of inducing a specific change in the self rating, and also begins to suggest conditions affecting the relative success of attempts to change the self-concept. Subjects were college students who volunteered to spend two consecutive Saturday mornings having various measures made of their personalities. They were asked to rate themselves on a number of personality traits, and then to indicate the ratings they thought they would be given by several others who were important (significant) in their lives. Subjects then filled out an extensive "personality profile" administered by an impressive man dressed in a white lab coat who was introduced as a psychologist from the National Institutes of Mental Health and the University of Nevada.

At the second session, individuals were given the "results" of the personality profile by the psychologist. Results were in terms of the same variables on which they had earlier been asked their self-rank, and with two exceptions, the psychologist's results indicated that their self-rank had been accurate. However their self-rankings on two traits were disputed by the psychologist's report. One of these traits was chosen to be one on which the individual perceived a high degree of agreement from his significant others, and the other, a trait upon which there was low agreement.

Immediately following this individuals were again asked to rate themselves on the same set of traits, and particular interest focuses upon whether the psychologist's reports induce changes in self-ratings. They did indeed. The average change in rank of the "low consensus" trait was 3.43; for the "high consensus" trait, 1.75. These results show both that it is possible to induce change in self-concept, and that the degree of change effected is inversely related to the amount of social support from significant others. Note also that the personality assessment came from an individual who would reasonably be expected to have a high degree of competence in this matter—we may assume that a psychologist in a white coat is a significant other in personality assessments. Probably it would have been considerably more difficult to induce an appreciable change in subjects' self-rankings if the individual were not so impressive. We shall return to this issue in the following section.

Videbeck conducted a similar study in which the attempt was made to alter individuals' self ratings. Subjects were college students in a speech class who were asked to rate themselves on 24 items involving adequacy of oral presentation. Next the students read poems for a "visiting speech expert," and were randomly assigned to one of two conditions: *approval*, or *disapproval*. In the approval condition, after each poem the "visiting expert" praised the performance; in the disapproval condition, the performance was criticized. Finally, subjects again rated themselves on the same set of 24 items.

As we might expect, these evaluations had a direct effect upon individuals' self-ratings. Those in the approval condition generally raised their self-ratings, and those in the disapproval condition generally lowered theirs. The results of this well controlled study are completely in accord with the ideas of the interactionist self, and they parallel the results of the Backman et al. study, while using an entirely different sort of self-rating and a different subject population.

Maehr and his colleagues report replications of the Videbeck study. Subjects for these studies were high school and junior high school age boys enrolled in physical education classes. Subjects rated themselves on 30 items having to do with body coordination and general physical fitness. Then they were asked to perform various athletic tasks (such as dribbling a basketball, doing sit-ups), for a "physical education expert."

The first study (Maehr et al. 1962) replicates all findings of the Videbeck study. Because of the vast differences in the concrete setting of the two studies, including (1) a very different subject pool, (2) different attributes for self-evaluation, and (3) a different set of specific manipulations, the replication adds considerably to confidence that may be placed in the findings.

The later study (Hass and Maehr, 1965) involved boys enrolled in eighth grade physical education classes. Essentially the design and the results of this study are the same as those from the previous study. The results were extended in the direction of studying persistence of changes in the self-rating induced by the "expert." Subjects answered the physical fitness question (1) immediately after receiving the evaluation, (2) the next day, (3) six days later, and (4) six weeks later. Changes induced were greatest immediately following the evaluations, but they remained detectable at approximately the same level on all of the following measurement occasions. This result shows that in the absence of additional evaluative information, the level of self-rating induced by a significant other tends to persist through time.

A series of highly controlled experiments by Jones investigates some of the evaluative conditions making for change in self-evaluation, and some of the behavioral consequences of given levels of self-evaluation at a specific task. Experiments all use a variant of a basic design that involves a group of three or four subjects sitting around a table with dividers so that they cannot see each other, and with a set of lights to receive positive or negative evaluations from every other individual. Communication through the lights may be intercepted and controlled by the experimenter, so that the nature of the evaluations between subjects may be manipulated. The task employed for these studies is one in which individuals are required to announce verbally their judgments about some set of problems; for example, their clinical judgments of psychological "case histories."

Results of these studies are complex, but two findings are especially interesting. Both concern behavioral effects of evaluations from others. First, subjects told by a psychologist that they are low on "clinical assessment ability" who later receive *positive* evaluations of their judgments from other subjects will usually send *negative* evaluations to those others. It appears that a cognitive consistency phenomenon is at work here: if I am poor at this sort of judgment, anyone who agrees with me probably has low ability also. Second, the proportion of positive evaluations supposedly sent from others directly affects a subject's future likelihood of talking in this judgment task. The more positive evaluations a subject receives, the more likely is she to offer her ideas in the future. In addition the likelihood of talking is completely independent of the actual quality of her (female subjects) suggestions, as judged by the researchers. This finding is clearly consistent with a prediction of expectation states theory (Chap. 6), and it parallels the results found by Bavelas et al., also discussed in Chap. 6.

Our task now its to organize the theoretical ideas and findings of the inter-actionist self in such a way that they may be presented in a systematic theory. It may be apparent already that many of the issues of interest in self-evaluation literature are parallel to issues of interest in the research on the development and consequences of performance expectations. In both there is a concern with ability and with evaluations of ability; in both the individual is assumed to base his observable behavior directly upon his conception of the ability of others with whom he is in interaction; and in both there is a considerable body of empirical data that is more or less closely tied to the theoretical concepts.

Within certain scope limitations it is possible to extend the concepts and propositions of expectation states theory to deal with many of the topics of interest in self evaluation literature. In many ways, the concept of a self-expectation state is similar to the concept of self-evaluation. Many of the (implicitly assumed) determinants of self-evaluation have counterparts in the unit evaluation process that is assumed to determine expectation states. Also many of the interaction consequences of self-evaluation, such as those studied by Jones and others, are roughly the same variables as consequences of expectation states.

There are at least two important differences between the concept self-expectation and the concept self-evaluation as it is usually used. First, ex-pectation states are *relative*. Actor A may have high expectations for success when he competes with Actor B, but not when he competes with Actor C. Most of the self-evaluation literature neglects any mention of this relative property. This is unfortunate for in many cases it makes the term "self-evaluation" meaningless. To say that a graduate student in psychology has a high evaluation of his knowledge of the field may tell us something about how he will interact with an undergraduate student, but it will not help us predict his interaction with a professor.

The second distinction between expectation state and self-evaluation is that the latter is frequently conceived of as a trans-situational characteristic of the individual: he "carries around" his self-evaluation with him into the various interaction situations. By contrast, expectation states are specific to a particular task. With these two restrictions—relativity of expectations, and task-specificity of expectations—assertions that would be made about expectations states are generally consistent with any assertions that would be made about self-evaluation.

A place where these conceptual differences become important is research on effects of school desegregation. In the last few years several investigators have administered various "self-esteem scales" to black and white children at either segregated or integrated schools. What they expect to find, of course, is lower self-esteem among blacks, since they are socially disad-vantaged, have the low state of a status characteristic, etc. What is usually found, especially comparing students from all black schools to students from all white schools, is no difference at all in self-esteem. Black students at integrated schools show higher self-esteem than whites on some questions, and lower on others. Unless we use a relative conception of self-evaluation, these findings are hard to interpret. But from the *relative* concept self-expectation the findings are easy to understand. Black children may have low self-expectations when they interact with white children, at certain types of tasks, in certain types of social situations. Black children definitely do not, however, always hold themselves in low esteem. What clearly is needed is a relative concept of self-evaluation which takes account of the task, the social situation, and the other actors involved.

The major contribution of the self-evaluation literature to the extension of expectation states theory is Sullivan's concept of a significant other. For Sullivan's clinical interests, significant others were such people as parents and teachers. But what *characteristics* do they possess? That is, what is it that can make an other a *significant* other? In Backman's experiment what was it about the psychologist in the white lab coat, and about Maehr's "visiting speech expert" that made their opinions significant? In most cases the answer seems to be "competence to evaluate." It seems reasonable to believe that evaluations from a highly competent other will be accepted. Evaluations from an other of low competence seem very likely to be ignored. These ideas are incorporated formally into the version of expectation states theory presented in Chart 15–1. The equivalent of a significant evaluating other is designated by the term *source*. There are two primary ways in which an individual could come to fulfill the condition of definition two. First, the actor *p* might have some reason to believe that *e* has unusually high ability to perform the task himself. Second, *p* might believe that *e* has access to evaluative information (such as an answer sheet) that is denied to *p*. In the second case, *e*'s actual ability level would be irrelevant, but the condition of definition two would still be fulfilled. Therefore this version of expectation states theory in Chart 15-1 could be used to predict the results of the experiment by Berger and Conner (reported in Chap. 6) in which the experimenter—who had an answer key—evaluated subjects' performances. Thus the version of the theory constitutes a generalization of earlier versions of the theory.

The "source version" of expectation states theory was initially tested in an experiment in which subjects had their performances evaluated by a third individual who was described as possessing either very high task ability himself or very low task ability. This manipulation was accomplished by telling subjects that the third person, the "evaluator," had arrived at the laboratory earlier than they had, and that his ability had been measured. They were told that he had scored either unusually highly or unusually poorly at this initial test. Results showed good support for the two major predictions: (1) subjects did form expectation states on the basis of evaluations from the "high ability evaluator"; and (2) the "low ability evaluator" was generally ignored.

Sobieszek extended the basic source theory to handle cases where two evaluators may agree or disagree with each other. Experimental results support this extension, which is a considerable widening of cases within the

CHART 15–1   The Source Theory:
Formal Statement of Propositions

389

*The
Social
Self*

DEFINITION 1

A situation is task-situation S if and only if it contains:

   a. at least two actors, p and o, making performance outputs;
   b. an actor, e, making unit evaluations of those performance outputs;
   c. no previous expectations held by p and o of their own or each other's abilities at the task;
   d. task orientation of all actors;
   e. collective orientation of all actors.

DEFINITION 2

e is a *source* for p in task-situation S if and only if p believes that e is more capable than p of evaluating performances.

ASSUMPTION 1

In task-situation S, if e is a source for p, then p will agree with e's unit evaluations of any actor's performances.

ASSUMPTION 2

In task-situation S, if p evaluates a series of performances of any actor, then he will come to hold an expectation state for that actor which is consistent with those evaluations.

ASSUMPTION 3

In task-situation S, if p holds higher expectations for any actor o_1 than for another actor o_2:

   a. p will be more likely to give o_1 action opportunities than o_2;
   b. p will be more likely to evaluate positively o_1's future performance outputs than o_2's;
   c. in case of disagreement between o_1 and o_2, p will be more likely to agree with o_1;
   d. p will be more likely to accept o_1 than o_2 as a source.

ASSUMPTION 4

In task-situation S, the higher the expectations an actor, p, holds for self relative to the expectations he holds for o:

   a. the more likely is he to accept a given action opportunity and make a performance output;
   b. in case of disagreement with o, the more likely is he to reject influence.

scope of the theory. As you might expect from reading Chap. 14, actors seem to combine all evaluations in forming expectation states and to give more weight to information from the highly competent evaluators.

Sobieszek and I extended the theory a bit further to include cases where the competence of the evaluator is unknown. In such cases the diffuse status of the evaluator determines whether his opinions will be influential. Subjects with no information about an evaluator's competence seem to treat him like a source if he has high status, and to ignore him if he has low status.

Let us consider one interesting application of the ideas of the source theory. Individuals generally pay attention more to evaluations from people they believe are more competent than themselves. On any evaluative scale, there will be a few people near the top; people who are generally acknowledged to be the most competent of anybody in the world, and who believe this evaluation of themselves. What would the source theory say about these people's self evaluations? One thing it suggests is that they rarely have access to any effective sources. Stated differently, there is no one else around whom they believe to be competent to evaluate their work, *and thus* their self-evaluations are likely to be insecure. Biographies of a surprisingly large number of extremely eminent people mention this very insecurity. They seem never to be satisfied that their work really is good. A graduate student in sociology who was attending a national meeting of sociologists was introduced to a man who is generally acknowledged to be the leading sociological thinker. The student, searching for an appropriate remark, commented that he had read one of the eminent man's recent papers. The surprising response from the eminent man was a genuine look of concern as he asked the question, "What did you think of my paper?" Here was the most famous living sociologist anxious to hear an evaluation from a student whose name he had never heard before. Why? Very possibly because the man has achieved a position of such eminence that there simply are no more sources for him. There is no one whose positive evaluation he trusts completely, and consequently, his opinion of his own work tends to be quite shaky. I have read reliable reports of just this phenomenon in comedian Groucho Marx, physicists Ernest Rutherford and Albert Einstein, athletes Billie Jean King and Joe Frazier, and many others. It usually gets described as "humility," with the implication it is insincere, but I think it is a genuine insecurity. These are the best people in the world at what they do—and therefore they have no effective sources.

Self-Evaluation in Education

It is in schools that research and theory in self-evaluation have their most important application. Literally thousands of studies of our educational systems involve the idea of self-evaluation, both as independent variable (for example, "the effects of self-evaluation on academic achievement") and dependent variable (as "effects of different teaching styles on self-evaluation"). From this variety of studies, let us examine some that represent many others treating development and consequences of performance expectations in the classroom.

We begin with the folk wisdom that a person who expects to do well at something probably will do better at it than someone who expects to fail. In terms a social psychologist uses, expectation level will effect actual performance level.

There seem to be two sorts of cases in which expectations are important determinants of actual performance. In the first case performance is highly variable and is easily affected by social circumstances. Alec's performance at bowling (Chap. 6) and Bobby Fischer's attempts to unnerve Boris Spassky by squeaking his chair and humming are examples of this sort of situation. In these cases the individual knows how well he can perform under "ideal" circumstances, but it is possible for others to have a negative effect upon his potential performance.

In the second type of case the individual does not know how well he can perform, and his confidence may affect the enthusiasm and openness which he brings to the task. When someone is learning a new skill, such as mastering a foreign language, if he expects to do well, he is likely to bring more energy to the task and to work harder at it—thus improving his actual chances for learning it.

Some dramatic effects of expected performance level upon actual performance were demonstrated a few years ago by Rosenthal and Jacobsen. This research employed a straightforward adaptation of some of the ideas in the preceding paragraph to a situation where the effects of anticipated success would be both marked and important for the individuals involved. The researcher began with the idea that what teachers think about the likely success of their various pupils will have an important effect upon the pupils' actual success in school. All children in several gradeschool classrooms were tested at the beginning of the year with a test purported to identify "potential academic bloomers." Teachers were told that the test was helpful in identifying children who would suddenly show unusual spurts of development during the school year. Shortly after the tests were administered, the researchers selected about 20 percent of the children at random and identified them to the teacher as possessing unusual potential for academic development during the year. That is, the teachers were told that some of these children, who in reality were picked at random, had been identified as likely candidates for real improvement.

There are two sorts of effects of this manipulation which are of interest to us. First, in some cases there were dramatic improvements in marks of these children throughout the school year. In most classrooms there was a decided tendency for children who had been identified as potential bloomers to receive higher grades from teachers during the school year. This finding is itself important, but because the teachers had been misled to believe that the identified students actually possessed higher ability than the others, perhaps it is not so surprising.

The second effect is surprising, although the evidence here is not quite so dramatic. At the end of the school year all the children took standardized IQ tests. Although the results are not perfectly consistent, there is decidedly a tendency for those children identified to show higher IQ gains, especially in the lower school grades.

Other researchers have replicated essential features of the Rosenthal and Jacobsen studies, but with mixed results. Sometimes the "teacher expectancy" effect appears, and sometimes it does not. Rosenthal and Rubin surveying the literature in 1973, conclude that overall, 39 percent of the studies report significant improvements as a consequence of simply misleading teachers as to the abilities of some of the students. Rosenthal calls this the Pygmalion effect after the mythical king who undertook to "remake" a person into what he thought she should be. The modern version of the myth is the play My Fair Lady.

Professor Doris Entwisle of Johns Hopkins University has conducted a large number of studies in the areas of cognitive development and structural conditions surrounding school achievement. She initially proposed the idea of applying the source version of expectation states theory to phenomena related to those demonstrated by Rosenthal and Jacobsen, and she and I developed a major research program from this initial idea.

What is crucial according to this analysis is not teachers' expectations, but their effects upon students' expectations. To test this analysis we developed a simple classroom experiment designed to study the effects of expectations in a naturalistic setting. The classroom experiments were based upon the source theory presented earlier in this chapter, and constitute a direct application of the theoretical ideas for the goal of producing practical results. In general we were concerned to show that childrens' expectations for their own performance could be raised by the theoretical process of controlling unit evaluations, and that the improved self-expectations would have an effect upon a behavior regarded by educators as a significant factor in learning. This experiment was designed to be a natural setting analogue to the basic expectation laboratory experiment described in Chap. 6.

Groups of four children are assembled, each with an experimenter. The task for the group is to make up a story by supplying missing words for each of twelve sentences in a "story skeleton" like the one shown in Chart 15–2. The experimenter reads the sentence, and then pauses when the blank

CHART 15–2 Story Skeleton with Words Supplied by Children

THERE WAS ONCE A VERY TALL PRINCE WHO HAD A ____(castle)____
THAT (HE, SHE) ____(lived in)____
ONE DAY (HE, SHE) HAD TO GO TO ____(the dungeon to see his prisoners)____
(HE, SHE) DID THIS VERY ____(angrily)____
BECAUSE (HE, SHE) WANTED TO ____(make sure they were there)____
THIS WAS VERY DANGEROUS BECAUSE OF THE ____(strong prisoners)____
WHO (WHICH) WAS (WERE) VERY ____(mean)____
IN ORDER TO FOOL THE (FILL IN) THE (FILL IN) DRESSED UP AS ____(another prisoner)____
IN SUCH A DISGUISE THE (FILL IN) LOOKED ____(mean)____
AND WHEN THE (FILL IN) SAW THE (FILL IN), THEY ____(welcomed him)____
THIS MADE THE (FILL IN) ____(feel pretty good)____
AND ____/COMPLETE STORY/ (he let his new friends go).____

The experimenter chooses from alternatives in parentheses the item consistent with the story line. For example, in this story the pronoun "he" is chosen because it refers to "prince."

space is reached. Children are instructed to think up "good" words to fill in the blank. (A good word is interesting and exciting; a bad word is dull or does not fit in well with the rest of the story.) Those children who feel they have a good word are instructed to raise their hands, and the experimenter will call on one of them to give the "team word." The proportion of times that each child raises his or her hand in phase one is taken as the measure of expectations. Hand raising is a classroom interpretation of the variable "accepting an action opportunity." In phase two, three of the children are sent to a separate room where they are read a story or play a game to pass the time. One child is asked to remain with the experimenter and to make up a second story all by himself. Every word that he gives is positively evaluated; by nodding, by smiling, by saying "very good," and in every way consistent with sincerity praising his performance. Phase three, the data collection phase, is exactly the same as phase one.

From the theory, two predictions for this situation may be drawn. First, we would expect a noticeable increase in the rate of hand raising between phase one and phase three for the child selected to receive the phase two expectation raising treatment. Second, we would expect that in phase three, the rate of hand raising (expectation state) for the child who has received the phase two treatment should be greater than the rate of hand raising for the "control group" children who did not receive this treatment. Table 15–1 shows the *increase* in hand raising for children in the experiment. The results shown in Table 15–1 support both predictions from the theory. Moreover the range of sociological subgroups represented is considerable. Groups were constituted of both sexes of children in grades one through four, who lived in widely differing social backgrounds. Some of the children are black and live in the city of Baltimore, some are white and live in rural Maryland, and some are white middle class suburban children. Although there are some fluctuations in the precise degree of effect of the procedure, there is by this time considerable evidence that the experiments are generally effective across a broad range of children in producing the desired improvement in expectation states.

Experiments with these children demonstrate the utility of the strategy of applying a confirmed, explicit theory for the purpose of practical intervention. We would expect this procedure to be most effective for children

TABLE 15–1 Typical Data from Expectation
Raising Experiment

Residential Locus	Suburban		Inner City		Rural	
Grade	3	4	3	4	3	4
Experimental Group	1.85	2.20	1.85	1.90	2.60	1.90
	(20)	(10)	(20)	(10)	(20)	(10)
Control Group	1.20	2.07	0.97	0.20	0.57	−0.07
	(60)	(30)	(60)	(30)	(60)	(30)
Difference Between Groups	0.65	0.13	0.88	1.70	2.03	1.97

(*n*'s in parentheses)

whose self-expectations are unrealistically low and therefore prevent them from engaging in learning activities. For children with very high self-expectations, it may not be possible with this procedure to improve their learning. But for those with low self-expectations or for those in the middle range, it seems very likely that the procedure holds great promise for producing practical results. These experiments which directly affect childrens' expectations are parallel in many ways to the work of E. G. Cohen (summarized in Chap. 7) with mixed-racial groups of children.

As a result of this research program, including other experiments not summarized here, we believe expectations develop, are maintained, and then affect behavior in many important classroom interactions. Children first arrive at school, we know, with fairly definite ideas of how well they expect to do at reading, arithmetic, and "conduct." (Typically these expectations are unrealistically high.) Expectations at this stage are probably determined almost entirely by parents' expectations for their children.

During the first semester children attempt to perform in class, and these performances are evaluated—both by the teacher and by other children. This evaluation process leads rather quickly to formation of a "structure of expectations" in the classroom: teacher and students all come to hold rather firm ideas of how "smart" each child is at various subjects.

The expectations initially assigned to children are terribly important, for once they form they change the pattern of classroom interaction in a fundamental way. *The higher the expectations held for a given child, the more likely is any given future performance to be evaluated positively, both by the teacher and by other students.* This means that once the expectation structure is set up, it is quite resistant to change. It is much more difficult for a recognized "bright" child to make a mistake than it is for a "slow" child. Both teachers and other children act to maintain the expectations originally assigned to each child, through their unit evaluations. You can recall instances of this circular expectation–evaluation process from your own experience. We shall see some consequences in a moment.

Besides early performance evaluations, there are two other sources of classroom expectations that have been documented. The first is informal information transmission within the school system. Teachers tell each other who they think are the bright and slow children and can thereby lead to expectation formation before a new teacher even meets his or her class. Consistent with this, the Pygmalion effect usually does not work too well with children above 3rd grade. Why not? Because, I think, by that time a child has attended the school long enough that expectations are firmly held for him. The teacher is not likely to believe it when an outside researcher tells her that the class dunce is a potential bloomer.

Expectations also get attached to families. Seaver has shown recently that children with an older sibling (brother or sister) get similar grades from teachers who taught them both, and get dissimilar grades from teachers who did not teach the older sibling.

The second additional way for expectations to form even before a child performs is on the basis of the child's diffuse status characteristics. For example, a teacher may think that all girls cannot do arithmetic, using the characteristic *sex* to form expectations. Or the teacher may assume that black children cannot handle schoolwork as well as white children, thus using the characteristic *race*.

An important study by Rist shows the effect of the characteristic *social class* in expectation formation. The setting was a school with all black students and teachers. Students differed in social class, and the difference was plainly visible in their clothing. As early as the first day of school, the teacher placed children at different tables, and the sitting arrangement reflected ideas about children's ability.[1] Rist observed that he could predict extremely well where each child would be placed by rating the social class background revealed by his clothing.

There is evidence from survey research to support a claim that children's expectations for their own success produce marked effects upon their later classroom behavior. For instance, Meyer (1970) has shown that the higher the actual ability level of other children in the class, the *less likely* is any given individual independent of his own ability to aspire to attend college.

Davis studied a group of college freshmen, all of whom had been National Merit Scholarship finalists, semifinalists, or winners. Even among this uniformly talented group of individuals, the higher the average ability of others in the freshmen class, the less likely was the student to choose "difficult" college courses and major fields of study. Davis has labeled this effect "the frog pond" effect: In intellectual pursuits, as in other activities, there is abundant evidence that how well the individual thinks he will do is affected by how well others about him are doing. From Davis' and Meyer's research, it appears that these expectations will have major, important effects upon the lives of the people involved. While the results of these studies may be interpreted using expectation states theory, at this stage we do not have all the necessary long range information to know how to intervene within the chain of events involving individuals' ability, beliefs, and career choices.

Summary on the Self

The *self*, by which we mean the more or less stable set of ideas we hold about who we are, develops only in a social context. The crucial processes are perceived opinions of others (the looking glass), being able to see oneself as an object (taking the role of the other), knowing opinions of the entire community (the generalized other), and paying special attention to certain others (significant others or sources).

---

[1] Grouping children by presumed ability is called "tracking," and it causes considerable controversy. Often the attempt is made to disguise the fact that tracking reflects differential evaluations of children, but the disguise is seldom successful. In Rist's study the "best" students were at the table closest to the teacher (and were called the "Eagles"), and the "slowest" (the "Clowns") were furthest.

Evaluations, which probably are the major portion of the self, develop in ways described in expectation formation in Chaps. 6 and 7: from performance evaluations, and through a burden of proof process utilizing either specific or diffuse status characteristics. Evaluations form quickly in social situations, and are specific to the task and other actors of each situation.

An individual's self-concept affects all of his waking behavior, and thus understanding what affects the self and what the self affects is a fundamental part of social psychology. We have touched on some of the findings in this area, but there is much more. I hope this introduction makes you interested in reading further.

16

Justice

Distributive Justice

More than any other topic, considerations of fairness and justice figure prominently in the lives of everyone. Besides those individuals whose work involves issues related to justice—such as lawyers, administrators, businessmen, and government officials—anyone who engages in sports, teaching, or any other type of interpersonal behavior must be concerned with questions of fairness.

As social psychologists we shall not be concerned in this chapter with defining what is fair, or what constitutes justice. What we ask is what people *think* is fair, where people get their ideas of fairness, and how they act as a consequence of perceptions of fairness.

Since antiquity, writers have expressed the feeling that particular types of relationships between actors and objects were fair or just, and other relationships were unfair. Certain people ought to get certain types of rewards for their efforts; other people ought to be punished for their acts. Of course just *which* people deserve *which* rewards or punishments depends upon interests and values: Do police narcotics agents deserve high pay and respect for performing dangerous and needed services, or should they be treated with contempt for limiting citizens' civil liberties? Were the American POWs in Vietnam heroes or war criminals? How about draft evaders who went to Canada? In these cases as in all cases involving justice, there is a feeling that certain personal characteristics of actors *are or ought to be* linked with certain positive or negative outcomes to those actors. This is the essence of issues of justice perceptions. Along with the feeling that certain characteristics and certain outcomes are linked, there are usually strong emotions which we term moral: this is the right and proper way for things to be, and they should not be otherwise.

The ways in which rewards and punishments are allocated to individuals are studied under the term *distributive justice*. Distributive justice is the relationship between actors with their personal characteristics and their perceptions of what constitutes a fair reward (or punishment) for someone with those characteristics.

A good place to look for justice concerns is in news stories describing a strike or a threatened strike. If you study the positions of both labor and management, you will find appeals on both sides to what they describe as a fair rate of pay for the workers involved. Let us look at a few illustrative examples, focusing on the reasons given by the unions for more pay.

In 1968 women seat cover stitchers employed at Ford in England struck demanding a 5¢ per hour raise, which they said was just because it would make their pay equal to that of male seat cover stitchers. They quickly won their 5¢ raise—and the men were immediately given a 1¢ per hour raise, maintaining inequality of the sexes.

In 1970 New York City cab drivers struck, demanding changes that would bring their pay up to the level of subway train drivers. They won their demand, and cab fares went up accordingly. The next year subway train drivers threatened to strike until their pay was brought up to the level of bus drivers. This demand was met. Also in 1971 firemen threatened to go on strike unless their pay was brought up to the level of policemen, which it was. (New York City is a gold mine of cases for anyone interested in strikes!)

All of the above cases involve a collective action on the part of individuals who feel that, *by comparison with some other individuals who are somehow similar to themselves,* they are underpaid. In other words, they feel that similar pay for individuals with similar jobs and similar characteristics is fair.

Some Justice Situations

In 1970, Anna Flores, an unmarried Navy enlisted woman, filed suit against the United States Navy. Miss Flores had given birth to a child fathered by a Navy enlisted man, and in accord with Navy regulations, she had been discharged as the result. She argued that in discharging women but not men for actions that similarly involved both, the Navy was practicing an unfair double standard of distributing punishments.

Women employees of the University of Wisconsin sued both the University and the U.S. Department of Health, Education, and Welfare in 1971 for distributing federal funds illegally. Specifically, they charged that the University practice—which they documented with figures—of paying women less than men for equivalent work was in violation of the 1964 Civil Rights Act, which prohibits discrimination on the basis of race or sex. They argued, in effect, that the sex characteristic is not a fair basis to use in allocating rewards differentially among individuals.

The court martial and conviction of Lieutenant William Calley was a justice situation which involved the whole nation in a controversy over morally right distribution of punishments. Some individuals felt he deserved prison punishment on account of his participation in the My Lai killings; some felt it would be more appropriate to honor and reward him; and some felt that it would be fair to punish Calley *only if* others who had performed similar acts also were punished. A Gallup Poll conducted immediately after the verdict reported that fully 79 percent of the American people disapproved of the court martial outcome. Either the act was thought praiseworthy—in which case punishment would be unfair—or punishment was considered unfair unless administered equally to all individuals who had engaged in the (from this point of view) wrongdoing. (Cases selected from Bobrow, 1972.)

However, conceptions of fairness, and strikes to achieve what is thought fair, can involve other things besides pay. In 1972 some California state college professors went on strike for reasons not involving money at all. Their complaint was that University of California faculty—who were like them in possessing a Ph.D. degree—taught fewer classes than they.

The Social Psychology of Fairness

Now we begin to be more precise as to what we mean by a situation of fairness. Actors look around at others whom they perceive to be similar to themselves in some respect such as ability, training, level of effort, or responsibility; and they feel that their pay, amount of work, and other benefits ought to be the same as those of the comparison others. Feelings of injustice never arise in a vacuum. There must be some social comparison of this sort before it is reasonable to talk about fairness or unfairness.

The second component of justice situations is that actors focus their attention on a small number of personal characteristics, such as age, training, loyalty, sex, or professional certification. Comparisons of actors are made in terms of what are perceived as relevant characteristics. People say, "I have as much skill or training as he does, and *therefore* I should be paid the same," or "She is a woman and I am a man, and *therefore* it is only fair that I be paid more than she is." The intriguing thing, which we will try to explain later, is that if you can get both individuals to focus on the same characteristic, you probably can get them to agree on what constitutes a fair wage.

Third, there are moral feelings associated with conceptions of justice and injustice. Individuals feel strongly and emotionally that justice, however they perceive justice, *ought to be* the way things are. An underpaid worker is dissatisfied; in fact he is morally indignant. An overpaid worker (we shall see some subsequently) is also dissatisfied; he feels guilty. And most telling, we find that individuals who are not directly involved themselves form strong emotional opinions about justice situations. What we call "disinterested outrage" at the shabby treatment of others, or at what looks like favoritism is a very common phenomenon. Think of how many people have opinions on the fairness of any contemporary strike, and the vehemence with which they express their opinions. These three elements—comparison, focus on a small number of personal characteristics, and moral feelings—accompany any situation of distributive justice, including strikes and other labor negotiations, and they can easily be seen if you look for them.

A useful term in studying justice situations is *relative deprivation*, meaning that in relation to some specific other individual or group of individuals, an actor feels deprived. As a working definition, relative deprivation is the state that the individual feels when comparing himself to members of a reference group who are better off than he is. (If the individual finds that he is better off than members of his reference group, we say he is "relatively gratified," but this term is not used very often.) The term *relative deprivation* was developed by Merton and Rossi (1950, 1968) to explain some puzzling findings from a monumental study of American soldiers by Stouffer et al. during World War II. Let us briefly examine some of the findings that become understandable through use of the idea of relative deprivation.

First, one effect of race involving relation deprivation. Stouffer found that blacks from the North in this country preferred to be stationed in the *South* rather than the *North*. Also Northern blacks who actually were stationed in the South were generally more satisfied than those stationed in the North. These findings are often mentioned, because they are counter to our intuitions. Intuitively we would expect that a black person during the 1940s would prefer to live in the North rather than the South, due to greater racial discrimination in the South. However if we assume that black enlisted men took as their reference group black civilians in the area where they were stationed, then the findings become understandable. In the North a black soldier comparing himself to black civilians may have felt relatively deprived, due to the greater restrictions the Army put on his own life. In the South a black soldier comparing himself to black civilians may have felt relatively gratified, due to the relatively unpleasant life of black civilians in the South. It is *relative* deprivation or gratification, produced by the types of social comparisons made by the individual, which determines his degree of satisfaction with life.

Second, an effect of actual chances for promotion upon perceived opportunities. Table 16–1 shows the *actual* chances for promotion of high school graduates and nongraduates in both the Military Police and the Air Corps (which is now the U.S. Air Force). For both graduates and nongraduates, the chances for promotion in the Air Corps were considerably greater; in fact chances of promotion in the MP were the worst in any branch of the Army, and they were about the best in the AC. Now look at Table 16–2, which shows the proportion of soldiers, both noncommissioned officers and enlisted men, who said they thought, "a soldier with ability has a very good chance of promotion in the Army." In every possible comparison the percentage saying they thought there was a very good chance is *greater* in the Military Police, exactly opposite to the actual state of affairs.

How are we to explain this difference? The idea of relative deprivation says that a soldier assesses his own probability of promotion by comparison with members of his own reference group. Consider the situation from the point of view of a private in the Air Corps (who has not been promoted) with a high school diploma. In actuality 56 percent of his reference group has been or will be promoted, but he has not; therefore it must be that a

TABLE 16–1 Actual Chances for Promotion

EDUCATIONAL LEVEL	MP	AF
High school graduate	34%	56%
Nongraduate	17%	47%

(Adapted from Stouffer et al., 1949.)

TABLE 16–2 Percent Saying "A Very Good Chance"
for Promotion

EDUCATIONAL LEVEL	MP	AC	MP	AC
High school graduate	27%	19%	21%	7%
Nongraduate	58%	30%	33%	20%
	Noncoms		Privates	

(Adapted from Stouffer et al., 1949.)

soldier with ability does not have a good chance for promotion. *Relatively*, he is doing poorly. Now consider the situation from the point of view of a noncommissioned officer (who has been promoted) in the MP without a high school diploma. In actuality only 17 percent of his reference group has been or will be promoted, but he has been; therefore there must be good opportunities for a soldier. *Relatively*, he is doing well. Now can you use a similar analysis to explain why nongraduates felt chances for promotion were better than graduates did?

Finally, education. Of the high school graduates in the Army, 79 percent either volunteered or thought they "should not have been exempted from the draft." Of the nongraduates, only 68 percent volunteered or felt they "should not have been exempted." In order to explain this using the idea of relative deprivation, you need to know that nongraduates were more likely to be deferred than graduates during World War II for reasons of health or defense-related occupations (farming and factory labor). Now can you explain the difference? And can you use the same principles to explain why, during the 1960s when many college students *were* deferred, it was college students who most often thought the draft was unfair?

Spector reports an experiment designed to test the idea of relative deprivation in a setting where choice of reference group can be controlled. The study involves a simulated army bureaucracy, with 36 teams of 4 members each. Two independent variables are involved: perceived probability of promotion, and actual promotion. Morale, attractiveness of the group, and desire to remain in the group were the dependent variables. During the group session, some subjects actually were promoted, and some were not. Table 16–3 shows the ordering of groups by these independent vari-

TABLE 16–3 Satisfaction as a Function of Perceived
and Actual Chances for Promotion

PERCEIVED PROBABILITY	ACTUAL PROMOTION?	"SATISFACTION WITH PROMOTION SYSTEM"
High	No	3.60
High	Yes	3.14
Low	No	2.87
Low	Yes	2.55

(Adapted from Spector, 1956, Table 3.)

ables on the three measures of satisfaction, where *low* satisfaction scores indicate more satisfaction. The ordering of groups is exactly as we would expect from the Stouffer results. Because the only comparisons possible for subjects in this study were within their groups (and thus Spector solved the problem of independently identifying reference groups), Spector's data provide an independent test, as well as a stronger test of the ideas of relative deprivation.

It is important to recognize that relative deprivation is a subjective thing. By the objective facts of his situation, an individual may or may not be actually deprived; what is important is that *he thinks* he is deprived. In addition to the idea of comparison, we note that individuals do not compare just to anyone. They choose others who are similar to themselves *in terms of* one or a few characteristics; that is, others who have similar education, age, job titles, and so on. Finally as can be seen particularly in cases of strikes, strong moral feelings such as anger and guilt also can accompany relative gratification.

Exchange Analyses of Distributive Justice

What an individual "brings" to his job, such as his level of skill or his training, may be looked at as what he "gives" the employer in exchange for the wage he is "given." Thus the exchange approach seems naturally well suited to justice situations. In some cases exchange analyses are perfectly satisfactory, and exchange theorists have produced some interesting empirical research, though as we shall see later on, for other situations an exchange approach does not give all the answers. Both historically and in terms of direct application, however, there are good reasons to begin theoretical analyses with an understanding of the work of exchange analysts.

During 1949 and 1950 Homans performed an observational and interviewing study of the Customer Accounting Department of a large eastern utility company. This department had the responsibility for keeping electric bills for customers in a city of about half a million people. There were four levels of employees, all females, in the office, with a clearly hierarchical relationship due to the fact that nearly all promotions to levels 2, 3, and 4 came from within the organization.

Level 1 was file clerks, whose job was to keep the address files up to date and to enter new accounts. It was dull, repetitive work, and employed the least senior women at the lowest pay scale.

Level 2 was cash posters, whose job was to take bundles of paid bills (called "stubs") to the files (called "ledgers"), and to pull the card records of paid accounts (called "arrears") to prevent a customer's being billed twice. The work, though requiring a level of skill and speed, was still repetitive; the pay was higher than that of the file clerks. Pay of the cash posters was $42.23 a week. (Remember this was quite some time ago.)

Level 3 was ledger clerks. Everything necessary for keeping accounts in order and up to date was their responsibility. In addition to tasks usually handled by the cash posters, this meant handling underpayment or overpayment of bills, changing type of service or rate charged a customer, and answering telephone questions about bills. The work was more interesting than that of the cash posters, and the pay was exactly the same as theirs: $42.23 a week. Normally we would expect level 3 employees to be paid more than level 2, but in this company in years past the cash posters had been males, and we have seen that men often get paid more than women for performing similar tasks. Thus the level 2 employees were paid a bit more than usual, and the level 3 employees were paid the "normal" rate.

Level 4 was cycle balance clerks. Once a month they had to find and correct errors in customers' accounts. This position had the greatest degree of responsibility and flexibility in the office, and it was generally filled by older women.

Table 16–4 summarizes some of the significant aspects of the jobs for these four positions. We shall be concerned primarily with the two middle levels, the cash posters and the ledger clerks. Members of one of these groups frequently complained about the "fairness" of their jobs. Can you tell from Table 16–4 which group it was? Notice that the ledger clerks differ from other positions in that the components of their jobs are noticeably "out of line" with each other; by comparison to others in the office they are high on two aspects and medium on others. What this inconsistency produced was a frequent complaint that, "We ought to get just a couple of dollars a week more to show that our job is more important" (Homans, 1962, p. 92). The ledger clerks were not dissatisfied with their jobs in general—in fact, they liked the general working conditions—just with the fairness of the pay. By comparison there were no fairness complaints by either the file clerks or the cycle balance clerks, although the latter liked their jobs and the former did not. What seems to have caused the trouble, therefore was not the total makeup of the job, but very specifically, the fact that the components of the job were not all in line with each other. The ledger clerks felt they ought to be paid enough to reflect their greater responsibility and the fact that their jobs had more variety than the jobs of the cash posters. A small pay increase, they felt, would produce distributive justice.

An exchange analysis of distributive justice is based upon calculating

TABLE 16–4 Comparative Job Aspects in Customer Accounting Division

Job Component	File Clerk	Cash Poster	Ledger Clerk	Cycle Balance Clerk
Variety	Low	Medium	High	High
Responsibility	Low	Medium	High	High
Seniority	Low	Medium	Medium	High
Pay	Low	Medium	Medium	High

(Adapted from Homans, 1964.)

a ratio for two actors of their "inputs" (such things as responsibility, skills, seniority, or loyalty) and their "outcomes" (such as wages or fringe benefits). Taking a pair of actors, p and his comparison o, and either by focusing upon a single input and a single outcome, or upon the entire set of inputs and outcomes, we construct these ratios as follows:

$$\frac{\text{Outcomes}_{(p)}}{\text{Inputs}_{(p)}} = \frac{\text{Outcomes}_{(o)}}{\text{Inputs}_{(o)}}$$

When the ratios are equal, as they are in this example, the situation is one of justice, and the comparing actor p feels neither relative deprivation nor relative gratification. Injustice to p's detriment, which produces the feelings of indignation we have seen in most of the above examples, would be:

$$\frac{\text{Outcomes}_{(p)}}{\text{Inputs}_{(p)}} < \frac{\text{Outcomes}_{(o)}}{\text{Inputs}_{(o)}}$$

Injustice to p's benefit, of which we shall shortly see several examples, would be:

$$\frac{\text{Outcomes}_{(p)}}{\text{Inputs}_{(p)}} > \frac{\text{Outcomes}_{(o)}}{\text{Inputs}_{(o)}}$$

In either type of injustice situation, either to p's benefits or to his detriment, we expect the actor to experience moral feelings that it is not right, and to take steps to produce justice. When justice fails to p's detriment, the most usual emotion is anger, and the anger motivates him to try to change things. When justice fails to p's benefit, the usual emotion is guilt, and again, he will try to change things to relieve his guilt feelings.[1] As suggested by these ratios, a p who perceives injustice has, at least theoretically, several options to reduce the injustice. If justice has failed to his detriment, he may try to increase his outcomes (for example, by a strike); he may reduce his inputs (for example, by putting less effort or care into the work); he may try to reduce o's outcomes (by drawing attention to the injustice); or he may try to increase o's inputs (by telling him to work harder). The exchange point of view analyzes justice situations in terms of the inputs and the outcomes of pairs of actors, and justice is defined as a situation in which the "equal" ($=$) sign may be placed between the two ratios.

One of the more famous unpublished studies was conducted by Clark in the late 1950s. He observed a supermarket chain, focusing on checkout

---

[1] Failure of justice to p's benefit—for example, by unfair overpayment—usually as unpleasant to p as failure to his detriment. This view is supported by Adams' experiments described in the next section. It is interesting to note, however, that this appears to differ from Homans' view in part b of his distributive justice proposition (5b in Chap. 9). This proposition states that overpayment is pleasing. Most of the evidence I know—and we shall see some here—indicates that overpayment produces *guilt* and subsequent attempts to restore fairness.

clerks. Each line had two clerks, the "ringer" who operated the cash register, and the "bundler" who put the food in bags. Since bundlers got less of the outcome "prestige"—they worked "for" ringers—only those bundlers who also had fewer inputs (such as age, sex, education) would feel the relationship was just. What could a bundler in an unjust relationship do? One thing is reduce his input "effort" by working slower.

Store #58 had the most consistent ringer–bundler pairs; store #6 had the fewest. Table 16–5 shows two measures of efficiency for these two stores, the percent profit made by the store after wages were paid, and the number of hours of operation for each check-out counter to earn $100 profit for the store. By both these measures, store #58 was more profitable. Incidentally though the differences in Table 16–5 may look small, remember that the margin of profit in supermarkets is smaller than in any other type of merchandising. It really is the case that supermarkets cannot operate without great volume, and small differences in profit can be crucial. Another way to interpret these figures is to say that it took 27 percent more hours in store #6 to make the same profit as in store #58, or that profits were 46 percent greater in store #58. The differences are considerable.

Another example of the same phenomenon, reducing injustice by reducing outputs, can occur in the type of restaurant usually called "coffee shops," characterized by a counter and several booths for customers. Cooks in these restaurants are usually males and older and more highly skilled than the female waitresses. Therefore if the waitress is given power over the cook, the situation will probably be perceived as unjust by the cook. Yet the waitress does have some power over the cook by virtue of their jobs. She transmits customers' orders to him, thus in effect telling him what to do. It turns out that letting waitresses give verbal orders directly to the cook is bad business. It produces feelings of injustice for the cook and can lead to fights with waitresses and to his deliberately reducing his inputs of speed and care in preparing orders. (The cook's strategy is a good one, incidentally, since the waitress is the one who gets blamed for slow or poorly cooked food.) The way most of these restaurants avoid this type of trouble is to keep the waitresses from giving verbal orders to the cook. They place their order sheets on the "wheel," which the cook then revolves *when he wants to*, to see the order. A small symbolic gesture, perhaps, but one with tremendous significance to the actors involved, and ultimately, to the customers and the owner of the coffee shop. This case was studied by Whyte.

TABLE 16–5 Effects of Injustice upon Supermarket Profits

	Store #6	Store #58
% Profit	3.89	5.67
Hours per $100 profit	3.85	3.04

(Figures computed from Adams, 1963.)

Adams' Exchange Experiments

Studies of the effects of injustice tend to focus on situations where justice has failed to the actor *p*'s benefit, rather than to his detriment. Naturally occurring situations and strikes provide ample instances of actors responding to perceived injustice to their detriment, but in experimental studies it is equally possible to tell subjects that they are unfairly the recipients of too much outcomes. The main reason for focusing on situations of unjust over-reward is that the expected behaviors of actors in these situations—such as reducing their own outcomes—are more unusual and more difficult to ascribe to any factors other than the predicted guilt and attempts to reduce it.

One of the early experiments, by Adams and Rosenbaum, involved hiring students from the New York University Placement Service for an interviewing task. There were two conditions: fair payment and unjust overpayment. In the fair payment condition, subjects were told that their inputs just matched the outcomes they were to receive. They were, that is, fully qualified for the rate of pay they were to get. In the unjust overpayment condition, the treatment is quite severe. The experimenter tells subjects angrily that they are unqualified for the job, but he will "have to" hire them anyway. He tells them to *please* pay attention to his instructions so they will have some hope of doing an adequate job.

All subjects in the study were paid $3.50 an hour; thus their outcomes were the same in both conditions. However the instructions were designed to make subjects in the fair condition believe that their inputs (skill) justified this outcome, while subjects in the unjust overpayment condition were expected to feel that their inputs were too small. By comparison with an *o* who was a qualified interviewer, subjects in the fair condition should have perceived justice:

$$\frac{\text{Outcomes}_{(p)}}{\text{Inputs}_{(p)}} = \frac{\text{Outcomes}_{(o)}}{\text{Inputs}_{(o)}}$$

Subjects in the unjust overpayment condition should have perceived injustice of the sort to make them feel guilty:

$$\frac{\text{Outcomes}_{(p)}}{\text{Inputs}_{(p)}} > \frac{\text{Outcomes}_{(o)}}{\text{Inputs}_{(o)}}$$

What could subjects in the unjust situation do? They could not very well reduce their outcomes, since these were set by the (rather hostile) experimenter. What they could do was to increase their inputs in the form of effort: they could work harder, longer, and faster, in hopes of making their inputs great enough to produce justice. Table 16–6 shows the average number of interviews completed by subjects (all of whom were paid for 2½ hours work) in both conditions. Those in the unjust condition produced nearly 50 percent more interviews than those in the fair condition!

TABLE 16–6   Average Number of Interviews Per Hour
as a Function of Distributive Justice or Injustice

Fair Payment	Unjust Overpayment
11.40	16.16

(Calculated from Adams and Rosenbaum, 1962, Table 1.)

In a second experiment, Adams and Rosenbaum assessed a second independent variable, method of payment. In one case subjects were paid as in the first experiment, by the hour. In the other they were paid 30¢ for each interview they completed, in a "piecework" fashion. Although the situation is similar, and the basic prediction is that subjects in the unjust conditions will try to produce justice, the empirical consequences are different. The way to produce justice in the piecework conditions is to produce *fewer* completed interviews, thus cutting down the total pay for the work. Table 16–7 presents the mean number of interviews completed per hour in each of the four conditions of the second experiment. In the hourly conditions the same results obtained as in the first experiment. In the piecework conditions subjects told their inputs were too small seem to have tried to decrease their outcomes by cutting down the number of interviews they completed. (The relevant comparisons are fair vs. unjust within each payment method; there is no particular reason to compare the number of interviews produced by the hourly and the piecework payment methods.)

Adams and Jacobson studied the same sorts of processes in a more refined experimental design using a different task. We shall look at three of their conditions, which we will call "High Injustice," "Reduced Injustice," and "Just." (These are not the names of conditions used by the authors, but I think these are less confusing. They also included a second independent variable, prospects for future exployment, but I have omitted it since it did not produce interesting effects and there is some question about success of operationalizing the variable.)

Subjects again were college students (from Columbia University) hired for a proofreading task. They were given a "test of proofreading ability" before being hired, and were told either that their ability was low (in both injustice conditions), or that it was just right (in the just condition). The difference between the high injustice and the reduced injustice con-

TABLE 16–7   Average Number of Interviews Per Hour
as a Function of Justice and Method of Payment

Method	Fair Payment	Unjust Overpayment
Hourly	13.65	16.34
Piecework	11.77	8.96

(Calculated from Adams and Rosenbaum, 1962, Table 2.)

ditions was in rate of pay. The rate for just and high injustice conditions was 30¢ per page; it was reduced to 20¢ in the reduced injustice condition.

If subjects accepted this manipulation, we would expect only those in the high injustice condition to feel the guilt. They had low qualifications, but were still receiving the rate of pay of others who had high qualifications. Subjects in the reduced injustice condition would feel that their qualifications were low, but so was their pay. Subjects in the just condition received high pay, and were told they were highly qualified. Thus we would expect only subjects in the high injustice condition to try to reduce their outcomes; and since it was a piecework experiment, they would do this primarily by decreasing the number of pages they proofread.

Table 16–8 shows the mean number of pages corrected by subjects in each of these three conditions. As we expected, those in the high injustice condition completed much less than those in either of the other two conditions, and the numbers are about the same for those in the latter two conditions.

Table 16–9 presents two measures of effort, which would be an input in this experiment: the number of errors correctly identified by subjects in each condition, and the number of nonerrors identified. (A nonerror is a word that is actually correct, but which the subject has thought is typed incorrectly. Anyone who has ever done proofreading recognizes finding of nonerrors as a result of tension and, perhaps, of effort.) Subjects in the high injustice condition found significantly more actual errors and more nonerrors than subjects in the other two conditions, and the figures for the other two conditions do not differ appreciably from each other. These findings are as expected.

There are several other experiments conducted within the exchange framework on the effects of injustice, but they all have the same basic design and they usually yield comparable results. Similar results have been obtained in a wide range of situations, including children as young as fourth grade (by Long and Lerner), and Austrian College students (by Mikula). The overpayment/equity effect apparently is quite general.

Lawler has proposed that the effect of telling subjects they are unqualified is to threaten their self-esteem: perhaps the greater effort produced is the result of subjects' trying to prove their ability to the experimenter, rather than trying to reduce injustice. As another alternative interpretation,

TABLE 16–8 Pages Corrected as a Function of
Distributive Justice

Condition	Pages
High Injustice	8.70
Reduced Injustice	11.30
Just	11.70

(Adapted from Adams and Jacobson, 1964, Table 5.)

TABLE 16–9 Identification of Errors and Nonerrors
as a Function of Distributive Justice

Condition	Errors Detected	Nonerrors
High Injustice	7.87	1.80
Reduced Injustice	4.70	.58
Just	4.90	.92

(Adapted from Adams and Jacobson, 1964, Tables 1 and 3.)

it has always impressed me that when subjects are told they are unqualified, the experimenter almost invariably asks them to try harder, a request omitted from the just conditions. Since we know that subjects generally want to please the experimenter—a point discussed more fully in Chap. 17—this instruction alone might be sufficient to produce the differences between conditions which we have seen.

However in spite of the criticisms against Adams' and related experiments, most experiments of this type have produced the effects we would expect from subjects trying to reduce injustice. These experimenters deserve credit for responding to the criticisms by designing new studies to eliminate design flaws or to give the alternative interpretations full chance to be supported. Most of the time, the redesigned experiments also produce the effects expected from attempts to reduce injustice—even though they sometimes show that many other, previously unrecognized, factors were operative in the situation as well as injustice. For instance, Moore and Baron, as well as Cook and others, have found that subjects sometimes change their self-esteem or self-evaluation as the result of overpayment or underpayment.

It is tempting to try to draw direct parallels from these experiments to the work situation. For instance if you hire somebody and tell him he is being overpaid, will this always induce guilt and insure that he will work harder and longer for you? There is good evidence that this technique will induce guilt and that people try to reduce guilt by increasing their inputs, but we must remember that these experiments are of short duration compared to most jobs people hold. It was one of Freud's great insights that guilt turns to hostility rather rapidly, so telling someone he is being overpaid may make him feel guilty and even grateful for a short time period, but it also seems likely that eventually he will get angry at you for making him feel guilty. He may try to get out of the situation by quitting his job, or the hostility may take the form of ridicule directed towards someone so stupid as to overpay his employees.

Consistency Analyses of Justice

Useful as the exchange approach is to problems of justice, it has some serious limitations. These limitations prevent applying the analysis to some of the most interesting sorts of cases (those involving status value), and they make precise specification of some of the central concepts difficult or impossible. Zelditch et al. describe four major difficulties with the exchange analysis, and suggest the outlines of an alternative, consistency-based, approach. We shall review these criticisms and describe the consistency theory of justice.

You recall that the exchange approach formulates justice as a relation of inputs (such as effort) to outcomes (such as pay). Fairness or justice is then defined as an equality sign between the ratios of two actors *p* and *o*. In case of injustice one actor is overpaid and the other is underpaid; the former feels guilt, the latter feels anger, and both will take steps to produce justice; that is, equality between their ratios.

The greatest problem is that it is extremely difficult to conceptualize *status value* in this way. Justice problems, especially those dealing with wages, very often focus upon "inputs" and outcomes that have little if any intrinsic value, yet which have acquired tremendous status significance for actors in a social system.

What do we mean by status value? We owe the term to the economist Veblen (1899; republished in 1973), who observed that once people attain and surpass a certain minimal level of wealth—that level necessary to supply enough food and shelter to survive—they begin to become concerned with *status value* as well as *consummatory value* of goods. To a starving person any sort of food has consummatory value. We have reports of people eating rats and insects, and occasionally, other people in order to survive. But beyond this extreme case, food acquires status value: it is satisfying to be able to eat expensive foods and to drink expensive beverages, *and part of the satisfaction comes from the fact that not everyone can afford these things.* This is status value. Status value is largely what makes a big house in an exclusive neighborhood more desired than a shack; it is what makes high priced American cars more desired than low priced cars; it accounts in large measure for the willingness to stay in expensive hotels, to fly in the first class section of planes, to eat at expensive restaurants, to buy expensive clothes, perfumes, and shaving lotions. The marginal utility of expensive objects over inexpensive is very small in terms of consummatory value; in terms of status value, it can be tremendous.

Virtually every object we possess, seek, or use has some consummatory value and some status value. The surprising thing, when you begin to look at objects in this way, is just how large a component the status value is. We live in an affluent culture, and for most objects we purchase it seems that the status value component is greater than the consummatory value component.

It has always surprised me how unaware people can be of status value; the implicit norm against being a snob has great strength in our culture. When I was in college and drove a big Detroit convertible, a friend once told me that his car (an old Volkswagen) performed just the same functions as mine—meaning transportation—and yet cost less. In terms of consummatory value he was correct, yet he couldn't have been more wrong. Those two cars did not perform the same functions at all! How many people do you know who claim to be able to recognize "good liquor" (meaning expensive) from bad (cheap) by taste? There is quite a bit of empirical evidence that most people cannot recognize any distinctions reliably even on the first drink—*after* one drink, not even an expert taster can do this. The extreme case of this in this country is vodka, which by law is nothing except grain alcohol and water; no flavoring of any sort whatsoever. Yet how many people do you know who claim they can tell good vodka from bad?

Status value is very important in justice phenomena, yet it cannot be conceptualized in the exchange theory because it is difficult to quantify. Such inputs as years of education or seniority can be quantified; for example, we might say that the following is just:

$$\frac{\$300/month}{4 \text{ years education}} = \frac{\$900/month}{12 \text{ years education}}$$

But how about

$$\frac{\$300/month}{female} \text{ ? } \frac{\$400/month}{male}$$

In many cases that would be considered fair by both parties, yet this doesn't make sense. Other characteristics—race, loyalty, age—could be substituted for sex here with the same result. There is status value attached to all these characteristics, yet they are difficult to quantify to make the ratios work out.

Status value inheres in outcomes as well. It is common in businesses to reward people with objects that have great status significance but almost no consummatory value: the key to the executive washroom was a prized object in many companies a few years ago. At Johns Hopkins we still have a washroom labelled "faculty women only," and most grade schools segregate teachers and students with separate washrooms, coat rooms, and lounges. A rug on the floor in a man's office has tremendous status significance, and thus constitutes a large outcome in justice situations. The size of one's desk in a large office indicates status within the organization, but again, it is difficult to conceptualize this significance in an exchange ratio. I know a man who was stationed in a large Navy office in this country. His rank was the lowest of all the people in that office, and accordingly, his desk was the smallest in the room. But he found that, through a perfectly legitimate procedure, he could request and obtain a much larger desk. When his larger desk arrived, the tension level in the office went up appreciably. Within 3 months every one of the desks in that office had been changed so that their relative sizes again reflected the Navy rank of their occupants! We laugh at a story like this one only when we do not fully appreciate the significance of the status value attaching to objects.

In terms of the exchange theory, only consummatory value can be incorporated in the ratios which define justice or injustice. Because a very large portion of justice concerns revolve about status value rather than consummatory value, an exchange analysis cannot be used for many of the most interesting cases.

The second problem with the exchange version is that *there is no unique and precise conceptualization of justice.* In many cases small differences in outcomes can have great importance to feelings of justice or injustice. Remember that the cash posters said they ought to get "just a few dollars more" to show that their position was superior to that of the ledger clerks. It really did not matter precisely *how much* more; presumably any one of a number of values would have produced feelings of justice in this case. In other words we cannot specify a unique or a precise value of wage which would produce justice for the cash posters. In the case of the British Ford seat cover stitchers, at first the 5¢ differential between men and women was perceived as just (at least by the men). When the women got their raise the men got only a 1¢ raise, and this was now perceived as justice. Thus apparently either a 1¢ or a 5¢ differential—or perhaps some other differential —would be perceived as just.

Third, *the exchange version gives no unique and empirically plausible definition of injustice.* That is, in many cases we have what looks like different situations which produce exactly the same outcome, or what looks like two identical cases producing different outcomes in terms of perceived fairness. The problem with defining injustice comes from the fact that the exchange ratios consider only two actors at one time, and this is not enough to know whether a situation is just or unjust; and if unjust, who is underpaid and who is overpaid.

Suppose we know that p is paid \$3.50 an hour; clearly this is not sufficient to know whether he feels this is just or not. Suppose p is paid \$3.50 an hour and o is paid \$4.30 an hour and p feels he is similar to o; does this solve the problem? A moment's thought should indicate that p could be underpaid, o could be overpaid, or perhaps even both are overpaid—there still is no basis for defining the outcome in terms of justice. Now suppose p is a skilled mechanic paid \$3.50 an hour; skilled mechanics typically make \$4.30 an hour; o is an unskilled mechanic; and unskilled mechanics typically make \$4.30 an hour. Now the question is resolved: p is underpaid and o is fairly paid. The difference is that we have finally added a stable frame of reference: we know how much skilled and unskilled mechanics typically make.

Suppose we know that skilled mechanics typically make \$4.30 an hour, and p and o are both skilled mechanics making \$3.50 an hour. In this case we know that both p and o are unfairly underpaid. But from simply looking at their ratios of input (skilled mechanic) and outcome (\$3.50/hr) we could not tell this. Suppose p is a skilled mechanic paid \$4.30 an hour and o is a skilled mechanic paid \$3.50 an hour. From simply comparing their ratios we could conclude that p is unfairly overpaid; yet because of the frame of reference we know that p is fairly paid and o is unfairly underpaid.

Note also that the empirical behaviors we would expect in various types of over- and underpayment differ considerably. In our second example where p and o are both unfairly underpaid, we might expect some sort of collective action, such as a strike. In the first example where *p* is unfairly underpaid and *o* is fairly paid, we might expect *p* to be angry, but there is no reason for him to be angry at *o*, and there is no reason for *o* to feel guilty when he compares himself to *p*. The empirical consequences we expect depend directly upon what type of injustice exists; that is, upon just how each actor is paid *in relation to* a stable frame of reference. There is no frame of reference in exchange analysis of justice.

The fourth problem with the exchange version of justice is that *it offers no way to explain either the acquisition of feelings of justice, nor the strong moral feelings (including anger, guilt, and disinterested outrage) regarding injustice.* We have already identified these feelings as being normative—that is, rules which individuals come to believe tell how things ought to be—and we would like to describe how people come to believe these norms. (We would suspect that justice is normative simply on the grounds that people become emotionally upset at injustice. See the discussion of emotional behavior as a consequence of norm violation in Chap. 2.) The exchange analysis mentions the importance of moral feelings, but the theory certainly does not imply them as a necessary consequence.

There are some striking cases of normatively defined justice which we would like to explain. For example, how does it come about that in some places *both black and white people* feel it is right and proper for whites to be paid more than blacks for identical work? Why is it that many women feel it is just for men to be paid more than women for identical work; why do some single people feel it is just for married people to be paid more than themselves for the same work? For that matter why should a college education be accepted as a relevant characteristic in differential pay for the many occupations which are only slightly related to skills developed in college?

More generally we would like to be able to explain the development and the effects of the strong moral feelings which people display in cases where injustice obtains. In order to do this we need a theoretical explanation of the formation of norms regarding justice: norms that tell what defines a just situation, and a theory that will enable us to predict consequences of various types of violation of a justice norm.

A Status Value Theory of Justice

In this section we shall construct an alternative view of justice phenomena, one designed to answer the four objections given to the exchange analysis considered earlier. Note that this theory is an alternative; we are not saying that the exchange version is incorrect, but only that it has limitations which we hope to remove by developing another theory. We will use standard balance diagrams to illustrate this theory. (These diagrams are described in Chap. 12.)

The theory begins by describing what we call the *referential structure*. This is the frame of reference which actors must use in order for any comparisons they make among themselves to have meaning in terms of justice or injustice. The referential structure is what defines the normative beliefs about what rewards and punishments "ought to" go with which actors in a given situation. It is the way the actor perceives things are in the world. This is represented in Fig. 16–1.

We assume that the actor p, when he observes the world, notes that there are two types of people whom we will call the X-type people and Y-type people. X-type people have characteristic a (denoted by subscript $_{ca}$) and Y-type people have characteristic b (denoted by subscript $_{cb}$). The X and Y could be any differentiating principle at all; for convenience, we might think of X-type people as being males and Y-type as females; or X as whites and Y as blacks; or X as highly skilled and Y as unskilled. (As the examples suggest, we are going to show later that X-type people come to be preferred, but at the beginning this is not necessarily the case.)

Second, p notes two types of *goal objects* in the world, GO_a and GO_b. Goal objects can be anything at all which are valued, either positively or negatively. This means they can be rewards, such as pay or status-valued objects; or they could be punishments such as years in prison or disgrace. We know that p prefers one state of GO to the other; (such as preferring high wages to low, or preferring a short prison term to a long one); for convenience we say he prefers GO_a to GO_b. This is indicated by the evaluated relations between p and both goal objects in Fig. 16–1.

Our first assumption is that if p perceives that a particular characteristic (for example, ca) is regularly associated with a particular state of a goal object (the a state), then he will come to think that "there must be a reason for it." In other words noticing that a characteristic and a goal object are usually associated will lead to p's forming the conclusion that the characteristic is *relevant* to the goal object. For example, he might come to think that being a male is *relevant* to receiving the high state of the goal object income. If p notices that certain relations regularly occur in the world, he will come to think that this is not chance; it is for some reason. This assumption we call the *Acquisition of Relevance*, and it is an outgrowth of Heider's attribution principle of Chap. 4. It is indicated by the unit relations between characteristics in Fig. 16–1.

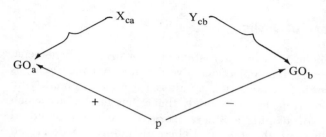

FIGURE 16–1 Evaluation of goal objects and acquisition of relevance

1. *Acquisition of Relevance.* If p perceives that a Characteristic X is associated regularly with particular states of a Goal Object X, then p will come to believe that Characteristic X is Relevant to Goal Object X.

As soon as characteristics have acquired relevance, we add a second assumption, called *Acquisition of Status Value.* We assert that p will complete his cognitive structure (in Fig. 16–1) in a balanced fashion; he will come to differentially evaluate the characteristics as the result of his earlier differential evaluation of the goal objects. For example, if he notes that men are regularly associated with high pay and women with low pay, he will conclude that the characteristic male is somehow preferable to the characteristic female. Acquisition of status value thus allows us to predict that individuals will come to evaluate characteristics as the result of noting that they are associated with already evaluated goal objects. The acquisition could also work in reverse: noting that a previously unvalued goal object (such as the key to the executive washroom) is regularly associated with actors who possess a particular characteristic (such as high pay) would make the goal object acquire status value.

2. *Acquisition of Status Value.* If Characteristic X has no value to p and if Characteristic X is perceived as relevant to an evaluated Goal Object X, then Characteristic X will acquire the same value to p as Goal Object X.

2'. *Acquisition of Status Value.* If Goal Object X has no value to p and if Goal Object X is perceived as relevant to an evaluated Characteristic X, then Goal Object X will acquire the same value to p as Characteristic X.

This assumption is illustrated in Fig. 16–2 where the referential structure is completely connected. Figure 16–2 represents the way p perceives relations between actors and goal objects in the world, and because of the two preceding assumptions, we assume a tendency for individuals to evaluate

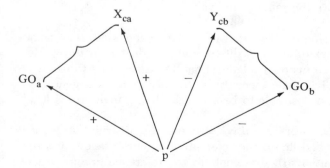

FIGURE 16–2   Balanced unitary referential structure

either characteristics or goal objects in a referential structure. The structure in Fig. 16–2 is *balanced* and *unitary*. You already know what a balanced structure is from Chap. 12. A unitary referential structure is one in which characteristics and goal objects are uniquely linked. If some men and some women *both* got the high state of the goal object wages, for instance, the referential structure would not be unitary. *Unless the referential structure is balanced and unitary, no justice process is possible.* Justice concerns arise only where characteristics and goal objects are uniquely related—or where people think they are uniquely related.

Now we need to tell how the referential structure produces feelings of justice and injustice. In addition to the referential structure—which is the way an actor perceives the larger world—we speak of the *local system.* The local system contains the other actors, goal objects, and relations perceived by the actor in his own life. It is the group of others with whom he spends his time. The local system is perceived in ways heavily determined by the referential structure. That is, the actor has a tendency to think things are the same in his local system as they are in the larger world, *and when things are not the same, there is a tendency to think that they ought to be.*

We add two assumptions describing how the referential structure affects the local system, using lower case letters to differentiate points in the local system from points in the referential structure.

3. *Spread of Relevance.* If characteristic x (in the local system) is perceived as an instance of Characteristic X (in the referential structure), and if Characteristic X is perceived as relevant to Goal Object X, then characteristic x will be perceived as relevant to goal object x.

This assumption says that if p has come to believe that the characteristic female is relevant to earning lower wages in the world, he will think it is relevant (that is, that the rule applies) to females in his own local system.

4. *Spread of Status Value.* If characteristic x (in the local system) is perceived as an instance of Characteristic X (in the referential structure), and if Characteristic X has acquired status value, then characteristic x will acquire the same status value.

This final assumption simply says that if p has concluded that some characteristic (such as sex or skill) is differentially evaluated in the world, then he will evaluate it in his own relationships the same as he thinks it is evaluated in the world. If female seems to be the disfavored sex generally, he will also think it is less desirable to be a female than a male in his local system.

Figure 16–3 shows the entire cognitive structure for distributive justice processes. Above the dashed line is the referential structure; below it is the local system. The referential structure contains the reference groups p perceives and the characteristics they possess. It also shows p's awareness of their respective states of goal objects. The local system contains p as

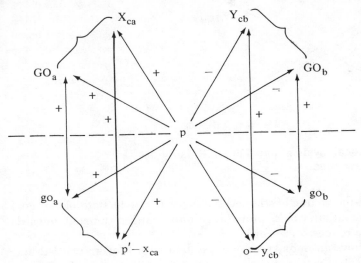

Local System

FIGURE 16–3   Balance diagram for distributive justice

viewed by himself (p') and another actor o. In this case, p perceives that p' possesses the high state of the characteristic and o possesses the low state. For example, p perceives that he is a male and o is a female; or that p is highly skilled and o has low skill. The assumptions in Fig. 16–3 are as follows: Assumption 1, acquisition of relevance, is indicated by the unit relations in the referential structure between the Characteristics and the Goal Objects. Assumption 2, acquisition of status value, is shown by the evaluations in the referential structure from p to the Characteristics and from p to the Goal Objects. Assumption 3, spread of relevance, is shown in the local system by the unit relations between the characteristics and the goal objects. Assumption 4, spread of status value, is shown in the local system by evaluations from p to the characteristics and from p to the goal objects.

Now we are in a position to give a precise definition of distributive justice, by reference to Fig. 16–3: *Justice is defined as balance in the local system.* When the relations in the local system constitute a balanced system, then p perceives justice in terms of characteristics and goal objects. If the local system is imbalanced, p perceives a state of injustice, and feels tension and pressures to change the system towards balance and justice. Happiness is a balanced local system.

The consistency approach to justice can distinguish several different types of injustice, in which we expect quite different responses on the part of p. For instance, Fig. 16–4 shows an imbalanced local system in which the cycle containing p' is balanced and hence just. The cycle containing o, however, is imbalanced, with o overrewarded. This is, o has the b (or dis-

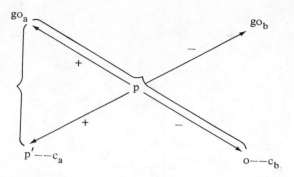

FIGURE 16–4   Local system imbalance: P fairly rewarded, O overrewarded

favored) state of the characteristic and the *a* (or favored) state of the goal
object. Such a situation would probably produce anger directed towards
o and attempts to reduce *o*'s reward.

Figure 16–5 shows an imbalanced local system with *p* overrewarded and
o fairly rewarded. In this case we expect *p* to feel guilty and to display the
sorts of behaviors observed in Adams' experiments.

In Fig. 16–6 the cycles containing both *p'* and *o* are imbalanced, and
both actors are unjustly underrewarded. Note that both *p'* and *o* have the
a state of the characteristic, and that both are receiving the *b* state of the
goal object. Note also that this sort of injustice could not be described without a referential structure. In particular we would think from an exchange-
type equation that *p* and *o* were in a state of justice. In the situation depicted
in Fig. 16–6 we expect some sort of collective action by *p* and *o* (such as
a strike) to gain redress against what they perceive as unfairness produced
by "the system," or whoever has allocated them the *b* state of the goal
object.

To summarize the status-value theory of distributive justice, the process
requires at the outset that *p* perceive a balanced, unitary referential structure before any justice process can be set in motion. Then the assumptions

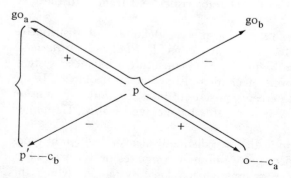

FIGURE 16–5   Local   system   imbalance: P   overrewarded, O fairly rewarded

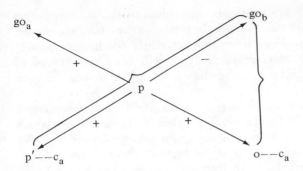

FIGURE 16–6 Local system imbalance: P and O both
underrewarded

say essentially that *p* will expect that the local system ought to mirror the referential structure. He will come to expect as right and proper (that is, as normative) that his local system will reflect the way things are in the world. If the local system is balanced, he will think this is just. If the local system is imbalanced, it is unjust. Finally, in cases of local system imbalance, *p* will take those actions that will balance the imbalanced cycles. The sort of action *p* takes in cases of perceived injustice can be predicted from the specific cycles that are imbalanced in the local system.

The status-value theory of justice is particularly interesting because it tells the conditions under which we expect justice processes to occur or not to occur, and it suggests some ways in which individuals' conceptions of what is fair can be changed. As we have already noted, justice conceptions will not occur in any situation unless the actor *p* perceives that one state of a characteristic is uniquely associated with a particular state of a goal object. Unless it is the case that females always (or nearly always) get lower wages than men, for instance, actors will not come to believe that sex is a relevant characteristic for forming justice conceptions. Note that the reverse is true also: Even actors possessing the low state of a characteristic, if that characteristic is uniquely associated with the low state of the goal object in the referential structure, will come to believe that it *should* be associated with the low state of the goal object in the local system.

Suppose that you are interested in using this analysis to find ways to change the conceptions people have about fair wages. For instance, how could we change a belief that blacks ought to get lower wages than whites for doing the same work? Because justice processes cannot take place without a balanced, unitary referential structure, one strategy would be to see that the referential structure changes to cease being unitary with respect to the characteristic race. If as the result of changes in laws and social programs, people come to believe that the referential structure is no longer unitary—that is, that race is no longer uniquely associated with wages; some blacks earn high wages and some whites earn low—then they cease to believe that that is the way things *ought to be* in the local systems. Such changes are very much in evidence now for the characteristic sex: more and more women are coming to earn as much as men do for equivalent work, and this means that sex is unlikely to continue to function in justice arguments that women ought to earn less than men. Even if sex characteristics continue to be differentially evaluated, which does seem likely, it will not be perceived as relevant; that is, as the basis for arguing that it *should be* associated with wage differential.

Before leaving the status-value theory, I would like to mention another problem area, one which at first looks totally different from justice, but which actually is quite similar. This is known as victim derogation studies. We hear, surprisingly often, people saying of the victim of some personal misfortune, "He probably deserved it." For instance, upon reading about a rape victim someone might say, "She probably led him on." Or a robbery victim "must have done something stupid." Obviously not everybody thinks this about every crime or misfortune, but these are not rare occurrences, either. Furthermore, the effect has been produced experimentally, and it appears regularly.

To understand the victim derogation phenomenon, refer to Fig. 16–3 and note that being a victim is the low status of a goal object (GO_b). Now if our actor believes that some characteristic, such as seductiveness or carelessness, is regularly associated with GO_b, the acquisition of relevance assumption tells us that he will perceive a causal link: "seductive people get raped; rape victims are seductive." Since we know that rape is the disfavored goal object assumption 2 tells us that seductiveness (or carelessness, and so on) will acquire a similar, negative value. Finally, assumptions 3 and 4 complete the explanation of why any particular case of rape should be taken as evidence of that victim's carelessness. Note also that we have an explanation why not everybody derogates the victim in this way. Unless the person believes in a balanced unitary referential structure—that is, no nonseductive person gets raped—the process does not operate.

Perspective on Fairness Conceptions

Investigators concerned with distributive justice, both from an exchange and from a consistency point of view, provide a starting point from which to analyze justice phenomena and some empirical support for their analyses. In certain cases the simpler exchange version permits us to make sorts of analyses we need, but for many other situations of interest—particularly those involving status value—the consistency approach seems preferable. Final acceptance of the status value theory, of course, will have to await the results of complete experimental tests, of which at this time only a few have been conducted.

One problem with designing distributive justice experiments has been that justice concerns seem to be a fragile phenomenon. By this I mean that it is difficult to design an experiment which incorporates all the features of naturally occurring justice situations and which allows the investigator to observe the behaviors predicted without confounding from other factors.

For example, justice experiments frequently involve some sort of payment to subjects, and it would be interesting to allow subjects to allocate money to themselves and others to see whether they would try to do so fairly. To date there has not been a very successful allocation experiment. Subjects either give themselves all the money they can, or else—what is more common—they try to be nice to others and give them most of the reward. What this indicates is not so much the failure of predictions of a justice principle, since we know that justice does function in real-life situations, but rather the difficulty of making a justice norm have force in a short-term experimental group. Other considerations such as a desire for money or a desire to buy approval from other subjects seem more important.

A second problem with designing justice experiments is also related to the short time duration of experimental groups. In natural settings actors seem to try to produce justice, not on every possible situation, but over the long run. If somebody is short-changed this time, others will try to give him a little more next time. There usually isn't enough time to observe this behavior in a laboratory. Another difficulty is we believe that some justice feelings, especially guilt, are not likely to endure for long in natural settings. Yet because of the short duration of experimental groups, it is currently impossible to study whether this is true, and what happens to guilt feelings in the experimental laboratory.

Finally, I would like to leave you with the conjecture that all distributive justice might be a cultural phenomenon, one which we just wouldn't see in a culture very different from ours. In many countries there are no fixed prices for goods, no regularly agreed upon wages for particular jobs or particular types of people. In these places, in other words, there can be no balanced, unitary referential structure at all. Thus we would not expect to see any evidence of either anger at underpayment or guilt at overpayment. If you can get away with paying someone too little, bigger fool he. It would be interesting to look for some anthropological data to test the conjecture that only in cultures like our own do we see justice phenomena at all.

17

The Experiment
and the Experimenter

Experiments as Social Situations

In this chapter we widen the scope of attention to include the experimenter as well as the experimental subjects and their behaviors. We shall be concerned with the experimenter in two senses: first, as his actions and attitudes affect the actions and attitudes of subjects in experiments; and second, as he views his own actions in terms of moral and ethical considerations.

Ideas and issues raised in this chapter are of necessity more subjective than those in previous chapters, and often there is no consensus on what is known or what should be done. However by describing the issues along with my own ideas about them, I hope to give you enough information to reach your own independent conclusions. Some readers of this book, I hope, will later become professional social psychologists, and early exposure to some of these concerns will give you time to reflect upon some problems and some solutions.

For the majority of readers who do not plan to become social psychologists, the purpose of this chapter is to give some acquaintance with issues of concern to practitioners in the field. Social psychologists sometimes have a reputation, for example, of being unconcerned about the lives and welfare of their human experimental subjects. In most cases this reputation is undeserved, but it persists because research reports and textbooks typically do not describe measures taken to protect the welfare or the rights of subjects. In addition some discussion of ethical issues may help to discourage practices by a few social psychologists which are not in the best interests of their subjects. An introduction to ethical concerns in experimentation can serve as a foundation for informed exercise of judgment by citizens to influence policy legislation on future research in social psychology.

Some of the discussions that follow might be construed as more critical than they are intended to be. As a cautionary note before we begin, remember that it always is easier to criticize than to offer constructive suggestions for changes. I am aware that there are some problems in experimental social psychology for which I cannot propose completely satisfactory solutions. This does not mean that the problems should be ignored; only that we should approach the critical task with an awareness of what we do not know. A simple criticism of experimental design, or the ethics of experimenting on people, is a cheap shot. An uninvolved spectator can always find some aspect of a situation which is vulnerable to criticism: the experimental results do not support the hypothesis with perfect certainty, the experimenter over-

423

*The
Experiment
and
the
Experimenter*

looked something in the design or forgot to control some factor that later proved troublesome, the rights of subjects were not guaranteed with 100 percent certainty. To point out problems in this way is simply to say that we live in an imperfect world. As Freud was fond of saying after hearing one of his colleagues describe a patient's neuroses, "Yes, but what is to be done?" By placing a chapter of criticism like this one at the end of this text, I hope that readers can bring to it some appreciation of the great difficulties of designing experiments and of respecting human subjects' rights and welfare. Experimental design requires considerable ingenuity and sustained, concentrated effort—things that are not oversupplied to social psychologists any more than they are to the rest of us. Social psychologists, being human, have as much difficulty with ethical and moral issues as anyone else. It is unreasonable to expect to find them all either incredibly brilliant experimentalists, or paragons of moral virtue.

Experimenter Effects

The experimental method was developed in the natural sciences, especially chemistry and physics, in which the investigator had few worries about interaction between himself and the materials being studied. Chemicals do not react to people; they react to other chemicals. Weights and magnets may be kept on the shelf with no attention until it is convenient to study them.

As the newer science of biology developed beyond the stage of observing animals in their environments to a stage where experimental control became necessary, investigators became aware that their materials were much more interactive and much more fragile than those studied by other scientists. How an animal behaves can be importantly influenced by the presence or the actions of the biologist—some animals will not eat or mate in the presence of humans or in captivity, for instance. Living cells die if not maintained in a favorable environment until they are studied. Quite often, the simple act of observation is impossible without doing something to the organism which destroys it—any frog gets dissected only once in biology class. The term biologists apply to this sort of investigation is *destructive observation;* we can study certain phenomena only by destroying the conditions which cause them to occur. (Interestingly, destructive observation became a problem in physics only after it had been recognized in biology. Study of subatomic particles, which has been conducted only in the 20th century, always requires major disturbance of the phenomena studied. We observe effects of electrons, for example, only by breaking up the atom in which they occur.)

Survey researchers who study social attitudes and behavior came to recognize a similar sort of problem. Surveys rely on asking people what they think and how they act (or how they would act in a hypothetical situation), and the way in which a question is phrased can have major effects on the answers people give. If you ask people what social class they think they belong to—upper class, middle class, lower class—virtually everyone will say "middle class" and hardly anyone will say upper or lower cass. If you substitute "working class" for "lower class"—the terms are equivalent to a sociologist—somewhere between 25 and 35 percent of the respondents will choose that alternative.

For certain advertising purposes—"Of those dentists replying, 9 out of 10 said they prefer sugarless gum for their patients who chew gum"—it may be desirable to bias respondents' answers, but presumably sociologists would like to avoid it. In survey research considerable effort is spent designing nonbiasing questions, which are called *nonreactive* or *unobtrusive measures*. When these are used, it is possible to study peoples' attitudes or behaviors without having to ask them anything, or without telling them they are being studied. We could ascertain preference among brands of gum by counting sales at a counter, or study groups of people by pretending to be members of the group rather than social scientists. We sometimes can tell which television programs are most popular by comparing water usage—caused by flushing toilets—to the time commercials are shown on different stations.

Within the past decade, experimentalists in social psychology have become aware that they exert influences—unintended, and sometimes strong influences—over subjects' behaviors in their experiments. When such influences are later recognized, as they were in Schulman's conformity experiment discussed in Chap. 3, they often give us valuable information beyond that gained in the original experiment. However what worries experimentalists is that such influences may creep into their designs to produce unwanted—or, what is worse, unrecognized—sorts of effects. What have come to be termed *experimenter effects* are regularly discovered in even the most careful experimental designs, and in some cases, we have evidence of dramatic strength of their effects.

Rosenthal conducted an extensive research program to study the strength and the generality of experimenter effects upon data. The basic research setting involves using two sets of experimenters, one told to expect the data to look one way, and the second told to expect the data to look another way. For example, one of the standard tasks is to present subjects a set of pictures of human faces, and to ask them to judge how "successful" each person depicted has been, on a scale ranging from -10 ("extreme failure") to $+10$ ("extreme success"). One set of experimenters is told to expect subjects' judgments to range between 0 and -5; the other experimenters are told to expect subjects' judgments to range between 0 and $+5$. Experimenters are told to be careful not to communicate their expectancies to subjects. However in most cases, experimenters with different expectancies about subjects' judgments actually do elicit statistically significant differences from them. The effect occurs strongly and repeatedly in a variety of situations and experimental tasks, and even in the face of efforts by the experimenters (who typically are *not* highly trained) to conceal their expectancies.

As the term is used, "experimenter effects" are always unwanted and unintended when they occur. If a particular effect were desired, the experimenter would design his study so as to guarantee that it would be included. Only those effects that the original investigator neither intends nor recognizes ahead of time are designated by the term experimenter effects.

425

*The
Experiment
and
the
Experimenter*

One way to view experimenter effects is to say that they are independent variables which produce some important influence over the measures of the dependent variables in a situation. You recall that experimental design revolves around the testing of hypotheses or knowledge claims of the form "If X, then Y." In such a hypothesis, the X becomes the manipulated independent variable in an experiment, and the Y is the predicted measure of the dependent variable. When experimenter effects occur, they affect the dependent variable Y; thus we may say that they function as unrecognized independent variables, or Xs. Something the experimenter does, even if it involves simply being in the room with the subjects (as in Schulman's study) or having an opinion about the empirical truth of the hypothesis (as in Rosenthal's studies), affects the dependent variable in the experiment. What is serious, of course, is that the effects of this unrecognized independent variable may incorrectly be attributed to the intended independent variable.

It is helpful to recognize that experimenter effects may operate in two basic ways: they may help to confirm the experimenter's hypothesis, or they may act to disconfirm it. Either result is undesirable, since to the extent that experimenter effects operate, the hypothesis does not actually receive the empirical test the experiment was designed to provide. When the hypothesis is believed to be supported as the result of experimenter effects, we say the outcome is a *false positive* result. When experimenter effects act to disconfirm the hypothesis, we say the outcome is a *false negative* result.

As Rosenthal's work suggests, false positive results are far more dangerous than false negatives, because to some extent false negatives tend to be self-correcting. Presumably the experimenter believes the truth of his hypothesis. Thus when it is disconfirmed by the experiment, he is likely to look around for some "reason" such as experimenter effects that could have produced the disconfirmation and still allow him to believe in the hypothesis. When a believed hypothesis is confirmed as a false positive, such additional investigation is much less likely. In this case, the search for experimenter effects is likely to be undertaken by others than the person originally designing the experiment. Let us examine these two types of biasing in more detail.

False Negative Results

Something almost guaranteed to produce unexpected effects is strong emotions on the part of subjects, particularly feelings of hostility. Experimental social psychologists have so far directed little systematic attention to causes and consequences of hostility, and so they are unlikely to recognize features of their experiments which can produce it. As we shall see, strong emotion can alter subjects' behaviors enough to disconfirm falsely the experimental hypotheses.

Mills (1962) reanalyzed the Schachter experiment on the reactions of members of different types of groups to an actor who expresses deviant opinions. Mills' analysis shows quite clearly that in three out of the four conditions of the experiment, behavior was not what would be expected from

Schachter's conceptualization, and that the behavior in those three conditions is consistent with an interpretation that the experimenter produced hostility in subjects.

You recall from Chap. 5 that Schachter's discussion groups all contained a confederate, the deviate, who expressed views opposite from those of most members. There were two other independent variables. "Cohesiveness" was manipulated by putting subjects either in a group they had requested, or in another group. "Relevance" was manipulated by making their assigned discussion topic apply either directly or not at all to the group's interests.

Schachter expected that the same basic pattern of communication would appear in all groups: beginning low, then rising rapidly, and finally falling off as he was rejected. This pattern, which *was* observed in the "hi cohesive, hi relevance" groups is shown in Fig. 17–1. But the actual communication patterns for the groups are shown in Fig. 17–2, which I constructed from data in Schachter's Table 7.

How are we to make sense of these results? Mills argues persuasively that it is reasonable to suppose that the experimenter inadvertently induced hostility in subjects by the procedures to manipulate the independent variables. The Low Cohesive manipulation involved first asking people which groups they wanted to join, and then putting them in other groups. In other words it may have looked to subjects in these conditions as though they were asked their preferences, and then deliberately ignored. Quite reasonably, they might become angry at this. Similarly the nonrelevant manipulation involved interrupting the normal business of the club and forcing members to discuss an irrelevant topic. Again it is reasonable to suppose that this procedure would make them angry. The HR condition, by comparison, probably was very enjoyable to subjects. Not only did

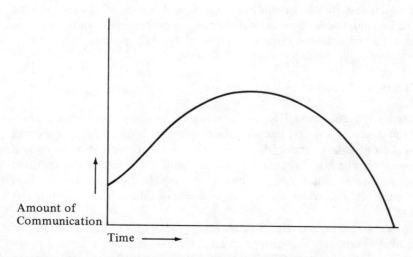

FIGURE 17–1 Communication and rejection of deviate

427

*The
Experiment
and
the
Experimenter*

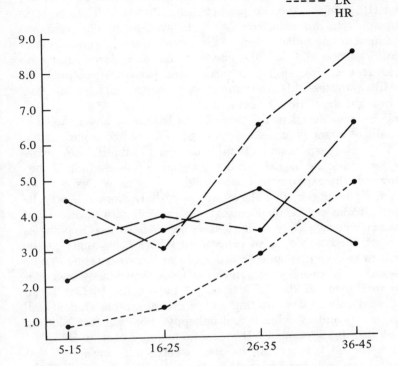

FIGURE 17–2 Actual communication to deviate,
"mild" and "strong" rejectors combined. (Calculated
from Schachter, 1951, Table 7.)

they get the group they preferred, but the experimenter flattered them by asking for their opinions on Johnny Rocco.

Though Mills indicates that it was the experimenter who induced the anger, it would be difficult for subjects to express hostility towards him. Norms of politeness, the status of the experimenter, and lack of opportunity prevented this. What subjects could do in the three conditions where they may have been angry is to displace anger from the experimenter to the most available and reasonable scapegoat: the deviate. The amount of communication directed towards the deviate, which we may suppose consisted largely of criticism and attempts to make him admit he was wrong, thus reflected anger produced, not only by his opinions, but by the experimenter's earlier treatment of subjects. Most other evidence presented by Schachter—such things as number of interruptions per group, choices for various committees, and desire to remain in the group—are consistent with Mills' hostility interpretation.

It would be a mistake to conclude from this either that the Schachter experiment was poorly designed, or that the results are unreliable. The most useful result of the experiment, the pattern of communication to the deviate in the HR group, is the one predicted, and the hostility interpretation does not apply to this condition. With the wisdom of hindsight, we would not manipulate the independent variables *cohesiveness* and *relevance* the same way Schachter did, but the effects of his procedures are by no means obvious. It was, after all, eleven years after Schachter published his results that Mills published his alternative interpretation, and in that time nobody else brought these ideas to general attention.

The general problem faced in this experiment is that of anger, and the most usual result of anger is to disconfirm hypotheses of the experimenter. Sometimes in simpler experiments than Schachter's, subjects can figure out with some accuracy the hypotheses being tested in the research. If they feel hostile towards the experimenter, one good way to show this is to *try* to disconfirm his predictions, to behave just oppositely from the way he seems to expect. It may not be obvious that it is possible also to disconfirm hypotheses rather well even if you don't know just what those hypotheses are. All a subject needs to do in an experiment where he is angry at the experimenter is to behave psychotically—to act in as bizarre a fashion as he can imagine—and he is virtually guaranteed success. Any bizarre behavior is very likely to disconfirm the "If X then Y" hypothesis. In fact I can remember from my college days waiting with a group of other students, all of us about to be involuntary subjects and unhappy about the fact, plotting to try to "mess up his experiment." It was frighteningly easy to do.

Hostility is produced, most often, in cases where individuals feel that some important norm is being violated. In the Schachter experiment, the norm might be one which says you don't ask people's preferences and then totally disregard them. Looking for possible norm violations in the design of contemplated experiments is a good place to begin attempts to avoid hostility problems.

There is a practice which is so widely followed that to criticize it may be ineffective, but it produces large amounts of hostility, and very probably, unreliable experimental results. This is requiring students enrolled in introductory psychology and sociology classes to act as unwilling participants in experimental research. At many colleges it is a requirement of the introductory course to serve as a subject in a number of hours of experiments, and this involuntary servitude induces considerable hostility among a sizable portion of the subjects. The alternative of using paid volunteer subjects exclusively may increase the costs of research, but it is probably money well spent. The consequences of hostility among subjects can negate the most careful theoretical work and experimental design.

Finally, there is the less concrete but equally important matter of doing everything in the experimenter's power to minimize unpleasant aspects of the experiment for subjects. It is unfortunately too easy to become so wrapped up in the theory or the experimental design that little things like keeping subjects waiting beyond the scheduled time, or treating them coldly, get overlooked by the experimenter. The experimental situation

429

*The
Experiment
and
the
Experimenter*

resembles an elaborate testing procedure to many subjects, and they are understandably anxious about their performance in it. Explaining (when appropriate) that they are not being tested, that their actions and attitudes will be treated confidentially, and in general showing respect for subjects as individuals are important.

Tension-producing aspects of experimentation should be minimized wherever possible (a point discussed more fully later). Often a simple matter like choosing a neutral word in place of an evaluative or a threatening word can make the experiment more pleasant. I prefer the words "participant" to "subject"; "study" to "experiment"; and "session" to "test." If this reduces the chances of producing hostility, it is a worthwhile change.

False Positive Results

It may be surprising that the greater danger in experimentation is biasing of results *in favor of* predictions. Most subjects (and this is also true of respondents in survey research) will, if given the chance, try to "help" the experimenter by confirming his hypotheses. People seem to want to help out when they can, and what looks like helping out to a subject can be false positive results to a social psychologist. Especially in research with volunteer subjects, a major motivation for participating in the research is to contribute to knowledge. I have heard subjects say this repeatedly over the years; some even try to refuse payment for their time, and in any case the amount of payment is not large enough to induce anyone to participate against his will. As we have already noted, false positive results are particularly dangerous because the experimenter is less likely to search for them than he is for false negatives.

Just how cooperative subjects are willing to be, and just how much they want to "help" an experimenter is demonstrated dramatically in experiments by Orne (1962). Orne was originally interested in studying some effects of hypnosis, particularly the extent to which hypnotized subjects are more willing to obey suggestions than nonhypotized subjects. (Hypnosis, I am sure you have heard, is a state characterized by heightened suggestibility. However this bit of lore is not particularly well supported by empirical evidence. People are not much more receptive to suggestions while hypnotized, providing they have volunteered to participate in the study.)

To study differences in suggestibility, Orne needed to find a task which was rather unpleasant for subjects, so that at some point they would refuse to comply with his instructions to do it. Then he could compare how long hypnotized subjects persisted to how long the same or similar subjects persisted when not hypnotized. The task he tried was to ask subjects to add up columns of numbers on sheets; each sheet contained enough numbers for over 200 separate additions, and the subject was presented a stack of 2000 sheets. The numbers were random digits, which a computer will generate obligingly for researchers. We might expect that subjects would try to comply with the request for a short time, but boredom at the senseless task, and despair at ever completing 2000 sheets would cause them to quit after awhile. In fact after almost *six hours* the experimenter had to terminate the study—subjects continued to work away at the addition!

To make the task more unpleasant, Orne then tried a variation on the task. This time, the subject was given two stacks: one stack of sheets filled with random digits, and one stack of "instruction cards" face down, as in a Monopoly game. The task was to take a sheet of numbers, perform the additions, and then take an instruction card to learn what to do next. *Every single instruction card said:*

> You are to tear up the sheet of paper which you have just completed into a minimum of 32 pieces and go on to the next sheet and continue working as you did before; when you have completed this piece of paper, pick up the next card which will instruct you further. Work as accurately and as rapidly as you can. (Orne, 1962, 777.)

Orne does not report exact data from this variant, but there is again no evidence of subjects' refusing to comply. Orne concluded:

> Thus far, we have been singularly unsuccessful in finding an experimental task which would be discontinued, or indeed, refused by subjects in an experimental setting. Not only do subjects continue to perform boring, un-rewarding tasks, but they do so with few errors and little decrement in speed. (Orne, 1962, 778.)

From our point of view, the significance of these results is to show the degree to which experimental subjects are willing to put up with what must appear to be ridiculous and senseless requests from the experimenter. If they will try this hard to comply with obviously meaningless requests, we may infer that they will try even harder to help an experimenter when they believe his work and his hypotheses are worthwhile.

As as first step towards minimizing bias in favor of hypotheses, experimenters can try not to reveal hypotheses to subjects. Insofar as possible, the experimenter must try to maintain a neutral manner; accepting of any response which seems natural to subjects in the experiment, not smiling or otherwise indicating when they act "correctly." Keeping hypotheses of the study from subjects is certainly not a unique problem for experimentalists; in no type of social science research—surveys, participant observation, simple observation, and so on—are subjects told the hypotheses being tested in a study. Beyond this it seems wise to test ideas in the simplest imaginable experimental design. Making an experimental design more complicated or "rich" than absolutely necessary for the sake of making it interesting or real-life brings along a great danger of introducing unwanted independent variables.

Even in the absence of complete information about all the possible ways in which an experimenter might influence subjects, sometimes it is possible to minimize these effects by essentially taking the experimenter out of the situation. A relatively sophisticated technique for doing this is the double-

431

*The
Experiment
and
the
Experimenter*

blind design, which has long been a standard practice in pharmacological research, but which has only recently been adapted for social psychological experimentation. For example, a doctor testing a new drug may not know whether he is administering the new drug or the old one to a given patient. When this method of safeguarding is applied, experimenters who come into direct contact with subjects do not know the hypotheses being tested. For example, the person running the experiment may be unaware to which treatment condition particular subjects have been assigned. This technique requires a study design in which the manipulation of independent variables may be accomplished in a separate phase from that in which data are collected on the dependent variable.

Although the double-blind approach is an extremely useful technique for some types of studies, it is not such a universal solution for problems of biasing in social psychology as it has been for medical research. One reason for this is that quite often it is difficult to design a two-phase experiment for certain types of problems. For example, it would be impossible that the experimenter in the basic Asch conformity experiment would not know who was the subject and who were the confederates. Similarly many studies require slightly different physical arrangements of laboratory equipment for the different conditions, and some require that at some point during the experiment the subject will respond in a way that his treatment condition is made known to the experimenter. As a practical matter, even when the logic of the design can be preserved in a two-phase experiment, the amount of time and the size of the experimental staff required for the study are increased sharply. However when it is possible to eliminate the experimenter from the situation, the double-blind technique is a particularly effective way of minimizing the risk that some inadvertent act of his will produce biased data.

Including the Experimenter

If the experimenter cannot be eliminated as by the double-blind technique, the alternative is to build him in by including him explicitly in the conceptualization of the study. By this approach the presence of the experimenter becomes one of several independent variables recognized ahead of time in the interaction situation. For example, when subjects are asked to play a bargaining game with each other for points, we recognize that they also are playing a game with the experimenter for his approval: what will the experimenter think of them if they adopt a particular strategy? Our analysis of the Mintz experiment on panics in Chap. 11 indicated that subjects in his No Reward condition probably responded to the possibilities for approval or disapproval from the experimenter in deciding how to act, and Alexander and Weil (Chap. 13) show similar effects in a prisoner's dilemma situation.

We have already seen one example of explicitly including the experimenter, in the decision-making model first presented by Camilleri and

Berger (Chap. 11). This model predicts acceptance of influence under conditions of disagreement between pairs of subjects as a function of three utilities or rewards. The utility u_3 is the way in which the experimenter is explicitly conceptualized as part of the experimental situation.

As the example indicates, explicitly including the experimenter in making predictions for subjects' behavior requires a precise conceptualization and a fairly advanced level of theory. No longer is it possible to define all factors except the independent variables as extraneous, and to try to eliminate them. Instead the experimenter who employs this approach must state explicitly all factors he can see in the situation, and then predict how they will affect the dependent variables of interest. Besides theoretical understanding, this implies a need for a familiar experimental situation, so that the experimenter can be reasonably certain that subjects' interpretations of the situation will be quite close to that intended in the design. An important aid in this method is test groups in which procedures may be tested for clarity and workability, and in which subjects may be interviewed about their understanding of features of the situation.

Concern with experimenter effects has had, on the whole, a beneficial effect on social psychological experimentation. It has forced investigators to be concerned with factors prior to those deliberately built into the experimental design, and to recognize that these pre-experimental factors can have important consequences for behavior in the experiment. The attitudes and experiences subjects bring to the laboratory can have effects quite as strong as the independent variables built into the social situation. How subjects react to the experimenter can be just as important a topic for social psychology as how they react to an experimental situation.

Experimenter Responsibility

Anyone who studies human subjects takes on enormous responsibilities not needed in other types of research. He has the usual responsibilities of careful research design and the rules of permissible inference, but in addition, he must protect the welfare of subjects while they are studied.[1] Protection of what is studied is not at all an issue in physics or chemistry, only occasionally is it an issue in biology, fairly often it is a concern in zoology and veterinary medicine, and it should always be the primary concern in sociology, psychology, and social psychology. Sometimes it is better not to have knowledge if it can be had only by sacrificing the human subjects—on those grounds we reject the (sometimes scientifically valuable) medical research performed in Nazi concentration camps, or in American prisons.

Deciding just what constitutes concern for subjects' welfare sometimes is

---

[1] Concern for subjects' *privacy* approaches fetishism in behavioral research; it is virtually impossible to link any individual with data from any study. While I believe privacy of subjects is vital, this concern should not receive all the attention of the investigator. My impression is that subjects are much less concerned with maintaining their anonymity than they are about honesty and understanding purposes of research.

433

*The
Experiment
and
the
Experimenter*

not a clearcut matter. Clearly it was morally wrong for Nazi physicians to study the limits of endurance by working, starving, or freezing people to death. Clearly it was wrong to allow American convicts to live with syphilis for decades beyond the development of penicillin—a project begun quite legitimately in the days before there was any general cure for syphilis, and one that has yielded some useful knowledge about the natural course of that disease. But suppose a psychologist has a procedure which he is sure will produce vast improvement in children's reading. To demonstrate success, he selects one classroom of children to receive the treatment, and one room to serve as a control and not receive the treatment. We might expect, especially if the treatment were a simple one, that parents of the control group children would be unhappy that their children were (relatively) deprived. Would this be a legitimate objection on moral grounds? How about the use of convict volunteers to try out new pharmaceutical drugs? I do not have all the answers as to which sorts of experiments are morally defensible, or even a complete set of criteria for deciding questions of morality. However I do have opinions about some of the more familiar issues faced in social psychological research.

The vast majority of social psychological experimentation involves some sort of deception. Subjects are told something that is not true about themselves or about the social situation of the experiment: confederates are presented as real subjects; interaction is controlled so that it looks like others are doing something they are not doing. Most situations that have been studied experimentally have been studied this way precisely because the investigator needed to produce a situation that does not occur frequently in the natural setting; and producing any controlled social situation—an experiment in social psychology, or a smooth, pleasant dinner party—involves some degree of deception.

Deception research is particularly susceptible to problems of secrecy. Subjects, when they appear for an experiment, must not know about certain key features of the design, or else they cannot participate in any meaningful way in the study. Nobody who has read this text, for example, can ever be a subject in the Asch conformity experiment or in the Sherif experiment on formation of norms. In a psychological sense, then, deception research produces its own particular form of destructive observation—participation in it makes the subject unfit for further participation in other related experiments.

Maintaining secrecy about the deceptive features of a study is essential during the time it takes to complete the experiments. If subjects who have participated in the study tell their friends about it before they participate, these friends are likewise unfit for the research. As you can well imagine, in principle it would be possible for a single subject to render an entire potential subject population unfit simply by telling them all about his experiences immediately after the experiment. The word social psychologists use when a subject pool becomes unfit due to information about an experiment is *contamination*. It conjures up pictures of sewage in a swimming pool, and to an experimentalist it is about as undesirable.

One way some have tried to avoid problems of contamination is not to reveal the deception to subjects after the experiment. Perhaps for example, subjects who have participated in a conformity experiment do not need to be told about the social situation and the confederates. I find this solution unacceptable. Deception experimentation is lying, and anyone who lies to someone has a moral obligation to set him right. Every subject in a deception experiment should have a full explanation of all arrangements and the reasons for them as soon as possible after the experiment.

In my experience, contamination has not been a problem when subjects receive a full and complete explanation immediately following an experiment. If the experimenter is completely honest about the experimental arrangments and the reasons for them, most people can understand the importance of not talking to others about the study and will keep confidence. When the experiment *is* explained fully—as I believe it must be—lack of contamination problems is a good indication of success at minimizing unpleasantness for subjects and explaining the importance of the research. Any subject who feels he has been misused can quickly put the experimenter out of business by telling others about his experiences. With a well designed study, fully explained, this will not happen.

Exactly how to protect human subjects from harmful or potentially harmful experiences is a very complex and difficult issue. Within the past decade, the National Institutes of Health, which is the branch of the federal government which funds most research involving humans, has imposed the "informed consent" criterion for studies using human subjects. This criterion requires that potential subjects be informed as fully as possible about both the gains from the research and any potential harmful side-effects to themselves. The criterion of informed consent became law after a particularly frightening story of hospital patients who were injected with live cancer cells without their knowledge, and it is designed to prevent such cases in future medical research.

Unfortunately, however, informed consent is much more applicable to medical research than to social psychological experimentation. There are two primary reasons for this. First, informed consent to any deception experimentation such as the conformity experiment is impossible. There is no way to conduct such experimentation after informing the subject of all deceptive features of the experimental design. Second, and more important in my opinion, exactly what constitutes psychological stress, and how much of it a person can stand, are not at all well understood. *Most people simply do not know* how they will respond to social situations involving deception or tension. If anything, people seem to overestimate their own capacities to tolerate stresses. To ask a subject to give his informed consent in such matters is to ask him to make a judgment for which he is not equipped by knowledge. It is putting on the subject a judgmental matter which is rightly the experimenter's: if anyone is competent to decide whether a given subject is able to endure a given experiment, it is the experimenter who has seen many other subjects and who knows the situation—not the subject who has never encountered the situation before.

435

*The
Experiment
and
the
Experimenter*

Although it is not a perfectly satisfactory solution, a thorough review of procedures of any experiment, including plans for explanation to subjects, by professionals not associated with the research project has been adopted in most places for social science research. A "peer review" committee composed of others who understand the nature and the risks of experimentation must approve any social science research project before it is undertaken in most universities and research institutes. The peer review committee procedure guarantees that a disinterested but competent group of professionals will evaluate potential projects, and that the experimenter will be held accountable to a specific body of individuals for any unpleasant side effects of his research.

Before the peer review committee meets, the individual experimenter should take all possible steps to minimize stress in research, and to watch carefully for signs of unexpected reactions to the experimental arrangements. Although the vast majority of individuals are able to undergo experimentation with no ill effects whatsoever—literally millions of people have been subjects in social science research by now—to be on the safe side the experimenter should treat every subject as if he were highly unstable, apt to suffer psychic damage from very little stress. It is better to err on the side of too much caution when using human subjects.

During the actual running of an experiment, some member of the research staff must exercise surveillance over the procedures and over the subjects. For example, during a conformity experiment there should be an observer watching the subject for undue signs of stress, and the observer should be ready to interrupt the experiment if it appears necessary. Although I have watched hundreds of conformity experiments without ever seeing one in which it was necessary to terminate the group, there has invariably been an observer who was prepared to do so if necessary.

In an ideal experimental situation, the investigator has planned the research carefully to eliminate and to minimize as much as possible any deception and psychological stress for the subjects. He has subjected his research proposal and experimental procedures to a competent peer review committee for approval, and has made whatever modifications he and the committee work out together. Recruiting of volunteer subjects, and scheduling of them for groups is accomplished in a way which reflects concern for their welfare and for their rights as individuals. Immediately after the experiment each subject receives a full explanation of all features of the design and the reasons for them, all false information is corrected, and any questions he has are answered fully. Under these conditions, careful research can be conducted, subjects will generally find participation in the research to be an interesting and an enjoyable experience, and social psychological experimentation can earn deservedly high esteem as a means of increasing knowledge.

Bibliography

The bibliography was compiled by the author and D. Randall Smith. Its aim is to extend the range of the text beyond what is contained in its chapters. Time and space limitations preclude a *complete* bibliography, but such an encyclopedia would be of little use anyway. The titles listed treat subjects of the chapters of *Actions and Actors* in more detail than the book. In some cases they provide an alternative view to the one expressed in the book. In all cases the attempt is to select those articles and books which can provide the foundation for a thorough knowledge of these topics.

Entries are selected on three bases. First, research specifically mentioned in the text is included and indicated by an asterisk (*). Second, "classic" articles, those generally recognized as providing significant contributions to knowledge, are included. Third, recent research on topics in the text are included. Entries in the first two categories are selected on the basis of the compilers' judgment that it is important for a student to be familiar with the research described. For the third category, recent research, it is much more difficult to assess significance without the perspective of history. Consequently, very recent articles and books constitute the largest proportion of the references to most chapters. It is the latest information available, but it must be left to future readers to evaluate its usefulness.

The reference style used is the standard style of the American Psychological Association and the American Sociological Association, as revised in 1975.

A Note to the Reader and Chapter 1

Ball-Rokeach, S. J. From pervasive ambiguity to a definition of the new situation. *Sociometry*, 1973, *36* (September):378–389.

Batchelor, J. P., & Goethals, G. R. Spatial arrangements in freely formed groups. *Sociometry*, 1972, *35* (June):270–279.

*Bauer, E. A. Personal space: A study of blacks and whites. *Sociometry*, 1973, *36* (September):402–408.

*Bovard, E. Social norms and individual. *Journal of Abnormal and Social Psychology*, 1948, *43*:62–69.

Boyanowsky, E. O., & Allen, V. L. Ingroup norms and self-identity as determinants of discriminatory behavior. *Journal of Personality and Social Psychology*, 1973, *25* (March):408–418.

*Como, P. A hubba-hubba-hubba. (Song by Adamson and McHugh, released 1945.)

*Durkheim, E. *Suicide*. New York: The Free Press, 1963. (Originally published, 1897).

*Festinger, L. A theory of social comparison processes. *Human Relations*, 1954, *7*:117–140.

Gamson, W. A. *Power and discontent*. Homewood, Ill.: Dorsey Press, 1968.

*Hare, A. P., Borgatta, E. F., & Bales, R. F. *Small groups.* New York: Alfred A. Knopf, 1965.

*Hood, W. R., & Sherif, M. Verbal report and judgment of an unstructured stimulus. *The Journal of Psychology,* 1962, *54* (July):121–130.

*Jacobs, R. C., & Campbell, D. T. The perpetuation of an arbitrary tradition through several generations of a laboratory microculture. *Journal of Abnormal and Social Psychology,* 1961, *62,* 649–658.

Jones, E. E. Conformity as a tactic of ingratiation. In E. P. Hollander and R. G. Hunt (Eds.), *Current perspectives in social psychology.* New York: Oxford University Press, 1971.

Kiesler, S. B., Preference for predictability or unpredictability as mediator of reactions to norm violations. *Journal of Personality and Social Psychology,* 1973, *27* (September):354–359.

Labovitz, S., & Hagedorn, R. Measuring social norms. *Pacific Sociological Review,* 1973, *16* (July):283–303.

Machiavelli, N. *[The prince and selected discourses: Machiavelli.]* (D. Donno, Ed. and trans.). New York: Bantam Books, 1966.

*Potter, S. *The theory and practice of gamesmanship; or, the art of winning games without actually cheating.* New York: Henry Holt & Co., 1948.

*Rohrer, J. H., Baron, S. H., Hoffman, E. L., & Swander, D. V. The stability of autokinetic judgments. *Journal of Abnormal and Social Psychology,* 1954, *49* (October):595–597.

*Rosenthal, R. *Experimenter effects in behavioral research.* New York: Appleton-Century-Crofts, 1966.

*Sherif, M. Group influences upon the formation of norms and attitudes. In E. Maccoby, T. Newcomb, & E. Hartley (Eds.), *Readings in social psychology.* New York: Holt, Rinehart and Winston, 1958.

Stone, W. F. Patterns of conformity in couples varying in intimacy. *Journal of Personality and Social Psychology,* 1973, *27* (September):413–418.

*Sumner, W. G. *Folkways.* Boston: Ginn Publications, 1940. (Originally published, 1906.)

Thibaut, J. W., & Kelley, H. H. On norms. In E. P. Hollander & R. G. Hunt (Eds.), *Current perspectives in social psychology.* New York: Oxford University Press, 1971.

*Townsend, R. *Up the organization.* New York: Alfred A. Knopf, 1970.

*Wolfe, Tom. *The kandy-kolored tangerine-flake streamline baby.* New York: Pocket Books, Inc., 1971.

Chapter 2

Allen, V. L., & Newtson, D. Development of conformity and independence. *Journal of Personality and Social Psychology,* 1972, *22* (April):18–30.

*Asch, S. Effects of group pressure upon the modification and distortion of judgments. In E. Maccoby, T. Newcomb, & E. Hartley (Eds.), *Readings in social psychology.* New York: Holt, Rinehart and Winston, 1958.

Crawford, J. L., & Haaland, G. A. Predecisional information seeking and subsequent conformity in the social influence process. *Journal of Personality and Social Psychology,* 1972, *23* (July):112–119.

Darley, J. M., Morarity, T., Darley, S., & Berscheid, E. Increased conformity as a function of prior deviation. *Journal of Experimental Social Psychology,* 1974, *10* (May):211–223.

°Deutsch, M., & Gerard, H. B. A study of normative and informational social influences upon individual judgment. *Journal of Abnormal and Social Psychology,* 1955, *51* (November):629–636.

°Dittes, J. E., & Kelley, H. H. Effects of different conditions of acceptance upon conformity to group norms. *Journal of Abnormal and Social Psychology,* 1956, 53:100–107.

Hollander, E. P., & Willis, R. H. Some current issues in the psychology of conformity and nonconformity. In E. P. Hollander & R. G. Hunt (Eds.), *Current perspectives in social psychology.* New York: Oxford University Press, 1971.

°Jung, C. G. *Man and his symbols.* New York: Dell Publishing Co., 1971.

°Kelley, H., & Shapiro, M. An experiment on conformity to group norms where conformity is detrimental to group achievement. *American Sociological Review,* 1954, *19*:667–677.

°Lawrence, D. H. *The virgin and the gypsy.* New York: Bantam Books, 1971.

Nosanchuk, T. A. & Lightstone, J. Canned laughter and public and private conformity. *Journal of Personality and Social Psychology,* 1974, 29 (January): 153–156.

Riesman, D., Glazer, N., & Denney, R. *The lonely crowd.* New York: Doubleday, 1953.

°San Francisco Chronicle. July 6, 1972, p. 1.

Toder, N. L., & Marcia, J. E. Ego identity status and response to conformity pressure in college women. *Journal of Personality and Social Psychology,* 1973, 26 (May):287–294.

Willis, R. H. The basic response modes of conformity, independence, and anticonformity. In E. P. Hollander & R. G. Hunt (Eds.), *Classic contributions to social psychology.* New York: Oxford University Press, 1972.

Wolosin, R., Sherman, S. J., & Mynatt, C. R. Perceived social influence in a conformity situation. *Journal of Personality and Social Psychology,* 1972, 23 (August):184–191.

Chapter 3

°Back, K., Bogdonoff, M. D., Shaw, D. H., & Klein, R. F. An interpretation of experimental conformity through physiological measures. *Behavioral Science,* 1963, 8 (January):34–40.

Berger, J., Cohen, B. P., Snell, J. L., & Zeldith, M., Jr. *Types of formalization.* Boston: Houghton Mifflin Co., 1962.

°Cohen, B. P. *Conflict and conformity.* Cambridge: M.I.T. Press, 1963.

°Costell, R. H., & Liederman, P. H. Psychophysiological concomitants of social stress: the effects of conformity pressure. *Psychosomatic Medicine,* 1968, 30 (May-June):298–310.

°Dittes, J. E., & Kelley, H. K. Effects of different conditions of acceptance upon conformity to group norms. *Journal of Abnormal Social Psychology,* 1956, 53 (July):100–107.

Lewis, S. A., Langan, C. J., & Hollander, E. P. Expectation of future interaction and the choice of less desirable alternatives in conformity. *Sociometry,* 1972, 35 (September):440–447.

*Schulman, G. Asch conformity studies: Conformity to the experimenter and/or to the group? *Sociometry*, 1967, *30* (March):26–40.

Chapter 4

Bavelas, A. Leadership: man and function. In E. P. Hollander & R. G. Hunt (Eds.), *Current perspectives in social psychology*, New York: Oxford University Press, 1971.

*Chowdhry, K., & Newcomb, T. The relative abilities of leaders and non-leaders to estimate opinions of their own groups. *Journal of Abnormal and Social Psychology*, 1952, *47*, 51–57.

Fiedler, F. E. Leadership and leadership effectiveness traits: A reconceptualization of the leadership trait problem. In E. P. Hollander & R. G. Hunt (Eds.), *Classic contributions to social psychology*. New York: Oxford University Press, 1972.

Fiedler, F. E. Styles of leadership. In E. P. Hollander & R. G. Hunt (Eds.), *Current perspectives in social psychology*. New York: Oxford University Press, 1971.

Gallagher, J., & Burke, P. J. Scapegoating and leader behavior. *Social Forces*, 1974, *52* (June):481–488.

*Heider, F. *The psychology of interpersonal relations*. New York: John Wiley and Sons, 1958.

*Hollander, E. P. Conformity, status, and idiosyncrasy credit. *Psychological Review*, 1958, 65:117–127.

Kern, A. G., & Bahr, H. M. Some factors affecting leadership climate in a state parole agency. *Pacific Sociological Review*, 1974, *17*, (January):108–118.

*Merei, F. Group leadership and institutionalization. *Human Relations*, 1949, 2:23–29.

Nemeth, C., & Markowski, J. Conformity and discrepancy of position. *Sociometry*, 1972, *35* (December):562–575.

*Newcomb, T. Attitude development as a function of reference groups: The Bennington study. In H. Proshansky & B. Seidenberg (Eds.), *Basic studies in social psychology*. New York: Holt, Rinehart and Winston, 1965.

*Newcomb, T. Persistence and regression of changed attitudes: Long-range studies. *The Journal of Social Issues*, 1963, *19*, 3–14.

Read, P. B. Source of authority and the legitimation of leadership in small groups. *Sociometry*, 1974, *37* (June):189–204.

Roistacher, R. C. A microeconomic model of sociometric choice. *Sociometry*, 1974, *37* (June):219–238.

*Schachter, S. Deviation, rejection, and communication. *Journal of Abnormal and Social Psychology*, 1951, *46* (April):190–207.

Sorrentino, R. M. An extension of theory of achievement motivation to the study of emergent leadership. *Journal of Personality and Social Psychology*, 1973, *26* (June):356–368.

Stein, R. T., Geis, F. L., & Damarin, F. Perception of emergent leadership hierarchies in task groups. *Journal of Personality and Social Psychology*, 1973, *28* (October):77–87.

*United States Army. Field Manual FM 22–100, 1972.

Wahrman, R., & Pugh, M. D. Competence and conformity: Another look at Hollander's study. *Sociometry*, 1972, *35* (September):376–386.

Wahrman, R., & Pugh, M. Sex, nonconformity and influence. *Sociometry,* 1974, 37 (March):137–147.

*Weber, M. The sociology of charismatic authority. In H. Gerth and C. W. Mills (Eds.), *From Max Weber,* New York: Oxford University Press, 1958. (First published in *Wirtschaft und Gesellschaft,* 1922).

Chapter 5

Berkanovic, E. Lay conceptions of the sick role. *Social Forces,* 1972, *51* (September):53–64.

Block, J. H. Generational continuity and discontinuity in the understanding of societal rejection. *Journal of Personality and Social Psychology,* 1972, *22* (June):333–345.

Bonacich, P., & Lewis, G. H. Function specialization and sociometric judgment. *Sociometry,* 1973, *36* (March):31–41.

Chemers, M. M., & Skrzypek, G. J. Experimental test of the contingency model of leadership effectiveness. *Journal of Personality and Social Psychology,* 1972, *24* (November):172–177.

Cole, S. G. Conflict and cooperation in potentially intense conflict situations. *Journal of Personality and Social Psychology,* 1972, *22* (April):31–50.

*Cooley, C. H. *Human nature and the social order.* New York: Schocken Books, Inc., 1954. (Originally published, 1902.)

Curtis, R. L., Jr. Parents and peers: Serendipity in a study of shifting reference sources. *Social Forces,* 1974, *52* (March):368–375.

Cvetkovich, G., & Baumgardner, S. R. Attitude polarization: The relative influence of discussion group structure and reference group norms. *Journal of Personality and Social Psychology,* 1973, *26* (May):159–165.

Ellis, L. J., & Bentler, P. M. Traditional sex-determined role standards and sex stereotypes. *Journal of Personality and Social Psychology,* 1973, *25* (January): 28–34.

*Festinger, L., Schachter, S., & Back, K. The operation of group standards. In H. Proshansky & B. Seidenberg (Eds.), *Basic studies in social psychology.* New York: Holt, Rinehart and Winston, 1965.

Frey, R. L., Jr., & Adams, S. J. The negotiator's dilemma: Simultaneous in-group and out-group conflict. *Journal of Experimental Social Psychology,* 1972, *8* (July):331–346.

*Glazer, N., & Moynihan, D. P. *Beyond the melting pot* (2nd ed.). Cambridge: M.I.T. Press, 1974. (Originally published, 1964.)

Hunt, R. G. Role and role conflict. In E. P. Hollander & R. G. Hunt (Eds.), *Current perspectives in social psychology.* New York: Oxford University Press, 1971.

Hyman, H. H., & Singer, E. An introduction to reference group theory and research. In E. P. Hollander and R. G. Hunt (Eds.), *Current perspectives in social psychology.* New York: Oxford University Press, 1971.

*James, W. *Psychology.* New York: Fawcett Publications, Inc., 1963. (Originally published, 1890.)

*Kelley, H. H. Two functions of reference groups. In G. E. Swanson, T. M. Newcomb, & E. L. Hartley (Eds.), *Readings in social psychology.* New York: Henry Holt & Co., 1952.

Kelley, H. H., & Grzelak, J. Conflict between individual and common interest in an n-person relationship. *Journal of Personality and Social Psychology,* 1972, *21* (February):190–197.

*Killian, L. The significance of multiple group membership in disaster. *American Journal of Sociology,* 1952, *67* (January):309–314.

*Merton, R. K., & Rossi, A. S. Contributions to the theory of reference group behavior. In R. K. Merton (Ed.), *Social theory and social structure.* New York: Free Press, 1968.

Messe, L. A., Aronoff, J., & Wilson, J. Motivation as a mediator of the mechanisms underlying role assignments in small groups. *Journal of Personality and Social Psychology,* 1972, *24* (October):84–90.

Moore, H. A., Schmitt, R. L., & Grupp, S. E. Observations on the role-specific and orientational other. *Pacific Sociological Review,* 1973, *16* (October):509–518.

*Ofshe, R. Reference conflict and behavior. In J. Berger, M. Zelditch, & B. Anderson (Eds.), *Sociological theories in progress* (Vol. 2). Boston: Houghton Mifflin Co., 1972.

Rollins, J. H. Reference identification of youth of differing ethnicity. *Journal of Personality and Social Psychology,* 1973, *26* (May):222–231.

Shibutani, T. Reference groups as perspectives. In E. P. Hollander & R. G. Hunt (Eds.), *Classic contributions to social psychology.* New York: Oxford University Press, 1972.

*Shils, E. A. The study of the primary group. In H. D. Lasswell & D. Lerner (Eds.), *The policy sciences, recent developments in scope and methods.* Stanford: Stanford University Press, 1951.

*Siegel, S., & Siegel, A. E. Reference groups, membership groups, and attitude change. *Journal of Abnormal Social Psychology,* 1957, *55* (November):360–364.

Smith, K. H. Changes in group structure through individual and group feedback. *Journal of Personality and Social Psychology,* 1972, *24* (December):425–428.

Smith, S., & Haythorn, W. W. Effects of compatibility, crowding, group size, and leadership seniority on stress, anxiety, hostility, and annoyance in isolated groups. *Journal of Personality and Social Psychology,* 1972, *22* (April):67–69.

Tajfel, H., & Billig, M. Familiarity and categorization in intergroup behavior. *Journal of Experimental Social Psychology,* 1974, *10* (March):159–170.

Works, E. Role violations and intergroup prejudice. *Pacific Sociological Review,* 1972, *15* (July):327–344.

Chapter 6

*Bales, R. F. *Average interaction percentage matrices.* Unpublished mimeographed paper circulated in Department of Social Relations, Harvard University, 1953.

Bales, R. F. The equilibrium problem in small groups. In T. Parsons, R. F. Bales, & E. A. Shils, (Eds.), *Working papers in the theory of action.* Glencoe: The Free Press, 1953.

*Bales, R. F. *Personality and interpersonal behavior.* New York: Holt, Rinehart and Winston, 1970.

Bales, R. F., & Slater, P. E. Role differentiation in small decision-making groups. In T. Parsons & R. F. Bales (Eds.), *Family, socialization, and interaction process.* Glencoe: The Free Press, 1955.

Bales, R. F., Strodtbeck, F., Mills, T. M., & Roseborough, M. Channels of communication in small groups. *American Sociological Review*, 1951, *16*, 461–468.

*Bavelas, A., Hastorf, H., Gross, A. E., & Kite, W. R. Experiments on the alteration of group structure. In J. L. Freedman, J. M. Carlsmith, & D. O. Sears (Eds.), *Readings in social psychology*. Englewood Cliffs, N.J.: Prentice-Hall, 1971. Also in *Journal of Experimental Social Psychology*, 1965, *1*:55–70.

*Berger, J., & Conner, T. L. Performance expectations and behavior in small groups. *Acta Sociologica*, 1969, *12*, 186–197.

*Berger, J., Conner, T. L., & McKeown, W. L. Evaluations and the formation of performance expectations. *Human Relations*, 1969, *22* (December):481–502.

Berger, J., Fisek, M. H., & Conner, T. L. (Eds.). *Expectation states theory*. Cambridge: Winthrop Publishers, 1974.

Black, T. E., & Higbee, K. L. Effects of power, threat, and sex on exploitation. *Journal of Personality and Social Psychology*, 1973, *27* (September):382–388.

Blumstein, P. W. Subjective probability and normative evaluations. *Social Forces*, 1973, *52* (September):98–107.

Burkett, S. R. Self-other systems and deviant career patterns. *Pacific Sociological Review*, 1972, *15* (April):169–183.

Crawford, J. L. Task uncertainty, decision importance, and group reinforcement as determinants of communication processes in groups. *Journal of Personality and Social Psychology*, 1974, *29* (May):619–627.

Davis, J. H., Cohen, J. L., & Hornik, J. Dyadic decision as a function of the frequency distributions describing the preferences of members' constituencies. *Journal of Personality and Social Psychology*, 1973, *26* (May):178–195.

*Fisek, M. H. A model for the evolution of status structures in task-oriented discussion groups. In J. Berger, M. H. Fisek, & T. L. Conner (Eds.), *Expectation states theory*. Cambridge: Winthrop Publishers, 1974.

*Fisek, M. H., & Ofshe, R. The process of status evolution. *Sociometry*, 1970, *33* (September):327–346.

Fontaine, G. Social comparison and some determinants of expected personal control and expected performance in a novel task situation. *Journal of Personality and Social Psychology*, 1974, *29* (April):487–496.

Freese, L. Conditions for status equality in informal task groups. *Sociometry*, 1974, *37* (June):174–188.

Gjesme, T. Achievement-related motives and school performance for girls. *Journal of Personality and Social Psychology*, 1973, *26* (April):131–136.

Gustafson, D. P., & Gaumnitz, J. E. Consensus rankings in small groups: Self-rankings included and excluded. *Sociometry*, 1972, *35* (December):610–618.

*Harvey, O. J. An experimental approach to the study of status relations in informal groups. *American Sociological Review*, 1953, *18* (August):357–367.

Heinecke, C., & Bales, R. F. Developmental trends in the structure of small groups. *Sociometry*, 1953, *16* (March):7–38.

Kadane, J. & Lewis, G. H. The distribution of participation in group discussions. *American Sociological Review*, 1969, *34* (October):710–723.

Kipnis, D. Does power corrupt? *Journal of Personality and Social Psychology*, 1972, *24* (October):33–41.

Leik, R. Comment on Kadane and Lewis. *American Sociological Review*, 1969, *34* (October):723–724.

*Lewis, G. H. Role differentiation. *American Sociological Review*, 1972, *37* (August):424–434.

*Lorenz, K. *On aggression*. New York: Harcourt Brace Jovanovich, 1966.

*Mayhew, B., & Levinger, R. L. *On the emergence of oligarchy in human inter-

action. Unpublished manuscript, Temple University, 1974. (Available from Department of Sociology, Temple University, Philadelphia, Pa. 19122.)

*Michels, R. [*Political parties.*] (E. Paul & C. Paul, Trans.). New York: Free Press, 1966.

Mulder, M., Veen, P., Hijzen, T., & Jansen, P. On power equalization: A behavioral example of power-distance reduction. *Journal of Personality and Social Psychology,* 1973, *26* (May):151–158.

Mulder, M., Veen, P., Rodenburg, C., Frenken, J., & Tielens, H. The power distance reduction hypothesis on a level of reality. *Journal of Experimental Social Psychology,* 1973, *9* (March):87–96.

Olsen, M. E. The process of social power. In E. P. Hollander & R. G. Hunt (Eds.), *Current perspectives in social psychology.* New York: Oxford University Press, 1971.

Orcutt, J. D. Societal reaction and the response to deviation in small groups. *Social Forces,* 1973, *52* (December):259–267.

Reynolds, P. Comment on "the distribution of participation in group discussions" as related to group size. *American Sociological Review,* 1971, *36* (August): 704–706.

Seaver, W. B. Effects of naturally induced teacher expectancies. *Journal of Personality and Social Psychology,* 1973, *28,* (December):333–342.

Shannon, J., & Guerney, B., Jr. Interpersonal effects of interpersonal behavior. *Journal of Personality and Social Psychology,* 1973, *26* (April):142–150.

*Sherif, M., White, B. J., & Harvey, O. J. Status in experimentally produced groups. *American Journal of Sociology,* 1955, *60,* 370–379.

*Whyte, W. F. *Street corner society.* Chicago: University of Chicago Press, 1955. (Originally published, 1943.)

Willard, D., & Strodtbeck, F. L. Latency of verbal response and participation in small groups. *Sociometry,* 1972, *35* (March):161–175.

Chapter 7

*Bales, R. *Personality and interpersonal behavior.* New York: Holt, Rinehart and Winston, Inc., 1970.

*Berger, J., Cohen, B. P., & Zelditch, M. Status characteristics and expectation states. In J. Berger, M. Zelditch, Jr., & B. Anderson (Eds.), *Sociological theories in progress* (Vol. 1). Boston: Houghton Mifflin Co., 1966.

*Berger, J., Cohen, B. P., & Zelditch, M., Jr. Status characteristics and social interaction. *American Sociological Review,* 1972, *37* (June):241–255.

*Caudill, W. A. *The psychiatric hospital as a small society.* Cambridge: Harvard University Press, 1958.

*Cohen, B. P., Kiker, J. E., & Kruse, R. J. *The formation of performance expectations based on race and education: a replication.* (Technical Report No. 30). Stanford, Calif., 94305: Stanford University, Laboratory for Social Research, February 1969.

*Cohen, E. G., & Roper, S. Modification of interracial interaction disability. *American Sociological Review,* 1972, *37* (December):643–657.

Deaux, K., & Emswiller, T. Explanations of successful performance on sex-linked tasks: What is skill for the male is luck for the female. *Journal of Personality and Social Psychology,* 1974, *29* (January):80–85.

Edwards, D. W. Blacks versus whites: When is race a relevant variable? *Journal of Personality and Social Psychology*, 1974, *29* (January):39–49.

Fisek, M. H. A model for the evolution of status structures in task oriented discussion groups. In J. Berger, T. L. Conner, & M. H. Fisek (Eds.), *Expectation states theory*. Cambridge: Winthrop Publishers, 1974.

°Freese, L., & Cohen, B. P. Eliminating status generalization. *Sociometry*, 1973, *36* (June):177–193.

Green, J. A. Attitudinal and situational determinants of intended behavior. *Journal of Personality and Social Psychology*, 1972, *22* (April):13–17.

Hadley, T. R., & Jacob, T. Relationship among measures of family power. *Journal of Personality and Social Psychology*, 1973, *27* (July):6–12.

Hughes, E. C. Dilemmas and contradictions of status. *American Journal of Sociology*, 1945, *50* (January):353–359.

°Katz, I. Experimental studies in Negro-white relationships. In L. Berkowitz (Ed.), *Advances in experimental social psychology* (Vol. 5). New York: Academic Press, 1970.

°Katz, I., & Benjamin, L. Effects of white authoritarianism in biracial work groups. *Journal of Abnormal and Social Psychology*, 1960, *61* (November):448–556.

°Katz, I., & Cohen, M. The effects of training Negroes upon cooperative problem solving in biracial teams. *Journal of Abnormal and Social Psychology*, 1962, *64* (May):319–324.

Katz, I., Epps, E. G., & Axelson, L. J. Effect upon Negro digit-symbol performance of anticipated comparison with whites and other Negroes. *Journal of Abnormal and Social Psychology*, 1964, *69* (July):77–83.

°Katz, I. J., Goldston, & Benjamin, L. Behavior and productivity in biracial work groups. *Human Relations*, 1958, *11* (May):123–141.

Katz, I., Roberts, O., & Robinson, J. Effects of task difficulty, race of administrator, and instructions of digit-symbol performance of Negroes. *Journal of Personality and Social Psychology*, 1965, *2* (July):53–69.

°Kervin, J. B. Extending expectation states theory: A quantitative model. *Sociometry*, 1974, *37* (September):349–362.

°Moore, J. C. Status and influence in small group interaction. *Sociometry*, 1968, *31* (March):47–63.

°Seashore, M. J. The formation of performance expectations for self and other in an incongruent status situation. (Doctoral dissertation, Stanford University, 1968).

°Smith, J. *Gospel doctrine*, 1929. (Cited in Strodtbeck, 1951.)

°Strodtbeck, F. L. Husband-wife interaction over revealed differences. *American Sociological Review*, 1951, *16* (August):468–473.

°Strodtbeck, F. L., James, R. M., & Hawkins, C. Social status in jury deliberations. *American Sociological Review*, 1957, *22* (December):714–719. (Reprinted in A. P. Hare, E. F. Borgatta, & R. F. Bales (Eds.), *Small groups* (Rev. Ed.) New York: Alfred A. Knopf, 1965.)

°Strodtbeck, F. L., & Mann, R. D. Sex role differentiation in jury deliberations. *Sociometry*, 1956, *19* (March):3–11.

°Torrence, E. P. Some consequences of power differences on decision making in permanent and temporary three-man groups. In A. P. Hare, E. F. Borgatta, & R. F. Bales (Eds.), *Small groups*. New York: Alfred A. Knopf, 1955.

Vidmar, N. Effects of decision alternatives on the verdicts and social perceptions of simulated jurors. *Journal of Personality and Social Psychology*, 1972, *22* (May):211–218.

*Whyte, W. F. *Street corner society: The social structure of an Italian slum.* Chicago: The University of Chicago Press, 1942.

Zillman, D. Rhetorical elicitation of agreement in persuasion. *Journal of Personality and Social Psychology,* 1972, *21* (February):204–218.

Chapter 8

*Allard, A. *The human imperative.* New York: Columbia University Press, 1972.

*Ardrey, R. *The territorial imperative.* New York: Atheneum, 1966.

*Ardrey, R. *African genesis.* London: Collins, 1961.

*Bandura, A., & Kupers, C. Transmission of patterns of self-reinforcement through modeling. *Journal of Abnormal and Social Psychology,* 1964, *69* (January): 1–9.

*Bandura, A., Ross, D., & Ross, S. A comparative test of the status envy, social power, and secondary reinforcement theories of identificatory learning. *Journal of Abnormal and Social Psychology,* 1963, 67:527–534.

*Bandura, A., & Walters, R. H. Principles of social learning. In E. P. Hollander & R. G. Hunt (Eds.), *Classic contributions to social psychology.* New York: Oxford University Press, 1972.

*Bandura, A., & Walters, R. H. *Social learning and personality development.* New York: Holt, Rinehart and Winston, 1963.

*Barchas, P., Fisek, M. H. *Rhesus and freshmen: Studies in status structures.* Unpublished paper, 1969, Department of Sociology, Stanford University, Stanford, Calif., 94305.

Baron, R. A. Reducing the influence of an aggressive model: The restraining effects of peer censure. *Journal of Experimental Social Psychology,* 1972, *8* (May):266–275.

*Becker, H. S. Becoming a marijuana user. *American Journal of Sociology,* 1953, 59:235–242.

*Becker, H. S., & Geer, B. The fate of idealism in medical school. *American Sociological Review,* 1958, *23:*50–56.

Brim, O. G., Jr. Socialization in later life. In E. P. Hollander & R. G. Hunt (Eds.), *Current perspectives in social psychology.* New York: Oxford University Press, 1971.

Brim, O., & Wheeler, S. *Socialization after childhood.* New York: Wiley, 1966.

Chapman, A. J. Social facilitation of laughter in children. *Journal of Experimental Social Psychology,* 1973, *9* (November):528–541.

*Coleman, J. S. The adolescent subculture and academic achievement. *American Journal of Sociology,* 1960, 65:337–347.

Coleman, J. S. *The adolescent society.* New York: The Free Press, 1961.

Darley, J. M., & Batson, C. D. "From Jerusalem to Jerico": A study of situational and dispositional variables in helping behavior. *Journal of Personality and Social Psychology,* 1973, *27* (July):100–108.

Darley, J. M., Teger, A. I., & Lewis, L. D. Do groups always inhibit individuals' responses to potential emergencies? *Journal of Personality and Social Psychology,* 1973, *26* (June):395–399.

*Davis, K. Final note on a case of extreme isolation. *American Journal of Sociology,* 1947, 52:432–437.

*Dornbusch, S. M. The military academy as an assimilating institution. *Social Forces,* 1955, *33* (May):316–321.

Dorr, D., & Fey, S. Relative power of symbolic adult peer models in the modification of children's moral choice behavior. *Journal of Personality and Social Psychology*, 1974, *29* (March):335–341.

°Goffman, E. *Asylums*. Garden City, N.Y.: Doubleday Anchor, 1961.

°Goldstein, J., & Arms, R. Effects of observing athletic contests on hostility. *Sociometry*, 1971, *34* (March):83–90.

Greenberg, M. S., & Frisch, D. M. Effects of intentionality on willingness to reciprocate a favor. *Journal of Experimental Social Psychology*, 1972, *8* (March):99–111.

Grusec, J. E. Demand characteristics of the modeling experiment: altruism as a function of age and aggression. *Journal of Personality and Social Psychology*, 1972, *22* (May):139–148.

Grusec, J. E., & Brinker, D. B., Jr. Reinforcement for imitation as a social learning determinant with implications for sex-role development. *Journal of Personality and Social Psychology*, 1972, *21* (February):149–155.

Haier, Richard. *A comparison of two models of moral development*. (Unpublished doctoral dissertation, Johns Hopkins University, 1975.)

°Hartshorne, H., & May, M. A summary of the work of the character education inquiry. *Religious Education*, 1930, *25*:607–619.

Hildebrandt, D. E., Feldman, S. E., & Ditrichs, R. A. Rules, models, and self-reinforcement in children. *Journal of Personality and Social Psychology*, 1973, *25* (January):1–5.

Hilgard, E. R., & Bower, C. *Theories of learning*. New York: Appleton-Century-Crofts, 1966.

°Hogan, R. T. Moral conduct and moral character. *Psychological Bulletin*, 1973, *79* (April):217–232.

Hogan, R. T. *The personological tradition*. Englewood Cliffs, N.J.: Prentice-Hall, 1975.

Hogan, R., & Dickstein, E. Moral judgment and perceptions of injustice. *Journal of Personality and Social Psychology*, 1972, *23* (September):409–413.

Keasey, C. B. Experimentally induced changes in moral opinions and reasoning. *Journal of Personality and Social Psychology*, 1973, *1* (April):30–38.

°Kohn, M. Bureaucratic man: A portrait and an interpretation. *American Sociological Review*, 1971, *36* (June):461–474.

Levy, P., Lundgren, D., Ansel, M., Fell, D., Fink, B., & McGrath, S. E. Bystander effect in a demand-without-threat situation. *Journal of Personality and Social Psychology*, 1972, *24* (November):166–171.

°Logan, C. General deterrent effects of imprisonment. *Social Forces*, 1972, *51* (September):64–73.

Maccoby, E. *The development of sex differences*. Stanford: Stanford University Press, 1966.

Masor, H. N., Hornstein, H. A., & Tobin, T. Modeling, motivational independence, and helping. *Journal of Personality and Social Psychology*, 1973, *28* (November):236–248.

McClintock, C. G. Development of social motives in Anglo-American and Mexican-American children. *Journal of Personality and Social Psychology*, 1974, *29* (March):348–354.

°Merton, R. Bureaucratic structure and personality. In R. Merton (Ed.), *Social theory and social structure*. New York: The Free Press, 1968.

°Meyer, J., & Sobieszek, B. Effect of a child's sex on adult interpretations of its behavior. *Developmental Psychology*, 1972, *1*:42–48.

*Mischel, W. Theory and research on the antecedents of self-imposed delay of reward. In B. A. Maher (Ed.), *Progress in experimental personality research* (Vol. 3). New York: Academic Press, 1966.

Mischel, W., Ebbesen, E. B., & Zweiss, A. R. Cognitive and attentional mechanisms in delay of gratification. *Journal of Personality and Social Psychology,* 1972, *21* (February):204–218.

Morris, S. C., III, & Rosen, S. Effects of felt adequacy and opportunity to reciprocate on help seeking. *Journal of Experimental and Social Psychology,* 1973, *9* (May):265–276.

Noble, G. Effects of different forms of filmed aggression on children's constructive and destructive play. *Journal of Personality and Social Psychology,* 1973, *26* (April):54–59.

*Pavlov, I. P. *Conditioned reflexes.* New York: Oxford University Press, 1927.

Piliavin, J. A., & Piliavin, I. M. Effect of blood on reactions to a victim. *Journal of Personality and Social Psychology,* 1972, 23 (September):355–361.

Powers, P. C., & Geen, R. G. Effects of the behavior and the perceived arousal of a model on instrumental aggression. *Journal of Personality and Social Psychology,* 1972, 23 (August):175–183.

Ross, A. S., & Braband, J. Effect of increased responsibility on bystander intervention II: The cue value of a blind person. *Journal of Personality and Social Psychology,* 1973, 25 (February):254–258.

Schleifer, M., & Douglas, V. Effects of training on the moral judgment of young children. *Journal of Personality and Social Psychology,* 1973, *28* (October): 62–68.

Schwartz, S. H. Normative explanations of helping behavior: a critique, proposal, and empirical test. *Journal of Experimental Social Psychology,* 1973, *9* (July):349–364.

*Scott, J. F. *Internalization of norms.* Englewood Cliffs, N.J.: Prentice-Hall, 1971.

*Skinner, B. F. *Science and human behavior.* New York: Macmillan, 1953.

*Skinner, B. F. *Beyond freedom and dignity.* New York: Alfred A. Knopf, 1971.

*Skinner, B. F. *The behavior of organisms.* New York: Appleton-Century-Crofts, 1938.

Skinner, B. F. *About behaviorism.* New York: Alfred A. Kopf, 1974.

Smith, R. E., Smythe, L., & Lien, D. Inhibition of helping behavior by a similar or dissimilar nonreactive fellow bystander. *Journal of Personality and Social Psychology,* 1972, 23 (September):414–419.

*Sobieszek, B. *Adult interpretations of child behavior: A replication and extension.* Unpublished paper, 1974, Department of Sociology, University of Rochester, Rochester, N.Y. 14627.

Stumphauzer, J. S. Increased delay of gratification in young prison inmates through imitation of high-delay peer models. *Journal of Personality and Social Psychology,* 1972, *21* (January):10–17.

Thelen, M., McGuire, D., Simmonds, D. W., & Akamatsu, T. J. Effect of model-reward on the observer's recall of the modeled behavior. *Journal of Personality and Social Psychology,* 1974, 29 (January):140–144.

*Tiger, L., & Fox, J. *Men in groups.* New York: Random House, 1969.

*Verplanck, W. The control of the content of conversation. *Journal of Abnormal and Social Psychology,* 1955, *51*:668–676.

White, G. M. Immediate and deferred effects of model observation and guided and unguided rehearsal on donating and stealing. *Journal of Personality and Social Psychology,* 1972, *21* (February):139–148.

Yarrow, M., & Scott, P. M. Imitation of nurturant and nonnurturant models. *Journal of Personality and Social Psychology*, 1972, *23* (August):259–270.

Zube, M. J. Changing concepts of morality: 1948–69. *Social Forces*, 1972, *50* (March):385–393.

Introduction to Theory in Social Psychology and Chapter 9

*Abrahamson, B. Homans on exchange: Hedonism revised. *American Journal of Sociology*, 1970, *76* (September):273–285.

*Blau, P. M. *The dynamics of bureaucracy*. Chicago: University of Chicago Press, 1954.

*Blau, P. M. *Exchange and power*. New York: John Wiley and Sons, 1964.

*Coleman, J. S. Collective decisions. *Sociological Inquiry*, 1964 (Spring):166–181.

*Coleman, J. S. Foundations for a theory of collective decisions. *American Journal of Sociology*, 1966, *6* (May):615–625.

*Coleman, J. S. *The mathematics of collective action*. Chicago: Aldine Publishing Co., 1973.

*Emerson, R. M. Exchange theory, part I: A psychological basis for exchange. In S. Berger, M. Zelditch, Jr., & B. Anderson (Eds.), *Sociological theories in progress* (Vol. 2). Boston: Houghton Mifflin Co., 1972.

*Emerson, R. M. Exchange theory, part II: exchange relations and network structures. In S. Berber, M. Zelditch, Jr., & B. Anderson (Eds.), *Sociological theories in progress* (Vol. 2). Boston: Houghton Mifflin Co., 1972.

*Emerson, R. M. Power-dependence relations. *American Sociological Review*, 1962, *27* (February):31–41.

*Fort, C. *The book of the damned*. New York: Boni and Riverright, 1919.

Homans, G. Fundamental processes of social exchange. In E. P. Hollander & R. G. Hunt (Eds.), *Current perspectives in social psychology*. New York: Oxford University Press, 1971.

Homans, G. C. Social behavior as exchange. *American Journal of Sociology*, 1958, *62* (May):597–606.

*Homans, G. *Social behavior: Its elementary forms*. New York: Harcourt Brace Jovanovich, 1961. (Revised edition, 1974.)

Popper, K. *The poverty of historicism*. New York: Harper & Row, 1964. (Originally published, 1957.)

*Thibaut, J. W., & Kelley, H. H. *The social psychology of groups*. New York: John Wiley and Sons., 1959.

*Von Dahnieken, E. *Chariots of the gods*. New York: Putnam, 1970.

Chapter 10

*Anderson, R. E. Status structures in coalition bargaining games. *Sociometry*, 1967, *30* (December):393–403.

Bem, D. J., Wallach, M. A., & Kogan, N. Group decision making under risk of aversive consequences. In J. L. Freedman, J. M. Carlsmith, & P. O. Sears

(Eds.), *Readings in social psychology.* Englewood Cliffs, N.J.: Prentice-Hall, 1971.

Burnstein, E., & Vinokur, A. Testing two classes of theories about group induced shifts in individual choice. *Journal of Experimental and Social Psychology,* 1973, *9* (March):123–137.

*Caplow, T. A theory of coalitions in the triad. *American Sociological Review,* 1956, *21* (August):489–493.

*Caplow, T. *Two against one, coalitions in triads.* Englewood Cliffs, N.J.: Prentice-Hall, 1968.

*Conviser, R. H. Toward a theory of interpersonal trust. *Pacific Sociological Review,* 1973, *16* (July):377–400.

*Crosbie, P. Social exchange and power compliance: a test of Homans' propositions. *Sociometry,* 1972, *35* (March):203–222.

*Crosbie, P. *The process of decreasing marginal utility and the exercise of power: an experimental test.* Unpublished manuscript, 1969. (Available from Humbolt State College, Arcata, Calif. 95521.)

*Crosbie, P. *The process of decreasing marginal utility and the exercise of power: an experimental test.* Unpublished doctoral dissertation. Stanford University, 1970.

Derlega, V. J., Harris, M. S., & Chaikin, A. L. Self-disclosure reciprocity, liking and the deviant. *Journal of Experimental Social Psychology,* 1973, *9* (July): 277–284.

*Deutsch, M. Trust and suspicion. *Journal Conflict Resolution,* 1958, *3* (September):265–279.

*Emerson, R. M. Power-dependence relations: Two experiments. *American Sociological Review,* 1962, *27* (February):31–41.

*Fromm, E. *Escape from freedom.* New York: Holt, Rinehart and Winston, 1941.

*Gamson, W. A. A theory of coalition formation. *American Sociological Review,* 1961, *26* (June):565–573.

*Hobbes, T. Leviathan. In E. A. Burtt (Ed.), *The English philosophers from Bacon to Mill.* New York: The Modern Library, 1939. (Originally published, 1651.)

*Hoffman, P. J., Festinger, L., & Lawrence, P. H. Tendencies toward group comparability in competitive bargaining. *Human Relations,* 1954, *1*:141–159.

Horne, W. C., & Long, G. Effect of group discussion on universalistic-particularistic orientation. *Journal of Experimental Social Psychology,* 1972, *8* (May): 236–246.

*Kelley, H. H., & Arrowood, A. J. Coalitions in the triad: Critique and experiment. *Sociometry,* 1960, *23* (September):231–244.

Kelley, H. H., Beckman, L. L., & Fischer, C. S. Negotating the division of a reward under incomplete information. *Journal of Experimental Social Psychology,* 1967, *3* (September):361–398.

*LaPiere, R. T. *A theory of social control.* New York: McGraw-Hill, 1954.

Michener, H. A., & Lyons, M. Perceived support and upward mobility as determinants of revolutonary coalitional behavior. *Journal of Experimental and Social Psychology,* 1972, *8* (March):180–195.

Michener, H. A., & Zeller, R. A. The effects of coalition strength on the formation of contractual norms. *Sociometry,* 1972, *35* (June):290–304.

Nagle, J. A. Power, stability, and friendship in coalitions. *Pacific Sociological Review,* 1973, *16* (October):519–536.

Pilisuk, M., & Skolnick, P. Inducing trust: a test of the Osgood proposal. *Journal of Personality and Social Psychology,* 1968, *8* (February):121–133.

°Simmel, G. [*The Sociology of Georg Simmel*] (K. Wolff, Ed. and Trans.). Glencoe: The Free Press, 1964. (Originally published, 1890–1916.)

°Vinacke, W. E., & Arkoff, A. An experimental study of coalitions in the triad. *American Sociological Review*, 1957, 22 (August):406–414.

Walker, M. B. Caplow's theory of coalitions in the triad reconsidered. *Journal of Personality and Social Psychology*, 1973, 27 (September):409–412.

°Weber, M. *The theory of social and economic organization.* New York: Oxford University Press, 1947.

°Weil, H. G. *Distributive justice in a coalition game.* Master's thesis, 1970. Department of Sociology, Stanford University, Stanford, Calif. 94305.

Chapter 11

°Balkwell, J. W. A structural theory of self-esteem maintenance. *Sociometry*, 1969, 32 (December):458–473.

Baranowski, T. A., & Summers, D. A. Perception of response alternatives in a prisoner's dilemma game. *Journal of Personality and Social Psychology*, 1972, 21 (January):35–40.

Baron, R. S., Monson, T. C., & Baron, P. H. Conformity pressure as a determinant of risk taking: replication and extension. *Journal of Personality and Social Psychology*, 1973, 28 (December):406–413.

°Bartos, O. J. Foundations for a rational-empirical model of negotiation. In J. Berger, M. Zelditch, & B. Anderson (Eds.), *Sociological theories in progess* (Vol. 2). Boston: Houghton Mifflin Co., 1972.

Bedell, J., & Sistrunk, F. Power, opportunity costs, and sex in a mixed-motive game. *Journal of Personality and Social Psychology*, 1973, 25 (February): 219–226.

Benton, A. A., Kelley, H. H., & Liebling, B. Effects of extremity of offers and concession rate on the outcomes of bargaining. *Journal of Personality and Social Psychology*, 1972, 24 (October):73–83.

Berkowitz, N. H., Hylander, L., & Bakaitis, R. Defense, vulnerability, and co-operation in a mixed-motive game. *Journal of Personality and Social Psychology*, 1973, 25 (March):401–407.

°Berne, E. *Games people play.* New York: Grove Press, 1964.

Blascovich, J., & Ginsburg, G. P. Emergent norms and choice shifts involving risk. *Sociometry*, 1974, 37 (June):205–218.

Bonacich, P. Norms and cohesion as adaptive responses to potential conflict: an experimental study. *Sociometry*, 1972, 35 (September):357–375.

Bonoma, T. V., Tedeschi, J. T., & Helm, B. Some effects of target cooperation and reciprocated promises on conflict resolution. *Sociometry*, 1974, 37 (June): 251–261.

°Brown, R. *Social psychology.* New York: The Free Press, 1965.

Burnstein, E., Vinokur, A., & Trope, Y. Interpersonal comparison versus persuasive argumentation: A more direct test of alternative explanations for group-induced shifts in individual choice. *Journal of Experimental Social Psychology*, 1973, 9 (May):236–245.

°Camilleri, S. F., Berger, J., & Conner, T. L. A formal theory of decision-making. In J. Berger, M. Zelditch, & B. Anderson (Eds.), *Sociological theories in progress* (Vol. 2). Boston: Houghton Mifflin Co., 1972.

Clark, R. D., III, & Word, L. E. Why don't bystanders help? Because of ambiguity? *Journal of Personality and Social Psychology,* 1972, *24* (December): 392–400.

Dawes, R. M., Singer, D., & Lemons, F. An experimental analysis of the contrast effect and its implications for intergroup communication and the indirect assessment of attitude. *Journal of Personality and Social Psychology,* 1972, *21* (March):281–295.

*Deutsch, M., & Krauss, R. M. Studies of interpersonal bargaining. *Journal of Conflict Resolution,* 1962, *6* (March):52–76.

*Deutsch, M., & Krauss, R. M. The effect of threat upon interpersonal bargaining. *Journal of Abnormal Social Psychology,* 1960, *61* (September):181–189.

*Foy, E., & Halow, A. F. *Clowning through life.* New York: E. P. Dutton & Co., 1928.

Friedland, N. Arnold, S. E., & Thibaut, J. Motivational bases in mixed-motive interactions: The effects of comparison levels. *Journal of Experimental Social Psychology,* 1974, *10* (March):188–199.

Gardin, H. Kaplan, K. J., Firestone, I. J., & Cowan, G. A. Proxemic effects on cooperation, attitude, and approach-avoidance in a prisoner's dilemma game. *Journal of Personality and Social Psychology,* 1973, *27* (July):13–18.

Gross, D. E., Kelley, H. H., Kruglanski, A., & Patch, M. E. Contingency of consequences and type of incentive in interdependent escape. *Journal of Experimental Social Psychology,* 1972, *8* (July):360–377.

Hamner, W. C. Effects of bargaining strategy and pressure to reach agreement in a stalemated negotiation. *Journal of Personality and Social Psychology,* 1974, *30* (October):458–467.

Harnett, D. L., Cummings, L., & Hamner, W. C. Personality, bargaining style and payoff in bilateral monopoly bargaining among European managers. *Sociometry,* 1973, *36* (September):325–345.

Harvey, J. H., & Johnston, S. Determinants of the perception of choice. *Journal of Experimental Social Psychology,* 1973, *9* (March):164–179.

Hoyt, M. F., Henley, M. D., & Collins, B. E. Studies in forced compliance: Confluence of choice and consequence on attitude change. *Journal of Personality and Social Psychology,* 1972, *23* (August):205–210.

*Humphreys, L. C. Acquisition and extinction of verbal expectations in a situation analogous to conditioning. *Journal of Experimental Psychology,* 1939, *25* (September):294–301.

*Huston, T. L. Ambiguity of acceptance, social desirability, and dating choice. *Journal of Experimental Social Psychology,* 1973, *9* (January):32–42.

Johnson, D. F., & Tullar, W. Style of third party intervention, face-saving and bargaining power. *Journal of Experimental Social Psychology,* 1972, *8* (July): 319–330.

Kahn, A. S., & Kohls, J. W. Determinants of toughness in dyadic bargaining. *Sociometry,* 1972, *35* (June):305–315.

Kogan, N., Lamm, H., & Trommsdorff, G. Negotiation constraints in the risk-taking domain: effects of being observed by partners of higher or lower status. *Journal of Personality and Social Psychology,* 1972, *23* (August):143–156.

*Luce, R. D. *Individual choice behavior.* New York: John Wiley and Sons, 1959.

Luginbuhl, J. E. R. Role of choice and outcome on feelings of success and estimates of ability. *Journal of Personality and Social Psychology,* 22 (April): 121–127.

Marwell, G., & Schmitt, D. R. Cooperation in a three-person prisoner's dilemma.

Journal of Personality and Social Psychology, 1972, *21* (March):376–383.

McClintock, C. G., Messick, D. M., Kuhlmann, D. M., & Campos, F. T. Motivational bases of choice in three-choice decomposed games. *Journal of Experimental Social Psychology,* 1973, *9* (November):572–590.

McNeel, S. P. Training cooperation in the prisoner's dilemma. *Journal of Experimental Social Psychology,* 1973, *9* (July):335–348.

McNeel, S. P., McClintock, C. G., & Nuttin, J. M., Jr. Effects of sex role in a two-person mixed motive game. *Journal of Personality and Social Psychology,* 1972, *24* (December):372–380.

*Mintz, A. Non-adaptive group behavior. *Journal of Abnormal and Social Psychology,* 1951, *46* (April):150–159.

Mogy, R. B., & Pruitt, D. G. Effects of a threatener's enforcement costs on threat credibility and compliance. *Journal of Personality and Social Psychology,* 1974, *29* (February):173–180.

Myers, D. G., Bach, P. J., & Schreiber, B. F. Normative and informational effects of group interaction. *Sociometry,* 1974, *37* (June):275–286.

Nisan, M. Dimension of time in relation to choice behavior and achievement orientation. *Journal of Personality and Social Psychology,* 1972, *21* (February):175–182.

*Ofshe, R., & Ofshe, S. L. Social choice and utility in coalition formation. *Sociometry,* 1969, *32* (September):330–347.

*Ofshe, S. L., & Ofshe, R. *Utility and choice in social interaction.* Englewood Cliffs, N.J.: Prentice-Hall, 1970.

Rubin, J. Z., & DiMatteo, M. R. Factors affecting the magnitude of subjective utility parameters in a tacit bargaining game. *Journal of Experimental Social Psychology,* 1972, *8* (September):412–426.

Sales, S. M. Economic threat as a determinant of conversion rates in authoritarian and nonauthoritarian churches. *Journal of Personality and Social Psychology,* 1972, *23* (September):420–428.

Schlenker, B. R., Helm, B., & Tedeschi, J. T. The effects of personality and situational variables on behavioral trust. *Journal of Personality and Social Psychology,* 1973, *25* (March):419–427.

*Scodel, A., Minas, J. S., Ratoosh, P., and Lipetz, M. Some descriptive aspects of two-person non-zero sum games. *Journal of Conflict Resolution,* 1959, *3* (June):114–119.

*Scodel, A., & Minas, J. S. The behavior of prisoners in a prisoner's dilemma game. *Journal of Psychology,* 1960, *50* (July):133–138.

*Siegel, S., Siegel, A. E., & Andrews, J. M. *Choice strategy and utility.* New York: McGraw-Hill, 1964.

Slack, B. D., & Cook, J. O. Authoritarian behavior in a conflict situation. *Journal of Personality and Social Psychology,* 1973, *25* (January):130–136.

Swingle, P. G., & Santi, A. Communication in non-zero-sum games. *Journal of Personality and Social Psychology,* 1972, *23* (July):54–63.

Tedeschi, J. H., Horai, J., Lindskold, S., & Faley, T. The effects of opportunity costs and target compliance on the behavior of a threatening source. *Journal of Experimental Social Psychology,* 1970, *6* (April):205–213.

Tedeschi, J. T., Schlenker, B. A., & Bonoma, T. V. *Conflict, power, and games: The experimental study of interpersonal behavior.* Chicago: Aldine Publishing Co., 1973.

Toomey, M. Conflict theory approach to decision making applied to alcoholics. *Journal of Personality and Social Psychology,* 1972, *24* (November):199–206.

Turner, R. H., & Killien, L. M. *Collective behavior.* Englewood Cliffs, N.J.: Prentice-Hall, 1974. (First published, 1957.)

Vinacke, W. E., Mogy, R., Powers, W., Langan, C., & Beck, R. Accommodative strategy and communication in a three-person matrix game. *Journal of Personality and Social Psychology,* 1974, *29* (April):509–525.

°Walster, E., Berscheid, E., & Walster, G. W. New directions in equity research. *Journal of Personality and Social Psychology,* 1973, *25* (February):151–176.

Wiley, M. G. Sex roles in games. *Sociometry,* 1973, *36* (December):526–541.

Wood, D., Pilisuk, M., & Uren, E. The martyr's personality: An experimental investigation. *Journal of Personality and Social Psychology,* 1973, *25* (February):177–186.

Yuhl, G. A. Effects of situational variables and opponent concessions on a bargainer's perception, aspirations, and concessions. *Journal of Personality and Social Psychology,* 1974, *29* (February):227–236.

Zajonc, R. B., Wolosin, R. J., & Wolosin, M. A. Group risk-taking under various group decision schemes. *Journal of Experimental Social Psychology,* 1972, *8* (January):16–30.

Zanna, M. P., Lepper, M. R., & Abelson, R. Attentional mechanisms in children's devaluation of a forbidden activity in a forced-compliance situation. *Journal of Personality and Social Psychology,* 1973, *28* (December):355–359.

Chapter 12

Abelson, R. P. Modes of resolution of belief dilemmas. *Conflict Resolution,* 1959, *3* (December):343–352.

°Abelson, R. P., & Rosenberg, M. J. Symbolic psycho-logic: a model of attitudinal cognition. *Behavioral Science,* 1958, *3* (January):1–13.

Albrecht, S. L., DeFleur, M. L., & Warner, L. G. Attitude-behavior relationships: a reexamination of the postulate of contingent consistency. *Pacific Sociological Review,* 1972, *15* (April):149–168.

Aronson, E. Dissonance theory: progress and problems. In E. P. Hollander & R. G. Hunt (Eds.), *Current perspectives in social psychology.* New York: Oxford University Press, 1971.

Bleda, P. R. Toward a clarification of the role of cognitive and affective processes in the similarity-attraction relationship. *Journal of Personality and Social Psychology,* 1974, *29* (March):368–373.

°Cartwright, D., & Harary, F. Structural balance: a generalization of Heider's theory. *Psychological Review,* 1956, *63* (September):277–293.

Crano, W. D., & Cooper, R. E. Examination of Newcomb's extension of structural balance theory. *Journal of Personality and Social Psychology,* 1973, *27* (September):344–353.

°Davis, J. A. Clustering and structural balance in graphs. *Human Relations,* 1967, *20*:181–187.

°Feather, N. T. The prediction of interpersonal attraction: The effects of sign and strength of relations in different structures. *Human Relations,* 1966, *19*: (May):213–237.

Feldman, S. *Cognitive consistency: Motivational antecedents and behavioral consequences.* New York: Academic Press, 1966.

*Festinger, L. *A theory of cognitive dissonance*. Stanford: Stanford University Press, 1964. (Originally published, 1957.)

*Harary, F. On the measurement of structural balance. *Behavioral Science, 4,* 1959 (October):316–323.

*Harary, F. "Cosi fan tutte": A structural study. *Psychological Reports,* 1963, *13*:466.

*Harary, F. Structural study of "a severed head." *Psychological Reports,* 1966, *19*:473–474.

*Harary, F., Norman, R. Z., & Cartwright, D. *Structural models: An introduction to the theory of directed graphs*. New York: John Wiley and Sons, 1965.

*Heider, F. Social perception and phenomenal causality, *Psychological Review,* 1944, *51* (November):358–374.

*Heider, F. Attitudes and cognitive organization. *Journal of Psychology,* 1946, *21* (January):107–112.

*Heider, F. *The psychology of interpersonal relations*. New York: John Wiley and Sons, 1958.

Hovland, C. I. Reconciling conflicting results derived from experimental and survey studies of attitude change. *The American Psychologist,* 1959, *14* (January):8–17.

*James, W. *The principles of psychology*. New York: Holt, 1890.

*Lewin, K. *A dynamic theory of personality*. New York: McGraw-Hill, 1935.

*Lewin, K. Field theory and experiment in social psychology: conceptual methods. *American Journal of Sociology,* 1939, *44* (May):868–896.

*McGuire, W. J. The current status of cognitive consistency theories. In S. Feldman (Ed.), *Cognitive consistency: Motivational antecedents and behavioral consequences*. New York: Academic Press, 1966.

*Mead, G. H. *Mind, self, and society*. Chicago: University of Chicago Press, 1934.

*Morrissette, J. O., Jahnke, J. C., & Baker, K. Structural balance: A test of the completeness hypothesis. *Behavioral Science,* 1966, *11*:121–125.

*Newcomb, T. M. An approach to the study of communicative acts. *Psychological Review,* 1953, *60* (November):393–404.

*Norman, R. Z., & Roberts, F. S. A measure of relative balance for social structures. In J. Berger, M. Zelditch, & B. Anderson (Eds.), *Sociological theories in progress* (Vol. 2). Boston: Houghton Mifflin Co., 1972.

*Osgood, C. E., & Tannenbaum, P. H. The principle of congruity in the prediction of attitude change. *Psychological Review,* 1955, *62*:42–55.

*Stanton, R. G. 'A midsummer night's dream': A structural study. *Psychological Reports,* 1967, *20*:687–658.

*Taylor, H. F. *Balance in small groups*. New York: Van Nostrand Reinhold Co., 1970.

*Triandis, H. C., & Fishbein, M. Cognitive interaction in person perception. *Journal of Abnormal and Social Psychology,* 1963, *67*:446–453.

*Weinberg, G. *The action approach*. New York: New American Library, 1969.

Chapter 13

Ajzen, I., & Fishbein, M. Attitudinal and normative variables as predictors of specific behaviors. *Journal of Personality and Social Psychology,* 1973, *27* (July):41–57.

Alwin, D. F. Making inferences from attitude-behavior correlations. *Sociometry,* 1973, *36* (June):253–278.

Apsler, R. Effects of the draft lottery and a laboratory analogue on attitudes. *Journal of Personality and Social Psychology,* 1972, *24* (November):262–272.

*Aronson, E., & Mills, J. The effect of severity of initiation on liking for a group. *Journal of Abnormal and Social Psychology,* 1959, *59* (September):177–181.

Banikiotes, P. G., Russell, J. M., & Linden, J. D. Interpersonal attraction in simulated and real interactions. *Journal of Personality and Social Psychology,* 1972, *23* (July):1–7.

Barton, L., & Cattell, R. B. Marriage dimensions and personality. *Journal of Personality and Social Psychology,* 1972, *21* (March):369–375.

Brickman, P. Rational and nonrational elements in reactions to disconfirmation of performance expectancies. *Journal of Experimental Social Psychology,* 1972, *8* (March):112–123.

Brickman, P., & Horn, C. Balance theory and interpersonal coping in triads. *Journal of Personality and Social Psychology,* 1973, *26* (June):347–355.

Brickman, P., Redfield, J., Harrison, A. A., & Crandall, R. Drive and predisposition as factors in the attitudinal effects of mere exposure. *Journal of Experimental Social Psychology,* 1972, *8* (January):31–44.

Bridgeman, W. Student attraction and productivity as a composite function of reinforcement and expectancy conditions. *Journal of Personality and Social Psychology,* 1972, *23* (August):249–258.

*Byrne, D. Authoritarianism and response to attitude similarity-dissimilarity. *Journal of Social Psychology,* 1965, *66*:251–256.

*Byrne, D., Griffitt, W., & Stefaniak, D. Attraction and similarity of personality characteristics. *Journal of Personality and Social Psychology,* 1967, *5* (January):82–90.

*Byrne, D., London, O., & Reeves, K. The effects of physical attractiveness, sex, and attitude similarity on interpersonal attraction. *Journal of Personality,* 1968 *36*:259–271.

*Byrne, D., & McGraw, C. Interpersonal attraction toward Negroes. *Human Relations,* 1964 *17*:201–213.

*Byrne, D., & Wong, T. J. Racial prejudice, interpersonal attraction and assumed dissimilarity of attitudes. *Journal of Abnormal and Social Psychology,* 1962 *65*:246–253.

*Carlsmith, J. M., Collins, B. E., & Helmreich, R. L. Studies in forced compliance I: The effect of pressure for compliance on attitude change produced by face-to-face role-playing and anonymous essay writing. *Journal of Personality and Social Psychology,* 1966, *4* (January):1–13.

Chaikin, A. L., & Cooper, J. Evaluation as a function of correspondence and hedonic relevance. *Journal of Experimental Social Psychology,* 1973, *9* (May):257–264.

*Cohen, A. R. A study of discrepant information in betrothal. In J. W. Brehm & A. R. Cohen, *Explorations in cognitive dissonance.* New York: John Wiley and Sons, 1962.

Collins, B. E. The effect of monetary inducements on the amount of attitude change induced by forced compliance. In A. Elms (Ed.), *Role playing, reward and attitude change.* New York: Van Nostrand Reinhold, 1969.

Cooper, J., & Goethals, G. R. Unforeseen events and the elimination of cognitive dissonance. *Journal of Personality and Social Psychology,* 1974, *29* (April):441–445.

Cooper, J., Jones, E. E., and Tuller, S. M. Attribution, dissonance, and the illusion of uniqueness. *Journal of Experimental Social Psychology*, 1972, 8 (January):45–57.

Cooper, J., & Scalise, C. J. Dissonance produced by deviations from life styles: The interaction of Jungian typology and conformity. *Journal of Personality and Social Psychology*, 1974, 29 (April):566–571.

Cooper, J., & Zanna, M. P. Mistreatment of an esteemed other as a consequence affecting dissonance reduction. *Journal of Experimental Social Psychology*, 1974, 10 (May):224–233.

Cozby, P. C. Self-disclosure, reciprocity and liking. *Sociometry*, 1972, 35 (March):151–160.

Crockett, W. H. Balance, agreement, and subjective evaluations of the P-O-X triads. *Journal of Personality and Social Psychology*, 1974, 29 (January):102–110.

Darley, S. A., & Cooper, J. Cognitive consequences of forced noncompliance. *Journal of Personality and Social Psychology*, 1972, 24 (December):321–326.

*DeSoto, C. B. Learning a social structure. *Journal of Abnormal and Social Psychology*, 1960, 60:417–421.

*Desoto, C. B., Henley, N. M., & London, M. Balance and the grouping schema. *Journal of Personality and Social Psychology*, 1968, 8.

Dinner, S. H., Lewkowicz, B. E., & Cooper, J. Anticipatory attitude change as a function of self-esteem and issue familiarity. *Journal of Personality and Social Psychology*, 1972, 24 (December):407–412.

Dutton, D. G. Effect of feedback parameters on congruency versus positivity effects in reactions to personal evaluations. *Journal of Personality and Social Psychology*, 1972, 24 (December):366–371.

Eagly, A. H., & Telaak, K. Width of the latitude of acceptance as a determinant of attitude change. *Journal of Personality and Social Psychology*, 1972, 23 (September):388–397.

Farina, A., Chapnick, B. Chapnick, J., & Misiti, R. Political views and interpersonal behavior. *Journal of Personality and Social Psychology*, 1972, 22 (June): 273–278.

*Festinger, L. *A theory of cognitive dissonance*. Stanford: Stanford University Press, 1964. (Originally published, 1957.)

*Festinger, L., & Carlsmith, J. M. Cognitive consequences of forced compliance. *Journal of Abnormal and Social Psychology*, 1959, 58:203–210.

*Festinger, L., Riecken, H. W., & Schachter, S. *When prophecy fails*. Minneapolis: University of Minnesota Press, 1956.

Fischer, E. H. Consistency among humanitarian and helping attitudes. *Social Forces*, 1973, 52 (December):157–168.

Freedman, J. L. Long-term behavior effects of cognitive dissonance. *Journal of Experimental Social Psychology*, 1965, 1 (May):145–155.

*Gerard, H. B. and Mathewson, G. C. The effect of severity of initiation on liking for a group: A replication. *Journal of Experimental Social Psychology*, 1966, 2 (July):278–287.

Goethals, G. R., & Cooper, J. Role of intention and postbehavioral consequence in the arousal of cognitive dissonance. *Journal of Personality and Social Psychology*, 1972, 23 (September):293–301.

Goethals, G. R., & Nelson, R. E. Similarity in the influence process: The belief-value distinction. *Journal of Personality and Social Psychology*, 1973, 25 (January):117–122.

Goethals, G. R., & Reckman, R. F. The perception of consistency in attitudes. *Journal of Experimental Social Psychology*, 1973, 9 (November):491–501.

Goldstein, M., & Davis, E. E. Race and belief: A further analysis of the social determinants of behavioral intentions. *Journal of Personality and Social Psychology*, 1972, 22 (June):346–355.

Gormly, J., Gormly, A., & Johnson, C. Consistency of sociobehavioral responses to interpersonal disagreement. *Journal of Personality and Social Psychology*, 1972, 24 (November):221–224.

Granberg, D., & Brent, E. E., Jr. Dove-hawk placements in the 1968 election: Application of social judgment and balance theories. *Journal of Personality and Social Psychology*, 1974, 29 (May):687–695.

*Griffith, W., & Veitch, R. Preacquaintance attitude similarity and attraction revisited: Ten days in a fall-out shelter. *Sociometry*, 1974, 37 (June):163–173.

Gutman, G. M., & Knox, R. E. Balance, agreement, and attraction in pleasantness, tension, and consistency ratings of hypothetical social situations. *Journal of Personality and Social Psychology*, 1972, 24 (December):351–357.

Gutman, G. M., Knox, R. E., & Storm, T. F. Developmental study of balance agreement, and attraction effects in the ratings of hypothetical social situations. *Journal of Personality and Social Psychology*, 1974, 29 (March):201–211.

*Halberstam, D. *The best and the brightest*. New York: Random House, 1972.

Heilman, M. E., Hodgson, S. A., & Hornstein, H. A. Effects of magnitude and rectifiability of harm and information value on the reporting of accidental harm-doing. *Journal of Personality and Social Psychology*, 1972, 23 (August): 211–218.

Heslin, R., & Amo, M. F. Detailed test of the reinforcement-dissonance controversy in the counterattitudinal advocacy situation. *Journal of Personality and Social Psychology*, 1972, 23 (August):234–242

Hewitt, J. Liking and the proportion of favorable evaluations. *Journal of Personality and Social Psychology*, 1972, 22 (May):231–235.

Hodges, L. A., & Byrne, D. Verbal dogmatism as a potentiator of intolerance. *Journal of Personality and Social Psychology*, 1972, 21 (March):312–317.

Hoyt, M. F., & Centers, R. Temporal situs of the effects of anticipated publicity upon commitment and resistance to countercommunication. *Journal of Personality and Social Psychology*, 22 (April):1–7.

Insko, C. A., Songer, E., & McGarvey, W. Balance, positivity, and agreement in the Jordan paradigm: A defense of balance theory. *Journal of Experimental Social Psychology*, 1974, 10 (January):53–83.

Insko, C. A., Thompson, V. D., Stroebe, W., Shaud, K. F., Pinner, B. E., & Layton, B. D. Implied evaluation and the similarity attraction effect. *Journal of Personality and Social Psychology*, 1973, 25 (March):297–308.

Insko, C. A., Worchel, S., Songer, E., & Arnold, S. E. Effort, objective self-awareness, choice, and dissonance. *Journal of Personality and Social Psychology*, 1973, 28 (November):262–269.

Jackman, M. R. Social mobility and attitude toward the political system. *Social Forces*, 1972, 50 (June):462–472.

Jellison, J. M., & Davis, D. Relationships between perceived ability and attitude extremity. *Journal of Personality and Social Psychology*, 1973, 27 (September):430–436.

Johnson, D. W., & Johnson, S. The effects of attitude similarity, expectation of goal facilitation, and actual goal facilitation on interpersonal attraction. *Journal of Experimental Social Psychology*, 1972, 8 (May):197–206.

Jones, E. E., & Wein, G. A. Attitude similarity, expectancy violation, and attraction. *Journal of Experimental Social Psychology*, 1972, 8 (May):222–235.

*Jordan, N. Behavioral forces that are a function of attitudes and of cognitive organization. *Human Relations*, 1953, 6 (August):273–287.

Kahn, A., & Tice, T. E. Returning a favor and retaliating harm: the effects of stated intentions and actual behavior. *Journal of Experimental Social Psychology*, 1973, 9 (January):43–56.

Kanfer, F. H., Karoly, P., & Newman, A. Source of feedback, observational learning and attitude change. *Journal of Personality and Social Psychology*, 1974, 29 (January):30–38.

Kaplan, K. J. From attitude formation to attitude change: Acceptance and impact on cognitive mediators. *Sociometry*, 1972, 35 (September):443–467.

Kian, M., Rosen, S., & Tesser, A. Reinforcement effects of attitude similarity and source evaluation on discriminating learning. *Journal of Personality and Social Psychology*, 1973, 27 (September):366–371.

Kleinke, C. L., Bustos, A. A., Meeker, F. B., & Staneski, R. A. Effects of self-attributed and other-attributed gaze on interpersonal evaluations between males and females. *Journal of Experimental Social Psychology*, 1973, 9 (March):154–163.

Kleinke, C. L., Staneski, R. A., & Weaver, P. Evaluation of a person who uses another's name in ingratiating and noningratiating situations. *Journal of Experimental Social Psychology*, 1972, 8 (September):457–466.

*Kogan, N., & Tagiuri, R. Interpersonal preference and cognitive organization. *Journal of Abnormal and Social Psychology*, 1958, 56:113–116.

Konecni, V. J. Some effects of guilt on compliance: A field replication. *Journal of Personality and Social Psychology*, 1972, 23 (July):30–32.

Kukla, A. Attributional determinants of achievement related behavior. *Journal of Personality and Social Psychology*, 1972, 21 (February):166–174.

Layton, B. D., & Insko, C. A. Anticipated interaction and the similarity-attraction effect. *Sociometry*. 1974, 37 (June):149–162.

Lepper, M. R. Dissonance, self-perception, and honesty in children. *Journal of Personality and Social Psychology*, 1973, 25 (January):65–74.

Liebhart, E. H. Empathy and emergency helping: The effects of personality, self-concern, and acquaintance. *Journal of Experimental Social Psychology*, 1972, 8 (September):404–411.

Liska, A. E. The impact of attitude on behavior: Attitude-social support interaction. *Pacific Sociological Review*, 1974, 17 (January):83–97.

Lombardo, J. P., Weiss, R. F., & Buchanan, W. Reinforcing and attracting functions of yielding. *Journal of Personality and Social Psychology*, 1972, 21 (March):359–368.

Lombardo, J. P., Weiss, R. F., & Stitch, M. H. Effectance reduction through speaking in reply and its relation to attraction. *Journal of Personality and Social Psychology*, 1973, 28 (December):325–332.

Mascaro, G. F., & Graves, W. Contrast effects of background factors on the similarity-attraction relationship. *Journal of Personality and Social Psychology*, 1973, 25 (March):346–350.

Matefy, R. E. Attitude Change induced by role playing as a function of improvisation and role-taking skill. *Journal of Personality and Social Psychology*, 1972, 24 (December):345–350.

Mazen, R., & Leventhal, H. The influence of communicator-recipient similarity upon the beliefs and behavior of pregnant women. *Journal of Experimental Social Psychology*, 1972, *8* (July):289–302.

Mazis, M. B. Cognitive tuning and receptivity to novel information. *Journal of Experimental Social Psychology*, 1973, *9* (July):307–319.

Mazur, A. Increased tendency toward balance during stressful conflict. *Sociometry*, 1973, *36* (June):279–283.

McGinnies, E. Initial attitude, source credibility, and involvement as factors in persuasion. *Journal of Experimental Social Psychology*, 1973, *9* (July):285–296.

Metee, D. R., & Wilkins, P. C. When similarity "hurts": Effects of perceived ability and a humorous blunder on interpersonal attractiveness. *Journal of Personality and Social Psychology*, 1972, *22* (May):246–258.

Michener, H. A., & Schwertfeger, M. Liking as a determinant of power tactic preference. *Sociometry*, 1972, *35* (March):190–202.

Miller, H., & Geller, D. Structural balance in dyads. *Journal of Personality and Social Psychology*, 1972, *21* (February):135–138.

Mills, J. & Harvey J. Can self-perception theory explain the findings of Harvey and Mills (1971)? *Journal of Personality and Social Psychology* 1972, *22* (May):271–272.

Mitchell, H. E., & Byrne, D. The defendant's dilemma: Effects of jurors' attitudes and authoritarianism on judicial decisions. *Journal of Personality and Social Psychology*, 1973, *25* (January):123–129.

°Morrissette, J. O. An experimental study of the theory of structural balance. *Human Relations*, 1958, *11*:239–254.

Nemeth, C., & Wachtler, J. Consistency and modification of judgment. *Journal of Experimental Social Psychology*, 1973, *9* (January):65–79.

°Newcomb, T. M. *The acquaintance process*. New York: Holt, Rinehart and Winston, 1961.

°Newcomb, T. M. The prediction of interpersonal attraction. *American Psychologist*, 1956, *11* (November):575–586.

°Newcomb, T. M. Stabilies underlying changes in interpersonal attraction. *Journal of Abnormal and Social Psychology*, 1963, *66*:376–386.

Pallak, M. S., Muller, M., Dollar, K., & Pallak, J. Effect of commitment of responsiveness to an extreme consonant communication. *Journal of Personality and Social Psychology*, 1972, *23* (September):429–436.

Pallak, M. S., & Pittman, T. S. General motivational effects of dissonance arousal. *Journal of Personality and Social Psychology*, 1972, *21* (March):349–358.

Potter, D. A. Personalism and interpersonal attraction. *Journal of Personality and Social Psychology*, 1973, *28* (November):192–198.

Regan, D. T., & Cheng, J. B. Distraction and attitude change: A resolution. *Journal of Experimental Social Psychology*, 1973, *9* (March):138–147.

Rokeach, M., & Kliejunas, P. Behavior as a function of attitude-toward-object and attitude-toward-situation. *Journal of Personality and Social Psychology*, 1972, *22* (May):194–201.

Rosen, N. A., & Wyer, R. S., Jr. Some further evidence for the "Socratic effect" using a subjective probability model of cognitive organization. *Journal of Personality and Social Psychology*, 1972, *24* (December):420–424.

°Rosenberg, M. J. When dissonance fails: On eliminating evaluation apprehension from attitude measurement. *Journal of Personality and Social Psychology*, 1965, *1*:28–42.

Ross, M., & Shulman, R. F. Increasing the salience of initial attitudes: Dissonance versus self-perception theory. *Journal of Personality and Social Psychology,* 1973, *28* (October):138–144.

°Runkel, P. J. "Equilibrium" and "pleasantness" of interpersonal situations. *Human Relations,* 1956, 9:375–382.

°Saegert, S., Swap, W., & Zajonc, R. B. Exposure, context, and interpersonal attraction. *Journal of Personality and Social Psychology,* 1973, *25* (February): 234–242.

Sample, J., & Warland, R. Attitude and prediction of behavior. *Social Forces,* 1973, *51* (March):292–304.

°Schick, C., McGlynn, R. P., & Woolam, D. Perception of cartoon humor as a function of familiarity and anxiety level. *Journal of Personality and Social Psychology,* 1972, *24* (October):22–25.

°Schopler, J., & Bateson, N. A dependence interpretation of the effects of a severe initiation. *Journal of Personality and Social Psychology,* 1962, *30* (December):633–649.

Schwarz, J. C. Effects of peer familiarity on the behavior of preschoolers in a novel situation. *Journal of Personality and Social Psychology,* 1972, *24* (November):276–284.

Schwartz, S. H., & Tessler, R. C. A test of a model for reducing measured attitude-behavior discrepancies. *Journal of Personality and Social Psychology,* 1972, *24* (November):225–236.

Seyfried, B. A., & Hendrick, C. Need similarity and complementarity in interpersonal attraction. *Sociometry,* 1973, *36* (June):207–220.

Seyfried, B. A., & Hendrick, C. When do opposites attract? When they are opposite in sex and sex-role attitudes. *Journal of Personality and Social Psychology,* 1973, *25* (January):15–20.

Shaffer, D. R., & Hendrick, C. Dogmatism and tolerance for ambiguity as determinants of differential reactions to cognitive inconsistency. *Journal of Personality and Social Psychology,* 1974, *29* (May):601–608.

Sherif, M., & Hovland, C. I. Judgmental processes and problems of attitude. In E. P. Hollander and R. G. Hunt (Eds.), *Current perspectives in social psychology.* New York: Oxford University Press, 1971.

Sherman, S. J. Effects of choice and incentive on attitude change in a discrepant behavior situation. *Journal of Personality and Social Psychology,* 1970, *15* (July):245–252.

Sherman, S. J. Internal-external control and its relationship to attitude change under different social influence techniques. *Journal of Personality and Social Psychology,* 1973, *26* (April):23–29.

Silverman, B. I. Consequences, racial discrimination, and the principle of belief congruence. *Journal of Personality and Social Psychology,* 1974, *29* (April): 497–508.

Smith, A. J., & Clark, R. D., III. The relationship between attitudes and beliefs. *Journal of Personality and Social Psychology,* 1973, *26* (June):321–326.

Smith, R. E., & Campbell, A. L. Social anxiety and strain toward symmetry in dyadic attraction. *Journal of Personality and Social Psychology,* 1973, *28* (October):101–107.

Snyder, M., & Ebbesen, E. B. Dissonance awareness: A test of dissonance theory versus self-perception theory. *Journal of Experimental Social Psychology,* 1972, *8* (November):502–517

Staats, A. W., Minke, K. A., Martin, C. H., & Higa, W. R. Deprivation-satiation and strength of attitude conditioning: a test of attitude-reinforcer-discriminative theory. *Journal of Personality and Social Psychology*, 1972, *24* (November):178–185.

Stang, D. J. Effect of interaction rate on ratings of leadership and liking. *Journal of Personality and Social Psychology*, 1973, *27* (September):405–408.

*Stapleton, R. E., Nacci, P., & Tedeschi, J. T. Interpersonal attraction and the reciprocation of benefits. *Journal of Personality and Social Psychology*, 1973, *28* (November):199–205

Tessler, R. C., & Schwartz, S. H. Help seeking, self-esteem, and achievement motivation: An attributional analysis. *Journal of Personality and Social Psychology*, 1972, *21* (March):318–326.

Touhey, J. C. Comment on Harvey and Mills' "Effect of a difficult opportunity to revoke a counterattitudinal action upon attitude change." *Journal of Personality and Social Psychology*, 1972, *22* (May):269–270.

Touhey, J. C. Comparison of two dimensions of attitude similarity on heterosexual attraction. *Journal of Personality and Social Psychology*, 1972, *23* (July):8–10.

Touhey, J. C. Individual differences in attitude change following two acts of forced compliance. *Journal of Personality and Social Psychology*, 1973, *27* (July):96–99.

Trope, Y. Inferential processes in the forced compliance situation: A Bayesian analysis. *Journal of Experimental Social Psychology*, 1974, *10* (January):1–16.

Watts, W. A. Intelligence and susceptibility to persuasion under conditions of active and passive participation. *Journal of Experimental Social Psychology*, 1973, *9* (March):110–122.

Willis, R. H., & Burgess, T. D., II. Cognitive and affective balance in sociometric dyads. *Journal of Personality and Social Psychology*, 1974, *29* (January):145–152.

Worchel, S., & Arnold, S. E. The effects of censorship and attractiveness of the censor on attitude change. *Journal of Experimental Social Psychology*, 1973, *9* (July):365–377.

Worchel, S., & Brand, J. Role of responsibility and violated expectancy in the arousal of dissonance. *Journal of Personality and Social Psychology*, 1972, *22* (April):87–97.

Wyer, R. S., Jr. Test of a subjective probability model of social evaluation processes. *Journal of Personality and Social Psychology*, 1972, *22* (June):279–286.

Yang, K. S., & Yang, P. H. L. The effects of anxiety and threat on the learning of balanced and unbalanced social structures. *Journal of Personality and Social Psychology*, 1973, *26* (May):201–207.

*Zajonc, R. B. Attitudinal effects of mere exposure. *Journal of Personality and Social Psychology Monograph Supplement*, 1968, *9* (Pt. 2) (June):1–27.

*Zajonc, R. B., Shaver, P., Tavris, C., & Kreveld, D. V. Exposure, satiation, and stimulus discriminability. *Journal of Personality and Social Psychology*, 1972, *21* (March):270–280.

Chapter 14

Ajzen, I. Effects of information on interpersonal attraction: Similarity versus affective value. *Journal of Personality and Social Psychology*, 1974, *29* (March):374–380.

Alexander, C. N., Jr., & Sagatun, I. An attributional analysis of experimental norms. *Sociometry,* 1973, *36* (June):127–142.

⁕Alexander, C. N., & Weil, H. G. Players, persons, and purposes: Situational meaning and the prisoner's dilemma game. *Sociometry,* 1969, *32* (June):121–144.

⁕Anderson, N. H. Two learning models for responses measured on a continuous scale. *Psychometrika,* 1961, *26*:391–404.

⁕Anderson, N. H. Linear models for responses measured on a continuous scale. *Journal of Mathematical Psychology,* 1964, *1*:121–142.

⁕Anderson, N. A simple model for information integration. In R. P. Abelson, E. Aronson, W. J. McGuire, T. M. Newcomb, M. J. Rosenberg, & P. H. Tannenbaum (Eds.), *Theories of cognitive consistency: A sourcebook.* Chicago: Rand McNally & Co., 1968.

⁕Anderson, N. H. Application of a linear-serial model to a personality-impression task using serial presentation. *Journal of Personality and Social Psychology,* 1968, *10* (December):354–362.

Anderson, N. H. Functional measurement of social desirability. *Sociometry,* 1973, *36* (March):89–98.

Anderson, N. H., & Farkas, A. J. New light on order effects in attitude change. *Journal of Personality and Social Psychology,* 1973, *28* (October):88-93.

Anderson, N. H., Lindner, R., & Lopes, L. L. Integration theory applied to judgments of group attractiveness. *Journal of Personality and Social Psychology,* 1973, *26* (June):400–408.

Aronson, E., & Linder, D. Gain and loss of esteem as determinants of interpersonal attractiveness. *The Journal of Experimental Social Psychology,* 1965, *1* (May):156–171.

⁕Berger, J., & Fisek, M. H. Consistent and inconsistent characteristics and the determination of power and prestige orders. *Sociometry,* 1970, *33* (September): 278–304.

Calder, B. J. Informational cues and attributions based on role behavior. *Journal of Experimental Social Psychology,* 1974, *10* (March):121–125.

Calder, B. J., Ross, M., & Insko, C. A., Attitude change and attitude attribution: Effects of incentive, choice, and consequences. *Journal of Personality and Social Psychology,* 1973, *25* (January):84–99.

Campus, N. Transituational consistency as a dimension of personality. *Journal of Personality and Social Psychology,* 1974, *29* (March):593–600.

Collins, B. E., & Hoyt, M. F. Personal responsibility-for-consequences: An integration and extension of the "forced compliance" literature. *Journal of Experimental Social Psychology,* 1972, *8* (November):558–593.

Costanzo, P. R., Grumet, J. F., & Brehm, S. S. The effects of choice and source of constraint on children's attributions of preference. *Journal of Experimental Social Psychology,* 1974, *10* (July):352–364.

Dienstbier, R. A. The role of anxiety and arousal attribution in cheating. *Journal of Experimental Social Psychology,* 1972, *8* (March):168–179.

⁕Dion, K. Physical attractiveness and evaluation of children's transgressions. *Journal of Personality and Social Psychology,* 1972, *24* (November):207–213.

⁕Dion, K., & Berscheid, E. Physical attractiveness and peer perception among children. *Sociometry,* 1974, *37* (March):1–12.

⁕Dion, K., Berscheid, E., & Walster, E. What is beautiful is good. *Journal of Personality and Social Psychology,* 1972, *24* (December):285–290.

Dutton, D. G. Attribution of cause for opinion change and liking for audience members. *Journal of Personality and Social Psychology,* 1973, *26* (May):208–216.

*Duval, S., & Wicklund, R. Effects of objective self-awareness on attribution of causality. *Journal of Experimental Social Psychology*, 1973, 9 (January):17–31.

Einhorn, H. J., Komorita, S. S., & Rosen, B., Multidimensional models for the evaluation of political candidates. *Journal of Experimental Social Psychology*, 1972, 8 (January):58–73.

Eiser, J. R., & Tajfel, H. Acquisition of information in dyadic interaction. *Journal of Personality and Social Psychology*, 1972, 23 (September):340–345.

Feldman, J. M. Stimulus characteristics and subject prejudice as determinants of stereotype attribution. *Journal of Personality and Social Psychology*, 1972, 21 (March):333–340.

Fishbein, M., & Ajzen, I. Attribution of responsibility: A theoretical note. *Journal of Experimental Social Psychology*, 1973, 9 (March):148–153.

Girodo, M. Film-induced arousal, information search, and the attribution process. *Journal of Personality and Social Psychology*, 1973, 25 (March):357–360.

Goethals, G. R. Consensus and modality in the attribution process: The role of similarity and information. *Journal of Personality and Social Psychology*, 1972, 21 (January):84–92.

Gollob, H. F., & Rossman, B. B. Judgments of an actor's "power and ability to influence others." *Journal of Experimental Social Psychology*, 1973, 9 (September):391–406.

Gollob, H. F., Rossman, B. B., & Abelson, R. P. Social inference as a function of the number of instances and consistency of information presented. *Journal of Personality and Social Psychology*, 1973, 27 (July):19–33.

Hamilton, D. L., & Fallot, R. D. Information salience as a weighting factor in impression formation. *Journal of Personality and Social Psychology*, 1974, 30 (October):444–448.

Hamilton, D. L., & Zanna, M. P. Context effects in impression formation: Changes in connotative meaning. *Journal of Personality and Social Psychology*, 1974, 29 (May):649–654.

Harrison, A. A., & Crandall, R. Heterogeneity-homogeneity of exposure sequence and the attitudinal effects of exposure. *Journal of Personality and Social Psychology*, 1972, 21 (May):234–238.

Hendrick, C. Effects of salience of stimulus inconsistency on impression formation. *Journal of Personality and Social Psychology*, 1972, 22 (May):219–222.

Himmelfarb, S. Integration and attribution theories in personality impression formation. *Journal of Personality and Social Psychology*, 1972, 23 (September):309–313.

Himmelfarb, S. General test of a differential weighted averaging model of impression formation. *Journal of Experimental Social Psychology*, 1973, 9 (September):379–390.

Jellison, J. M., Broll, L., & Riskind, J. Attribution of ability to others on skill and chance tasks as a function of level of risk. *Journal of Personality and Social Psychology*. 1972, 22 (May):135–138.

*Jones, E. E., & Davis, K. E. From acts to dispositions. In L. Berkowitz (Ed.), *Advances in experimental social psychology* (Vol. 2). New York: Academic Press, 1965.

Jones, S. C., & Regan, D. T. Ability evaluation through social comparison. *Journal of Experimental Social Psychology*, 1974, 10 (March):133–146.

Kaplan, M. F. Stimulus inconsistency and response dispositions in forming judgments of other persons. *Journal of Personality and Social Psychology*, 1973, 25 (January):58–64.

Kaplan, M. F., & Anderson, N. H. Information integration theory and reinforcement theory as approaches to interpersonal attraction. *Journal of Personality and Social Psychology*, 1973, *28* (December):301–312.

Katz, I., Atchison, C. O., Epps, E. G., & Roberts, S. O. Race of evaluator, race of norm, and expectancy as determinants of black performance. *Journal of Experimental Social Psychology*, 1972, *8* (January):1–15.

Kelley, H. H. The warm-cold variable in first impressions of persons. *Journal of Personality and Social Psychology*, 1950, *18* (June):231–329.

*Kervin, J. B. An information processing model for expectation states theory. *Sociometry*, 1974, *37* (September):349–362.

Kruglanski, A. W., Alon, S., & Lewis, T. Retrospective misattribution and task enjoyment. *Journal of Experimental Social Psychology*, 1972, *8* (November): 493–501.

Kruglanski, A. W., & Cohen, M. Attributed freedom and personal causation. *Journal of Personality and Social Psychology*, 1973, *26* (May):245–250.

Landy, D. The effects of an overhead audience's reaction and attractiveness on opinion change. *Journal of Experimental Social Psychology*, 1972, *8* (May): 276–288.

Landy, D., & Sigall, H. Beauty is talent: Task evaluation as a function of the performer's physical attractiveness. *Journal of Personality and Social Psychology*, 1974, *29* (March):299–304.

Lay, C. H., Burron, B. F., & Jackson, D. N. Base rates and information value in impression formation. *Journal of Personality and Social Psychology*, 1973, *28* (December):390–395.

Leon, M., Oden, G. C., & Anderson, N. H. Functional measurements of social values. *Journal of Personality and Social Psychology*, 1973, *27* (September): 301–310.

Lindskold, S. & Bennett, R. Attributing trust and conciliatory intent from coercive power capability. *Journal of Personality and Social Psychology*, 1973, *28* (November):180–186.

Lopes, L. L. A unified integration model for "prior expectancy and behavioral extremity as determinants of attitude attribution." *Journal of Experimental Social Psychology*, 1972, *8* (March):156–160.

McArthur, L. A. The how and what or why: Some determinants and consequences of causal attribution. *Journal of Personality and Social Psychology*, 1972, *22* (May):171–193.

McMahan, I. D. Relationships between causal attributions and expectancy of success. *Journal of Personality and Social Psychology*, 1973, *28* (October): 108–114.

Messick, D. M., & Reeder, G. Perceived motivation, role variations, and the attribution of personal characteristics. *Journal of Experimental Social Psychology*, 1972, *8* (September):482–491.

Newtson, D. Attribution and the unit of perception of ongoing behavior. *Journal of Personality and Social Psychology*, 1973, *28* (October):28–38.

Pagano, D. F. Information-processing differences in repressors and sensitizers. *Journal of Personality and Social Psychology*, 1973, *26* (April):105–109.

Peevers, B. H., & Secord, P. F. Developmental changes in attribution of descriptive concepts to persons. *Journal of Personality and Social Psychology*, 1973, *27* (July):120–128.

Regan, D. T., Straus, E., & Fazio, R. Liking and the attribution process. *Journal of Experimental Social Psychology*, 1974, *10* (July):385–397.

Reisman, S. R., & Schopler, J. An analysis of the attribution process and an application to determinants of responsibility. *Journal of Personality and Social Psychology,* 1973, *25* (March):361–368.

Rodin, M. J. The informativeness of trait descriptions. *Journal of Personality and Social Psychology,* 1972, *21* (March):341–344.

Ross, L., Bierbrauer, G., & Polly, S. Attribution of education outcomes by professional and nonprofessional instructions. *Journal of Personality and Social Psychology,* 1974, *29* (May):609–618.

Rump, E. E., & Delin, P. S. Differential accuracy in the status-height phenomenon and an experimenter effect. *Journal of Personality and Social Psychology,* 1973, *28* (December):343–347.

Samuel, W. On clarifying some interpretations of social comparison theory. *Journal of Experimental Social Psychology,* 1973, *9* (September):450–465.

Schmidt, C. F., & Levin, I. P. Test of an averaging model of person preference: Effect of context. *Journal of Personality and Social Psychology,* 1972, *23* (August):277–282.

Schopler, J., & Layton, B. Determinants of the self-attribution of having influenced another person. *Journal of Personality and Social Psychology,* 1972, *22* (June):326–332.

Sears, D. O. The paradox of de facto selective exposure without preferences of supportive information. In R. P. Abelson, E. Aronson, W. J. McGuire, T. M. Newcomb, M. J. Rosenberg, & P. H. Tannenbaum, (Eds.), *Theories of cognitive consistency: A sourcebook.* Chicago: Rand McNally & Co., 1968.

*Shelly, R. K. On "accepting significant others." *American Journal of Sociology,* 1974, *79* (May):1477–1480.

Shoemaker, D. J., South, D. R., & Lowe, J. Facial stereotypes of deviants and judgments of guilt or innocence. *Social Forces,* 1973, *51* (June):427–433.

*Sigall, H., & Landy, D. Radiating beauty: Effects of having a physically attractive partner on person perception. *Journal of Personality and Social Psychology,* 1973, *28* (November):218–224.

Sloan, L. R., & Ostrom, T. M. Amount of information and interpersonal judgment. *Journal of Personality and Social Psychology,* 1974, *29* (January):23–29.

Slovic, P. Information processing, situation specificity, and the generality of risk-taking behavior. *Journal of Personality and Social Psychology,* 1972. *22* (April):128–134.

Sorrentino, R. M., & Boutilier, R. C. Evaluation of a victim as a function of fate similarity/dissimilarity. *Journal of Experimental Social Psychology,* 1974, *10* (January):84–93.

Steffensmeir, D. J., & Terry, R. M. Deviance and respectability: An observational study of reactions to shoplifting. *Social Forces,* 1973, *51* (June):417–426.

Steiner, I. D., Rotermund, M., & Talaber, R. Attribution of choice to a decision maker. *Journal of Personality and Social Psychology,* 1974, *30* (October): 553–562.

Stephan, C. Attribution of intention and perception of attitudes as a function of liking and similarity. *Sociometry,* 1972, *36* (December):463–475.

Thompson, D. D. Attributions of ability from patterns of performance under competitive and cooperative conditions. *Journal of Personality and Social Psychology,* 1972, *23* (September):302–308.

*Triandis, H. C., & Fishbein, M. Cognitive interaction in person perception. *Journal of Abnormal and Social Psychology,* 1963, *67* (November):446–453.

*Triandis, H. C., Tanaka, Y., & Shanmugam, A. V. Interpersonal attitudes among American, Indian, and Japanese students. *International Journal of Psychology,* 1966:177–206.

Warr, P. B., & Smith, J. S. Combining information about people: Comparisons between six models. *Journal of Personality and Social Psychology,* 1970, *16* (September):55–65.

*Webster, M., Jr., Roberts, L., & Sobieszek, B. I. Accepting significant others: Six models. *American Journal of Sociology,* 1972, *78* (November):576–598.

*Webster, M., Jr., Roberts, L., & Sobieszek, B. I. Reply to Shelly. *American Journal of Sociology,* 1974, *79* (May):1480–1483.

Weiner, B., Heckhausen, H., Meyer, W., & Cook, R. E. Causal ascriptions and achievement behavior: A conceptual analysis of effort and reanalysis of locus of control. *Journal of Personality and Social Psychology,* 1972, *21* (February): 239–248.

Weitz, S. Attitude, voice, and behavior: A repressed affect model of interracial interaction. *Journal of Personality and Social Psychology,* 1972, *24* (October): 14–21.

Wolosin, R. J., Sherman, S. J., & Till, A. Effects of cooperation and competition on responsibility attribution after success and failure. *Journal of Experimental Social Psychology,* 1973, *9* (May):220–235.

Worchel, S., & Andreoli, V. A. Attribution of causality as a means of restoring behavioral freedom. *Journal of Personality and Social Psychology,* 1974, *29* (March):237–245.

Wortman, C. B., Costanzo, P. R., & Witt, T. R. Effect of anticipated performance on the attributions of causality to self and others. *Journal of Personality and Social Psychology,* 1973, *27* (September):372–381.

Wyer, R. S., Jr. Effects of information inconsistency and grammatical context on evaluation of persons. *Journal of Personality and Social Psychology,* 1973, *25* (January):45–49.

Zadny, J., & Gerard, H. B. Attributed intentions and informational selectivity. *Journal of Experimental Social Psychology,* 1974, *10* (January):34–52.

Zahm, G. L. Cognitive integration of verbal and vocal information in spoken sentences. *Journal of Experimental Social Psychology,* 1973, *9* (July):320–334.

Zander, A., Fuller, R., & Armstrong, W. Attributed pride or shame in group and self. *Journal of Personality and Social Psychology,* 1972, *23* (September): 346–352.

Zanna, M. P. On inferring one's beliefs from one's behavior in a low-choice setting. *Journal of Personality and Social Psychology,* 1973, *26* (June):386–394.

Zanna, M. P., & Cooper, J. Dissonance and the pill: An attribution approach to studying the arousal properties of dissonance. *Journal of Personality and Social Psychology,* 1974, *29* (May):703–709.

Chapter 15

*Backman, C., Secord, P., and Peirce, J. Resistance to change in self-concept as a function of consensus among significant others. *Sociometry,* 1963, *26* (March):102–111.

*Cooley, C. H. *Human nature and the social order.* New York: Schocken Brothers, 1964. (Orginally published, 1902.)

*Davis, J. A. The campus as a frogpond. *American Journal of Sociology,* 1966, *72* (July):17–31.

Deaux, K. Anticipatory attitude change: A direct test of the self-esteem hypothesis. *Journal of Experimental Social Psychology,* 1972, *8* (March):143–155.

Dion, K. L., & Miller, N. Determinants of task-related self-evaluations in black children. *Journal of Experimental Social Psychology*, 1973, *9* (September): 466–479.

Eagly, A. H., & Whitehead, G. I., III. Effect of choice on receptivity to favorable and unfavorable evaluations of oneself. *Journal of Personality and Social Psychology*, 1972, *22* (May):223–230.

Eisen, M. Characteristic self-esteem, sex, and resistance to temptation. *Journal of Personality and Social Psychology*, 1972, *24* (October):68–72.

Ellison, C. W., & Firestone, I. J. Development of interpersonal trust as a function of self-esteem, target status, and target style. *Journal of Personality and Social Psychology*, 1974, *29* (May):655–663.

*Entwisle, D. R., & Webster, M. Raising children's expectations for their own performance: A classroom application. In J. Berger, T. L. Conner, & M. H. Fisek (Eds.), *Expectation states theory*. Cambridge: Winthrop Publishers, 1974.

Gecas, V. Parental behavior and contextual variations in adolescent self-esteem. *Sociometry*, 1972, *35* (June):332–345.

*Haas, H. T., & Maehr, M. L. Two experiments on the concept of self and the reaction of others. *Journal of Personality and Social Psychology*, 1965, *1* (February):100–105.

Hewitt, J., & Goldman, M. Self-esteem, need for approval, and reactions to personal evaluations. *Journal of Experimental Social Psychology*, 1974, *10* (May): 201–210.

Ickes, W. J., Wicklund, R. A., & Ferris, C. B. Objective self awareness and self esteem. *Journal of Experimental Social Psychology*, 1973, *9* (May):202–219.

*Jones, S. C. Some determinants of interpersonal evaluating behavior. *Journal of Personality and Social Psychology*, 1966, *3* (April):397–403.

*Jones, S. C. Some effects of interpersonal evaluations on group process and social perception. *Sociometry*, 1968, *31* (June):150–161.

*Jones, S. C., and Pines, H. A. Self-revealing events and interpersonal evaluations. *Journal of Personality and Social Psychology*, 1968, *3* (March):277–281.

*Jones, S. C., and Ratner, C. Commitment to self-appraisal and interpersonal evaluations. *Journal of Personality and Social Psychology*, 1967, *6* (August): 442–447.

*Jones, S. C., and Schneider, D. J. Certainty of self-appraisal and reactions to evaluations from others. *Sociometry*, 1968, *31* (December):395–403.

Levine, J. M., Ranelli, C. J., & Valle, R. S. Self-evaluation and reaction to a shifting other. *Journal of Personality and Social Psychology*, 1974, *29* (May): 637–643.

Liebling, B. A., & Shaver, P. Evaluation, self-awareness, and task performance. *Journal of Experimental Social Psychology*, 1973, *9* (July):297–306.

*Maehr, M. L., Mensing, J., & Nafzger, S. Concept of self and the reaction of others. *Sociometry*, 1962, *25* (December):353–357.

Marecek, J., & Mettee, D. R. Avoidance of continued success as a function of self-esteem, level of esteem certainty, and responsibility for success. *Journal of Personality and Social Psychology*, 1972, *28* (April):98–107.

*Mead, G. H. *Mind, self, and society*. Chicago: University of Chicago Press, 1934.

*Meyer, J. High school effects on college intentions. *American Journal of Sociology*, 1970, *76* (June):59–70.

Millimet, C. R., & Gardner, D. F. Induction of threat to self-esteem and the arousal and resolution of affect. *Journal of Experimental Social Psychology*, 1972, *8* (September):467–481.

Mischel, W., Ebbesen, E. B., & Zeiss, A. R. Selective attention to the self: Situational and dispositional determinants. *Journal of Personality and Social Psychology*, 1973, 27 (July):129–142.

°Miyamoto, S. F., & Dornbusch, S. M. A test of interactionist hypotheses of self-conception. *American Journal of Sociology*, 1956, 41 (March):399–403.

°Moore, J. C. A *further test of interactionist hypotheses of self-conception.* (Tech. Rep. 6). Stanford, Calif.: Stanford University, Laboratory for Social Research, May 1964.

°Reeder, L. G., Donohue, G. A., & Biblarz, A. Conceptions of self and others. *American Journal of Sociology*, 1960, 66 (September):153–159.

°Rist, R. C. Student social class and teacher expectations: The self-fulfilling prophecy in ghetto education. *Harvard Educational Review*, 1970, 40 (Winter):411–451.

Rosenberg, M. and Simmons, R. G. *Black and white self-esteem.* Washington, D.C.: American Sociological Association, 1972.

°Rosenthal, R., & Jacobson, L. *Pygmalion in the classroom.* New York: Holt, Rinehart and Winston, 1968.

Schneider, D. J., & Eustis, A. C. Effects of ingratiation motivation, target positiveness, and revealingness on self-presentation. *Journal of Personality and Social Psychology*, 1972, 22 (May):149–155.

°Seaver, W. B. Effects of naturally induced teacher expectancies. *Journal of Personality and Social Psychology*, 1973, 28 (December):333–342.

Shrauger, J. S. Self-esteem and reactions to being observed by others. *Journal of Personality and Social Psychology*, 1972, 23 (August):192–200.

°Sobieszek, B. Multiple sources and the formation of performance expectations. *Pacific Sociological Review*, 1972, 15 (January):103–122.

Stebbins, R. A. Modesty, pride, and conceit: Variations in the expression of self-esteem. *Pacific Sociological Review*, 1972, 15 (October):461–481.

°Sullivan, H. S. *Conceptions of modern psychiatry.* Washington, D.C.: W. H. White Psychiatric Foundation, 1947.

Tognoli, J., & Keisner, R. Gain and loss of esteem as determinants of interpersonal attraction: A replication and extension. *Journal of Personality and Social Psychology*, 1972, 23 (August):201–204.

°Videbeck, R. Self-conceptions and the reactions of others. *Sociometry*, 1960, 23 (December):351–359.

°Webster, M. and Sobieszek, B. *Sources of self-evaluation.* New York: Wiley-Interscience, 1974.

Wicklund, R. A., & Ickes, W. J. The effect of objective self-awareness on predecisional exposure to information. *Journal of Experimental Social Psychology*, 1972, 8 (July):378–387.

Youngleson, M. L. The need to affiliate and self-esteem in institutionalized children. *Journal of Personality and Social Psychology*, 1973, 26 (May):280–286.

Chapter 16

Adams, J. S. Toward an understanding of inequity. *Journal of Abnormal and Social Psychology*, 1963, 67 (November):422–436.

°Adams, J. S. Inequity in social exchange. In L. Berkowitz, *Advances in experimental social psychology* (Vol. 2). New York: Academic Press, 1965.

°Adams, J. S., & Jacobson, P. R. Effects of wage inequities on work quality. *Journal of Abnormal and Social Psychology*, 1964, 69 (July):19–25.

*Adams, J. S., & Rosenbaum, W. B. The relationship of worker productivity to cognitive dissonance about wage inequities. *Journal of Applied Psychology,* 1962, *46* (June):161–164.

Aderman, D., Brehm, S. S., & Katz, L. B. Empathetic observation of an innocent victim: The just world revisited. *Journal of Personality and Social Psychology,* 1974, *29* (March):342–347.

*Berger, J., Zelditch, M., Jr., Anderson, B., and Cohen, B. P. Structural aspects of distributive justice: A status-value formulation. In J. Berger, M. Zelditch, Jr., and B. Anderson, *Sociological theories in progress* (Vol. 2). Boston: Houghton Mifflin Co., 1972.

*Bobrow, S. B. A balance theory of distributive justice and experimental tests of consequences. (Doctoral dissertation, Johns Hopkins University, 1972).

Chaikin, A. L., & Darley, J. M. Victim or perpetrator?: Defensive attribution of responsibility and the need for order and justice. *Journal of Personality and Social Psychology,* 1973, *25* (February):268–275.

*Clark, J. V. A preliminary investigation of some unconscious assumptions affecting labor efficiency of eight supermarkets. DBA thesis, Harvard Graduate School of Business, 1958.

Cohen, R. L. Mastery and justice in laboratory dyads: A revision and extension of equity theory. *Journal of Personality and Social Psychology,* 1974, *29* (April):464–474.

Collins, B. E. Four components of the Rotter internal-external scale: Belief in a difficult world, a just world, a predictable world, and a politically responsive world. *Journal of Personality and Social Psychology,* 1974, *29* (March):381–391.

Cook, K. S. Expectations, evaluations, and equity. *American Sociological Review,* 1975.

Deci, E. L. Intrinsic motivation, extrinsic reinforcement, and equity. *Journal of Personality and Social Psychology,* 1972, *22* (April):113–120.

Dorris, J. W. Reactions to unconditional cooperation: A field study emphasizing variables neglected in laboratory research. *Journal of Personality and Social Psychology,* 1972, *22* (June):387–397.

Druckman, D., Solomon, D., & Zechmeister, K. Effects of representational role obligations on the process of children's distribution of resources. *Sociometry,* 1972, *35* (September):387–410.

Dweck, C. S., & Reppucco, N. D. Learned helplessness and reinforcement responsibility in children. *Journal of Personality and Social Psychology,* 1973, *25* (January):109–116.

Garrett, J., & Libby, W. L., Jr. Role of intentionality in mediating responses to inequity in the dyad. *Journal of Personality and Social Psychology,* 1973, *28* (October):21–27.

*Homans, G. Status among clerical workers. *Human Organization,* 1953, *12,* 5–10. (Reprinted in G. Homans, *Sentiments and activities.* New York: Free Press, 1962.)

*Homans, G. The cash posters. *American Sociological Review,* 1954, *19,* 724–733. (Reprinted in G. Homans, *Sentiments and activities.* New York: Free Press, 1962.)

Jones, C., & Aronson, E. Attribution of fault to a rape victim as a function of respectability of the victim. *Journal of Personality and Social Psychology,* 1973, *26* (June):415–419.

Kahn, A. Reactions to generosity or stinginess from an intelligent or stupid work partner: A test of equity theory in a direct exchange relationship. *Journal of Personality and Social Psychology*, 1972, *21* (January):116–123.

Katz, I., Glass, D. C., & Cohen, S. Ambivalence, guilt, and the scapegoating of minority group victims. *Journal of Experimental Social Psychology*, 1973, *9* (September):423–436.

Landy, D., & Aronson, E. The influence of the character of the criminal and his victim on the decisions of simulated jurors. *Journal of Experimental Social Psychology*, 1969, *5* (April):141–152.

Lane, I. M., & Messe, L. A. Distribution of insufficient, sufficient, and oversufficient rewards: A clarification of equity theory. *Journal of Personality and Social Psychology*, 1972, *21* (February):228–233.

°Lawler, E. Effects of hourly overpayment on productivity and work quality. *Journal of Personality and Social Psychology*, 1968, *10* (November):306–314.

Legant, P., & Mettee, D. R. Turning the other cheek versus getting even: Vengeance, equity, and attraction. *Journal of Personality and Social Psychology*, 1973, *25* (February):243–253.

Lerner, M. J. The justice motive: "Equity" and "parity" among children. *Journal of Personality and Social Psychology*, 1974, *29* (April):539–550.

Lerner, M. J. Observer's evaluation of a victim: Justice, guilt, and veridical perception. *Journal of Personality and Social Psychology*, 1971, *20* (November): 127–135.

Leventhal, G. S., Michaels, J. W., & Sanford, C. Inequity and interpersonal conflict: Reward allocation and secrecy about reward as methods of preventing conflict. *Journal of Personality and Social Psychology*, 1972, *23* (July): 88–102.

Leventhal, G. S., & Whiteside, H. D. Equity and the use of reward to elicit high performance. *Journal of Personality and Social Psychology*, 1973, *25* (January):75–83.

°Long, G. T., & Lerner, M. J. Deserving, the "personal contract," and altruistic behavior by children. *Journal of Personality and Social Psychology*, 1974, *29* (April):551–556.

°Merton, R., & Rossi, A. K. Contributions to the theory of reference groups behavior. In R. K. Merton, *Social theory and social structure.* New York: Free Press, 1968.

Messe, L. A., Dawson, J. E., & Lane, I. Equity as a mediator of the effect of reward level on behavior in the prisoner's dilemma game. *Journal of Personality and Social Psychology*, 1973, *26* (April):60–65.

Meux, E. P. Concern for the common good in an N-person game. *Journal of Personality and Social Psychology*, 1973, *28* (December):414–418.

°Mikula, G. Nationality, performance, and sex as determinants of reward allocation. *Journal of Personality and Social Psychology*, 1974, *29* (April):435–440.

Mills, J., & Egger, R. Effect on derogation of a victim of choosing to reduce his distress. *Journal of Personality and Social Psychology*, 1972, *23* (September): 405–408.

°Moore, L. M., & Baron, R. M. Effects of wage inequities on work attitudes and performance. *Journal of Experimental Social Psychology*, 1973, *9* (January): 1–16.

Regan, D. T., Williams, M., & Sparling, S. Voluntary expiation of guilt: A field experiment. *Journal of Personality and Social Psychology*, 1972, *24* (October): 42–45.

Schmitt, D. R., & Marwell, G. Withdrawal and reward reallocation as responses to inequity. *Journal of Experimental Social Psychology,* 1972, *8* (May):207–221.

Shaver, K. G. Defensive attribution: Effects of severity and relevance on the responsibility assigned for an accident. *Journal of Personality and Social Psychology,* 1970, *14* (February):101–113.

Shaver, K. G. Redress and conscientiousness in the attribution of responsibility for accidents. *Journal of Experimental Social Psychology,* 1970, *6* (January): 100–110.

Shaw, J. T., & Skolnick, P. Attribution of responsibility for a happy accident. *Journal of Personality and Social Psychology,* 1971, *18* (June):380–383.

Simons, C. W., & Piliavin, J. A. Effect of deception on reactions to a victim. *Journal of Personality and Social Psychology,* 1972, *21* (January):56–60.

*Spector, A. J. Expectations, fulfillment, and morale. *Journal of Abnormal Social Psychology,* 1956, *52* (January):51–56.

Stokols, D., & Schopler, J. Reactions to victims under conditions of situational detachment: The effects of responsibility, severity, and expected future interaction. *Journal of Personality and Social Psychology,* 1973, *25* (February): 199–209.

*Stouffer, S. A., Suchman, E. A., DeVinney, L. C., Starr, S. A., and Williams, R. M. *The American soldier: Adjustment during army life* (Vol. 1). Princeton: Princeton University Press, 1949.

Taynor, J., & Deaux, K. When women are more deserving than men: Equity, attribution, and perceived sex differences. *Journal of Personality and Social Psychology,* 1973, *28* (December):360–367.

Veblen, T. *The theory of the leisure class.* New York: Macmillan, 1973. (Originally published, 1899.)

Walster, E. Assignment of responsibility for an accident. *Journal of Personality and Social Psychology,* 1966, *3* (January):73–79.

Walster, E., & Prestholdt, P. The effect of misjudging another: Over-compensation or dissonance reduction? *Journal of Experimental Social Psychology,* 1966, *2* (January):85–97.

*Zelditch, M., Jr., Anderson, B., Berger, J., and Cohen, B. P. Equitable comparisons. *Pacific Sociological Review,* 1970, *13* (Winter):19–26.

Chapter 17

Adair, J., & Schachter, B. "To cooperate or to look good?": The subjects' and experimenters' perceptions of each others' intentions. *Journal of Experimental Social Psychology,* 1972, *8* (January):74–85.

Adler, N. E. Impact of prior sets given experimenters and subjects on the experimenter expectancy effect. *Sociometry,* 1973, *36* (March):113–126.

Barber, T. X. Invalid arguments, postmortem analyses, and the experimenter bias effect. *Journal of Consulting and Clinical Psychology,* 1969, *33*:11–14.

Barber, T. X. Five attempts to replicate the experimenter bias effect. *Journal of Consulting and Clinical Psychology,* 1969, *33*:1–6.

Barber, T. X., and Silver, M. Fact, fiction, and the experimenter bias effect: Pitfalls in data analysis and interpretation. *Psychological Bulletin Monograph Supplement,* 1968, *70*:1–29 and 48–62.

Baumrind, D. Some thoughts on ethics of research after reading Milgram's "behavioral study of obedience." *American Psychologist,* 1964, *19*:421–423.

Campbell, D. Factors relevant to the validity of experiments in social settings. *Psychological Bulletin,* 1957, *54* (July):297–312.

Foddy, W. H. *Compliance to rational-legal authority.* Paper presented at annual meeting, Canadian Sociological-Anthropological Association, 1969.

Holmes, D. S., & Bennett, D. H. Experiments to answer questions raised by the use of deception in psychological research. *Journal of Personality and Social Psychology,* 1974, *29* (March):358–367.

Kruglanski, A. W. Much ado about the "volunteer artifacts." *Journal of Personality and Social Psychology,* 1973, *28* (December):348–354.

Marquis, P. C. Experimenter-subject interaction as a function of authoritarianism and response set. *Journal of Personality and Social Psychology,* 1973, *25* (February):289–296.

°McCord, J. Effects of experimenter status on influence. (Doctoral dissertation, Stanford University, 1969.)

°Mills, T. M. A sleeper variable in small groups research: The experimenter. *Pacific Sociological Review,* 1962, *5* (Spring):21–28.

Newberry, B. H. Truth telling to subjects with information about experiments: Who is being deceived? *Journal of Personality and Social Psychology,* 1973, *25* (March):369–374.

°Orne, M. T. On the social psychology of the psychological experiment: With particular reference to demand characteristics and their implications. *American Psychologist,* 1962, *17* (November):776–783.

°Rosenthal, R. *Experimenter effects in behavioral research.* New York: Appleton-Century-Crofts, 1966.

Rosnow, R. L., & Aiken, L. S. Mediation of artifacts in behavioral research. *Journal of Experimental Social Psychology,* 1973, *9* (May):181–201.

Rosnow, R. L., Suls, J. M., Goodstadt, B. E., & Gitter, A. G. More on the social psychology of the experiment: When compliance turns to self-defense. *Journal of Personality and Social Psychology,* 1973, *27* (September):337–343.

Silverman, I., Shulman, A. D., & Wiesenthal, D. The experimenter as a source of variance in psychological research: Modeling and sex effects. *Journal of Personality and Social Psychology,* 1972, *21* (February):219–227.

Straits, B. C., Wuebben, P. L., & Majka, T. J. Influences on subjects' perceptions of experimental research situations. *Sociometry,* 1972, *35* (December):499–518.

Index